Tax Factors

in

Real Estate Operations

Fifth Edition

Tax Factors in Real Estate Operations

Fifth Edition

Paul E.
Anderson

Prentice-Hall, Inc.
Englewood Cliffs, N.J.

Prentice-Hall International, Inc., *London*
Prentice-Hall of Australia, Pty. Ltd., *Sydney*
Prentice-Hall of Canada, Ltd., *Toronto*
Prentice-Hall of India Private Ltd., *New Delhi*
Prentice-Hall of Japan, Inc., *Tokyo*
Prentice-Hall of Southeast Asia Pte. Ltd., *Singapore*
Whitehall Books, Ltd., *Wellington, New Zealand*

©1978, 1976, 1969, 1965, 1960 by

Prentice-Hall, Inc.
Englewood Cliffs, N.J.

All rights reserved. No part of this book may be reproduced in any form or by any means, without permission in writing from the publisher.

"This publication is designed to provide accurate and authoritative information in regard to the subject matter covered. It is sold with the understanding that the publisher is not engaged in rendering legal, accounting or other professional service. If legal advice or other expert assistance is required, the services of a competent professional person should be sought."

—From the Declaration of Principles jointly adopted by a Committee of the American Bar Association and a Committee of Publishers and Associations.

Library of Congress Cataloging in Publication Data

Anderson, Paul Edward
    Tax factors in real estate operations.

    Includes index.
    1. Real property and taxation--United States.
I. Title.
KF6540.A95 1978   343'.73'054   77-27901
ISBN 0-13-884890-4

Printed in the United States of America

PREFACE TO THE FIFTH EDITION

This book is written for one purpose: to explain and detail the vital essentials of the federal income, estate and gift tax consequences of real estate transactions. It discusses ownership in all forms: individual, joint tenancy, community property, partnership, limited partnership, corporation and Subchapter S corporations. It analyzes leases, purchases and sales with leasebacks. The benefits and burdens of accelerated depreciation are explored.

The book has been revised to reflect the changes made by the Tax Reform Act of 1976, and the Tax Amendment Act of 1977. These include a new classification of real estate known as vacation homes. Included is a discussion of the new treatment of home office expenses. Changes in the minimum tax on capital gains and accelerated depreciation are noted. Attention has been given by the author to the new basis on death provisions, including "Fresh Start," but the author admits candidly that more examples are needed, especially in the case of community property. A new section covering tax exemptions for qualified Homeowner's Associations, under the Tax Reform Act of 1976, has also been added.

Special emphasis is given to sales and the questions of postponing the tax on the gains realized: whether by election of the installment method, use of options or the deferred payment method. Almost one-half of the contents of this book deal with property subject to debt, whether recourse or non-recourse. Seldom is real estate purchased or sold (or inherited, for that matter) free and clear of debt against it. And what happens when substituted security is used by the buyer?

What is a "wrap-around" or "all-inclusive" loan agreement? If the "wrap-around" is challanged by the Internal Revenue Service as a "device" for creating artificial interest deductions, what happens to the sales price? Or is a "wrap-around" sale incomplete?

Leases are analyzed. When are tenant's improvements deductible? What is the tax consequence of a lessee who buys off his lessor's obligation to restore? And does the lessor have ordinary income? When are options to renew considered part of the lease term? Does it make a difference if the tenant has made substantial improvements? Are security deposits always treated as non-taxable loans? Or can the landlord elect to treat them as income and take a deduction on repayment?

When is a real estate corporation collapsible? What are the consequences?

Interest, and the pre-payment of interest, on debt obligations are discussed. Also discussed are "points." Does it make a difference whether the points are paid to the seller or a third party lending institution?

Repossessions and foreclosures are treated in depth. Condominium and cooperative ownership of property is explored. What is a syndicate? What is meant by a "joint venture"?

The author has deliberately selected what he considers the pertinent citations. "String citations" are meaningless. *Malat v. Riddell*, cited in the text, must be cited in well over 500 published decisions.

The author has also included detailed realistic examples, in numerical terms, of the principles set forth. This book has been built on four prior editions; each of which had more than one printing; and each of which had more than one criticism and correction. All of which adds to this edition.

This book is dedicated to the memory of my father, Anders Johann Theodor Andersson, born April 18, 1878, in Landshult, Sweden.

January, 1978.

Paul E. Anderson

About the Author

Paul E. Anderson is nationally known as a lecturer before business and professional groups on the subject of real estate taxation. A practicing attorney since 1951, he is a member of the California Bar, former Chairman of the State Bar of California Tax Committee, and past President of the Metropolitan Bay Area Section of Taxation, San Francisco Tax Club and Estate Planning Council. He formerly served as real estate editor for the Journal of Taxation. He is an Emeritus Professor of Law (Federal Income, Estate and Gift Taxation) of Hastings College of Law, University of California, a former Instructor of Law at Stanford University School of Law and Mayor of San Mateo, California. He is the author of *Tax Planning Of Real Estate* (Joint Committee, ALI-ABA) now in its seventh edition. He is listed in *Who's Who Among American Lawyers*.

Contents

1. GENERAL PRINCIPLES **19**

    Tax Advantages in the Ownership of Real Estate   19

    Depreciation, equity financing and tax-free exchanges. Treatment of sale of property. Postponed capital gain. Expenses of repair and maintenance. Casualty losses. Election to capitalize interest, taxes and carrying charges. Tenants' improvements. Leasing vs. ownership of real estate. Title to real estate.

    Tax Classification of Real Property   23

    Real estate held as a personal residence. Property held for production of income. Real estate held for use in a trade or business. Real estate held for sale to customers.

    Problems of Classification of Real Property   26

    When is a house a home? Quasi-business use: Office at home or vacation property rented out occasionally. When does rental property constitute a trade or business? When is an investor a dealer? Can a dealer hold real estate for investment? Principal purpose test.

2. HOW TO ACQUIRE REAL PROPERTY **35**

    How Should Title Be Taken?   35

    Individual ownership. Corporate ownership. Comparison of corporate and individual ownership. Husband and wife ownership. Husband and wife: estate and gift taxes. Husband and wife: basis after death. Husband and wife: termination of joint tenancy. Husband and wife: comparison of ownership. Tenancy in common. Joint tenancy. Partnership form of ownership.

    Tax Basis of Property Upon Acquisition   45

    Basis of property acquired by purchase. Basis of property acquired by tax-free exchange. Basis of property acquired by gift. Basis of property acquired by inheritance. Basis of property acquired by gift in contemplation of death. Basis of property ac-

HOW TO ACQUIRE REAL PROPERTY *(cont.)*

quired as surviving joint tenant. Basis of property acquired as community property. Basis of property acquired as compensation. Basis of property acquired for a debt. Basis of property acquired on a corporate distribution. Basis of property acquired subject to a mortgage.

Allocation of Tax Basis on Acquisition 52

Basis allocation in general. Basis allocation by contract. Basis allocation to structure to be demolished.

Purchase Under Option 54

Purchased option. Inherited option. Option to buy from estate. Failure to exercise or sale of option. Allocation of basis. Holding period.

Purchase for Bargain Price 56

Exception for pre-existing relationship. Purchase by broker for price without commission.

Apportionment of Real Estate Taxes on Acquisition 57

Apportionment of current real property taxes. Time for deducting the allocated tax. Treatment of excess tax paid. Treatment of reimbursement for taxes paid. Apportionment of real property taxes on acquistion other than purchase.

3. **OWNERSHIP AND OPERATION OF REAL PROPERTY** 64

Depreciation 64

Types of improvements qualifying for depreciation. Apportionment of basis. Measuring the depreciation allowance. Methods of allocating the depreciation allowance. Limitations on use of accelerated depreciation methods. Change of method. Useful life. Salvage value. Use of accelerated methods of depreciation. Effect on tax preference item tax or selection of depreciation alternatives. Who is entitled to depreciation?

Obsolescence 76

Demolition, Abandonment or Removal of Improvements 77

Owner intends to rebuild. Owner intends to lease. Owner acquires with intent to demolish.

Repairs, Maintenance Expenses, and Capital Improvements 78

Contents

OWNERSHIP AND OPERATION OF REAL PROPERTY *(cont.)*

Repair or capital improvement? Expenses of maintenance and operation.

Protection of Income or Defense of Title?   79

Taxes, Interest, and Carrying Charges   81

Taxes on real property. Interest. Special assessments. Election to capitalize taxes and other carrying charges.

Casualty Losses on Business Property   85

Measure of the loss. Cost of restoration. Reduction for insurance received.

Soil and Water Conservation Expenses   87

Limitation upon the deduction. Land used in farming. Limitation upon the amount deductible. Election to deduct conservation expenses. Soil and water conservation districts. Fertilizer and land clearing expenditures.

4. SALES, EXCHANGES, CONVERSIONS AND ABANDONMENTS ... 91

Sales of Real Property   91

Computation of gain or loss on sale. Computation of the gross sales price. Time for reporting gain or loss on sale. Basis allocation between portions of tract. Nature of gain or loss on sale. Treatment of ordinary gains or losses. Treatment of Section 1231 gains or losses. Treatment of capital gains or losses. Holding period of property. Recapture of depreciation: Generally. Recapture of depreciation: Real estate improvements. Recapture: Farm improvements. Sale of depreciable property to related parties. Timing the sale. Sale of property subject to a favorable mortgage.

Tax-Free Exchanges of Like Property   111

What is like property? How is the nature of the property determined? Losses on a tax-free exchange. Basis on tax-free exchange. Holding period on tax-free exchange. Effect of receiving "boot." Losses if "boot" received. Effect of giving "boot." Basis of property if "boot" received. Effect of a mortgage. Effect of offsetting mortgages. Three-cornered exchanges. Techniques for holding open a three-party exchange. Planning for a tax-free exchange.

Taxable Exchanges of Real Property   129

SALES, EXCHANGES, CONVERSIONS AND ABANDONMENTS *(cont.)*

Involuntary Conversions of Real Property   129

Tax-free exchange of converted property for similar property. Tax-free conversion of property into cash. What constitutes an involuntary conversion? Single economic unit rule. Proceeds that can be sheltered. Replacement property. "Like kind" property. Period of replacement. Election on tax return. Successor to owner of condemned property. Effect of a mortgage on converted property. Use and occupancy insurance. Condemnation expenses and severance damages. Taking of flowage and other non-exclusive easements.

Inverse Condemnation   139

Nature of action. Tax consequences. No prior loss deduction. Application of Section 1033. Partial destruction: the usual case. Loss previously taken.

Gains and Losses on Involuntary Conversions
       Under Section 1231.   145

Depreciation Recapture under Section 1033   146

Abandonment of Property   147

5. HOW TO POSTPONE TAX ON THE SALE OF REAL PROPERTY   148

Installment Sales   149

How to qualify sales for the installment method. Payments received in the year of sale. Readily tradable bonds of corporate seller. Constructive receipt of payment in year of sale. Planning for an installment sale. How to report gain on the installment method. Installment sales of mortgaged property. Use of "wrap-around" or "all inclusive" mortgage. Selling expenses: dealer vs. investor. Type of sales qualifying for installment method. Sale of installment contract. Pledge of installment obligations. Other dispositions of installment contracts. Substituted security on installment sale. Guarantees by financial institution. Repossession of property sold on installment method.

Deferred Payment Sales   168

Sales qualified for the deferred payment method. Non-negotiable contract sale. Negotiable contract of sale. Sale subject to note secured by mortgage. Sale subject to personal note. Sales by an accrual basis taxpayer. Deferred payment sale subject to

HOW TO POSTPONE TAX ON THE SALE OF
REAL PROPERTY *(cont.)*

mortgage. Sale of deferred payment obligation. Pledge of deferred payment obligation. Repossession of property sold.

Sale for an Indeterminate Price   175

Sales for a contingent price. Sales measured by production. Sales for a private annuity.

Option Sales   178

Option distinguished from sales contract. Effect of exercise or failure of option. Advantages to seller of option.

Escrow Sales   180

General rule: closing of escrow. Exception: deposit of purchase price. Exception: transfer of possession.

6. TAX ASPECTS OF MORTGAGE FINANCING 183

Placing a Mortgage upon Property   183

Effect upon income. Effect upon basis. Effect to owner on disposition. Release of liability as disposition. Costs of placing a mortgage on property.

Acquiring Mortgaged Property   187

Basis of property acquired. Effect on basis if mortgage liability not assumed. Basis for the purpose of subsequent sales. Payments made by owner on the mortgage debt. Payment of condemnation proceeds on mortgaged property. Reinvestment of condemnation proceeds received on mortgaged property. Effect of a reduction in the mortgage debt (other than by payment).

Mortgage Payments, Penalties and Commissions   193

Payment of interest or principal. Failure to provide for interest on deferred payments. Apportionment of lump sum payments. Delinquent interest on mortgage debt. Prepayment penalties. Commissions, fees, and other expenses.

Liabilities in Excess of Basis   197

Sale of property mortgaged in excess of basis. Taxable exchange of property mortgaged in excess in basis. Non-taxable exchange of property mortgaged in excess of basis. Abandonment of property mortgaged in excess of basis. Gift of property mortgaged in

TAX ASPECTS OF MORTGAGE FINANCING *(cont.)*

excess of basis. Inheritance of property mortgaged in excess of basis.

Partnership Transactions in Property Mortgaged in
      Excess of Basis   202

Contribution of property to a partnership. Possibility of gain on contribution. Contribution of partner not personally liable for mortgage debt. Receipt of contribution by partnership. Distribution by partnership. Tax-planning the contribution of property mortgaged in excess of basis to a partnership. Sale of contributed property by partnership. Distribution of contributed property by partnership. Conclusions on partnership transactions.

Corporate Transaction in Property Mortgaged in Excess of Basis   209

Contribution of property to corporation. Distribution of property by corporation. F.H.A. "windfall" profits.

Conclusion: Tax Advantages of Mortgage Financing   212

7. REPOSSESSIONS, MORTGAGE FORECLOSURES AND CANCELLATIONS 214

Reacquisitions by a Seller in Partial or Full Satisfaction of the
      Indebtedness Arising from the Sale   215

General rule: gain on reacquisition. Loss on reacquisition. Bad debt loss. Extent of gain on reacquisition. Character of gain on reacquisition. Basis of reacquired property. Holding period of property reacquired under Section 1038. Section 1038 rules personal to seller. Legal fees on repossession.

Foreclosure by Sale to a Third Party   219

Bad debt loss of the mortgagee. Business or non-business bad debt? Time for deducting the bad debt: effect of a deficiency. Determining the amount of the mortgagee's loss. Mortgagee's deduction for previously reported income. Possibility of gain or income to the mortgagee. Mortgagor's loss on foreclosure sale. Nature of mortgagor's loss on foreclosure. Time for deducting the mortgagor's loss on foreclosure. Mortgagor's gain on foreclosure sale. Gain or loss of a non-assuming mortgagor. Suggestions on foreclosure of mortgage by sale to third party.

Strict Foreclosure: Involuntary Conveyance to Mortgagee   232

Loss on involuntary conveyance to mortgagee. Gain to mortgagee

REPOSSESSIONS, MORTGAGE FORECLOSURES AND CANCELLATIONS *(cont.)*

on involuntary conveyance of property. Basis of acquired property to mortgagee. Mortgagor's loss on strict foreclosure. Mortgagor's gain on strict foreclosure. Suggestions on strict foreclosure.

Foreclosure by Sale to the Mortgagee   238

Loss to mortgagee who bids in. Nature of loss to mortgagee who bids in. Reduction of loss to mortgagee who bids in. Gain to mortgagee who bids in. Income to mortgagee who bids in. Gain or loss to the mortgagor. Suggestions on foreclosure of mortgage when the mortgagee bids in.

Voluntary Conveyance of Mortgaged Property   242

Gain or loss to the mortgagee on a voluntary conveyance. Basis to mortgagee of property received. Gain or loss to the mortgagor on a voluntary conveyance. Gain to insolvent mortgagor. Gain to purchase-money mortgagor. Voluntary conveyance by non-assuming mortgagor. Abandonment of mortgaged property. Suggestions on voluntary conveyance of mortgaged property.

Compromise of the Mortgage Debt   249

Loss to mortgagee on compromise of mortgage debt. Income to mortgagor on compromise of mortgage debt. Income to purchase-money mortgagor. Income to an insolvent mortgagor. Gift cancellation of a mortgage debt. Postponement of income by reduction of basis. Income to non-assuming mortgagor. Suggestions on compromise of mortgage debt.

Loss of Second Mortgagee   252

Expenses of Foreclosure   253

Assignment of Rents to the Mortgagee   254

Disposition of Property Acquired by Mortgagee   255

8. TAX TECHNIQUES AND ADVANTAGES IN LEASING REAL PROPERTY 256

Tax Consequences of Lease Clauses   256

Covenant to pay rent. Covenant to pay rent in advance. Covenant to pay bonus. Covenant to pay decreasing fixed or minimum rental. Covenant for true security deposit by tenant. Covenant for security deposit applicable to future rents. Covenant to pay property taxes. Covenant to pay mortgage service. Covenant to pay

**TAX TECHNIQUES AND ADVANTAGES IN LEASING
REAL PROPERTY** *(cont.)*

insurance premiums. Covenant to paint, repair and maintain. Covenant to reimburse landlord for expenses. Covenant to guarantee landlord against loss. Effect of net lease on landlord's interest deduction. Covenant to restore property: wear and tear not excepted. Covenant to restore: wear and tear excepted. Release of covenant to restore. Covenant to restore: failure either to restore or to pay. Restoration or reimbursement covenant. Covenant to demolish existing improvements. Covenant by landlord to improve the leased property: turn key lease. Covenant by landlord to reimburse tenant for improvements made by tenant. Covenant for tenant's improvements as allowance against rent. Covenant to reduce rent. Covenant to terminate: payment by landlord. Covenant to terminate: payment by tenant.

Depreciation of Improvements on Leased Property   271

Landlord's improvements. Trade fixtures installed by tenant. Permanent improvements to leased premises by tenant. Term of lease: option to renew. Month-to-month tenancy. Premature termination of lease or failure to renew option. Tenant's improvements as income to lessor.

Costs of Acquiring a Lease   274

Lease expenditures made by landlord. Allocation of cost to outstanding lease on acquisition of property. Allocation of carry over basis on death of lessor. Allocation of cost to depreciable improvements on acquisition of property subject to outstanding lease. Expenses paid by tenant to obtain lease.

Cancellation or Sale of Lease   280

Lessor's payment to cancel lease. Lessee's payment to cancel lease. Proceeds on sale or assignment of lease. Sublease vs. sale of lease.

Lease or Purchase?   282

Leasing vs. purchasing. Lease with option to purchase.

9. HYBRID FINANCING THROUGH SALES AND LEASEBACKS AND THE ABC TRANSACTION 287

Sales and Leasebacks   288

Advantages of sale and leaseback. Gain or loss on sale of property. Tax-free exchange and leaseback. Losses on tax-free ex-

HYBRID FINANCING THROUGH SALES AND LEASEBACKS AND THE ABC TRANSACTION *(cont.)*

change and leaseback. Rental deduction to seller-lessee. Rental income to buyer-lessor.

Sales and Leasebacks with Option to Repurchase   292

Reacquisition by seller-lessee on exercise of option. Loan with security or sale and leaseback with option to repurchase?

Sales and Leasebacks Between Related Parties   294

Gain or loss on sales between related parties. Gifts and leasebacks. Family leasebacks as income splitting devices. Requirements of a valid family leaseback. Rental deduction on leaseback between related parties.

The ABC Transaction   299

The ABC Transaction Applied to Real Estate Acquisitions   300

10. PARTNERSHIPS, SUBDIVISIONS, SYNDICATES, AND REAL ESTATE INVESTMENT TRUSTS 302

Real Estate Held by Partnerships   302

Problems of organizing a partnership. Problems of depreciation. Problems of gain. Undivided interests in contributed property. Partnership distributions. Collapsible partnerships.

Special Problems Relating to Limited Partnerships   312

Basis of limited partner's interest. "At Risk" basis for deductions. Association taxable as a corporation.

Subdivisions   316

Effect of subdividing. Subdivision during liquidation. Sale of unsuitable parts. Subdivisions under Section 1237.

Real Estate Syndicates   320

Unincorporated associations. Unincorporated associations taxed as corporations. Limited partnerships. Common ownership of income real estate.

Real Estate Investment Trusts   324

Election to be taxed as a real estate investment trust. Qualification as a real estate investment trust. Taxation of a real estate investment trust. Taxation of beneficiaries of trust. Evaluation of a real estate investment trust. Loss of qualified status.

11. CORPORATIONS 331

Problems of Incorporation   331

Tax-free incorporation. Taxable incorporation. "Thin" incorporation.

Problems of Operation   336

Accumulated earnings surtax. Personal holding company tax. Treatment of dividends paid. Treatment of distributions out of accelerated depreciation reserves. Treatment of distribution of "excess F.H.A. mortgage proceeds." Dividend in kind.

Problems of Sales and Liquidations   346

Sale of stock. Collapsible corporation rules applied to sales of stock. Liquidation of corporation and sale of property by stockholders. Sale of property in Section 337 liquidation. Distribution of property in "one month liquidation." Problem of accelerated depreciation in "one month liquidation." Liquidation of a collapsible corporation.

Problems on Acquisition of Property   357

Purchase of property by issuing stock. Tax-free reorganization. Statutory merger or consolidation. Other types of tax-free reorganizations. Acquisition of stock and liquidation.

Use of Corporation in Tax Planning   361

Comparison of the advantages and disadvantages of corporate ownership. Conclusion.

12. SUBCHAPTER S AND STRAW CORPORATIONS 363

Subchapter S.   363

Elections. Result of election. Basis as a tax problem. Conclusion.

Straw Corporations.   366

The "why" of non-recourse liability. Straw corporations as a useful device. Straw corporations as tax non-entities. Internal Revenue Service position. Ensurance of straw corporation position.

13. COOPERATIVE AND CONDOMINIUM HOUSING 369

Cooperative Housing Corporation   369

Benefits of Section 216: deductions. Requirements of Section 216.

Contents

COOPERATIVE AND CONDOMINIUM HOUSING *(cont.)*

Other tax aspects of ownership. The problem of non-qualifying income. Allowable commercial use. Non-exempt status of corporation.

The Condominium Owner as Property Owner   375

Definitions. Correlated rights and duties.

Condominium Unit Held for Personal Residential Use   375

Deductions. Sale of unit. Character of gain or loss. Gift of joint interest to spouse.

Condominium Units Held for Business Use   378

Depreciation. Limitation on interest deduction. Gain or loss on disposition of unit.

Condominium Management Agreements   379

Management, maintenance and servicing agreements. Restrictive covenants. Recreational facilities. Rental to outsiders.

Corporate Status of a Management Association   381

Continuity of life. Centralization of management. Limited liability. Free transferable interests.

Tax Consequences of Corporate Taxation.   383

Co-ownership of rental units. Loss of deductions. Section 216 availability. Section 528 availability: exempt homeowners association. Overassessments by a homeowners association. Separate entity for recreational purposes. Separate business entity alternative.

TABLE OF CASES **389**

INDEX **407**

1
General Principles

The tax factors in real estate operations today loom large in determining the relative advantage or disadvantage of a given investment, operation, or transaction. While tax consequences should never be the sole criterion of any transaction, the wise investor can afford to forgo consideration of the tax consequences inherent in any move he may contemplate. In fact, the tax factors in an investment in real estate can sometimes make the investment either extremely advantageous or quite disadvantageous, depending on the circumstances of acquisition and ownership.

The purpose of this chapter is to explore the field of real estate operations to locate some of the more common areas of advantage, disadvantage or difficulty. Accordingly, it is divided as follows:

A. *Tax Advantages in the Ownership of Real Estate;*
B. *Tax Classification of Real Property;*
C. *Problems of Classification of Real Property.*

A. TAX ADVANTAGES IN THE OWNERSHIP OF REAL ESTATE

Real estate presents a number of important tax advantages that make it an extremely desirable investment for the purposes of capital growth. The most important of these advantages are in the areas of depreciation, equity financing, and tax-free exchanges. By a shrewd combining of these advantages, a personal estate may be built up more rapidly in real estate than in any other type of investment property (save, perhaps, in more risky oil investments).

There are a number of other collateral, but significant, advantages that also add to the desirability of real estate as an investment vehicle. Among these are the following:

• Sales of real estate may qualify for capital gains treatment if sold for a profit, but for ordinary loss treatment if sold for a loss.

• Sales of real estate may be arranged in such manner that the gain is reportable over a number of years.

- Expenses of repair and maintenance are currently deductible.
- Casualty losses are deductible as ordinary losses.
- Interest and taxes on unproductive property may be capitalized or deducted at the option of the owner.
- A lessor of real property may receive additions to his capital without tax effect by the receipt of tenant's improvements.
- Use of real estate can be acquired either through outright ownership or through leasing.
- Title to real estate may be taken in a number of different ways, depending upon which presents the most favorable tax picture.

1. Depreciation, Equity Financing, and Tax-free Exchanges

In the ownership of real property *held for investment, for use in a trade or business,* or *for the production of income,* the owner is entitled to an allowance for depreciation deductible against income. This allowance permits him to recover the cost attributable to improvements on the land over their useful life. Thus, an investor in real estate is able to deduct a large portion of the total cost of his investment over its life.

Equally important is the fact that the investor's depreciation allowance is measured not only by the investment of his own funds, but also by the investment of borrowed funds that have been used to purchase property. Under the accelerated methods of depreciation, it is possible for the owner to build up his annual allowance for depreciation to an amount equal to the annual amounts required to amortize the purchase price loan. In other words, it is possible for an owner to build up his equity in the property out of tax-free funds.

And if the owner desires to switch his investment in one parcel of investment, or trade or business property, to another, he can make the switch without paying a capital gains tax. All he need do is to designate the switch as a tax-free exchange under the Code. Thus, if the owner comes toward the end of his depreciation allowance on one parcel of property, he can arrange to trade his equity in the property for another, more expensive parcel, to be financed by the equity he has built up in the first parcel plus a new mortgage loan. There is no limit to the number of times he can repeat the procedure so long as he holds each parcel for investment or trade or business use.

Compare this picture with that of an investor in the stock market. In the first place, an owner of stock or securities is not entitled to any allowance for depreciation. Consequently, his build-up of capital must be made solely out of tax-paid funds. And, in the second place, when the owner of securities wishes to switch his investment from one stock to another, he must pay a capital gains tax on any profit he realizes on the sale of his original investment. He does not have the privilege of designing the switch as a tax-free exchange.

For purposes of comparison, let us analyze the fortunes of two young men, each age 30, who are seeking a mode of investment to build up their capital. Let us assume that each of them starts with $25,000. One of them, A, decides to buy a small apartment. The other, B, decides to buy a small portfolio of common stocks. Let us further assume that values in the real estate market and the stock market double every 10 years.

TAX ADVANTAGES IN THE OWNERSHIP OF REAL ESTATE

A buys a new apartment for $80,000, paying $25,000 and obtaining financing for the $55,000 balance. He anticipates an annual income of $8,000, of which $3,000 goes to pay deductible interest and $3,000 to pay off the mortgage. His interest charge would accordingly drop to $1,500 per year after 10 years, or an average charge of $2,250 per year over the first 10 years of ownership. His annual depreciation allowance on a straight line basis over 30 years, assuming a land cost of $20,000, would be $2,000 per year. On an accelerated method of depreciation, his allowance would be $4,000 in the first year, dropping to $2,000 after 10 years, or an average charge of $3,000 per year over the 10-year period. Consequently, the loan amortization payments will be fairly well matched by A's allowance for depreciation.

B buys stock for $25,000, receiving annual dividends of $1,000. If the stock doubles in value in 10 years, the dividends should increase to $2,000 at the end of 10 years, or an average of $1,500 per year over the 10-year period. If we assume that each young man is in a 30-percent income tax bracket, let us see where each man will be after 10 years, at age 40.

1. Income Received in First 10 Years

	A	B
Gross	$80,000	$15,000
Less interest and depreciation	52,250	
Net income (exclusive of repairs and other expenses)	27,750	15,000
Tax at 30%	8,325	4,500
	$19,425	$10,500

2. Capital Value–End of First 10 Years

	A	B
Gross value (doubled)	$160,000	$50,000
Less encumbrance	25,000	
Net equity	135,000	50,000
Plus income after taxes	19,425	10,500
	$154,425	$60,500

If it becomes necessary or desirable for A and B to change their investments, A's advantage immediately increases. Let us assume that at the beginning of the second 10-year period, both A and B decide that their respective investments must be changed. B sells stock costing $25,000 for $50,000. His capital gain tax would be at one-half his normal rate of 30 percent, or an effective rate of 15 percent. Consequently, he would pay a tax of approximately $3,750, leaving him with only $56,750 to reinvest.

On the other hand, let us suppose A exchanges his $135,000 equity in the apartment plus his tax-paid income of $19,425 for a $154,425 equity in a new apartment costing $450,000, of which $295,575 is financed by borrowing. The exchange would be tax-free and, accordingly, A would have his entire capital build-up available for reinvestment.

If our projections continue, it is obvious that A is well on his way to becoming a millionaire, while B has only the possibility of accumulating sufficient capital after another 20 years to live comfortably. The difference is due to the combination of the leverage of equity financing, the benefits of accelerated depreciation, and the availability of tax-free exchanges.

2. Treatment of Sale of Property

Real estate held for purposes other than sale to customers can be sold under circumstances in which gain will be taxed as capital gain. This treatment is, of course, available to investors in other types of property.

But suppose the property is sold for a loss. Usually such a loss is treated as a capital loss. However, if the property is "property used in the trade or business" the loss realized on the sale may be treated as the equivalent of an ordinary loss. One of the advantages of investing in real estate lies in the fact that if the real estate is held for rental income it becomes "property used in the trade or business" of producing rental income. The benefits of these special rules are limited to real or depreciable property used in the trade or business and, accordingly, are not extended to investments in intangible wealth such as stocks or bonds.

3. Postponed Capital Gain

Sales of real estate may be handled in such manner that the gain realized will be spread over a number of years. This benefit can be realized by handling the sale on the installment or the deferred payment method, as outlined in Chapter 5.

While a sale of stock may qualify for installment treatment, ordinarily the sale of a listed stock is a cash transaction; accordingly, the entire gain would be taxed in the year of sale.

4. Expenses of Repair and Maintenance

All expenses of repairing, operating and maintaining investment, trade, or business real estate are deductible currently against ordinary income. To the extent that a policy of continual repair and constant maintenance will result in the build-up of capital value, the owner of real estate will have an advantage over an investor in other types of property not requiring repair.

5. Casualty Losses

Casualty losses to real estate, whether held for personal or for business purposes, are deductible as ordinary losses in the year sustained. No such similar tax benefit is available to the owners of intangible property.

6. Election to Capitalize Interest, Taxes, and Carrying Charges

The owner of unproductive real estate has an election either to deduct or to capitalize interest, taxes, and other carrying charges incurred on the property. Thus, he is in a position to choose the type of treatment that will give him the greatest tax benefit. Such an election is not available for other types of investments.

7. Tenants' Improvements

Improvements added by a tenant to leased property are not ordinarily income to the landlord even if he takes over these improvements at the end of the term of the

TAX CLASSIFICATION OF REAL PROPERTY

lease. The only exception to this rule is the case in which the tenant's improvements are intended as a substitute for rent.

Thus, in the ordinary case, the landlord can receive the benefit of an accretion to his capital without paying an income tax on the accretion.

8. Leasing vs. Ownership of Real Estate

Real estate can be leased as well as owned. This characteristic of real estate permits a taxpayer who requires the use of real estate to choose between ownership and leasing on the basis of the alternative offering him the least tax cost. In the case of property leased for business purposes, the rent paid will be fully deductible. In such a case, it may turn out that leasing is less expensive after taxes than outright ownership of the property would be.

9. Title to Real Estate

Title to real estate as an investment or business property can be held in a multiplicity of different ways. Each type of ownership involves its own peculiar tax consequences; accordingly, the prospective owner can choose the type of ownership that will give him the greatest tax benefit.

B. TAX CLASSIFICATION OF REAL PROPERTY

As we pointed out in the preceding part of this chapter, the character of a taxpayer's holding of real property will often control the incidence of the federal income, estate, and gift taxes. For example, the gain on a sale of property held for sale to customers will be taxed as ordinary income.

For this reason, the problem of classifying the various types of holdings of real property for tax purposes becomes extremely important. Unless the taxpayer knows what the tax character of his holding of the property is, he will not be in a position to predict what the tax consequences of a proposed transaction will be.

For our purposes, real estate can be classified into four types of holdings. These are the following:

1. Real estate held as a personal residence;
2. Real estate held for the production of income;
3. Real estate held for use in a trade or business;
4. Real estate held for sale to customers.

1. Real Estate Held as a Personal Residence

Real estate held as a personal residence has a number of peculiarities which distinguish it from other types of holdings. Under Section 262 of the Internal Revenue Code,[1] all expenses incurred for personal, living, or family purposes are non-

---

[1] Unless otherwise specified, all references to the Code or to Section numbers, I.R.C. are to Sections of the Internal Revenue Code of 1954 (26 U.S. Code, Sections 1-8023). The Commissioner refers to the Commissioner of Internal Revenue.

deductible. Consequently, expenses of repair, maintenance, and care are non-deductible; similarly, the owner is not permitted to deduct an allowance for depreciation. In the case of sale, any loss incurred is non-deductible; but a gain is taxed as capital gain, short or long term as the case may be.

But certain items of expense may be deductible independently of the personal nature of the holding of the property. Interest paid on a mortgage loan and real property taxes incurred on a home are of themselves deductible, provided the owner forgoes the benefit of the optional standard deduction. And if a loss is caused by theft, storm, or other casualty, the loss will be deductible regardless of the personal nature of the property lost.

Under certain circumstances, the owner of a personal residence is permitted (indeed, required) to defer part or all of the gain realized on its sale if he purchases a new home. The new home must be purchased within the two-year period beginning one year before the date of sale of the old residence and ending one year after the sale. If, however, the new home is to be constructed, construction must be started within eighteen months before or after the sale and completed by two years after the date of sale. If the purchase price of the new residence equals or exceeds the sale price of the old, no gain will be recognized on the sale. If the price of the new is less than the sale price of the old, taxable capital gain will be recognized, but not in excess of the amount of the difference in prices. The basis of the new residence is its cost less any gain not recognized on the sale of the old residence.[2]

Similar benefits also apply where a personal residence has been condemned or otherwise involuntarily converted.[3] In other words, the owner is permitted to postpone gain realized on the "destruction . . . seizure, requisition, or condemnation . . . or the sale of exhange . . . under threat or imminence thereof . . ." if he reinvests the proceeds of the conversion in a new home.[4]

Also, if a taxpayer is 65 or older, he may elect not to be taxed at all on the profit (up to a limit) from the sale of his principal residence.[5] For this purpose, the term "principle residence" is defined as a home owned by the taxpayer and used as his home for at least five of the last eight years. The amount of the gain excluded from taxation is all of the gain, provided the selling price does not exceed $35,000. If the selling price exceeds $35,000, the amount of gain that may be excluded from tax bears the same ratio to the total gain as $35,000 bears to the total sale price. The benefits of this exclusion may be used only once.

2. Property Held for Production of Income

Property held for the production of income includes real estate held for the purpose of capital growth through an increase in real estate prices[6] as well as property

---

[2]Section 1034, I.R.C. The gain can be further reduced by "fixing-up" expenses made within 90 days of sale. I.R.C. Reg. Sec. 1.1034-1(b)(6). The date of sale is the date of the sales contract, unless the sales contract does not close. Rev. Rul. 72-118, 1972-1 C.B. 227.
[3]Section 1034(i), I.R.C., Reg. Sec. 1.1034-1(h). Unless otherwise specified all references to "Reg. Sec." are to the Regulations issued by the Treasury Department under authority vested in it by the Internal Revenue Code and can be found under Title 26 of the Code of Federal Regulations.
[4]Section 1033, I.R.C.
[5]Section 121, I.R.C.
[6]George W. Mitchell, 47 T.C. 120 at 128 (1966), acq. 1967-1 C.B. 2

producing current income but not used in a trade or business. The owner of such property is entitled to deduct all of the expenses of management and conservation of the property.[7] Furthermore, if the property is unimproved, the owner is granted an election between deducting or capitalizing taxes and carrying charges incurred on the property.

The owner of improved investment property (which is not property used in the trade or business) is also permitted to deduct an allowance for depreciation.[8]

Gains and losses realized on the sale or exchange of such property are taxed as capital transactions, short or long term as the case may be. Losses on the sale of such property are allowable as capital losses arising out of a transaction entered into for profit.[9] The owner of such property also has the privilege of utilizing the tax-free exchange provisions of Section 1031.

For the purposes of classification, property is held for the production of income if that is the purpose of its ownership. Merely because the property may not have actually produced any current income in a taxable year will not deprive the owner of a deduction for depreciation.[10] All the owner need do is to establish the fact that he was holding the property for income purposes during the taxable year in which he seeks to deduct an allowance for depreciation.

3. Real Estate Held for Use in a Trade or Business

Real estate held for use in the taxpayer's trade or business receives under the tax laws the most favorable treatment afforded to the various categories of property. The owner is entitled to deduct all of his expenses of care and maintenance, as in the case of investment property, and he is also entitled to deduct an allowance for depreciation, as in the case of income-producing property.

On the sale of trade or business property held for more than twelve months, the owner is entitled to treat his gain or loss as a Section 1231 transaction. Accordingly, if the gains from such transaction exceed the losses, the net gain is taxed as long-term capital gain, subject to possible depreciation recapture under Section 1250. But if the losses exceed the gain, the owner is entitled to deduct the net loss as an ordinary loss.

Because such a loss is incurred in the taxpayer's trade or business, the owner is entitled to treat it as a part of his net operating loss for the purpose of carryover, if the loss is not entirely used up in the year incurred.[11]

4. Real Estate Held for Sale to Customers

Real estate held for sale to customers in the ordinary course of the owner's trade or business is treated similarly to real estate held for investment purposes, except that all

---

[7]Section 212(2), I.R.C., Reg. Sec. 1.212-1(b).
[8]Section 167(a)(2), I.R.C.
[9]Section 165(c), I.R.C.
[10]William C. Horrmann, 17 T.C. 903, 907 (1951), acq. 1952-1 C.B. 2. The term "production of income" under Section 212 is broadly construed to include "not merely income of the taxable year but also income which the taxpayer has realized in a prior taxable year or may realize in subsequent taxable years; and is not confined to recurring income but applies as well to gains from the disposition of property." This broad definition has been held to be applicable under Section 167, and therefore there is no difference between property held for investment and property held for the production of income. George W. Mitchell, 47 T.C. 120 at 128 (1966), acq. 1967-1 C.B. 2.
[11]Section 172(d)(4)(A), I.R.C.

sales are treated as ordinary income, not capital, transactions. Thus, any gain realized is taxed as ordinary income and any loss incurred is deductible as an ordinary loss.

The owner of property held for sale is entitled to deduct all of his expenses incurred on the property, including taxes, interest, repairs, maintenance, and casualty losses. But he is not entitled to deduct an allowance for depreciation unless the property also produces income or is held for the purpose for producing income.[12]

C. PROBLEMS OF CLASSIFICATION OF REAL PROPERTY

One of the basic problems facing anyone who wishes to predict the tax consequences of a proposed transaction in real estate is the problem of determining the nature of the owner's holding of the property. Is the property held for sale to customers? Or is it held for the production of income? Or is it trade or business property?

Probably more judicial blood has been shed over the ramifications of these problems than over any other single problem in tax jurisprudence. For this reason it may be worthwhile to spend a page or two on some of the more difficult problems of classification that have plagued taxpayers, the courts, and the Commissioner.

1. When Is a House a Home?

If a house is used as the owner's personal residence, the owner is not permitted to deduct any of his expenses of maintenance or repair, nor is he permitted to deduct an allowance for depreciation. If he sells his home, he is taxable on the gain as capital gain (unless he qualifies for postponement of the gain under Section 1034); if he realizes a loss, the loss is non-deductible.

But a house can be rented by the owner to others. If it is rented, the house becomes property held for the production of income. As such, the owner is entitled to deduct expenses of maintenance and repair and also to take an allowance for depreciation. On a sale of the property, any gain realized is taxed as capital gain; but if a loss is realized, the loss is allowable as a capital or Section 1231 loss.

Ordinarily, the problem of deciding whether or not a house is held as a home or as income property would not seem difficult. But suppose the owner had originally acquired the house as a home. After living in it for a number of years, he decides to sell the property. He finds, however, that he will incur a substantial loss on its sale. Accordingly, he decides to rent the property for a year before sale. By his action in renting the property, he converts it into property held for the production of income. Is a subsequent loss on its sale deductible in whole or in part?

If the conversion of the residence to income producing (e.g., rental) use was bona fide, and if it was actually so used (rented) prior to sale, a loss may be deductible. However, the amount of the loss deduction is limited to the difference between the sale price and either (1) the value of the house at the time of conversion or (2) cost, whichever is lower.[13] In effect, the owner is allowed a loss deduction only to the extent

---

[12]Camp Wolters Enterprises, Inc., 22 T.C. 737, 754 (1954), aff'd on other grounds, 230 F.2d 555 (5th Cir. 1956), cert. den. 352 U.S. 826. Homann v. Commissioner, 230 F.2d 671 (9th Cir. 1956).
[13]Heiner v. Tindle, 276 U.S. 582 585 (1928) Reg. Sec. 1.165-9(b)(2).

loss was incurred after conversion to income-producing use. Of course, allowable depreciation taken during the period of rental must be deducted from basis for the property at the time of conversion.

Example: Owner buys a home for $50,000. After living in it for for five years, he converts it to rental property. The house has a value of $40,000 at the time of conversion. Two years later, Owner sells the property for $35,000. In this period, he deducted $2,000 of depreciation. How much is his deductible loss?

Sales price received			$35,000
Less adjusted basis			
Original basis	$50,000		
Or value on conversion	$40,000		
Whichever is lower		$40,000	
Less depreciation allowable		2,000	38,000
Loss recognized by taxpayer			$ 3,000

Once a personal residence is converted into income-producing property, the owner is also entitled to deduct an allowance for depreciation. The basis for depreciation is the lesser of the owner's adjusted basis for the property or its value at the time of conversion.[14] Expenses of maintenance and repair are also deductible after the date of conversion.

One of the more difficult problems that arises in regard to homes converted into income-producing property is the determination of the date on which the conversion is actually made. Naturally, if the owner abandons his personal use of the house and immediately rents it to strangers, the house is immediately reclassified from property held for use as a residence to property held for the production of income.

But suppose the owner is not so successful. Suppose he abandons his personal use of the house, but then has trouble in finding a suitable tenant. If he immediately lists the house for *rent*, the date of listing will be date of conversion for the purpose of allowance of deductions for depreciation and for repair and maintenance expenses.[15] If he lists it for *sale*, the Tax Court has held, but the Commissioner disagrees, that the same result obtains: the date of listing is the date of conversion.[16] However, he must show a clear abandonment not only of residential use by him but also of the possibility of such use. For example, the failure to remove furniture and the failure to secure another permanent place of residence were held sufficient to deny deductions for depreciation and caretaking.[17]

For the purpose of deducting a loss on the sale of the property, however, the courts have been more strict. A mere listing of the property for rent after its abandon-

---

[14] Reg. Sec. 1.167(f)-1. Parsons v. United States, 227 F.2d 437 (3rd Cir. 1955).

[15] William C. Horrmann, 17 T.C. 903 (1951) acq. 1952-1 C.B. 2; Mary Laughlin Robinson, 2 T.C. 305 (1943) acq. 1944 C.B. 23.

[16] Hulet P. Smith, 1967 P-H T.C. Memo 67-165 (1967) affirmed per curiam, 22 AFTR 5096 (9th Cir. 1968).; Briley v. United States, 189 F. Supp. 510 (N.D. Ohio, 1960), reversed on another issue, 298 F.2d 161 (6th Cir. 1962).

[17] Charles F. Neave, 17 T.C. 1237, 1243 (1946). Compare Warren Leslie, Sr., 6 T.C. 488, 493 (1946), which denied the deductions on the ground that a mere listing for sale and abandonment of personal use did not convert the property to investment use; Frank A. Newcombe, 54 T.C. 1298 (1970); George W. Mitchell, 47 T.C. 120 (1966), acq. 1967-1 C.B. 2.

ment as a personal residence is not sufficient to convert the property from a residential to a business use.[18] The property must be actually rented for a substantial period prior to sale. If the actual period of rental has been relatively short the Commissioner may refuse to permit deduction of any part of a loss on the sale of the property.[19] Where, however, the house has actually been rented for a respectable period of time, many courts and the Commissioner will permit deduction of any loss incurred on a sale after conversion to rental use.[20]

Why the difference? Theoretically, it is due to the difference in the language of the sections of the Code relating to deductions. Section 212 allows a taxpayer to deduct "all the ordinary and necessary expenses . . . for the management, conservation, or maintenance of property held for the production of income." But Section 165 permits an individual to deduct a loss (other than a trade or business loss or a casualty loss) only if it is incurred "in a(ny) transaction entered into profit. . . ."

While the courts are willing to admit that an abandonment of the residential use of property, followed by its listing for rental, is sufficient to convert the house into property held for the production of income, the same acts are not sufficient to convert a transaction which originally was personal in nature into one entered into for profit.

This distinction is unfair. If property is held for income-producing purposes, this very fact characterizes the transaction as having been converted into a transaction for profit. Whether one purchases new property for rental purposes or converts existing property into real property, his motive is the same; that is, to make a profit.[21]

And because the owner's basis for measuring the loss on a sale is limited to the difference between the sales price and the value of the property on the date of conversion, there is no need for a distinction between the two rules of conversion. Any loss attributable to the owner's holding of the property for personal purposes is automatically eliminated by the write-down of his basis for the business property to its value on the date of the conversion.

2. Quasi-business Use: Office at Home or Vacation Property Rented out Occasionally

There is another problem in classification. Suppose a homeowner has an office in his house? To what extent are his expenses deductible?

First, let's consider the home office. Generally the taxpayer can take no deduction for that portion of his home expenses (e.g., depreciation, maintenance, cleaning, utilities, and repairs) attributable to the business use of his home.[22] Interest, casualty losses and real and personal property taxes are deductible whether business or personal if the taxpayer itemizes.[23] The only two exceptions are (1) if the home office is the taxpayer's principal place of business or (2) if the taxpayer normally meets with

---

[18] William C. Horrmann, 17 T.C. 903 (1951), acq. on another issue, 1952-1 C.B. 2.
[19] Morgan v. Commissioner, 76 F.2d 390 (5th Cir. 1935), cert. den. 296 U.S. 601; Rowena S. Barnum, 19 T.C. 401, 408 (1952).
[20] Leland Hazard, 7 T.C. 372 (1946), acq. 1946-2 C.B.
[21] Section 183.
[22] Section 280(A)(a).
[23] Section 280(A)(b).

customers, patients or clients in his home.[24] In either case, the taxpayer must use the home office premises exclusively for business; any personal use of the same premises will vitiate the deduction for expenses.[25] The amount of the deductible expense, in any event, cannot exceed the amount of gross income attributable to the home office less the allocable proportion of deductions (taxes, interest and casualty losses) allowable whether or not the real estate is used in a trade or business.[26]

Second, the renting out of vacation property does not result in a full deduction of expenses. As in the case of a home office, taxes, interest and casualty losses are fully deductible on vacation property provided the taxpayer itemizes his deductions. The question relates to depreciation, maintenance, repair and utility expenses, deductible only if attributable to a trade or business. The rules are:

(1) If the vacation home is rented out for less than 15 days, the rental income received is excludable from income and no deduction for business expenses is allowed. Taxes, interest and casualty losses are unaffected.[27]

(2) If the taxpayer holds the vacation property primarily for rental to strangers, then he will be entitled to all business deductions on the property. For this purpose, the words "primarily for rent to strangers" mean that the taxpayer's own use (including the use by relatives) be less than 15 days in any one year or, if greater, less than 10 percent of the total days the property is rented to strangers at a fair rental.[28] Even in this case, the taxpayer may suffer a limitation on his deductions if he fails to show a net profit on his vacation property in two out of five years.[29]

(3) But suppose the most normal case: the taxpayer holds the vacation property primarily for his own use, but rents it out as well.[30] What result? The taxpayer must allocate his annual depreciation, maintenance, repair and utility expense between personal and business use on the ratio of daily use for personal and business use during the year.[31] The taxpayer's allocable business expenses are deductible only to the extent of the taxpayer's gross rental income less taxes and interest attributable to the vacation property.[32]

One of the problems met by Section 280A was the co-use of vacation properties by persons otherwise unrelated. As the Senate Committee stated: "In addition, certain arrangements have been devised whereby an individual owner of a condominium unit is entitled to exchange the time set aside for the personal use of his own unit (typically three to six weeks) for the use of a different unit under the same general management at another location."[33]

---

[24] Section 280(A)(c). There is also an exception for a separate or detached building on the taxpayer's home property.

[25] Section 280(A)(d)(2). Examples of disallowed home office expenditures are a taxpayer who uses a den in his home for writing legal briefs or preparing tax returns. Similarily, a teacher who prepares lessons and grades exams at home is out. S. Rept. No. 94-938, 94th Cong. 2nd Sess., p. 147-148.

[26] Section 280(A)(c)(4).

[27] Section 280(A)(g).

[28] Section 280(d),(f)(3).

[29] Section 183.

[30] Personal use, including that of relatives, exceeds 14 days or 10 percent of total days rented to strangers Section 280A(e).

[31] Section 280A(e).

[32] Section 280(A)(c)(4).

[33] S. Rept. 94-938, 94th Cong. 2nd Sess. p. 152.

How will Section 280A affect the character of a vacation home or a home used partially for an office on the sale of the property? If a gain is realized, it will be taxable. Suppose, however, a new vacation property or home with an office is acquired. Partial business use of residential property has been held not to qualify the sale of it as a deductible business loss.[34] It has also been held that a temporary rental of a principal residence is not sufficient to deny the owner of the benefits of Section 1034.[35]

3. When Does Rental Property Constitute a Trade or Business?

Is property held for rental purposes classified as property held for the production of income or is it property held for use in a trade or business?[36] The resolution of this question is important only for one purpose, that of determining the treatment to be afforded to a sale of the property.[37]

For all other purposes the results of classifying rental property as one or the other are the same. Whether the property be held for income or for use in trade or business, the owner is entitled to deduct a reasonable allowance for depreciation and to deduct his expenses of maintenance, interest, taxes, repair, and management.

When the property is sold the question of classification arises. Is the sale to be treated as a capital transaction (property held for the production of income) or as a Section 1231 transaction (property held for use in a trade or business)? In the case of a gain on the sale, the result will ordinarily be the same; the only difference will arise in the case of an owner who has offsetting Section 1231 losses in the same year. Must he apply the gain on the sale to offset the Section 1231 losses, or is he permitted to report the gain as a capital gain while deducting the Section 1231 losses against ordinary income?

Example: Owner purchases a small apartment consisting of four rental units. The property cost him $40,000, but after 10 years of rental, its basis is reduced to $20,000. Owner then sells the apartment for $30,000, realizing a $20,000 gain. In the same year, he has reported the sale of two meat coolers used in his business for more than six months at a loss of $5,000. What result?

	Apartment Held As Income Producing	*Apartment Held for Use in Business*
Capital Gain	$10,000	$10,000
Section 1231 Gain		
Section 1231 Loss	(5,000)	(5,000)
Net Section 1231 Gain or Loss	$(5,000)	$ 5,000

Obviously, Owner is better off if he can classify the apartment as an income-producing asset. In that event, he is entitled to deduct the net Section 1231 loss of $5,000 as an ordinary loss while reporting the $10,000 gain on the apartment as a capital gain. But if

---

[34] Russell T. Smith, 1972, P-H T.C. Memo ¶72,046.
[35] Ralph L. Trisco, 29, T.C. 515 (1957), acq. 1959-1 C.B. 5; Arthur R. Barry, 1971 P-H T.C. Memo ¶ 71,179; Rev. Rul. 59-72, 1959-1 C.B. 203. Compare H.V. Watkins, T.C. Memo, 1973-167 (1973).
[36] Russell T. Smith, 1972 P-H Memo T.C. ¶72,046.
[37] Ralph L. Trisco, 29 T.C. 515 (1957), acq. 1959-1 C.B. 5; Arthur R. Barry 1971 P-H Memo T.C.; Rev. Rul. 59-72, 1959-1 C.B. 203. Compare H.V. Watkins, 1973 P-H Memo T.C. ¶73,167, in which it was held that a loss was deductible on an inherited house even though the owner had lived in it for four months.

PROBLEMS OF CLASSIFICATION OF REAL PROPERTY 31

the property is held for use in his trade or business, he must offset the $10,000 gain by the $5,000 loss, leaving a net gain of $5,000 to report.

The difference in classification becomes even more important if the sale of the apartment is at a loss. If the loss is incurred on the sale of property held for the production of income, the loss would be subject to the limitations of the capital loss provisions of the Code. But if it is incurred on the sale of trade or business property, it would qualify for treatment under Section 1231.

And if the loss is incurred on the sale of trade or business property, it also qualifies for the benefits of the net operating loss carryover provisions of Section 172.[38] But if the loss in incurred on property held for the production of income, the loss would qualify for carryover only under the capital loss provisions of Section 1212.[39]

These problems have been analyzed by the courts in terms of the owner's activities in renting the property. Are these activities sufficient in themselves to constitute a trade or business? Or are they merely incidental and sporadic acts associated with a taxpayer's investment activities?

Both the courts and the Commissioner agree that any owner who devotes a substantial portion of his time to the management of a number of rental units is engaged in a trade or business within the meaning of the Code.[40] Hence, his losses on sales are Section 1231 losses, for which he is entitled to the benefits of the net operating loss carryover.

But suppose the owner rents out only one unit. Are his rental activities sufficient to constitute a trade or business? The Tax Court[41] and the Commissioner[42] think that one rental unit is sufficient to constitute a trade or business.

But the logic of this position seems questionable. To equate the rental of one unit to a trade or business is to deny that rental property can ever be held for merely the production of investment income. And this equation is obviously a fallacy. The purchase of rental units for investment is fully as common as the purchase of common stocks or other intangible securities. Consequently, not all courts have followed the lead of the Tax Court. In more than one case, it has been held that the ownership of only one apartment unit does not in itself constitute a trade or business.[43]

There is no conflict if the property rented is unimproved. In this case, the rental activities of the owner are not sufficient to constitute a trade or business.[44]

What is the status of property held for rental on a "net-net" lease? Ordinarily, leases of this type provide that the lessee is to maintain the property, pay taxes, pay mortgage principal and interest directly to the mortgagee, and in effect discharge all of

---

[38] Adolph Schwarcz, 24 T.C. 733, 739; Reiner v. United States 222 F.2d 770,772 (7th Cir. 1955).

[39] Grier v. United States 120 F.Supp. 395, 398 (D. Conn. 1954), aff'd per curiam, 218 F.2d 603 (2d Cir. 1955).

[40] Gilford v. Commissioner, 201 F.2d 735, 736 (2d Cir. 1953); Maloney v. Spencer, 172 F.2d 638, 640 (9th Cir. 1949); Fackler v. Commissioner, 133 F.2d 509 (6th Cir. 1943); I.T. 3711, 1945 C.B. 162, 164.

[41] Anders I. Lagreide, 23 T.C. 508 (1954). It has been held that a loss on the sale of a residence converted into rental property is a Section 1231 loss. Stephen T. Wasnok, P-H Memo T.C. ¶71,906 (1971).

[42] Acq. to Leland Hazard, 7 T.C. 372 (1946), published in 1946-2 C.B. 3.

[43] Grier v. United States, 120 F.Supp. 395, 398 (D.Conn. 1954), aff'd per curiam, 218 F.2d 603 (2d Cir. 1955); Cole v. United States, 141 F.Supp. 558 (D.Wyo. 1956); Rylander v. United States ¶72,881 P-H Fed. 1956 (D Cal. 1956); Martin v. United States, 119 F.Supp. 468 (D.Ga. 1954).

[44] Susan P. Emery, 17 T.C. 308, 311 (1951).

the obligations of owner during the term of the lease. The only relationship that the lessor has to the property is to deposit his net rental checks as he receives them and to assume the risk of loss in the case of condemnation or physical damage. He also has the right of reversion. Under these circumstances, are his activities with respect to the property sufficient to characterize him as being engaged in a "trade or business"? Arguably not. If an owner of real estate is engaged in a trade or business only because of his extensive activities in managing the property, then it would follow that an owner who shifts these responsibilities of management to his lessee has lost his position as being engaged in a trade or business.[45] The owner of property leased on a "net-net" basis *may* therefore be treated as an investor in real estate held for the production of income. While he would be entitled to depreciation and all other expenses, gains and losses on his sales would be capital, not Section 1231, gains and losses.

4. When Is an Investor a Dealer?

Where the owner of property holds it "primarily for sale to customers in the ordinary course of his trade or business,"[46] he is said to be a "dealer" in such property. On the other hand, a person who holds property primarily as an investment for the production of income or for use in his trade or business is termed an "investor."

The basic difference in tax treatment between a dealer and an investor in real estate is the treatment of sales. The sales of a dealer are ordinary transactions, giving rise to capital gain or loss or Section 1231 gain or loss. An investor has another important advantage over a dealer; he can use the benefits of the tax-free exchange provisions of the Code, which are expressly denied to a dealer.

There are other collateral differences between the status of a dealer and an investor. A dealer is permitted to deduct as ordinary business expenses all of his expenses of sale; hence these expenses are deductible in the year when paid or incurred, regardless of the method of reporting the sale which he uses. But an investor is not permitted to deduct the expenses of sale as a business expense; these expenses must be used to offset the sales price received for the property. Accordingly, if the transaction is reported as an installment sale, these expenses are recoverable only on a *pro rata* basis over the life of the installment contract.

For these reasons it is important to determine whether a particular owner of real estate is a dealer or an investor. And this determination is not always easy. The problems lie not so much in the case of a real estate dealer who holds himself out as such,[47] as in the case of an investor who engages so heavily in real estate transactions that he may become a dealer without being fully aware of his changed status. The

---

[45] See, for example, Bauer v. United States, 144 Ct. Cl. 308, 168 F. Supp. 539 (Ct. Cl. 1958) and Grier v. United States, 120 F. Supp. 395 (D.C.Conn. 1954), aff'd per curiam, 218 F.2d 603 (2d Cir. 1955). Union National Bank of Troy v. United States, 195 F. Supp. 382, 384 (N.D.N.Y., 1961). It is interesting to note that the Commissioner does *not* appeal his losses in this area. He may be lying in wait for an unsuspecting net lease landlord who tries to take a Section 1231 loss. But he may have more to lose under Sections 163(d)(4) and 543(a)(3) than he has to gain.

[46] Section 1221(1), I.R.C. "Primarily" means "of first importance" or "principally." Malat v. Riddell, 383 U.S. 569 (1966).

[47] White v. Commissioner, 172 F.2d 629 (5th Cir. 1949).

frequency of sales and other transactions in real estate may in itself be sufficient to characterize an investor in real estate as a dealer for tax purposes.[48]

The frequency of sales is not necessarily conclusive. If the frequency of sales is traceable to some circumstances beyond the control of the owner, then the investor may retain his investment status. For example, the frequency of sales may be due to the necessity of liquidating extensive holdings in real estate.[49] Thus, it is necessary to consider all the factors that may be present in a given situation before a determination can be made. Among the factors that should be taken into account are the following:

Status as Dealer	*Status as Investor*
Frequent sales	Occasional sales
Sales for purpose of realizing appreciation	Sale for purpose of liquidation of investment
Reinvestment of sales proceeds in new real estate	No reinvestment in real estate
Sales after subdivision and improvement	Sale of property without improvements added by seller to enhance value
Listing and advertising of property for sale	Purchaser sought out seller
Property not actually used in owner's trade or business	Property formerly used in owner's trade or business
Owner's major source of income from sales	Gain on sale a minor item of owner's total income
Property not income-producing	Substantial rentals received from property
Originally purchased for resale	Originally acquired for rental or income purposes

In this area, each case turns on its own facts. The investor must carefully limit and protect each sale transaction so that he does not build a record of frequent sales, fast turnover, and immediate reinvestment in saleable properties against himself. Each sale should be explainable in terms of economic need, failure of contemplated project, or some other reason not related to a simple desire to buy and sell real estate at a profit.

5. Can a Dealer Hold Real Estate for Investment? Principal Purpose Test:

Ordinarily any sale of real estate by a dealer is a sale of property held for sale to customers in the ordinary course of business,[50] and is thus an ordinary-income transaction.

Nevertheless, it is possible, but difficult, for a dealer to sell some real estate on which he will be entitled to tax treatment as an investor. The sale, in order to be classified as a sale of investment property, must be a sale other than in the ordinary

---

[48]Ehrman v. Commissioner, 120 F.2d 607, 610 (9th Cir. 1941), cert. den. 314 U.S. 668.

[49]McGah v. Commissioner, 210 F.2d 769, 771 (9th Cir. 1954); Garrett v. United States, 120 F.Supp. 193 (Ct.Cl. 1954). U.S. v. Winthrop, 417 F.2d 905 (5th Cir. 1969).

[50]Jones v. Commissioner, 209 F.2d 415 (9th Cir. 1954); Robert K. Fronk, par.57,240 P-H Memo T.C. (1957), aff'd per curiam 265 F.2d 930 (6th Cir. 1959).

course of the seller's sales business. One example is the sale by a real estate dealer of his own home. On such a sale he would be entitled to report his gain as qualified for capital gain treatment.[51]

The answer depends upon the *primary purpose* for which the dealer acquired and held the property. For example, if the principal purpose of a dealer in acquiring property is to develop it for apartment use, then his later sale of the property, because of the frustration of the plan for development, gave rise to capital gain, notwithstanding the fact that the land was subdivided and the dealer had a secondary purpose of selling the property if that should be more profitable.[52] Similarly, if a real estate dealer sells property that has been extensively used in his trade or business before sale, he is entitled to the benefits of being treated as an investor on that particular property. The typical situation here is that of a dealer who sells rental units which he had purchased and rented for income for a substantial time prior to sale.[53]

Thus, it appears that the mere fact that a taxpayer is an admitted dealer with respect to certain property does not necessarily prove him to be a dealer with respect to the property sold. Accordingly, we can conclude that a dealer can segregate certain of his real estate acquisitions from property held for sale for the purpose of characterizing the segregated real estate as property held for investment or for use in a trade or business. Thus, property acquired by a dealer for use in his rental trade or business will qualify for section 1231 gain or loss.[54] Similarly, unimproved property acquired for long term investment purposes can be held by a dealer and give rise to capital gain or loss, despite the fact that the property does not produce current income.[55]

The test is simple: what is the primary purpose for the holding of the property? If it is for sale, the result is ordinary income. If it is for rental, the result is capital gain. If it is for investment, the result is based on facts and circumstances.[56]

---

[51]Walter R. Crabtree, 20 T.C. 841, 848 (1953), acq.1954-1 C.B. 4.
[52]Malat v. Riddell, 383 U.S. 569 (1966). Maddux Const. Co., 54 T.C. 1278 (1970); William B. Howell, 57 T.C. 546 (1972); Casalina Corp., 60 T.C. No. 72 (1973).
[53]Smith v. Commissioner, 232 F.2d 142 (5th Cir. 1956); Heller Trust v. Commissioner, 382 F.2d 675 (9th Cir. 1967).
[55]Charles E. Meig. 32 T.C. 1314 (1959), acq. 1960-2 C.B. 6. Scheuber v. Commissioner, 371 F.2d 996 (7th Cir., 1967). In the latter case, the court emphasized that the gain from the sale of an unimproved tract held by a licensed dealer for eight years was much more substantial than his ordinary profits in his real estate business; for this, and other reasons, the gain was not part of his ordinary business income.
[56]William I. Nash, 60 T.C. 503 (1973). Morris Cohen, 39 T.C. 886 (1963), acq. 1965-1 C.B. 4.

2
How to Acquire Real Property

This chapter deals with the problems of handling the acquisition of real property. The emphasis, as in all chapters of this book, is upon the tax consequences that flow from the various types of acquisition. Accordingly, the chapter is divided into six main parts, as follows:

A. *How Should Title be Taken?*
B. *Tax Basis of Property upon Acquisition;*
C. *Allocation of Tax Basis upon Acquisition;*
D. *Purchase under Option;*
E. *Purchase for Bargain Price;*
F. *Apportionment of Real Estate Taxes on Acquisition.*

A. HOW SHOULD TITLE BE TAKEN?

One of the most important problems facing a taxpayer who plans to acquire real property is the form of ownership in which he should take title. In making this determination, he may find that the tax consequences of the various forms of ownership will have an important bearing. For this reason, we find it necessary to analyze the various forms of ownership and their tax effects.

Obviously, if the owner is an existing corporation, partnership, or trust, the problem will solve itself. The form of ownership will be dictated by the form of the business entity. An exception to this conclusion would, of course, arise in the case of a joint or common ownership of land with another business entity.

But in the case of an individual, several alternative forms of ownership are available. If the taxpayer is unmarried, he may select between the individual or corporate form of ownership. If married, his choice of ownership is broadened. Should he take title solely in his own name? Or in the name of himself and his wife as joint tenants? Or as tenants in common? Or by the entireties? Or as community property? Or should he and his wife incorporate the ownership of the property?

And suppose an individual plans to own property with another person. Should they use the partnership form of ownership? Or should they hold the property as tenants in common? Or as joint tenants? Or should they incorporate?

1. Individual Ownership

If an individual holds title to trade or business property or to property held for the production of income, he must report all of the gross income in his individual tax return for the year in which the income is received or accrued; correspondingly, he is entitled to deduct all of the expenses on the property, including an allowance for depreciation, in the year paid or incurred.

As a result the net income from the property is taxed to the owner at his personal rate of taxation on ordinary income. The net income will be taxed to him in the year received or accrued even though it all may have been reinvested in the property by expenditure for improvements or by payments to reduce a mortgage indebtedness. The only shelter available to him against the incidence of the income tax is the annual allowance for depreciation on the property.

Similarly, if the property yields a net loss for tax purposes, the amount of the loss is deductible by the taxpayer on his personal income tax return, normally as a loss from a trade or business.

2. Corporate Ownership

But an individual who transfers the property to a corporation will find that this tax picture is changed considerably. The corporation will report the gross income from the property as its own. Correspondingly, the corporation will be entitled to take all of the deductions for expenses, including depreciation, paid or incurred on the property. Thus, the net income realized on the property will be taxed at corporate income tax rates. As in the case of an individual, all of the net income will be taxed whether or not it is reinvested in the property.

Thus, the question of the advisability of the corporate or individual form of ownership appears to be one of choosing between the respective tax rates imposed upon net income of an individual as compared with the corporate rate. The corporate rate is 20 percent of the first $25,000 of net income, 22 percent on the next $25,000 and 48 percent on all net income in excess of $50,000. The individual rate increases from 14 percent on the first $500 of taxable income to a maximum of 70 percent on income over $100,000.

But the simple comparison of rates is far from the full picture. If the income is earned by an individual, he free to use the income after taxes for whatever purpose he desires. On the other hand, income earned by a corporation can be used only for corporate purposes; if it is used for the personal benefit of a stockholder, the amount so used will be taxed to him as a dividend received. The amount of the dividend will be included in the stockholder's ordinary income in the year received, subject to a small dividends-received deduction.

Obviously, then, if the owner of the property needs the income for current living or personal expenses, he will be much better off taking title in his own name. In this manner, he will escape a double tax on the income: a first tax at the corporate level and a second tax at the individual level.

If the owner is willing to permit the corporation to accumulate net income from the property, he may find the corporate form less expensive taxwise. But the accumulation of income by a corporation involves in itself many problems (these will be considered in a separate chapter). And even if the accumulation of earnings is proper, the owner can enjoy the benefit of the earnings only by borrowing on his stock.[1] If he attempts to distribute out the earnings, he will be taxed on the receipt of a dividend, unless the distribution is in liquidation of the corporation.

On liquidation, or on sale of the stock, the owner will be faced with at least the imposition of a capital gains tax on the amount received in excess of his basis for the stock.

Reference is made to Chapter 10 for a more detailed discussion of these and other problems.

3. Comparison of Corporate and Individual Ownership

For purposes of comparing the advantages of individual ownership of real property as against corporate ownership, the following schedule may be useful (1968-69 "temporary" surcharge not included):

Factor of Comparison	Individual Ownership	Corporate Ownership
Tax rates on current income: (Individual rates computed on basis of separate return: on joint return brackets would be doubled)	14% on first $500 15% on next 500 16% " " 500 17% " " 500 19% " " 500 22% " " 2,000 25% " " 2,000 28% " " 2,000 32% " " 2,000 36% " " 2,000 39% " " 2,000 42% " " 2,000 45% " " 2,000 50% " " 4,000 Maximum rate on earned income above $26,000, rate rises from 53% to 70% on excess over $100,000	20% on first $25,000 22% on next $25,000 Above $50,000, rate is 48%
Other income earned by individual	Added to income from property	Not added
Depreciation deduction	Taken by individual	Taken by corporation

---

[1] Obviously, if the corporation pays off any part of such a borrowing, the payments will be taxed as dividends to the shareholder. Siphoning out earnings by means of fictitous "loans" from the corporation to its shareholder will also be treated as the payment of dividends, taxable to the shareholder.

Factor of Comparison	Individual Ownership	Corporate Ownership
Use of moneys for personal purposes of individual	No further tax liability	Dividend, taxed as ordinary income to individual
Sale of property	Section 1231 gain or loss available	Section 1231 gain or loss available, unless in liquidation
Use of sale proceeds by individual	No further tax liability	Dividend, or liquidation distribution giving rise to capital gain or loss
Net current losses from property	Can be offset against other individual income	Can be offset only against corporate income
Deduction of loss on sale of property	Section 1231 loss available	Section 1231 loss available; if loss on liquidation, captial loss to individual
Additional penalty taxes	None	Personal holding company tax; Surtax on excessive accumulations
Accumulated earnings credit	Unlimited	$150,000
Death of individual	Basis for property adjusted to value	Basis for property not adjusted; only basis for stock adjusted to value

While corporate and individual rates on ordinary income have not been changed, at least two significant changes have been made which should be taken into consideration in choosing between the corporate or individual form of ownership. These changes include the following:

(1) Fifty percent maximum on earned income.
(2) Tax preference items.

(1) *Fifty Percent Maximum Rate on Earned Income*: The maximum *marginal* tax rate to be applied to an individual's earned income cannot exceed 50 percent.[2] For this purpose, earned income generally includes wages, salaries, professional fees, and other compensation for personal services. If a taxpayer is engaged in a business in which both capital and services contribute to earnings, then a reasonable amount may be attributed to services, but not in excess of 30 percent of the total earnings. Pensions, annuity payments, and profit-sharing plan distributions are not considered to be earned income.

The provision will be of no help to real estate developers and subdividers because their income is derived from dealing in real property; it consists of gains realized on the turnover of their capital investment in real estate and not from services rendered. Hence, the use of the corporate form of ownership of such businesses is likely to continue to be favored. The individual rates set forth in the table will be fully effective to such taxpayers to the extent their income is derived from capital.

---

[2]Section 1348, I.R.C.

On the other hand, this limitation on high tax rates should be helpful to Realtors provided they are careful to segregate their investment activities from their commissions and other earnings derived from personal services. Other professional persons, such as lawyers and accountants who participate in real estate transactions, should also benefit from this limitation.

(2) *Tax Preference Income*: A flat 15 percent tax is levied on a taxpayer's tax preference income to the extent it exceeds $10,000 or one-half the normal income tax, whichever is greater.[3] The provision applies to both individuals and corporations.

In the case of real estate ownership, the most important of the tax preference items are one-half of capital gains and the excess of accelerated depreciation over straight line depreciation. But, because these items are to be added to other tax preference items in order to see if the minimum has been exceeded, a listing of them all is necessary, as follows:

a. Excess of accelerated depreciation on real property over straight line depreciation;

b. In the case of personal property, only if leased on a net basis, the excess of accelerated depreciation over straight line depreciation;

c. Excess of amortization of rehabilitation expenditures in excess of straight line depreciation;

d. Excess of amortization of certain pollution control facilities and railroad rolling stock over accelerated depreciation;

e. In the case of qualified stock options, the excess of the fair market value of the stock at the time of the exercise of the option over the option price;

f. Certain bad debt deductions of financial institutions;

g. Depletion deductions to the extent they exceed the cost or other basis of the mineral or oil producing property;

h. Capital gains; in the case of an individual one-half of the gain; in the case of a corporation 18/48's of the gain.

i. Excess of certain itemized deductions over 60 percent of adjusted gross income.

j. Intangible drilling costs on productive properties in excess of 10 years amortization.

What effect will these provisions have on real estate investment? Obviously, they will lessen the tax advantage of real estate as a tax shelter to taxpayers enjoying substantial incomes from other sources. But the smaller investor will still be able to utilize accelerated depreciation losses against other income without penalty so long as the tax preference income limitation is not exceeded. In the case of a taxpayer who uses depreciation write-off to reduce his taxable income to zero, the limitation will be a flat $10,000.

Example: Owner has $70,000 of taxable income from his medical practice. O owns an apartment building which, if depreciated on a straight line method, would throw off $35,000 of depreciation. O elects to use an accelerated method of depreciation and takes a 1977 depreciation deduction of $70,000. This deduction reduces his taxable income to zero. Even if we assume O

---

[3]Sections 56, 57 and 58, I.R.C.

has no other tax preference income (such as capital gains), he will be required to pay a tax of 15 percent on $25,000 or $3,750.

Why? His tax preference income is $35,000, which is the amount by which his deduction for accelerated depreciation of $70,000 exceeded the normal straight line depreciation on the property. But tax preference income is taxed only to the extent it exceeds $10,000. Here the normal tax was zero. Hence, the tax privilege income ceiling is the base $10,000. To the extent that the excess of accelerated depreciation over straight line depreciation ($35,000) exceeds the ceiling ($10,000), O has realized a "tax privilege" of $25,000, subject to a minimum tax of 15 percent, or $3,750.

What would happen if O in the preceding example had other tax privileged income?

Example: Suppose O also had sold a parcel of real estate in 1977 and had realized a capital gain of $100,000 on it. What result? One-half of the capital gain of $50,000 would be a second item of tax privileged income. Thus, the total tax privileged income would be $75,000 ($25,000 from the preceding example and $50,000 from this example).

But now the ceiling on tax privileged income has changed. If we assume that O paid a federal income tax of $13,000 on the capital gain (assuming a joint return and appropriate exemptions), then the ceiling is $13,000. Thus the taxable portion of the tax privileged income is the excess over $13,000 or $62,000. Thus, O would have to pay a minimum tax of $9,300.

Because of this minimum tax on tax privileged income, it will be impossible in the future for high income taxpayers to eliminate completely their income from tax.

What is the effect of this minimum tax on the form of ownership? The minimum tax on priveleged income applies equally to both individuals and corporations. On the surface, therefore, it should have no effect.

But we have also seen that, all other things being equal, individual ownership is preferable to corporate ownership. Why? Simply because income earned and taxed at the individual level can be enjoyed for personal purposes without any further tax. Income earned and taxed at the corporate level can be used only for the reasonable needs of the corporate business, or it becomes subject to a second tax. If it is retained at the corporate level without a proper business justification, it may be subject to certain penalty taxes. If it is used for the personal purposes of the shareholders, it becomes a dividend to them, taxable at ordinary income tax rates.

Because the minimum tax on tax privileged items is levied at the same rate on individuals and corporations, individual ownership would generally be more favorable under our principles of comparison. The corporate exemption is the greater of $10,000 or its normal tax.

One exception becomes readily apparent. Each taxpayer has his own exemption of $10,000 from the minimum tax. If two or more exemptions become of value to a taxpayer, the use of corporate ownership in conjunction with individual ownership may be worthwhile.

4. Husband and Wife Ownership

Ordinarily, it makes little difference from the standpoint of the federal income tax whether husband and wife own property in the name of the husband alone, in the name of both husband and wife as joint tenants, tenants by the entireties, tenants in common, or as community property. The net income realized from property may be split between the husband and wife in any case through the mechanics of a joint return; the form of ownership does not affect this right to the splitting of income.

5. Husband and Wife: Estate and Gift Taxes

But the federal estate and gift taxes may affect the form of ownership to be chosen. If the property is acquired by one spouse from his own funds, the creation of a tenancy in common (or the transfer into community property) is treated as a taxable gift of one-half of the property. The tax incidence at the time of the gift may be lessened by the availability of the marital deduction.

But if the property is retained in the sole name of the spouse who paid for it, the gift tax liability would be completely eliminated.

What if the property is taken by husband and wife as joint tenants? Under the Code, the transfer of real property into the names of the husband and wife as joint tenants (or as tenants by the entireties) will escape gift tax liability at the time the tenancy is created, provided the following conditions are present:[4]

1. The tenancy is created in real property;
2. The tenancy is between husband and wife;
3. The right of survivorship is given the surviving spouse; and
4. The creation of the tenancy is not reported as a taxable gift.

Under these circumstances the law gives the donor spouse the election to decide whether or not he wishes to treat the creation of the tenancy as a taxable gift; if he fails to file a timely gift tax return that reports the gift, he is deemed to have elected to treat the creation of the tenancy as non-taxable.[5]

In the event that the joint tenancy so created is severed during the lifetime of the spouses and no gift tax had been paid on its creation, the severance itself may be treated as a taxable gift. To the extent that the donee spouse receives an interest in excess of her proportionate share of the property as measured by the percentage of her original contribution to the original cost of the property, she will be the recipient of a taxable gift. The amount of the gift is measured by values on the date of termination, not on the date of creation.

What if the joint tenancy is terminated by death? The entire property, less the proportionate share attributable to the surviving spouse's original contribution, will be included in the deceased spouse's estate for federal estate tax purposes. If the creation of the joint tenancy were reported as a taxable gift only one-half the value thereof will be included in the estate of the first spouse to die.

6. Husband and Wife: Basis after Death

Basis after death is generally its adjusted cost to the decedent. It is the carryover basis of the decedent. His heirs take over the property at his adjusted cost or other basis

---

[4]Section 2515, I.R.C.
[5]Reg. Sec. 20.2515-2

on the date of death. Any appreciation in value will be taxed to their heirs at such time as they make a taxable disposition of the property.

There are several exceptions to this general rule. If the property were acquired by the decedent prior to January 1, 1977, then his estate or heirs is entitled to add to the decedent's carryover basis a pro-rata portion of the increase in value at the time of death over his adjusted cost. The pro-ration of the appreciation is measured by the ratio of the number of days the property was held by the decedent prior to January 1, 1977 to the total number of days it was held by him. For example, if the decedent acquired the property 900 days before January 1, 1977, and his estate sold the property 300 days thereafter, his estate could add 900/1,200 or ¾ of any excess of the date of death value to the decedent's carryover basis for the purpose of determining the gain or loss to the estate. This exception only applies to sales; no similar basis adjustment is available to the estate for measuring depreciation.[6]

A second exception is to allow an increase of the carryover basis by $60,000 for the purpose of eliminating gains on sales by the estate or heirs. Also up to $10,000 of household goods and personal effects may be sold without the recognition of gain.

Finally, the federal and state estate taxes attributable to the *appreciation in value* is an addition to the decedent's carryover basis. State death taxes paid by the transferee or heir may also be an addition to basis.[7]

7. Husband and Wife: Termination of Joint Tenancy

Because of the disadvantages inherent in joint tenancy ownership of depreciable real property, the spouses may wish to terminate the joint tenancy by converting it into a tenancy in common. If the creation of the joint tenancy was reported as a gift, this conversion may be made without gift tax liability. But if the spouses elected not to report the creation of the joint tenancy as a gift, the conversion into the tenancy in common will be treated as a taxable gift. Suppose, then, the donor spouse dies within three years of the conversion; will the conversion be treated as a gift in contemplation of death, and so, includable in the donor's estate?

Under the 1939 Code the conversion was held not to be a gift in contemplation of death because it was not a gift; it was considered to be an exchange of a vested one-half interest in joint tenancy property for a vested one-half interest in tenancy in common property. Thus, the exchange was supported by a full and adequate consideration that removed it from the category of gifts.[8]

The regulations under the Code make no reference to this problem.[9] Obviously, if the parties to the joint tenancy had reported the original creation of the tenancy as a

---

[6]Section 1023(h).
[7]Section 1023(c), (d), (e). See discussion at Part B, 3 of this Chapter.
[8]Sullivan's Estate v. Commissioner, 175 F.2d 657 (9th Cir. 1949); United States v. Heasty, 370 F.2d 525 (10th Cir. 1966); Glaser v. United States, 306 F.2d 57 (7th Cir. 1962); Estate of D.M. Brockway, 18 T.C. 488, 498 (1952), non-acq. 1962-1 C.B. 4(acq.1955-2 C.B. 4 withdrawn), aff'd on other grounds, 219 F.2d 400 (9th Cir. 1954); Estate of A. Carl Borner, 25 T.C. 584 (1955) non-acq. 1962-1 C.B. 4. The Commissioner's published non-acquiescences to the Tax Court decisions indicate he will not follow these precedents.
[9]Reg. Sec. 20.2040-1. Significantly, the proposed regualtions contained a subsection (d) which stated that a joint tenancy termination could not be treated as a gift in contemplation of death because it was an exchange. This subsection was dropped from the final regulation.

taxable gift, their position should be no different under the present Code from what it was under the 1939 Code. The conversion of the joint tenancy into a tenancy in common would not constitute a taxable gift; hence the conversion should not be treated as a gift in contemplation of death even if it is made within the statutory period.

But suppose that the parties had failed to treat the creation of the joint tenancy as a taxable gift. In that event, the gift would be reportable for gift tax purposes at the time the tenancy is terminated and the donee spouse receives an interest in excess of her original contribution. If the donee spouse made no contribution, the conversion would result in the transfer of a gift of one-half of the value of the property at the time of conversion.

Because the conversion constitutes a taxable gift, it has been held that the conversion under these circumstances constitutes a gift in contemplation of death if made within the three-year period. Thus the total value of the property would fall in the donor spouse's estate just as if title had been retained in joint tenancy to the date of death.[10]

8. Husband and Wife: Comparison of Ownership

For the purpose of comparing the several modes of property ownership, we can best illustrate the tax consequences by an example. Suppose Husband purchases an apartment for $100,000. His wife makes no contribution to its purchase price. He receives an annual net income from the property of $5,000, which is reported on a joint return with his wife. After holding the property for five years, Husband dies. In the five-year period let us assume that he took $15,000 of depreciation. On his death the property is valued at $95,000. The property passes on his death to his wife. What are the respective tax consequences?

	In Husband's Sole Name	As Tenants In Common	As Joint Tenants	As Community Property
Gift to W on purchase	None	$50,000	None*	None**
H's annual income	$ 2,500***	2,500	$ 2,500	2,500
W's annual income	2,500***	2,500	2,500	2,500
H's gross estate	95,000	47,500	95,000****	47,500
W's basis for H's share after death	85,000	42,500	85,000	42,500
W's basis for her own share	None	42,500	None	42,500
W's basis for total after death	85,000	85,000	85,000	42,500

*H has an election whether or not to report a taxable gift of 50,000 to W.
**If purchased with community funds (e.g. H's earnings after marriage). $50,000 gift if purchased with H's separate funds.
***Only if H files jointly with W.
****W made no original contribution.

---

[10] Harris v. United States, 193 F.Supp. 736 (D.Neb. 1961). But see Glaser v. United States, 306 Fed.2d 57 (7th Cir. 1962).

The effect of the 1976 amendments to the basis provisions on property transferred at death (or by way of gift) has been to eliminate much of the differences in form of ownership. Reference is made to prior editions of this book for purposes of comparison.

9. Tenancy in Common

Each tenant in common is entitled to report his proportionate part of the gross income from the property less his proportionate part of the deductible expenses paid or incurred. Even if he pays a larger share of the total expenses, he is entitled to deduct only his proportionate share of the expenses as measured by his interest in the property.[11] The payment in excess of his proportionate share is treated as an advance to his co-owners.

Similarly, gain or loss incurred on the sale or other disposition of the property is allocated among the co-owners in proportion to their interests in the property. Absent proof of actual ownership to the contrary, the proportionate share attributed to each owner will be governed by their respective interests in legal title to the property.[12]

10. Joint Tenancy

Each joint tenant is required to report his proportionate share of the gross income from the property as measured by his interest in the property.[13] However, he is permitted to report so much of the deductible expenses as he actually pays. If one of his joint tenants pays the expense in full, the deduction for the expense is allowable only to the joint tenant who pays it.[14]

The reason for this difference in treatment between joint tenants and tenants in common is found in the nature of the liability of each; each joint tenant is liable personally for the whole of the expense incurred on the property. But a tenant in common is personally liable only for his proportionate share of the expense.[15]

Gain or loss on the sale or other disposition of the property is allocated among the joint tenants in proportion to their respective interests in the property. Ordinarily, they are presumed to have equal undivided interests, and the gain or loss is, therefore, divided equally among themselves.[16]

11. Partnership Form of Ownership

Suppose the owners of a parcel of property decide to contribute the property to a partnership. What will be the tax consequences of the partnership form of ownership?

The partnership itself is not a taxpaying entity; it is merely an income-reporting entity which is not itself subject to tax.[17] For this reason, no additional tax liability is

---

[11] Estate of Eugene Merrick Webb, 30 T.C. 1202 (1958).
[12] Allen v. Beazley, 157 F.2d 970, 973 (5th Cir. 1946).
[13] Frederick J. Haynes, 7 B.T.A. 465 (1927) acq. VII-1 C.B. 14; [but if local law allocates all the income to H, this rule will be followed for federal purposes].
[14] I.T. 3785, 1946-1 C.B. 98, 99.
[15] Rev. Rul. 71-268, 1971-1 C.B. 58.
[16] I.T. 3754, 1945 C.B. 143, 14+ . James R. Bass.
[17] Section 701, I.R.C.

incurred on current income than would be the case if the property were owned directly by the individual partners.

All the income and deductions on the property, including depreciation, will be attributed to the partners for inclusion in their respective individual tax returns.[18] Except for a number of specially-enumerated deductions, the partnership is entitled to net its deductions against its gross income; each partner need report only his proportionate share of partnership net income, together with his share of the specially-stated items of deduction. These items of net income and deductions are reportable by the partners as if they had been realized by themselves personally.[19]

But despite the apparent simplicity of the partnership form of ownership, we must remember that the partnership constitutes an additional business entity which lies between the partners and the property. And the interposition of this extra entity by itself can give rise to a number of complicating factors and disadvantages. For example, it is the partnership, not the partners, which owns the property. Therefore, if one of the partners dies, only his partnership interest, not the property, will be taxed in his estate; consequently, only his partnership interest, not the property itself, will receive a basis adjustment equal to value.[20] Because only the property, not the partnership interest, is depreciable, the beneficiary of the partner's estate may find that he will not be entitled to the larger allowance for depreciation that he would have received had the property itself been owned directly by the partners, including his decedent, as tenants in common.

And other differences exist. For example, the property may be a capital asset in the hands of the partners but an ordinary asset in the hands of the partnership. Or the allowance for depreciation may be allocated among the partners in proportion to their interests in partnership capital or profits rather than in accordance with their investments in the property.

Thus, the mere fact that the partnership constitutes a separate tax-reporting entity interposed between the property and the partners will in itself give rise to complications. These problems and their ramifications will be discussed in a separate chapter.

B. TAX BASIS OF PROPERTY UPON ACQUISITION

Property may be acquired by an owner in a number of different ways. Purchase, inheritance, gift, compensation for services, satisfaction of indebtedness, dividend, and corporate distribution are all examples of ways in which property may be acquired.

But the way in which property is acquired will control its original basis to its new owner. Basis is, of course, important to the new owner because it measures the amount of the depreciation allowance which he will be entitled to recover on the property. Basis will also determine the amount of gain or loss to be realized by the owner on a disposition of the property; it will control the amount of the loss that can be deducted by the owner if the property is damaged or destroyed; and, if new property is acquired

---

[18] To be included in each partner's gross income in the taxable year in which or with which the partnership taxable year ends. Section 70b(a), I.R.C.

[19] Section 702, I.R.C.

[20] Subject to the possibility that the partnership may elect to adjust basis for the property under Section 743, I.R.C.

in a tax-free exchange, the basis for the former property will control the basis for the new property.

All of these factors make it necessary to study the effect that various methods of acquisition have upon the tax basis of the property to be acquired.

1. Basis of Property Acquired by Purchase

The basis of property acquired by purchase is its cost.[21]

If the property is purchased for cash, the amount of money paid measures its cost. And if the property is acquired for other property in a taxable exchange, the cost is measured by the fair market value of the property transferred.[22] If the exchange is an arm's-length bargain, the value of the two parcels exchanged will be assumed to be equal; consequently, if the value of one parcel is known, that value can be attributed to the other parcel for the purpose of measuring its cost.[23]

Suppose the property purchased is acquired subject to an indebtedness. In other words, all the purchaser is buying is an equity in the property. His cost is not only the amount paid for the equity but also the amount of the debt outstanding against the property at the time of its acquisition, whether or not the debt obligation is assumed by the purchaser.[24]

Cost, however, does not include any real estate taxes imposed against the property if these taxes will be deductible by the purchaser,[25] nor does it include any items of deductible interest which might be owing on an indebtedness against the property.[26]

Cost does include a number of other items of expenditure made by the purchaser on the acquisition of property, to the extent that these items are not currently deductible. Among these items of expenditure are the following:

1. Broker's commission;
2. Cost of title search or title insurance;
3. Delinquent real estate taxes, if not deductible;
4. Legal fees;
5. Option payments;
6. Cost of acquiring outstanding leases;
7. Appraisal fees;
8. Payments to clear title;
9. Survey expenses;
10. Inspection fees.
11. Rezoning or variance or rezoning costs and fees.[27]

---

[21] Section 1012, I.R.C.
[22] Reg. Sec. 1.1012-1; Estate of Isadore L. Myers, 1 T.C. 100,111 (1942) acq. 1943 C.B. 17. Proof of cost or other basis is on the owner. Joseph P. Abraham, 1970 P-H Memo T.C. ¶70,304
[23] United States v. Davis, 370 U.S. 65 (1962). Philadelphia Park Amusement Company v. United States, 126 F.Supp. 189 (Ct. Cl. 1954).
[24] Crane v. Commissioner, 331 U.S. 1, 11 (1947); Manuel D. Mayerson, Jr. 47 T.C. 348 (1969), acq. 1069-2 C.B. XXIV; The debt must be enforceable and have value to the creditor or lien holder. Edna Morris 59 T.C. 21 (1972) acq. on another issue, 1973-2 C.B. 3.
[25] Section 1012, I.R.C.
[26] Colonial Enterprises, Inc., 47 B.T.A. 518, 521, (1942), acq. on another issue, 1942-2 C.B.
[27] Ackerman Buick, Inc. T.C. Memo 1973-224 (1973).

2. Basis of Property Acquired by Tax-free Exchange

The basis of property acquired in a tax-free exchange is related to the basis of the property given up in order to acquire the new property. In general, the basis of the new property equals the basis of the old property diminished by the amount of any "boot" received, and increased by the amount of any gain recognized in the exchange.

This rule applies in the case of exchanges of property of like kind,[28] in the case of the acquisition or replacement property similar or related in use to property that has been involuntarily converted,[29] and in the case of an exchange of property for stock in a corporation controlled by the transferor of the property.[30] For detailed examples of the various basis rules, reference should be made to the discussion herein of these various types of exchanges.

3. Basis of Property Acquired by Gift

The basis of property acquired by the gift is the basis of the donor for the property immediately before the gift. In other words, the donee takes over his donor's basis for the property.[31]

This general rule is subject to two exceptions. First, if the property is worth more than its basis to the donor, the donee is entitled to add to his donor's basis the amount of any gift tax attributable to the appreciation paid on the gift. But the amount of the increase in basis due to the gift tax paid cannot exceed the difference between the value of the property and its basis to the donor. In short, this adjustment cannot increase the donee's basis above the market value of the property at the time of the gift.[32] This adjustment is allowed to the donee regardless of whether he or his donor paid the gift tax. The adjustment is available only for federal, not state, gift taxes paid.

Example: Donor gives his Son an apartment worth $100,000. At the time of the gift, Donor's unrecovered basis for the property is $98,000. Donor pays a gift tax of $5,000 on the transfer of which 2 percent is allocable to the appreciation over the donor's basis. Thus 2 percent of the $5,000 gift tax (or $100) is an addition to basis. What is Son's basis for the property?

Donor's basis at the time of gift		$98,000
Adjustment for gift tax paid:		
Total gift tax	$5,000	
Two percent thereof	100	100
Son's basis for property after gift:		$98,100

Had the apartment been worth $98,000 or less, Son would have been entitled to no adjustment for the gift tax paid.

The second exception to the general rule relates to the case in which the value of the property is less than the donor's basis at the time of the gift. In this case, the donee takes over his donor's basis for all purposes other than for the purpose of measuring the donee's loss on a sale or other disposition of the property. The donee's basis for

---

[28] Section 1031(d), I.R.C.
[29] Section 1033(c), I.R.C.
[30] Section 358(a), I.R.C.
[31] Section 1015(a), I.R.C.
[32] Section 1015(d), I.R.C.

measuring loss is the *lesser* of his basis or the value of the property at the time of the gift.[33]

Example: Donor gives his Son an apartment worth $50,000 which has a basis to him of $60,000. Donor pays a gift tax of $1,000 on the transfer. Son's basis for the property is computed as follows:

1. For the purposes of depreciation,

Donor's basis at the time of gift		$60,000
Adjustment for gift tax paid:		
Gift tax paid	$1,000	
Less excess of tax paid over value less basis	1,000	-0-
Son's basis for depreciation		$60,000

2. For the purposes of a loss,

Donor's basis at time of gift	$60,000
Value of property at time of gift	$50,000
Lesser of value or basis (Son's basis for purpose of loss)	$50,000

If the Son in our example immediately sold the property for $55,000 he would have neither gain nor loss. His basis for loss purposes is $50,000 and so he suffered no loss in selling for $55,000. Similarly, as his basis for calculating gain is $60,000, he had no gain on a sale for $55,000. But if he sells for $49,000, his loss is only $1,000, being the difference between his basis for loss ($50,000) and the amount realized ($49,000).

We can draw general conclusions from these rules. If an owner intends to make a gift which will be subject to tax, it is generally a good idea for him to give property that has appreciated in value. In this way the donee will be permitted to increase his basis for the gift tax attributable to the appreciation in value at the time of the gift. He will thereby be able to recover part of the gift tax paid through the mechanics of his allowance for depreciation or through a later disposition of the property. The gift tax itself is a non-deductible payment by the donor.

But if the property has depreciated in value below the basis to the donor, the donor should sell the property, deduct his loss, and give the proceeds to his donee. A gift of the property itself would require the donee to write his donor's basis down to value when the donee sells it. In other words, the donor's loss cannot be transferred to the donee; unless the donor takes the loss himself, it will be forfeited without any tax benefit. The only exception to this rule arises when the tax benefit of the higher basis (e.g., for depreciation) to the donee is greater than the tax benefit of the loss to the donor—an unusual situation.

4. Basis of Property Acquired by Inheritance

Property acquired by inheritance has a carryover basis; the heirs take over the decedent's basis as adjusted to the time of death.[34] However, if the property was subject to federal or state estate taxes (or to state inheritance taxes imposed on the heir),

---

[33] Section 1015(a), I.R.C.
[34] Section 1023(a)(1).

TAX BASIS OF PROPERTY UPON ACQUISITION   49

then the carryover basis of the decedent is increased by the amount of such taxes attributable to the appreciation. The increase is not the full amount of the death taxes; it is merely that portion of the death taxes imposed on the appreciation of the value of the property at the time of the decedent's death over his carryover basis.[35]

How is this adjustment computed? The adjustment required four steps, as follows:

(1) Total the qualified federal and state death taxes.

(2) Subtract from the gross value of the estate subject to tax the decedent's total carryover basis for the estate: this amount is the appreciation in value.

(3) Divide the appreciation in value determined under step (2) by the gross value of the estate; this percentage measures the amount of appreciation in value subject to the death taxes.

(4) Multiply the total death taxes by the percentage determined under step (3): this is the total upward basis adjustment available to the heirs or estate.

The upward basis adjustment is applied to the assets of estate individually. For example, properties that are worth less than the carryover basis are not netted against appreciated properties.[37] Nor can the upward adjustment exceed the date of death value of any particular item of property.[38] This adjustment to basis is available for both depreciation and sale purposes.

If the property were acquired by the decedent prior to January 1, 1977, there may be a further upward adjustment. This second adjustment has nothing to do with the amount of death taxes paid. It merely tries to reflect pre-January 1, 1977 appreciation in value as being a proper increase in basis.[39] In the case of real property, the amount of the upward adjustment is measured by allocating the appreciation over the carryover basis over the decedent's holding period for the property. The total appreciation is allocated to the pre-January 1, 1977 period by dividing the number of days the property was held by the decedent prior to January 1, 1977 by his total holding period of the property.

5. Basis of Property Acquired by Gift in Contemplation of Death

If an owner makes a gift of property within three years of his death, the gift is conclusively made in contemplation of his death.[40] The presumption can not be rebutted. The amount of the gift includes gift taxes paid.[41]

Thus the rules relating to basis of property acquired by inheritance apply. The donee's basis is the carryover of the property at the time of the owner-donor's death.[42] The only exception is for gifts made within the three-year period that have a value of less than $3,000.[43]

---

[35] Section 1023(c).
[37] Sen. Rept. No. 94-938, 94th Cong. 2nd Sess. p. 822
[38] Section 1023(f).
[39] Section 1023(h). This adjustment stems from the pre-January 1, 1977 rule that property includable in a decedent's estate for estate tax purposes got a new basis equal to the date-of-death value.
[40] Section 2035, I.R.C.
[41] Section 2035(c).
[42] Section 1014(b)(9).
[43] Section 2035(b)(z).

6. Basis of Property Acquired by a Surviving Joint Tenant

Property acquired by a surviving joint tenant takes a basis in the hands of the survivor equal to the carryover basis of the deceased joint tenant to the extent that the property was includable in the decedent's estate for estate tax purposes.[44]

Thus, if only one-half of the property were includable, only one-half would take a carryover basis but if the total were includable, the entire property would take the carryover basis which is subject to adjustment. And all of the property held in joint tenancy is presumptively includable in the decedent's gross estate, less any portion of the property that the survivor can show was attributable to his original contribution.[45]

The same adjustments to the carryover basis that are available to inherited property are available to joint tenancy property.[46] See Part C, 4 above.

7. Basis of Property Acquired as Community Property

The community property interest of a decedent in property owned by him and his spouse takes a carryover basis in the hands of the person who receives it on his death. It makes no difference whether the taker is the decedent's spouse or another heir.[47]

The interest of the surviving spouse in the community property is not adjusted as a result of the decedent spouse's death; its basis is unchanged.[48] The reason for this 1976 change in the law is that property qualifying for a marital deduction does not receive any basis adjustment in the death of the decedent spouse.[49] Since neither the surviving spouse's interest in community property nor property passing under the marital deduction are subject to tax, neither receives a basis adjustment.

8. Basis of Property Acquired as Compensation

Compensation for services, whether paid in money or in property, is taxable as income to the recipient when received or accrued.[50]

If property is paid, the amount of the taxable compensation is the fair market value of the property. Accordingly, the fair market value at the time of receipt becomes the tax basis of the property to the new owner on its receipt.[51]

9. Basis of Property Acquired for a Debt

Property acquired in payment of a debt takes its fair market value on the date of transfer as its basis to the creditor who acquires it.[52]

The basis of the debt to the creditor is not ordinarily transferred to the property, because the creditor is entitled to deduct any excess of his basis for the debt over the

---

[44] Section 1014(b)(9),1023.
[45] Section 2040, I.R.C.
[46] Section 1014(b)(9), I.R.C.; Reg.Sec. 1.1014-6(a)(2).
[47] Section 1023(a).
[48] Sen. Rept. No. 94-938, 94th Cong. 2nd Sess., p. 822.
[49] Section 1023(f)(4).
[50] Section 61(a)(1), I.R.C.
[51] William T. Bivin, 21 B.T.A. 1051 (1930), acq.X-1 C.B. 6.
[52] Herbert N. Fell, 18 B.T.A. 81,84 (1929); first National Bank, 43 B.T.A. 456 (1941).

TAX BASIS OF PROPERTY UPON ACQUISITION 51

value of the property received as a bad debt in the year in which the debt is satisfied or becomes uncollectable.[53] Even though the value of property received does not equal the amount of the debt canceled, the creditor's basis is therefore limited to its fair market value at the time of receipt.

Example: Creditor lends Debtor $10,000 in cash. Debtor fails to repay the loan. Creditor talks to Debtor about this delinquency, and Debtor agrees to convey a lot worth $8,000 to Creditor if Creditor will give him a full satisfaction of the loan. Creditor agrees. He receives the property and discharges the loan. His basis for the lot would be $8,000 and the amount of his bad debt deductible in the year of release would be determined as follows:

Basis for loan	$10,000
Less value of property received	8,000
Bad debt	$ 2,000

One exception to this rule should be mentioned. If the property received in satisfaction of the debt has no *ascertainable* fair market value (as distinguished from being provably worthless), the creditor must transfer his basis for the loan to the property.[54] In effect, the creditor must postpone his bad debt deduction, if any, to the year in which he disposes of the property.

10. Basis of Property Acquired on a Corporate Distribution

The basis of property acquired by an individual stockholder as a dividend is its fair market value at the time of receipt.[55]

Similarly, if property is acquired by a stockholder who is an individual on a taxable liquidation of a corporation, its basis to the stockholder will be its fair market value at the time of distribution.[56] This rule is limited to distributions under which gain or loss is recognized to the stockholder. Thus, exception must be made for special types of liquidation in which the total gain or loss realized is not recognized for tax purposes.[57]

11. Basis of Property Acquired Subject to a Mortgage

The basis of property acquired subject to a mortgage includes the amount of the mortgage debt outstanding at the time of acquisition. This rule holds true whether the acquisition is by purchase,[58] exchange,[59] inheritance,[60] or other methods. And the rule holds true whether or not the new owner is personally liable for the mortgage debt. Even if he merely takes the property subject to the debt, his basis for the property includes the amount of the debt outstanding on the date of acquisition.

These rules apply even if the mortgage debt is later reduced by negotiation among

---

[53]Kohn v. Commissioner, 197 F.2d 480 (2d Cir. 1952); I.T. 3548, 1942-1 C.B. 74.
[54]Society Brand Clothes, Inc., 18 T.C. 304, 317 (1952), acq. 1952-2 C.B. 3.
[55]Section 301(d)(1), I.R.C.
[56]Section 334(a), I.R.C.
[57]See Sections 322, 333, 334(b),(c), I.R.C. and Chapter 10, *infra*.
[58]See Strollberg Hardware Co., 46 B.T.A. 788, 794 (1942).
[59]Reg. Sec. 1.1031(d)-2, Example (2)(b).
[60]Crane v. Commissioner, 331 U.S. 1, 13 (1947).

the parties.[61] The rules apply to purchasers in states in which the purchaser is by statute non-liable for a deficiency on foreclosure.[62]

C. ALLOCATION OF TAX BASIS ON ACQUISITION

On every acquisition of improved real estate, the owner is compelled to make an allocation of his total basis for the property between the improvements on the land and the land itself. This allocation is necessary because only the improvements are depreciable; thus, the owner is entitled to recover the portion of the basis allocable to the improvements over their useful life through his allowance for depreciation. The remainder of the basis, allocable to the land is not depreciable. The owner can recover this portion of his basis only on the sale or other disposition of the property.

The proper allocation of basis between land and improvements is a matter of judgment. But we should remember that it is the Commissioner's judgment, not the owner's, that enjoys the benefit of a presumption of correctness.[63]

1. Basis Allocation in General

As a general rule, the basis on acquisition should be apportioned between land and buildings in proportion to their respective market values on the date of acquisition.[64]

Objective indications of the relative market values, such as the assessed valuations placed upon land and improvements by the local tax assessor, will be given weight in determining the proper allocation of basis to be made.

Example: Purchaser buys a store building for $40,000. The property is assessed on the tax assessor's books at $10,000, of which $2,000 is land value and $8,000 is improvement value. Purchaser allocates his cost basis between land and building on the same ratio:

$$\frac{\text{Basis for building}}{\text{Total basis}} :: \frac{\text{Assessed value of building}}{\text{Total assessed value}}$$

$$\frac{x}{\$40,000} :: \frac{\$8,000}{\$10,000}$$

$$x = \$32,000$$

Thus, the basis for the building would be $32,000 and the basis for the land would be the remainder, or $8,000.

2. Basis Allocation by Contract

Suppose the parties attempt to set a market value on each item in the contract of sale. Will such a recital of respective market values control the purchaser's allocation

---

[61] Manuel D. Mayerson, 47 T.C. 348(1969), acq. 1969-2 C.B.XXXIV.
[62] The use of a straw corporation to defeat personal liability did not deprive the shareholders of the inclusion of non-recourse debt in their basis. David F. Bolger, 59 T.C. 760 (1973).
[63] See Twin Ports Bridge Co., 27 B.T.A. 346, 359 (1932).
[64] Reg. Sec. 1.167(a)-5; Thomas J. Avery, 11 B.T.A. 958, 962 (1928), acq. on another point, VII-2 C.B. 3.

ALLOCATION OF TAX BASIS ON ACQUISITION

of basis between land and buildings? Or will the Commissioner be free to disregard the allocation?

The answer depends upon whether or not the contractual allocation had a substantial effect upon each party to the contract. If the contractual allocation was a matter of arm's-length bargaining that affected both parties, then the allocation will be controlling for tax purposes.[65]

But suppose the allocation is important only to the purchaser. In this case, the Commissioner would be free to disregard the allocation, because it did not represent a true part of the bargain between the buyer and seller. It would be nothing but "window dressing" put into the contract for no purpose other than the tax benefit to the purchaser.[66]

Example: Purchaser buys an apartment from Seller for $80,000. Purchaser asks Seller to place a clause in the contract that allocates $70,000 of the purchase price to the building and $10,000 to the land. Seller agrees. If his gain is taxed as capital gain in any event, it is a matter of indifference to him how the price is allocated. Obviously, if Purchaser attempts to allocate $70,000 of the price to the building and $10,000 to land on his books for tax purposes, he had better be in a position to prove the relative values of the land and buildings. The contractual allocation, under these circumstances would have no more than make-weight value. But just as obviously, any contractual allocation found in a contract of purchase would constitute a harmful admission against the Purchaser if he attempts to allocate a greater proportion of the purchase price to the building than the amount stated in the contract.

On the other hand, if part of the gain is taxable as ordinary income under Section 1250, an arm's-length agreement between buyer and seller for the purpose of allocating the sales price between land and improvements may well be controlling; it certainly should control in any case in which the allocation converts any portion of the seller's gain into ordinary income. See Chapter 4, Part A, 10.

3. Basis Allocation to Structure to be Demolished

If land and buildings are purchased or acquired by an owner who, at the time of purchase,[67] *intends* to demolish the buildings in order to clear the land for a new development, the owner cannot allocate any part of the cost of acquisition to the buildings. The entire cost of both the land and the buildings must be allocated to the land.[68]

Suppose the owner incurs an additional cost in razing the structures on the land. The amount of such expense must be added to his basis for the land. Any salvage received by the owner on demolition is treated as an offset to the cost of demolition.[69]

However, even if the owner purchases the property with the intention of demolishing the improvements, he is permitted to allocate a portion of his basis to the improve-

---

[65] Commissioner v. Gazette Telegraph Co., 209 F.2d 926 (10th Cir. 1954); Hamlin's Trust v. Commissioner, 209 F.2d 761 (10th Cir. 1954).

[66] Particelli v. Commissioner, 212 F.2d 498, 501 (9th Cir. 1954).

[67] It is the intent at the time of purchase which controls, even where this intent is frustrated for years by wartime conditions. Lynchburg National Bank and Trust Co., 20 T.C. 670 (1953), aff'd on another issue 208 F.2d 757 (4th Cir. 1953).

[68] Reg. Sec. 1.165-3(a)(1).

[69] *Ibid.*

ments for one limited purpose. If the owner actually rents the improvements or otherwise uses them in his trade or business prior to demolition, he may deduct an allowance for depreciation during the time he so uses the improvements. His basis for depreciation in this case is the present value of the rentals to be collected (or which could be collected, where the owner uses the property himself) over the period until the intended time of demolition.[70] Furthermore, it has been held that where there exists an intent to rent the building or operate it in the trade or business for an indefinite but substantial length of time, the intent to demolish may be ignored and basis allocated as usual.[71] If it later turns out that the building is demolished before its basis is fully depreciated, a loss deduction is allowable for the undepreciated part of the basis of the building.[72]

Of course, if there exists no intent to demolish the improvements at the time of purchase, basis is allocated in accordance with the normal rule, unaffected by a subsequently arising intent to demolish.[73]

D. PURCHASE UNDER OPTION

If property is acquired by the exercise of an option, the owner's basis for the property includes the cost to him of the option as well as the cost of the property.[74] The cost of the option is treated as part of the cost of the property.

1. Purchased Option

If an owner acquires property by the exercise of an option, the cost of the option is part of the owner's basis for the property.

If the owner fails to exercise the option and loses his option payment, his loss is realized as an ordinary, capital, Section 1231, or personal loss, depending upon the nature of the holding of the property in the owner's hands had he acquired it.

2. Inherited Option

If an option is inherited from a decedent, it will have value to the extent that it permits the holder of the option to purchase the property at a price less than its fair market value. Because the option is acquired from a decedent, it has a basis in the hands of the holder equal to its carryover basis on the date of the decedent's death. Therefore, if the holder of the option sells it to a third party, his gain or loss is recognized by the difference between the sales price and the basis of the option.[75] And, if the holder of the option exercises it, he is entitled to add the carryover to the price he pays for the property for the purposes of determining his total basis in the property.[76]

---

[70] Reg. Sec. 1.165-3(a)(2).
[71] Mechanics and Merchants Bank v. United States, 164 F. Supp. 246 (Ct. Cl. 1958).
[72] Reg. Sec. 1.165-3(a)(2)(ii).
[73] Reg. Sec. 1.165-3(b)(1).
[74] Stires Corporation, 28 B.T.A. 1,6 (1933). Rev. Rul. 58-234, 1958-1 C.B. 279.
[75] W. Einnie Cadby, 24 T.C. 899 (1955), acq. 1965-1 C.B. 3.
[76] Rev. Rul. 67-96, 1967-1 C.B. 195; Kalbac v. Commissioner, 298 F.2d 251 (8th Cir. 1962).

PURCHASE UNDER OPTION

Example: Owner receives distribution of an option to purchase real property from the estate of a decedent. The option has a carryover basis of $10,000 on the date of the decedent's death. Owner, therefore, has a basis of $10,000 for the option if he sells it to a third party. But Owner chooses to exercise the option. Owner pays $190,000 to acquire the property. His basis for the property is $200,000, consisting of the purchase price plus the carryover basis for the option.

3. Option to Buy from Estate

If an option is not inherited from the optionee, but is merely an option in an heir to buy from a decedent's estate, the exercise of the option is meaningless. The basis to the optionee will be zero.[77]

Therefore, unlike a purchased option, the holder of an inherited option is not entitled to any loss deduction if he fails to exercise his option. The expiration of the option is treated as a lapse or disclaimer of a bequest and, therefore, the holder is not entitled to any deduction.

4. Failure to Exercise or Sale of Option

If the holder of an option fails to exercise it, he is entitled to deduct its cost or other basis as a loss incurred in the year in which the option expires. Similarly, if the holder of an option sells it, he realizes gain or loss measured by the difference between the proceeds received on the sale and the basis of the option to him at the time of sale.[78]

Had the property that would have been acquired had the option been exercised been a capital asset in the hands of the optionee, the optionee's gain or loss on the sale or forfeiture of the option would be capital gain or loss; if the property had been a non-capital asset in his hands, the gain or loss would be ordinary gain or loss.[79]

5. Allocation of Basis

If a taxpayer purchases buildings and takes an option on the underlying land which he later exercises, he cannot allocate any part of the cost of the *option* to his basis for the buildings; it must all be added to his basis for the land.[80]

6. Holding Period

The holding period for property acquired by the exercise of an option commences the day after the option is exercised;[81] the owner's holding period for the option cannot be tacked on to his holding period for the property.[82]

On the other hand, if the option itself is sold, the length of time the option was held is the holding period for the option.

Thus, where sale of the property under option is contemplated, the gain on the sale will be short-term gain even where a simultaneous closing is arranged, since techni-

---

[77] Compare, Rev. Rul. 71-265, 1971-1 C.B. 223.
[78] Section 1234, I.R.C.
[79] Reg. Sec. 1.1234-1.
[80] Carnegie Center Company, 22 T.C. 1189 (1954), acq. on another issue, 1955-1 C.B. 4.
[81] E.T. Weir, 10 T.C. 996 (1948), aff'd per curiam, 173 F.2d 222 (3rd Cir. 1949).
[82] Helvering v. San Joaquin Fruit & Investment Co., 297 U.S. 496 (1936).

cally the option holder will hold the land, albeit fleetingly, prior to sale. This is true even though the property is deeded directly to the ultimate purchaser.[83] To avoid this result it is necessary that the option itself be sold, or, if exercised, that the property be held after exercise at least six months prior to sale.

E. PURCHASE FOR BARGAIN PRICE

No income is realized by a purchaser on the purchase by him of property at a bargain price *from a stranger*; the fact that the property is worth more than its cost does not create any tax consequences to the purchaser, provided the transaction is with a stranger at arm's length.[84]

1. Exception for Pre-existing Relationship

But if there is a relationship between the buyer and seller other than the one arising out of the sale itself, the bargain purchase may have tax consequences to either the buyer or seller, depending upon the pre-existing relationship. If, for example, the seller is a corporation and the buyer its stockholder, the difference between the value of the property and the purchase price may be a taxable dividend to the purchaser.[85] Or, if the seller is the employer of the purchaser, the difference may constitute additional compensation to the buyer.[86] If the buyer and seller are members of a family group, the difference between value and selling price may be a taxable gift from the seller to the buyer.

2. Purchase by Broker for Price without Commission

If a real estate salesman purchases real property for his own account and his employer receives a broker's commission on the purchase which he turns over to the salesman, the salesman has ordinary income to the extent of the payment he receives. Even though the commission was returned to him out of the purchase price he put up, the commission is not treated as a reduction of the purchase price; it is treated as compensation for services.[87]

What about a broker who purchases real estate for his own account? Does he have income when he receives a payment from his escrow for his share of the commission, or, alternatively, when he receives a credit against the purchase price due for his share of the commission? In the absence of an employer-employee relationship between the buyer and seller, we would think not. But in the related field of insurance brokerage, the Commissioner has ruled that an insurance broker realizes income to the extent of the commissions normally charged on policies that he buys commission-free from an

---

[83] Blick v. Commissioner, 271 F.2d 928 (3rd Cir. 1959).
[84] Fred Pellar, 25 T.C. 299 (1955), acq. 1956-1 C.B. 5.
[85] See Shunk v. Commissioner, 173 F.2d 747 (6th Cir. 1949).
[86] Commissioner v. LoBue, 351 U.S. 243, 76 S.Ct. 800; Ostheimer v. United States, 264 F.2d 789 (3rd Cir. 1959); Commissioner v. Minzer, 279 F.2d 338 (5th Cir. 1960).
[87] Commissioner v. Daehler, 281, F.2d 823 (5th Cir. 1960).

insurance company, whether or not the company is his employer.[88] The Commissioner's theory is that the insurance broker renders the same services and benefit to the insurance company for which he is paid a commission whether he writes a policy for himself or for someone else. Is not the same theory applicable to brokers in real estate? Does not the buying broker render the seller the same valuable services for which he is paid a commission whether or not the buyer is himself? But before concluding that the insurance ruling is applicable here, we should note that in the case of insurance the price is frequently set by law. A renegotiated price at a lower figure without commission would be more easy to defend against an attack by the Commissioner than would a sale at the original price with the payment of a cash commission to the purchaser, even though the latter payment was made from the purchaser's own escrow deposits.

F. APPORTIONMENT OF REAL ESTATE TAXES ON ACQUISITION

Real property is generally subject to local taxes imposed by the state, city, or county. These taxes, known generically as real property taxes, are levied at a uniform rate on the assessed value of all the real property located in the taxing jurisdiction. Customarily, the taxes are levied once a year, although collection of the amount due may be in two or more installments. In theory, the tax is levied against the property, not the owner; hence, the amount of tax levied against each parcel of property is considered to be a lien against that property. This lien arises on some arbitrary date set by law, which may be on the first of the real property tax year, in the middle of the year, or even prior to or subsequent to the tax year.

Because the real property tax is deemed against the property, not the owner, the tax is collectable against the property by foreclosure of the tax lien, even though it may have been sold or transferred by the owner after the lien date. In recognition of this fact, contracts for the sale of real estate normally provide for a proration between buyer and seller of outstanding real property taxes that have become a lien against the property. The seller is charged with the amount of the tax from the beginning of the real property tax year to the date of sale, and the buyer is charged with the balance of the tax to the end of the year.

But the proration of tax between buyer and seller is simply a matter of contract; it may be ignored completely by the parties. In this event, the party holding the property when the taxes become due will pay them in full without the benefit of reimbursement from the other party to the sale.

From the standpoint of the federal income tax, real property taxes are a deductible expense, deductible when paid or accrued.[89] But if the property is purchased subject to delinquent real property taxes, the amount of the delinquency is treated as an additional cost to the purchaser that must be capitalized as a payment to clear title.[90]

---

[88]Rev. Rul. 55-273, 1955-1 C.B. 221. See, also, Commissioner v. Minzer, 279 F.2d 1572 (5th Cir. 1960) Ostheimer v. United States, 264 F.2d 789 (3rd Cir. 1959); cert. den. 361 U.S. 818; George E. Bailey, 41 T.C. 663 (1964).
[89]Section 164(a), I.R.C.
[90]Magruder v. Supplee, 316 U.S. 394, 398 (1942).

What happens, then, if a taxpayer purchases property during the course of the real property tax year? If the taxes for the current year have already become a lien against the property, are they considered to be delinquent? Or may the purchaser take a deduction for the amount which he pays or reimburses the seller? Or is he entitled to prorate his deduction with the seller in a manner similar to the proration of taxes provided by contract?

l. Apportionment of Current Real Property Taxes

Under the 1954 Code, the buyer and seller are compelled to apportion the deduction for current real property taxes between themselves if the sale is made on a date other than the first of the real property tax year.[91]

This rule is mandatory. It applies to buyer and seller whether or not they have prorated the tax by contract. Under the statute, so much of the real property tax as is allocable to the period from the first of the tax year to the day before the date of sale is apportioned to the seller and may be deducted by him. The balance of the tax is apportioned to the buyer and is deductible by him. The regulations indicate that the allocation should be made on the basis of a 365-day real property tax year.[92]

Example: Seller sells a parcel of real estate to Purchaser on September 28, just 90 days after the beginning of the real property tax year which commenced on July 1. The tax for the entire year is $730. How much is deductible by the Seller? By the Purchaser?[93]

Seller's portion	= Total tax ×	$\dfrac{\text{Number of days to sale}}{365}$
	= $730 × 90/365	
	= $180	
Purchaser's portion	= $550	

The regulations extend the same rule to all types of combinations of the lien date and real property tax year. If, for example, the tax year begins after the lien date, the apportionment is made on the basis of the respective periods of ownership during the real property tax year just as in any other case. Thus, if the seller disposes of the property after the lien date but before the first of the real property tax year, the total tax for the year is deductible by the purchaser.[94]

Example: A California seller owns property on the first Monday in March when the real property taxes for the coming fiscal year become a lien. On July 1 he sells the property to Purchaser. The real property tax begins on July 1. Because Purchaser will own the property 365 days of the real property tax year, he is entitled under the regulations to deduct the total tax to be paid for the entire year.

But it should be noted that such a sale in a state like California would also involve apportionment of the preceding year's real property taxes. Since the sale was made on June 1, just after 11 months after the preceding year had commenced, 335/365 of the

---

[91] Section 164(d), I.R.C.
[92] Reg. Sec. 1.164-6(b), Ernest A. Pederson, 46 T.C. 155 (1966).
[93] Reg. Sec. 1.164-6(b)(3), Example (1).
[94] Reg. Sec. 1.164-4(b)(1)(ii).

preceding year's taxes would be apportioned to Seller and 30/365 to Purchaser. Because the statute refers only to the apportionment of real property taxes for the year of sale, the regulations may be in error in attempting to provide apportionment for a case not comprehended by the statute.

The regulations also attempt to cover the converse situation. The rule of allocation is applied to sales made after the conclusion of the real property tax year if the lien securing the tax arises after the expiration of the taxable year. Thus, if a seller sells property after the conclusion of the taxable year but before the lien date, the regulations state that the entire real property tax for the past year is to be allocated to him because he owned the property during the full year.[95]

2. Time for Deducting the Allocated Tax

In what year is the seller's allocated share of the real property tax to be deducted? And in what year should the purchaser deduct his share?

The answer depends upon a number of variables. First, are the seller and the purchaser on the cash or the accrual method of accounting? And if either party is on the accrual method, does he accrue the tax at the time the liability arises or does he accrue it monthly under the provisions of Section 461(c)? Second, who pays the tax to the taxing jurisdiction? Is it the seller? Or the purchaser? And, third, who owned the property when the tax became a lien?

1. Cash basis purchaser; purchaser pays the tax: the purchaser is entitled to deduct his portion of the tax in the year in which he pays it to the taxing authority.

2. Cash basis purchaser; seller pays the tax: the purchaser deducts his portion of the tax on the date of the sale or on the date that he reimburses the seller for the tax paid on his behalf.[96]

3. Cash basis seller; seller pays tax: the seller deducts his portion of the tax when he pays it to the taxing authority.

4. Cash basis seller; purchaser pays the tax: the seller deducts his portion of the tax on the date of sale or on the date he reimburses the purchaser for the tax paid on his behalf.[97]

5. Accrual basis purchaser; tax becomes a lien after sale: the purchaser deducts his portion of the tax on the lien date.[98]

6. Accrual basis purchaser; tax became a lien before sale: the purchaser deducts his portion of the tax on the date of sale.[99]

7. Accrual basis seller; tax became a lien before sale: the seller deducts his portion of the tax on the lien date.

---

[95]Reg. Sec. 1.164-6(b)(1)(iii). There is no statutory warrant for this, or the preceding regualtion. The statute authorized the purchaser to deduct real property taxes that become a lien before sale only if the purchase is "during any real property tax year," not before the commencement of that year. Similarly, a seller is permitted to deduct real property taxes becoming a lien after sale only if the sale is "during any real property tax year," not after the close of such year.
[96]Reg. Sec. 1.164-6(d)(2).
[97]Reg. Sec. 1.164-6(d)(1).
[98]Reg. Sec. 1.164-6(d)(6), Example.
[99]Reg. Sec. 1.164-6(d)(6).

8. Accrual basis seller; tax becomes a lien after sale: the seller deducts his portion of the tax on the date of sale.[100]

The theory underlying these rules is easy to state: if the taxpayer is on the cash method of accounting and he pays the tax, the date of his deduction is the date of payment; but if he does not actually pay the tax, the date of deduction is arbitrarily made the date of sale or the date he reimburses the other party to the sale.[101]

Similarly, if the taxpayer is on the accrual basis of accounting, and he holds title to the property at the time of the liability for payment or lien arises, the date of his deduction is the date of the liability or lien; but if he does not own the property when the liability or the lien arises, the date of the deduction is arbitrarily set at the date of sale.[102]

Under Section 461, an accrual basis owner of real property may elect to deduct real estate taxes ratably over the real property tax year. The election requires the consent of the Commissioner if it was not made in the first taxable year following the adoption of the Code. If the election was made, the party to the sale would merely accrue his deduction to or from the date of sale, with proper adjustment in the month of sale to take into account any fractional part of a month involved.

3. Treatment of Excess Tax Paid

The apportionment formula of Section 164(d) often can leave a party to a sale in the awkward position of having incurred a liability or having paid real property taxes in an amount in excess of the amount properly deductible by him. How must he treat the non-deductible portion of the taxes which have been paid or for which he has incurred a liability?

First, if the party paying the tax is the purchaser, the amount of the non-deductible taxes paid by him becomes a capital expenditure to be added to his basis for the property.[103]

But suppose the party paying the tax is the seller. The non-deductible portion of the tax will be treated in one of two ways. If the taxes were paid and deducted in the year of sale, the seller is entitled to add the non-deductible portion of the tax to his basis for the purpose of computing gain or loss realized on the sale. But if the tax has been deducted in full in a prior taxable year, then the seller is required to include as ordinary income the amount of the real property tax that became non-deductible because of the sale.[104] And if he has actually paid the tax, the amount now includable in income may be added to his basis for the property sold for the purpose of computing his gain or loss.[105]

---

[100]Reg. Sec. 1.164-6(d)(6), Example.
[101]Section 164(d)(2)(A), I.R.C.
[102]Section 164(d)(2)(D), I.R.C.
[103]Section 1012, I.R.C.
[104]The inclusion in income of the non-deductible portion of previously-deducted taxes is subject to the tax benefit rule. Reg. Sec. 1.164-6(d)(5).
[105]Section 1012, I.R.C.

4. Treatment of Reimbursement for Taxes Paid

Customarily, real estate sales contracts require that taxes be prorated between buyer and seller to the date of sale. The proration is normally accomplished through an adjustment of the agreed purchase price; either the price is increased to reflect taxes paid by the seller or the purchaser is allowed a partial credit for taxes to be paid by him for the seller. Thus, the parties prorate the economic incidence of the tax between themselves according to the time that each party holds the property during the real property tax year. A typical example of such a contract provision would be the following:

> Taxes for the fiscal year ending June 30, 19——shall be prorated to the date of closing.[106]

Under such a clause, if the seller has paid the tax in full before the sale, the purchase price will be increased by the amount of the tax allocable to the purchaser. But if the buyer is required to pay the tax in full, he will be entitled to a credit against the purchase price for the amount of the tax allocable to the seller.

How does the reimbursement clause affect the federal income tax picture? The regulations[107] specifically provide that the presence or absence of such a clause has no effect. The amount realized on the sale of the property is to be determined for this purpose without regard to the labels (e.g., reimbursement for taxes) attached by the parties.

This does not mean that a reimbursement clause has no significance for tax purposes. Since it may have the effect of changing the amount received by the seller, and paid by the buyer, it will affect the amount of gain or loss on the sale.

However, Code Section 1001(b) does require that amounts received as reimbursement for taxes by the seller be excluded in determining the amount he realized on the sale. It also requires that the seller take into account taxes allocable to him but to be paid by the purchaser.

Thus, the rule is that so much of the purchase price as equals real property taxes *paid by the seller but allocable to the purchaser* under Section 164 (discussed above) is excluded from the amount received by the seller in determining the amount realized on the sale. Conversely, an amount equal to the real property taxes allocable to the seller must be added to the amount otherwise realized by the seller if the purchaser has paid the tax.

The logic of these rules may be understood by considering the amount of real property taxes allocable to either party as the personal obligation of that party. If the seller pays or has paid all the taxes for the year of sale, he is treated as having loaned the purchaser the latter's share thereof. Then the same amount is excluded from the sale proceeds as a repayment of the "loan." If the purchaser pays or will pay all of the

---

[106]If the proration date is other than the date of sale, it would be advisable to change the contractual provision to the date of sale in order that the contractual apportionment corresponds with the income tax apportionment.

[107]Reg. Sec. 1.1001-1(b).

taxes, the seller is receiving the additional benefit of having his obligation paid by the purchaser, and so is treated as receiving additional sale proceeds.

Example: Let us assume that Seller sells a parcel of real property to Purchaser ninety days after the beginning of the real property tax year. The tax bill for the year on the property is $730, which Purchaser is to pay. Seller's portion of the tax will be $180 and Purchaser's is $550. Let us assume that the total price for the property is $40,000 and that the contract of sale requires proration to the date of sale.

Purchaser's Statement

	Dr.	Cr.
Gross price	$40,000	
Pro rata taxes		180
Down payment		2,000
Amount to close		37,820
	$40,000	$40,000

Seller's proceeds on the sale would, therefore, be only $39,820, the amount of cash received. To determine the amount realized for computing taxable gain or loss, however, Seller must add $180, representing his share of tax to be paid for him by the purchaser. Thus, Seller would realize $40,000 less costs on the sale for tax purposes.

If there had been no proration clause in the sale contract, seller would have received $40,000 cash, and the amount realized would be $40,180 less costs.

In either case, as indicated earlier, Seller will be entitled to a deduction of $180 on his return for the year of sale.

What about Purchaser? The $180 credit under the proration agreement merely goes to reduce his purchase price. Accordingly, his basis on acquisition is only $39,820, which will be increased to $40,000 when he pays the total $730 in taxes for the year. The balance of the tax ($550) will be deductible by him when paid.

Had Seller not reimbursed Purchaser by allowance of the credit, Purchaser's cost on acquisition would have been $40,000; later, when the tax had been paid, his cost would have been increased to $40,180 to reflect the payment of the Seller's tax.

Hence, Purchaser's basis for the property will always equal the amount Seller is considered to have realized on the sale (once the property taxes are paid).

Example: Let us assume the same facts as in the foregoing example, except that the Seller has paid $730 in real property taxes before the date of sale. Suppose, then, that Purchaser agrees to reimburse Seller for $550 of taxes paid on his behalf on a $40,000 purchase. What result?

Purchaser's statement

	Dr.	Cr.
Gross price	$40,000	
Pro rata taxes	550	
Down payment		$ 2,000
Amount to close		38,550
	$40,550	$40,550

Purchaser's total price is $40,550, of which $550 is currently deductible under Section 164(d). Since Code Section 1012 provides that the cost basis of real property shall not include amounts treated under Section 164(d) as imposed on the purchaser, his basis on acquisition is $40,000.

What are Seller's gross proceeds? As we have seen, Section 1001(b) prohibits inclusion in the amount realized of "reimbursement for real property taxes which are treated under Section 164(d) as imposed on the purchaser." Thus, Seller's gross proceeds for tax purposes are only $40,000 of the total $40,550 received. The $550 is received as a tax-free payment.

5. Apportionment of Real Property Taxes on Acquisition Other than Purchase

There is no indication in the regulations that the apportionment rules of Section 164(d) are to be applied to acquisitions of property other than by purchase. The statute itself creates the inference that its terms are limited only to sales.[108]

Thus, as to acquisitions by gift or by inheritance the rules under the 1939 Code would seem to be excluded, whether or not the exchange is taxable. [109]

Under these rules, real property taxes are deductible only by the person who held title at the time the taxes became a lien against the property or became a liability of the owner. If the owner is on the accrual basis, he can deduct the tax at that time; if he is on the cash basis, he may deduct the taxes when paid. Thus, if the tax became a lien before sale, only the seller can deduct the tax, either when paid by the purchaser (if on the cash basis) or when the tax became a lien or liability (if on the accrual basis).[110]

---

[108]Section 164(d), I.R.C.
[109]In general, throughout the Code, sales are distinguished from exchanges. The former is a transfer for money and the latter is a transfer for property other than money. Had Congress intended to include exchanges under the apportionment rules of Section 164(d), it could easily have said, "sale or exchange." The commissioner has ruled that the apportionment rules of Section 164 have no application to distributions of real property in liquidation of a corporation. Rev. Rul. 62-45; 1962-1 C.B. 2. He may, however, reach the same result by applying Section 482 to the transaction. Tennessee Life Insurance Co. v. Phinney, 280 F.2d 38 (5th Cir. 1960), cert. den. 364 U.S. 914. Contra, Simon J. Murphy Co. v. Commissioner, 231 F.2d 639 (6th Cir. 1956).
[110]Magruder v. Supplee, 316 U.S. 394, 398 (1942).

3

Ownership and Operation of Real Property

In this chapter we shall be concerned with expenses incurred and expenditures made in connection with the ownership and operation of real estate. The fundamental problem to be discussed will be whether a particular expenditure of funds constitutes an expense deductible currently or a capital expenditure that must be added to the owner's basis for the property. The discussion also will include an analysis of the techniques for recovering an allowance for the cost of property, or its other basis, over the useful life of the property.

Accordingly, the plan of this chapter is as follows:

A. *Depreciation*;
B. *Obsolescence*;
C. *Voluntary Demolition, Alteration, or Removal of Structure*;
D. *Repairs, Maintenance Expenses, and Capital Improvements*;
E. *Protection of Income or Defense of Title*;
F. *Taxes, Interest, and Carrying Charges*;
G. *Casualty Losses on Business Property*;
H. *Soil and Water Conservation Expenses*.

A. DEPRECIATION

The owner of business or rental real estate[1] is normally entitled to deduct an annual allowance for depreciation for the loss in value of improvements on the land due to the passage of time. The allowance for depreciation is measured by the cost of the

---

[1] Section 167(a), I.R.C., limits the allowance for depreciation to "property used in the trade or business (and) property held for the production of income." Improved property held for sale only and not being used for the production of rental income was held not depreciable in Camp Wolter Enterprises, Inc., 22 T.C. 737, 754 (1954), aff'd on another point, 230 F.2d 555 (5th Cir. 1956), cert. den. 352 U.S. 826. Homan v. Commissioner, 230 F.2d 671 (9th Cir. 1956); F.B. Cooper, 31 T.C. 1155 (1959); John P. Vidican, 1969 P-H Memo T.C. ¶69,207.

DEPRECIATION

improvements on the owner's land; it does not, however, include any allowance for the land itself. Land, being considered indestructible, is not depreciable.[2]

1. Types of Improvements Qualifying for Depreciation

Buildings and structures erected on the owner's land are depreciable.[3] Similarly, improvements such as paving, private streets, curbs and gutters,[4] railroad spur tracks,[5] and other installations that have limited useful life are subject to the allowance for depreciation.

Orchards,[6] oranges[7] and lemon groves[8] and fruit- and nut-bearing trees are depreciable if the owner can show they have a limited useful life. But the owner may run into trouble if he is unable to show any determinate life for an orchard, or if he expensed the cost of replacements; under these conditions he may lose his right to deduct any allowance for depreciation.[9]

Land itself is not depreciable because it has no determinable useful life. Similarly, land preparation costs are non-depreciable, unless the preparation costs are in connection with a depreciable improvement.[10] Landscaping with permanent shrubbery and trees is also non-depreciable unless it can be shown that the shrubbery and trees will have to be destroyed at the end of the useful life of other improvements. In such case, the trees and shrubbery are depreciable over the same useful life as the other improvements.[11]

What about pasture land? At least one court has held that pasture land is depreciable.[12] But in the similar case of a golf course, the Commissioner has ruled that the initial expense of installation is non-depreciable because the life of the greens is permanent if ordinary care and maintenance are provided.[13]

Even if a showing is made that land is deteriorating, the cost of the land is non-depreciable; for example, farm lands which are becoming progressively less useful due to subsidence are not depreciable.[14]

2. Apportionment of Basis

Because land is not depreciable, the owner of improved real property must apportion his total cost between land and improvements; only the portion of the basis

---

[2]Reg. Sec. 1.167(a)-5.
[3]Reg. Sec. 1.167(a)-2. The cost of grading land is non-depreciable, although the cost of excavating land for building foundations or grading for paved roadways is part of the cost of the improvement and therefore depreciable. Rev. Rul. 65-265, 1965-2 CB. 52; Rev. Rul. 68-193 I.R.B. 1968-17,6.
[4]Clinton Cotton Mills, Inc. v. Commissioner, 78 F.2d 292, 296 (4th Cir. 1935).
[5]G.C.M. 25503, 1948-1 C.B. 40.
[6]Ribbon Cliff Fruit Co., 12 B.T.A. 13, 17 (1928), acq. VII-2 C.B. 34; L.O. 797, 1 C.B. 130.
[7]Redlands Security Co., 5 B.T.A. 956 (1926), acq. VI-2 C.B. 6.
[8]Kaweah Lemon Co., 5 B.T.A. 992 (1927), acq. VI-2 C.B. 4.
[9]Thomas Palmer, 23 B.T.A. 296, 300, acq. X-2 C.B. 54; Chester B. Knox, 2 B.T.A. 1107, acq. V-1 C.B. 3; Isabelle B. Krome, Par. 50,064 P-H Memo T.C. (1950).
[10]See Rev. Rul. 72-96, 1972-1 C.B. 66.
[11]Rev. Rul. 74-265, I.R.B. 1974-23, p.7. Annual flowers are currently deductible.
[12]Johnson v. Westover, 48 A.F.T. R1671, 1675 (S.D. Cal. 1955).
[13]Rev. Rul. 55-290, 1955-1 C.B. 320
[14]Rev. Rul. 55-730, 1955-2 C.B. 53.

allocable to the improvements will be recoverable over its useful life out of the annual allowance for depreciation. The basis for depreciation is generally that portion of the basis of the entire property which bears the same ratio to the entire basis as the value of the depreciable portion of the property (at the time of acquisition) bears to the value of the whole property.[15]

The problem of allocation of basis on the acquisition of property with the intent of demolishing improvements is treated in detail in part C of Chapter 2.

3. Measuring the Depreciation Allowance

The total amount of depreciation allowable over the useful life of property is its original cost (or other basis) plus the cost of any additions less the amount of the salvage value at the end of its life.[16] The amount of the total allowance deductible in any given taxable year may be determined on the basis of any "reasonable consistent plan (not necessarily at a uniform rate)."[17]

Neither the statute nor the regulations permit the owner to use the estimated cost of replacement as his basis for depreciation; he is limited to the amount of his actual investment in the property.[18]

The owner's basis for the purpose of determining his gain or loss on its disposition *must be reduced* by the amount of the depreciation actually allowable to him under the plan of depreciation he adopts. Thus, if the owner fails to take a deduction for depreciation allowable in any given year, he loses the benefit of the depreciation deduction for that year. He is not permitted to increase his depreciation deduction in later years to make up for the lost depreciation,[19] and, furthermore, he must reduce his basis by the amount of the allowable but not taken deductions.

Even if the depreciation allowance taken by the owner resulted in no tax benefit to him, he is not permitted to postopne his deduction to a later year in which he may have taxable income, and his basis must be reduced by the amount of depreciation properly allowable.[20]

But suppose the owner took excessive depreciation in a year in which he had a net loss: must he reduce his basis for the purpose of determining gain or loss on a subsequent disposition by the excessive depreciation or only by the amount of depreciation which was properly allowable? According to the regulations, basis is reduced only for the amount of allowable depreciation. As long as the excessive depreciation resulted in no tax benefit to him, he need not reduce his basis for it.[21]

The problem of determining the amount of depreciation properly allowable in any given year is twofold: first, the owner must adopt a reasonably consistent plan of

---

[15] Reg. Sec. 1.167(a)-5. But in Rev. Rul. 68-362, 1968-2 C.B. 334, the Commissioner stated the rule differently: first the basis is allocated to improvements to the extent of fair market value; the balance is then allocated to land.
[16] Reg. Sec. 1.167(f)-1.
[17] Reg. Sec. 1.167(a)-1(a).
[18] National Packing Co., 24 B.T.A. 952, 956 (1931), acq. on another issue, XI-1 C.B. 5; O.D. 283, 1C.B. 138.
[19] Reg. Sec. 1.167(a)-10(a).
[20] Sec. 1016(a)(2), I.R.C.
[21] Sec. 1016(a)(2)(B), I.R.C.

DEPRECIATION

apportioning the total depreciation allowance over the useful life of the property and, second, he must estimate the useful life of the property and a reasonable salvage value for the property after the expiration of that useful life.

4. Methods of Allocating the Depreciation Allowance

The owner is given the choice of adopting any of several reasonably consistent plans of allocating his total allowance for depreciation over the life of the property; if he fails to adopt any plan, his depreciation allowance will be spread evenly over the life of the asset under the straight-line method.[22]

Among the methods of apportioning depreciation over the life of the property are the following:

(1) *Straight-Line Method*: The lifetime depreciation allowance (basis less slavage value) is prorated equally over the life of the property. For example, a building has a total cost of $10,000 with an estimated salvage value of $1,000 after a ten-year useful life. One-tenth of the total depreciation allowance of $9,000 would be allocated to each year, making an annual depreciation deduction of $900.[23]

(2) *Double-Declining Balance Method*: Under the double-declining balance method, the owner is permitted to allocate the bulk of his depreciation allowance to the earlier years of ownership. For this reason the method is known as a method of accelerated depreciation. The method is available only for property newly-constructed or acquired as new property after December 31, 1953, and having a useful life of three years or more.[24] Under this method, the owner is entitled to apply a uniform rate of depreciation (not to exceed double the straight-line rate) to the unrecovered basis of the property during the year. Although salvage value can be ignored in figuring the rate, the property can not be depreciated below its salvage value.[25] If we refer back to the preceding example, we find that the rate of depreciation on the straight-line method was 10 percent. Thus, under the double-declining balance method the owner would be entitled to use a rate of 20 percent. If he chooses this maximum, his depreciation deduction for the first year would be 20 percent of his unrecovered basis of $10,000, or $2,000. The next year, the same rate would be applied to the remaining basis after adjustment for the prior year's depreciation ($8,000), resulting in a depreciation deduction of $1,600. For the entire ten-year period, the depreciation deduction would decrease annually as follows:

Year	Rate	Unrecovered Basis	Depreciation
1st	20%	$10,000.00	$2,000.00
2nd	20%	8,000.00	1,600.00
3rd	20%	6,400.00	1,280.00
4th	20%	5,120.00	1,024.00

---

[22] Reg. Sec. 1.167(a)-10(a).
[23] Reg. Sec. 1.167(b)-1.
[24] Sec. 167(c), I.R.C. Property acquired in a tax-free exchange from an original user is not qualified for accelerated depreciation in the hands of the acquirer. Rev. Rul. 56-256, 1956-1 C.B. 129. The first use must be the owner claiming the benefits of accelerated methods of depreciation. Reg. Sec. 1.167(c)-1.
[25] Reg. Sec. 1.167(b)-2.

Year	Rate	Unrecovered Basis	Depreciation
5th	20%	4,096.00	819.20
6th	20%	3,276.80	655.36
7th	20%	2,621.44	524.29
8th	20%	2,097.51	419.43
9th	20%	1,677.72	335.54
10th	20%	1,324.18	324.18[26]
Actual Salvage value		$ 1,073.74	
Total depreciation			$8,926.26

If the reasonably anticipated salvage value of the asset in this example were $2,000, the depreciation allowable would remain the same through the eighth year. In the ninth year, however, depreciation would be only $97.15, reducing the recovered basis to $2,000. When it is ascertained in the tenth year that actual salvage will be $1,000.00, a depreciation deduction of $1,000.00 would be allowable.

(3) *Sum-of-the-Years' Digits Method*: This is an alternative method of accelerated depreciation. Again, the use of this method is restricted to property newly-constructed or acquired as new property after 1953, and having a useful life of three years or more. The total depreciation allowance is apportioned at a rate measured by the number of years of life remaining, divided by the sum of all the years' digits in the useful life of the property.[27] For example, in the case of property having a useful life of 10 years, the sum of the years' digits (1+2+3 . . .+ 10) is 55. If the salvage value of the property is $1,000, the $9,000 depreciation allowance would be apportioned as follows:

Year	Rate of Depreciation	$9,000.00 + basis to be = depreciated	Amount of Depreciation
1st	10/55		$1,636.36
2nd	9/55		1,472.73
3rd	8/55		1,309.09
4th	7/55		1,145.45
5th	6/55		981.82
6th	5/55		818.18
7th	4/55		654.55
8th	3/55		490.91
9th	2/55		327.27
10th	1/55		163.64
		Total depreciation	$9,000.00

(4) *Other Methods*: Any other consistent method of apportioning depreciation will be permitted, provided it does not permit recovery of a greater allowance for depreciation in the first two-thirds of the useful life of the property than would be permitted under the double-declining balance method.[28]

---

[26]Twenty percent of $1,342.18 is $268.44, but the regulations permit the owner to deduct the unrecovered balance of the depreciation account as part of the depreciation allowance in the year of retirement. Reg. Sec. 1.167(b)-2(b).
[27]Reg. Sec. 1.167(b)-3.
[28]Reg Sec. 1.167(b)-4.

DEPRECIATION

(5) *One Hundred Fifty Percent-Declining-Balance Method*: The 150%-declining-balance method is specifically permitted by the regulations,[29] and is not restricted to new property, as are the methods of accelerated depreciation discussed above. It is similar to the double-declining balance method, but is not as valuable because the depreciation rate is limited to one and one-half times the straight-line rate. It is, however, the method that produces the fastest recovery of basis for a taxpayer who acquires used property that does not qualify for the double-declining or sum-of-the-years' digits methods of accelerated depreciation.

(6) *One Hundred Twenty-Five Percent-Declining-Balance Method*: One hundred twenty-five percent-declining depreciation is figured in the same manner as the double-declining balance method of depreciation (known alternatively as the 200 percent-declining balance method of depreication). Under this method, the owner is entitled to apply a uniform percentage rate of depreciation (not to exceed 125 percent) to the unrecovered basis of the property during the year.

Thus, if the rate of depreciation on the straight-line method is 10 percent, the rate under this alternative method would be 12½ percent. The 12½ percent rate can be applied only to the basis of the property reduced by prior year's depreciation, not to the original cost or basis.[30]

5. Limitations on Use of Accelerated Depreciation Methods

The use of accelerated methods of depreciation is confined to newly acquired or newly constructed property; the taxpayer claiming the right to use an accelerated method of recovery must establish the fact that the first productive use of the property commenced with him.[31]

But even if the property is newly acquired or constructed and is in the hands of the first user, there are other limitations of the use of accelerated methods of depreciation, as follows:

a. *New Residential Housing*: New residential housing is the *only* property that qualifies for the 200 percent-(or double) declining-balance and sum-of-the-years' digits methods of depreciation.

New residential housing is defined as residential rental property but only if 80 percent or more of the gross rental income of the property is derived from the rental of dwelling units. The property must be "new" in the sense that its original use commenced with the taxpayer.[32]

b. *Other New Improvements*: All other new improvements, including commercial and industrial buildings, cannot be depreciated at a method faster than the 150 percent-declining-balance method.[33] In other words, the owner can choose between the straight-line method, the 150 percent-declining method, or any other method which

---

[29] Reg. Sec. 1.167(b)-0(b).
[30] Section 167(j)(5)(B), I.R.C.
[31] Reg. Sec. 1.167(c)-1.
[32] Section 167(j)(2), I.R.C.
[33] Section 167(j)(1), I.R.C.

will not exceed the depreciation deductible under the 150 percent-declining-balance method.

If the original use of the property commenced with the owner, it is new.

c. *Used Residential Housing*: If "residential rental property," as defined in (a) above, is acquired by an owner from another user, it can qualify for the 125 percent-declining-balance method. The owner has an election between this limited accelerated method or straight-line depreciation.

The used property must have a useful life of at least 20 years to qualify for the 125 percent-declining-balance method.[34]

d. *Other Used Improvements*: All other structures and improvements to land, if acquired from another user, are depreciable only on the straight-line method. Included in this classification are used residential income properties of a useful life of less than 20 years.

e. *Rehabilitation Expenditures*: If used rental housing is acquired by an owner, he may be entitled to a five-year amortizaion deduction of any capital expenditures he makes to improve the property.[35] In other words, he can deduct the cost of rehabilitating the property over a period of five years, provided the useful life of the property exceeds five years; if the useful life is less than five years, the useful life itself may be used. The allowance must be made on a straight-line basis, that is, one-fifth of the total expenditures is deductible in any 12-month period.

This accelerated write-off is allowable only for rehabilitation expenditures on "low-cost rental housing." What is low-cost rental housing? The Code defines it as housing which is rented to families or individuals of low or moderate income as determined under the policies of the Housing and Urban Development Act of 1968.

The amount or rehabilitation expenditures qualifying for the special five-year amortization allowance is subject to both a floor and a ceiling. The floor is $3,000 per unit over a two-year period. If the rehabilitation expenditures in two years do not exceed $3,000 per unit they can be depreciated only over the useful life of the property. If these rehabilitation improvements exceed $3,000 over two years, the entire amount is amortizable over the five-year period except to the extent it exceeds the ceiling. The ceiling is $15,000 per unit. Any excess expenditure over the $15,000 per unit ceiling can be depreciated only over the useful life of the property.

Again we must note that the excess of the five-year amortization allowance for rehabilitation expenditures over straight-line depreciation must be accounted for in at least two other places. First, the excess is an item of tax preference income,[36] and second, it may be subject to recapture if the property is sold.[37]

These provisions relating to rehabilitation expenditures do not affect the rules relating to repairs. Repairs are decuctible currently whether made to low-cost housing or to luxury penthouses. Rehabilitation expenditures refer only to items of capital improvements, the cost of which must be added to basis and recovered only through the allowance for depreciation or five-year amortization.

---

[34] Section 167(j)(5), I.R.C.
[35] Section 167(k), I.R.C.
[36] Section 57(a)(2), I.R.C.
[37] Section 1250(b)(4), I.R.C.

DEPRECIATION

6. Change of Method

The owner may use different methods of depreciation for different properties; he is not restricted to the use of only one method for all of his properties.[38] Once however, he has selected the use of one method of depreciation for a particular property, he is stuck with it.[39] He can change from one method to another only with the permission of the Commissioner, except that he may change from the double-declining-balance method to the straight-line method at any time.[40]

The privilege of switching from double-declining-balance to straight-line depreciation is a useful tool for the purpose of eliminating the "built-in" salvage value that is a concomitant of the double-declining method. However, once the taxpayer has switched to straight-line depreciation for a given property or account he cannot switch back without the consent of the Commissioner.[41]

When the change is made, the unrecovered basis of the property, less a reasonable estimate of salvage value, is divided by the number of years of remaining life to determine the new annual depreciation allowance. It is important to note that both life[42] and salvage value[43] must be estimated in accordance with the circumstances existing at the time of the change.

Obviously, if it appears at the proposed time of change, that the original estimate of useful life was too short, the change may be undesirable. The result may be reduced depreciation deductions for the balance of the useful life of the property. On the other hand, if the circumstances at the proposed time of change show that a shorter life is reasonably to be expected, or that the salvage value is zero, the change will be beneficial to the owner.

7. Useful Life

The useful life of real estate or other depreciable property is the period during which it is expected to be used in the trade or business or held for the production of income. This is not necessarily the same as the physical life of the property.[44]

If it is expected that the property will be used indefinitely or that it will be held for use so long as it is usable, physical life will probably be useful life. However, where the owner has a regular policy or practice of disposing of a given type of asset before the end of its physical life, useful life will be taken to be the length of time the owner *usually* holds such assets, even though this period may be much shorter than its physical life.[45]

---

[38]Reg. Sec. 1.167(c)-1(c).
[39]Reg. Sec. 1.167(e)-1.
[40]Sec. 167(e), I.R.C. Additionally, he may change from either the double-declining balance method or the sum-of-the-years' digits method to the straight-line method with respect to Section 1245 property if he does it in his first taxable year after December 31, 1962. Section 167(e)(2). The procedure for obtaining the Commissioner's consent in other cases is set forth in Rev. Proc. 67-40 I.R.B. 1967-43, 32. But a taxpayer cannot reserve the right to change from straight-line to accelerated depreciation in the event the useful life is extended. Rev. Rul. 74-154, I.R.B. 1974-14, 9.
[41]Reg. Sec. 1.167(e)-1(b).
[42]*Ibid.*
[43]Rev. Rul. 58-420, 1958-2 C.B. 83.
[44]Reg. Sec. 1.167(a)-1(b).
[45]Massey Motors, Inc. v. United States, 364 U.S. 92 (1960).

The Internal Revenue Service has promulgated certain guidelines for useful lives of real estate, as follows:[46]

(1) Pavement, sidewalks, and sewers	20 years
(2) Apartment buildings	40 years
(3) Bank buildings	50 years
(4) Single-family duplex rentals	45 years
(5) Factories	45 years
(6) Garages	45 years
(7) Hotels	40 years
(8) Loft buildings	50 years
(9) Office buildings	45 years
(10) Store buildings	50 years
(11) Theater buildings	40 years
(12) Warehouses	60 years
(13) Farm buildings	25 years

The categories stated above do not take into account the type of construction; they do seem to take into account an economic obsolescence factor, such as the 20-year difference in useful life between a warehouse and a hotel or theater building and the 35-year difference between a warehouse and a farm building.

Despite these anomalies, some courts have held the guidelines to be conclusive on useful life. The apparent theory is that the Internal Revenue Service's guidelines were to eliminate disputes over useful life by fiat.[47] But useful life cannot be established by fiat: the Tax Court has expressly recognized that fact when the shoe was on the Service's foot. The guidelines are merely that: a guideline, not a fiat.[48]

The guidelines are merely aids in that determination. Past experience, of others in the industry or community, expert opinion (both engineering and economic), and reasonable projections of the future all may assist the taxpayer in estimating the useful life of the property, or in defending that estimate if it is later challenged by the Commissioner.

Expert opinion is particularly useful for improvements on real estate. Every building has a probable life turning on its own more or less unique set of factors and conditions, many of which can best be appraised by experts. Some of these factors are the date and nature of construction, materials, design, past maintenance, improvements, present condition and use, location and character of the building and environs, future maintenance requirements, and business prospects.[49]

The estimates of average life on a national basis contained in the depreciation guidelines of the Revenue Service will thus be of little assistance in this area, except, perhaps, to have the effect of setting upper limits on useful life. Moreover, the useful lives listed there for buildings are generally rather longer than those listed in Bulletin F,[50] the predecessor of the guidelines, and probably longer than most now being used by taxpayers.

---

[46]Rev. Proc. 62-21, 1962 C.B. 418, 419-20.
[47]Stevens Realty Co., 1967 P-H Memo T.C. ¶67,113. Colin M. Peters, 1969 P-H Memo T.C. ¶69,052. *Contra* Richardson v. United States, 330 F. Supp 109 (D.C. Tex. 1971).
[48]The Tax Court ignored its prior division memorandum opinions cited in footnote 48 in its decision in Pacific Fruit Express Co., 60 T.C. no. 68 (1973).
[49]Laura Massaglia, 33 T.C. 379 (1959), acq. 1960-1 C.B. 5, aff'd 286 F.2d 258 (10th Cir. 1961).
[50]I.R.S. Publication No. 173 (1955), expressly withdrawn by Rev. Proc. 62-21, 1962-2 C.B. 418.

DEPRECIATION

Following are listed several guideline categories of buildings[51] with their guideline lives and, for comparison, the Bulletin F lives for "good" and "cheap" construction of the same categories of buildings.

Category	Guideline Life (yrs.)	Bulletin F Life Good	Bulletin F Life Cheap
Apartments	40	40	33 1/3
Dwellings	45	50	33 1/3
Factories[52]	45	40	33 1/3
Garages	45	50	33 1/3
Office Buildings	45	50	33 1/3
Stores	50	50	40
Warehouses	60	67 2/3	30

Once the estimated useful life of a depreciable asset has been determined it may be changed "only when the change in the useful life is significant and there is a clear and convincing basis for the redetermination."[53] However, the taxpayer may act at his peril if he fails to redetermine useful life at any time conditions warrant. When it becomes apparent that the actual useful life of the asset will be more or less[54] than that estimated originally, the depreciation allowance for the current and future years should be recomputed. Failure to do so may result in loss of allowance deductions currently and decreased basis when the property is eventually sold.

8. Salvage Value

The salvage value to be attributed to any piece of property is the estimated value that the property will have at the end of its useful life.[55] Salvage value can be estimated only after useful life is determined, and conversely, "salvage value is not a factor for determining useful life."[56]

Just as useful life is not necessarily the physical life of the asset, so salvage value is not always scrap value. If the taxpayer regularly disposes of property of the type in question before its useful life is exhausted, salvage value may amount to a substantial part of the original basis of the asset.[57]

The expected cost of removal and sale of the property at the end of its useful life may be deducted from the anticipated proceeds to arrive at net salvage value. It is this figure which is usually used in determining depreciation allowable, particularly in regard to real estate improvements.

Salvage value cannot be changed from the amount estimated on acquisition

---

[51] Defined to include "the structural shell of the building and all integral parts thereof. Includes equipment which services normal heating, plumbing, air conditioning, fire prevention and power requirements, and equipment such as elevators and escalators." Rev. Proc 62-21, 1962-2 C.B. 418.

[52] In the first court decision on the guideline life for a building, a District Court held that 45 years was too long for a factory building and allowed a life of 33 years. Frito-Lay, Inc. v. United States, 209 F.Supp. 886 (N.D.Ga. 1962).

[53] Reg. Sec. 1.167(a)-1(b).

[54] For example, extraordinary obsolescence resulting from unforeseen technological advances. See Reg. Sec. 1.167(a)-9.

[55] Reg. Sec. 1.167(a)-1(c).

[56] Reg. Sec. 1.167(a)-1(b).

[57] Reg. Sec. 1.167(a)-1(c); Massey Motors, Inc. v. United States, 364 U.S. 92 (1960).

merely because of changes in price levels. However, if useful life is redetermined, salvage value may also be redetermined to accord with the facts then known.[58]

In no event may an asset be depreciated below its reasonably estimated salvage value. However, the mere fact that an asset is sold at a gain (that is, in excess of its depreciated basis) does not mean that salvage value can automatically be redetermined for the purposes of disallowing depreciation in the year of sale.[59] Salvage value can be readjusted only in the light of relevant facts known or fairly ascertainable which indicate that the taxpayer's estimate of salvage value was unreasonable.[60]

9. Use of Accelerated Methods of Depreciation

The methods of accelerated depreciation made available under the 1954 Code will result in the recovery of a larger depreciation allowance in the earlier years of ownership than the straight-line method would permit. In general, the accelerated methods will permit approximately two-thirds of the total depreciation allowance to be recovered in the first half of the useful life of the property; under the straight-line method, one-half of the total allowance would be recovered in the first half of the useful life.

Thus, if the property is sold after having been depreciated for half of its life, the owner will be required to pay a tax on a larger gain if an accelerated method of depreciation has been used than if the straight-line method had been employed, assuming that the property has maintained a constant value. But in the case of trade or business property or of an asset held for the production of income, the gain so realized will be taxed as capital gain except for depreciation recapture, as discussed below. Because the owner would have deducted the depreciation allowance against ordinary income, he will normally be financially ahead by using an accelerated method of depreciation, to the extent that his taxable rate on ordinary income exceeds his capital gains rate. In effect, the sale of the asset after being held for one-half of its useful life may result in the conversion of ordinary income into capital gain. The exact nature of the gain realized on the sale of a depreciable real estate investment is analyzed in Chapter 4.

10. Effect of Tax Preference Item Tax on Selection of Depreciation Alternatives

The excess of accelerated depreciation over straight-line depreciation is defined as a tax preference item and may be subject to a 15 percent minimum tax if it, when added to other tax preferences, exceeds the limitations set forth in Chapter 1, Part 3. Therefore, if the owner is subject to the possibility of a tax preference item tax, he should eschew the use of accelerated depreciation.

Example: Owner acquires a new apartment house for $5,000,000 in 1974. In 1974, he reports gross rentals of $500,000 less cash expenses of $350,000. His depreciation deduction on an accelerated method totals $150,000, twice the allowance ($75,000) on a straight-line basis. Because the use of accelerated depreciation reduced *O's* 1974 income to zero, his tax preference

---

[58]Reg. Sec. 1.167(a)-1(c).
[59]Fribourg Navigation Co., 383 U.S. 272 (1966), overruling Cohn v. United States, 259 F.2d 371 (6th Cir. 1958).
[60]Rev. Rul. 67-272, 1967-2 C.B. 99 overruling Rev. Rul. 62-92, 62-1 C.B. 29.

DEPRECIATION

tax on the excess of accelerated depreciation over straight-line depreciation is computed as follows:

Accelerated depreciation	$150,000
Straight line depreciation	75,000
Excess depreciation	$ 75,000
Less exemption	10,000
Tax preference income	$ 65,000
Minimum tax thereon	$ 9,750

The minimum tax is not an addition to the basis of the property, nor is it deductible. It is a simple waste of money.

11. Who Is Entitled to Depreciation?

Generally, only the one who has a capital investment in the property is entitled to deduct the allowance for depreciation on the property.[61]

As between two or more persons, each having an economic investment in the property, the depreciation allowance follows the income. Thus, the owner of a mere security interest in the property will not usually be entitled to depreciation; only the equitable owner enjoying the beneficial use of the property will be allowed to deduct the depreciation. As between mortgagor and mortgagee, for instance, the mortgagor is entitled to the depreciation deduction.[62] Similarly, under a security deed of trust[63] or land purchase contract,[64] the party who has the benefits and burdens of ownership is permitted to take the deduction for depreciation. And a lessor of land is not entitled to take depreciation on a building constructed by his lessee and paid for by the lessee. The lessor has no economic interest in the building.[65]

If the ownership of the property is split between a life tenant and remainderman, the life tenant is allowed to deduct for depreciation during his lifetime.[66] But if the property is held in trust, the deduction is allocated between the income beneficiaries and the trustee on the basis of the trust income allocable to each unless the trust instrument, local law, or the trustee pursuant to discretion granted by either, establishes a reserve for depreciation. In that event, the deduction is allocated to the trust to the extent of the reserve and the rest to the income beneficiaries.[67]

In the case of an estate, the depreciation deduction is to be allocated among the estate and the income beneficiaries in accordance with their respective shares of the estate's income.[68]

---

[61] Helvering v. F.R. Lazarus & Co., 308 U.S. 252 (1939).

[62] E.J. Murray, 21 T.C. 1049, 1062 (1954), acq. 1954-2 C.B. 5, aff'd on another ground, 232 F.2d 742 (9th Cir. 1956), cert. den. 352 U.S. 872.

[63] Helvering v. F.R. Lazarus & Co., 308 U.S. 252 (1939).

[64] T.K. Harris Co., 38 B.T.A. 383, 387 (1938), aff'd on another point, 112 F.2d 76 (6th Cir. 1940). Rev. Rul. 69-89, 1969-1 C.B. 59.

[65] Catherine B. Currier, 51 T.C. No. 49 (1968).

[66] Sec. 167(g), I.R.C.

[67] Reg. Sec. 1.167(g)-1(b). The trust instrument cannot allocate a greater portion of the depreciation deduction to an income beneficiary than his share of the income would entitle him to receive. It can, however, authorize the trustee to maintain a reserve for depreciation even though all the income after depreciation be distributed.

[68] Reg. Sec. 1.167(g)-1(c).

Depreciation on property held in joint tenancy, tenancy in common, or tenancy by the entireties is allocable among the owners in proportion to their interests in the property.

Depreciation on property held by a straw corporation is allowable to the equitable owners of the property.[69]

B. OBSOLESCENCE

Ordinarily, an allowance for obsolescence of a building or improvement on real property is considered to be part of the owner's allowance for depreciation.[70] Consequently, the anticipated useful life of a building or improvement should be estimated by the owner in light of both its physical life and the possibilities that the asset may be discarded or replaced because of obsolescence that may be expected to occur. If the owner is able to show that the improvement may be discarded or replaced in a relatively short time, he is entitled to use an estimated useful life for the purposes of depreciation that may be considerably shorter than its physical life.[71] The "expectation" of obsolescence must be more than possibilities of economic loss. It must be based on realities.[72]

For example, an owner may be permitted to revise an estimated useful life for an improvement if changing economic or technological circumstances have intervened to shorten its expected useful life.[73] For example, a manufacturer was entitled to shorten the depreciable life of a manufacturing plant to two and one-half years upon a showing that competition was forcing him to build a more modern facility at a better location to replace his old plant.[74] In the extraordinary case of technological or economic circumstances which intervene to make the owner's improvements completely valueless, he may be entitled to deduct the entire unrecovered basis as a loss under Section 165, I.R.C.[75] How can the owner establish his loss resulting from extraordinary obsolescence? Obviously, if he demolishes,[76] alters substantially to fit the structure for another use,[77] or removes the structure,[78] his loss will be fixed for tax purposes. But domolition or removal is not necessarily required to justify a write-off of the remaining basis. If the owner can show that he has permanently devoted the structure to a radically different use, which was caused by the intervention of unforeseen external forces, he is entitled to write off the amount of his loss of value.[79] Similarly, an abandonment of the building will support a deduction of the entire remaining basis for the structure.[80]

---

[69]David E. Bolger, 59 T.C. No. 75 (1973), appeal not authorized.

[70]Reg. Sec. 1.167(a)-1(a). "Section 167(a) provides that a reasonable allowance for the exhaustion, wear and tear, and obsolescence of property used in the trade or business or of property held by the taxpayer for the production of income shall be allowed as a depreciation deduction."

[71]W.A. Graeper, 27 B.T.A. 632, 638 (1933), acq. XII-1 C.B. 5. See Real Estate Land Title & Trust Co. v. United States, 309 U.S. 13 (1940).

[72]Colin M. Peters, 1969 P-H Memo T.C. ¶69,052.

[73]Reg. Sec. 1.167(a)-9.

[74]American Valve Co., 4 B.T.A. 1204 (1926), acq. VII-1 C.B. 2.

[75]Section 165(b), I.R.C.; Reg. Sec. 1.165-2.

[76]Jack M. Chesboro, 21 T.C. 123, 130 (1953), aff'd per curiam, 225 F.2d 674 (2d Cir. 1955), cert. den. 350 U.S. 995.

[77]Parma Co., 18 B.T.A. 429 (1929), acq. IX-1 C.B. 42.

[78]Ingle v. Gage, 52 F.2d 738, 740 (W.D.N.Y. 1931).

[79]Reg. Sec. 1.167(a)-8(a)(3).

[80]Reg. Sec. 1.167(a)-8(a)(4).

In all cases, the amount of the deductible loss is limited to the owner's basis; if a partial loss in value is suffered, only a similar proportion of the owner's remaining basis may be written off.[81]

C. DEMOLITION, ABANDONMENT OR REMOVAL OF IMPROVEMENTS

If the improvements are held for a trade or business purpose, the demolition, abandonment, or removal is a deductible loss under Section 165. Whether or not the demolition, abandonment, or removal is voluntary or forced is immaterial.

If a building is voluntarily demolished,[82] substantially altered,[83] or removed[84] because of economic circumstances, the owner will be entitled to a loss deduction. The measure of the deduction will be the adjusted basis of the portion of the property destroyed or abandoned,[85] the amount of the loss will be increased by any expenses of removal or demolition and decreased by the amount of any salvage realized.[86]

But there are three areas of complication: *first*, suppose the owner intends to rebuild for his own purposes; *second*, suppose the owner plans to rebuild for a new tenant; and *third*, suppose the owner bought the property with the idea of demolishing all improvements? What are the tax consequences?

1. Owner Intends to Rebuild

It has been argued that if a building is demolished or removed to make way for a new building, the unrecovered basis for the old structure should be added to the new building which replaces it. Thus, no loss would be incurred in the year of demolition or removal; the unrecovered basis of the old structure would be recovered over the life of the new as a part of the owner's depreciation allowance.[87]

But the Commissioner has refused to accept this theory. The unrecovered basis of the old structure must be deducted in the year of demolition or removal; it cannot be added to the cost basis of the new structure. The Tax Court, as well as other courts,[88] has held to the contrary. Apparently, the owner can take it either way.

2. Owner Intends to Lease

The basis of the demolished or abandoned improvement is added to the cost of the lease and is amortized over the life of the lease acquired.[89]

---

[81] See Reg. Sec. 1.165-1(c).
[82] First National Bank of Evanston, 1 B.T.A. 9 (1924), acq. IV-1 C.B. 2.
[83] Union Bed & Spring Co. v. Commissioner, 39 F.2d 383 (7th Cir. 1930); The Winter Garden, Inc., 10 B.T.A. 71 (1928), acq. VII-2 C.B. 43.
[84] Herbert Burwig, Par. 53,339 P-H Memo T.C. (1953).
[85] Section 165(b), I.R.C., Reg. Sec. 1.165-1(c).
[86] Cf. Rev. Rul. 55-110, 1955-1 C.B. 280.
[87] Non-acq. 1946-2 C.B. 6 to Henry Phipps Estates, 5 T.C. 964 (1954).
[88] Commissioner v. Appleby's Estate, 123 F.2d 700 (2d Cir. 1941); Henry Phipps Estates, 5 T.C. 964 (1954), non-acq. 1946-2 C.B. 6; A. Raymond Jones, 25 T.C. 1100, 1103 (1956), reversed on other grounds 259 F.2d 300 (5th Cir. 1958). Nicholl's Estate v. Commissioner, 282 F.2d 895 (7th Cir. 1960).
[89] The problem is one of timing. See Chapter 8. How much time must elapse between the date of demolition and the date of the new lease? Donald S. Levinson, 59 T.C. 676 (1973). The fact that the tenant demolishes the landlord's improvements does not create a loss to the landlord. Landerman v. Commissioner, 454 F.2d 338 (7th Cir. 1972), cert. den. 406 U.S. 967.

3. Owner Acquires with Intent to Demolish

If a taxpayer purchases real property with the intention of razing, removing, or altering the existing structure, the unrecovered basis of the existing structure cannot be deducted as a loss.[90] The amount of the basis for the structure must be added to the cost of the land.[91] Any expense of removal or demolition incurred in such a case, less salvage received, is also treated as a part of the purchaser's cost for the land and cannot be deducted.[92]

On demolition or removal, the cost of the improvement becomes part of the cost of the land. But if, however, in the interim, the owner had rented the property; he would be entitled to allocate that portion of his cost to the improvements that would offset the "present value" of the rentals at the date of demolition on a straight-line depreciation deduction.[93] The difference between the reduced basis for the improved property after the depreciation deduction is disallowed as a loss.

But is the disallowed loss necessarily added to the basis of the land? Treasury Regulations so state.[94] There is some difference of opinion.[95]

D. REPAIRS, MAINTENANCE EXPENSES, AND CAPITAL IMPROVEMENTS

Expenses of operating, maintaining, and repairing real property are deductible by the owner in the year paid or incurred. If the owner is an individual, the deduction for costs of repair, maintenance, and operation is limited to property used in his trade or business,[96] property held for the production of income,[97] or property held for sale.[98]

On the other hand, expenditures that result in new structures or in permanent improvements or betterments to existing structures are not currently deductible; such expenditures are treated as capital improvements, the cost of which must be added to the owner's basis for the property.[99] The cost of these improvements can be recovered only through the owner's allowance for depreciation or upon a taxable disposition of the property.

1. Repair or Capital Improvement?

One of the most difficult problems faced by an owner of real estate is the drawing of the line between deductible repairs and non-deductible capital improvements. If the

---

[90] Lynchburg National Bank & Trust Co., 20 T.C. 670 (1953), aff'd on another ground, 208 F.2d 757 (4th Cir. 1953); Reg. Sec. 1.165-3(a).
[91] N.W. Ayer & Sons, Inc., 17 T.C. 631 (1951), acq. 1952-1 C.B. 1; Reg. Sec. 1.165-3(a).
[92] Rev. Rul. 55—110, 1955-1 C.B. 280. William I. Nash, 60 T.C. 503 (1973).
[93] Reg. Sec. 1.165-3(a). The "present value" of the rentals until demolition is the inverse factor of the current interest rate. The result is that the demolition-intending owner can offset rental income by all but the interest he pays (or would pay). Basis is correspondingly reduced. William I. Nash, 60 T.C. 503 (1973).
[94] Reg. Sec. 1.165-3(a).
[95] Piedmont National Bank of Spartanburg v. U.S., 162 F.Supp. 919 (W.D.S.Cal. 1958).
[96] Section 162(a), I.R.C.
[97] Section 212(2), I.R.C.
[98] S. Rose Lloyd, 32 B.T.A. 887, 890 (1935), acq. XIV-2 C.B. 13.
[99] Section 263(a), I.R.C.

expenditure does no more than keep the property "in an operating condition over its probable useful life for the uses for which it was acquired," it will be classified as a repair.[100] Thus, expenditures that merely maintain value or useful life are deductible repairs.[101]

On the other hand, if the expenditure results in prolonging the useful life of the property or results in increasing its value it will be classified as a capital improvement.[102] Merely because an expenditure does not add either life or value to the property will not in itself prove that it is a repair; a substantial alteration of property made merely to preserve value and useful life has been classified as a capital improvement.[103]

Repairs properly classified as such may be considered as capital improvements if they are made at the same time as, and as a part of, *a general plan to rehabilitate* or improve the property. For example, expenses of repair and moving partitions were capitalized because they were made at the same time with, and as a part of, a plan to remodel the floors of a building to add to its useful life.[104]

2. Expenses of Maintenance and Operation

Expenses of maintaining and operating both property used in the taxpayer's trade or business and property held for the production of income are deductible.[105] Examples of deductible expenses would be such items as the cost of painting and decorating, the expense of hiring a manager or agent to collect rents, janitorial and caretaker services, insurance, advertising expenses, and other similar or related expenses.

E. PROTECTION OF INCOME OR DEFENSE OF TITLE?

A similar problem arises in the case of an expenditure to protect the owner's interest in income-producing property. Was the expenditure made to protect title? Or was it an expenditure to conserve income? Only expenditures of the latter type are deductible.[106] Expenditures to perfect or to protect title must be capitalized as part of the cost of the property.[107]

If the expenditure involves protection of title, the owner must capitalize it even though his defense is unsuccessful.[108] If the unsuccessful litigant receives a cash award in his suit or in its settlement, he is permitted to offset the award received by the

---

[100] Illinois Merchants Trust Co., 4 B.T.A. 103, 106 (1926), acq. V-2 C.B. 2.

[101] Reg; Sec. 1.162-4.

[102] Section 263(a), I.R.C. Rev. Rul. 73-377, I.R.B. 1973-38, 6.

[103] Honigman v. Commissioner, 466 F.2d 69 (6th Cir. 1972), affirming the Tax Court on this point. Jason L. Honigman, 55 T.C. 1067 (1971).

[104] Phillips & Easton Supply Co., 20 T.C. 455, 460 (1953); Home News Publishing Co., 18 B.T.A. 1008 (1930).

[105] Section 162(a), I.R.C. Section 212(2), I.R.C. Insurance is deductible only as it furnishes benefits to the owner. Prepayment of insurance must be amortized over the term of the insurance. Rev. Rul. 70-413 1970-2 C.B. 103.

[106] Kornhauser v. United States, 276 U.S. 145 (1928); Allen v. Selig, 200 F.2d 487 (5th Cir. 1952); The Alleghany Corporation, 28 T.C. 298 (1957), acq. 1957-2 C.B. 3.

[107] Reg. Sec. 1.212-1(k).

[108] See Marion A. Burt Beck, 15 T.C. 642, 669 (1950), aff'd per curiam, 194 F.2d 537 (2d Cir. 1952), cert. den. 344 U.S. 821. J. Bryant Kasey, 54 T.C. 1642 (1970), aff'd, 457 F.2d 369 (9th Cir. 1972).

80 OWNERSHIP AND OPERATION OF REAL PROPERTY

amount of expenses incurred in protecting his interest.[109] But suppose he receives nothing; even in this event he must capitalize his expenditure.

What constitutes defense of title is not always easy to determine: for example, no costs and fees incurred in an unsuccessful attempt to limit the scope of a condemnation have been held deductible.[110]

Suppose the expenditure involves both defense of title to the property and defense of the right to income produced from the property. Will the owner be permitted to deduct any part of the expenditure?

If the owner recovers an award which includes an allowance for income, he is entitled to deduct a portion of his total expenditure as a defense of income. The amount of the deduction is measured by the proportion of the total expenditure which bears the same ratio to that total as the amount of income recovered bears to the total award recovered.[111]

Example: Owner sues to establish a one-half interest in an apartment that was devised to him and his co-owner. Owner also sues to recover one-half of the rents received since the date of his testator's demise. Owner wins judgment, entitling him to a one-half interest in the apartment and to $8,000 in back rents. His litigation expenses total $12,000. If the value of his one-half interest in the apartment is $40,000, he would be permitted to deduct the following portion of his expense:

$$\frac{\text{Deductible portion of fee}}{\text{Total fee}} = \frac{\text{Income recovered}}{\text{Total recovery}}$$

$$\frac{x}{\$12,000} = \frac{8,000}{\$40,000 + \$8,000}$$

$$\frac{x}{\$12,000} = \frac{\$8,000}{\$48,000}$$

$$x = \frac{\$96,000}{\$48,000}$$

$$x = 2,000$$

Thus, $2,000 of the fee would be deductible as expense of recovering income, and $10,000 would be capitalized as an expenditure to perfect title.

Suppose the owner recovers no income; suppose, for example, the suit is merely defensive. The owner makes an expenditure both to protect his title to the property and to preserve his right to income previously received. Under these circumstances, the courts are chary of permitting any portion of the total fee or expenditure to be deducted. It has been held that if the principal purpose of the suit is protection of title, the owner will not be permitted to allocate any portion of the fee to defense of income even though income may have been incidentally involved. All of the expenditure must be capitalized.[112]

---

[109]Johnson & Co. v. United States, 149 F.2d 851 (2d Cir. 1945); William Justin Petit, 8 T.C. 228, 236 (1947), acq. on another point, 1947-1 C.B. 3.
[110]Madden Blaine M. 56 T.C. 513 (1972).
[111]Helvering v. Stormfelz, 142 F.2d 982 (8th Cir. 1944); Reg. Sec. 1.212-1(k).
[112]Safety Tube Corp., 8 T.C. 757, 763 (1947), acq. on another point, 1947-2 C.B. 4, aff'd, 168 F.2d 787 (6th Cir. 1948); E.E. Shipp v, Commissioner, 217 F.2d 401 (9th Cir. 1954); Midco Oil Corporation, 20 T.C. 587 (1953).

F. TAXES, INTEREST, AND CARRYING CHARGES

Taxes and interest incurred on business or investment property are deductible currently, although under certain circumstances, outlined below, these charges may be capitalized at the option of the owner. Taxes and interest charges incurred on residential property may also be deducted by a taxpayer but only if he elects to itemize his personal deductions in lieu of the optional standard deduction.

1. Taxes on Real Property

Real estate taxes are deductible by the owner in the year paid or incurred.[113] In the case of property held for personal use, taxes are deductible as such only if the owner forgoes the use of the optional standard deduction.[114]

The deduction for real estate taxes does not include any amount of taxes that are treated as being apportioned to the seller on the purchase of property.[115]

2. Interest

Interest paid or incurred on an indebtedness arising in connection with the purchase or ownership of real property is deductible as a current expense.[116] If the interest is paid or incurred on a debt relating to property used for personal purposes, it is deductible only if the owner does not elect the benefits of the optional standard deduction.

(1) *Limitation on Investment Interest:* A limitation is placed on the interest deductible if it is considered investment interest.[117] The amount deductible is the sum of the following:

(1) $10,000; plus

(2) Net investment income; plus

(3) The excess of interest, repairs, maintenance and property tax deductions on a net leased property over the rental income for the property.

Investment interest is defined as being interest paid on an indebtedness incurred to purchase or carry investment property. Investment property is property held for profit or income which is not held in a trade or business. Examples of such property would be stocks, bonds, overriding royalties, and similar properties in the hands of an investor.

Generally, rental real estate would not be considered investment property for this purpose because the operation of rental real estate is a trade or business within the meaning of the Internal Revenue Code. But two exceptions exist: first, if the property is unimproved, the owner's activities with respect to the property may be so limited that he is not engaged in a trade or business. Second, property which is leased on a net basis is treated as investment property. For this purpose, property is deemed to be leased on a net basis if the owner's Section 162 (trade or business) deductions are less than 15 percent of the rental income produced by the property. Similarly, if the lessor is

---

[113] Section 164(a), I.R.C.
[114] Section 63(b), 144, I.R.C.
[115] Section 164(b)(7) I.R.C.
[116] Section 163, I.R.C.
[117] Section 163(d), I.R.C.

guaranteed a specific return on his investment, or if he is guaranteed against loss of income, the property will be treated as investment, property.[118]

In no event will interest incurred on an indebtedness used to pay the cost of construction of property be used in a trade or business.

Example: Owner purchased an improved parcel of land for $1,000,000. He financed his purchase with a 6 percent loan for the full purchase price. His annual interest cost is, therefore, $60,000. The property is leased on a net basis under the terms of which the lessee pays all taxes, repairs, cost of improvements, and similar charges. Owner, however, pays his own interest charges. Let us assume that O receives an $80,000 annual rental. Depreciation charges against this income reduce it to a net income of $15,000 before the interest deduction. O has no other investment income, but he does have $200,000 of trade or business income. He does not realize any capital gains in the year in question. What result?

O's investment interest is $60,000. His ceiling on investment interest is computed as follows:

(1) $10,000;

(2) $15,000 (net investment income);

(3) —0— (rental income of $80,000 exceeds the cash deductions, i.e., repairs, maintenance interest and taxes).

The ceiling is, therefore, $25,000. Accordingly, $35,000 of O's interest expense for the year is disallowed as a deduction.

The statute permits the disallowed portion of the investment interest expense to be carried forward to the subsequent years as an offset to investment income then received.[119]

(2) *"Points."* "Points" are an extra charge frequently made by mortgage lenders at the time of making a loan. Each point is one percent of the total amount borrowed. For example, if a person borrows $200,000, a two-point charge by the lender would be $4,000. The charge is technically referred to as a "loan processing fee."[120]

Because this charge is in addition to the agreed rate of interest to be charged and because it may be paid for various "services" rendered by the lender (such as checking credit, title to security, or preparing or recording security instruments), the Internal Revenue Service has previously required that the amount thereof be capitalized. If the borrower were engaged in a trade or business, he could amortize it over the life of the loan by taking an annual deduction equal to the amount of points paid divided by the number of years of the loan. If the borrower were not engaged in business but used the loan proceeds for personal purposes such as the purchase of a home, then he was not entitled to any deduction for the payment because the Service had ruled "points" were not interest.

But the Service has been forced to recognize that these loan-processing fees are principally hidden interest and, therefore, should be deductible as interest paid.[121]

---

[118]Section 163(d)(4)(A), I.R.C.

[119]Section 163(d)(2), I.R.C.

[120]The term "points" is also used to express the effective rate above the prime interest rate. For example, the expression "two points" above a prime interest rate of 9 percent would mean that the effective rate of interest was 11 percent, all of which would be deductible. The term "points" used in this book is different: it means a percentage of the amount borrowed.

[121]Revenue Ruling 69-188, 1969-1 C.B. 54.

Clearly, if the lender's "services" are charged for separately, the entire amount of the points will be deductible as interest. If the lender's "services," if any, are not charged for separately, the borrower should ask for a breakdown of the charge between the lender's "services" and the amount charged "for the use of forbearance of money per se . . .," i.e., interest.

Points paid by a cash method taxpayer on a loan secured by a mortgage on the taxpayer's principal residence for the purpose of its purchase or improvement are deductible when paid.[122]

(3) *Prepaid interest*. Prepaid interest is deductible only in the taxable year in which the prepaid amount is applied to the borrower's obligation to pay interest. This rule is applicable both to cash and accrual method taxpayers.[123]

Prepaid interest is taxable to the lender when received, it cannot be pro-rated over the life of the loan.

(4) *Construction period interest and taxes*. In the case of an individual (or Subchapter "S" corporation, or a personal holding company) construction period interest and real property taxes must be capitalized and recovered through an amortization deduction spread over a period of from 4 to 10 years.[124] The applicable table is:

If the amount is paid or accrued in a taxable year beginning in—			The percentage of such amount allowable for each amortization year shall be the following percentage of such amount
Non-residential real property	Residential real property (other than low-income housing)	Low-income housing	
1976			see subsection (f)
. . . .	1978	1982	25
1977	1979	1983	20
1978	1980	1984	16-2/3
1979	1981	1985	14-2/7
1980	1982	1986	12-1/2
1981	1983	1987	11-1/9
after 1981	after 1983	after 1987	10

This limitation does not apply to a personal residence.[125] Such interest in deductible currently, provided the taxpayer itemizes his deductions.

3. Special Assessments

The cost of any special assessment, whether paid immediately or over a period of time, is not deductible.[126]

---

[122] Section 461(g)(2).
[123] Section 461(g).
[124] Section 189.
[125] Section 189(d). See Chapter III, Part 10.
[125] That the Courts will agree with the Commissioner's 1968 ruling is clear from its decision in Jefferson Standard Life Insurance Co. v. United States, 408 Fed.2d 842, (4th Cir. 1969).
[126] Section 164(b)(5), I.R.C.

The amount of any such special assessment paid is added to the owner's basis for the property for the purpose of determining his gain or loss on a subsequent sale or exchange.[127] Are special assessment improvements depreciable by the members of the special assessment district? Because the improvements are those of the district, depreciation has been denied.[128] But where the district is small and the improvements have a limited useful life, the Service has allowed the members to depreciate their assessments.[129]

The disallowance of the deduction for taxes extends only to special assessments that result in benefiting the owner's property.[130] Assessments imposed for the general benefit of the entire district, such as assessments for parks, schools and water works, are deductible as taxes on real property.[131] Similarly, a special sprinkling tax was held deductible because it did not result in any permanent improvement to the owner's property.[132] And an assessment to cover expenses incurred in setting up a special sewer district which was abandoned before construction began was held deductible; the owner's property was not benefited by the assessment paid.[133]

If the special assessment district levies a tax to pay current maintenance expenses and interest charges incurred by the district, the portion of the assessment will be currently deductible; only the portion of the annual assessment that relates to the construction of the special improvement will be required to be capitalized.[134]

4. Election to Capitalize Taxes and Other Carrying Charges

Interest, taxes, and other carrying charges paid or incurred on certain real property held for business or income-producing purposes may be deducted or, at the election of the owner, may be capitalized and added to his basis for the property.[135]

This election is available for carrying charges incurred on vacant or unimproved property before it is devoted to a productive use, and for carrying charges on real property in the process of being improved. The election is limited to the period of time that the property is held in a non-productive state by the owner. As soon as the property is used for the production of income, or as soon as the improvement project is completed, the taxpayer loses the right to an election. He must then deduct the carrying charges against income produced from the property.[136]

For example, the election has been allowed to the owner of unproductive timber lands,[137] to the owner of real property on which a building is being constructed,[138] and

---

[127] National Lumber & Tie Co. v. Commissioner, 90 F.2d 216 (8th Cir. 1937).
[128] F. M. Hubbell & Son Co. v. Burnet, 51 F.2d 644 (8th Cir. 1931), cert. den. 284 U.S. 664; G.C.M. 11330, XI-2 C.B. 247.
[129] Rev. Rul. 73-188, 1973-62 C.B. 62. Assessments to store owners to convert a downtown street into a pedestrian mall. Interest payments on the City's bonds are deductible as taxes.
[130] Section 164(c), I.R.C.
[131] See Caldwell Milling Co., 3 B.T.A. 1232, 1236 (1926).
[132] Oscar Mitchell, 27 B.T.A. 101, 105 (1932, non-acq. XII-1 C.B. 19.
[133] Thomas H. Thatcher, 45 B.T.A. 64 (1941), acq. 1941—2 C.B. 12.
[134] Section 164(c), I.R.C. Rev. Rul. 73-188, 1973-1 C.B. 62.
[135] Section 266, I.R.C.
[136] Reg. Sec. 1.266-1.
[137] Warner Mountains Lumber Co., 9 T.C. 1171 (1947), acq. 1948-2 C.B. 4.
[138] Jackson v. Commissioner, 172 F.2d 605 (7th Cir. 1949), cert. den. 338 U.S. 4.

to the holder of a non-productive oil and gas lease.[139] The election does not, however, extend to a residence.[140]

The type of charge for which the election is available includes real property taxes, mortgage interest, fire insurance premiums,[141] social security and employment taxes, sale taxes, if incurred in connection with the construction of an improvement, and other necessary expenditures incurred in the development or the preservation of the property.[142]

If an owner desires to elect to capitalize carrying charges, he must file a statement with his income tax return which (1) sets forth the amount of the charges and (2) states an election to add them to basis. The election, once made, is binding for the year of election.[143] And, if the election is made for an improvement project, it is binding for the duration of the project. However, on unimproved and unproductive real estate, the election may be made each year, and it does not bind the owner to a similar election in a following year.[144]

G. CASUALTY LOSSES ON BUSINESS PROPERTY

The term "casualty losses" is somewhat misleading. A loss (not compensated for by insurance or otherwise) to business property caused by an external force beyond the control of the owner is deductible whether or not the occurrence is a "casualty" as that term is defined in connection with losses on residential property.

For example, termite damage that occurs "suddenly" is deductible as a loss. Similarly, damage due to an insect infestation of commercial trees has been held to constitute a deductible loss.[145] Also, destruction of grape vines from plant disease has been held deductible.[146] Erosion is not ordinarily thought of as a casualty; but repairs to correct erosion damages to farm land have been held deductible.[147] Rotting due to seepage is not a casualty; but the cost of repairing timbers rotted from seepage is deductible.[148]

It appears that a loss from external forces incurred on business property is deductible whether or not the force causing the loss qualifies as a "casualty." But the owner must be in a position to prove that the loss was caused by some unforeseen external force; a mere showing of loss in value would not of itself be deductible. The owner

---

[139] Rev. Rul. 55-118, 1955-1 C.B. 320.
[140] Megibow v. Commissioner, 218 F.2d 687 (3rd Cir. 1955).
[141] Warner Mountains Lumber Co., 9 T.C. 1171, 1176 (1947), acq. 1948-2 C.B. 4.
[142] Reg. Sec. 1.266.1.
[143] See Jackson v. Commissioner, 172 F.2d 605 (7th Cir. 1949), cert. den. 338 U.S. 716; Kentucky Utilities Co. v. Glenn, 21 AFTR 1263 (6th Cir. 1968).
[144] Reg. Sec. 1.266-1(c).
[145] Oregon Mesabi Corp., 39 B.T.A. 1033, 1038 (1939), acq. 1944-C.B. 22, appeal dismissed, 109 F.2d 1014 (9th Cir. 1940).
[146] F.H. Wilson, 12 B.T.A. 403, 406 (1928), acq. VIII-1 C.B. 49.
[147] J.H. Collingwood, 20 T.C. 937 (1953), acq. 1954-1 C.B. 4.
[148] Farmers Creamery Co. of Fredericksburg, 14 T.C. 879 (1959), acq. 1954-1 C.B.4. Compare Honingman v. Commissioner, 466 F.2d 69 (6th Cir. 1972) where salt water seepage repair was non-deductible because the beams replaced were steel. Business casualties are deductible in full whether or not they exceed $100. Section 165, I.R.C.

must also show that the sudden loss was not due to ordinary wear and tear or to age. In the absence of such proof, the owner's deduction for the loss must wait for realization through some "completed transaction," such as a sale, exchange, abandonment, demolition, alteration, or removal.[149]

1. Measure of the Loss

Under the regulations, the measure of the loss from casualty is the difference between the fair market value of the property immediately before and immediately after the casualty.[150] Evidence of the difference in values before and after is normally established by appraisals.[151]

Example: Owner of an apartment suffers damage from a landslide. His adjusted basis for the property at the time of the landslide was $120,000. Appraisals show that the value of the property immediately before the casualty was $150,000 and immediately after is only $100,000. His casualty loss would therefore be $50,000.

The maximum loss allowable is limited to the owner's adjusted basis for the property at the time of the casualty. Even though the loss in market value may exceed the owner's adjusted basis for the property, his loss is limited to his adjusted basis.[152]

2. Cost of Restoration

Suppose the amount of the loss in value is difficult to determine. If the owner expends a certain amount for repair and restoration of the damage, can he use the cost of restoration as the proper measure of his loss?

Although, technically, the cost of restoration is not the proper measure of the loss, many courts, and now the Regulations, have permitted the owner to deduct such cost as being the best evidence of the loss suffered in the absence of other proof.[153] The cost of restoring damage to a building caused by oil seepage has thus been allowed as a deduction.[154] Similarly, the cost of terracing to prevent erosion has been allowed as the proper measure of a loss from erosion.[155] And the cost of repairing hurricane[156] or fire[157] damage has been allowed as a deductible expense. Clean-up expenses are deductible.

But if the cost of restoration constitutes a major proportion of the entire value of the structure, the owner may face difficulty in using it as the measure of his loss. The cost of restoration may include expenditures for permanent improvements to the structure. If so, the total, including the amount to repair the damage, may be capitalized as being a part of a plan of improvement to the structure to increase its useful life.[158]

---

[149]Reg. Sec. 1.165-7(b).
[150]Reg. Sec. 1.165-7(b).
[151]Reg. Sec. 1.165-7(a)(2).
[152]Reg. Sec. 1.165-7(b).
[153]Harris Hardwood Co., 8 T.C. 847, 881 (1947), acq. 1947-2 C.B. 2; Reg. Sec. 1.165-7(a)(2)(ii).
[154]Midland Empire Packing Co., 14 T.C. 635 (1950), acq. 1950-2 C.B. 3.
[155]J.H. Collingwood, 20 T.C. 937 (1953), acq. 1954-1 C.B. 4; Rev. Rul. 54-191, 1954-1 C.B. 68.
[156]Tampa Electric Co., 12 B.T.A. 1002, 1007 (1928), acq. VII-2 C.B. 39.
[157]Ticket Office Equipment Co., 20 T.C. 272,279 acq. 1953-2 C.B. 6, aff'd per curiam, 213 F.2d 318 (2d Cir. 1954).
[158]Hubinger v. Commissioner, 36 F.2d 724 (2d Cir. 1929), cert. den. 281 U.S. 741. Louis v. Coughlin, T.C. Memo. 1973-243 (1973).

SOIL AND WATER CONSERVATION EXPENSES

The regulations qualify the use of the cost of restoration as a measure of the amount of the loss; the cost of restoration may be used only to the extent that (1) it restores the property to the condition that it was in before the loss; (2) it is not excessive; (3) it does no more than take care of the damage; and (4) the repairs were necessary.[159]

3. Reduction for Insurance Received

The amount of the loss deductible under Section 165 must be reduced by the amount of insurance or other compensation for the loss received by the owner.[160]

If the insurance proceeds exceed the owner's adjusted basis for the property, he will not be entitled to any deduction; in this case he suffers no loss.[161] The transaction will, in fact, be treated as a taxable disposition of the property that may qualify for special benefits as an involuntary conversion, if it results in a gain.[162]

If the recovery of insurance is indefinite in the year of the loss, the owner is well advised to deduct the full loss in the year it occurred.[163] If a recovery is later received through insurance on the property, the amount of the recovery will be taxed as income in the year received.[164] If the owner fails to deduct the loss in the year of damage, he may find that he has forfeited his right to a deduction for the difference between the amount of the loss and the insurance recovery.[165]

But where the owner is able to show that he has good reason to expect recovery of the *full amount* of the loss, he is entitled to postpone his deduction to the year in which he receives a compromise payment, to the extent that it is less than the loss suffered.[166] The rule is that no deduction is allowable for any portion of the loss for which there exists a reasonable prospect of reimbursement.[167]

H. SOIL AND WATER CONSERVATION EXPENSES

Certain expenditures made by a farmer for soil or water conservation purposes are currently deductible under Section 175, even though the expenditure is in the nature of a capital improvement.[168] The law defines deductible soil and water expenditures to include:

> ... the treatment or moving of earth, including (but not limited to) leveling, grading and terracing, contour furrowing, the construction, control, and protection of diversion channels,

---

[159] Reg. Sec. 1.165-7(a)(2)(ii).

[160] Section 165(a), I.R.C.; Reg. Sec. 1.165-1(c)(4); Federal benefits to casualty victims must also be taken into account. Lee R. Chronister, T.C. Memo 1973-237 (1973).

[161] United States v. Koshland, 208 F.2d 636, 639 (9th Cir. 1953).

[162] Sections 1231, 1033 I.R.C.

[163] Cahn v. Commissioner, 92 F.2d 674 (9th Cir. 1937); Commissioner v. Highway Trailer Co., 72 F.2d 913 (7th Cir. 1934), cert. den. 293 U.S. 626; Coastal Terminals, Inc., 25 T.C. 1053 (1956).

[164] See South Dakota Concrete Products Co., 26 B.T.A. 1429 (1932). B.C. Cook & Sons, 59 T.C. 516 (1972).

[165] Harry Brown, 23 T.C. 156 (1954).

[166] Commissioner v. Harwick, 184 F.2d 835 (5th Cir. 1950).

[167] Reg. Sec. 1.165-1(d)(2); Scofield's Estate v. Commissioner, 266 F.2d 154 (6th Cir. 1959); Rev. Rul. 59-388, 1959-2 C.B. 76; Rose Licht, 37 B.T.A. 1096 (1938), acq. 1963-2 C.B. 4.

[168] See Mim. 6030, 1946-2 C.B. 45, and Mim 6030, Supp. 1, 1948-1 C.B. 42 (applicable under the 1939 Code).

drainage ditches, earthen dams, watercourses, outlets, and ponds, the eradication of brush, and the planting of windbrakes . . .[169]

Expenditures for these purposes are deductible at the election of the owner of farm property. Once made, the election is binding.[170]

1. Limitation upon the Deduction

If the expenditure results in the creation of an improvement to the property of a character subject to an allowance for depreciation, the expenditure is not deductible under Section 175. The owner must recover his cost for the improvement out of his depreciation allowance.[171] For example, the cost of a concrete or masonary dam to aid in water conservation is not deductible under Section 175; the owner is required to capitalize the cost which would then be recoverable through the mechanics of depreciation. But an earthen dam constructed for the same purpose would be a currently deductible expense.[172]

Similarly, if the expenditure is deductible under some other provision of the Code, it will not qualify for deduction under Section 175. For example, the cost of repairs to conservation improvements on the farmer's property would be deductible as repairs, not as additional soil or water conservation expenses.[173]

2. Land Used in Farming

Soil and water conservation expenditures are deductible under Section 175 only if made on "land used in farming."[174] The regulations define this statutory phrase to require that the land be used for production of some agricultural crop or for the grazing of livestock.[175] The land must be currently devoted to such a use or must have been so used in the past.

An owner will not be permitted to deduct conservation expenditures made on virgin land in order to prepare it for a farming use. Similarly, if he acquires grazing land from another and prepares it for the growing of crops, he will not be entitled to the benefits of Section 175.[176]

In view of this limitation upon Section 175, a farmer would be well advised to postpone any soil or water conservation expenditures for a year or two after acquiring new land or after cultivating a parcel of virgin land. In this manner, he can plant and harvest a crop or two from the land before undertaking his conservation program. Such action will protect his right to a deduction for the expenditures under Section 175.

---

[169] Section 175(c), I.R.C. In addition expenditures made by farmers for clearing land to be used in farming are deductible under Section 18) up to the amount of $5,000 or 25 percent of the taxable income from farming, whichever is the lesser.

[170] Rev. Rul. 73-394, I.R.B. 1973-39, 10.

[171] Section 175(c)(1)(A), I.R.C.

[172] Reg. Sec. 1.175-2(b)(1); see Winfield A. Coffin, 41 T.C. No. 10 (1963).

[173] Reg. Sec. 1.175-2(b)(2).

[174] Section 175(a),(c)(2), I.R.C.

[175] Reg. Sec. 1.175-4(a).

[176] Reg. Sec. 1.175-4(b), except that land-clearing expenses qualify for a limited deduction under Section 182.

SOIL AND WATER CONSERVATION EXPENSES

3. Limitation upon the Amount Deductible

The deduction permitted under Section 175 is not unlimited. In any one year, a farmer is allowed to deduct soil and water conservation expenses up to a ceiling amount of 25 percent of his gross income from farming.[177]

Any expenditure in excess of the 25 percent ceiling can be carried forward by him to following years. In each subsequent year, he is also entitled to deduct up to 25 percent of his gross income from farming for expenditures made in the current year, together with any portion of the carry-forward expense from past years. This carry-forward may be made for an indefinite period until it is completely used up. Any unused carry-forward will not survive the death or dissolution of the taxpayer.[178]

The farmer's gross income from farming, which imposes the ceiling upon the deductible expenditure, includes all his income from farming whether realized from the farm on which the conservation expenses are incurred or not. But gross income from farming does not include gain from the sale or exchange of farm property or equipment; nor does it include income from non-farm sources.[179]

4. Election to Deduct Conservation Expenses

If a farmer wishes to take advantage of Section 175, he must manifest an election to deduct these expenses in the tax return that he files for the first year in which he makes expenditures for soil or water conservation purposes. Once made, the election becomes binding upon him and cannot be changed except with the Commissioner's consent.[180]

5. Soil and Water Conservation Districts

The election to deduct soil and water conservation expenses is also extended to assessments paid to soil or water conservation districts, to the extent that the assessments are used for expenditures similar in nature to those which would be deductible under Section 175 if made by the farmer himself.[181]

The deduction for such an assessment is subject to the same limitations as if the expenditure had been made directly by the owner. Thus, the amount of the assessment in excess of 25 percent of the owner's gross income from farming cannot be deducted in the year of payment but must be carried forward for possible deduction in future years.[182]

6. Fertilizer and Land Clearing Expenditures

Capital expenditures made by a farmer for fertilizer, lime, ground limestone, marl, or other materials to enrich, neutralize, or condition land for farming purposes

---

[177] Section 175(b), I.R.C.
[178] Reg. Sec. 1.175-5(b). It will, however, survive dissolution of a partnership.
[179] Reg. Sec. 1.175-5(a).
[180] Reg. Sec. 1.175-6; Rev. Rul. 73-394, I.R.B. 1973-39, 10.
[181] Section 175(c)(1), I.R.C.
[182] Reg. Sec. 1.175-2(c).

can be deducted currently if the farmer makes an election on his tax return so to do.[183] Otherwise, these expenditures would be capitalized and a depreciation recovery of their cost would be available only if the expenditures could be properly associated with the development of an orchard, vineyard, or other crop-producing asset having a limited useful life. Needless to say, fertilizer expenses incurred in producing annual crops are deductible currently.

A similar rule applies to land-clearing expenditures incurred by a farmer. If the expenditures for clearing land are for the purpose of making it suitable for farming they are deductible if the farmer makes an appropriate election on his tax return.[184] The amount qualifying for deduction is limited to a ceiling of $5,000 per annum or 25 percent of taxable income from farming, whichever is the lesser.

---

[183] Section 180, I.R.C.
[184] Section 182, I.R.C.

4

Sales, Exchanges, Conversions and Abandonments

In this chapter we shall discuss the tax consequences of sales, exchanges, conversions and abandonments of real property. The measure of the gain or loss on the transaction will depend upon the owner's tax basis for the property, the nature of his holding of the property, the length of time he held it, and the amount of consideration received for its disposition. In addition, certain dispositions, such as exchanges and conversions, may qualify for special tax benefits if handled properly.

The discussion of the tax aspects of real estate dispositions will be presented in the following sequence:

A. *Sales of Real Property;*
B. *Tax-Free Exchanges of Like Property;*
C. *Taxable Exchanges of Real Property;*
D. *Involuntary Conversions of Real Property;*
E. *Inverse Condemnations;*
F. *Gains and Losses on Involuntary Conversions under Section 1231;*
G. *Depreciation Recapture under Section 1033;*
H. *Abandonment of property.*

The various techniques for postponing the taxability of gain on the sale or real property will be outlined in Chapter 5.

A. SALES OF REAL PROPERTY

The sale of property for cash or its equivalent is a taxable transaction; the seller must account for the gain or loss realized on the sale in the year the property is sold. But in order to understand the tax treatment of sale, we must find the answers to a number of additional questions. How is a gain or a loss to be computed? In what manner is a gain to be taxed or a loss to be deducted? And in which year must the gain or loss be reported? These are the questions to be considered in this section.

1. Computation of Gain or Loss on Sale

As a general rule, the amount of gain or loss realized on a sale is the difference between the seller's cost or other basis for the property and the amount realized on the sale.[1]

Except in the case of a dealer, the amount realized on a sale of real property is the gross sales price less expenses of the sale.[2] Selling expenses include costs of commissions, advertising, transfer and stamp taxes, legal, escrow, and recording fees, and other similar payments if made by or charged to the seller.

In the case of a dealer in real property, selling expenses are deductible independently of the sale as business expenses; the amount realized by a dealer consists of the entire gross sales price.[3]

Example: Seller sells an apartment to Buyer for $40,000. The apartment had cost S $30,000 and he has taken $7,500 of depreciation on it. S's selling expenses amount to $2,000 for broker's commission, $50 for advertising and $44 for revenue stamps. His gain is computed as follows:

Gross selling price		$40,000
Less selling expenses:		
Commissions	$ 2,000	
Advertising	50	
Stamps	44	2,094
Amount realized on sale		$37,906
Less adjusted basis for property:		
Cost	$30,000	
Less depreciation	7,500	22,500
Gain realized on sale		$15,406

One of the effects of this method of computation is to force the seller to use his selling expenses as an offset to the sales price; thus, if the gain qualifies for capital gain treatment, the selling expenses will appear as an offset to the seller's capital gain, rather than being deductible as a business expense against ordinary income.

If S in the above example had been a dealer, the $2,094 of selling expenses would have been deductible separately as a business expense. Hence, the gain realized on the sale would have been computed as follows:

Gross sales price		$40,000
Less adjusted basis for property:		
Cost	$30,000	
Less depreciation	7,500	22,500
Gain realized on sale		$17,500

In the case of a loss, the same computation is used; the only difference is that the final figure is negative, representing a loss and measured by the amount by which the seller's basis for the property exceeds the amount realized on the sale.

---

[1] Section 1001(a), I.R.C.
[2] Mrs. E.A. Giffin, 19 B.T.A. 1243 (1930); I.T. 2340, VI-1 C.B. 43; Rev. Rul. 54-380, 1954-2 C.B. 155.
[3] I.T. 2305, V-2 C.B. 108.

2. Computation of the Gross Sales Price

The gross sales price is readily measurable if the total sales price is paid in cash; it is the total amount of cash paid by the purchaser for the property.

But suppose all or a portion of the total price is paid in property other than cash. In this event, the gross sales price consists of the cash paid, if any, plus the fair market value of the other property received.[4]

If the other property received is tangible property, the problem of valuation is normally met by an appraisal of the property as of the date of its receipt by the seller. The same rule applies to intangible property other than the notes or obligations of the purchaser.

But if the intangible property received by the seller consists of the note or obligation of the purchaser, then the rule to be followed depends upon the seller's method of accounting. If the seller uses the cash method, he is entitled to measure the gross sales price by the fair market value of the buyer's obligations. In the event that these obligations are worth less than face value, he need include in the sales price only the discounted value of the obligation.[5]

The burden of showing that the buyer's note or other obligation is worth less than face value is upon the seller. In the absence of such a showing by him, the note will be presumed to be worth its face value.[6]

What evidence, then, will be sufficient to establish a value less than face? For example, if the seller shows that he immediately sold the purchaser's notes at a discount, the notes need be included in the sales price for only the amount of the discount proceeds.[7] And if the notes are without interest, the seller may properly discount them to take into account the going rate of interest.[8] The value of the collateral behind the note may also establish a lower value for the note.[9] If the buyer's obligation is subject to a contingency, that too should be taken into account in measuring the fair market value.[10]

Under certain circumstances the obligation of the buyer may be so uncertain and contingent that it is not capable of valuation. If so, the seller is not required to include any portion of the face value of the obligation in the sales proceeds until the amounts represented by the obligation are actually paid over to him.[11]

An accrual method seller is subject to a different set of rules; normally a seller on the accrual method must include the full face value of his buyer's notes in the sales price in the year of sale.[12]

---

[4]Section 1001(b), I.R.C.

[5]Ives Dairy, Inc. v. Commissioner, 65 F.2d 125 (5th Cir. 1933); Michelin Corp. v. McMahon, 137 F.Supp. 798 (D.C.N.Y. 1956); C.S. Forve, 20 B.T.A. 861 (1930), acq. X-1 C.B. 22.

[6]Owen v. United States, 8 F.Supp. 707 (Ct.Cl. 1934); Whitlow v. Commissioner, 82 F.2d 569 (8th Cir. 1936); Shubin v. Commissioner, 67 F.2d 199 (9th Cir. 1933), cert. den. 291 U.S. 664.

[7]T.F. Sanford, 22 B.T.A. (1931), acq. X-2 C.B. 63.

[8]John Q. Shunk, 10 T.C. 293, 305 (1948), reversed on another point, 173 F.2d 747, 750 (6th Cir. 1949).

[9]George Antonoplos, 3 B.T.A. 1236 (1926), acq. V-2 C.B. 1.

[10]Carling Dinkler, 22 B.T.A. 329 (1931), acq. X-2 C.B. 19; William Parris, 20 B.T.A. 320, 326 (1930), acq. X-1 C.B. 50.

[11]Burnet v. Logan, 283 U.S. 404 (1931). This possibility is discussed in detail in Chapter 5.

[12]Spring City Foundry Co. v. Commissioner, 292 U.S. 182 (1934). Jones Lumber Co. v. Commissioner, 22 AFTR 2d 5924 (6th cir. 1968).

To this general rule of accrual one exception exists.[13] If the note or other obligation of the purchaser is worthless or uncollectable when received, it need not be reported as part of the sales price until payment is made or the obligation becomes valuable.[14] The same exception would apply to notes or other obligations that are subject to a contingency.[15]

The term "other property" received by the seller on the sale of property also includes any liabilities against the property sold, whether assumed by the buyer or taken subject to by the buyer. Thus, if property is sold subject to a mortgage, the sale proceeds include the amount of the outstanding mortgage debt, whether or not the buyer assumes the debt and whether or not the seller was personally liable for it.[16] Similarly, accrued mortgage interest and delinquent real estate taxes on the property assumed or paid by the buyer constitute part of the gross sales price realized by the seller.[17]

Example: Seller sells a parcel of real estate which is held subject to a mortgage debt of $20,000. Buyer agrees to pay $15,000 for S's equity, payable $5,000 in cash and $10,000 within two years of the date of sale. S figures that the note has a present value of $9,000. The property is also subject to a special assessment lien for $250 for street work. The amount realized on the sale by S, if he uses the cash method of accounting, is as follows:

Cash received on sale	$ 5,000
Value of note receivable	9,000
Outstanding mortgage indebtedness	20,000
Lien for special assessment	250
Gross sales price	34,250

Collection on B's note will be treated as the receipt of principal and of discount in the proportion that the total discount bears to total value.[18] Thus, if S collects $5,000 on the note in the following year, ten percent, or $500, will represent the collection of discount taxable as ordinary income; the balance, or $4,500, will be treated as the tax-free recovery of a portion of the seller's basis for the note.

If the transaction were a capital transaction giving rise to gain, S's action in valuing the note at less than face would have the effect of converting part of his capital gain otherwise realized on the sale into ordinary interest income. Except in unusual circumstances, therefore, it would not seem wise to value a note received in payment of a sales price resulting in capital gain at less than its full face value.

The place of current real property taxes in the measure of the gross sales price is discussed in Chapter 2, Part F. In general, current taxes on real estate are part of the

---

[13]Merely because the seller immediately discounts the note for less than its face value does not protect him; he is still required to report the entire face value as ordinary income. Hansen v. Commissioner, U.S. (1958); Shoemaker-Nash, Inc., 41 B.T.A. 17 (1940); G.C.M. 9571, X-2 C.B. 153.

[14]Clifton Mfg. Co. v. Commissioner, 137 F.2d 290 (4th cir. 1943); Corn Exchange Bank v. United States, 37 F.2d 34 (2d Cir. 1930); American Central Utilities Co., 36 B.T.A. 688 (1937), acq. 1938-1 C.B. 2.

[15]Commissioner v. Edwards Drilling Co., 95 F.2d 719 (5th Cir. 1938); C.W. Titus, Inc., 33 B.T.A. 928, 930 (1936), non-acq. XV-1 C.B. 46. See Lucas v. North Texas Lumber Co., 281 U.S. 11, 13 (1930).

[16]Crane v. Commissioner, 331 U.S. 1, 13 (1947).

[17]Norman Cooledge, 40 B.T.A. 1325 (1939), acq. 1940-1 C.B. 2; S.M. 4122, V-1 C.B. 55.

[18]Shafpa Realty Corp., 8 B.T.A. 283 (1927). *Accord,* Hatch v. Commissioner, 190 F.2d 254 (2d Cir. 1951); Victor B. Gilbert, 6 T.C. 10, 13 (1946), acq. 1946-1 C.B. 2.

gross sales price only to the extent that the seller is entitled to a deduction for them under the apportionment provisions of Section 164.[19]

Section 483, added to the Code in 1964, forces buyers and sellers to convert part of the selling price of property sold on a time basis into interest if the deferred payment contract itself fails to provide a reasonable rate of interest. Such imputed interest will be taken out of the purchase price of the property (reducing the gain or increasing the loss to the seller) and will be treated as interest to both the buyer (deductible to him) and to the seller (ordinary income). The reasonable rate of interest set by the Commissioner was 6 percent. In the event that the sales contract fails to provide for at least 6 percent interest, imputed interest of 7 percent will be charged to the parties.

Example: Seller sells 10 acres of unimproved land to Buyer for $100,000. Buyer agrees to pay $10,000 and the balance on or before 5 years from the date of sale. No interest is provided. Prior to January 1, 1964, Seller's gain assuming his basis for the property to be $40,000, would have been computed as follows:

Amount realized	$100,000
Less basis	40,000
Gain	$60,000

But if Section 483 were applicable to the sale and the reasonable rate of interest established by the Treasury were 6 percent then Seller's gain would be computed as follows:

Proceeds payable		$100,000
Less interest element:		
Deferred balance	$90,000	
Interest at 7%		
(5 years)	× .35	31,500
Amount realized on sale		68,500
Less basis		40,000
Gain on sale		28,500

Thus Seller would realize $31,500 of interest income and $28,500 of gain on the sale. Buyer would have a cost for the property of $68,500 and would be entitled to deduct $31,500 of interest under the contract.

Section 483 applies only to sales for a price in excess of $3,000 which are for a period of more than one year. If the sale would give rise to ordinary income in any event (i.e., a sale by a dealer), Section 483 does not apply. It does, however, apply to a sale of a capital or Section 1231 asset, whether the sale is at a gain or for a loss. Interestingly, while Section 483 forces the parties to provide for a reasonable rate of interest if too low a rate is used, the statute says nothing if the parties select an excessively high rate of interest.

3. Time for Reporting Gain or Loss on Sale

Gain or loss is reportable by the seller in the year the sale becomes a completed transaction. In the case of a seller on the cash method of accounting, gain or loss is

---

[19] Section 1001(b)(2), I.R.C.

ordinarily reported in the year of receipt of the sales proceeds.[20] For this purpose, constructive receipt is the equivalent of actual receipt of the sales proceeds.[21] In the case of a seller on the accrual method of accounting, gain or loss is ordinarily reported at the time the seller becomes entitled to receive the sales price and the buyer becomes unconditionally obligated to pay.[22]

For this purpose we must remember that an unconditional promissory note or other obligation of the seller is treated as the equivalent of cash, to the extent of its *fair market value* to a *cash method* seller, or to the extent of its *face value* to an *accrual method* seller. Hence, the fact that part or all of the sales price is not immediately paid over in cash will not ordinarily prevent the sale from being considered a completed transaction.

But suppose the note or obligation of the seller is conditioned upon some event that has not occurred at the time that sales escrow is closed and title is delivered to the buyer. Under such circumstances, the seller may be entitled to postpone the reporting of the gain to be realized on the sale to the date when the cash represented by the obligation becomes due or is actually paid over.[23]

The same analysis applies to losses. Losses are deductible only in the year in which they are sustained, "as evidenced by closed and completed transactions and as fixed by identifiable events occurring in such taxable year."[24]

Ordinarily, the effective date of the sale will be the proper time for deducting the loss,[25] but if the note or obligation of the buyer is contingent or conditional, the time for deducting the loss may be postponed to the date that the final payment is made or becomes due.[26]

4. Basis Allocation between Portions of Tract

Where a portion of property which had been acquired as a unit is sold it becomes necessary to allocate basis between the portion sold and that remaining. The Treasury Regulations provide that when a part of a larger property is sold, the cost or other basis of the entire property shall be equitably apportioned among the several parts, and the gain realized or loss sustained on the part of the entire property sold is the difference between the selling price and the cost or other basis allocated to such part.[27]

The key word in this regulation is "equitably." Although this does not necessarily mean ratably,[28] a ratable allocation frequently is applied. Various criteria have been used to determine an "equitable" apportionment, including appraisals, expert opinion, assessed valuation, selling price, and mere rough approximation of relative value.

---

[20] Harold W. Johnston, 14 T.C. 560, 565 (1950); Milton S. Yunker, 26 T.C. 161, 170 (1956).
[21] Williams v. United States, 219 F.2d 523 (5th Cir. 1955); Reg. Sec. 1.451-2(a).
[22] Lucas v. North Texas Lumber Co., 281 U.S. 11 (1930).
[23] See Chapter 5, Parts B & C.
[24] Reg. Sec. 1.165-1 (d)(1).
[25] See Chapter 5, Part E.
[26] First Nat. Corp. v. Commissioner, 147 F.2d 462 (9th Cir. 1945); Stiver v. Commissioner, 90 F.2d 505, 508 (8th Cir. 1937); Brandeis v. Allen, 60 F.2d 1004 (D.C.Neb. 1932), app. dis., 61 F.2d 1018 (8th Cir. 1932); Solomon Silberblatt, 28 B.T.A. 73 (1933), acq. 1938-1 C.B. 27; I.T. 1594, II-1 C.B. 91.
[27] Reg. Sec. 1.61-6(a).
[28] I.T. 1843, II-2 C.B. 72.

SALES OF REAL PROPERTY

In any event, the real meaning of "equitable" is relative fair market values, and the Tax Courts[29] and the Regulations[30] have so held. Furthermore, and importantly, it is relative market value at the time of the original purchase, not relative value at the time part is sold, which controls the apportionment.[31]

On the other hand, if it is not practical to make an allocation of basis between the property sold and the property retained *because of the character of the interest sold*, then basis is allocated to the interest sold in an amount sufficient to equal the sales proceeds received. The most common example of such a sale is a sale of an easement for roadway, pipeline, or power purposes under the terms of which the seller retains fee ownership and rights of user not inconsistent with the easement granted. Gain is, therefore, not realized on the sale of an easement except in the unusual case of a sale the proceeds of which exceed the seller's total basis for the property in which the easement is granted.[32] But if the easement affects only a portion of the land owned by the seller, only the basis for *that* portion can be used to offset the proceeds received on a sale of an easement.[33]

5. Nature of Gain or Loss on Sale

Gains realized on the sale of real property may be taxed as ordinary income or as capital gain, depending upon the character of the property in the hands of the seller and the time of its holding prior to sale. Similarly, the deductibility of a loss depends upon the character of the property in the seller's hands and the period of holding.

As we saw in the chapter relating to ownership of real property, the nature of the seller's ownership depends upon the use to which he put the property prior to sale, as follows:

1. Property held for use as a personal residence;
2. Property held for investment or the production of income;
3. Property held for use in trade or business;
4. Property held for sale to customers in the ordinary course of business.

Gains realized on the sale of a personal residence are capital gains: if the property has been held for more than one year, the gain qualifies for long-term capital gain treatment; if the holding has been for one year or less, the gain is reportable as short-term capital gain. Losses incurred on the sale of a home are not deductible, regardless of the period of the seller's holding.

Gains and losses realized on the sale of investment or income-producing real estate are capital gains or losses. If the seller's holding period has been more than one year, the sale is a long-term capital transaction; if it has been one year or less, it is a short-term transaction.

Gains and losses realized on the sale of the trade or business property are treated

---

[29] Fairfield Plaza, Inc., 39 T.C. 706 at 712-714 (1963).
[30] Reg. Sec. 1.61-6(a) example (2).
[31] W.A. Ayling, 32 T.C. 704 (1959), acq. 1959-2 C.B. 3.
[32] Inaja Land Co., 9 T.C. 727 (1947), acq. 1948-1 C.B. 2. Cf. Rev. Rul. 54-575, 1954-2 C.B. 145 (air rights) with Rev. Rul. 59-121, 1959-1 C.B. 212 (right to deposit waste).
[33] Rev. Rul. 68-291, 1968-23 IRB 24.

specially under Section 1231 of the Code; if the property has been held for one year or less, gain or loss is ordinary in nature. But if the property has been held for more than one year, Section 1231 gains and losses realized in a particular year must be netted and the result treated as a long-term capital gain, if a gain, or an ordinary loss, if a loss.

Gains and losses realized on the sale of property held for sale to customers in the ordinary course of business are ordinary gains or losses, regardless of the holding period.

6. Treatment of Ordinary Gains or Losses

Ordinary gains or losses realized on the sale of real estate are treated just like any other item of income or deduction. If a gain, the full amount is taxable as ordinary income; if a loss, the full amount is deductible against ordinary income.

Ordinary gains or losses are realized on the sale of property which is not a Section 1231 or a capital asset in the hands of the seller.

7. Treatment of Section 1231 Gains or Losses

The benefits of Section 1231 extend only to "property used in the [seller's] trade or business" which has been held for more than one year.

Trade or business property covers such diverse properties as real estate used for commercial or manufacturing purposes, lands used for farming or ranching,[34] and apartments and other types or rental real estate.[35]

The property need not actually be devoted to a trade or business use *if it was purchased for that purpose* and the owner can show that his sale of the property was due to unexpected circumstances arising afterwards that prevented the planned use of the property.[36] But this liberal rule does not apply to property purchased by the owner which was unsuitable for trade or business use at the time it was purchased. For example, property zoned residentially cannot be considered trade or business property even if the owner was ignorant of its zoning classification at the time he bought.[37] Similarly, if property was once used for trade or business purposes, a mere cessation of that use before sale would not disqualify the property from the benefits of Section 1231,[38] so long as other circumstances (including the passage of time) do not indicate a change in the character of the holding.

The interest of the owner in the real estate need not be a full-fee interest in order for the sale to qualify. For example, a sale of water rights which had previously been used in the owner's trade or business was a Section 1231 sale.[39] Also, the sale of a

---

[34]Olin Alexander, Par. 55,029 P-H Memo T.C., aff'd on other grounds, 234 F.2d 915 (6th Cir. 1956).
[35]Gilford v. Commissioner, 201 F.2d 735, 736 (2d Cir. 1953); Leland Hazard, 7 T.C. 372, 375 (1946), acq. 1946-2 C.B. 3.
[36]Rev. Rul. 58-133, I.R.B. 1958-13, 33; Carter-Colton Cigar Co., 9 T.C. 219 (1947), acq. 1947-2 C.B. 1.
[37]Montell Davis, 11 T.C. 538, 541 (1948), acq. on another ground, 1949-2 C.B. 1.
[38]Graves Bros. Co., 17 T.C. 1499 (1952); Solomon Wright, Jr., 9 T.C. 173 (1947), acq. 1947-2 C.B. 5.
[39]Rev. Rul. 55-295, 1955-1 C.B. 373.

depreciable leasehold in property is a Section 1231 sale.[40] And the interest of a lessee in an oil and gas lease qualifies for the benefits of that section.[41]

Under a special statutory rule, the sale of an unharvested crop qualifies for Section 1231 treatment if it has been sold at the same time and to the same purchaser as the underlying farm land and if the land itself had been held for more than six months.[42]

In the event only one Section 1231 sale is made by the seller in the taxable year, the seller is entitled to treat the sale as a capital transaction if a gain has been realized; thus, the gain would qualify for long-term capital gain treatment. But if a loss is incurred, the loss is deductible in full as an ordinary loss.

If the seller has more than one Section 1231 transaction in a taxable year, his treatment of these transactions depends upon whether or not the gains realized exceed the losses. If the gains exceed the losses, all of the transactions are treated as long-term capital transactions; in effect, the net gain is taxed to the seller as long-term capital gain. But if the losses exceed the gains, all of the sales are treated as non-capital transactions; in effect, the net loss is deductible by the seller as an ordinary loss.

Example: Seller, in the manufacturing business, sells two factory buildings which are no longer needed in his manufacturing operations. Parcel 1 is sold for a gain of $10,000 and Parcel 2 for a loss of $6,000. Both parcels were held for more than one year before sale.

Gain on Parcel 1	$10,000
Loss on Parcel 2	(6,000)
Net gain on sales	$ 4,000

Because gain exceeded loss, both transactions would be treated in S's tax return as capital transactions. Had loss exceeded gain, both transactions would have been treated as non-capital transactions.

Property similar in nature and use to that described above but held for one year or less will not qualify for Section 1231 treatment. The sale of trade or business property held for one year or less constitutes the sale of an ordinary asset, giving rise to *ordinary income or loss* as the case may be.[43]

The tax objective when selling property used in the trade or business is to realize all gains in one taxable year and all losses in another. In this way, the gains (if held more than one year) will be taxed at capital gain rates, and the losses will be deductible in full. Otherwise, gains that might qualify for capital gain treatment will have the effect of ordinary gains because they will offset fully deductible losses.

8. Treatment of Capital Gains or Losses

Gains and losses incurred on the sale of capital assets are treated in a different manner from gains and losses resulting from sale of ordinary assets. The rules governing the treatment of capital gains and losses are found in Section 1201-1223 of the Internal Revenue Code.

---

[40]See 512 West Fifty-Sixth Street Corp. v. Commissioner, 151 F.2d 942 (2d Cir. 1945).
[41]I.T. 3693, 1944 C.B. 272, 274.
[42]Section 1231(b)(4), I.R.C.
[43]Rev. Rul. 54-607, 1954-2 C.B. 177.

These rules require the taxpayer to report all of his gains and losses from the sale of capital assets, together with other transactions giving rise to capital gain or loss, in a schedule separate from other gains and losses. These capital transaction are classified according to the length of the taxpayer's holding period prior to sale. If the asset has been held for more than one year, the sale is reported as a long-term capital transaction. If the holding period was one year, or less, the sale is a short-term transaction. Gain or loss from capital transactions is then computed as follows:

1. All short-term transactions are added together, resulting in either net short-term gain or net short-term loss.

2. All long-term transactions are added together, resulting in either net long-term gain or net long-term loss.

3. If there is neither net short-term loss nor net long-term loss, the net short-term gain is taxed as ordinary income and the net long-term gain is taxed as capital gain.

4. If there is net short-term gain and net long-term loss, the difference is treated as ordinary income if gain exceeds loss, and a capital loss if loss exceeds gain.

5. If there is net short-term loss and net long-term gain, the difference is treated as capital gain if gain exceeds loss, and as capital loss if loss exceeds gain.

6. If there is both net long-term loss and net short-term loss the sum is treated as a capital loss.

The following examples illustrate these computations:

Example: Seller sold four parcels of property, two of which, Parcels A and B, were held for more than one year, and the other two of which, Parcels C and D, were held for one year or less. S realized a gain of $4,000 on Parcel A, a loss of $2,000 on Parcel B, a gain of $3,000 on Parcel C and a loss of $500 on Parcel D. S should report the transactions as follows:

Long-term transactions:		
Parcel A	$4,000	
Parcel B	(2,000)	$2,000
Short-term transactions:		
Parcel C	$3,000	
Parcel D	(500)	2,500
Capital gain		$2,000
Ordinary income		$2,500

Example: Parcel B has been sold for a loss of $8,000. S would report the transactions as follows:

Long-term transactions:		
Parcel A	$4,000	
Parcel B	(8,000)	(4,000)
Short-term transactions:		
Parcel C	$3,000	
Parcel D	(500)	2,500
Capital loss		($1,500)

Example: A similar result would occur if the large loss were incurred in a short-term transaction. Suppose, for example, Parcel B were sold for a gain of $1,000, but Parcel D for a loss of $10,000:

SALES OF REAL PROPERTY

Long-term transactions:		
Parcel A	$4,000	
Parcel B	1,000	$5,000
Short-term transactions:		
Parcel C	$3,000	
Parcel D	(10,000)	(7,000)
Capital loss		($2,000)

Example: Had the large short-term loss in the preceding example been insufficient to offset completely all of the gain realized, it would first be applied to short-term gain and any remainder to long-term gain. Suppose, for example, the loss on the sale of parcel D was $6,000:

Long-term transactions:		
Parcel A	$4,000	
Parcel B	1,000	$5,000
Short-term transactions:		
Parcel C	$3,000	
Parcel D	(6,000)	(3,000)
Capital gain		2,000

Example: The converse would hold true equally as well. Suppose the large loss were incurred on a long-term sale, Parcel B being sold for a loss of $5,000 and Parcel D for a gain of $500:

Long-term transactions:		
Parcel A	$4,000	
Parcel B	(5,000)	(1,000)
Short-term transactions:		
Parcel C	$3,000	
Parcel D	500	3,500
Ordinary income		$2,500

As indicated above, net short-term gains that result after all capital losses have been used up are taxed as ordinary income.[44]

(1) *Excluded one-half as tax preference item*: If the result of the computation is a long-term capital gain, the Code permits taxpayers other than corporations to exclude one-half of it from income; the remaining one-half is included in the taxpayer's income and is taxable at ordinary income tax rates.[45]

But the excluded one-half may be subject to a special penalty. It is treated as an item of tax preference.[46] As such it must be aggregated with other tax preference items. If the total exceeds $10,000, or one-half the normal federal income tax paid then a minimum income tax of 15 percent is levied on the excess.[47] A similar rule applies to corporations, except that the excluded percentage treated as a tax preference item is different.

---

[44] Section 61(a)(3), I.R.C.
[45] Section 1202, I.R.C.
[46] Section 57(a)(9), I.R.C. the tax preference tax applies to capital gains even though the alternative tax is elected.
[47] Section 56, I.R.C.

102   SALES, EXCHANGES, CONVERSIONS AND ABANDONMENTS

(2) *Alternative tax*: If the result of the foregoing computations is a long-term capital gain, the taxpayer has a limited privilege of computing the tax on an alternative basis under which the tax is measured by a percentage of the gain.

In the case of individuals, an alternative tax of 25 percent is available only on their first $50,000 of gain.[48] All of the gain in excess of $50,000 qualifies for an alternative tax of 35 percent.

The alternative tax in the case of corporations is 30 percent of the gain.[49] Corporate taxpayers must include 100 percent of their net long-term capital gains in income, so that the alternative tax has meaning to them.

(3) *Treatment of capital losses*. If the result of the capital gain and loss computation is a net capital loss, it is deductible only to a limited extent. In the case of an individual, he can deduct a net short-term capital loss against ordinary income only to a ceiling amount of $3,000. Long-term losses can also be deducted up to a ceiling of $3,000 but, in making the deduction against ordinary income, only 50 percent of the long-term loss may be taken into account.[50] Thus, it takes $6,000 of a net long-term capital loss to offset $3,000 of ordinary income, but only $3,000 of a short-term loss to achieve the same effect.

If a portion of the loss is unused after this computation, the balance may be carried forward to following years first, to offset capital gains and then to offset ordinary income in the limited manner described above. The benefits of the carry-forward of a capital loss are available to an individual taxpayer until used up or until his death.

If the taxpayer is a corporation, a net capital loss is not deductible against ordinary income. It can be used only to offset the corporation's capital gains. Any excess capital loss can be carried back three years or carried forward five years to offset capital gains incurred in those years.[51]

If married persons file separate returns, the $3,000 ceiling on the deduction of capital losses against ordinary income is lowered to $1,500.[52]

9. Holding Period of Property

The holding period is the period of time between the date of acquisition of the property and the date of its sale. For the purpose of counting the period between these dates, the seller must exclude the date of acquisition, but he is entitled to count the date of sale.[53]

The simple rule is the "first day after the anniversary date of purchase."[54] For example, if an asset is purchased on April 14, 1977, its sale should not be made until

---

[48]Section 1201(b), I.R.C.
[49]Section 1201(a), I.R.C. If the corporation's tax rate is at 20 or 22 percent, it may apply that rate to its capital gains.
[50]Section 1211(b), I.R.C.
[51]Section 1212(a)(1).
[52]Section 1211(b)(2), other than in community property states.
[53]E. T. Weir, 10 T.C. 996 (1948), aff'd per curiam, 173 F.2d 222 (3rd Cir. 1949); I.T. 3287, 1939-1 C.B. (part 1) 138; I.T. 3705, 1945 C.B. 174.
[54]See I.T. 3985, 1949-2 C.B. 51. A capital asset acquired on the last day of a month (whether or not of 31 days) must be held until, on or after the first day of the seventh succeeding month in order to obtain long term gain treatment on its disposition. Rev. Rul. 66-7, 1966-1 C.B. 188. In 1977 only the period is nine months.

SALES OF REAL PROPERTY

April 15, 1978. Similarly, if a property is purchased on February 28, a March 1 selling date a year later is recommended. What about a February 29 purchase? Theoretically, the March 1 date a year later should suffice, even though the period is only 364, not 365 days. Caution, however, would suggest a March 2 sales date.

The holding period begins to run the day after the day on which property is "acquired." If the property is purchased, the date of acquisition would be the date on which title is taken.[55] Ordinarily, the date of acquisition is the date on which a deed to the property is delivered to the owner out of escrow; the date on which the deed is conditionally deposited in escrow is immaterial.[56] This date may, however, be advanced to an earlier date if the owner takes possession of the property and assumes the benefits and burdens of ownership under an unconditional contract of sale prior to receiving legal title; the date of taking possession would then constitute the date of acquisition.[57]

The taking of an option to purchase the property prior to acquiring title will not advance the date of acquisition.[58] Even if the purchaser takes possession of the property under an option agreement, the date will not be advanced; acquisition will occur either on the date that the optionee takes title or enters into possession under an unconditional contract of sale.[59]

If the property has been acquired from a decedent, the date of acquisition to the distributee is the date of the decedent's death, not the date on which the property is formally distributed out of the decedent's estate to him.[60]

Property acquired by gift has a holding period which may be measured either by the date of the gift or the date of the donor's acquisition, depending upon whether or not the donee is entitled to use the donor's basis for the property. If the property is worth more at the time of the gift than its basis to the donor, the donee must use his donor's basis as his own; consequently, he is entitled to measure his holding period from the date of his donor's acquisition of the property.[61]

But if the property is worth less at the time of the gift than its basis to the donor, the donee must use the value of the property as his basis if he sells at a loss; consequently, the date of the gift is the date of acquisition to the donee.[62]

Suppose improvements are constructed within one year before sale upon land which has been held by the seller for more than the required year. Do the improvements take the same holding period as the underlying land? Or must separate holding periods be used for the land and the improvements?

In *Dunigan v. Burnet*[63] it was held that separate holding periods must be com-

---

[55] Helvering v. San Joaquin Fruit & Investment Co., 297 U.S. 496 (1936).
[56] Howell v. Commissioner, 140 F.2d 765 (5th Cir. 1944), cert. den. 322 U.S. 735.
[57] Rev. Rul. 54-607, 1954-2 C.B. 177; Ted F. Merrill, 40 T.C. 66 (1963); Vernon Hoven, 56, T.C. 50 (1971), acq. 1971-2 C.B. 3.
[58] Helvering v. San Joaquin Fruit & Investment Co., 297 U.S. 496 (1936).
[59] Rev. Rul. 54-607, 1954-2 C.B. 177.
[60] Helvering v. Gambrill, 313 U.S. 11, 14, (1941); McFeely v. Commissioner, 296 U.S. 102, 108 (1935); This rule applies even though the donee's carryover basis may be adjusted upwards for federal estate taxes paid.
[61] Helvering v. New York Trust Co., 292 U.S. 455 (1934); Section 1223(2), I.R.C.
[62] I.T. 3453, 1941-1 C.B. 254; Rev. Rul. 59-416, 1959-2 C.B. 159.
[63] 66 F.2d 201 (D.C. Cir. 1933).

puted; hence, the portion of the gain allocable to the land was taxed as long-term capital gain, but the portion allocated to the improvements was short-term gain.

This rule requiring separate holding periods for land and improvements was extended in *Paul v. Commissioner*.[64] There the owner started construction of a building more than the required period before sale but it was not completed until a date less than such period. The Court held that the gain allocated to the building should be allocated between long-term and short-term gain in proportion to the amount of construction completed on the day before the anniversary date. The gain attributable to construction completed by then was to be taxed as long-term gain and the remainder as short-term capital gain. The Commissioner now agrees with the *Paul* rule.[65]

10. Recapture of Depreciation: Generally

One of the important advantages in depreciating property as rapidly as possible lies in the fact that depreciation is deductible against ordinary income. The tax cost of a depreciation deduction is that basis must be reduced by depreciation allowable. But if the property is a capital asset or property used in the trade or business, and is held for more than one year, the gain on the sale of it, including the gain attributable to reduction of basis for depreciation, is taxed at capital gain rates. Hence, the owner may obtain deductions against ordinary income while he owns the property at the cost of only a capital gains tax when he disposes of it.

In 1962, Congress attempted partially to close this "loophole" by enacting Section 1245 of the Code. This provides that any gain on the disposition of "Section 1245 property" will be taxed as ordinary income to the extent of depreciation taken after December 31, 1961. If the disposition is other than a sale, exchange or involuntary conversion (e.g., corporate distribution) the recapture of depreciation rule will apply, limited to the difference between basis and fair market value at the time of disposition if this difference is less than post-1961 depreciation taken.

There are several exceptions to the application of Section 1245. Chief among these are transfers by gift, transfers at death, and certain tax-free transactions in which the basis of the property in the hands of the transferee is determined by the transferor's basis. In the latter situation, ordinary income is recognized under Section 1245 only up to the extent gain would be recognized on the transfer anyway (e.g., boot.)

Example: M, a manufacturer, sells machinery used in his trade or business on January 1, 1964, for $11,000. He had purchased the machinery for $12,000 at the beginning of 1960. It then had a 12-year life and M chose to apply straight-line depreciation. What is his ordinary income and capital gain on the sale?

Total gain on the sale:		
S Selling price		$11,000
Less Basis:		
Cost	$12,000	
Less Depreciation	4,000	8,000
Total gain		$ 3,000

---

[64] 206 F.2d 763 (3rd Cir. 1953).
[65] Commissioner v. Williams, 256 F.2d 152 (5th Cir. 1958); Fred Draper, 32 T.C. 545 (1959), acq. 1960-2 C.B. 4.

SALES OF REAL PROPERTY

```
Amount taxed as ordinary income:
  "Recomputed basis":
    Adjusted basis                    $8,000
    Plus post '61 deprec.              2,000        10,000
    Less adjusted basis                             8,000
  Ordinary income                                  $ 2,000
Amount taxed as capital (§1231) gain:
  Total gain                                       $ 3,000
  Less taxed as ordinary income                      2,000
  Capital (§1231)gain               $ 1,000
```

What, then, is "Section 1245 property"? The code says it is all personal property of a character subject to depreciation (except livestock) and all other depreciable property used in manufacturing, production, extraction, transportation, and communication *except a building or its structural components*. In the real estate field, this means that furniture, furnishings, and most fixtures (even though considered part of the realty under local law) are subject to Section 1245 if they (or the building they are in) are used in manufacturing, production, extraction, transportation, or communication. Only those fixtures which are "structural components" are excluded. On the other hand, all fixtures would be excluded if the real estate were not used in manufacturing, production, extraction, transportation, or communication.

In 1964, Congress added Section 1250 to the Code. Its purpose is to effect a limited recapture of accelerated depreciation on real property in any case in which the property is sold. But the rules on recapture differ from those relating to real estate improvements.

11. Recapture of Depreciation: Real Estate Improvements

In the case of real estate, the amount of recapture income on the sale of capital gain or Section 1231 property is only the excess of accelerated depreciation over straight-line depreciation taken by the seller during the period of his ownership of the property.[66]

Recapture income occurs only if the property is sold for a gain. If it is sold for a loss, no recapture occurs. The amount of recapture income is thus the lesser of (1) the excess of acclerated depreciation over straight-line depreciation or (2) the amount of the gain.

Example: Owner buys a building at a cost of $150,000, of which $100,000 is allocable to improvements. If we assume a useful life of 33-1/3 years, his annual straight-line depreciation for three years would be $3,000. Let us assume that he elected a method of accelerated depreciation that produced depreciation deductions of $4,300. The amount of recapture is, therefore, $1,300, the amount by which the $4,300 of depreciation taken exceeds straight-line depreciation of $3,000.

After a reduction in basis of $4,300 for the depreciation taken, O's basis for the improvements is $95,700 ($100,000 less $4,300). If O sells the property for less than $95,700, he will have no recapture. If he sells the improvements for more than $95,700 but not more than $100,000 (his original cost), the entire gain will be recapture income. And if he sells the

---
[66] Section 1250, I.R.C.

improvements for more than $100,000 (say $120,000), part of the gain will be recapture income and the balance Section 1231 gain as follows:

Amount realized	$120,000
Less basis	95,700
Gain	$ 24,300
Recapture income	$ 4,300
Section 1231	20,000
	$ 24,300

Recapture income is taxed as ordinary income. Normally, it is limited to the excess of accelerated depreciation (200 percent, 150 percent and 125 percent declining-balance methods, sum-of-the-years' digits method or other accelerated methods) over straight-line depreciation. However, if the property is held for one year or less, all depreciation is recaptured if the property is sold at a gain equal to or in excess of the depreciation.[67]

Before 1970, recapture income was taxed on a sliding scale which phased out the recapture income over a 10-year period. The Revenue Act of 1969 eliminated this phase out, except in two cases discussed below. Now, all excess depreciation is recaptured if the sale is made at a gain sufficient to cover the excess depreciation taken *regardless of the length of the holding period of the property*.[68] Thus even if property is held for a full 10 years after purchase, the excess of accelerated depreciation over straight-line depreciation will be recaptured if the gain realized on a sale is sufficient.

Naturally, if the property is held for the full period of its useful life, there will be no recapture. Why? Methods of accelerated depreciation cannot produce a greater amount of total depreciation than straight-line depreciation because both are limited to the cost or other basis allocable to the improvements. If $100,000 is allocated to the improvements, only $100,000 can be recovered by way of depreciation over its useful life, regardless of what method of depreciation is used. Thus, at the end of the useful life of the improvements, the amount of depreciation recovered under an accelerated method will be exactly to straight-line depreciation; hence, there is no "excess" to recapture.

What accelerated methods of depreciation do is to permit a faster recovery of the *total* depreciation allowance over the useful life of the property than does the straight-line method of depreciation. It has been estimated, for example, that both the double-declining (200 percent) balance and sum-of-the-years' digits methods recover two-thirds of the total depreciation allowance in the first one-half of the useful life of the property.

Hence, these accelerated methods would produce depreciation allowances in the last one-half of the useful life which would be *less* than the allowances available under the straight-line method. Only one-third of the depreciable base would be available as a

---

[67] Section 1250(b)(1), I.R.C.

[68] Section 1250(a)(1)(C)(v), I.R.C., effective July 25, 1969, except for sales under binding contracts executed prior thereto. Pre-1969 Revenue Act recapture rules apply to the recapture of pre-January 1, 1970 depreciation even on sales made after July 24, 1969. That is to say, pre-1970 accelerated depreciation can be recaptured only on a sliding scale percentage basis: if the property is held for 20 months or less, 100 percent is subject to recapture; for each month it is held beyond 20 months, 1 percent less is subject to recapture. Thus if the property is held 120 months (i.e., 10 years) nothing is subject to recapture.

SALES OF REAL PROPERTY

write-off under the accelerated method, whereas one-half would be available under the straight-line method. Therefore, in the last one-half of the useful life of the property, the "excess" depreciation under the accelerated methods built up in the first one-half of the useful life would be steadily decreased until it reached zero at the end of the useful life.

There are two exceptions to the general rule that excess accelerated depreciation is subject to recapture regardless of the length of the seller's holding period. *The first exception* is in the case of improved residential real estate that is rented out and that had qualified for mortgage insurance under Sections 221 (d)(3) or 236 of the National Housing Act (or similar State enactments). The excess of accelerated depreciation (200 percent declining balance in the case of new property and 150 percent declining balance in the case of used property) over straight-line depreciation is subject to complete recapture for the first 100 months (8 years and 4 months) it is held. Thereafter, the amount of potential recapture is reduced 1 percent per month that the property is held beyond the first 100 months. If, for example, the property is held for 140 months, the amount subject to recapture is only 60 percent (100 percent less 40 percent) of the excess of accelerated depreciation. Naturally, if the property is held for 200 months (16 years and 8 months), then the amount subject to recapture is reduced to zero.

The second exception pertains to rehabilitation expenditures. Rehabilitation expenditures can be amortized over a five-year period if incurred in connection with low-income rental housing. In order to qualify, the amount of rehabilitation expenditures must exceed $3,000 per unit in a period of 2 years but cannot exceed $20,000 per unit. Low-income rental housing is defined in accordance with the leased Housing Program under Section 8 of the United States Housing Act of 1937.

The excess of rehabilitation improvement 5-year amortization over straight-line depreciation is subject to complete recapture if the property is sold in the first 100 months of ownership. Thereafter, it is subject to recapture under the same sliding scale applied to residential rental property. For each month the property is held beyond 100 months, the amount of recapture is reduced one percent. Thus, if the property is held for 150 months, the excess of rehabilitation expenditure amortization over straight-line depreciation is subject to recapture only to the extent of 50 percent. If the property is held for 200 months, no part of the excess is subject to recapture.

12. Recapture: Farm Improvements

If losses from farming operations are used to offset non-farming income, recapture of expenditures may occur in a number of ways. The first recapture occurs in the case of a gentleman farmer whose income from other sources exceeds $50,000 and whose farming loss exceeds $25,000. Deductions for farming expenses in excess of $25,000 are allowed in full, but the amount of such excess deductions must be kept recorded in an "excess deductions account." This account is subject to adjustment, if for example, farm income is produced by the gentleman farmer.

If farming property is sold by a gentleman farmer at a gain, the gain is treated as ordinary income to the extent of the balance in the "excess deductions account" at the time of sale.[69] The balance of the gain would be Section 1231 gain, taxable as capital gain to the extent it exceeded Section 1231 losses.

Another farm recapture provision applies to regular working farmers who are not reliant upon other income as well as to gentlemen farmers. Special benefits have been allowed to them under Section 175 and 182 of the Code. Capital expenditures for soil and water conservation and for land clearing are deductible as a current expense if the farmer so elects. These deductible capital expenditures are now subject to recapture on the sale of the farmland.[70]

The amount of recapture income is, of course, limited to the gain derived on the sale of the property as in other recapture income situations. But if the gain realized equals or exceeds the deductions taken by the farmer for conservation and land clearing expenditures, then the gain is treated as ordinary income to the extent of these deductible expenditures[71] if the sale occurs within five years of acquisition. If the farm is held more than five years, the amount of recapture is reduced step-by-step to zero after ten years. The schedule is as follows:

Year	Percentage of Recapture
Within 5 years	100 percent
Within 6 years	80 percent
Within 7 years	60 percent
Within 8 years	40 percent
Within 9 years	20 percent
Within 10 years	-0- percent

13. Sale of Depreciable Property to Related Parties

Section 1239 of the Code provides that the gain on the sale of depreciable property by a husband to his wife or by a more than 80 percent shareholder[72] to his corporation is ordinary income regardless of the character of the property in the hands of the seller. Ordinary income is also incurred on the sale of depreciable property between two corporations each controlled (80%) by the same individual, directly or indirectly. The purpose of this statutory rule is to prevent related sellers and buyers from increasing the basis of the property for depreciation purposes by paying a capital gains tax on a sale between themselves.

Example: Husband owns as his separate property an apartment building that has a fair market value, not including land, of $250,000, but a depreciated basis of only $120,000. He sells it to his wife who pays him $250,000. Her basis is now $250,000. But the $130,000 of his gain realized by H is ordinary income.

---

[69] Section 1251, I.R.C. No additions are to be made to the excess deductions account after December 31, 1975.

[70] Section 1252, effective January 1, 1970.

[71] Items of repair are not included in this computation.

[72] For this purpose shareholder ownership is direct and indirect. The family and other attribution rules of Section 318 apply. The 80 percent test is based on value, not number of shares. Rev. Rul. 69-339, 1969-1 C.B. 203. A sale of depreciable property converts any gain on the property into ordinary income. Rev. Rul. 69-109, 1969-1 C.B. 202.

SALES OF REAL PROPERTY

Because all the gain is ordinary income there is no purpose to the transaction. The rule effectively prevents related parties from realizing a gain at capital gain rates for the purpose of increasing their depreciation deductions against ordinary income.

14. Timing the Sale

If a gain is anticipated on the sale of trade or business property, or on the sale of a capital asset, the seller should be sure that his holding period for the property will exceed one year. He may, however, grant an option to the purchaser covering the property during the minimum one-year period without causing an interruption in his holding which will later disqualify the sale from long-term capital gain treatment.[73]

If the seller plans to sell two or more parcels of trade or business property, or if he has other Section 1231 transactions, he should be aware of the fact that the gains and losses from these transactions must be netted. The benefits of a Section 1231 loss incurred on one transaction may be partially lost if another 1231 transaction occurs in the same year which produces a gain; the loss incurred on the first transaction, which otherwise would be deductible in full, must be used to offset the long-term gain realized on the second transaction. If the two transactions had been spaced carefully so that each occurred in a separate taxable year, the loss from the first would be deductible in full and the gain from the second would be taxed as long-term capital gain.

Suppose, however, that the seller does not have sufficient income from other sources to offset a loss incurred on the sale of trade or business property. Will this fact deprive him of the full use of the loss? Since the enactment of the 1954 Code, the answer is no. A loss incurred on the sale of Section 1231 property qualifies for carryover as a net operating loss deduction, whether the taxpayer is an individual or a corporation.[74] Such a loss may be carried back three years and carried forward seven years to offset income earned by the seller in these other years unless an election not to carry back is made.

The loss incurred in the sale of trade or business property will qualify for the net operating loss carryover even if the sale is a disposition of all of the seller's trade or business assets and amounts to a termination of his trade or business activities.[75]

These rules give the owner of high-basis, low-value trade or business property considerable latitude in timing the sale to take maximum advantage of the loss. For this purpose, the seller should keep in mind that the net operating loss deduction is first carried back to the three preceding years before it is carried forward to offset future income.[76]

A word of caution is in order in connection with the use of the net operating loss carryover. For the purpose of computing the amount of the carryover, the taxpayer must add back the amount of any long-term capital gains excluded from income by virtue of the rules relating to capital gains.[77] Thus, if the taxpayer expects to incur a net

---

[73] Rev. Rul. 54-607, 1954-2 C.B. 177.
[74] Section 172(d)(4)(A), I.R.C.
[75] Reg. Sec. 1.172-3(a)(3)(ii); Sen. Rep. No. 1622, 83rd Cong., 2d Sess. 212-213 (1954).
[76] Section 172(b), I.R.C.
[77] Section 172(d)(2)(B), I.R.C.; Reg. Secs. 1.172-3(a)(1)(iii).

operating loss, he should be careful to postpone the taking of any capital gains to a later year; if he fails to observe this warning, he may find that part or all of his anticipated carryover loss is used up in the year of the loss by application against capital gains already excluded from income.

Example: Seller, an individual, sells a parcel of real estate for a long-term capital gain of $80,000. At the end of the year, he discovers that he has incurred a net loss of $70,000 in the operations of his business. His income tax for the current year would, of course, be zero. But how much of the loss could be carried back to an earlier year? None. For the purpose of computing the net operating loss carryover, S must add back the $40,000 of excluded capital gains, the total of which ($80,000) more than offsets the entire operating loss.

Taxable Income in Current Year:		
Net loss from business		($70,000)
Long-term capital gain	$80,000	
Less one-half excluded	40,000	40,000
Net taxable income in current year		($30,000)
Net operating loss carryover:		
Net taxable income	($30,000)	
Adjustment for excluded capital gain	40,000	
Net operating loss carryover	—0—	

Had S waited until a later year to take the $80,000 capital gain, his net operating loss of $70,000 would have been fully available for carryback to earlier years.

15. Sale of Property Subject to a Favorable Mortgage

If the owner of property holds it subject to a mortgage debt that bears an attractive rate of interest, he should consider the possibility of selling it subject to a purchase money wrap-around mortgage.[78] In this manner he can retain for himself the benefits of the favorable rate of interest and make an additional profit on the differential between current interest rates and his more favorable rate.

Example: Owner owns property subject to a $1,000,000 first-mortgage note bearing interest at 6 percent. For purposes of simplicity, we will assume that no principal amortization payments are required. At the time O decides to sell the property, the going interest rate is 8 percent. Suppose O sells it for $1,100,000. If he conveys the property subject to the first-mortgage debt and takes back a second-mortgage note of $100,000 for his equity, his annual interest income will be $8,000.

Suppose, instead, the owner agrees to retain primary liability on the first-mortgage note after the sale. The buyer agrees to assume a purchase-money mortgage for the entire sales price, provided the owner will discharge the first-mortgage note as it becomes due. If the owner can charge the buyer with interest at current rates on the entire balance of the purchase-money wrap-around note, his interest income will be substantially enhanced.

Example: If, under the facts of the prior example, O were to sell the property for a $1,100,000 wrap-around note, his annual interest income would now be $88,000. Not all of this

---

[78]Stonecrest Corp. 24 T.C. 659 (1955), non-acq. 1956-1 C.B. 6.

is net, however. Because O has agreed to pay the obligations under the first-mortgage note, he must pay interest on it at 6 percent, or $60,000. His net interest income is, therefore, $28,000 ($88,000 less $60,000), or $20,000 more than if he had made the sale in the conventional way.

B. TAX-FREE EXCHANGES OF LIKE PROPERTY

Owners of real property held for investment or held for use in trade or business have the privilege of deferring the potential gain to be realized upon a disposition of the property by exchanging it for another parcel of real property "of a like kind."[79]

Thus, an owner of business real estate which is worth more than its basis may exchange the property for another parcel of business real estate without paying a tax on the gain represented by the excess of the value over basis. Similarly, a farmer may exchange his farm or ranch for another farm or ranch and qualify the exchange as a tax-free transaction. The same benefits are extended to owners of apartments who exchange their interest in one apartment for an interest in another.

The benefits of a tax-free exchange are expressly denied to owners of real property held for sale to customers in the ordinary course of business[80] or to owners of property used for residential purposes.[81]

If the exchange and the property involved fit the definition of a tax-free exchange, the rules apply automatically; the provisions of Section 1031 are not elective.[82] Hence, we find it important to know exactly what the rules are and how they are applied.

1. What Is Like Property?

The first requirement that we must keep in mind is that the property received in the exchange must be "of a like kind" to the property disposed of. The regulations define this requirement broadly, stating,

> . . . the words "like kind" have reference to the nature or character of the property and not to its grade or quality. One kind or class of property may not under (Section 1031) be exchanged for property of a different kind or class. The fact that any real estate involved is improved or unimproved is not material, for that fact relates only to the grade or quality of the property and not to its kind or class. Unproductive real estate held by one other than a dealer for future use or future realization of the increment in value is held for investment and not primarily for sale.[83]

For example, an exchange of city real estate held for rental purposes qualifies under Section 1031 even if it is exchanged for a farm.[84] Also, a commercial building rented for store use has been held to be like unimproved city lots.[85] An exchange of mineral rights in property for hotel property is an exchange of like property.[86]

---

[79] Section 1031(a), I.R.C.
[80] Section 1031(a), I.R.C.
[81] Section 1034, I.R.C. may be applicable.
[82] See Mrs. C.B. Staton, 1 B.T.A. 1222 (1925); Frederick R. Horne, 5 T.C. 250, 256 (1945).
[83] Rec. Sec. 1.1031(a)-1(b).
[84] E.R. Braley, 14 B.T.A. 1153 (1929), acq. VII-2 C.B. 6.
[85] Burkhard Inv. Co. v. United States, 100 F.2d 642 (9th cir. 1938).
[86] Commissioner v. Crichton, 122 F.2d 181 (5th Cir. 1941), aff'g Kate J. Crichton, 42 B.T.A. 490 (1950), acq. 1952-1 C.B. 2.

Exchanges of a fee interest in trade or business property for a leasehold interest of 30 years or more in the same or like property is treated as an exchange of like property.[87] An exchange of a fee interest in land for perpetual water rights has also qualified as a tax-free exchange.[88] An exchange of an oil and gas lease for a ranch is an exchange of like property.[89] But a similar exchange of a ranch for an oil payment limited in duration does not qualify as an exchange of like property.[90] Domestic real estate can be exchanged for foreign.[91] Timberland held for a trade or business use can be exchanged for timberland held for investment.[92] But a life estate in one farm cannot be exchanged for a remainder interest in another farm.[93]

An exchange of real estate for any type of personal property,[94] or for intangible property, such as stocks, bonds, or promissory notes, constitutes a taxable exchange.[95] Land is not of the same character as a building, even though the term covers both.[96] Thus, the exchange of land for a building to be constructed on other land owned by the taxpayer would not be tax free.

2. How Is the Nature of the Property Determined?

As pointed out in the opening of this chapter, the benefits of Section 1031 are expressly denied to dealers or to the owners of homes. This limitation imposes a second requirement that must be met in order for a transaction to qualify as a tax-free exchange; both the property exchanged and the property received must be held by the taxpayer for investment purposes or for use in his trade or business.[97]

This requirement, like the first requirement that the properties be of like kind, has been interpreted broadly. Thus, the owner of property held for a trade or business use may exchange it for property to be held for investment purposes; and, conversely, property held for investment may be exchanged for trade or business property.[98]

The nature of the holding of property is judged from the point of view of the party to the transaction who is claiming the benefits of the tax-free exchange rules. Thus, the fact that the taxpayer exchanges business or investment property for property held by a dealer will not deprive the taxpayer of the benefits of a tax-free exchange, provided he holds the new property for a business or investment use.

The taxpayer must be careful to hold the new property acquired in the exchange for business or investment purposes. If he immediately resells the property acquired, he

---

[87]Reg. Sec. 1.1031(a)-1(c); Century Electric Co. v. Commissioner, 192 F.2d 155 (8th cir. 1951), cert. den. 342 U.S. 954.
[88]Rev. Rul. 55-749, 1955-2 C.B. 295.
[89]Rev. Rul. 68-331, I.R.B. 1968-26, 15.
[90]Commissioner v. P.G. Lake, Inc., 356 U.S. 260 (1958).
[91]Rev. Rul. 68-363, 1968-28 I.R.B. 18.
[92]Rev. Rul. 72-515, 1972-2, C.B. 466.
[93]Rev. Rul. 72-601, 1972-2, C.B. 467.
[94]Rev. Rul. 72-151, 1972-1 C.B. 225.
[95]Section 1031(a), I.R.C.; Reg. Sec. 1.1031(a)-1(d). However, exchanges of partnership interests may qualify. Miller v. United States, 12 AFTR 5244 (S.D. Ind. 1962). In Rollin E. Meyer's Estate, 58 T.C. 311 (1972) on appeal it was held that partnership interests could be exchanged except that a general partnership interest could not be exchanged for a limited partnership interest.
[96]Rev. Rul. 67-255, 1967-2 C.B. 270.
[97]Section 1031(a), I.R.C.
[98]Reg. Sec. 1.1031(a)-1(a).

TAX-FREE EXCHANGES OF LIKE PROPERTY

may unwittingly create an inference that the property received in the exchange was acquired for the purposes of resale. In this event, the exchange would be converted into a taxable transaction by the intention to resell held at the time of the property was acquired.[99]

3. Losses on a Tax-free Exchange

The rules relating to tax-free exchanges work both ways; neither gain nor loss will be recognized if the exchange is tax-free.[100]

Thus, if business or investment property is exchanged for similar property worth less than the basis of the former property, the owner will be denied the right to take a deduction for the difference between the basis of the old property and the value of the new.

This rule may be avoided by arranging a separate sale of the old property and a separate purchase of the new. Nevertheless, (1) if the purchaser of the old is the seller of the new, (2) if the transactions are consummated concurrently or if their consummation is interdependent, (3) if the prices reflect unusual values (as in "trade-in" pricing), or (4) if other circumstances exist tending to indicate that the sale and the purchase are reciprocal and mutually dependent transactions, the sale and purchase may be treated as an exchange, and the loss deduction disallowed.[101]

4. Basis on Tax-free Exchange

If property is acquired in a tax-free exchange, the owner must transfer his remaining basis for the property disposed of to the new property received in the exchange. The basis of the property carries over to become the owner's basis for the new property.[102]

Example: Owner holds title to an apartment worth $50,000 which has a depreciated basis to him of $30,000. O makes an agreement with X to exchange his apartment for an unimproved ranch also worth $50,000. O's basis for the ranch will be $30,000.[103]

Basis of apartment	$30,000
Adjustment for gain recognized:	
Value of ranch	$50,000
Basis of apartment	30,000
Potential gain	$20,000
Gain recognized	—0—
Basis of ranch	$30,000

If two properties are received in a tax-free exchange, the old basis is allocated between them in proportion to their respective fair market value.[104]

---

[99] Regals Realty Co. v. Commissioner, 127 F.2d 931 (2d Cir. 1942); Ethel Black, 35 T.C. 90 (1960).
[100] Section 1031(a), I.R.C.
[101] Rev. Rul. 61-119, 1961-1 C.B. 395.
[102] Section 1031(d), I.R.C.
[103] If the apartment was Section 1250 property, then gain would be recognized to the extent of the potential depreciation recapture and basis of the ranch (non-Section 1250 property) would be increased in a corresponding amount.
[104] Rev. Rul. 68-36, 1968-4 IRB 14.

5. Holding Period on Tax-free Exchange

The owner of property acquired in a tax-free exchange is entitled to add his holding period for the property disposed of to the holding period of the property acquired, provided the property disposed of was a capital asset or qualified as trade or business property prior to the exchange.[105]

6. Effect of Receiving "Boot"

In almost every exchange, the values of the properties to be exchanged will not be identical. One party to the exchange will be forced to give a little "sweetener" in order to balance the exchange. If this "sweetener" consists of cash or other unlike property, it is termed "boot" and will affect the tax treatment of the exchange. But if the "sweetener" is additional property "of like kind," it will not affect the tax treatment of the exchange, except that the carryover basis must be apportioned among more than one parcel.

Suppose boot, or unlike property, is received in an otherwise tax-free exchange. What effect does the boot have? It does not make the entire transaction taxable. Rather, it converts only a portion of the transaction into a taxable exchange. To the extent of the boot received, the transaction constitutes a taxable sale or exchange if a gain is realized.[106]

Example: Owner exchanges an apartment worth $50,000 but having a basis to him of $30,000, for an apartment worth $40,000 and $10,000 in cash. Because O receives $10,000 boot, his total gain of $20,000 is taxed to the extent of $10,000, and the remainder is untaxed:

Amount realized on the exchange:		
Value of apartment received	$40,000	
Cash received	10,000	$50,000
Less basis of apartment transferred		30,000
Potential gain realized on exchange		$20,000
Amount of gain taxed on exchange:		
Total gain	$20,000	
Boot received	10,000	
Gain taxed to extent of boot received		$10,000
Gain on exchange not taxed (remainder)		10,000

If the boot were received in property other than cash, the measure of the boot received would be the fair market value of the so-called "other property."[107]

Suppose the amount of the boot received exceeds the total gain realized on the exchange. In that event, the total gain is taxed in full. The excess amount of boot is received tax-free as the recovery of part of the owner's basis for his former property.

Example: Owner exchanges an apartment worth $50,000, having a basis to him of $30,000, for an improved lot worth $20,000 plus cash of $10,000 and promissory notes worth $20,000. O's total gain of $20,000 would be taxed in full:

---

[105] Section 1223(1), I.R.C.
[106] Section 1031(b), I.R.C.
[107] Section 1031(b), I.R.C.

TAX-FREE EXCHANGES OF LIKE PROPERTY

Amount realized on exchange:		
Value of lot received	$20,000	
Cash received	10,000	
Value of notes received	20,000	$50,000
Less basis of apartment transferred		30,000
Potential gain on exchange		$20,000
Amount of gain taxed:		
Total potential gain	$20,000	
Amount of boot received	30,000	
Gain taxed to extent of boot		$20,000
Remainder of boot (applied against basis)		10,000

Thus, boot received in an exchange is taxed only to the extent of the gain realized, and, conversely, the gain realized is taxed only to the extent of the boot received.

7. Losses if "Boot" Received

Even if boot is received, the owner is not entitled to deduct a loss realized on a tax-free exchange. The receipt of boot in addition to like property does not convert the transaction into a taxable transaction when a loss is incurred,[108] although it will affect basis.

Example: Owner exchanges an investment lot worth $10,000, having a basis to him of $15,000, for a second lot worth $7,500 and $2,500 in cash. No part of O's potential loss of $5,000 is recognized for tax purposes. O's basis for the second lot is $12,500 ($15,000 old basis less $2,500 cash received).

8. Effect of Giving "Boot"

Suppose you represent the party to the exchange who is giving the boot. Is his position changed by the fact that the party with whom he deals may have, in part, a taxable transaction because of the receipt of boot? No. The giving of boot does not affect the tax position of a party to an exchange; it is only the receipt of boot that may convert the exchange into a partially taxable exchange from the point of view of the recipient.[109]

Example: Owner exchanges an apartment worth $50,000, having a basis to him of $30,000, for another apartment worth $60,000. O also agrees to pay an additional $10,000 to balance the exchange. No part of O's potential $20,000 gain on the exchange will be recognized for tax purposes. O's basis will be $40,000, consisting of his old basis of $30,000 plus the additional $10,000 cash paid.

9. Basis of Property if "Boot" Received

If boot is received in a tax-free exchange, the taxpayer must adjust the carryover basis for the property received, to reflect both the amount of cash or other property received and the amount of gain taxed. He is required to reduce the carryover basis by

---

[108] Section 1031(c), I.R.C.; Reg. Sec. 1.1031(c)-1.
[109] Reg. Sec. 1.1031(a)-1(c).

the amount of boot received and is permitted to increase the carryover basis for the amount of gain taxed on the exchange.[110]

Example: Owner exchanges an apartment worth $50,000, having a basis to him of $30,000 for an apartment worth $40,000 and $10,000 in cash. Because O receives $10,000 boot, his total gain of $20,000 is taxed to the extent of $10,000. His carryover basis of $30,000 from the old apartment must first be reduced by the $10,000 boot received and then increased by the $10,000 gain taxed:

Amount realized on exchange:		
Value of apartment received	$40,000	
Cash received	10,000	$50,000
Basis of apartment transferred		30,000
Total gain realized		$20,000
Gain taxed (equal to boot received)		$10,000
Basis of new apartment:		
Carryover basis of old apartment		$30,000
Less cash received		10,000
		$20,000
Plus gain taxed on exchange		10,000
Basis of new apartment acquired		$30,000

The theory underlying this allocation of the carryover basis is simple. Obviously, part of the carryover basis must be allocated to the cash received as well as to the new apartment acquired. Since cash has a basis equal to value, $10,000 of the carryover basis is assigned to the $10,000 of cash acquired; the remainder is allocated to the new apartment. To the extent of the cash received, the owner has liquidated his investment in the apartment property.

But because gain is recognized in part on the exchange, the owner is allowed to increase his basis for the new apartment in a like amount. In effect, the basis of the new property will equal its value less the amount of potential gain on the exchange of the old apartment that is not taxed.

Suppose the boot received consists of unlike property other than cash. How much of the carryover basis must be assigned to it? The regulations require that the carryover basis be allocated first to the unlike property to the extent of its fair market value; only the remainder of the carryover basis is available for allocation to the new property received.[111]

Example: Owner exchanges an apartment worth $50,000, with a basis of $30,000, for an unimproved lot worth $20,000 plus cash of $10,000 and the other party's promissory notes worth $20,000. O's total gain of $20,000 on the exchange will be taxed in full because boot in excess of $20,000 was received. Consequently, O's carryover basis of $30,000 will be reduced by the $30,000 boot received, but it will be increased by the $20,000 gain, taxed as follows:

Amount realized on exchange:		
Value of lot received	$20,000	
Cash received	10,000	
Notes received	20,000	$50,000
Basis of apartment transferred		30,000
Gain taxed on exchange		$20,000

---

[110] Section 1031(d), I.R.C.
[111] Reg. Sec. 1.1031(d)-1(c).

TAX-FREE EXCHANGES OF LIKE PROPERTY

Basis of new property:			
Carryover basis		$30,000	
Less boot received:			
Cash	$10,000		
Notes	20,000	30,000	$—0—
Plus gain taxed on exchange			20,000
Basis of new property			$20,000

A similar rule applies in the case of an exchange of an apartment or other property for a loss. If cash or other unlike property is received in the exchange, the owner must allocate a portion of the carryover basis to the boot received to the extent of its value.[112]

Example: Owner exchanges an investment lot worth $10,000 which has a basis to him of $15,000, for a second lot worth $7,500 and $2,500 in cash. No part of O's potential loss is recognized. However, $2,500 of his carryover basis of $15,000 must be allocated to the boot received; only the balance of $12,500 constitutes his basis for the property acquired. No adjustment need be made for the potential loss because no part of it is recognized for tax purposes.

10. Effect of a Mortgage

If an owner of property subject to a mortgage exchanges it for an unencumbered parcel of property, the amount of the mortgage debt against the property is treated as the equivalent of boot received on the transaction. For this purpose it is immaterial whether the other party to the exchange assumes the mortgage debt or whether he merely takes the property subject to it.[113]

Correspondingly, the owner must reduce the carryover basis to be allocated to the new property by the amount of the outstanding mortgage debt just as if he had received an equivalent amount of cash with, of course, the right to make an offsetting adjustment for the amount of gain taxed.[114]

Example: Owner exchanges an apartment worth $70,000 which has a basis in his hands of $50,000 and which was held subject to a $30,000 mortgage debt. O receives in the exchange a new apartment worth $40,000 which is taken free of any liability. Because O is treated as having received $30,000 in cash on the transfer on account of his relief from the $30,000 mortgage debt, his entire gain of $20,000 is taxable. Correspondingly, O must make proper adjustment to reflect the receipt of boot and the recognition of gain:

Amount realized on exchange:		
Value of apartment received	$40,000	
Mortgage debt relief	30,000	$70,000
Basis of old apartment		50,000
Amount of gain (all taxed)		$20,000
Basis of new apartment:		
Carryover basis	$50,000	
Less boot (mortgage debt)	30,000	
Plus gain taxed on exchange		20,000
Basis of new apartment		$40,000

---

[112] Reg. Sec. 1.1031(d)-1(d).
[113] Section 1031(d), I.R.C.
[114] Reg. Sec. 1.1031(d)-2.

118   SALES, EXCHANGES, CONVERSIONS AND ABANDONMENTS

These rules apply not only to mortgage debts but also to other types of liabilities of the owner that the other party to the exchange agrees to assume in connection with the receipt of the taxpayer's property, or to which the property is subject.[115]

Suppose that the owner's property is free and clear. He agrees to exchange his unencumbered property for another property of like kind that is subject to a mortgage indebtedness. Does the fact that he accepts property subject to a mortgage debt affect his tax position? Not at all. The assumption of another's liabilities is treated in the same manner as the giving of boot, which, as we saw, does not affect the exchange from the viewpoint of the party giving the boot.

Example: Owner exchanges an apartment worth $50,000, which has a basis to him of $30,000 for a new apartment worth $75,000 but held subject to a mortgage debt of $25,000. No gain would be taxed to O on the exchange; however, he would be entitled to add the face amount of the new mortgage debt incurred (boot paid) to his carryover basis:

Amount realized on exchange:		
Value of new apartment	$75,000	
Less mortgage debt	25,000	$50,000
Basis for old apartment		30,000
Gain not recognized on exchange		$20,000
Basis for new apartment:		
Carryover basis	$30,000	
Plus boot paid (mortgage assumed)	25,000	
Basis for new apartment	$55,000	

11. Effect of Offsetting Mortgages

Suppose both parcels of property in the exchange are each transferred subject to mortgage debt. How are the mortgages handled? The regulations state that the amounts of the respective mortgage debts are to be offset one against the other and *only the net debt* need be treated as the receipt or the payment of boot.[116]

Example: Owner exchanges an apartment worth $70,000 subject to a $30,000 mortgage for an apartment worth $65,000 subject to a $15,000 mortgage. O also agrees to pay $10,000 cash to boot. If we assume that O's basis for the old apartment was $50,000, the gain recognized on the exchange and the basis of the apartment received are computed as follows:

1. Potential Gain Realized

Amount received on exchange:		
Value of apartment acquired	$65,000	
Liability against property transferred	30,000	$95,000
Less price paid for exchange:		
Basis of old apartment	$50,000	
Cash paid	10,000	
Debt against property acquired	15,000	75,000
Potential gain realized on exchange		$20,000

---

[115] Reg. Sec. 1.1031(d)-2.
[116] Reg. Sec. 1.1031(b)-1(c); G.C.M. 2641, VI-2 C.B. 16.

TAX-FREE EXCHANGES OF LIKE PROPERTY

2. Gain Taxed on Exchange

Amount of boot received:		
Liability against property transferred		$30,000
Less boot given:		
Debt on property received	$15,000	
Cash paid[117]	10,000	25,000
Net boot received		$ 5,000
Amount of gain taxed (equal to boot)		$ 5,000

3. Basis of Property Acquired

Carryover basis of apartment transferred		$50,000
Plus additional consideration paid:		
Cash	$10,000	
Debt assumed	15,000	25,000
Carryover basis plus boot given		$75,000
Less liability against property transferred		
(boot received)		30,000
Carryover basis adjusted for boot		$45,000
Plus gain taxed on exchange		5,000
Basis of apartment acquired		$50,000

If the liability assumed by the owner on the property received exceeds the liability against the property transferred, no boot will be received out of the exchange of liabilities. The exchange may be tax-free in its entirety, provided no other boot is received. The amount of the mortgage debt should, however, be taken into account in measuring the owner's basis for the new property acquired.[118]

Example: Suppose we analyze the exchange outlined in the preceding example from the point of view of the other party to the exchange. Let us assume that his basis for the original $65,000 apartment owned by him is $45,000. Then we have the following result:

1. Potential Gain on Exchange

Amount received on exchange:		
Value of apartment received	$70,000	
Debt against old property	15,000	
Cash received	10,000	95,000
Potential gain on exchange		$20,000

2. Gain Taxed on Exchange

Amount of boot received:	
Cash received[119]	$10,000

---

[117]Consideration given in the form of cash as well as in the form of a liability against the property acquired is an offset to consideration received in the form of a liability against the property transferred. Reg. Sec. 1.1031(d)-2, Example (2)(c).

[118]Reg. Sec. 1.1031(d)-2, Example (2). What we are really saying here is always trade up if you want to avoid tax. A trade down (i.e., a more valuable building for a less valuable one) invariably incurs tax because boot must make up the difference (whether in cash or debt relief).

[119]Cash received on an exchange is not offset against consideration given in the form of an assumption of liability against the property acquired. Reg. Sec. 1.1031(d)-2, Example (2)(c). Obviously, the thing to do is to use the cash to reduce the mortgage debt prior to the exchange. For example, had the $10,000 cash been

Excess of debt on property transferred over debt on property acquired		
Amount of gain taxed (equal to boot)	—0—	$10,000

3. Basis of Property Acquired

Basis of apartment transferred		$45,000
Liability against property acquired		30,000
		$75,000
Less		
Cash received	$10,000	
Debt on property transferred	15,000	25,000
Carryover basis adjusted		$50,000
Plus gain recognized on exchange		10,000
Basis of property acquired		$60,000

12. Three-cornered Exchanges

Exchanges involving three parties, as well as those involving only two parties, may be qualified for the benefits of Section 1031.

Example: Owner owns Lot A. He desires to acquire Lot B from Seller but he doesn't want to pay cash for it. Instead, he offers to exchange Lot A for Lot B.

Seller demurs. Seller doesn't want to acquire Lot A, but is willing to sell Lot B.

Owner then learns that Purchaser wants to buy Lot A. Owner suggests to Purchaser that Purchaser buy Lot B from Seller and then exchange it for Lot A.

Even if Seller deeds Lot B directly to Owner, Owner will be entitled to treat the transaction as a tax-free exchange of Lot A for Lot B.[120]

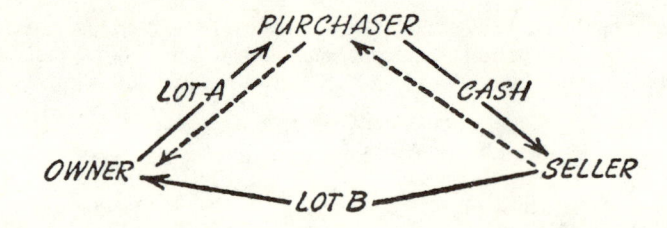

A three-cornered transaction involving a purchase for cash, as in the example illustrated, must be carefully arranged to avoid loss of tax-free status. If Purchaser had been under an obligation to pay cash to Owner for lot A when the purchase and exchange of lot B was arranged, the transaction might be considered a taxable sale of lot A, followed by a purchase of lot B by Owner through Purchaser as Owner's

---

used to pay off $10,000 of the $30,000 mortgage debt, the exchange would have been tax-free to the party in this example. The debt he was incurring ($20,000) still exceeded the $15,000 debt against the property he exchanged.

[120] W.C. Haden Co. v. Commissioner, 165 F.2d 588, 590 (5th Cir. 1948); Mercantile Trust Co., 32 B.T.A. 82 (1935), acq. XIV-1 C.B. 13. Rev. Rul. 73-476, I.R.B. 1973-43, 19.

agent.[121] The critical distinction appears to be whether Purchaser is buying lot B with money belonging to Owner, as opposed to buying lot B with his own money to obtain it for the purpose of completing an exchange. In the eyes of the Commissioner and the Tax court, the answer to this question depends upon whether or not the Owner had constructively received (that is, had the contractual right to receive) the cash sales proceeds. For example, if the Purchaser deposits his full purchase price in escrow and receives a deed to the property he wants to purchase, Owner has constructive receipt of the proceeds and will be taxed on a sale. The fact that he directs the escrow holder to pay the proceeds to Seller for a deed to seller's property does not convert the transaction into an exchange.[122]

On the other hand, the mere fact that an agreement for exchange also contains an agreement to sell if suitable like kind property cannot be found is immaterial, if an exchange is actually consummated.[123] An agreement of sale with the option in the seller to effect an exchange if suitable property can be found has also been approved in a case in which the exchange was consummated.[124]

But if only real property is involved, with no party "cashing-out," the exchange of three parcels of property by three owners causes no problem. The transactions will qualify as a tax-free exchange.

Example: A, B, and C each own lots. A conveys his lot to B, B conveys his lot to C, and C conveys his lot to A. These exchanges qualify for treatment under Section 1031 of the Code, regardless of the fact that the deeds may have been drawn in favor of a grantee other than the person who furnished the consideration.[125]

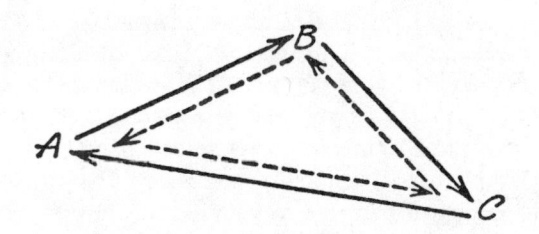

While the Commissioner has been strict in attacking tax-free, three-party exchanges, the court's have been more liberal. The test now appled by the court is one of "what was the net effect of the transaction?" Was it an exchange or was it a sale? For example, the fact that the original contract was one of sale is immaterial if it is

---

[121]James Alderson, 38 T.C. 215 (1962), *rev'd,* Alderson v. Commissioner, 317 F.2d 790 (9th Cir. 1963). A favorable result was reached in Coastal Terminals, Inc. v. United States, 320 F.2d 333 (4th Cir. 1963), although the purchaser not only had to acquire the new property, but also had to build new improvements. To the same effect, J.H. Baird Publishing Co., 39 T.C. 608 (1962).

[122]John M. Rogers, 44 T.C. 126 (1965), affirmed 377 F.2d 534 (9th Cir. 1967); Carlton v. United States, 20 AFTR 5376 (5th Cir. 1967).

[123]Antone Borchard, 1965 P-H Memo T.C. ¶65,297 (1965).

[124]Coastal Terminals, Inc. v. Commissioner, 320 F.2d 333 (4th Cir. 1963); Leo A. Woodbury, 49 T.C. 180 (1967).

[125]Rev. Rul. 57-244, 1957-1 C.B. 247; Rev. Rul. 73-476, I.R.B. 1973-43, 19.

rewritten as a contract of exchange before the transaction is consummated.[126] Even if the original contract of sale is not rewritten, the transaction may still qualify as an exchange, provided the original buyer is willing to accept a deed from the third party who obtained title to the taxpayer's property by way of exchange.

Example: A taxpayer contracted to sell his farm to a railroad for approximately $500,000. After signing the contract, the taxpayer contacted an attorney for the purpose of finding a replacement farm. The attorney tried to modify the contract with the railroad but without success. He did, however, arrange to purchase suitable farm property which he planned to sell to the railroad for its use in satisfying its purchase obligation. The railroad refused to comply because it did not want to be in the chain of title.

The attorney then consummated an exchange by means of the following steps: (1) the taxpayer conveyed his farm to the attorney; (2) the attorney sold the farm to the railroad for cash; (3) the attorney used the cash to buy the new farm he had contracted for; and (4) he conveyed the new farm to the taxpayer.

The Commissioner challenged the transaction as constituting a sale by the taxpayer, not an exchange. He argued, first, that the taxpayer had entered into a sales transaction and, second, the attorney was acting merely as the taxpayer's agent. Thus, the receipt of cash by him was receipt by the taxpayer.

His arguments failed. The Tax Court held that a true three-party, tax-free exchange had occurred.[127] It emphasized that (1) title to taxpayer's farm was transferred in consideration for the new farm received (not cash); (2) the attorney had acted as agent for the railroad as well as the taxpayer; (3) the transactions are to be viewed as a whole and the net result to be examined.[128]

The use, however, of an agent as a third party is fraught with difficulties. If the agent is the agent of the taxpayer, then the receipt of cash by him from the buyer is the equivalent of the receipt of cash by the taxpayer. The transaction is treated as a sale.[129] On the other hand, if the agent is an agent for others as well as the taxpayer, his receipt of cash is not the taxpayer's. The transaction is an exchange.[130]

How about title? With inconsistent logic, some courts have insisted that title pass from the taxpayer to the third party conveying title to him.[131] Such a test places formality over the net effect of the transaction. But as long as title is a problem, it is the course of wisdom to pass title to the exchange property through the person receiving title from the taxpayer.

Real property held for investment or for use in a trade or business can be exchanged for property of like kind without the recognition of gain for tax purposes. However, the benefits of this rule under Section 1031 I.R.C. are not available to a taxpayer who sells his property for cash even though he immediately reinvests the cash proceeds by purchasing property of like kind. He has made a taxable sale because he has received the cash proceeds and must pay a tax on his gain. Thus, the exchange, if

---

[126]Alderson v. Commissioner, 317 F.2d 790 (9th Cir. 1963).
[127]Leslie Q. Coupe, 52 T.C. 394 (1969), acq. 1970-2 C.B. xix.
[128]This rule is irreverently referred to as the "wait until the dust settles" rule.
[129]Rogers v. Commissioner, 377 F.2d 534 (9th Cir. 1967).
[130]Leslie Q. Coupe, 52 T.C. 394, (1969), acq. 1970-2 C.B. xix.
[131]Carlton v. United States (5th Cir. 1967); James Alderson, 38 T.C. 215 (1962) reversed Alderson v. Commissioner, 317 F.2d 790 (9th Cir. 1963).

TAX-FREE EXCHANGES OF LIKE PROPERTY

one is intended, should be clearly cast as an exchange. The price of ambiguity is a law suit.

13. Techniques for Holding Open a Three-party Exchange

If all the parties to a proposed three-cornered exchange are known at the time the transaction is made, no problem exists about holding the exchange open. It can close as soon as the proper instruments and payments have been deposited in escrow and title checking has been completed.

Example: A wants to buy B's property, B does not want to sell because of the capital gains tax, but is willing to trade for C's land. C is willing to sell for A's money. The parties enter into a three-party sale and exchange agreement which requires (1) A to pay the agreed purchase price for C's land into escrow to be released to C on delivery to A of a deed to B's property; (2) B to deposit a deed to his property in favor of A to be released on delivery to B of a deed to C's land; and (3) C to deposit a deed to his land in favor of B to be released on delivery to C of A's purchase money.

The foregoing can be diagrammed and will be followed throughout this part:

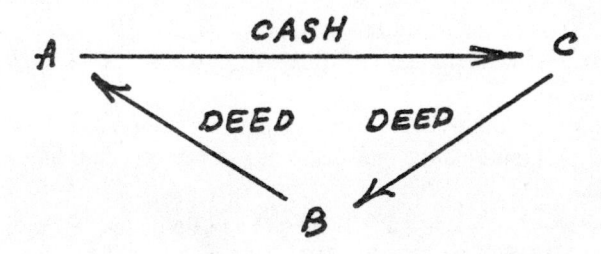

```
         CASH
   A ───────────────▶ C
      ◀         ╱
       DEED  DEED
         ╲   ╱
           B
```

A has cash that C wants. B has property that A wants. C has land that B wants.

What are the results? A is a purchaser of B's property and his basis for it is the money he paid into escrow. B has made a tax-free exchange of his property for C's land. C has sold his property to A for cash and has recognizable gain or loss as the case may be. What may be a taxable sale to one party to a transaction may be a tax-free exchange to another. It is possible, for example, for a taxpayer to enter into a tax-free trade with a real estate dealer although the benefits of tax-free treatment may be denied to the dealer because the property trade is held for sale to customers in his hands.

But suppose one of the parties is unknown. Can a three-cornered exchange be arranged?

Example: A wants to buy B's property. B does not want to sell, but is agreeable to an exchange if suitable like kind property can be found for him. A is anxious to obtain an immediate hold on B's property at a price agreeable to them both, but is willing to cooperate with B in trying to find like kind property in order to consummate the exchange.

One solution to the foregoing problem is to have A and B sign a contract to exchange. This contract is not a contract of exchange at the present because A does not presently own acceptable like kind property. It is a contract looking to the future acquisition by A of acceptable like kind property. In essence, A agrees to find suitable like kind property, acquire it and transfer it to B in exchange for B's property. The fact that A did not have title to the exchange property at the time he entered into the agreement will not result in denying B the benefits of a tax-free trade.[132]

Example: A and B enter into a contract to exchange B's property for land to be acquired by A but only if acceptable to B. The contract states an agreed value for B's property, and A commits himself to spend an equivalent amount in cash to buy land acceptable to C. Because A is not sure of what B wants, B does the looking and, six months later, finds land acceptable to him. The transaction is then closed by a deed by B to A, a deed from C to B and a cash payment by A to C.

As in the prior example, A is a purchaser, B a tax-free exchangor, and C a seller. The fact that A had C deed C's land directly to B does not alter the result. The net effect of the transaction to B is that he exchanged property for land.[133]

There are certain problems and pitfalls that must be avoided in using this technique. Obviously, the contract should be phrased in terms of exchange as far as B is concerned, not in terms of a sale.[134] Second, the contract should not permit B to obtain control of the funds either directly or constructively.[135] Third, A should not be required, or permitted,[136] to deposit his cash for the purchase price of the like kind land until the land has been selected and C has indicated his willingness to accept it. Fourth, if B finds he has inadvertently signed a contract of sale, he should do his best to renegotiate it to an exchange contract;[137] one-party escrow instructions delivered unilaterally will not suffice.[138]

All of the foregoing helps B to preserve his tax-free position. But what are A's risks? If A wants the property and is willing to pay B's price (including accommodating B on his desired tax-free exchange), how can A be assured of getting the property? Suppose, for example, B accepts a juicy deposit and thereafter turns down all properties proferred to him as being unacceptable. What can A do?

The most common solution is to provide in the contract to exchange that A has an option to acquire B's property for cash, but only in the event that agreeable exchange property cannot be found within a specified time.

Example: A wants B's farm. B is willing to sell, but, because he will invest the proceeds to buy a new farm, he insists on an exchange. A agrees. The parties place a value of $750,000 on B's farm. A agrees to attempt to purchase another farm agreeable to B for approximately $750,000 within 6 months of the contract to exchange. In the event A is not successful in acquiring a farm agreeable to B, then, at the end of six months, A has the option to purchase B's farm for $750,000. Prior to the end of the six-months period, A buys an acceptable farm for $750,000 and has it conveyed to B in exchange for B's conveyance of his farm to A.

The result is the same as in the preceding examples. A is a purchaser of B's farm. B has a tax-free exchange and the unknown owner of the farm received by B in the

---

[132]Alderson v. Commissioner, 317 F.2d 390 (9th Cir. 1963); Mercantile Trust Co., 32 B.T.A. 82 (1935).
[133]Leslie Q. Coupe, 52 T.C. 394 (1969), acq. 1970-2 IRB 5; Rev. Rul. 57-244, 1957-1 C.B. 247.
[134]Carlton v. United States, 385 F.2d 238 (5th Cir. 1967).
[135]Compare Alderson v. Commissioner, 317 F.2d 790 (9th Cir. 1963).
[136]Rogers v. Commissioner, 377 F.2d 534 (9th Cir. 1967).
[137]Alderson v. Commissioner, 317 F.2d 790 (9th Cir. 1963).
[138]Rogers v. Commissioner, 337 F.2d 534 (9th Cir. 1967).

exchange has made a taxable sale. The fact that A held a conditional and unexercised option to buy for cash does not affect the tax-free exchange to B.[139] It was what was done that counts, not what might have been done.

Finally, suppose A not only wants to tie B down but also wants to take possession of B's property while B looks around for acceptable like kind property. Can he move into B's property and put it to his own uses without jeopardizing B's potential tax-free exchange? The answer is yes. All that need be done is for B to execute a short-term lease of the property to A for the period that B has to find acceptable like kind property for A to buy in order to consummate the exchange.

Example: Suppose under the facts of the preceding example, A wanted immediate possession. B has six months to find acceptable like kind property. After that, A can exercise his option to buy for $750,000. B, therefore, leases the property to A for the six-months period in question with all rights to make whatever renovations and improvements A wants to do. Within the six-months period, B finds acceptable like kind property that A purchases and has conveyed to B in exchange for B's property.

What result? The same as in the preceding examples. A is a purchaser, B a tax-free exchangor and the unknown owner of the property conveyed to B a taxable seller.[140]

The solutions above put the pressure on B to find like kind property acceptable to him within the time limits prescribed. Suppose B is not willing to be tied down? What alternative does A have?

Example: A wants B's property. B is willing to convey it to A but only if A can find acceptable exchange property. B refuses to sign any contract until A obtains acceptable exchange property. What can A do? If A can find exchange property acceptable to B, A immediately makes an offer to the owner of the exchange property to buy it, subject to the condition that B enter into an exchange agreement therefor. Alternatively, A takes an option to buy the property and then negotiates with B to exchange the properties.

Another common transaction involves an exchange in which one of the parties desires to bail out for cash as soon as possible. Normally, this situation occurs when an owner of investment properties decides that he would like to sell out, except that he does not want to pay the capital gains tax. What he wants to do is to put the cash received into new property. What can he do?

Example: B had purchased 10 houses over the past 15 years and had always rented them to tenants. B's basis for the houses is only $35,000 because of depreciation allowances. The houses now have an average market value of $25,000 each, but B is convinced that raw land promises a much greater growth potential. C owns raw land that he has sat on for 8 years. He paid $175,000 for it and has deducted taxes which have continually risen. If he could get $250,000 for his land, C would sell immediately. B approaches C to get rid of his houses and C is agreeable, provided

---

[139] Alderson v. Commissioner, 317 F.2d 790 (9th Cir. 1963); Antone Borchard 24 T.C.M. 1643 (1965). A more dangerous variant of this technique is to have B enter into a contract of sale, but with the option, in B, to find suitable like kind property for A to buy to exchange for B's property. But such an exchange was upheld in Coastal Terminals, Inc. v. Commissioner, 320 F.2d 333 (4th Cir. 1963).

[140] J.H. Baird Publishing Co., 39 T.C. 608 (1962), acq. 1963-2 C.B. 4, involved a more risky factual situation than the foregoing. There B decided to exchange property to A immediately. A took possession, but A's money was channeled to a contractor who built a building to B's specifications on like kind land purchased by A and ultimately deeded to B.

A will be assured of $250,000 in cash. B and C enter into an agreement of exchange under which B exchanges his 10 rental houses for C's land. C immediately sells off the houses for $250,000.

What result? B has a non-taxable exchange. The fact that C immediately sold off the houses he received does not affect the character of the transaction to B.[141] Suppose, however, B had guaranteed the sales price of the houses to C. In this event, B would undoubtedly be treated as a seller of the houses and his potential gain therein would be recognized in full. It would be better for B to try to locate a purchaser and consummate the transaction through a three-party exchange.

Example: C has raw land, B has houses. C wants cash, B wants C's raw land. B locates A who has cash to buy B's houses. A agrees to buy C's land to exchange for B's houses. B agrees to convey his houses to A on receipt from C of a deed to C's land. C receives A's cash and reports a taxable sale of his land. A acquires B's land and records its purchase price as his cost. B enjoys a tax-free exchange.

14. Planning for a Tax-free Exchange

In any case in which an owner of real property contemplates its sale in order to finance the acquisition of a new parcel of property, he should look into the possibilities of an exchange. If the existing property is held at a gain, its value being in excess of its basis, he may be able to trade the property for the new parcel without paying a tax on the gain inherent in the old parcel. In this manner he will obtain the use of the entire value of his present property as consideration to be paid to acquire the new property. If he sells the old property first, he will have available for reinvestment only the net proceeds after the payment of the tax on the gain; thus, he will have a lesser amount to apply against the purchase price of the property than if he had arranged an exchange.

Example: Owner decides that he wants to sell apartment A in order to raise cash to pay for apartment B which is priced at $80,000. If apartment A is worth $65,000 and has a depreciated basis to O of $25,000, O will be required to pay a capital gains tax of $10,000 (25% of $40,000 gain) on its sale. Hence, he will net only $55,000 to use to buy apartment B. But if O arranges an exchange, he will be able to use the entire $65,000 value of apartment A as consideration for apartment B, without paying a tax on the gain.

Naturally, if Owner were able to offset the taxable gain realized on the sale by an existing capital loss, he would not need to worry about the tax on the gain. But, except under such special circumstances, Owner would normally be money ahead if he exchanges rather than sells.

On the other hand, if the owner holds the property at a potential loss, he normally would want to sell the property for cash in order to obtain a tax benefit from the realization of the loss. If he exchanged the property for other like property, he would be deprived of the loss deduction.

The owner should be aware that he pays a price for a tax-free exchange. Even though he may eliminate the payment of any tax on the transaction, he must apply his basis for the old property to the new property acquired in the exchange. If he holds property in which there is a great disparity between basis and value, he may find that he

---

[141] W.A. Mays v. Cambell, Jr., 246 F.Supp. 375 (N.D. Tex. 1965).

has acquired a new parcel of property with only a relatively small basis available for depreciation. The price of eliminating a capital gains tax on the sale may turn out to be the loss of a higher depreciation deduction against ordinary income resulting from the operation of the new property.

Example: Suppose we refer back to the facts of the preceding example. Let us assume that apartment B to be acquired has an expected life of 20 years and that 75 percent of the purchase price may be allocated to the building. Under these circumstances, O's annual allowance for depreciation on apartment B, if he acquires the property by exchange, would be only half his allowance if he sells and repurchases:

	Purchase	Exchange
Total price paid:		
Cash paid	$80,000	$15,000
Basis of apartment A		25,000
Basis of apartment B	$80,000	$40,000
Basis allocable to building	$60,000	$30,000
Annual depreciation (straight line method on 20 years)	$ 3,000	$ 1,500

Before deciding upon the exchange versus sale-and-repurchase method, the owner should always judge whether or not the immediate savings in tax on the exchange will outweigh the advantages of an enhanced depreciation allowance.

Correspondingly, the value of a greater allowance for depreciation tends to minimize the advantage of selling the property for cash if a potential loss is involved. Thus, if the owner is able to transfer a basis from his old property in excess of the value of the new property, he will have the benefit of a greater allowance for depreciation than if he had paid cash for the property. The fact that he may have forfeited an immediate loss deduction on the sale of the property may turn out to be a small price to pay for the higher depreciation allowance. In many cases, the owner may not be permitted to deduct the loss in full because of the limitations imposed upon capital losses; he may find that the preservation of his basis by use of an exchange is far more valuable to him than a current limited capital loss deduction.

These rules as to the transfer of basis in an exchange may also permit an owner of undepreciable land to exchange his investment for depreciable property, the carryover basis being allocated between the land and building acquired in proportion to their respective market values. Similarly, the owner of improved property which has been depreciated down to its salvage value may also exchange the property for another improved parcel and thereby acquire a new allowance for depreciation without paying a tax on the gain, provided the salvage value of the new property is lower than that of the old or additional indebtedness is incurred on the new property.

What about the question of boot? It is wise to keep in mind the fact that an exchange of property may involve the payment or receipt of boot even though no cash may change hands. Suppose, for example, a parcel of rental property is exchanged for a ranch on which the new owner plans to live. The party acquiring the ranch receives boot to the extent of the value of the residence because he plans to use it for personal purposes. As a corollary, the new owner of the ranch would be required to allocate a portion of his carryover basis to the residence *in an amount equal to its value*. Similarly, if a furnished apartment building is exchanged for an unfurnished apartment building, the recipient of the furnished apartments would be held to have realized gain to the extent of the value of the furniture.

In the case of exchanges of properties held subject to mortgages, there will normally be no tax liability incurred by the party who is "trading up." If he acquires a more valuable piece of property subject to an indebtedness that exceeds the mortgage debt against his old property, he will be giving, not receiving boot.

But in "trading up" the owner should be chary of taking any cash to balance out the exchange. Any cash offered to him should be applied against the existing mortgage indebtedness to reduce it to an amount commensurate with the debt against the property being traded away. In this manner the receipt of boot in cash can be avoided, so long as the mortgage debt is not reduced below the debt against the parcel being traded away.

Example: Owner holds apartment A, worth $50,000 subject to $10,000 mortgage and having a basis to him of $42,000. He exchanges his $40,000 equity in apartment A for a $35,000 equity in apartment B, which is worth $75,000 but is held subject to a $40,000 mortgage. To balance the exchange, Owner is also to be paid $5,000 in cash. Owner should insist that the $5,000 cash be applied to the mortgage against apartment B, reducing it to $35,000.

1. Amount of Potential Gain

	Cash received	Cash applied to debt
Value of apartment received	$75,000	$75,000
Mortgage against a mortgage	10,000	10,000
Cash Received	5,000	—0—
Total consideration received	$90,000	$85,000
Less mortgage against B	40,000	35,000
Net value received	$50,000	$50,000
Less basis of A	42,000	42,000
Potential gain on exchange	$ 8,000	$ 8,000

2. Gain Taxed on Exchange

Amount of boot received		
Excess of liabilities against A over B	$ -0-	$ -0-
Cash Received	5,000	-0-
Total boot received	$ 5,000	$ -0-
Gain taxed (equal to boot)	$ 5,000	$ -0-

Once the parties have decided how the transaction should be handled, that is, whether it should be cast in the form of a sale or of an exchange, they should be careful to follow the proper legal formalities so that the character of the transaction is preserved. If it is to be an exchange, both parties should deposit all deeds, payments, *etc.*, in the same escrow. The legal agreement between them should be drawn in terms of an exchange, not a sale.[142]

---

[142]Mercantile Trust Co., 32 B.T.A. 82, 87 (1935); W.D. Haden Co. v. Commissioner, 165 F.2d 588 (5th Cir. 1948). Alderson v. Commissioner, 317 F.2d 390 (9th Cir. 1963).

On the other hand, if the transaction is to be a sale, the contracts between the parties should speak in terms of a sale. If the legal formalities are carefully observed, it is possible to have a sale and purchase of like properties between the same parties.[143] The sales escrow covering one parcel should be closed and the sales proceeds distributed to the seller before he enters into an agreement of purchase of the new property and deposits the purchase price in an escrow newly opened for that purpose. It is doubtful, however, if this procedure could be used to force the recognition of a loss.

C. TAXABLE EXCHANGES OF REAL PROPERTY

Exchanges of unlike properties, of property for services[144] or exchanges of properties held by a dealer are treated as taxable sales. Any gain or loss realized on the exchanges is recognized for tax purposes just as if the property had been sold for cash. The measure of the price received on the sale is the fair market value of the property received.[145] Correspondingly, the owner's basis for the property acquired will be the price he paid for it, measured by the amount of any cash paid plus the fair market value of the property transferred.

D. INVOLUNTARY CONVERSIONS OF REAL PROPERTY

In general, the involuntary conversion of real property, regardless of its nature, is treated as a sale of the property. The measure of the sales price is the consideration received for the property, measured by the cash received plus the fair market value of any other property received. Gain or loss will be recognized for tax purposes, measured by the difference between the consideration received and the owner's basis for the property at the time of conversion.

However, because the owner has no control over the transaction, Congress has enacted special rules to spare the owner from the rigors of having the conversion treated as a sale under all circumstances. To ask an owner to pay a capital gains tax on the involuntary taking of his property would weaken his economic ability to make himself whole out of the conversion proceeds by reinvesting them into a new parcel of property. The law therefore permits the owner, under certain conditions, to reinvest the proceeds on conversion into new property without paying a tax on the gain realized on the conversion.

For similar reasons, the benefits of Section 1231 have been extended to include involuntary conversions of trade and business property and of capital assets.

1. Tax-free Exchange of Converted Property for Similar Property

If property is involuntarily converted into other property similar in nature and use, no gain will be recognized on the exchange.[146] The owner merely transfers his basis

---

[143] Bloomington Coca-Cola Bottling Co. v. Commissioner, 189 F.2d 14 (7th Cir. 1951); Detroit Egg Biscuit & Specialty Co., 9 B.T.A. 1365 (1928), acq. VII-2 C.B. 11; J. Fleet Cowden, 1965 P-H Memo T.C. ¶65,278.
[144] John D. Riley, 37 T.C. 932 (1962), appeal docketed, 5th Cir.
[145] Speedway Water Co. v. United States, 100 F.2d 636, 638 (7th Cir. 1938).
[146] Section 1033(a)(1), I.R.C.

over to the new property received in the conversion as if nothing has happened.[147] If the property was a capital asset or was used in the owner's trade or business, the owner will be entitled to tack the holding period for his old property onto the new.[148]

If the conversion into similar property resulted in a gain, the rule of non-taxability is mandatory. The owner has no election to choose between a taxable or a tax-free treatment of the conversion. By law, the transaction is tax-free if the conversion itself results in replacing the lost property with other property similar in nature and in use.[149]

If a loss resulted from the conversion, the owner is entitled to treat the loss as deductible without regard to the fact that the property has been replaced by substituted property.[150] However, the carryover basis to the substitute property must be reduced by the amount of loss recognized.[151]

2. Tax-free Conversion of Property into Cash

Suppose that the owner of the converted property receives cash for his property. Must he report the gain resulting from the conversion in taxable gross income?

Section 1033 of the Code grants the owner an option to defer the taxation of any gain realized on the conversion. All he need do is to reinvest the conversion proceeds into other property similar in nature and use to that converted. If the reinvestment is made within the proper time and under proper election, the owner will not be taxed on the gain.

Example: Owner owns farming acreage that is taken for highway purposes. The acreage cost him $2,000 and he received a net amount of $10,000 for it in the condemnation proceeding. Within a year after the condemnation, the owner reinvested the $10,000 received in other farming property. No part of $8,000 gain was taxable.

The owner's basis for the new property acquired with part or all of the proceeds of the conversion is the cost of the new property decreased by the amount of any gain not recognized under Section 1033. In the preceding example, for instance, Owner's basis for the new acreage acquired would be $10,000 cost less $8,000 gain not recognized, or $2,000.[152]

If two or more parcels of property are acquired by the owner to replace the converted property, the owner must allocate his basis, as calculated above, among the new properties in proportion to their respective costs of acquisition.[153]

On the other hand, the failure to reinvest the entire conversion proceeds will result in taxable gain. If the amount reinvested is less than the conversion proceeds, gain is recognized and taxed to the extent of the excess cash proceeds not reinvested. To this extent, the transaction is treated as a partially taxable exchange.

---

[147] Section 1033(c), I.R.C.
[148] Section 1223(1), I.R.C.
[149] Reg. Sec. 1.1033(a)-1(a); Reg. Sec. 1.1033(a)-2(b).
[150] Reg. Sec. 1.1033(a)-1(a).
[151] Section 1033(c), I.R.C.
[152] Section 1033(c), I.R.C.; Reg. Sec. 1.1033(c)-1(b).
[153] Reg. Sec. 1.1033(a)-2(b).

Example: Owner's apartment building is destroyed by fire. He recovers $220,000 in fire insurance and uses $200,000 to construct a new apartment. If his basis for the destroyed apartment was $100,000 his total gain is $120,000, of which $20,000 is taxable and $100,000 is not recognized. The basis of the new apartment is computed as follows:

Cost of new apartment	$200,000
Less gain not recognized	100,000
Basis of new apartment	$100,000

Suppose the owner invested more than the full amount of the conversion proceeds in the replacement property. Under these circumstances, no part of the conversion gain would be taxable.

Example: Modifying the facts of the proceeding example, let us assume that owner's cost of construction of the new apartment was $230,000. No part of the potential gain on conversion would be taxed. His basis for the new apartment would be computed as follows:

Cost of new apartment	$230,000
Less gain not recognized	120,000
Basis of new apartment	$110,000

3. What Constitutes an Involuntary Conversion?

The benefits of Section 1033 are extended to any conversion of property at a gain which results from "the destruction, theft, seizure, requisition, or condemnation of the converted property, or the sale or exchange of such property under threat or imminence of requisition or condemnation."

Destruction from fire,[154] loss by flood,[155] destruction by wind storm,[156] damage by lightning[157] are all examples of types of involuntary conversions that are qualified under Section 1033.

Taking of property pursuant to eminent domain proceedings obviously qualifies under the statute; similarly, a sale made by the owner under the threat of condemnation will also qualify. But if the owner decides to make the sale prior to court action, he must be in a position to prove that the sale was prompted by the threat of condemnation. Normally, if the sale is made directly to the public agency involved, the owner's right to use Section 1033 will be clear,[158] but if the sale is made to a party other than the condemning agency, the owner will have a much tougher burden of proof. For example, the sale of a fertilizer plant, because of the complaints of neighboring residents, to another private party was held not to be a sale under the threat of condemnation.[159]

On the other hand, the sale of a retail store site to a private party for the purpose of building a parking garage was held to be an involuntary conversion where the city had

---

[154]Cotton Concentration Co., 4 B.T.A. 121, 126 (1926), acq. V-2 C.B. 1.
[155]Rev. Rul. 56-436, 1956-2 C.B. 520.
[156]See Reg. Sec. 1.1033(a)-3(b)(1).
[157]Rev. Rul. 57-261, 1957-1 C.B. 262.
[158]Davis Regulator Co., 36 B.T.A. 437 443 (1937), acq. 1937-2 C.B. 7; Rev. Rul. 54-575, 1954-2 C.B. 145.
[159]Piedmont-Mt. Airy Guano Co., 8 B.T.A. 72 (1927), acq. on other grounds, VII-1 C.B. 25.

announced its intention of condeming the property unless the owner or someone else built thereon a parking garage of specialized size and characteristics.[160]

Sales made by an owner for reasons other than the threat of condemnation cannot be qualified under Section 1033. The fact that considerations other than the realization of a business profit prompted the sale will not qualify the sale. For example, a sale made by an owner at the urging of his local chamber of commerce to provide a site for new industry was not an involuntary conversion.[161] Sales made to satisfy the obligations of creditors, whether voluntary or involuntary, are not involuntary conversions.[162] Nor is a sale made pursuant to restrictions in the owner's title an involuntary conversion.[163]

Similarly, the courts have construed the term "condemnation" narrowly. A sale made to avoid repairing rental property condemned as being unfit for habitation is not an involuntary conversion.[164]

By statute, the sale of property lying within an irrigation district in order to comply with acreage limitations of federal reclamation laws is treated as an involuntary conversion.[165] The lands sold must be irrigable lands, all owned by one land owner and lying within an irrigation project or district.[166] Similarly, property lying within an urban renewal district will be treated as having been condemned even though the district gave the owner the choice of improving the property or having it condemned.[167] An alternative threat is also sufficient: a threat to condemn as soon as the district has sufficient funds so to do qualifies the owner for the benefits of Section 1033.[168]

4. Single Economic Unit Rule

If a taxpayer owns two separate parcels of property bearing substantial economic relationship to each other, and one parcel is condemned and the other sold by the taxpayer, the tax-free replacement benefits of Section 1033 may apply to both parcels. What is critical is that the separate parcels constitute a single economic unit so that the taking of one parcel destroys the economic value of the other.[169]

For example, in *Harry G. Masser*,[170] the taxpayer conducted a trucking business, using a warehouse and contiguous vacant lot for parking. The lot was condemned by a housing authority, but the warehouse was not condemned. The taxpayer then sold the warehouse, and the Commissioner sought to tax the gain realized from this sale. The

---

[160] S.H. Kress & Co., 40 T.C. 142 (1963); See Rev. Rul. 63-221, 1963-2 C.B. 332. Compare Edward Warner, 56 T.C. 1126 (1971), which held that a sale to a third party because of newspaper statements was not a sufficient threat.

[161] The Davis Co., 6 B.T.A. 281 (1927), acq. on another ground, VI-2 C.B. 2.

[162] Philip F. Tirrell, 14 B.T.A. 1399 (1929); I.T. 2247, IV-2 C.B. 2.

[163] Rev. Rul. 57-717, 1957-2 C.B.; Cooperative Publishing Co. v. Commissioner, 115 F.2d 1017, 1021 (9th Cir. 1940).

[164] Rev. Rul. 57-314, 1957-2 C.B. 523.

[165] Sec. 1033(d), I.R.C.

[166] Reg. Sec. 1.1033(d)-1.

[167] S. & B. Realty Co., 54 T.C. 863 (1970), acq. 1970-2 C.B. xxi; Dominguez Estate Co., P-H Memo T.C. ¶63,113.

[168] Rev. Rul. 69-303, 1969-1 C.B. 201.

[169] Rev. Rul. 59-361, 1959-2 C.B. 183.

[170] Harry G. Masser, 30 T.C. 741 (1958), acq. 1959-2 C.B. 5 459 F.2d 1043 (4th Cir. 1972).

INVOLUNTARY CONVERSIONS OF REAL PROPERTY 133

taxpayer argued that the warehouse and lot were operated as a single economic unit and thus the replacement of both should qualify for tax-free treatment. The court agreed and held that the series of transactions (condemnation, sale, and replacement purchase) gave rise to no tax liability. When one parcel of a single economic unit is condemned, thus rendering continued use of the other parcel impractical, replacement of both parcels by similar property is subject to IRC section 1033 tax treatment.

The single economic unit rule does not apply if the parcels are owned by separate parties. Nor, apparently, does it apply to contiguous parcels used for different purposes.[171]

5. Proceeds That Can Be Sheltered

In a condemnation, or threat of condemnation situation, the proceeds received from the buyer of the property can be sheltered from tax on any gain. Similarly, insurance proceeds or damages received by an owner for a casualty loss to his premises can be similarly sheltered from tax on any gain. But proceeds from other sources cannot be so sheltered. For example, if a hurricane uproots a taxpayer's timber and he then sells the timber thus damaged, he cannot shelter his gain under Section 1033.[172]

6. Replacement Property

In order for the owner to take advantage of Section 1033, the property must be converted directly or by purchase into property "similar or related in service or use to the property so converted."

What constitutes "property similar or related in service or use"? This statutory phrase has received varying construction.

The courts and the Commissioner seem generally agreed that where the owner is also the user of the property, the test to be applied is the so-called "functional" test. This requires a comparison of the physical use and character of the old property to that of the replacement.

If the owner leases out the property, it is the service or use which the owner-lessor, not his tenant, makes of the property which is the relevant factor. Hence, where both the converted and the replacement property are held for the production of rental income, and the lessor's duties are not materially different, the replacement property qualifies.[173]

Where the owner-lessor's duties, responsibilities or functions have changed substantially the replacement property may not qualify. The replacement of an office building by a hotel failed to qualify for this reason.[174]

Certain other rules appear well established. The replacement of a long-term leasehold with outright ownership of like property qualifies.[175] Two converted buildings replaced by one devoted to the same use is proper.[176] And the replacement of an

---

[171] Rev. Rul. 69-53, 1969-1 C.B. 199.
[172] Rev. Rul. 72-372, 1972-2 C.B. 471.
[173] Harvey J. Johnson, 43 T.C. 736 (1965), acq. 1965-2 C.B. 5.
[174] Clifton Investment Co. v. Commissioner, *supra* note 125.
[175] Davis Regulator Co., 36 B.T.A. 437 (1937), acq. 1937-2 C.B. 7.
[176] Cotton Concentration Co., 4 B.T.A. 121, 125 (1926), acq. V-2 C.B. 1.

unimproved city lot by another lot twice the size is a qualified replacement.[177] Similarly, the purchase of two lots to replace one lot converted is a qualified replacement.[178] And evidently it is irrelevant that the replacement property is in another city or state, at least so long as the owner was already doing business in the latter place.[179]

The statute permits the recipient of a cash award for converted property to purchase a controlling interest in a corporation owning property similar or related in service or in use to the converted property. For this purpose, the owner must acquire at least 80 percent of all classes of stock issued by the corporation.[180] But the recipient of such an award does not have the alternative of purchasing an interest in a partnership which owns and operates property similar or related in use or service to that converted.[181]

Suppose the owner already owns other property that can be improved and placed into use as similar or related property. Can he qualify the award proceeds on conversion for tax-free treatment under Section 1033 by investing the proceeds into improvements on existing property? If the result of the expenditure is to make the property usable for purposes similar or related in use, the expenditure will qualify as a permitted replacement under the statute.[182]

For example, the use of proceeds received on a condemnation of a portion of a factory to rearrange the existing factory improvements is a proper use.[183]

However, the owner cannot use the conversion proceeds to pay off a mortgage debt against property already owned by him, even though the mortgaged property may be used for similar or related purposes.[184]

7. "Like Kind" Property

In one area the requirement of a replacement by property similar or related in use or in service has been broadened by statute. Trade or business *real property*, or investment *real property* which has been condemned, or has been sold under the threat of condemnation, may be replaced by property of "like kind." In this limited situation, the replacement of property qualifying for the benefits of Section 1033 has been broadened to the tests of Section 1031 exchanges of property.[185] But its benefits are available only to owners of real property held for investment or for use in the owner's trade or business.

8. Period of Replacement

If the owner's property has been converted into cash, the owner has until the end of the second tax year following the year of conversion within which to purchase the replacement property. For this purpose, the year of conversion is defined by statute to

---

[177] Columbus Die, Tool & Machine Co., Par. 52,312 P-H Memo T.C. (1952).
[178] Rev. Rul. 58-396, 1958-2 C.B. 403.
[179] S.H. Kress & Co., 40 T.C. 142 (1963).
[180] Reg. Sec. 1.1033(a)-2(c); Rev. Rul. 69-241, 1969-1 C.B. 200.
[181] Rev. Rul. 55-351, 1955-1 C.B. 342. Only the partnership can replace.
[182] Rev. Rul. 271, 1953-2 C.B. 36; Rev. Rul. 58-396, 58-2 C.B. 403.
[183] Rev. Rul. 67-254, 1967-33 I.R.B. 14.
[184] Rev. Rul. 70-98, 1970-1 C.B. 169. See Reg. Sec. 1.1033(a)-2(c)(9)(ii).
[185] Section 1033(g), I.R.C. See discussion under tax-free exchanges.

occur in the "first taxable year in which any part of the gain upon the conversion is realized." Thus, if there is any delay in the receipt of the conversion proceeds, the owner will not be penalized. On the other hand, the unrestricted withdrawal of proceeds deposited in court will commence the running of the statutory period. The fact that title has not been transferred is immaterial.[186]

If the conversion occurred as a result of eminent domain, the owner's period of replacement is 3 years. It begins on the earliest date of the "threat or imminence of requisition or condemnation." Thus, in the case of property lost under condemnation proceedings, the owner is permitted to purchase replacement property before as well as after the date of the actual taking. If the purchase of the replacement property occurs before the loss of the condemned property, the owner must be in a position to show that the purchase was made after the threat of condemnation had appeared.

Suppose the owner is unable to replace the converted property within the time required by law. He is permitted to file an application with his District Director of Internal Revenue asking for an extension of the replacement period. The application must be filed before the end of the original period of replacement and must state "reasonable cause" for the owner's inability to replace within the statutory period.[187]

9. Election on Tax Return

The benefits of Section 1033 are not mandatory, but require an express election. The election may be exercised at any time during the period of replacement. Ordinarily, the election will appear in the owner's tax return for the year of conversion. It can be evidenced by a statement in the return of the details of the conversion, coupled with a showing that the conversion gain is not being included in gross income.[188]

If the owner decides not to replace the property after having elected to do so, or if the replacement property costs less than the total conversion proceeds, so that a part of the gain will be taxed, the owner should file an amended return for the year of conversion and report the proper amount of gain to be taxed in that year.

10. Successor to Owner of Condemned Property

The right to replace condemned property under the provisions of Section 1033 is not personal to condemnee. The right to postpone recognition of gain does not die with the condemnee but is available to his estate or other successor, provided the property is replaced within the required period.[189] The reason should be obvious. Replacement by the estate results in the same loss of cost basis that the decedent would have suffered.[190]

---

[186]Town Park Hotel Corp. v. Commissioner, 446 F.2d 878, (6th Cir. 1971), cert. den. 405 U.S. 1039.

[187]Section 1033(a)(3), I.R.C.; Reg. Sec. 1.1033(a)-2(c)(3). Theron M. Lemly, T.C. Memo Dec. 1973-147 (1973).

[188]Reg. Sec. 1.1033(a)-2(c)(2).

[189]Goodman v. Commissioner (3d Cir. 1952) 199 F.2d 895; Estate of Morris (1971) 55 T.C. 636 (completion of decedent condemnee's attempted replacement acquisition by trustees of testamentary trust satisfied requirements of I.R.C. §1033).

The Internal Revenue Service has ruled, however, that if a condemnee dies after condemnation but before acquisition of replacement property, the right to make the tax-free replacement is terminated; his estate does not stand in his shoes for this purpose. Rev. Rul. 64-161, 1964-1 C.B. 298; Estate of Resler (1952) 17 T.C. 1085. In light of the decisions in Goodman v. Commissioner, *supra*, and Estate of Morris, *supra*, the I.R.S. position is questionable.

[190]Section 1033(e), I.R.C.

One corporation can succeed to tax-free replacement rights of another whose property has been condemned. If *Corporation A* loses property through condemnation and *Corporation B* then acquires *A*'s assets in a tax-free exchange or liquidates its 80 percent subsidiary, *Corporation A*, *Corporation B* steps into the shoes of *Corporation A* for purposes of tax-free replacement.[191]

A corporation that owns condemned property and later adopts a plan of liquidation can qualify for nonrecognition of gain if replacement is completed by the liquidating corporation before expiration of the replacement period. On the other hand, if a corporation liquidates and goes out of existence, its shareholders do not succeed to the right to shelter the gain by purchasing qualified replacement property; a corporation is a different taxpayer from its shareholders. Gain on the condemnation is fully taxable to the liquidating corporation. Adoption of a plan of liquidation after the effective date of the condemnation does not shelter the gain.

11. Effect of a Mortgage on Converted Property

If the converted property is burdened by a mortgage, the conversion proceeds will normally be split between the mortgagee and the mortgagor-owner. Even if the mortgagee's portion of the conversion proceeds are paid directly to the mortgagee, the mortgagor-owner must take into account the mortgagee's share as part of the total amount realized on the conversion.[192] Hence the mortgagor-owner must acquire replacement property with a cost basis equal to or in excess of the gross conversion proceeds, including the mortgagee's share thereof.[193]

Example: Owner possesses property that cost him $100,000, subject to a $50,000 mortgage. The property is condemned for a gross price of $110,000, of which $60,000 is paid to the owner and $50,000 to the mortgagee. The owner must acquire replacement property with a cost basis equal to or in excess of $110,000 in order to qualify under Section 1033. The $110,000 expended can consist, for example, of $60,000 cash and $50,000 in borrowed funds secured by a mortgage. Or, for that matter, the entire reinvestment can be borrowed funds with Owner pocketing the cash.

12. Use and Occupancy Insurance

Are the proceeds of a policy of use and occupancy insurance, received on the destruction of business property, to be treated as amounts received on an involuntary conversion? Or are such proceeds taxable as income?

The answer depends upon the nature of the insurance contract. If the policy calls for the payment of a flat per diem allowance for the loss of use and occupancy for the period prior to replacement of the converted property, then the proceeds paid by the insurer are considered as part of the amount received on the conversion. Hence, the

---

[191] See Smith & Wiggins Gin, Inc. v. Commissioner (5th Cir. 1965) 341 F.2d 341; The subsidiary liquidation must be other than under Section 334(b)(2) I.R.C.; Rev. Rul. 55-517, 1955-2 Cum. Bul. 297.

[192] Commissioner v. Fortee Properties, Inc., 211 F.2d 915 (2d Cir. 1954), cert. den. 348 U.S. 826; Wala Garage, Inc. v. United States, F. Supp. (Ct.Cl. 1958).

[193] Reg. Sec. 1.1033(a)-2(c)(11). Contra, Frank W. Babcock, 28 T.C. 781 (1957), aff'd 259 F.2d 689 (9th Cir. 1958). It has been suggested that the Babcock-Fortee Properties conflict can be resolved: in Babcock, the owner was not personally liable on the mortgage debt; in Fortee Properties, the owner was personally liable. Harsh Investment Corp. v. United States, 323 F.Supp. 409 (D.C. Ore. 1970).

owner may elect to invest these proceeds in replacement property to avoid being taxed on a conversion gain.[194]

If the policy insures against loss of profits during the period that the owner is deprived of use and occupancy of the premises, then the policy proceeds will be taxed as income.[195] Hence, reinvestment of the policy proceeds in replacement property will not qualify them for the benefits of Section 1033.

Similarly, the compensation paid for a forcible taking of the owner's premises for a limited period of time cannot be qualified under Section 1033. The amount of the condemnation award will be taxed as rental income, even though the owner uses the award to lease replacement property.[196]

13. Condemnation Expenses and Severance Damages

Proceeds received on condemnation which represent the price paid for the property taken are treated as moneys received on an involuntary conversion, which may be qualified for the benefits of Section 1033.

Only the net amount of the award need be invested in replacement property. For this purpose, the gross amount of the award may be reduced by the owner's expenses incurred in the condemnation proceeding, including his attorney's fees. Deduction should also be made for the amount of any special assessment levied against the owner's remaining property that accompanies the award. The net amount remaining constitutes the net price realized.

Example: Owner of a city lot which cost $10,000 loses a ten-foot strip (approximately one-tenth of the lot) by condemnation for street widening. He receives $2,500 for the strip taken, out of which $500 is withheld to pay for the cost of a special assessment against the remainder of his lot. His condemnation expenses total $750. His net gain would be computed as follows:

Gross amount of award		$2,500
Less: Expenses	$750	
Special assessment	500	1,250
Net amount of award		$1,250
Less basis allocable to strip (1/10)		$1,000
Net gain realized		$ 250

If the owner fails to reinvest the net award of $1,250 in similar property he will be taxed on the $250 gain.

A condemnation award may also contain an allowance for damages to the property of the owner that remains after the condemnation, commonly referred to as severance damages. Because severance damages are not paid for the property taken, they need not be taken into account as part of the price received; rather, severance damages reduce the owner's basis for the remaining property. In this manner, severance dam-

---

[194]Piedmont-Mt. Airy Guano Co., 3 B.T.A. 1009 (1926), acq. VII-1 C.B. 25 Williams Furniture Corp., 45 B.T.A. 928 (1941), acq. 1942-1 C.B. 17.
[195]Reg. Sec. 1.1033(a)-2(c)(8); Miller v. Hocking Glass Co., 80 F.2d 436 (6th Cir. 1935), cert. den. 298 U.S. 659; Massillon-Cleveland-Akron Sign Co., 15 T.C. 79, 85 (1950), acq. on another point, 1950-2 C.B. 3; Oppenheim's, Inc. v. Kavanaugh, 90 F. Supp. 107, 112 (E.D.Mich. 1950); See Cappell House Furnishing Co. v. United States, 244 F.2d 525 (6th Cir. 1957). Rev. Rul. 73-477, I.R.B. 1973-45, p.20.
[196]Rev. Rul. 38, 1953-1 C.B. 16.

ages are normally recovered tax-free as compensation for the injury to the remaining property to the owner.

Only the net amount of the severance damages need be applied against basis. The owner is permitted to deduct an allocable share of his expenses of the condemnation proceeding and any special assessment against the gross amount of the severance damages in order to compute the net reduction in basis.[197]

Obviously, then, it is in the interest of the owner to obtain an allocation of the condemnation award between compensation for the property taken and severance damages for injury to the property remaining. In this manner the owner will be able to apply the basis of the entire property against the proceeds received and thus minimize the possibility of being taxed on any gain arising out of the forced sale of part of the property.[198]

If the award itself makes no provision for severance damages, the owner will not be permitted to allocate any portion of the recovery to damages to his remaining property.[199] Similarly, a settlement of the condemnation action which fails to allocate any amount to severance damages will bar the owner from making any such allocation for tax purposes.[200] For this reason, the owner should see that an express allocation to severance damages is incorporated in the award or in the settlement agreement.

In the unusual case of severance damages exceeding the owner's basis for his remaining property, the amount of the excess is treated as a taxable gain as if the property were sold.[201]

If severance damages affect only part of the remaining land, only the basis for the specific part affected can be applied against the damages.

14. Taking of Flowage and Other Non-exclusive Easements

Can a taking of non-exclusive easement be sheltered from tax on the gain? The answer is "Yes."

The Service ruled that a farmer could qualify even though he granted a flowage easement to a flood-control authority and retained the right to grow rice on the land subject to the flowage easement. The fact that the easement is non-exclusive is immaterial.[202]

It has also been ruled that the proceeds received on the condemnation of a utility power line and right-of-way easement can be shielded from tax by the purchase of rental property. The owner reserved the right to cultivate the property beneath the utility towers.[203]

---

[197]Rev. Rul. 68-37, 1968-1 C.B. 359.
[198]Pioneer Real Estate Co., 47 B.T.A. 886, 889 (1942), acq. 1943 C.B. 18. Interest, however, received on the award is taxable. Rev. Rul. 72-77, 1972-1 C.B. 28.
[199]Rev. Rul. 59-173, 1959-1 C.B. 201. In Rev. Rul. 64-183, 1964-1 C.B. (Part 1) 297, the Commissioner recognized that underlying work papers may be sufficient to provide an allocation. The Tax Court has been more liberal. L.A. Beeghly, 36 T.C. 154 (1961), acq. 1962-1 C.B. 3; Arch B. Johnson, 42 T.C. 880 (1964), acq. 1965-2 C.B. 5.
[200]Lapham v. United States, 178 F.2d 994 (2d Cir. 1950).
[201]Rev. Rul. 54-575, 1954-2 C.B. 145.
[202]Rev. Rul. 72-433 1972-2 C.B. 470.
[203]Rev. Rul. 72-549, 1972-2 C.B. 472.

E. INVERSE CONDEMNATION

Inverse condemnation is defined, for the purpose of this section,[204] as an action brought by an injured property owner against a municipality, political district or other county or state political body that has the power of condemnation over private property through its power of eminent domain. Because of this body's failure to exercise its power timely, a property owner has suffered a serious monetary loss. The result is that he brings suit for damages for the loss to his property. We assume he recovers substantial money damages and so the property owner becomes a taxpayer. Recovery, or lack of recovery, of money has tax consequences.

1. Nature of Action

The nature of the inverse condemnation action is one of implied warranty by the district that, because it possesses the power of condemnation, it will use that power to protect all members of the district from injury. To the extent it fails to do so, it is absolutely liable to the injured member of the district to make good his loss. The recovery is based on the constitutional provision granting the district eminent domain powers. In many fact situations, a tort will also be involved because of negligence or the commission of a nuisance. In such case, the injured party usually pleads in the alternative. But, unlike the tort cause of action, the cause of action for inverse condemnation does not require the showing of negligence or intent. All that is required to be shown is damage and proximate cause. His recovery will be the monetary value of the damages.

The leading case is *U.S. v. Causby*.[205] There a chicken farmer sued the United States for the injury done by low flying military aircraft to the air space above his chicken farm. Other examples of inverse condemnation recoveries are the following:

1. Recovery for water damage resulting from construction of irrigation facilities by public irrigation district;
2. Recovery for flood damage because a public district failed to modify its flood control works to take into account changed conditions;
3. Recovery for damage to land stability because of highway or rapid transit facility construction;
4. Recovery for imposition of zoning restrictions on use of properties near airport;
5. Recovery for noise and air pollution damage caused by airport district;
6. Recovery for loss of access;
7. Recovery for injury caused by escaping sewage;
8. Recovery for damaged inventory because of flooding; and
9. Recovery for impairment of view.

2. Tax Consequences

What are the income tax consequences of the recovery to the unwilling eminent dominee? First: the fact that the destruction or "taking" was involuntary, does not by

---

[204] Reprinted with the kind permission of the *The Journal of Taxation*.
[205] 328 U.S. 256 (1946).

that fact make it exempt from being treated as a sale. It, the destruction or "taking," may entitle the proceeds (or lack thereof) to special treatment. But in either event, a tax-reportable transaction has occurred. Second, if the taxpayer suffered a loss, he may be entitled to deduct it against ordinary income as a casualty loss.[206]

3. No Prior Loss Deduction

What are the tax consequences of the inverse condemnation award? Assuming that no prior casualty loss had been taken, what the taxpayer recovers is tax-free as a return of capital.[207] To the extent that the recovery exceeds basis, the amount is a taxable gain.[208]

Normally, the inverse condemnation award does not result in a complete taking of the property, but, instead, requires the granting of a "usage" or easement over the property. Examples are many, but two will suffice: first, a right to flood in any year the normal high water level exceeds a stated level; second, a right to fly take-off jet flights over prior established residential districts. For example, if an airport district is compelled to pay an award for noise pollution, the district will insist that it have the right in the future to re-do the damage. The most common example is the jet fly patterns over residential areas. First, the flyways are established by the airport district. No compensation is paid, or even offered, to the residents below. Second, the residents sue to enjoin the use of the flyways because of "nuisance" or whatever. Third, the district agrees to pay cash to the homeowners for their loss of enjoyment of their homes, provided the jets can use an agreed fly pattern. That is what is meant by the "granting of an easement." It is involuntary but compensated for.

The same is true in flooding cases. If a district is forced to pay damages to a disgruntled orchard owner who lost four acres of trees, it may well pay if the orchard owner agrees he will not again bring suit if he or his successors plant trees in the four flooded acres and a later flooding occurs.[209]

If the owner is persuaded to "grant" an easement or right to make a nuisance perpetually, the amount he receives is treated as recovery of basis. No gain is recognized until the entire cost basis of the subservient property is recovered.[210]

---

[206] Section 165. The loss is measured by the loss in value of the property not to exceed basis, plus clean-up expenses. Katherine B. Bliss, 27 T.C. 770 (1957), acq. 1957-2 C.B. 4 reversed on another point, 256 F.2d 533 (2nd Cir. 1958).

[207] Farmers & Merchants Bank of Cattlesburg, Ky., 59 F.2d 912 (CA-6, 1932). The only exception is for "loss of profits." Such recovery is taxable regardless of basis. Swastica Oil & Gas Co., 123 F.2d 382 (CA-6, 1941), cert. den.; Rev. Rul. 73-161, I.R.B. 1973-14, 18.

[208] Tortious or other injury to capital (i.e., basis) is not taxable until basis is recovered. Durkee, 162 F.2d 184 (CA-6, 1947); Raytheon Production Corporation, 144 F.2d 110 (CA-1, 1944).

[209] Prime examples are the rice farmers who plant their crops in the Yolo "By-Pass" just west of Sacramento, California. The "By-Pass" was deliberately dredged and levied to drain the flood waters of the Sacramento River away from the City of Sacramento just as soon as the flood crest reached levy height. The soil in the Yolo "By-Pass" is rich and easily irrigated because the water level of the river is considerably higher. But in a flood year, if the Yolo "By-Pass" is opened, the rice farmers, who have sown their crop, lose all. But they have no cause of action. Their land is subject to a perpetual servitude to be flooded. The author has been told that in Virginia, this servitude is called a "flood plain."

[210] Inaja Land Co., 9 TC 727 (1947), acq.; Rev. Rul. 68-291 1968-1 C.B. 351. If the amount received exceeds the basis of the property affected by the easement, the excess is taxable as gain. Rev. Rul. 59-121, 1959-1 C.B. 212. But any amount received in excess of the basis for the subservient land is taxable gain. All allocation between the subservient and the free land may be required. Scales, 10 BTA 1024 (1928). Rev.

INVERSE CONDEMNATION

If the "usage" is less than perpetual, the award is the equivalent of rent. For example, a money grant of "usage" for five years has been ruled by the Service to be rent.[211] Any "usage" or easement award in excess of 30 years should be the same as the conveyance of a fee; the award should therefore be treated as a non-taxable recovery of basis under which no gain would be taxed until basis was recovered.[212]

4. Application of Section 1033

Section 1033 entitles the taxpayer not to pay the tax on the gain provided he purchases qualified replacement property within the time limits prescribed.[213] The price he pays for the non-taxation of his gain is a decrease in his cost basis equal to the amount of the gain not taxed.[214]

Does Section 1033 cover inverse condemnations as well as direct condemnations? The triggering language of Section 1033 is:

"If property (as a result of its destruction in whole *or in part*, theft, seizure, or requisition or condemnation or threat or imminence thereof) is compulsory or involuntarily converted . . ." (Emphasis added.)

The answer is positive. A partial seizure, by way of easement or otherwise, is a Section 1033 seizure.[215] It is hard to visualize an inverse condemnation case not so covered. Either the property has been physically damaged or has been partially taken (easement granted) or has been threatened before any recovery is obtained.

5. Partial Destruction: The Usual Case

If a portion of the property is damaged but the remainder unharmed, a question of allocation of cost or other basis becomes important. Normally, the property is not taken

---

Rul. 54-575, 1954-2 CB 145. Rev. Rul. 68-291, 1968-1 CB 351. In Rev. Rul. 73-161, IRB 1973-14 18, the Commissioner required an allocation between lost profits (ordinary income) and damages to the land. Because only a 50-foot permanent oil pipe line easement was taken, only that portion of the total basis could be recovered tax free; to the extent the proceeds exceeded the allocable basis the excess was Section 1231 gain. But an allocation will not be required if it is impractical or impossible so to do. Trunk, 32 T.C. 1127 (1950), acq. The sale of a perpetual easement over a portion of the land without the retention of any beneficial interest is treated as the sale of the fee: gain or loss will be measured by the difference between the award and the owner's basis allocable to that portion. If a taxpayer is forced to report a gain or loss on the taking or granting of an "easement," the amount of the gain would be an upward adjustment to basis; any loss, which is the usual case, would be a downward adjustment. If the easement be less than perpetual, the price paid may be just ordinary rental income, with neither a negative nor a positive basis adjustment. Rev. Rul. 72-255, IRB 1972-21, 11.

[211]Rev. Rul. 38, 1953-1 C.B. 16. The taking there was only for five years. A taking between five and 30 years may be argued as being the equivalent of a sale of a leasehold interest because it is to a third party, not to a lessor. See Hort, 313 U.S. 28 (1941).

[212]See Section 1031 and Reg. 1031(a)-1(c)(2), which state that a 30 year lease is the equivalent of a fee for purposes of the "like kind" test of tax-free exchanges under Section 1031.

[213]Qualified replacement property is, in the case of a casualty or condemnation loss, property "similar or related in service or use," the cost of which equals or exceeds the proceeds, after all expenses, received for the property. If the property is real property held for investment or trade or business purposes, qualified replacement property includes "like kind" property. The period of replacement is the following two taxable years. Section 1033.

[214]Section 1033(c), last sentence. Despite the change in basis, the holding period of the old property is tacked onto the new. Section 1223(1)(A).

[215]Rev. Rul. 60-69, 1960-1 CB 294, ruling that the taking of easements by a public utility that had the effect of making the owner's property inoperable constituted a taking that qualified for Section 1033.

in the sense that the guilty authority acquires legal title to it. What happens is that the land is flooded, burned, depreciated, or polluted by noise, smoke, or other objectionable emmission. But the land is still there. An allocation is necessary.

How does the taxpayer make the allocation? Because no part of the land itself has been taken, the taxpayer is free to use respective fair market values at the date the inverse condemnation happened. If, for example, a peach orchard were destroyed by flooding, at least four approaches could be used.[216]

(1) *Relative cost method*. The taxpayer could use the relative cost method. The recovery would be allocated between the peach trees destroyed and the land on the ratio of the cost of the land and the cost of the trees. Because most of the cost of the trees has probably been expensed,[217] the relative cost method allocates recovery to land, not to the destroyed trees.

Obviously, this method is the best one, if the taxpayer intends to retire from the peach growing business. The taxable gain on the destruction of the trees is minimized because most of the proceeds are allocated to land. If the original cost of the land exceeds the proceeds allocated to the land, the money is received tax-free as a recovery of cost. Any excess is taxable as Section 1231 gain.[218] The amount allocated to the trees will be taxable as Section 1231 treatment.[219]

(2) *Lost income method*. The taxpayer could allocate the proceeds to "lost income" and then to relative costs of the trees and the land. Tax-wise, this is the most disadvantageous allocation he could make because the portion allocated to "lost income" is taxed just as if it were found income.[220] It cannot be sheltered from tax.

Too frequently, this is the accomplished fact when the recovery is received. The suit filed on behalf of the taxpayer demanded an amount of lost profits equal to or in excess of the damage to the trees[221] or to the land.[222] "Lost profits" may be a fruitful tool for high condemnation awards. But it also is contaminated with high taxes: the amount of the award for "lost profits" is taxable as ordinary income.[223] The only concession the Service makes is that the fees and costs of recovery are deductible currently in the ratio that the "lost profits" recovery bears to the recovery for the

---

[216] These four alternatives are suggested as possibilities for consideration by the reader. The only analysis made here is what is best for the taxpayer.

[217] And deducted as water, fertilizer, labor (for pruning, tying and staking) under Section 162. Exception is made for citrus and almond groves. Section 278. The two exceptions were made by Congress because of the complaint by citrus and almond growers that so many high bracket taxpayers were investing in citrus and almond groves for tax shelter that the prices of almonds and citrus were forced below cost.

[218] If soil and water conservation or land clearing expenditures had been deducted in the prior ten years, there may be partial recapture at ordinary rates under Section 1252.

[219] Naturally, if the owner does not want to retire from his peach tree operation, he can shelter the Section 1231 gain by planting new trees at a cost equal to or in excess of the portion of the award allocable to the trees.

[220] Rev. Rul. 73-161, I.R.B. 1973-14, 18; Reg. 1.161-14(a) taxes treasure trove and other found income as ordinary income. It is doubtful that the limit on earned income under Section 1348 of a maximum 50% rate applies.

[221] Section 1231 gain to the extent recovery exceeds basis, unless sheltered under Section 1033.

[222] Recovery of basis: excess is Section 1231 gain.

[223] Swastica Oil & Gas Co., *supra* note 2; Liebes, 90 F.2d 932 (CA-9, 1937); Booker 27 TC 932 (1957); General American Investors Co., 348 U.S. 434, 1955).

damage to the trees and the land.[224] In the absence of any allocation in the award, the allegations of damage in the complaint will control.[225]

If a settlement of the suit for inverse damages is made, it is wise to give up lost profits and get recovery for the trees and the land. It is usually a matter of indifference to the public district paying the claim in which form the settlement is cast. The district is not a taxable entity. But a sharp attorney for the condemning authority may well recognize the problem the taxpayer has because of the emphasis in the complaint on lost profits. He may insist on reducing the award for a concession in the allocation away from lost profits.

(3) *Fair market value allocation.* The third method is an allocation on the basis of relative fair market values at the time of injury. Obviously, the bearing trees are worth much more than their depreciated cost. The land value is normally pegged at cost because its value is in what it produces. The "highest and best use," in the definition of MAI appraisers, has to be the current crops. If the trees were beyond their mature years and were dying, the highest and best use would be a new planting or other new use.

The reason as much as possible is allocated to the destroyed trees is because the cost of the trees is minimal and the amount of the inverse condemnation proceeds allocated to them is likely to result in a heavy Section 1231 gain. But this gain can be sheltered from any tax if the proceeds allocated to the trees are spent on new trees.[226] Or, alternatively, spent to build dike and drainage systems in order to prevent the casualty damage from again occurring.[227] Or, if the proceeds are used to buy a new peach orchard on credit with a minimal down payment.[228] So the fair market value method of allocation may be the most favorable to the *owner who wants to continue* in the farming business.[229]

(4) *Gross receipts method allocation.* Another alternative is to allocate on the basis of gross receipts. The inverse condemnation proceeds should be allocated between the trees damaged and the land on the ratio of the gross receipts to be derived from each.[230] The gross receipts method eliminates the income problem attached to the "lost profits" method because gross receipts may or may not result in income. The question of income is dependent upon future expenses, which are as undeterminable on the land for raising hay as for the destroyed trees bearing the finest quality of peaches.

The gross receipts method of allocation is useful only if the peach tree orchard owner is anxious to plant more trees to purchase more orchards, and wants to retain as high a cost basis for his land as he can.

---

[224] See Vincent, 219 F.2d 228 (CA-9, 1955).
[225] See Rev. Rul. 59-173, 1959-1 CB 201.
[226] Or, for that matter, new vines or asparagus roots. The test of Section 1033 is "similar or related in service or use." The test is functional which means: "Do you tend the crops the same way you used to?"
[227] Rev. Rul. 271, 1953-2 CB 36.
[228] No tracing of funds is required. Section 1033(a)(3).
[229] The new trees will have a cost basis for depreciation reduced by the postponed gain.
[230] Obviously, the land, if untended, grows weeds and only the trees produce saleable peaches. A 0 to 100% ratio. Preferably the land should be taken in at its value in common hay acreage because that value can be supported if challenged. The result is a 15% to 25% ratio to land and the balance to the trees if new or mature. If the trees are over age and dying, the result is less favorable.

The considerable benefit of the gross receipts method of allocation is that the amount allocated to the trees cannot be treated as "lost profits." The amount allocated to the trees will therefore qualify for either Section 1231 gain treatment (if no purchase of or planting of new trees) or Section 1033 tax-free investment in new orchards or plantings. Since, as indicated, lost profits are taxed as ordinary income, the allocation should be to loss of gross receipts, not to lost profits.

6. Loss Previously Taken

Suppose the peach grower in the preceding analysis had taken a Section 165 casualty loss in the year the flood, fire or other pollution had occurred.[231] If the taxpayer later recovers an inverse condemnation award, the tax benefit rule (Section 111), requires him to include in ordinary income the amount of any previously deducted item.[232]

The fact that the recovery is not "lost profits" is immaterial. The recovery of an item of property previously deductible produces ordinary income, taxed at the rate in the year of recovery.[233]

Application of Section 1033. An ordinary loss deduction has been taken for damage to the owner's property. The owner receives an award (other than for lost profits) allocable to trees destroyed. The award, to the extent of the prior casualty loss, is ordinary income. Can the casualty loss recovered be sheltered under Section 1033 by using it to purchase new trees, thus meeting the functional use test of Section 1033 and eliminating the gain by a reduction in basis? For example, all the award received for the destroyed peach trees is used to plant new peach trees or, alternatively, is used to purchase another peach orchard which the taxpayer will handle (i.e., crop lease, term lease, or himself operate) in the same manner as in the past.

The tax recovery income from the prior deducted casualty loss is as surely sheltered under Section 1033 as the gains of a dealer in real estate whose property has been destroyed or condemned.[234] In the case of a dealer in real estate (whose gain, if realized, would be ordinary income), the re-investment must be in new "dealer" property. In the case of our casualty-loss taxpayer, he must also invest in property "similar or related in service or use" to shelter the tax benefit income resulting from his prior tax deduction. In both cases, the price paid by the taxpayer for sheltering the income from tax is a reduction in basis of the replacement property equal to the income not taxed. The income will be realized in a later taxable disposition of the property and so is merely postponed.[235] The purchase of qualified replacement property is referred to as a "roll over" of the income. The peach tree owner has a wider range of sheltering

---

[231] Obviously, the taxpayer has to prove a completed loss; if he has any substantial prospects of recovery, he must postpone the deduction to year his prospects of recovery become nil.

[232] Reg. 1.111-1 Anders, 414 F.2d 1283 (CA-9, 1969) (towels expensed). Application of the rule to cattle feed expenses is found in Spitalny, 430 F.2d 195 (CA-9, 1970).

[233] Alice Phelan Sullivan Corp., 381 F.2d 399 (Ct. Cls., 1969). Rev. Rul. 71-160, 1971-1 C.B. 75. Rev. Rul. 73-408, IRB 1973-41, p. 7.

[234] The Service has rejected this analysis under I.R.C. Section 1034. Rev. Rul. 74-206, I.R.B. 1974-18, p. 12.

[235] Of course if there is a subsequent change of basis due to death of an individual taxpayer, the income or gains may be ameliorated because of the carryover basis provisions. Sections 1014, 1023.

his tax benefit income. He can purchase a new orchard (not only of peaches but of other orchard crops, such as apples, oranges, nuts and even asparagus) provided he meets the functional use test. Alternatively, he can expend monies to plant new trees on his existing property.

Treatment of gain on subsequent sale. The second difference between our taxpayer and a real estate dealer is that the dealer will realize ordinary income when he later makes a taxable disposition of the replacement property; that property is held for sale to customers. But the inverse condemnee acquires Section 1231 property (real or depreciable property) used in his orchard business. On a later taxable disposition, the condemnee's gain should therefore be Section 1231 gain rather than ordinary income. In other words, does the roll over of the casualty loss avoid the application of the prior tax benefit rule? The author submits that it should. The effect is exactly the same as if, for example, a casualty loss is deducted for damage to a capital asset. If the damage is made good through the receipt of insurance proceeds, the insurance recovery is treated as ordinary income to the extent of the prior loss. But if no insurance is recovered, the basis of the capital asset must be reduced by the amount of the casualty deduction. When the property is later sold, the gain realized at the time due to the prior basis reduction is capital gain.

Other tax consequences. To the extent the inverse condemnation award results in proceeds that exceed the amount of the prior casualty loss, the excess will be treated under the tax rules discussed at "no prior loss deduction."

F. GAINS AND LOSSES ON INVOLUNTARY CONVERSIONS UNDER SECTION 1231

Section 1033 does not apply to involuntary conversions that result in a loss; nor does it apply to an involuntary conversion resulting in a gain if replacement property is not acquired. In either of these two cases, the conversion is a taxable transaction.

The conversion, even though taxable, may be entitled to special relief under the provisions of Section 1231. If the property converted is trade or business property, or a capital asset held for more than one year, the owner is permitted to report the gain or loss under Section 1231. Thus, if the gains from involuntary conversions and other Section 1231 transactions exceed the losses, all of the transactions will be treated as long-term capital sales, resulting in net capital gain. If losses from these transactions exceed gains, all of the transactions will be treated as ordinary sales, resulting in net ordinary loss.

For the purpose of aggregating the Section 1231 transactions, the gains and losses from the sale, exchange, and conversion of trade or business property are to be added to the gains and losses from the *conversion* of capital assets. Gains and losses from the sale and exchange of capital assets are not, of course, to be included in the computation of the net gain or loss under Section 1231.[236]

In situations where the foregoing rules are operative, a condemnation gain qualifying for §1231 treatment will (absent other Section 1231 losses) be taxed at capital gain

---

[236]Reg. Sec. 1.1231-1(b); John L. Sullivan, 17 T.C. 1420, 1425 (1952), acq. 1953-2 C.B. 6.

rates after depreciation recapture, while, a condemnation loss will (absent other Section 1231 gains) be deductible as an ordinary business loss. Hence the owner realizes the most favorable treatment available to taxpayers on recognized gains and losses.

Before this result can occur, however, the owner's condemnation gains and losses must be offset against all other gains and losses qualifying for Section 1231 treatment. Gains and losses arising out of other types of involuntary conversions (such as casualty destructions with or without insurance recovery) and voluntary sales of real or depreciable property used in the owner's trade or business must be taken into account and used as offsets.

If, however, involuntary conversion losses resulting from fire, storm, shipwreck, other casualty or theft (but not including condemnation losses) exceed gains on Section 1231 property, the losses can be deducted under the casualty loss provisions of IRC Section 165 rather than be used to offset Section 1231 gains. The result is a tax benefit, as gains are entitled to capital gains treatment without offset by casualty losses, while casualty losses are deductible in full against ordinary income.[237]

G. DEPRECIATION RECAPTURE UNDER SECTION 1033

Suppose the condemned property was depreciable real estate and the owner had been taking accelerated depreciation in excess of the straight-line allowance. Section 1250[238] will force recognition and taxation of depreciation recapture despite the tax free replacement rules of Section 1033, with one exception. To avoid recapture of excess depreciation, the owner of the condemned property must acquire replacement property that is also depreciable. In this manner the recapture taint can be transmitted on to the replacement property. But if the owner buys only nondepreciable property, the recapture rules of Section 1250 will apply and a tax will be generated.

Example: Owner has a depreciated cost of $150,000 in a store building and lot that is condemned, and an award of $250,000 is made to him. At the time of taking, his depreciation recapture (that is, the excess of accelerated depreciation over straight line reduced in accordance with the formulas of Section 1250) is $30,000. He then buys an unimproved commercial lot for $250,000 within the time period specified in Section 1033. The results are changed in two respects from the last preceding example. *First*, he must pay a tax on $30,000 of depreciation recapture, taxed as ordinary income. *Second*, his cost of $250,000 for the new property is reduced by only $70,000 because $30,000 of the potential $100,000 gain was taxed. His cost basis for the replacement property is, therefore, $180,000.

To avoid depreciation recapture, the owner must acquire only as much depreciable property as that which equals the amount of depreciation recapture that would have been taxed.[239]

If we refer back to the facts of the preceding example, we see that the amount of depreciation recapture is $30,000 out of a total gain of $100,000. To escape recapture, all Owner needs to do is to purchase replacement costing at least $250,000 which includes depreciable improvements of a value of $30,000 or more.

---

[237]Section 1231(a), I.R.C.
[238]Section 1250, I.R.C.
[239]Section 1250(d)(4), I.R.C.

Example: Owner, in the preceding example, buys an old wood-frame, corrugated steel warehouse building located on a one-acre commercial lot for $250,000. He allocates $30,000 to the structure and the balance of his purchase price to the land. The results are as follows: *First*, he has no depreciation recapture because he has bought depreciable improvements at a cost equal to his $30,000 recapture exposure on the condemned property. *Second*, he has a zero cost basis for the improvements so that the $30,000 recapture taint will carry over (subject to possible diminution with the passage of time, depending upon which Section 1250 formula is applicable). *Third*, he has no gain on the condemnation sale because he bought property that cost an amount equal to the net condemnation proceeds. *Fourth*, his cost basis for the land is the $220,000 purchase price allocated to the land less the balance of the gain not recognized ($70,000) or $150,000.

H. ABANDONMENT OF PROPERTY

Real estate abandoned by an owner may give rise to a deductible loss measured by the owner's adjusted basis at the time of abandonment. If the owner is an individual, the loss must have been incurred in his trade or business or in a transaction entered into for profit.[240]

For the abandonment of real estate to qualify as a deductible loss, the owner must take action to abandon the property permanently in the year in which the property becomes useless or valueless to him.[241] The owner is not permitted to postpone the taking of the loss by merely retaining legal title to worthless property; the property must be abandoned in the year of worthlessness in order to qualify as a deductible loss.[242]

The taxpayer must establish both elements of the loss: the fact that the property became valueless in the taxable year and a showing of an act of abandonment.[243] The mere showing that the property is worthless will not justify the deduction without there being proof of an abandonment. Acts which have been held sufficient to manifest an intention to abandon are the execution of a quit claim deed,[244] the write-off of the property on the owner's books of account,[245] the delivery of a defective notice of relinquishment,[246] the discontinuance of operations and the abandonment of possession,[247] and the failure to pay real estate taxes.[248]

The amount of the loss is measured by the owner's adjusted tax basis for the property at the time of abandonment.[249]

The loss on abandonment is deductible by the owner as an ordinary loss; the limitations upon capital losses do not apply, because an abandonment is not a sale or exchange of the property.[250]

---

[240] Section 165(c), I.R.C.
[241] Reg. Sec. 1.165-1(d).
[242] Rev. Rul. 54-581, 1954-2 C.B. 112; Rhodes v. Commissioner, 100 F.2d 966, 969 (6th Cir. 1939).
[243] Commissioner v. McCarthy, 129 F.2d 84 (7th Cir. 1942).
[244] William H. Jamison, 8 T.C. 173, 181 (1947), acq. 1947-1 C.B. 2.
[245] Denman v. Brumbach, 58 F.2d 128 (6th Cir. 1932).
[246] Bickerstaff v. Commissioner, 128 F.2d 366 (5th Cir. 1942).
[247] Helvering v. Gordon, 134 F.2d 685 (4th Cir. 1943).
[248] Intercounty Operating Co., 4 T.C. 55, 69 (1944), acq. 1944 C.B. 15.
[249] Section 165(b), I.R.C.
[250] William H. Jamison, 8 T.C. 173, 181 (1947), acq. 1947-1 C.B. 2.

5
How to Postpone Tax on the Sale of Real Property

With any sale of property in which payment is deferred for a period of time, the seller usually is caught in a financial bind under the income tax laws; he may be required to report and pay a tax on the entire gain realized on the sale in the year he transfers the property, although he may have received only a small portion of the total price from the buyer. Hence, he may be forced to pay the tax on the gain out of sources other than the sales price for the property.

Even if the down payment is large enough to cover the tax payment due on the gain, the seller may be reluctant to part with the money received for any of a number of reasons. He may have plans for the reinvestment of these funds in other property. Or he may dislike paying a tax on the entire gain when he has not recovered his total investment in the property. Or he may be fearful of the buyer's default. Or he may wish to postpone payment of the tax to a later year in which his personal tax picture will afford a more favorable treatment of the gain. Whatever the reason, most sellers have the common objective of wishing to postpone as long as possible payment of the tax to become due on the sale.

Several alternatives for realizing this objective are presented to the seller under the tax laws. Among these are the following, each of which is discussed below:

A. *Installment Sales;*
B. *Deferred Payment Sales*;
C. *Sale for an Indeterminate Price, Including a Sale for a Contingent Price and for a Private Annuity;*
D. *Option Sales*;
E. *Escrow Sales*.

A. INSTALLMENT SALES

Under Section 453 the seller of real property has an election to report the gain realized from time payment sales as if a pro rata portion of the total gain were realized on the receipt of each payment under the sales contract. In effect, the seller is entitled to spread the receipt of the gain over the life of the installment contract.

Obviously, the installment method of reporting taxable gain has a number of advantages over the ordinary method of reporting the entire gain in the year of sale:

1. Only a pro rata share of the down payment will be needed to pay the tax due in the year of sale; if the entire gain were taxable in the year of sale, the bulk of the down payment, or more, might be dissipated in payment of the tax on the gain. Thus, if the seller utilizes the installment method of reporting the gain, he will obtain the immediate use for his own purposes of a greater proportion of the down payment. And ordinarily the seller will be spared the necessity of finding money from other sources to pay the tax.

2. The seller is permitted under the installment method to postpone payment of tax on parts of the gain until the years in which he receives payments which include that proportionate share of the gain. He is not put in the position of paying the tax in full in the year of sale and of having to rely upon the solvency and promptness of the buyer to ensure that payment of the gain so reported is ultimately received.

3. The seller may also enjoy some saving in the total tax paid by electing the installment method. This advantage is readily apparent if the gain on the sale is taxed as ordinary income. As a result of the progressive tax rate structure the seller's gain will be taxed at lower rates if reported over a period of years than if it is reported all in one year. If the gain qualifies as capital gain, the advantage in spreading its receipt is minimized since only if the seller's effective capital gains rate is less than the maximum 35 percent will he receive a saving in total tax paid by spreading the gain over the life of the installment contract.

4. One risk the seller runs is the possibilty of a change in the rates of tax to be applied to the gain realized. If the tax rates are increased in subsequent years, his total tax may be increased; if the rates are subsequently decreased, his total tax will be less if he spreads it out. In any event, the tax will be computed by reference to the rates of tax in effect in the year in which the gain is reportable.[1]

By ruling of the Commissioner of Internal Revenue, the installment method of reporting is not available on an "interest only" type of contract under which the entire purchase price is to be paid at the end of the contract.[2] It is his position that the term "installment" implies payments in more than one year.[3]

This ruling opens a Pandora's Box of uncertainties. Could you qualify a sale for

---

[1] Snell v. Commissioner, 97 F.2d 891, 893 (5th Cir. 1938); Harry B. Golden, 47 B.T.A. 94 (1942). See G.C.M. 21714, 1939-2 C.B. 218.

[2] Revenue Ruling 69-462, 1969-2 C.B. 107, to be applied retroactively to sales in all open years.

[3] Thomas F. Pendergast, 22 B.T.A. 1259 (1931); James McCutcheon & Co., 30 B.T.A. 1177 (1934); Walnut Realty Trust, 23 B.T.A. 850 (1931). Baltimore Baseball Club, Inc. v. United States, 481 F.2d 1283 (Ct. Cl. 1973).

the installment method if you took a 15-year "interest only" contract in 1970 and provided for one-half the principal to be paid on December 31, 1984 and the other one-half on January 1, 1985? The ruling states that the installment method is applicable ". . . only to those sales of real property that, by their terms and conditions, provide for two or more payments of portions of the purchase price in two or more taxable years." Literally the foregoing contract qualifies. Is this what the Commissioner meant?

Suppose an installment contract calls for a down payment of five dollars, interest only for 15 years, and then a $300,000 principal payment? Literally, the purchase price is payable in two or more years. Does this contract qualify? If not, how much must the down payment be? Ten dollars? One hundred dollars? One, ten, or one hundred-thousand dollars?

Significantly, the Commissioner published this ruling on September 2, 1969. The House of Representatives version of the Revenue Act of 1969, published on August 2, 1969, contained a provision requiring that installment payments be "spread relatively evenly over the installment period."[4] This provision was rejected by the Senate in late August, 1969. Was the ruling of September 2, 1969, a reaction of disappointment on the part of the Commissioner?

In rejecting the House proposal, the Senate Finance Committee stated that the change would be "a significant departure from existing law" and "could have an undesirable effect on legitimate commercial transactions where payment is deferred because of the purchaser's lack of ability to make immediate payment."[5]

1. How to Qualify Sales for the Installment Method

In order to qualify a sale of real estate for the installment method the seller must comply with two conditions; (1) not more than 30 percent of the total sales price may be received by the seller in the year of sale,[6] and (2) the seller must specifically elect the installment method on a timely tax return for the year of sale.[7]

The election is made on the seller's return by a showing of all of the facts relating to the sale, including the total price paid, the total gain to be realized over the life of the contract, and the pro rata portion of the gain taxable in the year of sale.[8]

Usually, the courts and the Commissioner have been strict in requiring an express election on the seller's tax return for the year of sale. Thus, if a proper election is not

---

[4]House Report No. 91-413 (Part 1), 91st Congress, 1st Session (August 2, 1969), page 108. The formula used by the House was a minimum of 5 percent of the principal in the first quarter of the installment payment, 15 percent in the second quarter and 40 percent in the third quarter. Alternatively, payments should be made every two years in even (or declining balance) amounts over the installment period.

[5]Senate Report No. 91-552, 91st Congress, 1st Session (November 21, 1969), page 145. An "interest only" purchase of property does not qualify the seller for installment reporting. 10-42 Corporation, 55 T.C. 593 (1971), non-acq. on another point 1972-2 C.B. 4.

[6]Section 453, I.R.C.

[7]Reg. 1.453-8(b).

[8]John W. Commons, 20 T.C. 900, 903 (1953), acq. on another issue, 1954-1 C.B. 4. For example, an election made on the fiduciary income tax of the estate of a decedent was not effective for the benefit of the heirs who had received distribution of the property prior to sale. Carlos Marcello, 1968 P-H Memo T.C. ¶68-268 aff'd per curiam, 414 F.2d 268 (5th Cir. 1969).

made by the seller in the year of sale, he loses his right to elect the installment method on that particular sale.[9] However, certain courts have exhibited a spirit of leniency; for example, the reporting of the first installment received upon the sale of a farm as rent was held not to bar the seller from later using the installment method.[10] And, similarly, the failure to elect because the taxpayer believed the transaction to be a tax-free sale of a residence did not prevent him from claiming the benefits of installment reporting in his petition to the Tax Court,[11] or by timely amended return.[12]

Because of the continuing liberality of the courts in permitting delinquent elections,[13] the Commissioner has receded from his too strict position and will now accept delinquent elections if (1) made on a delinquent original return for the year of sale, or (2) made on an amended return for the year of sale if that year is not barred by the statute of limitations, no inconsistent election had previously been made[14] and the failure to elect was made in good faith.[15]

Ordinarily a seller cannot change his mind once he has started an election as to any particular sale. He cannot, for example, attempt to change his election not to use the installment method by filing an amended return for the year of sale.[16] Conversely, the election of the installment method, once made, is binding upon the seller for all tax purposes as relating to the particular sale or sales for which the election was made.[17]

2. Payments Received in the Year of Sale

A seller is entitled to elect the installment method for a sale even if no payment is received in the year of sale.[18] All the gain to be realized under such a sale will be postponed until the year or years in which installment payments are received.

But if a payment is received in the year of sale, it must not exceed 30 percent of the total sales price. In any case in which the payments in the year of sale exceed 30 percent, the election of installment method is denied to the seller.[19] This restriction on the installment method requires careful thought and planning. It is necessary to know not only what the "total sales price" is for this purpose, but also what constitute "payments" to the seller in the year of sale. "Payments" for this purpose, as we shall see, include certain indirect as well as direct payments to the seller or for his benefit.

How is the total sales price measured for the purpose of determining compliance

---

[9] Jacobs v. Commissioner, 224 F.2d 412 (9th Cir. 1955).
[10] Scales v. Commissioner, 211 F.2d 133 (6th Cir. 1954); Hornberger v. Commissioner, 289 F.2d 602 (5 Cir. 1961).
[11] John F. Bayley, 35 T.C. 288 (1962); Nathan C. Spivey, 40 T.C. 1051 (1963).
[12] Rev. Rul. 56-396, 1956-2 C.B. 298.
[13] Bookwalter v. Mayer, 345 F.2d 476 (8th Cir. 1965); Hornberger v. Commissioner 289 F.2d 602 (5th Cir. 1961); John P. Reaves, 42 T.C. 72 (1964), acq. 1965-2 C.B. 6; Holley v. United States, 246 F. Supp. 553 (D.Nev. 1965).
[14] Rev. Rul. 65-297, 1965-2 C.B. 152.
[15] Mamula v. Commissioner, 346 F.2d 350 (9th Cir. 1965); John Harper, 54 T.C. 1121 (1970), acq. another point 1971-2 C.B. 2.
[16] Pacific National Co. v. Welch, 304 U.S. 191 (1938); Rev. Rul. 93, 1953-1 C.B. 82. See Rev. Rul. 56-396, 1956-2 C.B. 298.
[17] Commissioner v. South Texas Lumber Co., 333 U.S. 496, 502 (1948).
[18] Section 453(b)(2)(A)(i), I.R.C.
[19] Section 453(b)(2)(A)(ii), I.R.C.

with the 30 percent rule? It includes not only the cash to be paid to the seller over the life of the contract but also the amount of any *existing* mortgage indebtedness against the property, whether or not the liability is assumed by the buyer.[20] Nor is the sales price to be reduced by any selling commissions or other expenses paid or incurred by the seller on the sale. The gross sales price is the proper measure to use.[21]

However, the total sales price must be reduced by the amount of any imputed interest under Section 483.[22] This may well be a trap for the unwary, because a seller who is unaware of the tax necessity of charging at least 6 percent interest is likely to ask for the maximum initial payment.

Thirty percent of the gross sales price measures the maximum amount of payments that safely may be received in the year of sale. For this purpose the amount of any installment payments received in the year of sale is added to the down payment; the total of all payments received in the year of sale constitutes the initial payment.[23] Also to be included as part of the initial payment are any deposits, earnest money, or option payments applied to the purchase price, even if such payments were received in prior taxable years.[24]

The initial payment may be made in property other than cash. For example, suppose the buyer transfers notes *of a third party* to the seller in the year of sale; the fair market value of these notes must be included in the initial payment.[25] But notes or other obligations *of the buyer*, regardless of their value, are *not* part of the initial payment.[26] The reason for this exception for the buyer's obligations should be clear; if they were not excluded, the installment obligation itself would prevent the seller from electing the installment method.

Also to be included in the initial payment are certain indirect payments to third parties for the seller's benefit. For example, any amounts paid into escrow to be used to discharge liabilities against the property, such as liens for taxes or special assessments are part of the initial payment.[27] But if these liabilities are discharged by the buyer after he takes title to the property and are made outside the escrow, they are not treated as part of the initial payment in the absence of circumstances showing that the seller had required such payment by contract.[28]

Example: Seller sells his equity in a parcel of real estate to Buyer for $20,000. B takes the property subject to a mortgage of $30,000. S's commissions and selling expenses total $2,700. B

---

[20] 53 West 72d St., Inc., 23 B.T.A. 164 (1931); Reg. Sec. 1.453-4(c).

[21] Kirschenmann v. Commissioner, 488 F.2d 270 (9th Cir. 1973).

[22] T.I.R. 557 (March 25, 1964). But if the sale once qualifies for the installment method based on imputed interest calculated on the terms of the installment contract, it will not be disqualified merely because the buyer is late on an installment and imputed interest is thereby increased. Rev. Rul. 68-247 1968-21 IRB 16.

[23] Mamie E. Eining, 19 B.T.A. 1105, 1107 (1930).

[24] Waukesha Malleable Iron Co. v. Commissioner, 67 F.2d 368, 371 (7th Cir. 1933); Rev. Rul. 73-369 I.R.B. 1973-37, p.8.

[25] Caldwell v. United States, 114 F.2d 995 (3rd Cir. 1940); J.W. Elmore, 15 B.T.A. 1210, 1212 (1929).

[26] Section 453(b)(2)(A)(ii), I.R.C.

[27] Corona Flushing Co., 22 B.T.A. 1344 (1931).

[28] Katherine H. Watson, 20 B.T.A. 270 (1930), acq. X-1 C.B. 68. If such liabilities for liens, accrued taxes and interest are expressly assumed by the buyer, the buyer's payment of these liabilities in the year of sale converts them into part of the initial payment to the seller. Rev. Rul. 60-52, 1960-1 C.B. 186. Rev. Rul. 71-543, 1971-2 C.B. 223 is contrary.

INSTALLMENT SALES

pays $10,000 down and executes a note and second mortgage to S for the $10,000 balance. After the sale, but before the close of the taxable year, B pays an additional $1,000 on the second mortgage note. Can S qualify the sale for the installment method?

Total sales price:		
Cash to be paid to S	$20,000	
Mortgage on property	30,000	$50,000
30 percent thereof		
Initial payment received:		
Cash down payment	$10,000	
Installment received	1,000	$11,000

The sale can properly be reported on the installment method, the initial payment being less than 30 percent of the gross sales price.

Also included in the initial payment are any obligations of the seller which the buyer satisfies in the year of sale either by payment in escrow or pursuant to the requirements of a contractual agreement to do so between him and the seller. An example of such a payment that becomes part of the initial payment is the buyer's payment or deposit in escrow of the seller's attorney's fees.[29] This rule does not reach, however, the amount of any mortgage indebtedness against the property, whether or not the buyer assumes this indebtedness.[30] The only time that any part of the mortgage indebtedness can become part of the initial payment is in a case in which the mortgage debt exceeds the seller's basis for his property.

The Commissioner has taken the position, and has been sustained by the Tax Court,[31] that the payment in the year of sale of trade liabilities by the buyer of a business constitutes additional payments to the seller, and, if made in the year of sale, constitutes part of the initial payment. He has attempted to apply this rule to the sale of real estate[32] despite the fact that the Regulations clearly state that in the sale of mortgaged property, the amount of the mortgage shall not be considered a payment, except to the extent it exceeds basis.[33] Apparently his position is that *payments* on the mortgage after the sale, but in the year of sale, are to be considered payments to the seller, even though the mortgage itself is to be disregarded. Thus far his efforts have been unsuccessful. If his position is ultimately sustained, it will mean that all sales designed for the installment method will either have to take place at the end of the taxable year, or that the cash payment will have to be reduced by anticipated mortgage or other liability payments falling due in the year of sale.

Commissions and other expenses paid by the seller in the year of sale do not reduce the initial payment received in the year of sale.[34] Nor can this rule be avoided by instructing the escrow holder to pay the commission directly to the broker as the buyer's payments come in; for tax purposes the seller has constructively received the

---

[29] Wagegro Corp., 38 B.T.A. 1225 (1938), acq. on another issue, 1939-1 C.B. 36.

[30] Reg. Sec. 1.453-4(c). United States v. Marshall, 357 F.2d 294 (9th Cir. 1966); Rev. Rul. 71-543, 1971-2 C.B. 223.

[31] Ivan Irwin, Jr., 45 T.C. 544 (1966), reversed 21 AFTR 2d 778 (5th Cir. 1968); J. Carl Horneff, 50 T.C. No. 10 (1968).

[32] United States v. Marshall, 357 F.2d 294 (9th Cir. 1966).

[33] Reg. Sec. 1.453-4(c).

[34] Kirschenmann v. Commisssioner, 488 F.2d 270 (9th Cir. 1973).

buyer's payments since they are being used to discharge the seller's liability to pay his broker a commission.[35]

What happens if the parties inadvertently exceed the 30 percent limitation? If it is discovered in the year of sale, a refund may be made by the seller of the excess to the buyer and thereby qualify for the installment method.[36] If it is discovered after the close of the year of sale, the sale is disqualified.

3. Readily Tradable Bonds of Corporate Seller

. Payments in the year of sale under the installment method include, *at face value*, bonds or other evidence of indebtedness of a corporation or government body if the bond, debenture, or note meets certain conditions.[37]

First, if it is *payable on demand*, it is treated as a payment at face in the year of sale. This result is understandable because the seller could, on demand at any time, request the face amount of the indebtedness.

Second, if the bond, debenture or note is issued by a corporation or a governmental agency with interest coupons attached or in any other form designed to make the bond, debenture, or note readily tradable in an established securities market, then the full principal amount is treated as a payment in the year of sale. If the bond is issued in registered form, it will be presumed to be readily tradable unless the seller proves that it is not. If readily tradable, the face amount of the bond will be treated as the payment received in the year of sale, regardless of terms of payment.

4. Constructive Receipt of Payment in Year of Sale

The mere fact that the buyer is financially capable of paying the entire purchase price in cash will not, by that fact alone, destroy the installment election of the buyer.[38] But if the seller insists on security for the normal purchase money of the buyer (other than against the property purchased) the buyer may have constructive receipt in the year of sale.

For example, if the note to the seller were secured by a cash deposit[39] or a certificate of deposit[40] or by a deposit of cash in escrow.[41] The amount of the "cash equivalents" has been treated as a payment received in the year of sale.[42]

Can the effect of constructive receipt be countered by conditions established on the escrow? It has been held that an escrow deposit is not constructively received in the year of sale if it is conditioned on additional performance by the seller.[43] But if the

---

[35] Roland W. Sholund, 50 T.C. No. 48 (1968).
[36] Lewis M. Ludlow, 36 T.C. 102 (1961), acq. 1961-2 C.B. 5.
[37] Section 453(b), I.R.C. effective May 27, 1969.
[38] See J. Earl Oden, 56 T.C. 569 (1971), appeal dismissed.
[39] Everret Pozzi, 49 T.C. 119 (1967).
[40] J. Earl Oden, 56 T.C. 569 (1971), appeal dismissed.
[41] Rev. Rul. 73-451, I.R.B. 1973-44, p.11.
[42] This author wonders why a buyer's first-mortgage note against the property is not a payment in the year of sale, yet the buyer's escrow can be so treated. Why should the form of the transaction make such a big difference? Does the buyer have to be "cash poor" for the seller to be entitled to the installment election?
[43] Gibbs & Hudson, Inc. 35 B.T.A. 205, 210 (1936), acq 1937-1 C.B. 10; Rebecca J. Murray, 28 B.T.A. 624, 628 (1933), acq. XII-2 C.B. 10; Minnie R. Ebner, 26 T.C. 962 (1956), acq. 1956-2 C.B. 5.

INSTALLMENT SALES

escrow has no other purpose than to postpone receipt of the initial payment, the escrow is ineffectual: the escrowed monies are received and taxable when deposited.[44]

5. Planning for an Installment Sale

An escrow of money equivalents will not shelter an installment sale, unless the payment thereof is conditioned on further performance by the seller. Are there other alternatives?

How about a loan made by buyer in favor of seller, but not credited against the purchase price? The buyer in effect pays less than 30 percent of the sales price to the seller but in addition lends the seller other amounts of cash which the seller is obligated to repay. Is the amount of this loan in the year of sale to be included in the initial payment so that the transaction is disqualified? Or is it treated as a separate transaction so that the seller may elect the installment method for the sale? On this question, authority is divided. If the so-called "loan" has been treated as the equivalent of an unconditional payment on the purchase price and therefore part of the initial payment.[45]

On the other hand, if the "loan" is evidenced by the personal unconditional obligation of the seller to repay, the loan will be treated as a separate and distinct transaction from the sale.[46] The seller will therefore not be denied the benefits of the installment election despite the receipt of the loan proceeds in the year of sale. And this has been the result reached, even though the loan was in fact later discharged by applying part of the contract price owed to the seller against the seller's obligation to repay the loan.[47]

Are there any other alternatives? One is not the assumption of debt.[48]

A third alternative for accomplishing this result has been given impetus by a decision of the Tax Court.[49] There, the seller owned a mercantile business which he desired to sell. His buyer was willing to meet his price but he could not pay the full price in cash. The amount he could pay down, however, exceeded 30 percent of the sales price. The seller was anxious both to receive all the cash he could as soon as possible and to elect to defer reporting the gain on the unpaid portion of the sale price on the installment basis. Accordingly, he designed the sale as two transactions between him and his buyer. The first was a sale of the business inventory for cash in full. The second was a sale of the business and all the remainder of its assets *to the same buyer* for a modest down payment and an installment contract that qualified for installment reporting. Naturally, the Commissioner attacked the two sales as being in reality only one; by adding the price for the inventory to the down payment for the business, the

---

[44]Williams v. United States, 219 F.2d 523 (5th Cir. 1955); Rev. Rul. 55-694, 1955-2 C.B. 299.
[45]James Hammond, 1 T.C. 198 (1942).
[46]Rev. Rul. 234, 1953-2 C.B. 29.
[47]Minnie R. Ebner, 26 T.C. 962 (1956), acq. 1956-2 C.B. 5.
[48]Big "D" Development Corp., 1971 P-H T.C. Memo ¶71, 148, aff'd on this ground, 453 F.2d 1365 (5th Cir., 1971), cert. den. 406 U.S. 945.
[49]Andrew A. Monaghan, 40 T.C. 680 (1963) acq. 1964-2 C.B. 6. Although the foregoing decision was based in part on the fact that inventory is disqualified from installment reporting under the express provision of Section 453(b)(1)(B) IRC, the holding would not seem to be restricted to such situations. See Rev. Rul. 57-434, 1957-2 C.B. 300 and, also, Lubken v. United States, 8 AFTR 2d 5073 (S.D.Cal. 1961). See, also, Nathan C. Spivey, 40 T.C. 1051 (1963); Rev. Rul. 68-13, 1968-1 C.B. 195.

initial payment exceeds the 30 percent limit. But here he was unsuccessful. Obviously, this technique would lend itself to the sale of real estate in any case in which the property to be sold can readily be segregated into more than one parcel. Whether the sale of a homogenous parcel by two transactions in which an undivided interest is sold for cash and the balance for a down payment and an installment obligation would pass challenge is doubtful.

The Commissioner now agrees that a sale may be fragmented for purposes of installment reporting of a portion of the sale.[50] If, for example, the sale consists of inventory, assets sold at a loss, other personal property and real property, the Commissioner insists each be treated separately. An allocation of both the selling price and the initial payment must be made among the four categories. Why? First, inventory cannot be sold on the installment method except by a dealer. Second, if an asset is sold at a loss, the loss must be recognized in full in the year of sale. Third, personal property can be sold and the gain reported on the installment method only if the sale price exceeds $1,000. The allocation of both the down payment and the sales price must be made on the basis of respective fair market values.[51]

Similarly, if the development requirements of the buyer require that the seller separate his property into several parcels, each parcel will be treated individually for the purpose of installment reporting.[52] But if the seller sells two parcels in one transaction, an attempted allocation of the sales price will not be sufficient to qualify one parcel for the installment method if the entire transaction does not qualify.[53]

And, finally, a fourth alternative has suggested itself in any case in which the seller is willing to put up with the inconvenience of a corporate intermediary. If the seller has a corporation available, or if he is willing to organize one, he can in theory sell his property to his corporation for its fair market value. His sale would be in consideration of a down payment of less than 30 percent of the sales price plus an installment obligation for the balance. Accordingly, he would be entitled to elect the installment method on his sale to his corporation. The basis of the property to the corporation would be its cost for the property. Because the corporation paid a price equal to the fair market value of the property, its cost would be equal to fair market value. Accordingly, when the corporation resells the property to an outsider, little or no further gain will be realized. If, therefore, the corporation's sale to the outsider is disqualified for one reason or another from the installment method, it makes no difference; the corporation has little or no gain on which to be taxed. The gain was realized at an earlier stage when the owner sold to his corporation.[54] And this earlier sale was carefully designed to give the owner the benefits of installment reporting. Thus, the owner receives all the benefits of installment reporting despite the fact that the ultimate sale to the outsider does not qualify.

---

[50]Acq. 1964-2 C.B. 6 to Andrew A. Monaghan, 40 T.C. 680 (1963).
[51]Rev. Rul. 68-13, 1968-2 IRB 7.
[52]Charles A. Collins, 48 T.C. 45 (1967), acq. 1967-40 IRB 6. The court noted, "We see in this transaction no sham or fragmenting the sale for tax purposes."
[53]Boyd A. Veenkant, 1968 P-H T.C. Memo ¶68,119; Blackstone Realty Co. v. Commissioner, 22 AFTR 2d 5156 (5th Cir. 1968).
[54]If the property is depreciable and the seller owns more than 80 percent of the stock, the gain is ordinary income. Section 1239. Also depreciation recapture must be recognized. Sections 1245, 1250.

INSTALLMENT SALES

Example: Seller owns unimproved real property with a basis of $20,000 that is reasonably worth $100,000. He sells it to his corporation in a transaction that qualifies as a taxable sale and not a tax-free exchange or contribution. The sales price is $100,000 of which $10,000 is paid down and $90,000 is to be paid in future years. He reports the transaction on the installment method and pays a tax on one-tenth or $8,000 of the gain in the first year. Seller's corporation then is successful in finding an outside buyer for the property for $100,000. The outsider is willing to pay 50 percent down and the balance over a period of time. Seller's corporation is delighted to accept even though the sale will not qualify for installment reporting because the sale will be at its cost, giving rise neither to gain nor loss.

Sales price	$100,000
Less cost to corporation	100,000
Gain	—0—

Thus, seller has the benefits of (1) the installment method, (2) the receipt of more than 30 percent of the sales price in his corporation without further tax cost, and (3) the right to draw out the balance of the sale price in the future as installment payments to him.

But the foregoing technique is fraught with pitfalls. The sale to the corporation will be scrutinized minutely to ascertain whether or not there is any weakness in the installment election. Additionally, the sale will be examined to see if it can be recast into a tax-free exchange between a controlling stockholder and his corporation under Section 351, I.R.C. If so, the corporation's basis for the property would be the same as that of its stockholder and it, the corporation, would be taxed on the entire gain without the benefit of any installment election.[55] And, finally, the corporation's temporary ownership of the property may be treated as being without any substance; accordingly, its sale of the property is in reality for the account of the stockholder and he must report and pay the tax on the gross proceeds received by the corporation.[56] If, however, these hurdles can be surmounted, the transactions will gain for the owner the benefits he seeks.[57]

6. How to Report Gain on the Installment Method

The use of the installment method involves three steps: first, the seller must compute the total gain to be realized on the sale; next, he should determine the ratio of total gain to the total "contract price," and, finally, he should multiply the payments received on the contract in any year by this ratio. The result is the amount of gain taxable in that particular year.[58]

Example: Seller sells a commercial lot to Buyer for $28,000, payable $7,000 down and $21,000 over a period of three years after the date of sale. S's expenses of sale are $1,500; after the sale, but before the close of the taxable year, S receives additional installment payments of $1,000. If we assume that the lot cost him $12,500, his taxable gain in the year of sale is computed as follows:

---

[55]Gus Russell, Inc., 36 T.C. 965 (1961); Estate of Herbert B. Miller, 24 T.C. 923 (1955), reversed 239 F.2d (9th Cir. 1956).

[56]McInerney v. Commissioner, 82 F.2d 665 (6th Cir. 1936); Jacobs v. Commissioner, 224 F.2d 412 (9th Cir. 1955), Hindes v. United States. F.2d 13 AFTR. 2d 376 (5th Cir. 1964).

[57]Estate of Henry H. Rogers, 1 T.C. 629 at 632 (1943), acq. on other grounds, 1943 C.B. 19, aff'd on other grounds, 143 F.2d 695 (2d Cir. 1944), cert. den. 323 U.S. 780.

[58]Reg. Sec. 1.453-5(a).

Sales (contract) price	$28,000	
Less expenses of sale	1,500	$26,500
Adjusted basis for property		12,500
Total gain on sale		$14,000
Percentage of gain to contract price		50%
Payments received in year of sale:		
Down payment	$ 7,000	
Installment payments	1,000	$ 8,000
Gain taxable in year of sale (50%)		$ 4,000

Had S not elected to report the gain on the installment method, the total gain of $14,000 would have been taxable in the year of sale. By using the installment method, S has postponed the tax on the additional gain of $10,000 until it is paid to him.

In each subsequent year, S will be required to report 50 percent of the total payments received by him as taxable gain. Thus, if $7,000 is received in a later year, $3,500 would be the measure of the gain taxed in that year.

7. Installment Sales of Mortgaged Property

If property is mortgaged at the time of sale, we find that the computation of the installment gain is changed to take account of the mortgage debt. Although the sales price includes the mortgage debt, the "contract price" is limited to only the payments to be made directly to the seller; mortgage payments owed to persons other than the seller are eliminated from the contract price.[59]

Example: Suppose the property described in the preceding example were sold subject to a mortgage of $7,000. Buyer agrees to pay $6,000 down and to give a three-year note secured by a second mortgage for the $15,000 balance. If only the down payment is received in the year of sale, S's taxable gain for that year is computed as follows:

Contract price:		
Sales price	$28,000	
Less mortgage debt	7,000	$21,000
Total gain (see preceding example)		$14,000
Percentage of gain to contract price		66 2/3%
Payment received in year of sale		$ 6,000
Gain taxable (66 2/3%)		$ 4,000

If the mortgage indebtedness exceeds the seller's basis for the property, the amount of the excess is included in the contract price as a constructive payment to the seller. This constructive payment is deemed to be received by the seller in the year of sale as a part of the intitial payment, and must be included in the computation of both qualification under the 30 percent requirement and amount of gain taxable in the year of sale.[60]

Example: An apartment having adjusted basis to Seller of $76,000 is sold, subject to an $80,000 mortgage. Buyer agrees to pay $28,000 for S's equity, payable $5,000 down and the

---

[59] Reg. Sec. 1.453-4(c).
[60] Burnet v. S. & L. Building Corp., 288 U.S. 406 (1933); Reg. Sec. 1.453-4(c).

INSTALLMENT SALES

balance on a four-year second mortgage note. If we assume that the only payment received by S in the year of sale is the down payment, S's taxable gain for that year is computed as follows:

1. Qualification

Total sales price:		
Installment contract	$28,000	
Mortgage debt outstanding	80,000	$108,000
Payment in year of sale:		
Down payment		5,000
Excess of debt over basis:		
Mortgage debt	$80,000	
Less adjusted basis	76,000	4,000
Total payment in year of sale		9,000

Qualification ratio $\frac{9,000}{108,000} = 8\ 1/3\%$

2. Contract price

Sales price (including mortgage)	$108,000	
Less mortgage debt	80,000	$28,000
Plus excess of debt over basis		4,000
Total contract price		$32,000

3. Total Gain Realized

Sales price		
Installment contract	$28,000	
Mortgage debt outstanding	80,000	$108,000
Less adjusted basis		76,000
Total net gain realized on sale		$ 32,000

4. Gain Taxed in Year of Sale

Percentage of gain to contract price		100%
Payment in year of sale:		
Down payment	$5,000	
Excess of debt over basis	4,000	$ 9,000
Gain taxable in year of sale		$ 9,000

Nor can seller avoid this adverse result by having the buyer substitute a new note and mortgage for the seller's existing note and mortgage. Such a substitution has been held to be the equivalent of an assumption of the seller's mortgage liability. To the extent that liability exceeds the seller's basis for the property, the excess is treated as a payment in the year of sale.[61]

Example: Seller owns property having a depreciated cost to him of $75,000 but held subject to a $140,000 mortgage note. The property is worth $160,000, or $20,000 more than the mortgage debt. Because the mortgage debt ($140,000) exceeds S's basis ($75,000) by $65,000, S cannot sell on the installment method. The excess of $65,000 is obviously more than 30 percent of the $160,000 selling price. So S asks the holder of the first mortgage to release him from all liability on S's note in consideration for Buyer's new note and mortgage payable to the mortgage holder in the amount of $140,000. S then sells his equity to B for $20,000 payable

---

[61] R.A. Waldrup, 52 T.C. 640, (1969) aff'g per curiam, 428 F.2d 1216 (5th Cir., 1970).

$1,000 down, the balance in 10 years and elects the installment method. Because the excess of liabilities over basis of $65,000 is treated as a payment in the year of sale, S cannot elect the installment method.

Because the new obligation of the buyer was for exactly the same amount as the old obligation of the seller, the Tax Court concluded that the buyer had "assumed" the seller's debt; hence the excess of that debt over the seller's basis was received in the year of sale and the sale was disqualified from installment gain reporting.

Nor would the result be different if the buyer "refinanced" the property by placing a new larger loan on it. Because the seller received relief from his existing debt, the excess of that debt over his basis for the property would be a payment in the year of sale.

Example: If we take the facts of the prior example, but assume that B deposits in escrow a note payable of $160,000 to the holder of the first mortgage in exchange for which the holder agrees to release S from all liability on S's note and to pay S the $20,000 extra in cash. What result to S?

Amount realized:		
Cash	$ 20,000	
Debt relief	140,000	$160,000
Less basis		75,000
Gain		$ 85,000
Installment election:		
Total sales price		$160,000
30 percent thereof		48,000
Payments received in year of sale:		
Cash	$ 20,000	
Excess of mortgage debt over basis	65,000	95,000

The installment method cannot be elected because the payments received in the year of sale ($95,000) exceeded 30 percent of the selling price of $160,000.

A useful exception to the above rule regarding property mortgaged in excess of basis arises where the purchaser *neither assumes the mortgage nor receives title* to the subject property in the year of sale. The excess becomes a payment only in the year in which the mortgage is assumed or title is transferred. It is necessary that the purchaser expressly not assume the mortgage (until some future time, if at all) and that the seller be obligated to continue meeting the mortgage payments until title is transferred or the purchaser assumes the mortgage.

Example: Seller had purchased and subdivided a parcel of land on which he erected homes built under F.H.A. financing. The mortgage debt on each lot exceeded its basis to S. S then sold a lot and home to Buyer on a land contract for $4,450, payable $100 down and $47.40 per month for 27 months. Thereafter, B agreed to pay $33.50 per month to S until the balance of S's purchase price, together with interest, was paid.

For the first 27-month period, S agreed to make the necessary payments of principal and interest on the F.H.A. mortgage. After completion of the payments for the first 27-month period, S then conveyed the property to B who agreed to assume personal liability for the balance of the F.H.A. mortgage debt while at the same time completing the payments to S on the land contract. The remaining balance of S's price was secured by a second mortgage.

S reported the sale on the installment method. In the year of the sale, he reported only the down payment plus installments received as the initial payment. The excess of the mortgage debt over basis was not reported by him until the end of the 27-month period when title to the property was conveyed to B. The Commissioner challenged this method of reporting the initial payment; he claimed that the excess of the F.H.A. mortgage over basis should have been included in the

INSTALLMENT SALES 161

initial payment. The Tax Court held that the taxpayer's method of computing the initial payment was correct. The excess of mortgage debt over basis could not be made a part of the initial payment because the buyer had neither assumed the mortgage nor taken the property subject to the mortgage until the end of the 27-month period.

This technique still has not received the approval of the Commissioner although the Tax Court has recently reiterated its view that the result reached in the example is sound.[62]

8. Use of "Wrap-Around" or "All-Inclusive" Mortgage

This technique has become popularly known as the "wrap-around" mortgage use because the seller's purchase money mortgage is literally wrapped around the first-mortgage note. The amount of the wrap-around note includes both the principal amount of the first-mortgage note and the selling price of the seller's equity in the property. It is also referred to as an "all-inclusive" mortgage.

Example: Seller owns an apartment building that has a sales price of $1,000,000 but is subject to a first mortgage loan of $750,000. S's equity is worth $250,000. For simplicity, let us assume S sells it to Buyer for a $1,000,000 note, receiving no down payment other than interest. Because B gives S a note for the entire $1,000,000, B will expect S to pay off the first-mortgage note so that B will not have to make any payments on it. If S cannot pay the first-mortgage note in full at the time of sale, it will be necessary for S to contract to pay the installments due on the first-mortgage note as they become due. Thus, the purchase money note is designed to mirror the provisions of the first-mortgage note. As each payment falls due on the first-mortgage note, the purchase money pays an equal or greater amount to S. In this way, S is able to meet his payments on the first-mortgage note. Escrow and other security provisions may be required by B to insure that his payments will actually be used by S to meet payments on the first-mortgage note.

Why would such a wrap-around note be used? The traditional method of selling would be for the seller to sell subject to the existing first-mortgage debt and take back a second-mortgage note for the value of his equity only. Certainly, the wrap-around technique can involve more risk to the buyer if he has to rely upon the seller's integrity to see that the first-mortgage note is paid rather than paying it off himself.

There are at least four reasons for using a wrap-around note. First, if the seller has a favorable rate of interest on the first-mortgage note that he wishes to retain he may want to sell the property on a wrap-around note. Second, the buyer may wish to maximize his deduction for pre-paid interest. Third, the first-mortgage financing may not be transferrable although title to the property can be conveyed. And, fourth, the property may be mortgaged in excess of basis, which would otherwise prevent the installment method from being used.

Example: If we refer to the facts of our preceding example, we find that S is selling property for $1,000,000 which is subject to a $750,000 liability. If S's basis for the property is less than $450,000, the installment method cannot be elected because the excess (more than $300,000) of the mortgage debt ($750,000) over basis (less than $450,000) is treated as a payment in the year

---

[62]United Pacific Corp., 39 T.C. 721 (1963), appeal dismissed (9th Cir. 1963); E.P. Lamberth Est., 31 T.C. 302 (1958), non-acq. on this issue, 1959-1 C.B. 6; Stonecrest Corp., 24 T.C. 659 (1955), non-acq. 1956-1 C.B. 6, appeal dismissed (9th Cir. 1958).

of sale. Under this example, no more than $300,000 can be received in the year of sale (30 percent of $1,000,000).

But if the seller sells for a $1,000,000 wrap-around note, nothing is received in the year of sale. The seller is still primarily liable on the first-mortgage note. Until he enjoys relief from that debt, the debt cannot be included in the amount realized by him.

Example: If we assume a sale for a $1,000,000 wrap-around note and a basis of $400,000, the total profit to be realized will be $600,000 or 60 percent of the total contract price. Accordingly, 60 percent of each payment of principal on the wrap-around note will be taxable gain and 40 percent non-taxable recovery of basis. If S receives a $100,000 payment on the wrap-around note in the year of sale, the payment will be treated as follows:

Taxable gain	$60,000
Basis recovery	40,000
Total payment	$100,000

Had S sold in the traditional way, permitting B to take over the first mortgage note and taking back a second mortgage for his equity the entire gain would be taxed in the year of sale, as follows:

Total sales price	$1,000,000
Payments in year of sale (Excess of mortgage debt over basis)	350,000
Percentage received in year of sale	35%

Because more than 30 percent of the sales price has been received in the year of sale, the installment method is not available. S's gain is as follows:

Amount realized	$1,000,000
Less basis	400,000
Taxable gain	$ 600,000

But the wrap-around purchase money mortgage would have permitted the seller to use the installment method of reporting.

9. Selling Expenses: Dealer vs. Investor

Dealers as well as investors may use the installment method for reporting the gain on sales of real estate. The gain reportable by a dealer will be ordinary income rather than capital gain; however, the income will be spread out over the period of the installment contract as in the case of any other sale qualifying for the installment method.

A dealer is entitled to report his expenses of sale in a different manner from that used by an investor. An investor is required to subtract his selling expense from the gross sales price for the property in order to compute his gain on the sale. In the case of an installment sale, this requirement forces him to recoup his selling expenses over the life of the installment contract; he cannot deduct the selling expenses against the initial payment.[63]

---

[63]Mrs. E.A. Griffin, 19 B.T.A. 1243 (1930).

INSTALLMENT SALES

But a dealer is entitled to deduct his selling expenses as a trade or business expense independently of the sale. As a result, he is permitted to deduct the entire amount of these expenses in the year of sale. The net effect is to permit a dealer to postpone a larger share of the total gain to the later years of the contract than in the case of a similar sale by an investor.

Example: Dealer sells a house for $20,000, payable $5,000 down and $15,000 over a ten-year period. D's selling expenses are $1,500. D's basis for the house was $14,000. In the year of sale, his reportable gain is computed as follows:

Sales price (contract price)	$20,000
Less basis	14,000
Total gain	$ 6,000
Percentage gain to contract price	30%
Initial payment	$ 5,000
Gain taxable in year of sale (30%)	$ 1,500

Offsetting the entire $1,500 gain, taxable as ordinary income, are $1,500 of deductible selling expenses. D need pay no tax on this sale in the first year.

10. Type of Sales Qualifying for Installment Method

There is no restriction upon the type of installment sales contract that can be qualified for the installment method. Sales in which title is immediately conveyed are covered as well as sales in which title is retained by the seller. Both executory land contracts and executed conveyances in which the seller takes back a note for the purchase price come within the provisions of the installment method.[64] Nor is there any restriction upon the seller's normal method of accounting; both cash basis and accrual basis taxpayers may qualify sales for the installment method.[65]

The seller may report the gain from one sale on the installment method and the gain from other sales on his normal method of accounting; the election of the installment method is an election available for each sale. All that is required is that the gain from a particular sale be reported in a consistent fashion.[66]

The installment method is not, however, available for the reporting of losses incurred upon the sale of real estate.[67] Any loss incurred is recognized in full in the year of sale.

11. Sale of Installment Contract

Suppose after receiving the installment note or contract from the buyer, the seller decides to sell his right to the installment payments to a third party. How is the receipt of money from the sale of his installment obligations to be treated?

The seller will be taxed on the consideration received for the sale of the obligation

---

[64] Reg. Sec. 1.453-4(a).
[65] Section 453(b), I.R.C.
[66] Lubken v. United States, 8 AFTR. 2d 5073 (S.D.Cal. 1961); Chick M. Farha, 58 T.C. 526 (1972), aff'd F.2d (10th Cir. 1973).
[67] Martin v. Commissioner, 61 F.2d 942 (2d Cir. 1932), cert. den. 289 U.S. 737 (1933); Rev. Rul. 68-13, 1968-1 C.B. 195.

in accordance with specific rules.[68] His gain will be the difference between the amount received on the sale of the obligation and the basis thereof. Basis, in turn, is here defined as face value less the amount which would have been reportable as income if the obligation were satisfied in full. If, for example, the seller receives the full face value for the obligation on its sale, he will be taxed on the entire postponed gain just as if the buyer had paid the full contract price to him.[69] On the other hand, if he receives *less* than the full face value, then he will be taxed on the difference between the sale price and his basis (being face value less unreported gain) for the obligation sold.

The two transactions are entirely separate and independent. Even if the seller of the property sells a portion of the installment notes to a third party in the same year in which he sold the property, the payment for the notes will not be included in his initial payment to disqualify the original property sale from the installment method.[70]

This principle gives the seller considerable leeway in using the installment method. He can sell the property for less than 30 percent of the contract price down and yet receive additional moneys from the sale of part of his installment notes without losing the right to report the gain from the sale on the installment method.

Example: Seller sells an apartment for $50,000, receiving $15,000 from the Buyer in the year of the sale. The remainder of the purchase price is paid to him in seven interest-bearing notes of $5,000 each. These notes mature serially in years after the close of the taxable year of sale.

Immediately after the close of the apartment sale, S decides that he needs additional cash of $9,000. If he asks for payment for an additional $9,000 from B in the year of sale, he will lose his election to use the installment method. S therefore takes two of the notes down to his bank and discounts them for $9,000. If we assume that S made a gross profit of $25,000 on the apartment sale, only $11,500 of that profit would be reportable in the year of the sale on the installment method:

1. Gain on Sale of Apartment

Sales price (contract price)	$50,000
Less basis and expenses	25,000
Total gain	$25,000
Percentage of gain to contract price	50%
Initial payment from buyer	$15,000
Gain taxable in the year of sale (50%)	$ 7,500

2. Gain on Sale of Notes

Sales price of notes		$ 9,000
Less basis for note:		
Face value of note	$10,000	
Less portion attributable to income (50%)	5,000	5,000
Gain on sale of note		$4,000

The gain or loss resulting from the sale of the installment note is treated in the same manner (capital gain or ordinary income) as if it were received in payment for the original property sold.[71]

---

[68] Section 453(d), I.R.C.; Reg. Sec. 1.459-9.
[69] Miller Saw-Trimmer Co., 32 B.T.A. 931, 937 (1935).
[70] Duram Bldg. Corp. v. Commissioner, 66 F.2d 253 (2d Cir. 1933); Robinson v. Commissioner, 73 F.2d 769 (9th Cir. 1934); Reg. Sec. 1.453 4(c).
[71] Section 453(d)(1), I.R.C.

12. Pledge of Installment Obligations

There is still another method open to an installment seller who wishes to realize cash on his installment contract prior to the time for the buyer's payments. If he sells the installment obligation, he will be taxed on a pro rata share of the gain just as if the buyer had paid him directly. But if he merely pledges the installment contract or notes to secure a loan of money from a third party creditor, the pledge will not accelerate the gain represented by the obligations pledged.

As long as title to the installment contract remains in the seller, the money borrowed on the security does not constitute money realized upon the disposition of the contract; hence, no part of the avails of the borrowing will be treated as taxable gain. Care must be taken in framing the terms of the pledge agreement to ensure that the installment obligation is not being sold but is merely being put up as security for the personal borrowing of the seller.[72] The fact that the seller remains contingently liable as a guarantor of the installment is not sufficient, standing alone, to characterize the transaction as a pledge, as distinguished from a sale.[73]

Example: Suppose S in the example in the preceding section takes two of the notes to his bank and pledges them as security for a loan of $10,000. If the transaction is a bona fide loan, no part of the $10,000 borrowed will be regarded as a consideration realized on the disposition of the notes. Hence, S's original position of realizing but $7,500 of gain on the down payment will stand unchanged. No further payments need be reported by him until the buyer pays off the notes or the notes are otherwise disposed of.

The Service has ruled, however, that a pledge of an installment contract to secure loan of the same amount as the installment contract is a disposition where the repayment is effected by collections from the installment purchaser.[74]

13. Other Dispositions of Installment Contracts

In general, other types of dispositions of installment contracts have the effect of accelerating the postponed gain in the hands of the seller just as if the contract were sold for its fair market value.[75] For example, a gift of an installment contract accelerates the gain; the donor will be required to pay a tax on all of the remaining gain (less the difference, if any, between face and fair market values) in the year of the gift.[76] But a transfer of an installment obligation to the seller's children in exchange for a life time annuity is a taxable disposition that accelerates the postponed gain.[77]

An exception to this general rule is found in the case of a transfer of an installment obligation by virtue of a tax-free transaction.[78]

---

[72]Contrast Stein v. Director, 135 F.Supp. 356 (E.D.N.Y. 1955) with East Coast Equipment Co. v. Commissioner, 222 F.2d 676 (3rd Cir. 1955). United Surgical Steel Co., 54 T.C. 1215 (1970), acq. 1971-2 C.B. 3.

[73]Discounting of the installment obligation with a financial institution has generally been held to reflect a sale even though the seller guarantees collection. Miller Saw-Trimmer Co., 32 B.T.A. 931, 938 (1935).

[74]Rev. Rul. 65-185, 1965-2 C.B. 153.

[75]Reg. Sec. 1.453-9(b).

[76]See Roger's Estate v. Commissioner, 143 F.2d 695 (2d Cir. 1944), cert. den. 323 U.S. 780 (1944).

[77]Harold W. Smith, 56 T.C. 263 (1971); A.W. Legg, 57 T.C. 164 (1971).

[78]Section 453(d)(4), I.R.C.; Portland Oil Co. v. Commissioner, 109 F.2d 479 (1st Cir. 1940), cert. den. 310 U.S. 650 (1940); Nebraska Seed Co. v. United States, 116 F.Supp. 740 (Ct.Cl. 1953), cert. den. 347 U.S. 1012 (1954). See Reg. Sec. 1.453-9(c)(2) lists the following transactions as being within this exception: "Certain transfers to corporations under sections 351 and 361; contributions of property to a partnership by a partner under section 721; and distributions by a partnership to a partner under section 731 (except as provided by section 736 and section 751)." See also Reg. Sec. 1.453-9(c)(1).

Another exception is found in the case of the death of the seller; death by itself does not accelerate the postponed gain. However, the holder of the installment contract after the seller's death, whether the seller's estate or his beneficiary, will be required to report the receipt of the remainder of the gain in the same manner as the seller would have reported it had he lived. The gain is received by the holder of the contract in the nature of income or gain in respect of a decedent, and the holder is not entitled to take a deduction for the estate tax attributed to the contract.[79]

What about the transfer of the buyer's obligation by the buyer? Does the substitution of a new buyer amount to a disposition of the contract?

The mere substitution of a new installment contract for the old obligation, without a change of the party obligated to make payments, does not accelerate the seller's installment gain.[80] This conclusion holds true even if the original selling price is reduced by the terms of the new obligation.[81]

But if the new contract is drawn with new parties as buyers, the gain in the old contract will be accelerated as if it were sold for face value.[82] The Commissioner has taken the position that the substitution of a new buyer under the terms of the original contract is the equivalent of a disposition of the contract,[83] but the courts have not necessarily agreed with his position.[84]

14. Substituted Security on Installment Sale

Suppose the buyer of real property on the installment method desires to receive title to the land free and clear of his installment obligation so that he can proceed with his development plans. He is willing to put up a cash deposit equal to the balance of the installment obligation to secure payment to the seller. Does the substitution of the deposit for the land as security for the installment obligation accelerate the payment of that obligation?[85]

The Commissioner has ruled that such substitution does not accelerate payment, provided that the buyer cannot demand immediate payment to him of the deposit. Even if the note payments are made out of the escrowed deposit, no acceleration occurs as long as the payments are not demandable before the notes become due.[86]

On the other hand, the escrow of cash cannot be used to convert a cash sale into an installment sale. For example, if a buyer is willing to pay cash on closing, the installment method is not available to the seller even though he refuses the cash and insists upon installment notes secured by an escrowed deposit of cash.[87]

---

[79] Section 453(d)(3), I.R.C.; Section 691(a)(4)(c), I.R.C. These rules apply to the surviving spouse's community interest in installment obligations as well as the decedent spouse's interest. Bessie Stanly, 40 T.C. 851 (1963) aff'd 338 F.2d 434 (9th Cir. 1964). But see Bath v. United States, 323, F.2d, 980 (5th Cir. 1963).

[80] Rev. Rul. 55-5, 1955-1 C.B. 331. Sam F. Soter, 1968 P-H T.C. Memo ¶68,043.

[81] Rev. Rul. 55-429, 1955-2 C.B. 252. Rev. Rul. 72-570, 1972-2 C.B. 241.

[82] Burrel Groves, Inc. v. Commissioner, 223 F.2d 526 (5th Cir. 1955).

[83] See non-acq., 1943 C.B. 42, to J.C. Wynne, 47 B.T.A. 731 (1942).

[84] Harold A. Jackson, 24 T.C. 1, 14 (1955), acq. 1955-2 C.B. 7, aff'd on another point, 233 F.2d 289 (2d Cir. 1956); J.C. Wynne, 47 B.T.A. 731 (1942), non-acq. 1943 C.B. 42.

[85] A substitution of notes on the same property (even though subdivided) is not a deposition that results in accelerating the gain. Rev. Rul. 74-157, I.R.B. 1974-14, p. 11.

[86] Rev. Rul. 68-246, 1968-21 IRB 15.

[87] Everett Pozzi, 49 T.C. 119 (1967). Notes of the buyer for the purpose of installment reporting are *not* the equivalent of cash. Rev. Rul. 73-396, I.R.B. 1973-39, p. 12.

INSTALLMENT SALES 167

15. Guarantee by Financial Institution

The foregoing analysis indicates that security is not the controlling issue. Security is usually established by a note secured by a first mortgage or deed of trust on the property. But if it is secured by an escrow deposit of money, the Internal Revenue Service and the Tax Court get uptight about "cash receipt" and "constructive receipt" of cash.

Instead of an escrow of "cash" or "money" or "certificates of deposit," the author of this book just asks the financing institution to put its own name on the line. That is, the bank, or savings and loan association, must guarantee the buyer's note with all defenses waived.[88]

16. Repossession of Property Sold on Installment Method

Section 1038 governs the tax rules for determining gain or loss in the case of the repossession of real property previously sold by the taxpayer. In order for Section 1038 to apply, the property must be reacquired in full or partial satisfaction of an indebtedness incurred on the sale that is secured by the property itself. Under these circumstances, the seller will realize gain on repossession to the extent that money or marketable property (other than the purchaser's obligation) previously received exceeds the amount of gain previously reported by him on the sale. In any event, the gain realized on repossession cannot exceed the net gain on the original sale less reacquisition costs and the amount of gain previously reported.[89]

Example: In 1967, seller sold real estate for $30,000, accepting a down payment of $5,000 and the deferred balance of $25,000 being secured by a purchase money mortgage on the property. His adjusted basis for the property was $24,000, so that his total gain is $6,000. In the year of sale, he reported the $5,000 down payment as consisting of $1,000 of gain (20 percent of the contract price) and $4,000 of recovery of basis (80 percent of the contract price). If he repossesses the property in 1968, and no further payments are made by the buyer, then his gain would be computed as follows:

Amount received on the contract	$5,000.00
Amount previously reported as income	1,000.00
Amount taxable as gain	$4,000.00

In this case, the total amount of gain realized on repossession ($4,000) is less than the total gain on the entire transaction ($6,000). Accordingly, the entire gain is recognized in the year of repossession.

On the other hand, had the amount of money received as recovery of basis exceeded the amount of total gain, then the gain recognized on repossession would be limited to the amount of the total gain.

Example: Suppose in the previous example seller had received an additional payment of $5,000 in 1968. He would have reported 20 percent, or $1,000, as additional gain and $4,000 as recovery of basis. Suppose in 1969 he repossesses and incurs $500 of repossession costs. His gain on repossession would be computed as follows:

---

[88]The guarantee of the largest private bank with all defenses waived has been ruled not to be the equivalent of cash, or an escrow of cash.
[89]Reg. Sec. 1.1038-1(b),(c).

Amount received on contract	$10,000.00
Amount previously reported as gain	2,000.00
Difference	$ 8,000.00
Limitation	
Total gain on sale	$6,000.00
Less gain previously reported	2,000.00
Difference	$4,000.00
Less repossession costs	500.00
Gain taxable on repossession	$3,500.00

The gain realized on repossession will be of the same character as the gain realized upon the original sale, except where the seller retained title and reported gain on the deferred payment method.[90]

The basis to the seller of the repossessed property will be the basis to him of the installment contract, increased by any gain recognized on the repossession and by any expenses incurred in the repossession.[91]

Example: Assume the same facts as used in the prior example. The repossessed property will have the following basis:

Basis for Installment Obligation	
Basis for property sold	$24,000.00
Less recovery of basis (two payments)	8,000.00
Basis for installment obligation	$16,000.00
Basis for Property Reaquired	
Basis of installment obligation	$16,000.00
Gain on repossession	3,500.00
Repossession costs	500.00
Basis of repossessed property	$20,000.00

The holding period of the repossessed property commences with the date of repossession. It does not include the period from the date following the date of the sale and ending on the date of repossession.

No loss is recognized on repossession of real property. If basis exceeds fair market value on repossession, it represents a potential loss that can be realized either through the deduction for depreciation or by disposition of the property to a third party.

No bad debt loss is realized on the purchaser's obligation as a result of the repossession because all of the basis for the installment obligation is transferred to the repossessed property. Accordingly, the installment obligation has a zero basis to the seller.

B. DEFERRED PAYMENT SALES

In some situations, an alternative to the installment method of deferring recognition of gain on a long-term sale is the deferred payment method. Under the latter

---

[90] Reg. Sec. 1.1038-1(d), 1.453-9(a). Repossession by a financial institution results in gain taxable as ordinary income if the repossessed property is sold. Similarly, a repossessed property sold at a loss would be fully deductible.

[91] Reg. Sec. 1.1038-1(g).

DEFERRED PAYMENT SALES

method, no gain is reported by the seller until the payments received by him equal the cost or other basis for the property transferred; once the seller has recovered his basis, all of the remaining payments received by him are reportable as capital gain.

Example: Seller sells property for $20,000 which had cost him $7,500 ten years ago. His selling expenses were $1,200. Suppose the down payment in the year of sale is $5,000. In the second year, he receives installment payments totalling an additional $5,000. The balance is paid in the third year. His gain would be taxable as shown in the following table.[92]

1. Year of Sale

Payment received in year of sale		$ 5,000
Unrecovered basis and expenses:		
Cost	$7,1500	
Selling expense	1,200	8,700
Gain taxed in year of sale		—0—
Unrecovered basis after payment		$ 3,700

2. Second Year

Payment received		$ 5,000
Unrecovered basis and expenses:		
Total amount	$8,700	
Less portion recovered	5,000	3,700
Gain taxed in second year		$ 1,300

3. Third Year

Payment received		$10,000
Less unrecovered basis and expenses:		
Total amount	$8,700	
Less portion recovered	8,700	—0—
Gain taxable in third year		$10,000

If we contrast the deferred payment method with the installment method, we find that the former defers the recognition of the gain of the final years to the sales contract; the installment method spreads the gain proportionately over the life of the contract according to the payments received. Thus, the deferred payment method has certain special advantages and disadvantages peculiar to itself:

1. The postponement of the gain until basis has been recovered normally means that no tax will be reported in the year of sale unless, of course, the down payment exceeds basis. The entire down payment will ordinarily be available to the seller for reinvestment without diminution by the payment of the tax.

2. Furthermore, the seller need report no gain until he has recovered the money he had invested in the property; he runs no risk of reporting any part of the gain realized on a sale before he is assured of getting it.[93]

3. On the other hand, all of the tax on the gain will be bunched in the last year or years of the sales contract; the spreading feature of the installment method is lost.

4. And, as in the case of an installment sale, the seller runs the risk of a change in the rate of tax to be applied to the gain. If the rate increases, he will pay more tax than if he had reported all the gain in the year of sale; if the rate decreases, he will pay less.

---

[92] See Burnet v. Logan, 283 U.S. 404 (1931).
[93] Warren Jones Company, 60 T.C. No. 70 (1973).

5. Unlike the installment method, there is no statutory restriction upon the amount of the total payment that can be received in the year of sale.

1. Sales Qualified for the Deferred Payment Method

Not all sales of property qualify for the deferred payment method of reporting gain. Two requirements must be met: first, the sales contract must call for the payment of installments in one or more future taxable years; and, second, the gain to be realized on the sale must not become immediately reportable under the seller's normal method of accounting.

The second requirement flows out of the fact that *the deferred payment method does not rest upon any special election by the taxpayer*, as in the case of the installment method. Rather, the deferred payment method is based upon the application of the principles of the seller's normal method of accounting to the terms of the particular sale.

Thus, we must analyze the principles of cash and accrual accounting in order to determine whether or not a particular sale fits the deferred payment method. For the purposes of our study, let us first turn to the cash basis seller. He can draw a sales contract calling for deferred or installment payments in any one of four ways, as follows:

1. Contract for sale, title to be retained by the seller until the price is paid and other conditions are fulfilled; contract not negotiable.

2. Contract for sale, title to be retained by the seller for security purposes; contract readily negotiable.

3. Title conveyed, subject to a note and mortgage; note has a fair market value.

4. Title conveyed, subject to an unsecured note or note which has no fair market value.

Which, if any, of these four types of land sales qualifies for the deferred payment method of reporting by a cash basis taxpayer? The following sections will attempt to spell out the answer.

2. Non-negotiable Contract Sale

This is the most common illustration of a sale meeting the requirements of the deferred payment method, provided the seller is on the cash basis. At the time of sale, the seller enters into a contract of sale, transferring possession to the purchaser but retaining title himself. Because of additional conditions in the land contract, the contract itself is not readily negotiable nor is it capable of easy valuation. It is not essentially equivalent to cash.

Sales made pursuant to an executory contract of this type may properly be reported on the deferred payment method; no gain need be reported until the seller has first recovered his basis for the property plus the expenses of sale.[94]

---

[94]Burnet v. Logan, 283 U.S. 404 (1931); Perry v. Commissioner, 152 F.2d 183, 187 (8th Cir. 1945); Sterling v. Ham, 8 F.Supp. 386 (S.D.Me. 1933); Cambria Development Co., 34 B.T.A. 1155 (1936), acq. 1937-1 C.B. 4. But see Heller Trust v. Commissioner, 382 F.2d 675 (9th Cir. 1967) where the Court upheld a determination that land purchase contracts had a value equal to 50 percent of face, despite the facts that (1) the seller was a cash basis taxpayer, (2) the contracts were non-negotiable, and (3) a related entity had to perform continuing services to the buyers.

Example: Seller agrees to sell a parcel of real estate to Buyer for $40,000. The lot sold is made subject to a right of way for the joint use of both parties. B pays $10,000 down and agrees to pay the balance within three years, at which time title will be conveyed to him. B also agrees to install an all-weather road on the joint right of way to be completed within the three-year period. In case of default of either condition, S has the right to forfeit the contract.

Because of the non-monetary obligation to construct the road, the land contract would not be salable and would be difficult to value. S could properly report the $10,000 down payment and succeeding installments as return of capital until his basis was recovered.

3. Negotiable Contract of Sale

Suppose the sale is made by the execution of a land contract in the usual form which calls for no performance by the buyer other than the timely payment of the installments as they fall due. Title is reserved by the seller as security to ensure the payment of the total contract price. Suppose, also, that the land contract is readily salable at a discount upon an exchange specializing in land contacts.

Can the seller report his gain on the deferred payment method? The Commissioner has ruled that such a land contract is the equivalent of cash to the extent of its fair market value at the time of execution; hence, a cash basis seller must include in the payments received in the year of sale not only the cash received but also the fair market value of the contract.[95] The rigid application of this ruling would effectively wipe out the use of the deferred payment method for the normal type of land contract.

But by and large the courts have refused to follow the Commissioner's ruling. For example, the Tax Court has consistently held that the seller under a land contract is entitled to report the installments on the deferred payment method despite a showing by the Commissioner, which the Tax Court refused to accept, that the contract had a readily ascertainable price on an established exchange dealing in such contracts.[96]

Despite his losses in court, the Commissioner has given no evidence of abandoning his position; hence, the use of the deferred payment method to report the gain realized upon a simple land contract sale will undoubtedly face a challenge upon audit.

4. Sale Subject to Note Secured by Mortgage

Under this type of sale, the seller conveys title to the purchaser at the time the sale is made. To secure future installments of the purchase price, the buyer executes a promissory note payable to the seller which is secured by a mortgage on the property conveyed. A secured note of this type is ordinarily salable and has a readily ascertainable market value.

For this reason the deferred payment method is not available on a sale of this type even to a cash basis taxpayer. He must report the receipt of both the down payment and the fair market value of the secured note in the year of sale.[97]

---

[95] Reg. Sec. 1.453-6(a).
[96] Estate of Clarence W. Ennis, 23 T.C. 799 (1955), non-acq. 1956-1 C.B. 6. See, also, Nina J. Ennis, 17 T.C. 465, 470 (1951); Estate of Coid Hurlburt, 25 T.C. 1286 (1956), non-acq. 1956-2 C.B. 10.
[97] Ruth Iron Co. v. Commissioner, 26 F.2d 30 (8th Cir. 1928); Owen v. United States, 8 F.Supp. 707 (Ct.Cl. 1934).

The entire gain realized on the sale of the property is thus reportable in the year of sale. Consequently, if any collection is subsequently made upon the note in excess of the value at which it was reported upon the sale of the property, the excess collection is taxable as ordinary income, not as gain realized on the sale of the property.[98] The excess collection is treated as the collection of a discount in the face value of the note.

If a note is reported at less than face value at the time of sale, the discount from face is deemed to be collected proportionately over the life of the note. Thus, each payment received on the note must be reported as representing in part the collection of the discount and in part the collection of principal in the same proportion that the total discount bears to the total value placed upon the note at the time of sale.[99]

Example: Seller sells a lot for $10,000, payable $2,500 down and $7,500 on an installment note maturing in five years. S reports as the gross proceeds realized on the sale the $2,500 down payment and two-thirds of the value of the note, or $5,000. Suppose, in the year after sale, S receives installment payments of $1,500. How is this amount reported?

Recovery of principal (66-2/3%)	$1,000
Collection of discount (33-1/3%)	500
Total payment received in year	$1,500

If the seller fails to collect the full value at which the note was returned in the year of sale, he will be entitled to a bad debt deduction for the amount of his undercollection in the year in which the note becomes worthless.[100]

Naturally, if the amount not collected on the note represents discount not previously included in income, the seller will not be entitled to a deduction in the year of worthlessness for this amount.

5. Sale Subject to Personal Note

Suppose property is sold for a price payable in part in cash, the balance to be paid at a later date as evidenced by the unsecured personal note of the purchaser. The seller transfers title to the purchaser upon the receipt of the down payment. Can the seller defer reporting the gain on the sale until he has recovered his basis and expenses out of the down payment and following installment payments? In other words, is the personal note of the purchaser equivalent to cash?

The regulations state that "only in rare and exceptional cases does property have no fair market value."[101] Ordinarily, therefore, the deferred payment method would be unavailable to a seller who receives a note for the deferred balance in the year of sale. But if the seller is able to show the irresponsibility of the purchaser, or other factors

---

[98] A.B. Culbertson, 14 T.C. 1421, 1424 (1950), acq. 1950-2 C.B. 1. See Lee v. Commissioner, 119 F.2d 946 (7th Cir. 1941).

[99] Shafpa Realty Corp., 8 B.T.A. 283 (1927). Accord, Hatch v. Commissioner, 190 F.2d 254 (2d Cir. 1951); Victor B. Gilbert, 6 T.C. 10, 13 (1946), acq. 1946-1 C.B. 2.

[100] State Bank of Alcester, 8 B.T.A. 878 (1927), acq. VII-1 C.B. 30. These rules do not apply to an investor who buys the notes from the land seller at a discount. Such an investor is entitled to recover his basis first out of the payments to him before he receives any discount income. Phillips v. Frank, 295 F.2d 629 (9th Cir. 1961); Liftin v. Commissioner, 317 F.2d 234 (4th Cir. 1963); Willhoit v. Commissioner, 308 F.2d 259 (9th Cir. 1962). Contra, Darbs Investment Co. v. Commissioner, 315 F.2d 551 (6th Cir. 1963).

[101] Reg. Sec. 1.453-6(a)(2).

tending to show that the note has no ascertainable market value, he will be able to use the deferred payment method.[102]

Under exceptional circumstances, the benefits of the deferred payment method have been extended to a seller who has transferred title on the strength of a second-mortgage note against the property.[103] The burden is, of course, upon the seller to establish the fact that the notes received are incapable of valuation; in the absence of such proof, the notes will be presumed to be worth their face value.[104]

If, on the other hand, the notes are negotiable, the Commissioner has taken the position that the notes are rarely incapable of valuation. Thus, the fair market value of the notes will be treated as part of the sales proceeds received in the year of sale.[105] Collections on the notes in excess of the amount reported in the year of sale will be ordinary income.[106] And the Commissioner has successfully taken the position that collections on a note reported at a value of zero are taxable as ordinary income.[107] It is only, therefore, in a case in which the notes are not capable of valuation that the deferred payment method is available to a cash basis seller.[108]

6. Sales by an Accrual Basis Taxpayer

Generally we find that it is extremely difficult, if not impossible, for an accrual basis taxpayer to qualify a land sale for the deferred payment method. The reason for this limitation lies in the nature of accrual accounting; ordinarily, the receipt of a note or other unconditional obligation to pay is taxed or reportable by the recipient to the extent of its face amount in the year of receipt.[109] Hence, no part of the purchase price is deferred for reporting in subsequent years when collection is made.

But at least one accrual basis seller has successfully challenged this rule. In *C. W. Titus, Inc.*,[110] an accrual basis taxpayer sold certain oil leases upon a long-term contract, the deferred payments to become payable on a fixed schedule once the seller had performed certain conditions. Because the contract had no fair market value when executed, the seller, although on the accrual basis, was permitted to use the deferred payment method.[111]

---

[102] R. V. Board, 18 B.T.A. 650 (1930), acq. IX-2 C.B. 6, Johnson v. Commissioner, 56 F. 2d 58 (5th Cir. 1932), cert. den. 286 U.S. 551; Dudley T. Humphrey, 32 B.T.A. 280 (1935), non-acq. XIV-2 C.B. 34 See Cowden v. Commissioner, 289 F.2d 20 at 24 (5th Cir. 1961).

[103] Commissioner v. Liftin, 317 F.2d 234 (4th Cir. 1963); Miller v. United States, 235 F.2d 553 (6th Cir. 1956); Joliet-Norfolk Farm Corp., 8 B.T.A. 824 (1927), acq. VII-1 C.B. 16.

[104] Owen v. United States, 8 F.Supp. 707 (Ct. Cl. 1934); Louis Rubino, Par. 49,288 P-H Memo T.C. (1949), aff'd on other grounds, 186 F.2d 304 (9th Cir. 1951), cert. den. 342 U.S. 814.

[105] Saunders v. United States, 101 F.2d 133 (5th Cir. 1939).

[106] A. B. Culbertson, 14 T.C. 1421, 1424 (1950), acq. 1950-2 C.B. 1.

[107] Miller v. United States, 262 F.2d 584 (6th Cir. 1958).

[108] Owen v. United States 8 F.Supp. 707 (Ct. Cl. 1934).

[109] Spring City Foundry Co. v. Commissioner, 292 U.S. 182 (1934). Jones Lumber Co. v. Commissioner, 29 A.F.T.R. 2d 5024 (6th Cir. 1968).

[110] C.W. Titus, Inc., 33 B.T.A. 928, 930 (1936), non-acq. XV-1 C.B. 46. See Lucas v. North Texas Lumber Co., 281 U.S. 11, 13 (1930). Contra, George L. Castner Co., Inc., 30 T.C. 1061 (1958).

[111] George L. Castner Co., Inc., 30 T.C. 1061 (1958) held to the contrary involving personal property. See, also, Baltimore Baseball Club, Inc. v. United States, 481 F.2d 1283 (Ct.Cl. 1973), which made the same distinction; personal property does not qualify for the deferred payment method of reporting. Prefabricated housing materials placed on a lot owned by the seller have for this purpose been classified as personal property. Jones Lumber Co. v. United States, 404 F.2d 764 (6th Cir. 1972).

7. Deferred Payment Sale Subject to Mortgage

Suppose the property sold under the deferred payment method is subject to a mortgage which pre-dated the sale. Does the fact that the property was sold subject to an encumbrance change the result?

Not usually. Gain, computed on the total price for the property, including the outstanding mortgage debt, will be deferred until the seller has recovered his basis and expenses in full. However, we must remember that the portion of purchase price evidenced by the mortgage debt is considered to be received by the seller in the year of sale; hence, if the mortgage debt itself exceeds the seller's basis for the property, the amount of the excess will become taxable in the year of sale.[112]

Example: In a sale qualifying for deferred payment treatment, Seller sells an apartment for $80,000, including an outstanding mortgage indebtedness of $60,000. S's basis for the property is but $50,000. Buyer pays S $10,000 in the year of sale and $10,000 a year later in full payment for S's equity. S realizes a total gain of $30,000 on the transaction, of which $20,000 is reportable in the year of sale, as follows:

Payment received in year of sale:		
Cash received	$10,000	
Outstanding mortgage debt	$60,000	$70,000
Unrecovered basis for property		50,000
Gain reportable in year of sale		$20,000

The remainder of the gain would be taxable in the subsequent year, in which the $10,000 installment payment would be received.

8. Sale of Deferred Payment Obligation

If the seller of property on the deferred payment method sells or otherwise disposes of the time payment obligation prior to reporting all of the gain to be realized upon the sale, he may become taxable upon the remainder of the deferred gain in the year in which he disposes of the obligation. Thus, if the deferred obligation is sold for its face amount, he will be taxed upon the total gain deferred on the sale.[113] If the price received is less than face, he will be taxed upon the reduced payment just as if the equivalent reduced amount were received from the purchaser of the property in payment of the deferred on the obligation.[114]

Example: Seller sells his home for $30,000 on a long-term land contract which calls for the immediate payment of $5,000 and the payment of the balance over a period of 25 years with interest. S retains title to the property. Suppose S collects $1,000 on principal and then sells the contract to a bank for $22,500. The sale of the contract takes place in a year later than the year of the property sale. If S's original basis for the home plus expenses of sale totalled $20,000, his gain on the sale of the deferred payment contract would be computed as follows:

Proceeds on sale of contract		$22,500
Less unrecovered basis:		
Original basis for property	$20,000	
Less payments received	6,000	14,000

---

[112] Reg. Sec. 1.453-4(c);-6(a)(2).
[113] Imperator Realty Co., 24 B.T.A. 1010 (1931).
[114] Reg. Sec. 1.453-6(a)(2).

SALE FOR AN INDETERMINATE PRICE 175

   Gain on sale of deferred pay-
    ment contract $8.500

9. Pledge of Deferred Payment Obligation

On the other hand, if the holder of a deferred payment obligation uses it as security to borrow money from a third party, the deferred gain would not be taxable, provided the holder is careful to retain title to the obligation.

Just as in the case of a pledge of an installment contract, the seller is able to convert the bulk of his investment in the property into cash in the year of sale by borrowing upon the strength of the security of the contract for sale; the tax on the gain to be realized on the sale will be postponed until the buyer's deferred payments come in.

10. Repossession of Property Sold

Repossession of property previously sold under the deferred payment method is treated in substantially the same manner as in the case of repossession of property sold on the installment method. Gain is recognized only to the extent of payments previously received but not taxed.[115]

It makes no difference whether or not title has been transferred on the repossessioned sale.[116] What counts is the nature of the holding and the time thereof.[117] What counts is the character of the holdings.[118]

C. SALE FOR AN INDETERMINATE PRICE

The sale of property for a price indeterminate in amount is accounted for in the same manner as a deferred payment sale. The seller is privileged to charge off all of his cost or other basis against the first payments received; until his basis plus expenses of sale are recovered, no gain will be taxable to him. After recovery of basis and expenses, the seller must report the balance of the payments received as gain realized on the sale.

Among the more common illustrations of sales for an indeterminate price are the following:

  1. Sales for a contingent price;
  2. Sales measured by production;
  3. Sales for a private annuity.

1. Sales for a Contingent Price

Suppose business property is sold to a purchaser in consideration of the purchaser's agreement to pay a percentage of its profits to the seller for a certain number of

---

  [115]Reg. Sec. 1.1038-1(a)(2).
  [116]Reg. Sec. 1.1038-1(3)(ii).
  [117]Reg. Sec. 1.1038-2(g).
  [118]If the repossessor quickly resells the property, the repossessor (whether a bank, savings and loan institution, or other loan or financing company) will realize ordinary loss or ordinary income.

years. The payment of the sales price is wholly contingent upon the purchaser's profits, the amount of which is not ascertainable at the time of sale.

The seller in such a case is permitted to use the deferred payment method of reporting the percentage of the purchaser's profits paid to him as the sales price; until he has recovered his basis and expenses, no part of the payments received is taxed. After recovery of basis and expenses, the remaining payments are reportable gain realized on the sale.

2. Sales Measured by Production

In *Burnet v. Logan*,[119] which furnishes the genesis of the deferred payment method the seller sold certain property to a purchaser for the price of 60 cents per ton of all iron ore mined from the property sold. Because the price was contingent and not capable of valuation, the seller was permitted to treat the first payments out of production as an offset to his basis for the property sold. In the year of sale, "the promise (of the purchaser to pay) was in no proper sense equivalent to cash. . . ."

Similarly, a sale of property for an oil payment payable out of future production from certain lands under lease was property reported on the deferred payment method.[120] The benefits of this rule have been extended to accrual basis sellers.[121]

3. Sales for a Private Annuity

Suppose property is sold for a price measured by a guaranteed monthly payment to be made by the purchaser to the seller for the seller's life. The property is, in effect, exchanged for an annuity for the seller's life to be paid by the purchaser.

If the purchaser is a recognized insurance or annuity company, the present value of the payments for the seller's life can be computed by reference to annuity tables; this present value will measure the gross sales price received by the seller, and his gain or loss on the transaction will be computed accordingly.

But if the purchaser is an individual or a corporation not engaged in the annuity or life underwriting business, the courts have held that the purchaser's obligation to pay the annuity is not capable of valuation.[122] The seller must assume the risk of both his own life expectancy and of the continued solvency of the purchaser.

How are the annuity payments to be reported by the seller? Because an annuity is involved, the seller must look to the rules regarding annuities for his answer. Under the 1954 Code, these rules permit him to recover his "investment" in the contract tax-free over the period of his life expectancy. Any portion of the payment in excess of his "investment" is treated as interest paid by the purchaser for the privilege of deferring payment of the sales price.[123]

---

[119] 283 U.S. 404, 413 (1931).

[120] Rocky Mountain Development Co., 38 B.T.A. 1303 (1938), acq. 1939-2 C.B. 32; Kay Kimbell, 41 B.T.A. 940, 951 (1940), non-acq. 1940-2 C.B. 12.

[121] Commissioner v. Edwards Drilling Co., 95 F.2d 719 (5th Cir. 1938).

[122] J. Darsie Lloyd, 33 B.T.A. 903, 905 (1936), acq. 1950-2 C.B. 3; Commissioner v. Kann's Estate, 174 F.2d 357 (3rd Cir. 1949). But see Rev. Rul. 62-136 which attempts to apply the rules of commercial annuities to annuities issued by tax exempt organizations which "from time to time" receive contributions of appreciated property in exchange for guaranteed life payments.

[123] Section 72, I.R.C. See Gillespie v. Commissioner, 128 F.2d 140 (9th Cir. 1942).

Example: Property is sold by Seller to Buyer for the Buyer's agreement to pay S $100 a month for S's life. Let us assume that S has a life expectancy of 20 years; consequently, the total return anticipated under the contract will be $24,000 ($100 × 12 × 20). If S's "investment" in the annuity is $20,000, each $100 monthly payment would be taxed as follows:

Recovery of "Investment":
$$\frac{\$20,000}{\$24,000} \times \$100, \text{ or } \$83.33$$
Payment of Interest:
$$\frac{\$ 4,000}{\$24,000} \times \$100, \text{ or } \$16.67$$

Thus, $16.67 of each monthly payment will be taxed as ordinary income.

How will the "investment" portion of the payment be treated? The answer depends upon how the seller's "investment" in the annuity contract is measured. Ordinarily, the "investment" in an annuity is the price that the annuitant paid for it. If this ordinary rule applies in this situation, under which the seller has purchased the annuity by the transfer of property, the "investment" in the annuity would be the fair market value of the property on the date of transfer. And this is the rule adopted by the Commissioner.[124]

But the value of the property may be in excess of its basis to the seller.[125] Hence, a portion of the "investment" to be recovered over the projected life of the annuity contract may represent the receipt of gain on the sale of the property; the remainder, of course, would represent the recovery of the seller's basis for the property.

Under these circumstances, the "investment" portion of each monthly payment is first assigned to the recovery of the seller's basis. Once the seller has recovered his basis in full, the investment portion of each subsequent annuity payment is taxed as gain realized on the original sale of the property.[126]

Example: Suppose, under the facts of the preceding example, S's basis for the property sold was but $12,000. If we assume the value of the property at the time of its exchange to have been $20,000, S's "investment" in the contract would be $20,000. Consequently, as we saw in the preceding example, $83.33 of each $100 monthly payment will represent the recovery of S's "investment." Thus, in 12 years, S would have recovered $12,000 of his "investment," all of which would be received tax-free as the recovery of his basis for the property sold. Thereafter, the $83.33 of each monthly payment attributed to S's "investment" would become taxable as gain realized upon the sale of the property. This allocation would govern the receipt of payments under the contract for the remainder of S's life expectancy. If S outlives that expectancy, the $83.33 portion of each subsequent monthly payment would again be tax-free income.[127]

Obviously, there are a number of advantages to the sale of property for a private annuity. For instance, the tax on the gain to be realized on the sale is postponed until the seller has recovered his basis for the property. If he dies before recovering his basis,

---

[124] Rev. Rul. 239, 1953-2 C.B. 53. See Raymond v. Commissioner, 114 F.2d 140 (7th Cir. 1940), cert. den. 311 U.S. 710. Rev. Rul. 69-74, 1969-1 C.B. 43 confirms this treatment under current law. The transfer of installment obligations to a private annuity is a "disposition" that results in accelerating the postponed income or gain under I.R.C. §453. Harold W. Smith, 56 T.C. 263 (1971).

[125] Estate of Lloyd G. Bell, 60 T.C. No. 52 (1973).

[126] Hills Estate v. Maloney, 58 F.Supp. 164 (D.C.N.J. 1944); Rev. Rul. 239, 1953-2 C.B. 53.

[127] Section 72(b),(c)(3), I.R.C.; Rev. Rul. 239, 1953-2 C.B. 53. Under Rev. Rul. 69-74, 1969-1 C.B. 43; the gain is to be recovered ratably over the seller's life expectancy. But no loss can be deducted if the fair market value is less than cost. Rev. Rul. 71-492, 1971-2 C.B. 127.

there is no tax; but of course, in that event, he or his estate never receives the payment for the portion of the sales price attributable to the gain. And, as in the case of the other deferred payment sales, the seller runs the risk of a change in the tax rates between the date of sale and the date on which the gain is reportable.

Private annuities have proved to be a useful tool for estate planners. An owner of property is able to transfer the property out of his estate by a sale for an adequate consideration and still be assured of receiving payments for life on the disposition of the property. He can use low-basis, high-value property for this purpose without incurring an immediate tax on the excess of value over basis. And the property may be sold to the natural beneficiaries of his bounty in such manner that the income from the property will in good part finance the purchaser's obligation to pay the annuity.

D. OPTION SALES

The granting of an option to purchase property is not treated as a taxable event to the owner even if consideration for the option is paid to him.[128]

This rule gives the seller of real property some leeway in timing the sale of property. If he wishes to postpone the date of receipt of gain to a future year, the option device may prove valuable to him. Instead of making an outright sale of the property, he may grant the prospective purchaser an option to purchase the property at an agreed price to be paid in the future. The realization of the gain will be postponed to the year in which the optionee exercises the option to purchase; this result holds true even if the consideration for the option is applied against the agreed purchase price for the property.[129]

1. Option Distinguished from Sales Contract

However, for this result to obtain, the option contract must evidence a bona fide option to purchase; if it is merely a subterfuge for a completed contract of sale, it will be treated as any other completed sale. Any consideration received will be taxed as part of the sales proceeds received in the year of execution of the so-called "option."[130]

What, then, are the distinguishing characteristics of an option contract? How does it differ from a sales contract?

In general, an option contract is unilateral; only one of the parties (the seller) is bound, the other party being free to exercise or forfeit the right to buy at his option.[131] A sales contract is bilateral; it binds both parties to the contract, one to buy and the other to sell. If an option had previously been granted, its exercise by the purchaser would give rise to a sales contract,[132] or in the alternative, a completed sale.[133]

---

[128]Lucas v. North Texas Lumber Co., 281 U.S. 11 (1930).

[129]Aiken v. Commissioner, 35 F.2d 620, 624 (8th Cir. 1929), aff'd on other grounds, 282 U.S. 277 (1931); Virginia Iron Coal & Coke Co. v. Commissioner, 99 F.2d 919 (4th Cir. 1938), cert. den. 307 U.S. 630; Rev. Rul. 57-40, 1957-1 C.B. 266.

[130]C.A. Cochran, 23 B.T.A. 616, 619 (1931), appeal dismissed, 67 F.2d 988 (6th Cir. 1933); Watson v. Commissioner, 62 F.2d 35 (9th Cir. 1932). See Deal v. Morrow, 197 F.2d 821, 827 (5th Cir. 1952).

[131]Rich Lumber Co. v. United States, 237 F.2d 424 (1st Cir. 1956); Estate of C. William Meinecke, 47 B.T.A. 634 (1942), acq. 1942-2 C.B. 13.

[132]Lucas v. North Texas Lumber Co., 281 U.S. 111 (1930); see John T. Morris, 15 B.T.A. 260 (1929), acq. VIII-2 C.B. 37.

[133]Aiken v. Commissioner, 35 F.2d 620, 624 (8th Cir. 1929), aff'd on other grounds, 282 U.S. 277 (1931).

OPTION SALES

Thus, if a contract denominated an option contract calls for the immediate transfer of possession and the payment of the full price over an agreed period in installments, the contract will be treated as a sales contract, which in reality it is.[134] Similarly, an option contract calling for a disproportionately large option payment may be treated as a sales contract.

Also, the terms of the option should provide for the disposition of the option payment, in the event the option is not exercised. If the contract does not spell out whether the option payment is to be forfeited or returned, the consideration for the option may be treated as an unconditional deposit on the sales price to be taxed in the year of receipt.[135]

2. Effect of Exercise or Failure of Option

If the option is exercised by the buyer, the price previously paid for the option will be taxed to the seller as a portion of the total price paid for the property in the same manner as the remainder of the purchase price received.[136]

If the optionee fails to exercise the option, the tax treatment of the option payment previously received depends upon whether or not the option payment is to be forfeited. If the seller retains the option consideration, it is taxed to him as ordinary income in the year the option expired.[137] But if the option payment is returned to the optionee, it is treated as the non-deductible return of a security deposit by the optionor, and as a non-taxable return of funds by the optionee.[138]

Example: Seller grants Buyer an option to buy an apartment building for a price of $70,000 exercisable at any time within six months. B pays $2,000 for the option. If we assume that S's basis for the apartment plus expenses of sale total $50,000, we find that S may have the following amounts of income or gain to report, depending upon whether or not the option is exercised:

1. Granting of Option
S reports neither gain nor income.

2. Failure of Option
Ordinary income to S $ 2,000

3. Exercise of Option

Price received on sale	$70,000	
Plus option consideration	2,000	$72,000
Less basis and expenses		50,000
Gain realized on sale		$22,000

---

[134] C.A. Cochran, 23 B.T.A. 616, 619 (1931), appeal dismissed, 67 F.2d 988 (6th Cir. 1933).

[135] Estate of Mary G. Gordon, 17 T.C. 427 (1951), aff'd per curiam, 201 F.2d 171 (6th Cir. 1952). See Hirsch Improvement Co. v. Commissioner, 143 F.2d 912 (2d Cir. 1944), cert. den. 323 U.S. 750; Gilken Corp. v. Commissioner, 176 F.2d 141, 145 (6th Cir. 1949).

[136] Aiken v. Commissioner, 35 F.2d 620, 624 (8th Cir. 1929), aff'd on other grounds, 282 U.S. 277 (1931). See Bourne v. Commissioner, 62 F.2d 648 (4th Cir. 1933), cert. den. 290 U.S. 650; Veenstra & DeHaan Coal Co., 11 T.C. 964, 967 (1948), acq. 1949-1 C.B. 4; Sophia M. Garretson, 10 B.T.A. 1381 (1928), acq. VII-2 C.B. 14.

[137] Reg. Sec. 1.1234-1(b).

[138] See Clinton Hotel Realty Corp. v. Commissioner, 128 F.2d 968 (5th Cir. 1942).

3. Advantages to Seller of Option

The use of an option contract may fill either of two basic objectives of a seller. First, it may permit him to receive a part of the total consideration for the property in a year prior to the year of sale without liability for a tax on the payment. No tax will become due until the later year in which the option is exercised or forfeited.

Of course, this device cannot be used to justify the tax-free receipt of an "option payment" that constitutes a substantial proportion of the total sales price for the property. The receipt of an unusually large option payment in relationship to the sales price would undoubtedly be attacked by the Commissioner as representing the down payment made by the buyer on the sale.

A second major objective that might be served by an option contract would be to postpone the date of sale until after the running of the one year holding period for capital gains. To achieve such a result the option contract must be carefully drawn so that the prospective buyer is not bound to pay all of the sales price; he must have a real choice between exercising the option and forfeiting his right to buy. In the absence of such a choice, the option payment would probably be challenged as the down payment of a completed sale entered into prior to the running of the holding period.[139]

E. ESCROW SALES

Intelligent use of an escrow will enable a seller to control the taxable year in which the sales proceeds are to be reported by him for tax purposes. The date of sale will establish the date on which the seller must account for the sales price. But in real estate transactions the date of sale is not always easily determined; it may be any one of the following:

Date of the contract of sale;
Date of the deposit of the deed in escrow;
Date of the deposit of the purchase price in escrow;
Date of title clearance;
Date of issuance of title insurance;
Date of close of escrow;
Date of recording deed; or
Date of transfer of possession.

Because the time involved in carrying out these steps in the sale may range from a minimum of one day to several months, the parties have it within their power to control the actual date of sale for tax purposes.

1. General Rule: Closing of Escrow

For most purposes, the date of the closing of the sales escrow is taken as the date of sale; title to the property passes to the purchaser and the sales price is delivered to the seller. The sale is complete for tax purposes and the seller must account for the sales

---
[139] Deal v. Morrow, 197 F.2d 821 (5th Cir. 1952).

price on that date.[140] The fact that the parties may previously have executed a contract of sale and the purchaser may have paid a deposit will not affect the date of sale; that date is controlled by the close of the escrow.[141]

Obviously, the general rule permits some latitude in timing the sale. As long as the escrow is held open, the seller will not be taxed on the gain to be realized. The seller may, for example, benefit from the closing of the escrow in the tax year following the year in which the contract of sale was executed; the tax on the gain from the sale would be reportable in the later year. Or the seller may wish to hold the escrow open until the one year holding period for long-term capital gains has expired. In either event, the escrow may permit him to realize his objectives.

But the misuse of the escrow device has given rise to some qualifying exceptions which we shall consider in the following sections. If the escrow is a device having no purpose other than the postponement of the receipt of gain by the seller, it will probably be found insufficient to accomplish its purpose. The escrow arrangement must be a bona fide one calling for the performance of substantial conditions by both parties; only under these circumstances will the seller be entitled to rely upon the date of the escrow closing as the date of sale.[142]

2. Exception: Deposit of Purchase Price

Suppose, for example, the buyer and seller have executed a contract of sale and the seller has placed a good and sufficient deed to the premises to escrow to be delivered just after the close of the taxable year. Prior to the close of the year, the purchaser approves the title to the property and deposits the purchase price in escrow. On the first business day of the new year, the escrow holder delivers the funds to the seller and the deed to the buyer.

Under these facts, the seller would be taxed on the sale as if it were completed in the earlier year, at the time the buyer put his money in escrow.[143] At that time, both parties had completed their performances under the contract of sale; nothing remained to be done except the formal closing of the escrow. Thus, the seller had an unconditional right to the sales proceeds in the earlier year; for the purposes of taxation he had constructively received these proceeds prior to the close of the earlier tax year.

How can the premature closing of the sale be avoided? Obviously, if the purchaser has not completed his examination of the title and has retained the right to withdraw his purchase price should title prove defective, the sale could not be considered closed merely because the seller has deposited his deed in escrow. Until the purchaser has indicated his satisfaction with the title he is buying, the sale would remain executory.[144]

---

[140]E. K. Wood Lumber Co., 25 B.T.A. 1013, 1024 (1932), acq. on another point, XI-2 C.B. 10 R.M. Waggoner, 9 B.T.A. 629 (1927), non-acq. VII-1 C.B. 41; L.O. 1082, I-1 C.B. 80.

[141]Newaygo Portland Cement Co., 27 B.T.A. 1097, 1105 (1933), acq. XII-1 C.B. 9, aff'd on other grounds, 77 F.2d 536 (D.C.Cir. 1935).

[142]Rev. Rul. 72-256, 1972-1 C.B. 222.

[143]Williams v. United States, 219 F.2d 523 (5th Cir. 1955); Commissioner v. Moir, 45 F.2d 356 (7th Cir. 1930); William Holden, 6 B.T.A. 605 (1927).

[144]Bedell v. Commissioner, 30 F.2d 622 (2d Cir. 1929); George I. Bumbaugh, 10 B.T.A. 672 (1928). R. M. Waggoner, 9 B.T.A. 629 (1927), non-acq. VII-1 C.B. 41.

Other conditions imposed upon the payment of the purchase price to the seller would also serve to prevent the sale from being treated as a closed transaction prior to the close of the escrow. For example, the seller's broker may have the right to take his commissions out of the escrow proceeds; until these commissions are determined and paid over to the broker, the sale will not be deemed to be closed.[145]

On the other hand, the right of the purchaser to satisfy himself as to the state of title need not necessarily postpone the effective date of the sale. If the seller can get the purchaser to agree to accept delivery of the deed, subject to the right of rescission in the event the title is found to be defective, the effective date of sale will be the date of the close of the escrow and the transfer of title. At that time, the seller receives the purchase price under a claim of right; the fact that he may later be compelled to restore the purchase price to the buyer on a rescission of the contract will not postpone the effective date of the sale for tax purposes.[146]

What he should do to protect himself is to refuse to execute the deed until the beginning of the new taxable year in which he wants the gain to be reported.[147]

3. Exception: Transfer of Possession

Suppose, for example, the buyer and the seller execute a contract of sale; pending the close of escrow, the purchaser takes possession of the premises under an informal agreement to pay taxes, interest and maintenance charges. The contract of sale calls for the payment of the purchase price just after the close of the taxable year. The purchaser places his money in escrow, and on the first business day of the new taxable year, the seller deposits his deed in escrow and receives payment of the purchase price.

Again, the sale would be treated as having been completed in the earlier taxable year.[148] The transfer of possession, coupled with the assumption of the burdens of ownership by the purchaser under an unconditional contract of sale are sufficient to close the sale for tax purposes. The retention of bare legal title in the seller will not be sufficient to hold the transaction open.

But the converse does not seem to be true. Even if the seller retains possession and continues to assume the burdens of ownership after transferring title, the sale will be deemed to have closed on the transfer of title.[149]

---

[145] Ruling superseded, Rev. Rul. 68-575, 1968-2 C.B. 603, p. 606; without explanation.
[146] Frost Lumber Industries, Inc. v. Commissioner, 128 F.2d 693 (5th Cir. 1942).
[147] Commissioner v. Union Pacific Ry Co., 86 F.2d 637, 639 (2d Cir. 1936); Dakota Creek Lumber & Shingle Co., 26 B.T.A. 940 (1932); Harris Trust & Savings Bank, 24 B.T.A. 203 (1928), acq. on another ground VII-2 C.B. 30.
[148] The doctrine of constructive receipt does not extend to constructive payment other than in the limited area of disallowances under Section 267, I.R.C.
[149] Bernard Long, 1 B.T.A. 792 (1925).

6
Tax Aspects of Mortgage Financing

In today's economy we find mortgage financing of transactions in real estate to be very popular. There are many reasons for this popularity, but we are here concerned only with the tax aspects of such financing. As we develop the rules relating to the tax consequences of using borrowed money, we shall find that part of the popularity of mortgage financing is due to the tax laws. Thus, our survey will be concerned with such matters as the following:

A. *The advantages of using borrowed money to purchase real estate: although the money borrowed is not taxed as income to the borrower, it may become taxable upon the sale or other disposition of the property;*

B. *The effect upon basis of property acquired subject to a mortgage: the mortgage debt can be included in the owner's basis for the property even though he is not personally liable for its payment;*

C. *Interest, penalties, and commissions paid by the owner of mortgaged property as qualifying for deduction as an expense or amortization allowance;*

D. *Property "mortgaged out" without tax liability at the time of borrowing: can such property be disposed of without a tax upon the amount borrowed in excess of basis?;*

E. *The usefulness of, and limitations upon, contributing property mortgaged in excess of basis to a partnership;*

F. *The disadvantages of attempting to contribute property mortgaged in excess of basis to a corporation;*

G. *And, in summary, the basic tax advantages of mortgage financing in real estate transactions.*

A. PLACING A MORTGAGE UPON PROPERTY

Suppose an owner of certain real property mortgages it to secure a loan of money borrowed by him. Does the act of mortgaging the property affect his basis for it? Does the transaction give rise to taxable income? Does it make any difference if the proceeds of the mortgage loan exceed his cost so that he "mortgages out" on the property? How are his costs of obtaining the mortgage loan treated? These and other related questions will concern us here.

1. Effect Upon Income

The placing of a mortgage upon property already owned by the mortgagor does not create taxable income. Although the mortgagor may have received cash out of the transaction, he is under obligation to repay the same amount to the mortgagee. Hence, the transaction is treated as any other loan which a debtor is obliged to repay.[1]

Nor is the result altered by the fact that the owner may have "mortgaged out" his entire cost basis in the property. Even if the debt secured by the property exceeds his basis for it, the borrowing does not create taxable income.[2]

2. Effect Upon Basis

Correspondingly, the owner's basis for the mortgaged property is not directly affected by the placing of the mortgage against it. This conclusion holds true not only for the normal situation but also for the unusual case where the owner mortgages the property to secure a loan larger than his basis for the property.[3]

The owner's basis may be indirectly affected by the loan if the borrowed money is used to improve the property; under these circumstances the increase in basis is due to the capitalization of the expenditures actually made for the improvements, not to the fact that the moneys used were borrowed funds secured by a mortgage against the property.[4]

3. Effect to Owner on Disposition

Because the owner's basis is not affected by the mortgaging of the property, he is deemed to receive the amount outstanding on the mortgage debt at the time he sells or otherwise disposes of the property.[5] The amount realized by him on the sale or other disposition includes not only the cash received, but also the amount of "debt reduction" enjoyed by the owner as a result of the transaction. To the extent his debts are reduced by transfer to the buyer, the seller has received the equivalent of cash. As a result, the gain to be realized out of the property is postponed from the time of mortgaging to the time of disposition.

---

[1] See Helvering v. Roth, 115 F.2d 239, 240 (2d Cir. 1940); Al Goodman, Inc., 23 T.C. 288, 302 (1954), acq. 1955-2 C.B. 4; Victor Shaken, 2 T.C. 785 (1945), acq. 1954-2 C.B. 5. And, see, James v. United States, 336 U.S. 213, 81 S.Ct. 1052 (1961).

[2] Woodsam Associates v. Commissioner, 198 F.2d 357, 359 (2d Cir. 1952); Mendham Corporation, 9 T.C. 320, 323 (1952).

[3] Woodsam Associates v. Commissioner, 198 F.2d 357, 359 (2d Cir. 1952).

[4] Marion A. Blake, 8 T.C. 546, 555 (1947), acq. 1947-2 C.B. 1.

[5] Mendham Corporation, 9 T.C. 320, 323 (1947); Lutz & Schramm Co., 1 T.C. 682, 688 (1943), non-acq. on another issue, 1943 C.B. 35; Woodsam Associates, 198 F.2d 357, 359 (2d Cir. 1952); Simon v. Commissioner, 285 F.2d 422 (3rd Cir. 1961); Smith v. Commissioner, 324 F.2d 725 (9th Cir. 1963).

Example: Assume Owner borrows $20,000 on certain unimproved real property that originally cost him $15,000. At the time of borrowing, O neither realizes the $5,000 of potential gain nor does he need to adjust his $15,000 cost basis. Later, O sells his remaining equity in the property for $7,000. O's gain is computed as follows:

Sales proceeds:		
Cash received	$ 7,000	
Outstanding indebtedness	20,000	$27,000
Basis for the property		15,000
O's gain on the sale		$12,000

Although O has had the use of $5,000 of the eventual gain on the property at the time of the mortgage, he is not taxed upon that portion of the gain until he sells the property. Then out of the relatively small payment he receives for his equity, he must pay a tax upon the entire gain, including the portion received earlier, because his liability for the $20,000 indebtedness has been transferred to the purchaser.

4. Release of Liability as Disposition

Suppose after "mortgaging out" a parcel of property, the owner obtains a release of liability. Is he taxable upon the potential gain at the time he obtains the release?

In *Woodsam Associates*[6] just this occurred. The owner had bought property at a cost of $325,000. Later, he refinanced the property by increasing the outstanding mortgage indebtedness to $400,000. At the same time, he obtained a release of personal liability on all the mortgages. In a subsequent transaction, the mortgagor claimed his basis should have been adjusted to $400,000 because the refinancing coupled with a release of personal liability was tantamount to a sale or exchange of the property. The court rejected the owner's analysis to hold that the release of liability was not a disposition of the mortgaged property for this purpose. The refinancing resulted in neither the realization of gain nor the increase of basis. The postponed gain is not realized for tax purposes until the property is sold, exchanged, or otherwise transferred.

5. Cost of Placing a Mortgage on Property

The costs of placing a mortgage upon property are not deductible as expenses in the year paid. But the owner may be entitled to amortize these costs over the life of the mortgage loan if the loan is made in connection with trade or business property or property used for the production of income.[7] For this purpose, mortgage costs include such items as commissions, bonuses, brokerage fees, and other expenses of obtaining the loan, including points except on a personal residence.

The amortization deduction is normally taken as an annual pro rata allowance of the mortgage costs over the projected life of the mortgage. Thus, if the property is sold

---

[6]198 F.2d 357, 359 (2d Cir. 1952). Accord, Lutz & Schramm Co., 1 T.C. 682, 689, non-acq. on another issue, 1943 C.B. 35.

[7]Julia Stow Lovejoy, 18 B.T.A. 1179 (1930); Emil W. Carlson, 24 B.T.A. 868 (1931); Sayers F. Harman, 4 T.C. 335, 347 (1944), acq. on another point 1945 C.B. 3.

prior to the date on which the mortgage loan is repaid, the unamortized remainder of the costs becomes deductible in full in the year of sale.[8] Whether or not the purchaser assumes the mortgage debt is immaterial to the owner's right to deduct the unamortized balance of his costs in the year of sale.[9]

These costs are not added to the owner's basis for the property but are amortized as a separate deduction against income. Thus, on the sale of the property, the unamortized balance is not treated as an offset to the gross proceeds received. This balance qualifies as a deduction against ordinary income in the year of sale.[10] Even if the proceeds from the sale are reported on the installment method, the unamortized balance of the costs will be deductible in full in the year of sale; they need not be prorated over the life of the installment contract.[11]

Example: Debtor borrows $40,000 repayment of which is secured by a mortgage against property to be developed as an apartment. D paid $500 as a commission for arranging the loan, $125 for title insurance in favor of Creditor, and $75 in legal fees. Suppose the life of the loan is ten years. His annual allowance for amortization of the total $700 cost of the loan is $70, or one-tenth per year. At the end of three years, D sells the property. His deduction for the unamortized balance is computed as follows:

Total mortgage costs	$700
Less portion allowed (3 × $70)	210
Deduction in year of sale	$490

But this favorable rule does not extend to sales under an executory contract of sale in which the seller reserves title pending complete payment. Under these circumstances, the seller must continue to take his regular amortization allowance until the contract of sale if fully executed.[12] The reason is the substantial possibility of reacquisition.

Costs of renewing[13] or extending[14] an existing mortgage loan are similarly recoverable by amortization over the life of the renewed or extended loan.

Suppose the mortgage loan is taken out against non-business property, such as a residence. If the loan is used for personal purposes, such as the purchase of the residence, then the costs of the mortgage will be neither deductible nor amortizable by the owner. These costs are treated as a personal expense to him.[15]

Nor are these mortgage costs to be added to the owner's basis for his residence. The mortgage fees "do not represent cost of property, but represent cost of the use of money borrowed."[16]

---

[8]S. & L. Building Corp., 19 B.T.A. 788 (1930), acq. X-1 C.B. 60, aff'd on another point, 288 U.S. 406 (1933); Longview Hilton Hotel Co., 9 T.C. 180 (1947), acq. 1947-2 C.B. 3 (dissolution of corporate borrower).

[9]See Metropolitan Properties Corp., 24 B.T.A. 220, 225 (1931), acq. XI-1 C.B. 5.

[10]S. & L. Building Corp., 19 B.T.A. 788, 795 (1930), acq. X-1 C.B. 60, aff'd on another point. 288 U.S. 406 (1933).

[11]S. & L. Building Corp., 19 B.T.A. 788, 795 (1930), acq. X-1 C.B. 60, aff'd on another point, 288 U.S. 406 (1933).

[12]Clinton Park Development Co. v. Commissioner, 209 F.2d 951 (5th Cir. 1954).

[13]Sigmund Spitzer, 23 B.T.A. 776, 778 (1931).

[14]M.P. Klyce, 41 B.T.A. 191, (1940), non-acq. on another point, 1940-1 C.B. 7.

[15]Section 262, I.R.C.

[16]S. & L. Building Corp., 19 B.T.A. 788, 795, (1930), acq. X-1 C.B. 60, aff'd on another point, 288 U.S. 406 (1933).

But the fact that residential property is used as security for the loan will not deprive the owner of his right to amortize the costs of the mortgage in any case in which the loan proceeds are used in his trade or business. Provided the loan is a business loan, he will be entitled to amortize his mortgage costs over its life regardless of the personal nature of the security he puts up.[17] The amortization amount is deductible.[18]

To the extent that "points" are paid in order to pay for service of the lender, the points must be capitalized at the time of payment; recovery of the cost of the points is by amortization over the life of the loan.[19]

B. ACQUIRING MORTGAGED PROPERTY

The problems to be discussed in this part concern the rules relating to the acquisition of property subject to an outstanding mortgage indebtedness. For instance, what is the basis of property so acquired to the purchaser? Does it make any difference if he does not assume personal liability for the indebtedness? And what happens if the indebtedness is subsequently reduced?

1. Basis of Property Acquired

Property purchased subject to a mortgage has a basis in the hands of the purchaser equal to the total purchase price paid, including both the purchaser's cash outlay and the principal amount of any liabilities against the property or assumed by the purchaser.[20] Property acquired in a *taxable* exchange takes a basis in the hands of the recipient equal to the *value* of the property given up, plus the principal amount of any indebtedness assumed or subject to which the property is taken.[21] If the *exchange* is tax-free, a different rule applies. The recipient's basis for the property acquired equals his *basis* for the transferred property formerly owned by him plus the amount of any mortgage indebtedness outstanding against the property acquired.[22]

Mortgaged property acquired by inheritance has a basis in the hands of the heir or devisee equal to its value at the time of the decedent's death, unreduced by the amount of any mortgage indebtedness outstanding.[23] Or, stated conversely, the basis to the heir includes both the value of the equity at the time of death plus the outstanding mortgage indebtedness.

2. Effect on the Basis if Mortgage Liability Not Assumed

Whether or not the acquirer of the property assumes the outstanding mortgage debt is immaterial for the purpose of determining his basis. In either case, the basis will

---

[17] See Corrine S. Koshland, 19 T.C. 860 (1953), aff'd per curiam, 216 F.2d 751 (9th Cir. 1954). Cf. United States v. Wharton, 207 F.2d 526 (5th Cir. 1953).
[18] Rev. Rul. 69-188, 1969-1 C.B. 54.
[19] Rev. Rul. 69-582, 1969-2 C.B. 29.
[20] Stollberg Hardware Co., 46 B.T.A. 788, 749 (1942), acq. 1942-1 C.B. 16. See United States v. Hendler, 303 U.S. 564 (1938).
[21] Victory Glass, Inc., 17 T.C. 381, 386 (1951).
[22] Section 1031(d), I.R.C.
[23] Crane v. Commissioner, 331 U.S. 1 (1947).

be the property's cost or other basis on acquisition, unreduced by the amount of the mortgage debt.[24] One of the important consequences of this rule lies in the matter of computing the owner's depreciation allowance upon property acquired subject to a mortgage debt.[25]

Example: Suppose Purchaser buys an apartment for a total cash outlay of $20,000. The apartment is taken subject to a mortgage of $80,000, which P does not assume. If we suppose that $30,000 of the total $100,000 invested in the apartment represents land cost, what will P's basis for the purpose of depreciation be?

P's basis for the property:		
Cash paid	$20,000	
Mortgage on property	80,000	$100,000
Less portion of basis allocable to land		30,000
Basis allocable to depreciable improvements		$ 70,000

These rules permit the owner of mortgaged property to depreciate the entire investment in the property (less the portion allocated to land), whether or not he himself made that investment or assumed liability for it. He is permitted to depreciate not only his cash outlay in the property but also the investment made by others.

3. Basis for the Purpose of Subsequent Sales

What happens on a sale of property by an owner who had not assumed liability for the mortgage debt? Is he treated as a seller of merely his equity or of the entire property?

Example: Suppose we take the facts of the preceding example. P's basis was determined to be $100,000, of which $70,000 was allocated to improvements. If the remaining life of the apartment is 35 years, P's annual depreciation allowance on the straight-line method would be $2,000. Suppose P holds the property for 12 years, recovering $24,000 of depreciation. He then sells his equity for $10,000. His basis for his equity will by then have been reduced to zero, because he has recovered $24,000 on an investment of his own of but $20,000. Unless he is required to pick up all of the depreciation taken by him in the sale, he will have received a free ride to the extent that the depreciation allowed to him exceeded his investment in the property:

Cash received for P's equity		$10,000
P's cost for his equity	$20,000	
Less depreciation taken	24,000	—0—
Gain on sale of equity		$10,000
Excess depreciation not charged to P		$ 4,000

Obviously, such a computation of P's gain is not proper. For this reason, P's gain is figured on the assumption that he sold the entire property. The proceeds of sale include not only the price received for his equity but also the amount of any indebtedness outstanding against the property at the time of sale.

---

[24]Crane v. Commissioner, 331 U.S. 1 (1947). It is necessary to show that the liability is against the particular property acquired and that it is not so contingent as to be unrealistic. Columbus and Greenville R.R., 42 T.C. 834, 848 (1964), aff'd 358 F.2d 294 (5th Cir. 1966), cert. den. 385. U.S. 827. However, a 99 year mortgage debt, even though not assumed, was held part of the owner's basis in Manuel D. Mayerson, 47 T.C. 340, 353 (1966), acq. 1969-1 C.B. 21. Rev. Rul. 69-77, 1969-1 C.B. 59.

[25]David F. Bolger, 59 T.C. 760 (1973), appeal by Commissioner dismissed.

ACQUIRING MORTGAGED PROPERTY

Example: The proper computation of P's gain in the preceding example is as follows:

Proceeds received by P on sale:		
Cash received	$10,000	
Debt against property	80,000	$90,000
Less P's basis for the property:		
Original basis	$100,000	
Less depreciation	24,000	76,000
Gain realized on sale		$14,000

For the purpose of computing his gain or loss on the sale of mortgaged property, the owner must take into account the principal amount of any indebtedness against the property as a part of the gross proceeds realized. The "amount realized" on the sale includes both the cash received and the balance owing on the mortgage.[26]

4. Payments Made by Owner on the Mortgage Debt

Because the owner's basis under these rules includes the entire amount of the mortgage indebtedness at the time of acquisition, any payments made by him on the debt after acquisition do not affect his basis.[27] These payments have already been taken into account in the determination of his original basis for the property.

But we should note, these payments will be reflected as a reduction in the amount of proceeds received on a later sale of the property. To the extent that the mortgage debt is paid off prior to sale, the amount realized on the sale will be correspondingly reduced.[28] Only the amount of debt reduced at *time of sale* becomes part of the sale proceeds.

Example: Owner inherited property having a value for estate tax purposes of $80,000. This property when inherited was subject to a mortgage of $70,000. O paid $20,000 in installments on the mortgage debt and then sold his equity for $40,000. In the interim O had the benefit of $25,000 of depreciation allowances. What is his gain?

Proceeds received on sale:		
Cash received		$40,000
Plus balance of mortgage debt:		
Original debt	$70,000	
Less payments	20,000	50,000
Total proceeds received		$90,000
Less O's basis for the property:		
Original basis	$80,000	
Less depreciation	25,000	55,000
O's gain on the sale		$35,000

5. Payment of Condemnation Proceeds on Mortgage Property

A startling illustration of the foregoing principle is provided by the condemnation of mortgaged property. If the property is completely taken, the condemning authority will normally cause the proceeds to be paid first to the mortgagee, to the extent of the

---

[26] Crane v. Commissioner, 331 U.S. 1, 13 (1947).
[27] Blackstone Theatre Co., 12 T.C. 801 (1949), acq. 1949-2 C.B. 1.
[28] See, e.g., Parker v. Delaney, 186 F.2d 455, 458 (1st Cir. 1950), cert. den. 341 U.S. 926.

outstanding mortgage debt, and the balance to the mortgagor owner of the property. Despite this splitting of the proceeds between himself and the mortgagee, the mortgagor is required for tax purposes to report the entire condemnation award as the proceeds realized on the sale.[29] Nor is the mortgagor entitled to increase his basis for the property by the mortgagee's share of the condemnation proceeds; the mortgagor has already had the benefit either of receiving the mortgage proceeds tax-free if he borrowed the money, or of including the outstanding mortgage debt in his basis if he acquired the property subject to it.

The mortgagor must, therefore, account for the entire condemnation award as a part of the amount realized upon the condemnation ". . . regardless of whether or not (he) was personally liable for the mortgage debt."[30]

Example: Owner acquired property worth $100,000 subject to a $50,000 mortgage. Owner paid $50,000 in cash for the equity and took the property subject to the mortgage which he did *not* assume. Thereafter, prior to any payments on the mortgage debt, the property was condemned. A value of $110,000 was placed on the property and a gross award of that amount was made to the parties. However, $50,000 was paid directly to the mortgagee, and owner received only $60,000. For the purposes of computing his gain or loss on the condemnation sale, owner must account for the entire $110,000 as follows:

Proceeds received on sale:		
Cash received	$60,000	
Mortgage debt relief	50,000	$110,000
Less basis for property		100,000
Gain on sale		$ 10,000

6. Reinvestment of Condemnation Proceeds Received on Mortgaged Property

It is possible to postpone taxation on gain realized on a condemnation sale or conversion by reinvesting the proceeds in property that qualifies as "similar or related in service or use" to the property taken or destroyed. Where the property taken was burdened by a mortgage, the owner must reinvest an amount equal to the gross proceeds realized including not only his share, but the share paid to his mortgagee.[31]

Example: Under the facts of the foregoing example, it would be necessary for the owner to acquire qualified replacement property for a cost of at least $110,000 in order to prevent being taxed on his gain. If, on the other hand, he merely reinvested the $60,000 actually received by him for his equity, he would be taxed on $10,000 of gain as follows:

Proceeds received on sale:		
Cash received	$ 60,000	
Mortgage debt relief	50,000	$110,000
Less basis for property		100,000
Gain on sale		$ 10,000

---

[29]Reg. Sec. 1.1033(a)-2(c)(11).

[30]Reg. Sec. 1.1033(a)-2(c)(11).

[31]Commissioner v. Fortee Properties, Inc., 211 F.2d 915 (2d Cir. 1954), cert. den. 348 U.S. 826. But in Commissioner v. Babcock, 259 F.2d 689 (4th Cir. 1958), the Court held that the mortgagor-owner (who had not assumed personal liability) was required to account merely for the share of the condemnation proceeds paid for his equity. The Commissioner has published a non-acquiescence to the decision below to the same effect. See Frank W. Babcock, 28 T.C. 781 (1957), non-acq. 1959-1 C.B. 6.

ACQUIRING MORTGAGED PROPERTY

Excess of proceeds over cost of replacement:		
Proceeds received	$110,000	
Replacement cost	60,000	$ 50,000
Gain taxed (not in excess of $50,000)		$ 10,000

Despite the conflict in the cases, the regulations are clear: reinvestment must be of the entire condemnation award including the mortgagee's share.[32] But this rule is no longer as harsh as it was before Congress liberalized the rules for reinvestment. At one time, it was necessary to trace the condemnation proceeds into the purchase price of the replacement property.[33] Since 1950, this requirement is no longer the law. At the present time, all that is required is that the owner acquire replacement property within the period established by law. It makes no difference whether the owner uses the condemnation proceeds, other funds, or his credit to acquire the replacement property. Accordingly, the mortgagor-owner can shelter his condemnation gain from immediate tax by using the amount received for his equity as a down payment on a property costing at least as much as the condemnation proceeds subject to a mortgage debt for the balance.[34]

Example: Owner in the preceding examples uses the $60,000 portion of the condemnation award received by him to purchase qualified replacement property that costs $120,000. O is able to arrange favorable financing and, accordingly, is required to pay only $40,000 down, financing the $80,000 balance on a first mortgage. Although O is able to pocket $20,000 of the cash condemnation proceeds for his equity on the transactions, no part of the $10,000 gain realized on the condemnation sale is immediately taxable. The $20,000 cash he pockets is received by him tax-free just as if he borrowed it.

Proceeds received on condemnation:		
Cash for equity	$60,000	
Mortgage debt relief	50,000	$110,000
Cost of replacement property:		
Cash paid	$40,000	
Mortgage debt	80,000	$120,000
Excess of proceeds received on replacement cost		—0—
Amount of $10,000 gain taxed		—0—

7. Effect of a Reduction in the Mortgage Debt (Other than by Payment)

What happens if the mortgage debt is reduced by forgiveness after the purchaser has acquired his property? Does such a reduction affect his basis for the property, and, if so, in what manner?

Generally, it has been held that a forgiveness in a purchase money mortgage does not produce income; the forgiveness merely has the effect of compelling the owner of the property to reduce his basis for the property by an amount which corresponds to the

---

[32] Reg. Secs. 1.1033(a)-2(c)(11), 1.033(a)-3(d).

[33] See Reg. Sec. 1.1033(a)-3(c) dealing with pre-1951 conversions. See, also, Wala Garage v. United States, 163 F.Supp. 379 (Ct.Cl. 1958).

[34] Reg. Sec. 1.1033(a)-2(c) provides ". . . gain, if any, shall be recognized, at the election of the taxpayer, only to the extent that *the amount realized* upon such conversion *exceeds* the *cost* of other (replacement) property."

amount of forgiveness in the purchase money obligation. This result has been reached not only in cases in which the obligation is owed to the seller,[35] but also in cases in which the purchase money mortgagee is a third party.[36]

The same rule has been applied to any forgiveness in the mortgage debt which occurs at a time that the property is owned by a mortgagor who is not personally liable on the mortgage debt. The only effect of the forgiveness to a non-assuming mortgagor is to require him to reduce basis by an equivalent amount.[37]

How has this basis reduction been put into effect? If the mortgagor has taken depreciation measured by his original basis up to the time of the reduction, is he required to file amended returns to adjust for excessive depreciation taken?

Blackstone Theater Co.[38] is a case which presents this problem. A purchaser had bought property subject to a number of outstanding tax liens which were correctly included in his basis for the property. After a year or two of operating the property, he was able to pick up the tax liens at a considerable discount. He reduced his basis for the property accordingly. But the Commissioner assessed a deficiency against him for earlier years on the ground that the depreciation then taken was overstated. On petition to the Tax Court, the taxpayer successfully argued that the adjustment to basis should not be made retroactive. The Commissioner subsequently acquiesced.[39]

Example: P purchased property for $20,000, subject to a $40,000 mortgage. Of his total $60,000 basis, $50,000 was allocated to improvements. Assuming a 25-year remaining life, P took depreciation at the rate of $2,000 a year. Four years later P was able to settle his $40,000 debt for $34,000. His original $60,000 basis was thereby reduced to $54,000, of which five-sixths, or $45,000, would be attributed to improvements. For all years subsequent to the basis reduction, his depreciation allowance would be computed as follows:

Remaining basis at time of adjustment:		
Original basis of improvements	$50,000	
Less depreciation taken	8,000	$42,000
Less basis reduction (5/6 of amount of mortgage reduction)		5,000
Remaining basis after reduction		$37,000
Remaining life		22 years
Annual depreciation allowance thereafter		$ 1,682

Even if the mortgage reduction did not qualify for exclusion from income as a

---

[35] Helvering v. A.L. Killian Co., 128 F.2d 433 (8th Cir. 1942); Allen v. Courts, 127 F.2d 127 (5th Cir. 1942); Gehring Publishing Co., 1 T.C. 345, 354 :1942), acq. 1943 C.B. 9; Pinkney Packing Co., 42 B.T.A. 823, 829 (1940), acq. 1941-1 C.B. 8. An exception to this rule has been made in the case of a settlement for less than face of a mortgagee against property worth the price originally paid for it, not having subsequently depreciated in value.

[36] Hirsch v. Commissioner, 115 F.2d 656, 658 (7th Cir. 1940); Commissioner v. Sherman, 135 F.2d 68, 70 (6th Cir. 1943). Contra, Frank v. United States. 44 F.Supp 729 (D.C. Pa. 1942), aff'd 131 F.2d 864 (3rd Cir. 1942).

[37] Fulton Gold Corp., 31 B.T.A. 519 (1934); Hotel Astoria, Inc., 42 B.T.A. 759, 762 (1940), acq. 1940-2 C.B. 4; P.S. Hiatt, 35 B.T.A. 292, 296 (1937), acq. 1937-1 C.B. 12.

[38] 12 T.C. 801, 805 (1949), acq. 1949-2 C.B. 1.

[39] Acq. 1949-2 C.B.I.

purchase price reduction,[40] the owner would probably be entitled to take an election to adjust basis downward in lieu of reporting the income as provided under Sections 108 and 1017, I.R.C. Under these sections, the adjustment to basis is made prospective in effect only; it has no effect upon depreciation taken upon the property in earlier years, relating only to the year of adjustment and all subsequent years.[41]

C. MORTGAGE PAYMENTS, PENALTIES AND COMMISSIONS

This part deals with the tax characteristics of various payments and charges made by either the mortgagor or the mortgagee during the life of the mortgage.

1. Payment of Interest or Principal

Repayment of the principal of a mortgage debt is neither income to the mortgagee[42] nor a deductible expense to the mortgagor.[43] The payment of interest on a debt is both income to the mortgagee[44] and a deductible item to the mortgagor.[45]

Interest paid by an owner of property on a mortgage debt is deductible by him, even though he may not have assumed personal liability for the debt. The protection of his equity in the property is sufficient foundation in itself to justify his right to a deduction for interest paid.[46] Similarly, where the seller of mortgaged property remains personally and primarily liable on the mortgage debt under local law, and he actually pays the interest, he is entitled to the deduction for interest paid.[47]

Whenever interest is paid as interest and principal as principal, we can readily determine the tax consequences of the payments. But when both payments are combined into one, we must first allocate it into its component parts in order to decide how much is deductible interest and how much loan amortization. If, as in the case of most long-term principal amortization loans, payment is made in periodic installments, we must look first to any agreement between the parties which allocates each installment between principal and interest. Any allocation made pursuant to such agreement will govern the tax consequences of the payment.[48]

---

[40] See Amphitrite Corp., 16 T.C. 1140 (1951), acq. 1951-2 C.B. 1, where the purchase indebtedness became outlawed in part by the running of the statute of limitations. Such debt relief would be taxable income, not reduction in the purchase price. Securities Co. v. United States, 85 F.Supp. 532 (S.D.N.Y. 1948).

[41] Reg. Sec. 1.1017-(b)(4).

[42] See Charles H. Howell, 21 B.T.A. 757, 781 (1930), acq. X-1 C.B. 30, dismissed, 59 F.2d 1053 (8th Cir. 1932). [An exception arises, of course, when the repayment represents the collection of an amount earlier written off by the mortgagee as a bad debt. See Section 111, I.R.C.]

[43] John L. Hawkinson, 23 T.C. 933, 943 (1955), aff'd on another ground, 235 F.2d 747 (2d Cir. 1956).

[44] Section 61(a)(4), I.R.C.

[45] Section 163, I.R.C.

[46] New McDermott, Inc., 44 B.T.A. 1035, 1040 (1941), non-acq. 1954-1 C.B. 8; Reg. Sec. 1.163-1(a).

[47] Walther v. Commissioner, 316 F.2d 708 (7th Cir. 1963). But, see to the contrary J. Simpson Dean, 35 T.C. 1083 (1961), appeal dismissed.

[48] Huntington-Redondo Co., 36 B.T.A. 116 (1937), acq. 1937-2 C.B. 14; Annie B. Smith, Par. 53,046 P-H Memo. T.C. (1953); Marsh and Marsh, Inc., 5 B.T.A. 902 (1926).

2. Failure to Provide for Interest on Deferred Payments

If the buyer and seller of property fail to provide for a reasonable rate of interest of deferred payments of over six months,[49] the Service has the authority under Section 483 to impute a reasonable rate of interest.[50] The effect is to convert a portion of the principal payments into interest for all purposes, including interest income to the seller,[51] an interest deduction to the buyer, and a reduction of the selling price for purposes of an installment election under Section 453.[52]

3. Apportionment of Lump Sum Payments

Lump sum payments of principal and interest not subject to an existing amortization agreement provide more trouble. This difficulty may be dispelled by the parties by merely agreeing at the time of payment how much represents interest and how much principal. Such an agreement, if contemporaneous with payment, will control the allocation of the payment for tax purposes,[53] even though it may be contrary to the usual custom.[54]

But suppose the parties forgot to allocate the payment. How then will it be treated? Here we must look to other aids to solve our problem. If, for example, the statutes of the local jurisdiction establish a presumption that an unallocated payment is to be applied first to interest due, that presumption will fix the allocation for tax purposes.[55]

Generally, we find in this situation that the debtor has the first right to make an allocation of the payment as he sees fit. If he actually makes an allocation upon his books, his allocation will govern the tax consequences of the payment to the creditor.[56] In the absence of an allocation by the debtor, the creditor normally has the right to credit the payment to interest and principal as he sees fit; if he makes such an allocation, it will control.[57]

But suppose neither party makes an allocation. In the absence of other controlling indicia of the purpose of the payment the Commissioner is free to make his own allocation for tax purposes on the basis of what to him seems to be "the manner which most accords with the equity and justice of the particular case."[58] Needless to say, what is "equity and justice" to the Commissioner will probably be the allocation that

---

[49] Section 483(c), I.R.C. The section applies only to sales in excess of $3,000. Section 483(f), I.R.C.
[50] If a six percent rate of interest is not stated, a seven percent will be attributed to the sale. Reg. Sec. 1.483-1(c)(d).
[51] Section 483(a), (f)(3), I.R.C.
[52] Raymond Robinson, 54 T.C. 772, aff'd Robinson v. Commissioner 439 F.2d 767(8th Cir. 1971).
[53] Huntington-Redondo Co., 36 B.T.A. 116 (1937), acq. 1937-2 C.B. 14.
[54] Robert Hays Gries, Par. 50-125 P-H Memo T.C. (1950); Rev. Rul. 63-57, 1963-1 C.B. 103.
[55] Theodore R. Plunkett, 41 B.T.A. 700, 709 (1940), acq. 1940-1 C.B. 3, aff'd on another ground, 118 F.2d 644 (1st Cir. 1941); Estate of Paul M. Bowen, 2 T.C. 1,5 (1943), acq. 1943 C.B. 3; Millar Brainard, 7 T.C. 1180, 1185 (1946).
[56] Local law will govern.
[57] Weldon D. Smith, 17 T.C. 135, 144 (1951), reversed on other grounds, 203 F.2d 310 (2d Cir. 1953), cert. den. 346 U.S. 816.
[58] G.C.M. 2861 VII-1 C.B. 255, 257, declared obsolete. Rev. Rul. 68-674, 1968-2 C.B. 609.

produces the greatest amount of tax revenue. His determination of the proper allocation to be made will presumptively be correct,[59] subject to rebuttal only by production of evidence of an actual intent to the contrary.[60]

A retroactive allocation by agreement of the parties after the year of payment will not be sufficient to rebut the presumptive correctness of the Commissioner's allocation.[61] Allocation by agreement after payment, but before the close of the taxable year, has been held sufficient to fix the tax consequences of the payment.[62]

4. Delinquent Interest on Mortgage Debt

Suppose, at the time taxpayer purchases property subject to a mortgage, interest on the mortgage debt is overdue. Will he get a deduction for interest paid if he pays this overdue interest after acquiring the property? Unfortunately, no. Only interest that becomes due after he acquires the property will be deductible by him.[63] Delinquent interest paid by him is treated as a part of his cost of acquisition, to be capitalized as an addition to his basis for the property.[64]

Example: Purchaser bought an apartment for $60,000, of which $20,000 was paid in cash and $40,000 by the assumption of a mortgage debt against the property. At the time of purchase $1,000 of interest was delinquent. On acquiring the property P paid $1,167 to the mortgagee, which represented payment for the delinquent interest plus the current month's interest. How much is P's deduction for interest, and what is his basis for the property?

                1. Interest Deduction

Total interest payment	$1,167
Less delinquent interest	1,000
Current interest deduction	$ 167

                2. P's Basis

Cash outlay for the property	$20,000
Mortgage debt against property	40,000
Delinquent interest paid off	1,000
P's basis for the property	$61,000

The delinquent interest so paid by the purchaser, however, is deductible by the prior owner, who held the property when the interest became due. If the interest has not previously been deducted by the prior owner, it becomes deductible in the year in which the successor owner pays it.[65] The amount of delinquent interest paid by the buyer is correspondingly treated as additional sales proceeds to the seller.

---

[59]Weldon D. Smith, 17 T.C. 135, 144 (1951), reversed on other grounds, 203 F.2d 310 (2d Cir. 1953), cert. den. 346 U.S. 816.

[60]George S. Groves, 38 B.T.A. 727, 737 (1938), acq. on another ground, 1939-C.B. (Part 1) 15.

[61]Central Cuba Sugar Co., 198 F.2d 214, 217 (2d Cir. 1952), cert. den. 344 U.S. 874.

[62]Huntington-Redondo Co., 36 B.T.A. 116 (1937), acq. 1937-2 C.B. 14. Rev. Rul. 72-2, 1972-1 C.B. 19.

[63]Joell Co., 41 B.T.A. 825, 827 (1940), acq. 1940-2 C.B. 4; Walter H. Rich, Par. 36, 166 P-H Memo B.T.A. (1936).

[64]Rodney, Inc. v. Commissioner, 145 F.2d 692 (2d Cir. 1944).

[65]Norman Cooledge, 40 B.T.A. 1325, 1328 (1939), acq. 1940-1 C.B. 2.

5. Prepayment Penalties

Penalties paid by a mortgagor to permit prepayment of the mortgage loan are treated as the equivalent of interest income to the mortgagee. The penalty represents "an additional charge for the use of (the mortgagee's) money for a short period of time, rather than for a longer period as originally agreed upon at the time the money was borrowed."[66]

Adopting this theory of the nature of the prepayment penalty, the Commissioner has ruled that a prepayment penalty paid by a mortgagor is deductible as interest.[67] And this remains true even where the purpose of prepayment is to refinance with another lender; the penalty need not be amortized over the period of the new loan.[68]

6. Commissions, Fees, and Other Expenses

Finders' fees and other commissions paid by a bank or other lending institution for the acquisition of a loan must be capitalized as a part of the loan's cost; this cost may be written off over the life of the loan through the mechanics of an annual allowance for amortization.[69] The same rule applies to legal fees and brokerage fees incurred by institutional lenders in the acquisition of a loan.[70]

Similarly, the fees and commissions paid by individual lenders would also be amortizable over the projected life of the loan, if incurred in the individual's business.

But with individual lenders another problem arises. These fees are deductible as a business expense only if the mortgagee is engaged in the business of lending money, or if the loan constitutes a transaction entered into for profit. An illustration of the importance of this qualification is afforded by the case of *Clara Driscoll*.[71] There, the mortgagee made a loan to assist a private organization of which she was a member. Subsequently, she forgave the indebtedness and canceled the mortgage as a contribution to the organization. She deducted the entire amount of legal fees incurred in drawing up the mortgage papers in the year of cancellation. The Commissioner promptly disallowed the deduction as representing an additional cost of making her contribution to the organization. The Tax Court found that she made the original loan as a transaction for profit; her intent to make a gift of the loan proceeds arose later. Hence, the legal fees were properly deducted by her.

Clara Driscoll also points out that the remaining unamortized balance of these fees and commissions is deductible in the year of settlement if the loan is canceled prior to maturity.

Commissions, fees, and other expenses paid or incurred by the borrower in connection with his mortgage debt are also amortizable over the life of the mortgage debt, provided the debt was incurred in the mortgagor's trade or business or was used for the production of income.[72]

---

[66] General American Life Ins. Co., 25 T.C. 1265, 1267 (1956), acq. 1956-2 C.B. 5.
[67] Rev. Rul. 57-198, 1957-1 C.B. 194. Rev. Rul. 73-137, 1973-1 C.B. 68.
[68] The 12701 Shaker Blvd Co., 36 T.C. (1961), aff'd 312 F.2d 749 (6th Cir. 1963).
[69] Rev. Rul. 57-400, 1957-2 C.B. 520.
[70] See Reg. Sec. 1.1016-9(c).
[71] Clara Driscoll, Par. 44,021 P-H Memo T.C. (1944), aff'd on another ground, 147 F.2d 493 (5th Cir. 1945).
[72] Rev. Rul. 69-118, 1969-1 C.B. 54.

D. LIABILITIES IN EXCESS OF BASIS

This part deals with the perplexing problems arising out of transactions involving property mortgaged to secure a debt in excess of the owner's basis for the property. This situation may arise in either of two basic ways:

(1) The owner may have increased the financing against the property to take advantage of an increase in its value.

Example: Suppose Owner purchases an unimproved lot for $20,000, paying $10,000 cash and assuming an existing mortgage of $10,000. After five years the property doubles in value because of developments in the neighborhood. O then refinances the mortgage, increasing his borrowing against the property to $25,000. Unless O devotes the mortgage proceeds to the improvement of the property, the amount of the borrowing will not be reflected in his basis. If we assume O's basis is unaffected by the borrowing, the liabilities against the property ($25,000) will exceed its basis ($20,000) by $5,000.

(2) The owner may have depreciated the property in an amount greater than his cash investment in it.

Example: Assume that Owner purchases an apartment subject to a $90,000 mortgage for a net cash outlay of $10,000. Suppose O holds the property for 12 years, taking $24,000 depreciation on it. In this same period O pays off $10,000 of the mortgage debt. At the end of the holding period the relationship between the mortgage debt and basis would be as follows:

Remaining mortgage debt:		
Original debt	$ 90,000	
Less payments	10,000	$80,000
Remaining basis for property:		
Original basis	$100,000	
Less depreciation	24,000	76,000
Excess of debt over basis		$ 4,000

1. Sale of Property Mortgaged in Excess of Basis

As we saw previously, a sale of property mortgaged in excess of basis results in the realization of gain by the seller to the extent of the excess. The same result is reached whether or not the seller is personally liable for the mortgage debt[73] and whether the sale is voluntary or involuntary.[74]

Example: Suppose the Owner in the preceding example sells his equity in the property for a net cash price of $5,000. His gain would be computed as follows:

Sales price realized:			
Cash paid for equity		$ 5,000	
Plus mortgage debt:			
Original debt	$90,000		
Less payments	10,000	80,000	$85,000

---

[73]The result is questionable. Why should a non-liable buyer include as part of his sales proceeds a debt that he did not assume? Reg. Sec. 1.752(d) and (e) rule to the contrary.

[74]Crane v. Commissioner, 331 U.S. 1 (1947).

Less O's basis:		
Original basis	$100,000	
Less depreciation	24,000	76,000
Gain realized		$ 9,000

Thus, the seller realizes as gain not only the cash received for his equity but also the amount by which the liabilities against the property exceed his remaining basis for it at the time of sale.[75]

2. Taxable Exchange of Property Mortgaged in Excess of Basis

The same result holds in the case of exchanges of mortgaged property for unlike property. The most common example of such an exchange is the transfer of mortgaged property for the mortgage note held by the mortgagee.[76]

Example: Let us again take the facts of the preceding example. However, instead of selling the property, O conveys it to his mortgagee in satisfaction of the mortgage debt. Again O is held to have realized a gain to the extent of the excess of liabilites over basis, computed as follows:

Amount realized on exchange:		
Original mortgage debt	$ 90,000	
Less payments	10,000	$80,000
Less O's basis for property:		
Original basis	$100,000	
Less depreciation	24,000	76,000
Gain realized		$ 4,000

3. Non-taxable Exchange of Property Mortgaged in Excess of Basis

Nor can the gain inherent in this situation be avoided by a tax-free exchange of the property for like property. Under Section 1031(d), I.R.C. the amount of the liability against the property exchanged is treated as "boot" received by the owner.[77] Hence, the full amount of the gain will be recognized, despite the fact that the transfer otherwise qualifies as a tax-free exchange.

Example: Suppose we again refer to the basic facts of the preceding example, except that this time Owner exchanges the mortgaged apartment for a new unencumbered apartment worth $20,000. His gain is computed as follows:

Amount realized on exchange:			
Value of apartment received		$ 20,000	
Plus outstanding mortgage:			
Original debt	$90,000		
Less payments	10,000	80,000	$100,000
Less adjusted basis for old apartment:			
Original basis		$100,000	
Less depreciation		24,000	76,000
Gain realized			$ 24,000

---

[75] R. O'Dell & Sons v. Commissioner, 169 F.2d 247 (3rd Cir. 1948); Woodsam Associates, Inc. v. Commissioner, 198 F.2d 357 (2d Cir. 1952); Simon v. Commissioner, 285 F.2d 422 (3rd Cir.).
[76] Parker v. Delaney, 186 F.2d 455 (1st Cir. 1950), cert. den. 341 U.S. 926.
[77] Reg. Sec. 1.1031(d)-2.

LIABILITIES IN EXCESS OF BASIS

All of the gain realized will be recognized because the boot received, $80,000 of the outstanding mortgage, exceeds the gain realized. Owner will pay a tax not only upon the value of the apartment received ($20,000) but also upon the $4,000 excess of liabilities over basis.

Under the regulations, the liability transferred is treated as "other property or money" only if it exceeds the amount of any liability against the property received in the exchange.[78] In the event the liability against the property received exceeds the liability transferred, no part of the liability transferred is treated as boot. Hence, the potential gain arising in the case of property held subject to a mortgage in excess of basis may be postponed by exchanging the property for a parcel subject to a greater liability.

Example: Owner exchanges his apartment, having an adjusted basis to him of $76,000, subject to an $80,000 mortgage debt, for an apartment worth $120,000, subject to a $100,000 mortgage debt. The gain realized on this exchange is computed as follows:

Amount realized on exchange:		
Value of apartment received	$120,000	
Outstanding mortgage debt	80,000	$200,000
Less:		
Adjusted basis of old apartment	$ 76,000	
Liability against new apartment	100,000	176,000
Gain realized		$ 24,000

But none of the gain realized is recognized for tax purposes. Because the consideration received by O in the form of a transfer subject to a liability of $80,000 is offset by consideration given in the form of a receipt of property subject to a $100,000 liability, no part of the liability transferred is treated as "boot."

4. Abandonment of Property Mortgaged in Excess of Basis

Can realization of the gain inherent in the property be escaped by abandoning the property prior to foreclosure? If the property is conveyed to the mortgagee, the gain, if any, is realized at the time of conveyance on the theory of a taxable exchange.

Nor does it seem to make any difference if the property is worth less than the amount of liabilities against it. In applying the theory of a taxable exchange, the courts have been willing to ignore the economic realities of the transaction. The owner is taxed upon the potential gain in the property even if the equity he sells or exchanges is worthless. Regardless of the value of the equity, the owner is held to have realized the full amount of the debt outstanding against the property upon its conveyance to the mortgagee.[79]

Example: Suppose, under the facts of our example, Owner's property is worth only $60,000 after several years of operation. O has had the benefit of $24,000 depreciation and his basis for the property has been reduced to $76,000. Because the outstanding mortgage indebtedness is

---

[78] Reg. Sec. 1.1031(d)-2, Example (2)(b).
[79] See Woodsam Associates, Inc. v. Commissioner, 16 T.C. 649, 654 (1951), aff'd 198 F.2d 357 (2d Cir. 1952), where it appeared that the property was worth $61,000 less than the mortgage debt at the time of foreclosure. Similar facts existed in Lutz & Schramm Co., 1 T.C. 682, 689 (1943), non-acq. on another ground, 1943 C.B. 35. But see Crane v. Commissioner, 331 U.S. 1 (1947), footnote 37.

$80,000, O's equity is less than worthless. Yet, if O conveys the property to the mortgagee, he is taxed upon the realization of $4,000 of gain.

What if the owner abandons his equity in the property on the ground it is worthless? Because his equity is worthless, he faces no economic hardship in abandoning it, other than the loss of a possible cancellation of the mortgage debt. If he was not personally liable upon the debt, he can walk away from the property without fear of a deficiency judgment. But will his act of abandonment incur a tax upon the gain inherent in the property?

This problem was referred to in a footnote in the *Crane* decision in the following language:

> Obviously, if the value of the property is less than the amount of the mortgage, the mortgagor who is not personally liable cannot realize a benefit equal to the mortgage. Consequently, a different problem might be encountered where a mortgagor abandoned the property or transferred it subject to the mortgage without receiving boot.[80]

In cases in which mortgaged property has been abandoned at a loss, the owner's basis for measuring his loss has been limited to his basis for his equity.[81]

Example: Owner buys an equity in an apartment for $10,000, subject to a mortgage of $50,000. After a year or two of operation, O has difficulty in finding tenants and has the apartment appraised. Its value is only $40,000. If O abandons the property, his loss will be measured by the adjusted basis for his equity at the time of abandonment. Assuming he has taken $4,000 of depreciation, we find his loss to be computed as follows:

O's basis for his equity	$10,000
Less depreciation taken	4,000
O's abandonment loss	$ 6,000

The same theory, if applied to our case of property mortgaged in excess of basis, would give rise to no gain or loss.

Example: In our hypothetical example of the apartment mortgaged in excess of basis, we would have the following computation:

O's basis for his equity	$20,000
Less depreciation taken	24,000
O's abandonment loss	—0—
O's theoretical gain	$ 4,000

Can abandonment cause the realization of this theoretical gain? No court has so held. All of the cases dealing with this problem thus far have presented situations in which the owner has sold the property,[82] has lost it through foreclosure,[83] or has conveyed it to the mortgagee.[84]

---

[80] Crane v. Commissioner, 331 U.S. 1 (1947), footnote 37.

[81] See James B. Lapsley, 44 B.T.A. 1105, 1108 (1941), acq. 1941-2 C.B. 7. This decision preceded Crane v. Commissioner, 331 U.S. 1 (1947), and may be an unreliable reed for that reason.

[82] Crane v. Commissioner, 331 U.S. 1 (1947).

[83] R. O'Dell & Sons v. Commissioner, 169 F.2d 247 (3rd Cir. 1948); Woodsam Associates, Inc. v. Commissioner, 198 F.2d 357 (2d Cir. 1952).

[84] Lutz & Schramm Co., 1 T.C. 682 (1943), non-acq. on another ground, 1943 C.B. 35; Parker v. Delaney, 186 F.2d 455 (1st Cir. 1950), cert. den. 341 U.S. 926; Mendham Corp., 9 T.C. 320 (1947).

There are dicta in *Parka v. Delaney*[85] to the effect that, because the owner has had the benefit of depreciation deductions in excess of his basis for his equity, he is required to report these excess deductions as income when he disposes of the property, whether by abandonment or otherwise. He may convert this income into capital gain by selling or exchanging the property, but if he merely abandons it, the gain will be taxed as ordinary income.

Until this problem is worked out, it would seem proper to report the abandonment of the property without showing the transaction as giving rise to either taxable gain or deductible loss. An owner of such property should be cautioned that abandonment is no certain method of avoiding the tax upon the gain locked into the property by virtue of the excess of mortgage debt over basis.[86]

5. Gift of Property Mortgaged in Excess of Basis

Suppose property mortgaged in excess of basis is given away. Will the making of the gift accelerate the tax on the potential gain to the donor? Or will the tax be paid by the donee when he ultimately disposes of the property? Can the tax on the potential gain be eliminated by giving the property to a charity?

Because the donee either assumes or takes the property subject to the mortgage debt, it is likely that the transfer will be treated as a sale to the extent of the mortgage liability.[87] If the property has a *value* in excess of the mortgage liability, the transfer of the excess value will be treated as a gift. But the gain inherent in the excess of the mortgage debt over basis will be recognized.

Example: Owner owns a shopping center that had both a cost and construction mortgage liability of $1,000,000 in 1960. In 1968, the mortgage debt had been reduced to $800,000, but basis had been reduced to $650,000 by virtue of accelerated depreciation. In 1968, the property has a value of $850,000. O decides to give the center to his favorite charity. What result?

1. Sale

Amount realized:		
Mortgage debt relief		$800,000
Less basis:		
Original basis	$1,000,000	
Depreciation taken	350,000	650,000
Gain		$150,000

2. Gift

Value of property	$850,000
Less debt relief received	800,000
Gift to charity	$ 50,000

While owner will receive a charitable deduction of $50,000 for the value of his property in excess of the mortgage debt, he will also be taxed on $150,000 of gain resulting from the excess of the mortgage debt over basis. And part of that gain may be

---

[85] 186 F.2d 455 (1st Cir. 1950). See, also, Mendham Corp. 9 T.C. 320, 324 (1947).
[86] The current terminology is a "Walk-away."
[87] Simon v. Commissioner, 285 F.2d 422 (3rd Cir. 1960); Magnolia Development Corp., 1960 P-H Memo T.C. No. 60-177 (1960).

ordinary income under Section 1250 to the extent that accelerated depreciation exceeds straight-line.

6. Inheritance of Property Mortgaged in Excess of Basis

The problems of property mortgaged in excess of basis do not vanish with death. Basis to the heir is a carryover basis.[88] For that reason, the heir is saddled with his ancestor's basis according to the Internal Revenue Service.

This author suggests that the answer may *not* be so facile for the Internal Revenue Service. The heir, or estate, has acquired the property subject to a mortgage debt that he, or the estate, must pay. Hence his basis must be *at least* the amount of the mortgage debt. If so, basis to the heir or estate is, at the minimum, equal to the amount of liabilities at death.

E. PARTNERSHIP TRANSACTIONS IN PROPERTY MORTGAGED IN EXCESS OF BASIS

This part deals with the problem of the contributing property mortgaged in excess of basis to a partnership. Is the potential gain recognized upon the contribution? What happens if the partnership distributes the property? Does the distribution also result in a tax upon the gain?

1. Contribution of Property to a Partnership

Ordinarily, the contribution of property by a partner to a partnership does not give rise to taxable gain or deductible loss, whether the property is worth more or less than the partner's basis for it.[89] Is the usual rule changed, because the property contributed is mortgaged in excess of the partner's basis for it?

Curiously, the answer must be a qualified maybe. The regulations give an example of such a transfer that results in the recognition of gain, but the amount of gain taxed is only a portion of the total gain inherent in the property.[90] The reason for this odd result lies in the tax treatment of the contribution of property subject to a liability. To the extent that a partner's share of the liability against the property is decreased as a result of the contribution, he is treated as if he received a cash distribution from the partnership in the same amount.[91]

Normally, a partner will be responsible for all of the liability before the contribution. After the contribution has been made, the contributing partner is considered responsible only for his share of the partnership's liabilities. To the extent of the decrease in liabilities, he is treated as having received a distribution in cash.

Example: A contributes a building which cost him $100,000 to a partnership. At the time of contribution the property was subject to a mortgage debt of $60,000. If A is but a one-third

---

[88] Section 1023. There is some upward adjustment for the death duties attributable to any appreciation in the property.
[89] Sections 721-723, I.R.C.
[90] Reg. Sec. 1.752-1(c).
[91] Section 752, I.R.C.

PARTNERSHIP TRANSACTIONS

partner, his share of the liability will be but one-third of $60,000 or $20,000. He will be considered to have received a distribution of the other $40,000 of liability which is attributed to the other partners.

The net effect of the presumed distribution of cash is ordinarily to require the contributing partner to reduce his basis for his partnership interest by an equivalent amount.[92]

Example: Suppose Owner contributes property to a partnership in exchange for a one-half interest in partnership capital and profits. O's basis for the property is $76,000, and the outstanding liability is $80,000. His basis for his partnership interest is computed as follows:

O's basis for property contributed		$76,000
Less presumed distribution of cash:		
Outstanding liability	$80,000	
Less O's portion (50%)	40,000	40,000
Remaining basis for partnership interest		$36,000

2. Possibility of Gain on Contribution

Under certain conditions, the mechanics of the implied distribution of cash may give rise to taxable gain. If the share of liabilities attributed to the other partners exceeds the contributing parnter's basis for the property, he will be taxed upon the amount of the excess as gain realized upon the contribution.

Example: A contributes property having a basis to him of $1,000 to the AB partnership, in exchange for a 50 percent interest in capital and profits. The property is burdened by a mortgage debt of $2,500. Because the 50 percent share of liability attributed to the remaining partner ($1,250) exceeds A's basis for the property ($1,000), A is taxed upon $250 worth of the total potential gain of $1,500, as follows:[93]

A's basis for contributed property		$1,000
Less presumed distribution of cash:		
Total liability	$2,500	
Less A's share (50%)	1,250	1,250
A's basis for partnership interest		—0—
Gain taxed on contribution		$ 250

3. Contribution by Partner Not Personally Liable for Mortgage Debt

If the contributing partner is not personally liable for the mortgage debt, these rules will apply to him only to the extent of the fair market value of the property; the value of the property places a ceiling on the amount of liability that can be attributed to him.[94]

---

[92]Under Section 731, I.R.C., a distribution of money not in excess of a partner's basis for his interest merely serves to reduce his basis for that interest in an equivalent amount. He does not have any taxable income.

[93]Reg. Sec. 1.752-1(c). Under Section 731, I.R.C., gain is recognized to the extent that cash is distributed to a partner in excess of his basis for his partnership interest. See Reg. Sec. 1.722-1, Example (2).

[94]Section 752(c), I.R.C.

Example: Suppose the property contributed in the preceding example was worth only $2,000, although subject to a mortgage debt of $2,500. If A contributes it to the AB partnership in exchange for a 50 percent interest in the partnership, neither gain nor loss will be realized, and his basis for his partnership interest will be zero, as follows:

A's basis for contributed property		$1,000
Liability against property	$2,500	
Market value of property	2,000	
Lesser of liability or value	2,000	
Less A's share (50%)	1,000	1,000
A's basis for partnership interest		—0—
Gain on contribution		—0—

4. Receipt of Contribution by Partnership

Obviously, if the property subject to a mortgage is contributed to a partnership, not all of the contributing partner's basis for the property will be reflected in his basis for his partnership interest. What happens to the portion of the basis which disappears from his account?

This question presents the opposite side of the coin. The presumed distribution to one partner is made up by a presumed contribution by the others. Thus, the amount of basis for the property taken from the contributing partner finds its way into the partnership capital accounts of the other partners.[95]

Example: If O contributes property having a basis to him of $76,000, but subject to an $80,000 mortgage, in exchange for a 50 percent interest in the OP partnership, partner P is deemed to have made a contribution equal to his share of the liability after the partnership receives the property. This amount is identical to the amount of presumed distribution received by O:

O's basis for property contributed		$76,000
Less distribution to O:		
Total liability	$80,000	
Less O's share (50%)	40,000	40,000
O's basis for partnership		$36,000
Increase in P's basis:		
Total liability	$80,000	
Less O's share (50%)	40,000	40,000
Total increase in both O and P basis for partnership interests		$76,000

5. Distribution by Partnership

The same rules, but in reverse, apply on the distribution by a partnership of mortgaged property. The partner receiving the property is deemed to have made a contribution to the partnership to the extent that his share of the liability against the property is increased. And conversely the other partners are deemed to have received a distribution of cash to the extent that their share of the liability is decreased.[96]

---

[95] Section 752(a), I.R.C.; Reg. Sec. 1.752-1(a)(2).

[96] Reg. Sec. 1.752-1. Again, if neither the partnership nor the partner has assumed liability for the debt against the property, the liability to be attributed to them under these rules is limited to the market value of the property. Section 752(c), I.R.C.

PARTNERSHIP TRANSACTIONS

Example: Partnership OP distributes to partner O property having a basis to it of $76,000, but subject to an $80,000 mortgage debt. The property is worth more than $80,000. If we assume that O had a 50 percent interest in the partnership, the amount of O's distribution is $36,000, computed as follows:

Property distributed to O (at basis)		$76,000
O's contribution to partnership:		
Total liability	$80,000	
Less partnership's share	40,000	40,000
Net distribution to O		$36,000
Distribution to P (P's share of liability transferred to O)		40,000
Total distribution to both O and P		$76,000

6. Tax-planning the Contribution of Property Mortgaged in Excess of Basis to a Partnership

These rules give the owner of property mortgaged in excess of basis some leeway in escaping the recognition of the potential gain in property mortgaged in excess of basis by contributing it to a partnership. Only in the exceptional case in which the other partner's share of the liability exceeds the contributing partner's basis will any gain be recognized; even then, only a fractional part of the total gain is taxed.

Although the contribution does not eliminate the potential gain, it may have the effect of permitting the owner to liquidate a portion of his investment in the property without paying a tax.

Example: Owner, holding an apartment worth $80,000, subject to an $80,000 mortgage debt, wishes to dispose of the property. His basis for the property is but $50,000. Because his equity in the property is zero (value of $80,000 less debt of $80,000), O will receive only a nominal price if he sells it. Yet the sale will force the recognition of $30,000 gain ($80,000 sales price less $50,000 basis), on which he will be taxed. The net result to him will be an economic loss to the extent that he is required to pay a tax on the gain.

Facing this situation, O consults you. He tells you that he has a party, P, who is willing to buy a half interest in his equity for $1,000. You suggest that O and P form a partnership, OP, to which O will contribute the property and P his $1,000. Each partner will take a one-half interest.

1. O's Basis

O's basis for the property		$50,000
Less distribution to him:		
Total liability	$80,000	
Less O's share (50%)	40,000	40,000
O's basis for partnership interest		$10,000

2. P's Basis

P's basis for money contributed		$ 1,000
Plus contribution of liability:		
Total liability	$80,000	
Less O's share (50%)	40,000	40,000
P's basis for partnership interest		$41,000

3. OP's Basis

Basis to O of property contributed	$50,000
Adjustment for gain or loss	—0—

Basis to OP for property	50,000
Basis to OP for money	1,000
Total basis to OP	$51,000

In effect, O has sold a half interest in the property to P without paying a tax on any of the potential gain. And O can draw out up to $10,000 of partnership capital without incurring a tax on the distribution. If, for example, O draws out the $1,000 P promised to pay him for a half interest in the property, he will not be compelled to pay a tax on any part of the potential gain. Thus, O has achieved part of his objective of selling a half interest to P for $1,000.

But O is not free of all difficulty in connection with the $30,000 potential gain in the property. The gain has merely been transferred to the partnership of which he remains a member. As long as the partnership continues to operate the property, O is safe and can enjoy the fruits of its operation. But if the property is sold by the partnership, his haven will be destroyed and the gain will be taxed to him.

7. Sale of Contributed Property by Partnership

Assume that the partnership sells the property for a net price of $1,000. The gain realized on the sale will be $31,000, computed as follows:

Sales price to OP		
Cash received	$ 1,000	
Plus outstanding debt	80,000	$81,000
Less OP's basis for property		50,000
Gain realized by OP on sale		$31,000

Without an agreement assigning all the gain to O,[97] the gain will be credited to the accounts of O and P in equal shares, as follows:

Gain credited to O	$15,500
Gain credited to P	15,000
Total gain realized	$31,000

As a result, each partner's basis for his partnership interest will be increased to reflect the credit for his portion of the gain realized.[98]

	O	P
Original basis for partnership interest	$10,000	$41,000
Plus share of gain	15,500	15,500
Adjusted basis for interest	$25,500	$56,500

Thus, O and P will each pay a tax on $15,500 of gain realized by the partnership on the sale of property.

But this is not all. Because the partnership has disposed of the property, its total liabilities have been decreased to reflect the fact that the mortgage debt against the

---

[97] See Section 704(c)(2), I.R.C.
[98] See Section 705(a), I.R.C.

PARTNERSHIP TRANSACTIONS

property has also been transferred. And, as we learned, any decrease in partnership liabilities is treated as a distribution in cash to each partner to the extent of his share of the liability transferred.[99] In our example, the total decrease in partnership liabilities is $80,000, the amount of the outstanding mortgage debt. Half of this amount is deemed to be distributed to each partner. Does any portion of this distribution give rise to additional gain?

	O	P
Amount deemed distributed	$40,000	$40,000
Less adjusted basis of interest	25,500	56,500
Gain recognized on distribution	$14,500	—0—
Remaining basis for interest	—0—	$16,500

Thus, O must pay a tax on the gain arising from two transactions in the year of sale: first, his share of the gain on the sale of $15,500 and, second, his gain on distribution of $14,500, or a total gain of $30,000. Interestingly, the total gain from the two transactions is $30,000, exactly the amount of the potential gain inherent in the property prior to contribution of it to the partnership.

But what about P's share of the gain realized on the sale of the property by the partnership? He has been required to pay a tax on $15,500 of gain in addition to the tax paid by O. Obviously, the total gain recognized under these transactions greatly exceeds the economic gain received by the partners. P's gain on the sale, however, can readily be offset. All he need do is to liquidate his interest in the partnership by distributing the cash on hand:

Total cash on hand:			
Cash contributed by P		$1,000	
Cash received on sale		1,000	$ 2,000
Distribution of cash to partners:		O	P
Cash distributed to each		$1,000	$ 1,000
Less remaining basis		—0—	16,500
Gain realized on liquidation		$1,000	
Loss realized on liquidation			$15,500

P's capital loss of $15,500 on liquidation of his partnership interest would wipe out his $15,500 share of the capital gain realized on the sale of the property by the partnership. P also has his original $1,000 back, as if he had never entered into the partnership in the first place.

O picks up an additional capital gain of $1,000 on liquidation. His total gain from the three transactions is $31,000, which is exactly the same as if he had sold the property directly to a third party for $1,000 at the first.

Obviously, then, the use of the partnership form will not permit the owner of property mortgaged in excess of basis to assign the gain to his partner for the purpose of a sale. Its only value to him lies in the use of the partnership form as a method of operating the property after liquidating a portion of his investment by the original contribution to the partnership.

---

[99] Reg. Sec. 1.752-1(b)(1).

8. Distribution of Contributed Property by Partnership

Nor can O arrange to have the property distributed to P by the partnership. Such a distribution will also result in the recognition to O of all of the potential gain in the property because the distribution transfers the liability from the partnership to P. Thus, the distribution consists not only of the property distributed but also of the amount by which each partner's share of the partnership's liability is decreased.[100]

If the property is distributed to P, the partnership's liability will be decreased by $80,000, of which $40,000 is deemed distributed to O and $40,000 to P. But P's total individual liabilities after distribution are increased by $80,000, which represents an additional contribution by him, increasing his basis for his partnership interest.[101] These rules work out as follows:

	O	P
Amount distributed:		
Basis of property		$50,000
Decrease in liability	$40,000	40,000
Total distribution	$40,000	$90,000
Amount contributed	—0—	80,000
Net distribution	$40,000	$10,000
Less original basis for partnership interest	10,000	41,000
Gain to partner	$30,000	—0—
Remaining basis for partnership interest	—0—	$31,000

Obviously, this alternative furnishes O no answer to his problem of avoiding the tax on the potential gain. The distribution of the property mortgaged in excess of basis will in itself accelerate the tax on the gain just as if the property had been sold.

And P is left holding the property with a basis of $50,000 subject to an $80,000 liability. Unless P takes steps to liquidate his interest in the partnership, he will be taxed a second time on the same gain. But if he liquidates his interest in the same transaction, both O and P will be placed in exactly the same position as if P had purchased O's equity for $500, as follows:

	O	P
Distribution on liquidation:		
Cash in partnership ($1,000)	$500	$ 500
Less adjusted basis for interest	—0—	31,000
Additional gain	$500	—0—
Basis transferred to property		$30,500

Thus, O will have realized a total gain of $30,500 on the distribution, and P will be holding property having a basis to him of $80,500 ($50,000 original partnership basis plus $30,500 basis for partnership interest), but subject to a liability of $80,000. All of the potential gain to the extent of the excess of liability over basis will have been taxed.

---

[100] Reg. Sec. 1.752-1(b)(1).
[101] Reg. Sec. 1.752-1(a)(2).

CORPORATE TRANSACTIONS

9. Conclusions on Partnership Transactions

From this example, we can draw four conclusions:

(1) In general, no tax will be incurred on the contribution of property mortgaged in excess of basis to a partnership. The only exception arises in the singular case in which the share of liability attributed to the non-contributing partners exceeds the contributing partner's basis for the property.

(2) The partnership may operate the property without accelerating the contributing partner's gain. Distributions out of income or the depreciation allowance may be made to the contributing partner up to the amount of his basis for his interest without any liability for tax.

(3) But the partnership cannot sell the property without forcing the contributing partner to pay a tax on the potential gain.

(4) Nor may the property be distributed out of the partnership to another partner without incurring the same tax liability as if the property had been sold by the contributing partner.

F. CORPORATE TRANSACTIONS IN PROPERTY MORTGAGED IN EXCESS OF BASIS

This part deals with the problem of contributing or distributing property mortgaged in excess of basis to or by a corporation. The problem again to be faced is whether or not the contribution or distribution has the effect of accelerating the potential gain so that the transferor becomes taxable upon it by virtue of the transaction.

1. Contribution of Property to Corporation

Under the 1954 Code, the contribution of property mortgaged in excess of basis by a shareholder will result in the realization by him of the potential gain inherent in the property. The gain is taxed to him whether the exchange of the property for stock is otherwise taxable or tax-free.[102] Assumption by the corporation of the liability against the shareholder's property is immaterial; if the liability exceeds basis, the gain is taxable.[103]

Example: Owner contributes the property described in our preceding examples to a wholly owned corporation in exchange for stock. At the time of contribution, the property has an adjusted basis of $76,000 and the outstanding mortgage against it is $80,000. The contribution will result in the recognition of $4,000 worth of gain, as follows:

Value of stock received	$ —0—
Plus mortgage debt against property	80,000
Total consideration received	$80,000
Less O's basis for property	76,000
O's gain on exchange	$ 4,000

---

[102] Section 357(c), I.R.C. The measure of gain recognized under this section is the excess of "the sum of the amount the liabilities assumed, plus the amount of the liabilities to which the property is subject, (over) the total of the adjusted basis of the property transferred pursuant to such exchange . . ."

[103] Reg. Sec. 1.357-2(a).

In the case of a wholly owned corporation, as in the above example, the gain realized would be converted from capital gain to ordinary income if the property exchanged is depreciable. Any transfer of depreciable property, whether by sale or taxable exchange, to a corporation more than 80 percent of whose stock is owned by the transferor is automatically classified as ordinary income.[104]

Thus, the penalties of contributing property mortgaged in excess of basis to a wholly owned corporation may be severe; it may be the course of wisdom to sell the property to an outsider and pay a capital gains tax on the built-in gain.

2. Distribution of Property by Corporation

A similar rule applies under the 1954 Code as to a dividend of property mortgaged in excess of basis. Gain is recognized to the distributing corporation at the time of distribution to the extent that the liability against the property exceeds its basis to the corporation.[105]

Example: C Corporation distributes property to its shareholders which has an adjusted basis of $80,000, subject to an $86,000 mortgage debt. The distribution creates $6,000 of taxable gain to C Corporation, just as if it had sold the property:

Liability against property distributed	$86,000
Less C Corporation's basis	80,000
Taxable gain on distribution	$ 6,000

But if the shareholders do not assume personal liability for the mortgage debt, this rule is subject to a limitation; gain is recognized on the distribution only if the fair market value of the property exceeds its basis.[106] Under these circumstances, the gain may be avoided at the corporate level, provided the property is worth less than basis:

Example: C Corporation distributes property having a value of $70,000 to its shareholders. The property has a basis to the corporation of $76,000 and is distributed subject to a mortgage debt of $80,000, which the shareholders do not assume. No gain is recognized to the corporation on the distribution.[107]

Liability against property distributed	$80,000
Less C Corporation's basis	76,000
Potential gain	$ 4,000
Excess of value over basis	—0—
Gain recognized on distribution	—0—

Will the gain so avoided by the corporation later be taxed to the shareholders? The shareholders take a basis for the property that is independent of the former basis to the corporation. It is measured by ". . . the fair market value of (the) property."[108] Does

---

[104] Section 1239, I.R.C.; Rev. Rul. 60-302, 1960-2 C.B. 223. For this purpose, stock which is owned by the transferor's spouse, minor children, and minor grandchildren is attributed to him. See Reg. Sec. 1.1239-1.
[105] Section 311(c), I.R.C.
[106] Section 311(c), I.R.C.
[107] Reg. Sec. 1.311-1(d).
[108] Section 301(d), I.R.C.; Reg. Sec. 1.301-1(h).

CORPORATE TRANSACTIONS   211

this language mean the fair market value of the shareholder's equity in the property, which is zero, or the fair market value of the total property? The regulations shed no light on the problem.

If it means the former, the tax on the gain will be avoided entirely. Some substance is given this contention by the fact that the amount of the taxable dividend received by the shareholders is measured by the value of the equity, rather than the value of the property.[109] Since the amount of the distribution cannot be reduced below zero for the purpose of taxing the distribution, it would appear unfair to permit the amount of the distribution to be reduced below zero for the purpose of measuring the shareholder's basis for the property distributed. Thus, the shareholder's basis for the total property, including each one's equity as well as the mortgagee's interest, would be equal to the outstanding indebtedness. In other words, the distribution would eliminate the potential gain, without tax either to the corporation or its shareholders, provided the property is worth less than the liabilities outstanding against it at the time of distribution and provided the shareholders do not assume the liabilities.

But this favorable conclusion is not free of doubt. The regulations concerning basis to the shareholders do not distinguish between the property and equity in the property.[110] Hence, the Commissioner is free to take the position that the shareholders too may have a basis less than the indebtedness on such a distribution. Basis would be measured by the value of the property, unreduced for the mortgage indebtedness. Because we have assumed in our example that the value of the property is less than the liability outstanding against it, the shareholders would also have to shoulder the burden of a basis less than liabilities after the distribution.

These rules apply to all current distributions of a corporation to its shareholders, whether by dividend or otherwise. But distributions in liquidation, whether complete or partial, are found in a different part of the Code.[111] No gain or loss is recognized to a corporation on a distribution in liquidation.[112] The shareholders receiving the liquidating distribution report as gain or loss the difference between the fair market value of the property received and their basis for their stock.[113] Basis for the property received is measured by its fair market value.[114]

Hence, it appears that property mortgaged in excess of basis can be distributed in partial or complete liquidation of the corporation in such manner that the tax upon the potential gain is never incurred, provided, of course, the property is worth less than the liability against it. Apparently, no tax is payable by the corporation at the time of distribution. However, the distribution wipes out that gain because the shareholders take a new basis for the property measured by its value at the time of distribution.[115]

---

[109] Section 301(b)(2), I.R.C.; Reg. Sec. 1.301-1(g).
[110] Reg. Sec. 1.301-1(h).
[111] Part I of Subchapter C, in which Sections 301 and 311 are found, deals with "Distributions of Corporations." Part II is titled "Corporate Liquidations" and contains its own rules for determining gain and measuring basis upon liquidating distributions.
[112] Section 336, I.R.C.; Reg. Sec. 1.336-1.
[113] Section 331, I.R.C.; Reg. Sec. 1.331-1.
[114] Section 334, I.R.C.; Reg. Sec. 1.334-1.
[115] See Lurie, Alvin D., "Causes and Effects of a Negative Basis in Mortgage Transactions," *Encyclopedia of Tax Procedures* (Prentice-Hall, 1956), pp. 1219, 1230.

3. F.H.A. "Windfall" Profits

Prior to the enactment of the 1954 Code the possibility existed of a tax-free distribution by a corporation of windfall mortgage proceeds obtained on governmentally secured loans. In the normal case, a construction corporation obtained an F.H.A.-secured mortgage to raise funds necessary for construction. Because of the liberality of the guaranteeing agency, the money borrowed on the mortgage loan may have exceeded the total cost of construction and of land acquisition. As a result, the corporation might have on hand cash in an amount that exceeded its needs. If this excess cash were distributed prior to the time that any portion of the property was sold or rented, the distribution could not be charged to earnings and profits of the corporation for the purpose of taxing the distribution as a dividend.

Section 312(j) was added by the 1954 Code to convert such distributions into taxable dividends. Even though the cash distributed was obtained by "mortgaging out" on the property, rather than from sales or rentals, it is treated under Section 312(j) as a dividend from constructive earnings and profits erected at the time of distribution. The section provides that the earnings and profits of a corporation are to be increased at the time of distribution by the excess of any loan "made, guaranteed or insured by the United States (or any agency or instrumentality thereof)" over the basis to the corporation of the property subject to the loan. The distribution, being presumed to be from corporate earnings and profits, is thereby converted into a taxable dividend to shareholders.

Example:[116] The C Corporation borrowed $1,000,000 on an F.H.A. guarantee. The loan proceeds were used to construct apartment housing. Construction costs and land acquisition costs totalled $900,000. If the excess $100,000 received on the mortgage loan is distributed to shareholders, Section 312(j) would compel the corporation to add $100,000 to its earnings and profits account as long as the liability exceeds basis by this amount. The distribution would be taxable as a dividend.

G. CONCLUSION: TAX ADVANTAGES OF MORTGAGE FINANCING

From the foregoing discussion we can see that mortgage financing of real property transactions has two fundamental advantages over cash financing. First, if property is being purchased, the purchaser can include the amount of any borrowed money used to finance the purchase as a part of his cost basis for the purpose of computing his allowance for depreciation. Although only a part of the money put up to pay for the property is his, he is entitled to take for his cost basis the entire price paid, including both the money put up by him and by his mortgagee. Thus, a substantial portion of the gross income from the property may be received by the purchaser as a tax-free allowance for depreciation. The purchaser is placed in the position of being able to increase his equity in the property by paying off the mortgage debt out of the moneys attributed

---

[116] Reg. Sec. 1.312-12(b), Example.

TAX ADVANTAGES OF MORTGAGE FINANCING

to the depreciation allowance. Obviously, he can increase his equity in the property much faster than if he were required to make his payments out of taxable income.

The second major advantage in the use of mortgages arises from the rule that the borrowing of money does not represent taxable income to the borrower. Thus, an owner who wishes to liquidate a portion of his investment in real property can accomplish the same result by borrowing against the property. The cash received on the borrowing will not be taxable, even though he may have borrowed in excess of the property's basis. The owner's price for this privilege is the payment of interest, an expense normally deductible.

These two principles constitute the major tax advantages in the use of mortgage money, which may in great part explain the current popularity of real estate investment as a vehicle for building up capital values.

7

Repossessions, Mortgage Foreclosures, and Cancellations

When we read case material relating to mortgage foreclosures and cancellations, we find that an analysis of these transactions is unduly complicated for at least two reasons: (1) the foreclosure or cancellation can be cast in any one of several forms, and (2) the relationship of each party to the foreclosure involves principles of law between debtor-creditor as well as principles of sales or exchanges. To make this material understandable and usable, we find it necessary first to divide it up in terms of the form of the transaction and then to analyze separately the tax position of the mortgagee and the mortgagor in each basic type of foreclosure.

In addition to analyzing foreclosures according to their form, we must classify them according to whether the mortgagee is a seller of property or a lender of money. If he is a seller, we must determine whether or not he has reacquired the property which he sold in partial or full satisfaction of the indebtedness arising from the sale (Part A). All foreclosures not involving the reacquisition of property previously sold by the mortgagee are handled under the general rules discussed in Parts B, C, D, E and F.

For our purpose we shall separate the various types of foreclosures and cancellations into the following categories:

A. *Reacquisitions by a seller in partial or full satisfaction of the indebtedness arising from the sale.*
B. *Foreclosure by sale to a third party.*
C. *Strict foreclosure: Involuntary conveyance to mortgagee.*
D. *Foreclosure by sale to the mortgagee.*
E. *Voluntary conveyance to the mortgagee.*
F. *Compromise of the mortgage debt.*

These various types of non-reacquisition foreclosures and cancellations will first be analyzed from the point of view of the mortgagee and the mortgagor followed by a list of suggestions to be borne in mind by anyone who faces such a transaction.

This development of the basic types of foreclosures and the tax rules relating to each will be followed by a discussion of several special problems arising in mortgage foreclosures as follows:

G. *Loss of second mortgagee.*
H. *Expenses of foreclosure.*
I. *Assignment of rents to the mortgagee.*
J. *Disposition of property acquired in foreclosure.*

A. REACQUISITIONS BY A SELLER IN PARTIAL OR FULL SATISFACTION OF THE INDEBTEDNESS ARISING FROM THE SALE

Section 1038 governs all reacquisitions by a seller-mortgagee. Among those forms included are:

1. Voluntary conveyance to the mortgagee.
2. Strict foreclosure: Involuntary conveyance to mortgagee.
3. Foreclosure by sale to the mortgagee.[1]

Section 1038 controls recognition of gain or loss on reacquisition, recognition of income on indebtedness previously charged off, and the basis of the purchaser's obligation and the reacquired property. Special provision is also made for reacquisitions of principal residences.

The Section applies only where there has been a sale of real property, giving rise to an indebtedness to the seller which is secured by the property sold. The seller must reacquire the property in full or partial satisfaction of the debt. Thus, the Section will not apply where the seller repurchases the property by paying the buyer consideration in addition to the discharge of the indebtedness unless this repurchase was provided for in the original sale contract. However, Section 1038 cannot be avoided by the payment of additional consideration by the seller when the purchaser has defaulted on his obligation, or when default is imminent.[2]

1. General Rule: Gain on Reacquisition

On reacquisition the seller will realize taxable gain measured by the payments he had previously received but had not reported as income or gain.

Example: In 1966, Seller sold real property for $30,000, $5,000 in cash and $25,000 note. His adjusted basis for the property was $15,000, or 50 percent of the total sales price. S elected to report the sale on the installment method. Accordingly, 50 percent ($2,500) of the down

---

[1] Reg. Sec. 1.1038-1(a)(3)(ii).
[2] Reg. Sec. 1.1038-1(a)(3)(i).

payment was reported as gain and 50 percent ($2,500) as recovery of basis. No further payments are made. In 1968, S repossesses.

What is his gain?

Payments received	$5,000
Gain reported	2,500
Gain on repossession	$2,500

2. Loss on Reacquisition

For reacquisitions under Section 1038, no loss will be realized by the seller. Any potential loss is postponed and is added to the seller's basis for the property reacquired, even though his basis will be in excess of the value of the property. The loss is realized only upon the resale of the property.

3. Bad Debt Loss

No bad debt loss will be realized on the purchaser's obligation as a result of the reacquisition, nor thereafter, because the note will emerge from the recovery of the property with a zero basis. On the contrary, to the extent the debt has previously been treated as worthless or partially worthless, the seller will realize income. He will be considered to have recovered that amount on the reacquisition, regardless of whether the entire transaction to that point has produced a gain or a loss. The basis of the reacquired property will reflect the increased basis of the purchaser's obligation resulting from this *recovery* of indebtedness previously charged off. All payments on the debt received by the seller subsequent to a Section 1038 reacquisition will be ordinary income.[3]

4. Extent of Gain on Reacquisition

The seller will realize gain, however, limited to the net gain on the original sale of the property less reacquisition costs and the amount of gain previously returned. The limitation does not apply where the original selling price could not be ascertained at the time of sale as, for example, where the price was stated as a percentage of the profits to be realized from the development of the property sold.

An example will illustrate the application of Section 1038(b) providing for recognition of gain on reacquisition.

Example: Assume S in 1966 sold real estate for $30,000. *Terms*: $5,000 cash plus $25,000 purchase-money mortgage payable $5,000 annually starting in 1967. His adjusted basis for the real estate was $24,000. Thus, the gain was $6,000 or 20% of the selling price. If S elected installment reporting he would report $1,000 gain for 1966 and assuming the 1967-69 payments were timely made, an additional $1,000 in each of those years, a total gain reported of $4,000.

Assume buyer defaults at the beginning of 1970 and S repossesses. Repossession costs are $500.

Result: Under the general rule, S's repossession gain would be $16,000, that is, the $20,000 cash received minus the $4,000 gain reported. But, under the limitation, S's repossession gain is

---

[3]Reg. Sec. 1.1038-1(g)(2).

limited to $1,500, that is, the $6,000 gain on the original sale minus the $4,000 income reported and minus the $500 repossession costs.

5. Character of Gain on Reacquisition

What is the character of the gain realized on reacquisition? While the Congressional Committee Reports indicated that the gain on repossession would have the same character as the gain realized on the original sale,[4] the Regulations take a different approach.[5]

If the sale were returned on the installment method, the gain on repossession has the same character as the gain on the original sale. For example, if the original sale created capital gain, the repossession gain will be capital. But if the sale were made by a dealer, the repossession gain will be ordinary.

If the sale were returned as a deferred payment sale, title was transferred to the purchaser, and if the reacquisition were by voluntary deed, the reacquisition gain is ordinary income. Presumably, this result is based on the fact that a voluntary conveyance is more like a collection on the note than an exchange of the note for the property. Capital gain can be realized only when a sale or exchange takes place.[6]

Is the rule different if the reacquisition is by foreclosure and title was transferred? Here we have a clear exchange of the note for the property;[7] hence, while the regulations are silent, the gain should be capital gain, except in the case of a dealer.

Finally, if title is not transferred, the regulations are also silent. But the rules should be no harsher than in the case of a title transfer. However, the Commissioner has the additional argument that because of the failure to transfer title, the gain is ordinary income since the original transaction was more like an option than a sale.[8]

6. Basis of Reacquired Property

The repossessed property will have for its basis the adjusted basis to the seller of the purchase obligation[9] increased by any gain recognized on reacquisition and by any expenses incurred by the selller in recovering the property. Because the seller's basis in purchaser's indebtedness becomes his basis for the property reacquired under Section 1038, the purchaser's obligation will have a zero basis, and any income recovered thereon after reacquisition of the property will be ordinary income. Adjusted basis of the debt is the balance of the debt due at the time of reacquisition, less gain (or plus loss) previously unreported, and plus any amount previously charged off by the seller as worthless.

Example: Assume S in 1966 sold real estate for $30,000. *Terms*: $5,000 cash plus $25,000 purchase-money mortgage payable $5,000 annually starting in 1967. His adjusted basis for the

---

[4] S. Rept. No. 1361, 88th Cong. 2d Sess. 8,9 (1964).
[5] Reg. Sec. 1.1038-1(d).
[6] Rev. Rul. 73-36, 1973-1 C.B. 372.
[7] See this Chapter, C, 2.
[8] Ralph A. Boatman, 32 T.C. 1188 (1959). See also Reg. Sec. 1.453-6(b).
[9] Section 1038(c). If any part of the debt has been written off in a prior year, the write-off becomes income at the time of reacquisition (Section 1038(d)) and basis is increased in a like amount.

real estate was $24,000. Thus, the gain was $6,000 or 20% of the selling price. If S elected installment reporting he would report $1,000 gain for 1966, and assuming the 1967-69 payments were timely made, an additional $1,000 in each of those years, a total gain reported of $4,000.

Assume buyer defaults at the beginning of 1970 and S repossesses. Repossession costs are $500. His repossession gain is $1,500.

Basis of the reacquired property will be as follows:

Balance on note	$10,000
Less unreported gain	2,000
Adjusted basis of note	8,000
Plus reacquisition gain	$ 1,500
Plus reacquisition costs	500
Basis of reacquired property	$10,000

If the seller had previously written off $1,000 on the purchaser's note as worthless, his basis in the reacquired property would be computed as follows:

Balance on note (amount due less amount charged off)	$ 9,000
Less unreported gain	(2,000)
Plus indebtedness previously charged off	1,000
	8,000
Plus reacquisition gain	1,500
Plus reacquisition costs	500
Basis of reacquired property	$10,000

7. Holding Period of Property Reacquired Under Section 1038

Section 1038 makes no provision relating to holding period. However, the Regulations set out the rules to be followed. The holding period will commence with the first acquisition of the property by the seller and end at the time of disposition following the reacquisition. In other words, the holding period includes the period that the seller held the property before the original sale. However, the period does not include the period from the date following the date of the original sale to the purchaser and ending on the date the property is reacquired.[10]

The general provision governing holding period for exchanges, Section 1223, are to be followed in computing the time the seller held the property before the original sale.

8. Section 1038 Rules Personal to Seller

If a seller dies after the sale of property and it becomes necessary for his estate to repossess the property, the estate is taxable on the deferred installment gain to the extent of the fair market value of the property.[11] This rule is extremely harsh because the estate cannot step-up its basis for the installment obligation equal to its value (which would be the value of the property repossessed). The deferred gain is income in

---

[10] Reg. Sec. 1038-1(g)(3).
[11] Rev. Rul. 69-83, 1969-1 C.B. 202.

respect of a decedent to which a basis adjustment to value on death is expressly denied by the Code.[12]

9. Legal Fees on Repossession

Legal fees incurred on repossession are not deductible; such fees must be added to the repossessing sellers' cost basis for the property.[13]

B. FORECLOSURE BY SALE TO A THIRD PARTY

This type of foreclosure is the classic illustration of a mortgage foreclosure. It normally involves sale be decree of court in a suit brought by the mortgagee to foreclose, or in the case of a deed of trust, a sale by the trustee under its power of sale. For the purposes of our analysis, we shall confine our discussion in this part to the case in which the foreclosed property is sold to an independent third party and the cash proceeds of the sale are turned over to the mortgagee in full or partial satisfaction of his mortgagee's and the mortgagor's rights in the property, subject to a possible right of redemption in the mortgagor. What are tax consequences of such a foreclosure sale, first to the mortgagee and then to the mortgagor?

1. Bad Debt Loss of the Mortgagee

Basically, the mortgagee in any foreclosure action is a creditor who is attempting to collect on his debt by taking steps to liquidate the security for his loan. His tax position must be analyzed from the viewpoint of a creditor, and he is subject to the rules relating to the collection of debts. Consequently, if the mortgagee receives less from the liquidation of his security than the amount of the mortgage debt, his loss is deductible only under the mechanics of the bad debt deduction under Section 166, I.R.C.[14]

2. Business or Non-business Bad Debt?

Whether or not the bad debt deduction suffered by the mortgagee is deductible in full depends upon the character of the debt in the hands of the individual. It qualifies as an ordinary deduction only if the individual mortgagee is in the business of lending money[15] or in some closely allied business, such as that of dealing in loans secured by real estate or in mortgage equities.[16] An individual mortgagee who makes only casual or occasional loans would be allowed to deduct his bad debt only as a non-business deduction.[17]

---

[12]Section 1014(c), I.R.C.
[13]Virginia M. Cramer, 55 T.C. 1125, 1132 (1971), acq. on another point, 1971-2 C.B. 2.
[14]Reg. Sec. 1.166-3(a). Rev. Rul. 73-36, 1973-1 C.B. 372.
[15]Estate of Theodore Gutman, 18 T.C. 112, 121 (1952), acq. 1952-2 C.B. 2 (lawyers engaged in the real estate and mortgage business).
[16]See Commissioner v. Smith, 203 F.2d 310, 312 (2nd Cir. 1953), cert. den. 346 U.S. 816.
[17]W.A. Dallmeyer, 14 T.C. 1282, 1289 (1950).

For example, an investor (as opposed to a "dealer") in mortgage equities is not engaged in the money lending business as such; consequently, his bad debt loss on foreclosure is a non-business bad debt.[18] Its deduction is subject to the limitations imposed by Section 1211, I.R.C., on the allowance of short-term capital losses to an individual taxpayer.[19]

Under the rules established by the 1954 Code, a debt owing to an individual is considered a business bad debt if connected with his business either at the time he made the loan or at the time the loan became worthless, or if the loss due to worthlessness is incurred in the business.[20] The fact that the mortgagee is no longer actively engaged in his business at the time of foreclosure will not affect his deduction for the bad debt; even a retired money lender or mortgage dealer is entitled to a business bad debt deduction for a loss on foreclosure.[21]

The distinction between business and non-business bad debts drawn above does not apply to a corporation; all bona fide loans made by a corporation are considered to be business loans. Hence, a corporate mortgagee is entitled to a deduction in full against ordinary income for the amount of its bad debt loss realized upon a mortgage foreclosure.[22]

However, a corporation, just as any other taxpayer, is subject to a further limitation on the deductibility of certain securities that become worthless. Any loan which is evidenced by a "bond, debenture, note, or certificate, or other evidence of indebtedness, issued by a corporation or by a government or political subdivision thereof, with interest coupons or in registered form" is treated as a security under Section 165(g), I.R.C. Hence, Section 166 (bad debt deductions) does not apply[23] and any loss incurred in foreclosing a mortgage guaranteeing such a corporate security is by definition, a capital loss, subject to the restrictions imposed upon the deductibility of capital losses.[24] A special exception to these rules is carved out by Section 582, I.R.C., for corporate securities held by a bank.

3. Time for Deducting the Bad Debt: Effect of a Deficiency

When is the mortgagee's bad debt loss deductible? Is it deductible in the year of foreclosure? Or at some other time? The answer depends upon (1) whether or not the mortgagee obtains an enforceable judgment for the deficiency against the mortgagor, and (2) whether or not the deficiency judgment has any value at the time it is obtained.

For example, if the mortgagee does not, or cannot, secure a deficiency judgment in the foreclosure proceedings for the amount of his loss, that loss is deductible in the year of foreclosure.[25] On the other hand, if the mortgagee does obtain a judgment against the mortgagor for the deficiency between the amount of his loan and the sale

---

[18]Thomas v. Obenchain, 185 F.2d 455 (5th Cir. 1950); see Whipple v. Commissioner, 373 U.S. 193 (1963).
[19]Section 166(d), I.R.C.; Reg. Sec. 1.166-5(a).
[20]Section 166(d)(2), I.R.C.; Reg. Sec. 1.166-5(b).
[21]Sen. Rep. No. 1622, 83rd Cong., 2nd Sess. (1954), p. 24.
[22]Section 166(a), I.R.C.; Reg. Sec. 1.166-5(a).
[23]Section 166(e), I.R.C.; Rec. Sec. 1.166-3(c).
[24]For individuals, see Section 1211(b), I.R.C.; for corporations, see Section 1211(a), I.R.C.
[25]G.C.M. 19573, 1938-1 C.B. 214.

FORECLOSURE BY SALE TO A THIRD PARTY 221

proceeds, the time for deducting his loss depends upon the date that the deficiency judgment becomes worthless.[26] Obviously, if the mortgagee can show that he has no hope of collecting the deficiency from the mortgagor, he is permitted to deduct his bad debt loss in the year of foreclosure.[27] Otherwise, the time for deducting his loss is postponed to the date on which the deficiency judgment becomes unenforceable or is shown to be worthless.[28]

What factors evidence the uncollectability or worthlessness[29] of a deficiency judgment obtained in foreclosure proceedings? The cases shed some light upon this problem. For example, proof of the fact that the mortgagor disappeared after foreclosure, leaving no distrainable property behind, would establish the worthlessness of any deficiency judgment against him.[30] Also, sufficient showing of unsuccessful attempts to collect the deficiency would entitle the mortgagee to his loss deduction.[31] And evidence that the expense of recovery of the deficiency would exceed the amount of possible recovery would justify a write-off for worthlessness.[32] Bankruptcy of the mortgagor may also be sufficient.[33] In the case of a corporation, evidence of insolvency coupled with foreclosure establishes the loss in the year of foreclosure.

Carelessness in handling the deficiency judgment may result in forcing the mortgagee to litigate to establish the year of his loss. And the result of his litigation may be a disallowance of his deduction if he is unable to show by affirmative evidence that the deficiency actually became worthless in the year of write-off. The government may disallow the write-off either on the ground that the deficiency should have been written off in a prior year[34] or on the ground that a subsequent year is correct[35] or both alternately. If the government wins, the mortgagee is plagued with the necessity of attempting to justify a write-off in a year other than the one first chosen.

The presence or absence of a right of redemption in the mortgagor to recapture the foreclosed property does not affect the time in which the mortgagee must deduct his worthless deficiency.[36] The right of redemption is a right exercisable by the mortgagor against the third party who purchased the property at the foreclosure sale. Hence, that right does not affect the finality of the write-off of the mortgagee's deficiency.

4. Determining the Amount of the Mortgagee's Loss

The mortgagee's loss is measured by the difference between the basis for his loan and the net sales price realized by him on the foreclosure sale. Both these amounts are

---

[26] Reg. Sec. 1.166-6(a).
[27] Doris D. Havemeyer, 45 B.T.A. 329, 330 (1941), acq. 1942-1 C.B. 8.
[28] Schoellkopf v. United States, 6 F.Supp. 225, 227 (Ct.Cl. 1934); Vancoh Realty Co., 33 B.T.A. 918, 926 (1936), non-acq. on another point, XV-2 C.B. 49; See O.D. 687, 3 C.B. 166.
[29] See Reg. Sec. 1.166-2.
[30] Edward F. Dalton, 2 B.T.A. 615 (1925), acq. IV-2 C.B. 2.
[31] Mt. Vernon National Bank, 2 B.T.A. 581 (1925), acq. V-1 C.B. 4 (return of execution unsatisfied).
[32] Estate of James R. Jewett, par. 49, 163 P-H Memo T.C. (1949).
[33] Reg. Sec. 1.166-2(c); Schoellkopf v. United States, 6 F.Supp. 225, 227 (Ct.Cl. 1934).
[34] Vancoh Realty Co., 33 B.T.A. 918 (1936), non-acq. on another point, XV-2 C.B. 49; O.D. 687, 3 C.B. 166; Little v. Helvering, 75 F.2d 436 (8th Cir. 1935).
[35] Larson v. Cuesta, 120 F.2d 482 (5th Cir. 1941); Estate of Eleanor H. Davidson, par. 46,259 P-H Memo T.C. (1946).
[36] William C. Heinemann & Co., 40 B.T.A. 1090, 1093 (1939).

subject to adjustment for events occurring after the loan has been made to the mortgagor. For example, any payments on principal made by him prior to foreclosure reduce the mortgagee's basis for his loan. Conversely, any additions to the loan made by the mortgagee increase the loan basis.

The starting point for determining the mortgagee's basis for his loan is the cost of the loan to him: if he was the original lender, it is the total amount outstanding at the time of foreclosure; if he purchased the loan, it is the amount he paid for the loan, plus any additional amounts he may have subsequently loaned to the mortgagor and less any payments on principal received by him.

To the basis for the loan thus computed, the mortgagee is entitled to add any charges against the mortgaged property that he paid prior to foreclosure. These charges are, in effect, treated as additional amounts loaned to the mortgagor.[37] Thus, taxes, special assessments, and other governmental liens paid by the mortgagee are treated as advances to the mortgagor to be added to his debt.

Correspondingly, the mortgagee's basis for the loan must be reduced for any payments received by him on principal. In addition, other reductions in basis may have to be made. If the mortgagee previously wrote off any part of the mortgage debt as worthless, his basis for the loan must be reduced by the partial write-off.[38] This reduction in basis for partial write-offs must be made even if the prior write-off resulted in no tax benefit to the mortgagee.[39] However, the mortgagee would then be entitled to a recovery exclusion for any amount previously written off without tax benefit.[40]

Against the basis for his loan, adjusted above, the mortgagee must set off the amount of the net proceeds received by him in the foreclosure sale. For this purpose, the net proceeds constitute the gross sales price paid by the purchaser at the foreclosure sale, reduced by the costs of foreclosure.[41] These expenses do not include any expenditures made by the mortgagee during the foreclosure to protect the property or to satisfy prior liens against the property.[42] Such expenditures to preserve and protect the property, if incurred during foreclosure, are added to the mortgagee's basis for whatever property he has left after foreclosure; in the case of a foreclosure by sale to a third party, the amounts of these expenditures are added to his basis for the deficiency judgment, to be written off when that judgment becomes worthless.

The net result of these adjustments is the measure of the mortgagee's loss. Whatever portion of his original basis for the loan remains after these adjustments and the application of the foreclosure proceeds constitutes his basis for any deficiency judgment obtained, to be written off when the deficiency becomes uncollectable or worth-

---

[37] Estate of Lucy S. Schieffelin, 44 B.T.A. 137, 140 (1941), acq. 1941-1 C.B. 9.

[38] Motor Products Corp., 47 B.T.A. 983, 1001 (1942), aff'd per curiam, 142 F.2d 449 (6th Cir. 1944); Ludlow Valve Mfg. Co. v. Durey, 62 F.2d 508, 509 (2nd Cir. 1933); see W.Z. Sharp, 8 B.T.A. 399 (1927), acq. VII-1 C.B. 28. Only business bad debts qualify for partial write-offs. Section 166 (d), I.R.C.; Reg. Sec. 1.166-5(a)(2).

[39] Bank of Newberry, 1 T.C. 374, 376 (1942), acq. on another point, 1943 C.B. 2; Bank of New York v. Commissioner, 147 F.2d 651 (2nd Cir., 1945), cert. den. 325 U.S. 872.

[40] Section 111, I.R.C., "Recovery exclusion" means an exclusion from income of an amount of bad debt recovery equal to the amount of prior bad debt deduction (for the same debt) which produced no tax benefit. This amount of the prior bad debt write-off is excluded from gross income when later recovered.

[41] See G.C.M. 19573, 1938-1 C.B. 214,216.

[42] Hadley Falls Trust Co. v. United States, 110 F.2d 887, 893 (1st Cir., 1940).

FORECLOSURE BY SALE TO A THIRD PARTY

less. Naturally, if the deficiency is later paid, no deduction for worthlessness is allowable, because no loss will have been suffered.

Example: Suppose Creditor loans Debtor $10,000, secured by a first mortgage on D's property. D pays back $1,000 before defaulting. In the year of default, C deducts a partial write-off of $2,000, on evidence that D's personal note is worthless and the mortgaged property is worth only $7,000. Prior to foreclosure C pays $200 of delinquent real property taxes on the property. C forecloses and pays an attorney's fee, court costs, brokerage, etc., of $500; the property is sold for $4,500. How much is C's loss?

C's original basis for loan		$10,000
Less: D's payments	$1,000	
Prior write-off	2,000	3,000
Basis after deductions		$ 7,000
Plus advances for taxes		200
C's adjusted basis for loan		$ 7,200
Foreclosure proceeds	$4,500	
Less expenses	500	$ 4,000
C's bad debt deduction		$ 3,200

C's bad debt deduction, business or non-business[43] as the case may be, is deductible immediately if no deficiency judgment was obtained; otherwise, the $3,200 bad debt is the basis of the deficiency judgment and becomes deductible in the year in which the judgment becomes worthless.

5. Mortgagee's Deduction for Previously Reported Income

If the mortgagee was on the accrual basis, he may have accrued interest on the debt as income in the year in which it became due. If any of the previously reported interest is delinquent when the mortgagee forecloses, he is entitled to a special adjustment for it. If the net amount realized on the foreclosure is less than his basis for the mortgage loan plus the accrued interest, the amount of the previously reported interest is deductible as a part of the mortgagee's bad debt loss.[44]

Example: Creditor loans Debtor $10,000 secured by a mortgage. D agrees to pay $500 a year interest. C, on the accrual basis, accrues two years' interest, or $1,000 prior to foreclosure as income. Assuming that no interest has been paid, we find that the amount of C's bad debt deduction is the difference between $11,000 (the principal of $10,000 and accrued interest of $1,000) and the net proceeds realized on the foreclosure sale.

Except in the above case, delinquent interest is not included in the measure of the mortgagee's bad debt deduction.[45] The fact that delinquent interest may be included as

---

[43] Of course, if the debt had been non-business in nature, there would have been no prior write-off of $2,000 for partial worthlessness. Only business bad debts qualify for partial worthlessness. Section 166(d)(1)(A), I.R.C.

[44] Reg. Sec. 1.166-6(a)(2).

[45] Tiscornia v. Commissioner, 95 F.2d 678, 683 (9th Cir. 1938); W.L. Moody Cotton Co. v. Commissioner, 143 F.2d 712, 714 (5th Cir. 1944); Henry v. Poor, 11 B.T.A. 781 (1928), aff'd per curiam, 30 F.2d 1019 (2nd Cir. 1929).

a part of the deficiency judgment is immaterial if that interest has not previously been reported as income.

6. Possibility of Gain or Income to the Mortgagee

Normally, the mortgagee will receive less than his basis for his mortgage loan in the foreclosure proceedings. However, it is possible that he may receive an amount in excess of his basis, due to one or more of the following circumstances:

(1) The mortgagee may have purchased the mortgage from the original lender at a substantial discount;

(2) The mortgage may have previously taken a deduction for partial worthlessness;

(3) The property may have appreciated in value sufficiently to affect its forced sale value.

Suppose the mortgagee does receive more than his adjusted basis for his loan. How is the excess recovery treated? An analysis of the possible allocations of the excess payment will make the answer clear. If, for instance, the excess payment is allocated to the recovery of a partial write-off of the mortgage debt in an earlier year, then it will be treated as the recovery of taxable income to the extent that the prior write-off had resulted in a tax benefit to the mortgagee.[46] To the extent that the prior deduction did not result in a tax benefit, the mortgagee will be entitled to exclude an equal amount of the recovery from income, under the provisions of Section 111, I.R.C.

On the other hand, the excess payment may represent the recovery of the discount at which a purchaser of the mortgage note bought the note from the original mortgagee. Here, again, the collection of the face amount of the mortgage note in excess of the price paid for it would represent ordinary income to the holder of the note. This result appears to be the general rule applied to collections on a note by a purchaser in excess of the price he paid for it.[47] Also, it has been held that collections by an estate upon a note owed to the decedent in excess of the estate tax valuation are ordinary income to the estate.[48] The decisions that require collections upon a purchase money note in excess of basis to be treated as ordinary income also bear out this conclusion.[49] However, special rules permitting capital gain treatment may be applicable in connection with the collection of an "original issue discount" on "bonds, debentures, notes

---

[46]See First National Bank of Lawrence County; 16 T.C. 147 (1951); Merchants National Bank of Mobile v. Commissioner, 199 F.2d 657, 659 (5th cir. 1952); National Bank of Commerce v. Commissioner, 115 F.2d 875 (9th Cir. 1940).

[47]Galvin Hudson, 20 T.C. 734 (1953), aff'd per curiam, 216 F.2d 748 (6th Cir. 1954); Peter Jung, Sr., par. 41,411 P-H Memo T.C. (1941).

[48]Herbert's Estate v. Commissioner, 139 F.2d 756 (3rd Cir. 1943), cert. den. 322 U.S. 752; Helvering v. Roth, 115 F.2d 239, 241 (2nd Cir. 1940); Estate of Ernst Zobel, 28 T.C. No. 97 (1957). The same is true of a note acquired in a corporate liquidation: Osenbach v. Commissioner, 198 F.2d 235, 237 (4th Cir. 1952). See the progenitor of these cases, Fairbanks v. United States, 306 U.S. 436 (1939).

[49]A.B. Culbertson, 14 T.C. 1421, 1424 (1950), acq. 1950-2 C.B. 1; Lee v. Commissioner, 119 F.2d 946 (7th Cir. 1941); Victor B. Gilbert, 6 T.C. 10, 13 (1946), acq. 1946-1 C.B. 2; Shafpa Realty Corp., 8 B.T.A. 283 (1927).

or certificates or other evidences of indebtedness . . . issued by any corporation, or government or political subdivision thereof."[50]

Similarly, any recovery on the mortgage note in excess of the face amount of the unpaid loan will be taxed as ordinary income to the extent of the interest in default; such an application of the excess payment represents the payment of interest.[51]

Presumably, any amount of the foreclosure price received in excess of the unpaid principal of the loan, plus interest in default, plus expenses of foreclosure, would be paid over to the mortgagor rather than to the mortgagee. Hence, there appears to be no possibility of a case in which the mortgagee could realize gain independently of these payments for prior write-offs, for discounts in the purchase price, and for overdue interest. We must conclude that all of the foreclosure gain paid to a mortgagee on a foreclosure sale to a third party will be taxed as ordinary income.

7. Mortgagor's Loss on Foreclosure Sale

Turning now to the position of the mortgagor, we find that he too may realize taxable gain or loss on the foreclosure sale of his property to a third party. Although the sale is made by decree of court (or by trustee's deed under a power of sale in a deed or trust), the tax law treats him as if he were a voluntary seller of the property. His gain or loss is measured in the same manner as gain or loss realized upon an ordinary sale.[52]

Let us first examine the more common situation in which the mortgagor suffers a loss on foreclosure. Here we are assuming that the net price realized on the foreclosure sale (gross proceeds less expenses of sale) is less than the mortgagor's cost or other basis for his property. The difference between his basis and the net price realized is the measure of his loss on foreclosure.[53]

Example: Assume that Debtor purchased a parcel of real estate for $25,000, paying $5,000 cash and a $20,000 note secured by a first deed of trust. Suppose D repaid $2,000 of the principal before default. On foreclosure, the net proceeds realized amounted to $18,000, just sufficient to pay off the mortgage debt in full. How much is D's loss?

D's basis for the mortgaged property	$25,000
Net price realized on foreclosure	18,000
Loss on foreclosure sale	$ 7,000

How is the loss to be computed if the net amount realized on foreclosure is not sufficient to discharge the mortgage debt in full? If the mortgage was taken or assumed in the acquisition of the property, we find that the net proceeds realized by the mortgagor must include the entire amount of the mortgage outstanding at the time of the foreclosure. This rule for measuring the amount realized on the sale of mortgaged

---

[50] Section 1232, I.R.C.
[51] Warner A. Shattuck, 25 T.C. 416, 422 (1955); Allen Tobey, 26 T.C. 610 (1956), acq. on another point, 1956-2 C.B. 8. See Fisher v. Commissioner, 209 F.2d 513 (6th Cir. 1954), cert. den. 347 U.S. 1014.
[52] Helvering v. Hammel, 311 U.S. 504 (1941); Electro-Chemical Engraving Co. v. Commissioner, 311 U.S. 513 (1941); I.T. 3135, 1937-2 C.B. 226.
[53] Section 1001, I.R.C.

property is a corollary to the rule which permits the mortgagor to include the entire amount of the mortgage debt in his basis for the property. Hence, the net amount realized includes the mortgage debt, whether or not the actual price is sufficient to discharge the debt in full.

Example: Assume in the above case that the property was knocked down to the highest bidder at $15,000. What then would be D's loss?

D's basis for the mortgaged property		$25,000
Net foreclosure sale proceeds (discharge of debt):		
Original mortgage debt	$20,000	
Less payments	2,000	18,000
Loss on foreclosure sale		$ 7,000

The amount of loss realized on the foreclosure is the same in this example as in the preceding one. In essence, the mortgagor's loss is limited to a write-off of his total investment in the property, regardless of the cash actually paid in the foreclosure action to the mortgagee. In both of the above cases, the mortgagor's total investment in the property is $7,000, consisting of his $5,000 down payment plus $2,000 of mortgage reduction. Consequently, you may find that most of the older cases measure the amount of the mortgagor's loss by his equity in the property.

But this measure may not be the full amount of the mortgagor's loss. He may also be compelled to pay a deficiency to the extent that the mortgagee's loan is not fully satisfied out of the foreclosure proceeds. If so, the amount of any deficiency later paid by the mortgagor is to be added to the payments previously made by him under the mortgage. In effect, the amount of any deficiency payment is added to his investment in the property for the purpose of ascertaining his loss.

Example: If we refer back to the above example we find that the net deficiency owing on the mortgage debt after application of the foreclosure proceeds would be $3,750, assuming foreclosure expenses of $750:

Original mortgage		$20,000
Less payments	2,000	$18,000
Foreclosure proceeds	$15,000	
Less expenses	750	14,250
Deficiency		$ 3,750

If D is required to pay the deficiency in full, the total amount of his loss on foreclosure is increased by $3,750, as follows:

D's basis for the mortgaged property			$25,000
Foreclosure sale proceeds:			
Original mortgage debt		$20,000	
Less payments	$2,000		
Less deficiency	3,750	5,750	14,250
Less on foreclosure			$10,750

If the mortgagor's loss was originally computed as the loss of his equity in the property, then the amount of the deficiency is added to his basis for his equity in order to ascertain the total amount of his loss.[54]

But suppose the mortgage loan bore no relationship to the mortgaged property at the time it was made. Suppose, for example, the loan had been taken out in order to engage in a certain line of business, not for the purpose of acquiring or improving the mortgaged property. In that event, it can be argued that the amount of any deficiency paid after foreclosure should not be added to the cost of the property for the purpose of determining the mortgagor's loss. Rather, the deficiency should be deductible on its own merits as a loss incurred in the conduct of the mortgagor's business.

There seems to be no direct authority on this point, but is has been held that a deficiency payment made in a taxable year after the foreclosure loss had been ascertained is deductible in the year paid; it need not necessarily be related back to the year of the foreclosure sale loss.[55]

Example: Debtor borrowed $30,000 in order to purchase inventory for his business. Creditor insisted upon security; so D gave him a first mortgage on certain real estate that constituted a capital asset in his hands. D defaulted. C foreclosed and realized a net amount of $20,000 on the foreclosure. If we assume that D's original basis for his property was $24,000, his loss on foreclosure would be computed as follows:

D's basis for the mortgaged property	$24,000
Amount realized on foreclosure	20,000
Loss on foreclosure	$ 4,000

In this example, the mortgage debt was not included in D's basis for the property; so D is not considered to have realized the outstanding mortgage debt on foreclosure; only the net proceeds actually applied to his debt are considered to have been received by him out of the foreclosure sale.

Suppose Creditor later collects the $10,000 deficiency from Debtor. The payment of the deficiency would be treated as the repayment of money previously borrowed; hence, no portion of the deficiency payment would be deductible. If any loss were incurred by Debtor on the sale of the inventory, that would be a loss deductible wholly independently of the foreclosure loss and the deficiency payment.

8. Nature of Mortgagor's Loss on Foreclosure

Because the mortgagor is treated as the seller of the mortgaged property on foreclosure, his loss is deductible only as a loss from the sale or exchange of property. Whether a deduction is allowed to the mortgagor for a capital or an ordinary loss depends upon the character of the property in his hands prior to foreclosure.[56] If the

---

[54] Harry H. Diamond, 43 B.T.A. 809, 812 (1941); see Richter v. Commissioner, 124 F.2d 412 (2nd Cir. 1942); Stamler v. Commissioner, 145 F.2d 37 (3rd Cir. 1954).
[55] Charles H. Black, 45 B.T.A. 204 (1941), acq. 1941-2 C.B. 2.
[56] Neils Shultz, 44 B.T.A. 146, 151 (1941), acq. 1941-1 C.B. 9.

property has been held by the mortgagor for use in his trade or business, then the loss would qualify for Section 1231, I.R.C., treatment.

For example, the full amount of the loss suffered by a farmer on the foreclosure sale of his farm was deductible (Section 1231) as a trade or business loss.[57] Similarly, the loss of improved rental real estate by foreclosure would be deductible as a Section 1231 loss.[58]

And if the mortgaged property were inventory property in the hands of the mortgagor, his loss would also be deductible in full against ordinary income.[59] For instance, any loss on foreclosure suffered by a real estate dealer on property held for sale to customers would qualify as an ordinary loss.[60]

Apart from these two categories of real property holdings, a mortgagor's loss on foreclosure sale is a capital loss. Because the property in his hands is a capital asset, his foreclosure loss is subject to allowance only under the restrictions imposed upon capital losses.[61]

9. Time for Deducting the Mortgagor's Loss on Foreclosure

When is the mortgagor's loss on foreclosure deductible? Because the transaction is considered to be a sale, the year of deduction is the year in which the sale becomes final. Thus, in any case in which the mortgagor has a right of redemption after foreclosure, the deduction for his loss must be postponed to the year in which his redemption right expires.[62] So long as he possesses the right to set aside the foreclosure sale by redeeming the property from the purchaser, the sale is not final and his loss is fixed for the purpose of a deduction.

Of course, if the mortgagor has no right of redemption under state law, the foreclosure sale itself would fix the year of loss.[63] Under these circumstances, if any payments are made on a deficiency after the year in which the foreclosure loss became final, these deficiency payments are deductible in the year made.[64]

But let us return to the more normal situation in which the mortgagor possesses the right to redeem. Suppose he decides not to exercise his right of redemption and he

---

[57]See McCarthy v. Cripe, 201 F.2d 679, 680 (7th Cir. 1953).
[58]Rothschild v. Berliner, 43 A.F.T.R. 1147 (N.D. Cal. 1950). See Leland Hazard, 7 T.C. 372, 375 (1946), acq. 1946-2 C.B. 3; Gilford v. Commissioner, 201 F.2d 735, 736 (2nd Cir. 1953). But cf. Susan P. Emery, 17 T.C. 308, 311 (1951), where the rented property was unimproved.
[59]Section 1221, I.R.C.
[60]Charles H. Black, 45 B.T.A. 204 (1941), acq. 1941-2 C.B. 2; Neils Schultz, 44 B.T.A. 146, 148, 151 (1941), acq. 1941-1 C.B. 9.
[61]Helvering v. Hammel, 311 U.S. 504 (1941); Harry H. Diamond, 43 B.T.A. 809 (1941).
[62]This rule applies whether the mortgagor retains possession during the period of redemption—Derby Realty Corp., 35 B.T.A. 335 (1937), acq. 1938-1 C.B. 9, appeal dismissed, 92 F.2d 999 (6th Cir. 1937); Sheldon Land Co., 42 B.T.A. 498, 505 (1940), acq. 1940-2 C.B. 6—or the purchaser takes immediate possession—J.C. Hawkins, 34 B.T.A. 918 (1936), acq. 1937-2 C.B. 13, aff'd 91 F.2d 354 (5th Cir. 1937); Nickoll v. Commissioner, 103 F.2d 619, 621 (7th Cir. 1939); G.C.M. 19367, 1937-2 C.B. 115. However, an exception may arise in any case in which the property is shown to be worthless in a year prior to foreclosure and evidence of abandonment in the earlier year is shown. James Petroleum Corp., 24 T.C. 509, 518 (1955), acq. 56-1 C.B. 4; see W.W. Hoffman, 40 B.T.A. 459, 462 (1939), acq. 1951-1 C.B. 2, aff'd 117 F.2d 987 (2d Cir. 1941).
[63]Nathan Schwartz, par. 51,125 P-H Memo T.C. (1951); see Helvering v. Hammel, 311 U.S. 504 (1941).
[64]Charles H. Black, 45 B.T.A. 204 (1941), acq. 1941-2 C.B. 2.

wishes to accelerate his loss. Can he take any steps to fix his loss prior to the date on which his redemption right will expire?

Obviously, if he quitclaims his interest in the property to the purchaser, he has released his equity of redemption; hence, his loss would be fixed in the year of release.[65] Thus, if a quitclaim deed is given in the year of the foreclosure sale, the mortgagor's loss will be deductible in the year of foreclosure.[66]

Can acceleration of the foreclosure loss be accomplished in any other manner? Suppose, after foreclosure, the mortgagor decides that he will not exercise his right of redemption on the ground that the property is not worth the price of redemption. Under these circumstances, the date of his loss may be fixed by evidence of an abandonment of the right of redemption.

For example, it has been held that a write-off of an investment in property as worthless on the owner's books was sufficient to justify a deduction for the loss in the year of a tax sale; the book entry evidenced an abandonment of the right of redemption.[67] Also, a showing of a deliberate decision on the part of a group of mortgagors to abandon the foreclosed property was sufficient to establish the deduction in the year of foreclosure.[68]

Although it is possible to accelerate the foreclosure loss by abandonment, the better procedure is the execution and delivery of a quitclaim deed to the mortgagee. Proof of the deed of relinquishment would be easier and stronger proof than the showing of an abandonment.

We should consider one further aspect of the rules governing the finality of foreclosure sales. Suppose the mortgagor contests the foreclosure proceeding by taking an appeal from the decree of foreclosure. As long as the decree has not become final, the loss is deductible. Until the mortgagor's appeal or suit to set aside the foreclosure is settled, his loss will not be fixed for purposes of a deduction.[69]

Naturally, if the mortgagor exercises his right to redemption by recovering the property, he realizes no deductible loss.[70] Any payment in excess of his original basis for the property would be added to his basis for the redeemed property.

10. Mortgagor's Gain on Foreclosure Sale

It is possible, though not probable, that the mortgagor may realize taxable gain on foreclosure. Suppose, for example, that the price received on the foreclosure sale

---

[65] Atmore Realty Co., par. 42,248 P-H Memo, B.T.A. (1942).
[66] See Sherwin A. Hill, 40 B.T.A. 376, 380, non-acq. on another ground, 1939-2 C.B. 53, 58 reversed on another ground, 119 F.2d 421 (6th Cir. 1941).
[67] See Commissioner v. Peterman, 118 F.2d 973, 976 (9th Cir. 1941).
[68] Jacob Abelson, 44 B.T.A. 98, 104, non-acq. 1941-2 C.B. 14.
[69] Morton v. Commissioner, 104 F.2d 534, 536 (4th Cir. 1939); Edward and John Burke, Ltd., 3 T.C. 1031, 1040 (1944), acq. 1944 C.B. 4.
[70] Ferdinand Hotz, 42 B.T.A. 432 (1940). Cf. Tompkins v. Commissioner, 97 F.2d 396, 401 (4th cir. 1938), in which one of the mortgagors purchased the property at the foreclosure sale. Its purchase at the sale was not treated as the equivalent as a redemption; hence the foreclosure loss was allowed to the mortgagor in the year of foreclosure. In McCarthy v. Cripe, 201 F.2d 679, 682 (7th Cir. 1953), a similar situation occurred and the government argued that Section 267, I.R.C. disallowing losses between related parties, would prevent the mortgagor from taking a deduction for his share of the foreclosure loss. The court allowed the loss, finding that Section 267 was confined to voluntary sales.

exceeded the mortgagor's basis for his property; the amount of the excess would be taxable gain to him just as if the sale were voluntary. For this purpose, it is immaterial whether any part of the proceeds are paid to the mortgagor. If the proceeds in excess of the mortgagor's basis are paid to the mortgagee, to be applied to the mortgage debt, the mortgagor is taxed for their receipt just as if he had received the cash directly.[71]

Example: Assume that Debtor purchased a parcel of real estate ten years ago for $40,000. The property has been used for rental purposes. Last year D borrowed $35,000 from Creditor, putting up the property as security. In the ten-year period, D took $10,000 depreciation on the property, reducing his basis to $30,000. Suppose D failed to make any payments on the mortgage and this year C foreclosed to collect the $35,000 principal together with $1,000 of delinquent interest. Let us assume the property was sold for $37,500 in the foreclosure proceeding, C being paid $36,000 on principal and interest, D receiving $500, and $1,000 being consumed in expenses. D's gain would be computed as follows:

Proceeds realized on foreclosure		$37,500
Less expenses of sale		1,000
Net proceeds realized on foreclosure		$36,500
D's original basis	$40,000	
Less depreciation	10,000	30,000
D's gain on foreclosure		$ 6,500

Of the $6,500 gain, $6,000 was realized by credit on D's liability for the mortgage loan; the remaining $500 was realized as cash in hand. If D had not previously taken a deduction for the interest paid in the foreclosure, he would be entitled to a deduction for $1,000 interest paid out of the foreclosure proceeds in the year of the sale.[72]

Nor is this the only case in which the mortgagor may realize gain on foreclosure. Assume, for example, that property is purchased for $20,000, the consideration being $5,000 cash and the assumption of a $15,000 mortgage. Prior to foreclosure, the property appreciates in value; thus, any amount received on the foreclosure sale in excess of the mortgagor's basis of $20,000, plus expenses of foreclosure, would be taxable gain to him.

If the property were a capital asset in the hands of the mortgagor, or if it were trade or business property held for more than six months, then the gain would be taxed as capital gain. Otherwise the gain would be included in ordinary income.[73]

11. Gain or Loss of a Non-assuming Mortgagor

Is the application of these rules affected by the fact that the mortgagor-owner may not have assumed personal liability for the mortgage debt? Because we must view the mortgagor as a seller of the mortgaged property, the rules for determining the nature of the mortgagor's loss and the time for its deduction are the same whether or not he was personally liable on the indebtedness.[74]

---

[71]The gain would not be taxed until the possibility of a deficiency recovery was barred. R. O'Dell & Sons, Inc., 169 F.2d 247, 249 (2nd Cir. 1948).
[72]See Harold M. Blossom, 38 B.T.A. 1136 (1938), acq. 1939-1 C.B. (Part 1) 4.
[73]See Peninsula Properties Co., Ltd., 47 B.T.A. 84, 91, acq. 1942-2 C.B. 14.
[74]Jacob Abelson, 44 B.T.A. 98, 103 (1941), non-acq. 1941-2 C.B. 14; Edward F.C. McLaughlin, 43 B.T.A. 528 (1941).

FORECLOSURE BY SALE TO A THIRD PARTY

Is there any difference in making the computation of his loss? Most of the earlier cases which discuss the problem of a non-assuming mortgagor measure his loss on foreclosure by the cost of his equity in the property.[75] These cases, however, antedate the decision of the Supreme Court in *Crane v. Commissioner*.[76] In that case, it was held that the entire amount of the mortgage indebtedness outstanding at the time of acquisition of the property must be included in the mortgagor's basis for the property. Hence, the corollary must follow that the price realized on a sale of the property includes the entire amount of the mortgage indebtedness outstanding at the time of foreclosure. Consequently, the computation of a mortgagor's loss is the same whether or not he is also the debtor liable for the mortgage debt.

Example: Owner purchases property from Debtor $5,000. The property is transferred to O subject to a $15,000 mortgage which O does not assume. Subsequently, the mortgage is foreclosed and the property is sold for $15,000, all of which is paid to the mortgagee. O's loss of $5,000 would be computed as follows:

O's basis for the property	$20,000
Proceeds realized	15,000
O's loss	$ 5,000

If the property were sold for only $12,000, O's loss would still be limited to his $5,000 investment, computed as follows:

O's basis for the property	$20,000
Proceeds realized (liability discharged)	15,000
O's loss	$ 5,000

Because no deficiency would be collectable from O, his loss could not be increased by any subsequent deficiency payments as in the case of the original mortgage debtor.

The importance of this method of computation appears in the case of a possible gain to the mortgagor. If the mortgagor's basis has been confined to his equity in the property, he will realize a gain only to the extent that he receives proceeds out of the foreclosure in excess of his investment in the property. But the courts have not let the non-assuming mortgagor off so easily. Because he is treated as having realized the entire amount of the outstanding mortgage, he may, in fact, be required to report a gain even in a case in which he actually receives no part of the sale proceeds.[77]

Example: Owner acquires property which is subject to a $300,000 mortgage, none of which is assumed by him. For the purpose of computing depreciation, O includes the entire mortgage debt in his basis. Prior to foreclosure, O takes the benefit of $45,000 of depreciation. During the period, he pays off $13,000 of the initial mortgage debt. Assume that the remainder of the debt is discharged in the foreclosure. What is his gain, if any?

---

[75] Edward F.C. McLaughlin, 43 B.T.A. 528 (1941); Welch v. Street, 116 F.2d 953, 955 (1st Cir. 1941); Commissioner v. Abramson, 124 F.2d 416 (2nd Cir. 1942). See Helvering v. Nebraska Bridge Supply & Lumber Co., 115 F.2d 288, 291 (8th Cir. 1940), reversed, 312 U.S. 666 (1941).
[76] 331 U.S. 1, 13 (1947).
[77] Woodsam Associates, Inc. v. Commissioner, 198 F.2d 357 (2d Cir. 1952). See Mendham Corp., 9 T.C. 320 (1947).

Proceeds realized ($300,000 − $3,000)		$287,000
O's basis for the property	$300,000	
Less depreciation	45,000	255,000
Gain realized		$ 32,000

In effect, the foreclosure sale forces him to recoup his depreciation as gain (usually capital or recapture gain) to the extent that it exceeds the payments made by him on the mortgage. Because the mortgagor has had the advantage of a deduction for this depreciation, he should not be heard to complain.[78]

12. Suggestions on Foreclosure of Mortgage by Sale to Third Party

The mortgagee's problem is simply stated: when should he deduct his loss? The answer depends upon when his deficiency judgment becomes worthless. Consequently, the mortgagee should be alert to collect evidence such as the following to sustain a write-off of the deficiency judgment:

(1) Proof of an unsuccessful attempt to collect;
(2) Proof of the mortgagor's insolvency;
(3) Proof of bankruptcy without assets to satisfy the deficiency;
(4) Proof of the mortgagor's disappearance without assets.

If such evidence is available in the year of foreclosure, the mortgagee's loss will be deductible in that year; otherwise, his loss deduction will be postponed to the year the deficiency judgment becomes unenforceable or worthless.

The mortgagor faces a similar problem in a foreclosure sale. His problem is one of determining whether his loss is deductible in the year of foreclosure or the year when his right of redemption expires. If he wishes to perfect his loss deduction prior to the date his redemption right expires, he may do so by releasing or abandoning that right. The facts showing the release or abandonment should be carefully marshalled for later proof, in case the timing of the deduction is challenged.

C. STRICT FORECLOSURE: INVOLUNTARY CONVEYANCE TO MORTGAGEE

In a strict foreclosure, the court orders the property to be conveyed to the mortgagee in full satisfaction of the mortgage debt. No sale of the property is held, nor is any deficiency judgment obtainable. The conveyance of the property is deemed to be payment of the mortgage debt in full.

This type of foreclosure creates three basic problems requiring analysis under the tax laws. First, does the mortgage realize a gain or loss at the time of foreclosure, and if so, how much? Second, and related to the first problem, what is the measure of the

---

[78]See Parker v. Delaney, 186 F.2d 455 (1st Cir. 1950), cert. den. 341 U.S. 926. The facts of the example in the text are akin to those of the Parker case, except that the court assumed the mortgagor's basis to be the amount of the mortgage outstanding at the time of foreclosure. Hence, the amount of the interviewing payments of principal was subtracted from the depreciation deducted by him for the purpose of ascertaining the net benefit realized by him from his ownership of the property.

mortgagee's basis for the property conveyed to him? And, third, does the mortgagor realize a gain or loss? If so, to what extent?

1. Loss on Involuntary Conveyance to Mortgagee

In a strict foreclosure, the mortgagee receives the mortgaged property in satisfaction of his debt; the value of the property measures the amount of his recovery on the mortgage debt. In effect, the debt is considered to be paid to the extent of the value of the property.[79]

Consequently, we find that the mortgagee realizes a loss in any case in which the value of the property received is less than his basis for his loan. Because the property is accepted in payment of the loan, the mortgagee's loss is deductible as a bad debt realized in the year of foreclosure.[80] No postponement of the time for deduction can occur because of the absence of any deficiency judgment.

The amount of the mortgagee's bad debt is the difference between the value of the property and the mortgagee's basis for his loan at the time of foreclosure. For this purpose, the basis of the mortgagee's loan must be adjusted in the same manner as in the case of a foreclosure by sale to a third party.

Similarly, the bad debt realized will be deductible as a business or non-business bad debt depending upon whether or not the debt, or its worthlessness, was incurred in the course of the mortgagee's trade or business.[81]

Example: Creditor had loaned Debtor $20,000 on a note secured by a first mortgage on D's property. C forecloses on his mortgage and the court orders the property conveyed to him in full satisfaction. After receiving the property, C has it appraised at a market value of $17,500. C's loss of $2,500 will be deductible by him as a bad debt, business or non-business, as the case may be.

The importance of establishing the value of the property at the time of foreclosure is obvious. If the mortgagee is unable to show the value of the property, he will not be entitled to any deduction for a bad debt.[82]

2. Gain to Mortgagee on Involuntary Conveyance of Property

What if the value of the property received in the foreclosure exceeds the mortgagee's basis for his loan? To the extent that the excess value can be allocated to delinquent interest, to prior write-offs for partial worthlessness, or to collections on the face of the mortgage note in excess of the price paid for the note, the excess will be taxed as the receipt of ordinary income.[83]

---

[79] See I.T. 3548, 1942-1 C.B. 74.
[80] See Commissioner v. Spreckles, 120 F.2d 517 (9th Cir. 1941); Rogan v. Commercial Discount Co., 149 F.2d 585, 587 (9th Cir. 1945), cert. den. 326 U.S. 764; Bingham v. Commissioner, 105 F.2d 971 (2d Cir. 1939); Commissioner v. National Bank of Commerce, 112 F.2d 946 (5th Cir. 1940); Harold S. Denniston, 37 B.T.A. 834, acq. 1942-2 C.B. 5.
[81] Section 166, I.R.C.
[82] Daniel Hecker, 17 B.T.A. 874, 876 (1929), acq. on another point, IX-1 C.B. 23. See Francis Perot's Sons Malting Co., 1 B.T.A. 562 (1925).
[83] Manufacturer's Life Insurance Co., 43 B.T.A. 864, 873 (1941), acq. 1947-1 C.B. 3; Edward A. Atlas, par. 45,044 P-H Memo T.C. (1945).

But what is the rule if the value in excess of the basis for the loan cannot be attributed to the collection of interest, discount, or prior write-offs? Is such excess value taxed as ordinary income or as capital gain? Or is it taxed at all?

The answer depends upon the analysis of the transaction by the courts. In all of these cases, with an exception noted below, the Commissioner appears to have set up the excess value as capital or recapture gain received by the mortgagee on the exchange of his mortgage note for the property. One defense, as yet unsuccessful, asserted by the mortgagee to this treatment is the defense that the mortgagee is the purchaser of the foreclosed property. The fact that a purchaser is able to buy property worth more than he paid for it is not considered to result in the receipt of taxable gain.

This defense has been rejected by the courts.[84] The mortgagee is treated as disposing of his note for the property in a taxable exchange. He is taxed on the excess value received just as if he had exchanged the note for property belonging to a third party. The value of the property received in excess of the mortgagee's basis for his note plus interest is, therefore, taxed as gain realized on an exchange by him.[85]

Ordinarily, the amount of the gain seems to qualify for capital gain treatment.[86] However, the Commissioner has been successful in taxing the gain as ordinary income in a case in which he was able to show that it represented consideration for a promise to extend time of payment of the mortgage note.[87] In view of the fact that the Commissioner has conceded that the foreclosure transaction is not a sale or exchange in the case of a loss, the treatment of the excess value as capital gain would seem to rest at present upon shaky grounds.[88] But the result of rejecting the sale or exchange theory would not necessarily cause the excess value to be converted into ordinary income. The ultimate result may be to permit the excess value to be received without being taxed if the bargain purchase analysis can be applied successfully to the transaction. Which answer will be adopted depends upon the course of future litigation in the area of the mortgagor-mortgagee relationship.

Example: Creditor loans Debtor $20,000, taking in exchange for the loan D's note secured by a mortgage on D's home. D fails to make any payments. C has D's home appraised and the value placed on the home is only $18,000. On the strength of the appraisal C writes off $2,000 of the loan as a deduction for partial worthlessness. In a later year C forecloses and acquires the property in a strict foreclosure action. At the time of foreclosure the property is worth $22,000. Assume that $1,000 of interest is in default at the time of foreclosure. What is C's gain, and how is it taxed?

Value of the property acquired	$22,000
Less basis for C's note	18,000
Excess value over basis	$ 4,000

---

[84]See, e.g., Elverson Corp. v. Helvering, 122 F.2d 295 (2d Cir. 1941), in which it was stated that only a bargain purchase for cash can result in unrealized gain; Henry Heldt, 16 B.T.A. 1035, 1036 (1929).

[85]Elverson Corp. v. Helvering, 122 F.2d 295, 297 (2d Cir. 1941); Kathryn Lammerding, 40 B.T.A. 589 (1939), aff'd 121 F.2d 80 (D.C. Cir. 1941). See Commissioner v. Sisto Financial Corp., 139 F.2d 253, 255 (2d Cir. 1943).

[86]See Neville Coke & Chemical Co., 3 T.C. 113 (1944), aff'd, 148 F.2d 599 (3rd Cir. 1945), cert. den. 326 U.S. 726.

[87]Elverson Corp., 40 B.T.A. 615, 634, aff'd 122 F.2d 295 (2d Cir. 1941).

[88]I.T. 3548, 1942-1 C.B. 74, revoking I.T. 3121, 1937-2 C.B. 138, which had ruled the mortgagee's loss to be one incurred upon the sale or other disposition of the mortgage note.

STRICT FORECLOSURE

Recovery of prior write-off	$2,000	
Recovery of interest	1,000	3,000
Remainder of gain		$ 1,000

Of C's total gain of $4,000, $2,000 will be taxed as ordinary income on the recovery of the partial write-off (subject to a possible recovery exclusion of the prior write-off if it produced no tax benefit[89]); $1,000 of the gain will be taxed as the payment of interest. The remainder of the gain, or $1,000, will represent gain realized on the disposition of the note. If the note is a capital asset in the hands of the mortgagee, the gain will be taxed as capital gain.

3. Basis of Acquired Property to Mortgagee

The mortgagee's basis for the property acquired by him in a strict foreclosure proceeding is the fair market value of the property when acquired.[90] In effect, only the portion of the mortgagee's basis for his loan which equals the value of the property is transferred to the property. The remainder of his basis for his loan, if any, is written off at the time of foreclosure as a bad debt deduction. This is true even when the mortgagee's bad debt deduction does not result in a tax benefit to the mortgagee in the year of deduction.[91]

Example: Assume that Creditor received property worth $10,000 in the foreclosure of a mortgage loan having a basis to him of $15,000. C's basis for the property received would be $10,000 and the remaining $5,000 of his loan basis would qualify for a bad debt write-off.

The same rule holds true in the case of a foreclosure resulting in the realization of income or gain to the mortgagee. The excess value of the property would be taxed to the mortgagee under the principles developed in the preceding section and, consequently, could be added to the mortgagee's basis for his loan for the purpose of determining his basis for the property.

Example: If Creditor forecloses upon property worth $10,000 in satisfaction of a mortgage debt that has a basis to him of only $8,000, his basis for the property would be $10,000. The additional $2,000 would be taxed to him as income or gain realized in the year of foreclosure.

4. Mortgagor's Loss on Strict Foreclosure

In a strict foreclosure proceeding, the mortgagor loses his property in exchange for the cancellation of his indebtedness. Although the conveyance is involuntary, the mortgagor is treated as if he had voluntarily sold his property and paid the proceeds to the mortgagee in full satisfaction.[92] The assumed price received for the property is the full amount of the debt canceled, including delinquent interest.

In any case in which the mortgagor's basis for his property exceeds the debt

---

[89] Section 111, I.R.C.
[90] See Kohn v. Commissioner, 197 F.2d 480 (2d Cir. 1952); Bennet v. Commissioner, 139 F.2d 961, 965 (8th Cir. 1944); W.D. Haden Co. v. Commissioner, 165 F.2d 588, 589 (5th Cir. 1948); Margery K. Megargel, 3 T.C. 238, 248 (1944), acq. 1944 C.B. 19; I.T. 3548, 1942-1 C.B. 74.
[91] First National Bank of Philipsburg, 43 B.T.A. 456 (1941).
[92] See E.F. Simms, 28 B.T.A. 988, 1030 (1933), acq. XV-2 C.B. 22.

canceled, he realizes a loss to the extent of the difference. This loss is one incurred upon the sale or exchange of the property. Consequently, the loss will be deductible only as a capital loss, unless the property is inventory property, or trade or business property.

The time for deducting the loss depends upon when the sale or exchange becomes final. If the mortgagor has the right to redeem the property from the foreclosure, the loss occurs in the year his redemption right expires, is released, or becomes worthless. In the absence of a right of redemption, the mortgagor's loss is fixed in the year of foreclosure.

Example: Debtor buys unimproved land for $40,000, paying $15,000 and borrowing the remainder from Creditor on his personal note secured by a mortgage on the land. Assume that C forecloses and acquires the property in a strict foreclosure proceeding. If the debt canceled in the foreclosure was $25,000, D's loss would be computed as follows:

D's basis for the property	$40,000
Amount of debt canceled	25,000
D's loss on foreclosure	$15,000

Suppose, however, the value of the property transferred to the mortgagee is sufficient to force the recognition of interest income to him. In view of the fact that the mortgagor has used part of his property to pay delinquent interest, ought not he be entitled to a deduction for interest paid in an amount equal to the interest reported by the mortgagee?[93] Part of the mortgagor's loss on the exchange of his property would thereby be converted into a deduction against ordinary income for interest paid.

Example: Let us refer to the facts of the preceding example, but assume that at the time of foreclosure $1,500 of interest is in default. The foreclosure proceeding cancels the mortgagor's liability both for principal and for interest due. Assume, further, that the value of the property equals or exceeds $26,500, so that C must report the entire $1,500 as interest income received on foreclosure. What is D's loss on the exchange and his interest deduction?

D's basis for the property		$40,000
Amount received:		
Debt canceled	$25,000	
Interest canceled	1,500	26,500
D's loss on the exchange		$13,500
D's deduction for interest paid		1,500

Thus, if D suffers a capital loss on the exchange, part of it would be converted into a deduction for interest against ordinary income. But not in the case of an insolvent debtor.[94]

5. Mortgagor's Gain on Strict Foreclosure

If we refer back to the beginning of the preceding section, we see that the foreclosure may result in the receipt of taxable gain to the mortgagor under certain cir-

---

[93] See Harold M. Blossom, 38 B.T.A. 1136 (1938), acq. 1939-1 C.B. (Part 1) 4; Helvering v. Midland Mutual Life Ins. Co., 300 U.S. 216, 224 (dictum) (1937).
[94] George R. Newhouse, 59 T.C. 783 (1973). The entire recovery is applied to principal.

cumstances. The measure of the gain or loss is the difference between the debt canceled and the mortgagor's basis for the foreclosed property; if the amount of the debt canceled exceeds the mortgagor's basis for the property, then the difference represents taxable gain to the mortgagor.[95]

The nature of the gain to the mortgagor will depend upon the nature and the period of the mortgagor's holding of the property. If the property had been a capital asset in his hands prior to foreclosure, his gain will be capital gain;[96] the same result would apply to trade or business property held for more than six months.[97] Gain from inventory property would, of course, be classified as ordinary income.

Example: Debtor mortgages property that originally cost him $40,000 to secure a loan of $30,000. Over a period of years D had taken $15,000 of depreciation on the property so that, at the time of foreclosure, his adjusted basis was only $25,000. If the property were foreclosed in a strict foreclosure proceeding which extinguished D's liability for the $30,000 loan, D's gain would be computed as follows:

Amount of debt canceled	$30,000
Less D's basis for the property	25,000
Gain realized by D on foreclosure	$ 5,000

If the mortgagor is faced with this possibility, it may be wise for him to attempt to reach a voluntary settlement of the mortgage loan prior to foreclosure. In this way, he may escape being taxed on the potential gain under any one of the following exceptions:[98]

(1) The transaction represented a gratuitous cancellation of indebtedness by the mortgagee.

(2) The transaction represented a cancellation of indebtedness which is not taxable because the mortgagor was insolvent both before and after the cancellation.

(3) The transaction represented a renegotiation of the original purchase price between the seller-mortgagee and the purchaser-mortgagor.

But when the settlement of the mortgage debt is obtained through the mechanics of a foreclosure proceeding that results in an involuntary conveyance of the property, the mortgagor will be in a much poorer position to claim the benefit of any of these exceptions to the general rule taxing his gain. By and large, these exceptions are based upon voluntary negotiations between the parties rather than upon the involuntary transaction resulting from the application of creditors' remedies available to the mortgagee.

6. Suggestions on Strict Foreclosure

The mortgagee's most serious problem in a strict foreclosure proceeding is one of proving the value of the property conveyed to him. His right to a bad debt deduction

---

[95] See E.F. Simms, 28 B.T.A. 988, 1030 (1933), acq. XV-2 C.B. 22; Lutz & Schramm Co., 1 T.C. 682 (1943), non-acq. on another point, 1943 C.B. 35; J.K. McAlpine Land & Development Co., 43 B.T.A. 520, 526 (1941), aff'd on another point, 126 F.2d 163 (9th Cir. 1942); Carlisle Packing Co., 29 B.T.A. 514 (1933); Twin Port Bridge Co., 27 B.T.A. 346 (1932).

[96] Peninsula Properties Co., 47 B.T.A. 84, 91 (1942), acq. 1942-2 C.B. 14.

[97] Section 1231, I.R.C.

[98] These exceptions are discussed below in more detail, Part E, *infra*.

depends upon proof that the value of the property is less than his basis for the canceled debt. Even if the property is equal to or greater in value than the basis for his loan, the amount of income or gain to be reported will again depend upon the value of the property. Then, too, the value of the property will constitute its basis to the mortgagee after foreclosure.

Because the foreclosure does not result in an actual sale, the proceeding itself will not usually produce any evidence of value; it is incumbent upon the mortgagee to prove that value by other evidence. Ordinarily, his best bet would be a contemporaneous appraisal of the property by an independent qualified appraiser. The transaction should be reported in conformity with the appraisal, which should be retained to prove the correctness of the reported figure should a question later arise.

Ordinarily, the matter of the value of the foreclosed property is of no concern to the mortgagor. His gain or loss is measured by the difference between his basis for the property and the debt canceled. His problem, if any, is one of escaping the possibility of a tax if the debt to be canceled exceeds his basis for the property. If this possibility faces him, the mortgagor would be well advised to attempt to settle the debt by voluntary negotiation under principles discussed in Part E.

C. FORECLOSURE BY SALE TO THE MORTGAGEE

Here we revert to the first type of foreclosure, namely foreclosure by sale. The only difference between this part and the first part is that we are now dealing with the case in which the mortgagee himself buys the property at the foreclosure sale.

Thus, the transaction is a hybrid between foreclosure by sale to a third party and strict foreclosure. A sale price is established by the proceeding and the mortgagee may obtain a deficiency judgment as in any other sale foreclosure. But the mortgagee ends up with the property as in the case of a strict foreclosure. As we might expect, the hybrid nature of the transaction has resulted in the development of a hybrid set of tax rules.

1. Loss to Mortgagee Who Bids in

A mortgagee who bids in at a foreclosure sale may realize two losses, each of them independently deductible. The first loss arises in any case in which the amount bid in is less than the basis for his loan. The amount of difference between the bid price and the loan is the measure of the loss, which is deductible as a bad debt realized in the year and to the extent that the deficiency becomes unenforceable or uncollectable.[99]

But the mortgagee received payment not in cash but in a conveyance of the property. Suppose the property is worth less than the amount for which it was bid in. Is the mortgagee entitled to an additional loss deduction for the difference between the value of the property received and the bid price?

By analogy to the strict foreclosure situation, the mortgagee ought to be entitled to disregard the bid price entirely; his bad debt deduction would then be measured by the difference between the amount of his debt and the value of the property.

---

[99] Reg. Sec. 1.166-6(a).

FORECLOSURE BY SALE TO THE MORTGAGEE

Unfortunately, this simple rule does not prevail. This factual variation to the normal foreclosure proceeding came to the Supreme Court before the rules relating to strict foreclosures had been worked out. And in *Helvering v. Midland Mutual Life Insurance Co.*,[100] the Supreme Court denied a mortgagee the right to deduct the difference between his bid price and the value of the property. The mortgagee's bid price was taken as conclusive of the value of the property. On this theory, the Supreme Court ignored the economic facts of the transaction and treated the mortgagee as if he had been paid off in property worth the price bid for it.

It was not long, however, before the courts and the Commissioner carved an exception to the *Midland Mutual* rule.[101] That decision was treated as if it merely established a presumption in favor of the correctness of the bid price; hence, if the mortgagee were able to show by "clear and convincing proof"[102] that the value of the property was less than the bid price, he was entitled to a deduction for the difference.[103]

Example: Creditor forecloses on a mortgage debt of $10,000. He bids in his debt at $8,000. At the time the property is sold to him, its value is fixed at $5,000. What is his loss?

Amount of mortgage debt		$10,000
Less value of property received		5,000
Mortgagee's total loss		5,000
Amount deductible as bad debt:		
Mortgage debt	$10,000	
Less bid price	8,000	2,000
Remainder of mortgagee's loss		$ 3,000

2. Nature of Loss to Mortgagee Who Bids In

Because of the interposition of the *Midland Mutual* rule, the amount of the mortgagee's additional loss was not added to the mortgagee's bad debt deduction as it should be. Instead, the additional loss was considered to be a separate deduction. On the curious theory that this additional loss was incurred on the disposition of the mortgagee's note for the property, the loss has uniformly been held to be a capital loss.[104]

The time for deduction of the additional capital loss occurs when the foreclosure proceeding becomes final. Thus, any right of redemption held by the mortgagor will operate to postpone the date of the mortgagee's deduction until the right expires, or is released or abandoned.[105]

---

[100] 300 U.S. 216 (1937).

[101] Elliot S. Nichols, 1 T.C. 328 (1942), reversed, 141 F.2d 870 (6th Cir. 1944). The Commissioner acquiesced in the result. Aug. 1943—C.B. 17.

[102] Reg. Sec. 1.166-6(b). What constitutes "clear and convincing proof" is well illustrated by comparing Helvering v. New President Corp., 122 F.2d 92, 97 (8th Cir. 1941) with Korth v. Zion's Savings Bank & Trust Co., 148 F.2d 170 (10th Cir. 1945).

[103] Nichols v. Commissioner, 141 F.2d 870, 876 (6th Cir. 1944); Hadley Falls Trust Co. v. United States, 110 F.2d 887, 893 (1st Cir. 1940).

[104] Larson v. Cuesta, 120 F.2d 482 (5th Cir. 1941); Hadley Falls Trust Co. v. United States, 110 F.2d 887, 892 (1st Cir. 1940); Nichols v. Commissioner, 141 F.2d 870, 876 (6th Cir. 1944); I.T. 3159, 1938-1 C.B. 188.

[105] G.C.M. 19573, 1938-1 C.B. 214, 216. The Tax Court holds to the contrary; a sheriff's sale establishes the date of deduction despite a right of redemption. Securities Mortgage Co., 58 T.C. 667 (1972).

3. Reduction of Loss to Mortgagee Who Bids In

Undoubtedly the Commissioner was influenced in his decision to limit the effect of the *Midland Mutual* case by the fact that its literal application would pave the way to widespread juggling of the bid price. By negotiating a low bid, a mortgagee would be able to write off most of his mortgage loan as a bad debt and yet acquire property worth considerably more than the bid price. Hence, if the Commissioner is able to show by "clear and convincing proof" that the property is worth more than the bid price, he can charge the mortgagee with capital gain on the transaction to offset in part the fictitiously large bad deduction.[106]

4. Gain to Mortgagee Who Bids In

Suppose the mortgagee bids in at the foreclosure sale to acquire property that is worth more than the remaining basis for the mortgage loan. If the Commissioner can set aside the rule of *Midland Mutual* by showing "clear and convincing proof" of value in excess of the loan basis, can he tax the excess value as gain realized by the mortgagee out of the foreclosure?

Although the courts have been reluctant to reach this conclusion, the answer appears to be yes.[107] Just as the Commissioner may use the value of the property to offset the mortgagee's bad debt, he can assess the mortgagee with a tax on the overall gain arising out of a foreclosure. To the extent, then, that the value of the property exceeds his loan basis, gain will be realized.[108]

For example, suppose the mortgage holder had purchased the mortgage at a substantial discount. He later foreclosed and bid in the entire amount of the mortgage debt. If the property is worth the bid price, the mortgage holder will be taxed upon the difference between the value of the property and his basis for the loan as a foreclosure gain.[109] The use of the mortgage debt acquired at a discount to purchase property worth more than the price paid by the mortgagee for the mortgage debt was in itself sufficient justification on which to tax the gain.[110]

Example: Creditor purchased a $30,000 first mortgage debt for $25,000. Later C is forced to foreclose to collect the debt. He bids in the entire amount of his debt and acquires the property in the foreclosure proceeding. If we assume that the property was worth $30,000 at the time of foreclosure, his taxable gain would be computed as follows:

Face amount of obligation bid in	$30,000
Less C's basis for mortgage debt	25,000
Gain realized on foreclosure	$ 5,000

---

[106]The withdrawal of I.T. 3159 indicates that the Service takes the position that the gain or loss on repossession is capital or ordinary, not part of both.

[107]See Helvering v. New President Corp., 122 F.2d 92, 97 (8th Cir. 1941); James J. Reilly, 46 B.T.A. 1246, 1251 (1942), acq. 1942-2 C.B. 15.

[108]Aaron W. Hardwick, Par. 47,060 P-H Memo T.C. (1947); contra, Egbert J. Henschel, Par. 38,187 P-H Memo B.T.A. (1938).

[109]Clarkson Coal Co., 46 B.T.A. 688 (1942); Commissioner v. West Production Co., 121 F.2d 9, 11 (5th Cir. 1941), cert. den. 314 U.S. 682.

[110]West Production Co., 41 B.T.A. 1043, 1049 (1940), aff'd, 121 F.2d 9, 11 (5th Cir. 1941), cert. den. 314 U.S. 682.

Could C avoid the gain by bidding in only $25,000 of the mortgage debt? If the realization of the gain is dependent upon the realization of the discount, he might avoid a tax upon the gain.

However, the Commissioner's theory of the realization of gain goes beyond the question of the discount. It rests not upon the bid price but upon the value of the property received. Gain will be realized if the value of the property received exceeds the mortgagee's basis for his note, whether or not that note was acquired at a discount.

Although this theory has not been spelled out clearly in the cases, the result squares with the holdings that permit the mortgagee to disregard the bid price for the purpose of computing his loss.

How is the gain taxed? Presumably, it will be taxed as ordinary income in any case in which it represents the collection of a discount.[111] Otherwise, the gain should qualify for capital gain treatment, being the result of a taxable exchange of the mortgage note for the mortgaged property.[112]

5. Income to Mortgagee Who Bids In

In *Helvering v. Midland Mutual Life Insurance Co.*[113] the mortgagee bid in the full amount of the mortgage obligation, including delinquent interest. On the assumption that the bid price was conclusive of value, the Supreme Court held that the property was received by the mortgagee in full settlement of both the principal and interest outstanding. Because the transaction resulted in the payment of interest, the mortgagee was compelled to report the outstanding interest as ordinary income realized in the foreclosure.

Can this result be prevented by showing that the property received is worth less than the amount bid in? From an economic point of view, such a transaction would not result in any benefit to the mortgage commensurate with the interest discharged in the foreclosure. It has been held that no interest income is realized on foreclosure if the property is worth less than the bid price.[114]

But the mortgagee faces the problem of rebutting the presumption that value is equal to the bid price. This difficulty can be obviated by an alternative course of action. All the mortgagee need do is to confine his bid to the principal portion of the mortgage obligation. If he does not bid in the delinquent interest, he is not charged with the realization of the interest on the foreclosure.[115]

The only exception to this alternative for eliminating interest income would be found in the case in which the mortgaged property actually exceeds in value the bid price. And we should remember that in any case in which interest has previously been reported as income, the rule of *Midland Mutual* would not apply. The receipt of

---

[111] To the extent of the discount, the excess value was treated as interest income in Clarkson Coal Co., 46 B.T.A. 688, 696 (1942). The remainder of the value in excess of the face amount of the note was capital gain.

[112] Clarkson Coal Co., 46 B.T.A. 688, 696 (1942).

[113] 300 U.S. 216 (1937).

[114] Nichols v. Commissioner, 141 F.2d 870, 876 (6th Cir. 1944).

[115] American Central Life Ins. Co., 30 B.T.A. 1182, 1190 (1934), acq. XIII-2 C.B. 1; John Hancock Mutual Life Ins. Co., 10 B.T.A. 736 (1928), acq. VII-2 C.B. 20.

delinquent interest would, then, be excluded from income in the year of foreclosure as the collection of income previously reported.

6. Gain or Loss to the Mortgagor

Gain or loss to the mortgagor in a foreclosure in which the mortgagee bids in is computed in the same manner as if the property had been sold to a third party and the proceeds paid to the mortgagor. His gain or loss is measured by the difference between the net amount of the mortgage obligation bid in and his basis for the property.

Example: Debtor borrowed $30,000, secured by a first mortgage. After default Creditor foreclosed and bid in the face amount of the mortgage of $30,000. If the property pledged to secure the loan had a basis to D of $40,000, D's loss would be computed as follows:

D's basis for the mortgaged property	$40,000
Amount realized on foreclosure	30,000
D's loss on foreclosure	$10,000

The loss would not be deductible by D until the sale became final by the release or expiration of his right of redemption.

7. Suggestions on Foreclosure of Mortgage when the Mortgagee Bids In

Here the problem faced by the mortgagee is one of deciding how much to bid. In view of the rule of *Midland Mutual*, the mortgagee should confine his bid to the principal of the mortgage debt. If he includes the amount of delinquent interest in the bid price, he runs the risk of being taxed upon the receipt of that interest.

The mortgagee may benefit in another way from making his bid as low as possible. By a low bid, he will be entitled to write off the difference between the basis of the mortgage debt and the bid price as a bad debt. Even if the value of the property exceeds the bid price, the offsetting gain to be realized will be treated as capital gain.

The mortgagee also faces the problem of timing his bad debt deduction. If a deficiency judgment is obtained, he should marshal evidence to show when the deficiency becomes worthless or unenforceable.

The mortgagor's problem is also one of determining the time for deduction. If he possesses a right of redemption, the time for deduction will be fixed in the year his right expires, unless he sooner abandons or releases that right.

E. VOLUNTARY CONVEYANCE OF MORTGAGED PROPERTY

An outstanding mortgage debt may be discharged in a manner other than by recourse to a foreclosure proceeding. For example, the mortgagee may be willing to accept a conveyance of the property in full settlement of the debt, in order to avoid the expense and bother of a foreclosure action. The tax consequences of such a voluntary conveyance by the mortgagor are discussed below.

1. Gain or Loss to the Mortgagee on a Voluntary Conveyance

The measure of the gain or loss realized by the mortgagee in accepting a deed to mortgaged property is the difference between the mortgagee's basis for his note and the value of the property at the time of conveyance. In effect, the mortgagee is treated as if he had received payment in cash on his debt to the extent of the value of the property.[116]

Example: Suppose Creditor, who has loaned $20,000 to Debtor on the strength of D's personal note secured by a mortgage on D's home, agrees to accept a quitclaim deed to the home in full settlement of the note. If we assume that the market value of the home is only $15,000 at the time of conveyance and no payments on the principal of the note were made, C's loss would be computed as follows:

Basis for C's loan	$20,000
Less value of property received	15,000
Loss realized	$ 5,000

Conversely, had D's home been valued at $22,000 at the time of the conveyance, C would have realized a gain of $2,000.

How is the gain taxed or the loss allowed? Again we are faced with a hybrid transaction. Is the mortgagee's gain or loss realized on an exchange of his note for the property, or is it realized as a collection upon his note? When this problem first came up, the Commissioner attempted to apply the rules of sales and exchanges to the transaction to limit the mortgagee's loss to a capital loss.[117] But in this attempt the Commissioner was unsuccessful. It has uniformly been held that the mortgagee's loss on the receipt of a voluntary conveyance of the property qualifies for deduction as a bad debt.[118] The Commissioner revoked his earlier ruling to concede that a mortgagee under these circumstances is entitled to deduct the difference between the basis for his loan and the value of the property as a bad debt.[119]

The only burden imposed upon the mortgagee, then, is one of proving the value of the property for the purpose of establishing the amount of his bad debt deduction. Without proof of value, no deduction for a bad debt will be allowed.[120]

How is gain realized on a voluntary conveyance of mortgaged property treated? If we assume that the loss transaction is properly analyzed, the mortgagee's gain ought to be classified as ordinary income to the extent that it represents the collection of delinquent interest, discount, or prior write-offs of the mortgage note.[121]

---

[116] I.T. 3548, 1942-1 C.B. 74.
[117] Elliot S. Nichols, 1 T.C. 328 (1942).
[118] Commissioner v. Spreckles, 120 F.2d 517 (9th Cir. 1941); Bingham v. Commissioner, 105 F.2d 971 (2d Cir. 1939); Commissioner v. National Bank of Commerce, 112 F.2d 946 (5th Cir. 1940); Rogan v. Commercial Discount Co., 149 F.2d 585, 587 (9th Cir. 1945), cert. den. 326 U.S. 764: Harold S. Denniston, 37 B.T.A. 834 (1938), acq. 1942-2 C.B. 5.
[119] I.T. 3548, 1942-1 C.B. 74.
[120] Daniel Hecker, 17 B.T.A. 874, 876 (1929), acq. on another point IX-1 C.B. 23; Francis Perot's Sons Malting Co., 1 B.T.A. 562 (1925).
[121] Manufacturer's Life Ins. Co., 43 B.T.A. 864, 873 (1941), acq. 1947-1 C.B. 3; Edward A. Atlas, par. 45,044 P-H Memo T.C. (1945).

In order for the delinquent interest, discount, or recovery of prior write-offs to be taxed as ordinary income, it must be shown that the property received was in fact worth at least as much as the principal of the mortgage note plus the interest, discount, or prior write-off. The mere fact that the mortgagor's liability for overdue interest has been discharged in the settlement will not in itself force the recognition of interest to the mortgagee.[122]

2. Basis to Mortgagee of Property Received

The fair market value of the property is the measure of the mortgagee's basis for it on receiving it from the mortgagor.[123] A determination of value is important, not only for the purpose of measuring the mortgagee's loss or gain on the conveyance but also for establishing his basis for the property after the conveyance.

3. Gain or Loss to the Mortgagor on a Voluntary Conveyance

How is the conveyance treated from the standpoint of the mortgagor? Does it amount to an exchange of the property for the note, or does it represent payment upon the debt?

Here we find that the sale or exchange theory has won out. What is an exchange of the property for one party is not an exchange for the other party to the transaction. Thus, the mortgagor is deemed to have sold the property for an amount equal to the debt discharged. A loss is suffered by the mortgagor if the amount of the outstanding debt is less than his basis for the property.[124] Conversely, a gain is realized if the mortgage debt exceeds his basis.[125]

Example: Suppose Debtor purchased property from Creditor for $40,000, paying $10,000 down and giving his note and a mortgage on the property for the balance. Assume that D defaults and C accepts a reconveyance of the property as full settlement of the $30,000 note. Regardless of the value of the property, D's loss would be computed as follows:

D's basis for the reconveyed property	$40,000
Less debt discharged	30,000
D's loss	$10,000

Had D taken the depreciation on the property of $15,000 prior to the reconveyance, he would have realized a gain of $5,000 on reconveyance, as follows:

Proceeds realized (debt discharged)		$30,000
Less D's basis:		
Original basis	$40,000	
Less depreciation	15,000	25,000
D's gain		$ 5,000

---

[122]Helvering v. Missouri State Life Ins. Co., 78 F.2d 778, 780 (8th Cir. 1934); Manhattan Mutual Life Ins. Co., 37 B.T.A. 1041, 1043 (1938), acq. 1938-2 C.B. 20.
[123]Kohn v. Commissioner, 197 F.2d 480 (2d Cir. 1952); Bennet v. Commissioner, 139 F.2d 961, 964 (8th Cir. 1944); W.D. Haden Co. v. Commissioner, 165 F.2d 588, 589 (5th Cir. 1948); I.T. 3548, 1942-1 C.B. 74.
[124]Kaufman v. Commissioner, 119 F.2d 901 (9th Cir. 1941).
[125]Lutz & Schramm Co., 1 T.C. 682, 689 (1943), non-acq. on another point, 1943 C.B. 35.

VOLUNTARY CONVEYANCE OF MORTGAGED PROPERTY 245

Except in the case of inventory property[126] the gain or loss on the conveyance of real property will be treated as a section 1231 or a capital gain or loss realized upon the sale or exchange of the property for the debt.[127] The same rule applies to personal property (if it is a Section 1231 or capital asset) except to the extent of depreciation taken on the property after 1961. Under Section 1245, gain, to the extent of such depreciation, is treated as ordinary income. Buildings and their structural components are, however, specifically excluded from the operation of Section 1245, but may be subject to depreciation recapture under Section 1250.

4. Gain to Insolvent Mortgagor

Suppose the mortgagor is insolvent both before and after the conveyance of the property to the mortgagee. Does this fact affect the taxability of any gain that may be realized by him upon the release of his indebtedness?

In the ordinary debtor-creditor situation, such an insolvent debtor would not be taxed on gain attributable solely to the cancellation of his indebtedness. He would be required to report the gain only to the extent that it made him solvent.[128]

Does this exception in favor of an insolvent debtor fit our case of an insolvent mortgagor? The mortgagor's gain is realized upon the exchange of his property, not upon the cancellation of the indebtedness. Despite this difference in facts, however, the courts have held that the gain realized upon a voluntary conveyance of mortgaged property is not taxable to the mortgagor unless he is solvent after the discharge of the mortgage debt.[129]

Example: Debtor mortgaged property that originally cost him $10,000 to secure a note of $40,000. Suppose D dissipated the money and at the time of foreclosure owed a total of $100,000 to creditors. D's only asset was the mortgaged property. Even if D conveyed the property to his mortgagee in full settlement of the mortgage debt, he would not be taxed on the amount of theoretical gain:

Amount of debt canceled		$40,000
D's basis for property		10,000
Amount of theoretical gain		$30,000
Excess of liabilities over assets	$90,000	
Less gain realized	30,000	60,000
Amount		—0—

5. Gain to Purchase-money Mortgagor

Another example of peculiar circumstances that may insulate a mortgagor from a taxable gain under these circumstances arises in the case of a purchase-money mortgage.

---

[126] Charles H. Black, Sr., 45 B.T.A. 204, 208 (1941), acq. 1947 C.B. 2.
[127] Kaufman v. Commissioner, 119 F.2d 901 (9th Cir. 1941); Rogers v. Commissioner, 103 F.2d 790, 792 (9th Cir. 1939), cert. den. 308 U.S. 580; Pender v. Commissioner, 110 F.2d 477 (4th Cir. 1940), cert. den. 310 U.S. 650.
[128] Lakeland Grocery Co., B.T.A. 289 (1937).
[129] Estate of Turney v. Commissioner, 126 F.2d 712 (5th Cir. 1942); Dallas Transfer & Terminal Warehouse Co. v. Commissioner, 70 F.2d 95 (5th Cir. 1934); Main Properties, Inc., 4 T.C. 364, 384 (1945), acq. 1945 C.B. 5; The Springfield Industrial Bldg. Co., 38 B.T.A. 1445 (1938), non-acq. 1941-2 C.B. 23.

Suppose, for example, that after purchasing certain property at a high price the owner discovers that the actual value is considerably less than the price he agreed to pay. Because a portion of the price is deferred on a purchase-money mortgage, he goes to the mortgagee to negotiate a reduction in the mortgage note. If the mortgagee cancels a portion of the note, the effect is the same as if the purchase price were reduced. If the transaction is a bona fide reduction in price, the cancellation of a part of the mortgage debt would not result in the realization of taxable income to the purchaser-mortgagor.[130]

But the overstated purchase price may be settled in another way. Suppose the mortgagor-purchaser agrees to reconvey the property to the mortgagee in exchange for a complete discharge of the purchase-money debt. If the mortgagor can show that the property was actually worth no more than its basis at the time of reconveyance, should he be taxed on gain merely because the debt canceled exceeded his basis?

Under similar circumstances it has been held that such a voluntary conveyance is tantamount to a rescission of the purchase; hence the discharge of the debt in excess of the mortgagor's basis does not give rise to taxable gain.[131]

6. Voluntary Conveyance by Non-assuming Mortgagor

Is the application of these rules affected by the absence of personal liability on the part of the mortgagor? Superficially, a non-assuming mortgagor would appear to be in the same position as any other mortgagor. But in the case of a loss, this conclusion is not necessarily true. Because he is not liable for the mortgage debt, a non-assuming mortgagor is in a much better position to qualify a loss on the reconveyance as an ordinary, rather than a capital, loss.

The reason for this benefit to a non-liable mortgagor lies in the theory of the mortgagor's loss on a conveyance of the property to the mortgagee. Ordinarily, the loss is analyzed as one growing out of the exchange of the property for the mortgage debt; hence, if the property is a capital asset in the mortgagor's hands, his loss will be a capital loss arising out of the exchange.

But how can there be any exchange of the property for the debt if the mortgagor is not liable upon the debt? Under these circumstances, the mortgagor ordinarily receives no consideration for his conveyance. The loss to him partakes of the nature of an abandonment loss. Consequently, the non-assuming mortgagor will be entitled to deduct his loss in full as an ordinary business loss.[132]

But any consideration paid to the mortgagor may nullify this benefit. If consideration is received, regardless of the amount, and the circumstances do not sufficiently suggest abandonment, the transaction will be converted into an exchange.[133] For example, an agreement by the mortgagee to assume delinquent real property taxes which were a personal liability of the mortgagor in exchange for the mortgagor's conveyance of the property has been held sufficient to deprive the mortgagor of his

---

[130]See discussion, *infra* (Part E, 3).
[131]Charles L. Nutter, 7 T.C. 480, 483 (1946), acq. 1946-2 C.B. 4.
[132]Stokes v. Commissioner, 124 F.2d 335 (3rd Cir. 1941); Commissioner v. Hoffman, 117 F.2d 987 (2d Cir. 1941); Bert B. Burnquist, 44 B.T.A. 484 (1941), appeal dismissed, 123 F.2d 64 (8th Cir. 1941).
[133]Blum v. Commissioner, 133 F.2d 447 (2d Cir. 1943).

VOLUNTARY CONVEYANCE OF MORTGAGED PROPERTY 247

right to treat the loss as an abandonment loss; if the property was a capital asset, his loss is converted by the mortgagee's agreement into a capital loss.[134]

7. Abandonment of Mortgaged Property

Can a mortgagor who is personally liable for the mortgage debt take advantage of the theory expressed in the preceding section to convert what would be a capital loss into an ordinary loss? As we saw, the acceptance of a discharge of the mortgage debt in exchange for a conveyance of the property results in characterizing the mortgagor's loss as a capital loss arising out of a taxable exchange. Suppose, then, he abandons the property without seeking a discharge of the debt. Is he entitled to an abandonment loss?

The cases have so held. Even a mortgagor who is liable for the mortgage debt may have the benefit of an abandonment loss, provided he receives no consideration for his act of abandonment.[135]

The mortgagor's right to take an abandonment loss faces two hurdles. First, he must show that he received no payment for his abandonment; and, second, he must show some fact or event fixing the abandonment.

The receipt of any consideration, regardless of how minute, may deprive the mortgagor of an abandonment loss. For example, in *Park Chamberlain*[136] the mortgagor abandoned the mortgaged premises by executing a quitclaim deed to his fellow mortgagor. The deed contained a recital of the receipt of $1.00 and other good and valuable consideration. The Commissioner claimed that this recital created a presumption of consideration sufficient to deny an abandonment loss to the mortgagor. On petition to the Board of Tax Appeals, the mortgagor proved that no consideration had in fact been received; his abandonment loss was reinstated, but the Commissioner has not accepted the decision.[137]

Naturally, if the mortgagor receives a discharge of the mortgage debt in exchange for his abandonment of the property, he cannot claim an abandonment loss; his loss is then one arising out of a taxable exchange of the property for this discharge.[138]

Suppose, however, that the mortgagor first abandons the property. Subsequently, by independent action, the mortgagee acquires the property through a foreclosure proceeding which has the effect of discharging the mortgage debt. Does the later foreclosure convert the mortgagor's abandonment loss into a capital loss? The answer depends upon a factual analysis of the transaction. If the abandonment and foreclosure are both part of but one transaction, then the mortgagor will be restricted to a loss resulting from an exchange of the property.[139] On the other hand, the mortgagor may be able to show that his abandonment was not motivated by the later foreclosure;

---

[134]Aberle v. Commissioner, 121 F.2d 726 (3rd Cir. 1941); Philips v. Commissioner, 112 F.2d 721 (3rd Cir. 1940).

[135]Rhodes v. Commissioner, 100 F.2d 966, 970 (6th Cir. 1939). See Bickerstaff v. Commissioner, 128 F.2d 366 (5th Cir. 1942). But see Commissioner v. Green, 126 F.2d 70 (3rd Cir. 1942); Compare Rev. Rul. 74-40, I.R.B. 1974-4, 11.

[136]41 B.T.A. 10, 16 (1940), non-acq. 1940-1 C.B. 6.

[137]Non-acq. 1940-1 C.B. 6.

[138]See discussion Part E, 3, *supra*.

[139]Stamler v. Commissioner, 145 F.2d 37, 39 (3rd Cir. 1944); Richter v. Commissioner, 124 F.2d 412 (2d Cir. 1942).

although the Commissioner has not agreed, the mortgagor should be permitted to take his abandonment loss.[140]

To justify an abandonment loss, the mortgagor must show that the property is worthless, in the sense that liens outstanding against it exceed its value.[141] The mortgagor must also take some action toward the property that demonstrates objectively an intent to abandon.[142] Relinquishment of title is one method fixing the abandonment loss.[143] For this purpose, however, a conveyance of title is not essential; a letter notice renouncing title has been held sufficient.[144] Cessation of use of the property has also been deemed sufficient to support an abandonment loss.[145]

It has been argued that if a taxpayer takes an ordinary loss based on the abandonment of his equity in the property, he may be saddled with that position should a court find that in fact he had made a sale or exchange; any gain realized on the sale or exchange would, then, presumably be ordinary income regardless of the nature of the taxpayer's holding of the property.

8. Suggestions on Voluntary Conveyance of Mortgaged Property

The mortgagee's problem in accepting a voluntary conveyance of the property in satisfaction of the mortgage debt is one of establishing the value of the property at the time of its conveyance. For it is value that fixes the amount of his bad debt deduction, or, alternatively, the amount of the gain or income realized on the transaction. Value also fixes his basis for the future. An independent written appraisal of the property at the time of the conveyance is almost essential to protect his subsequent tax position.

The mortgagor's problem is of a different nature. If the property is a capital asset in his hands, is he willing to settle for a capital loss? If he insists upon a discharge of liability, his loss will be subject to the restrictions upon capital losses. If he is willing to forego a release of the debt, he may obtain a deduction against ordinary income by abandonment of the property. In order to ensure an abandonment loss, the mortgagor must establish the following factors:

(1) The property was worthless at the time of abandonment.

(2) The property was in fact abandoned by some objective act disclosing an intent to abandon.

(3) The mortgagor received no consideration for the abandonment.

(4) In the event the abandonment is followed by a foreclosure, the two transactions were completely independent.

---

[140]Frederick S. Jackson, par. 41,131 P-H Memo B.T.A. (1941). See Bert D. Burnquist, 44 B.T.A. 484, 488 (1941), non-acq. 1941-1 C.B. 13, appeal dismissed, 123 F.2d 64 (8th Cir. 1941); Walter M. Priddy, 43 B.T.A. 18, 29 (1940), acq. on another point, 1941-1 C.B. 7; Enid Ice and Fuel Co. v. United States (W.D. Okla. 1956), 142 F.Supp. 486. Contra, Commissioner v. Green, 126 F.2d 70 (3rd Cir. 1942).

[141]See W.W. Hoffman 40 B.T.A. 459, 462 (1939), acq. 1951-1 C.B. 2, aff'd curiam, 117 F.2d 987 (2d Cir. 1941).

[142]Loss denied for failure to fix abandonment in year deduction taken: Commissioner v. Jones, 120 F.2d 828, 830 (8th Cir. 1941), cert. den. 314 U.S. 661.

[143]See A.J. Schwarzler Co., 3 B.T.A. 535 (1926), acq. V-1 C.B. 5.

[144]Realty Operators, Inc., 40 B.T.A. 1051, 1055 (1939), non-acq. 1940-1 C.B. 8, appeal dismissed, 118 F.2d 286 (5th Cir. 1941).

[145]Helvering v. Gordon, 134 F.2d 685, 687 (4th Cir. 1943).

F. COMPROMISE OF THE MORTGAGE DEBT

As an alternative to foreclosure, the mortgagee may release the mortgagor from the mortgage debt in consideration of the payment of a lesser sum. Upon paying the discounted amount, the mortgagor would be entitled to keep the mortgaged property free and clear of the mortgage lien.

Naturally, if the amount paid were equal to the amount due, there would be no adverse tax consequence. The payment would be received as the non-taxable repayment of a loan. But suppose the compromise payment is less than the amount due. Does the mortgagee realize a loss? And, correspondingly, does the mortgagor have a gain?

1. Loss to Mortgagee on Compromise of Mortgage Debt

If the mortgagee permits the mortgagor to settle his debt at a discount, the difference between his basis for the mortgage loan and the amount received is a bad debt, business or non-business as the case may be.[146] The full amount of this difference will be deductible in the year of compromise, provided a write-off for partial worthlessness had not been taken in a prior year.[147]

Example: Creditor loans Debtor $10,000 to buy a home. After a period of several years, the home depreciates in value and D is in financial straits. D offers to settle the $10,000 debt by paying C $8,000. C decides that he could realize no greater amount by foreclosure and therefore accepts the compromise payment. Provided C had not previously taken a deduction for partial worthlessness, his bad debt deduction in the year of compromise would be computed as follows:

C's basis for mortgage debt	$10,000
Less payment received	8,000
Amount of bad debt deduction	$ 2,000

The amount of the bad debt is measured by the difference between the basis for the note to the creditor and the amount received. Thus, if the holder of the note had purchased it at a discount, the measure of his bad debt deduction would be the difference between his cost for the note and the compromise payment.[148]

2. Income to the Mortgagor on Compromise of Mortgage Debt

To the extent that the mortgagor is able to settle his debt by a payment of less than the amount due, he will be charged with the realization of income.[149] The saving will be taxed as ordinary income arising out of the cancellation of indebtedness.[150]

Example: Creditor loaned $10,000 to Debtor, secured by a first mortgage on D's house. A year later C went to D to ask for immediate repayment because C needed the money. D offered to

---

[146] Hale v. Helvering, 85 F.2d 819, 822 (D.C.Cir. 1936).
[147] Reg. Sec. 1.166-1(d).
[148] See discussion Part B, 4, *supra*.
[149] Section 61(a)(12), I.R.C.
[150] Haden Co. v. Commissioner, 118 F.2d 285 (5th Cir. 1941), cert. den. 314 U.S. 622; Frank v. United States, 44 F.Supp. 729, 733 (E.D.Pa. 1942), aff'd per curiam, 131 F.2d 864 (3rd Cir. 1942); L.D. Coddon & Bros., Inc., 37 B.T.A. 393, 398 (1938).

pay $9,000, which C accepted in full settlement of the mortgage note. D realized $1,000 of ordinary income out of the compromise.[151]

3. Income to Purchase-money Mortgagor

But this rule taxing the forgiven debt to the mortgagor as income is not without exception. Assume, for example, that the mortgage debt arose between the buyer and seller of a parcel of property. The buyer paid a certain sum down and signed a note secured by a mortgage on the property for the balance. After obtaining possession of the property, the buyer discovers that the price he agreed to pay was too high. He calls the matter to the attention of the seller and after negotiation the seller agrees to take a lesser sum in full satisfaction of the mortgage note. Has the buyer realized income?

Under these circumstances, the buyer could probably escape taxation by showing that the reduction in the debt obligation reflected a reduction in the purchase price for the property.[152] Surely, no one ought to quarrel with this result if the property had actually been overpriced at the time of purchase. Nor would there be much reason to tax the purchaser with income if the property depreciated from the time of purchase so that it is worth no more than the scaled-down purchase price at the time of compromise.

However, suppose the property was not overpriced at the original sale and has not depreciated since the sale. Should the buyer be permitted to exclude the amount of forgiveness from his income on the theory that it represented a reduction in the purchase price? Obviously not. And this has been the position asserted by the Commissioner. A purchaser who settles a purchase-money obligation for less than face realizes income to the extent that the payment saved represents value in excess of the compromise payment.[153]

Does it make any difference if the purchase-money obligation is owed to a party other than the seller? Although the cases are not in accord, the purchase-reduction theory has been extended to prevent the taxability of the amount of a forgiven indebtedness owed to a third party on a purchase-money obligation.[154]

4. Income to an Insolvent Mortgagor

Another exception to the basic rule of income realization on the cancellation of a portion of the mortgage debt arises in the case of an insolvent mortgagor. Under the theory of the *Lakeland Grocery* case,[155] a mortgagor insolvent both before and after the mortgage compromise will realize no income on the cancellation of a portion of his mortgage debt.

---

[151]Commissioner v. Stanley Co. of America, 185 F.2d 979 (2d Cir. 1951).

[152]Helvering v. A.L. Killian Co., 128 F.2d 433 (8th Cir. 1942); Allen v. Courts, 127 F.2d 127 (5th Cir. 1942); Gehring Publishing Co., 1 T.C. 345, 354 (1942), acq. 1943 C.B. 9; Pinkney Packing Co., 42 B.T.A. 823, 829 (1940), acq. 1941-1 C.B. 8.

[153]Coddon Bros., Inc., 37 B.T.A. 393 (1938).

[154]Permitting the debtor to use the purchase reduction theory: Hirsch v. Commissioner, 115 F.2d 656, 658 (7th Cir. 1940); Commissioner v. Sherman, 135 F.2d 68, 70 (6th Cir. 1943). Contra, Frank v. United States, 44 F.Supp. 729 (D.C.Pa. 1942), aff'd 131 F.2d 864 (3rd Cir. 1942).

[155]Lakeland Grocery Co., 36 B.T.A. 289 (1937).

5. Gift Cancellation of a Mortgage Debt

Similarly, if the mortgage debt is canceled by way of a gift, the cancellation would not result in the creation of taxable income.[156] In order for the cancellation to qualify as gratuitous, the creditor must receive no consideration for it[157] and it must be voluntary.[158] The burden of showing the absence of consideration is, of course, upon the debtor-taxpayer.[159] But for there to bs a gift cancellation of a debt, it is essential that the parties prove some personal relationship to each other besides debtor-creditor.[160]

6. Postponement of Income by Reduction of Basis

If the mortgage debt was incurred for the purpose of acquiring specific property, the mortgagor has an option to treat the amount of debt canceled as income in the year of compromise or to reduce his basis for the property by a corresponding amount.[161] This election is available to corporate taxpayers on all their debts and to individuals on debts incurred in connection with their trades or businesses.[162] By reducing the basis of the property, the tax upon the cancellation of debt is, in effect, postponed until the property is sold or the reduced basis is fully recovered by depreciation.

Example: Debtor purchased property for use in his trade or business. Creditor had loaned D $30,000 to buy the property. D paid $40,000 for it. A year later D settled his debt with C by the payment of $25,000. D elected to reduce basis for the property as follows:

Original basis for property		$40,000
Less portion of debt canceled:		
Original debt	$30,000	
Compromise payment	25,000	5,000
Basis after reduction		$35,000

In effect, the election to reduce basis achieves the same result in this type of case as the application of the reduction-of-purchase-price theory.

The reduction of basis may be spread to other business property of the taxpayer in two situations: (1) the basis reduction required exceeds the remaining basis of the property in the hands of the mortgagor, or (2) the indebtedness forgiven was not incurred in connection with any specific property. In either of these two circumstances, the excess reduction of basis is spread ratably over all the trade and business property of the mortgagor, other than inventory and notes or accounts receivable.[163]

7. Income to Non-assuming Mortgagor

If the mortgagor is not personally liable upon the mortgagor debt, any reduction in that debt will not affect his liabilities. Hence, it has been held that no taxable income is

---

[156]Helvering v. American Dental Co., 318 U.S. 322 (1943), as modified by Commissioner v. Jacobson, 336 U.S. 28 (1949).
[157]Liberty Mirror Works, 3 T.C. 1018, 1022 (1944), acq. 1944 C.B. 17.
[158]Compare Shellabarger Grain Products Co. v. Commissioner, 146 F.2d 177, 185 (7th Cir.).
[159]Elizabeth Operating Corp., par. 43,434 P-H Memo T.C. (1943).
[160]Commissioner v. Duberstein, 363 U.S. 278 (1960).
[161]Sections 108, 1017, I.R.C.
[162]Reg. Sec. 1.108(a)-1.
[163]Reg. Sec. 1.1017-1.

realized by him on the compromise or settlement of the mortgage debt for less than face value. The only effect of the compromise is to cause a corresponding reduction in his basis for the property.[164]

8. Suggestions on Compromise of Mortgage Debt

If the mortgagee accepts a payment in compromise of the mortgage note, the difference between the mortgagee's basis for the note and the payment received is deductible by him as a bad debt.

The mortgagor's problem is one of dealing with the realization of income upon the settlement of his debt for less than the amount due. If the cancellation grew out of a purchase-money transaction, the mortgagor may be able to treat the reduction in the mortgage note in the original purchase price of the property. In order to qualify the debt reduction as a reduction as a purchase-price reduction, the mortgagor must be able to show the following:

(1) That the value of the property at the time of purchase or compromise is no greater than the reduced purchase price; and

(2) That the parties intended a reduction of the purchase price.

In the absence of a purchase-price reduction, the mortgagor may still be able to qualify the forgiven debt for treatment as a reduction in basis by filing a proper election under Sections 108 and 1017, I.R.C.

G. LOSS OF SECOND MORTGAGEE

What is the position of a second mortgagee if the first mortgage is foreclosed? Obviously, if the foreclosure of the first mortgage wipes out his interest in the property, his position as a secured creditor is destroyed. He is not necessarily entitled to a bad debt deduction for his second-mortgage note by virtue of this fact alone.[165] His loss, if any, is suffered on the failure of the mortgagor-debtor to pay the note. Hence, he must also show that the note is uncollectable. If he can make this additional showing, he will be entitled to deduct the remainder of his basis for the second-mortgage note as a bad debt.[166]

For example, if the foreclosure of the first mortgage is accompanied by the insolvency of the mortgagor, the second mortgagee will be allowed a bad debt deduction in the year of foreclosure.[167]

Because the second mortgagee's position is essentially that of a creditor, he may be entitled to a bad debt deduction for his note even in the absence of a foreclosure by the first mortgagee. It has been held, for instance, that a second mortgagee may deduct his debt as worthless upon a showing that the mortgagor-debtor is insolvent and that the

---

[164]Fulton Gold Corp., 31 B.T.A. 519 (1934); Hotel Astoria, Inc., 42 B.T.A. 759, 762 (1940), acq. 1940-2 C.B. 4; P.S. Hiatt, 35 B.T.A. 292, 296 (1937), acq. 1937-1 C.B. 12.

[165]Arthur Berenson, 39 B.T.A. 77 (1939), aff'd per curiam, 113 F.2d 113 (2d Cir. 1940); John Charney, par. 34,543 P-H Memo B.T.A. (1934).

[166]Edward S. Phillips, 9 B.T.A. 1016 (1927), acq. VII-2 C.B. 31; Wellman v. United States, 25 F.Supp. 868 (D.C.Mass. 1938).

[167]Waters F. Burrows, 38 B.T.A. 236 (1938), non-acq. 1938-2 C.B. 38.

H. EXPENSES OF FORECLOSURE

present value of the property is less than the amount outstanding on the first mortgage debt.[168]

Expenditures made by the mortgagee to protect the mortgaged property are not ordinarily deductible as such. Normally, these expenses are capitalized by adding them to the mortgagee's basis for his note or to his basis for the property, depending upon when the expenditures are made or incurred. If the expenses are added to the mortgagee's basis for his note, they will be recovered in the foreclosure proceeding; if added to the property, they will be recovered only upon the subsequent sale or depreciation of the property.

For example, if the mortgagee pays off charges or liens against the mortgaged property prior to foreclosure, the amount paid is considered to be an additional loan to the mortgagor. Hence, the amount paid out by the mortgagee to protect his security interest in the property is added to his loan for the purpose of computing the gain or loss realized by him on the foreclosure.[169]

But charges and liens against the property paid by the mortgagee during the course of the foreclosure proceeding are capitalized by adding them to the mortgagee's basis for the property.[170] The same rule applies to taxes or other charges paid after the foreclosure has been completed but which had become liens prior to foreclosure.[171] An exception would be made, however, to real property taxes for the year in which the foreclosure action occurs; the mortgagee would be entitled to a deduction for the pro rata share of these taxes that accrued during the portion of the tax year that he has title to the property.[172]

Naturally, if the mortgagee does not acquire the property in the foreclosure proceeding, these payments during the course of the proceeding cannot be added to his basis for the property itself; they are, under these circumstances, added to the basis of any deficiency judgment he obtains. As such, the amount of these expenditures will be deducted at the time the deficiency is written off.

What about the actual expenses of foreclosing, such as court costs, legal fees, etc? These expenses are treated differently. They are used to offset the gross proceeds received on foreclosure for the purpose of computing the net price received. Only the net price is taken into account in measuring the mortgagee's gain or loss on foreclosure; hence, these expenses are recouped in the foreclosure action itself.[173]

This rule has been applied not only to foreclosure proceedings in which the property is sold to an outsider, but also to proceedings in which the mortgagee bids in

---

[168] W.Z. Sharp, 8 B.T.A. 399 (1927), acq. VII-1 C.B. 28; George Leavenworth, 1 B.T.A. 754, 757 (1925).

[169] Estate of Lucy J. Schieffelein, 44 B.T.A. 137, 140 (1941), acq. 1941-1 C.B. 9.

[170] Hadley Falls Trust Co. v. United States, 110 F.2d 887, 893 (1st Cir. 1940).

[171] Hadley Falls Trust Co. v. United States (D.C.Mass. 1938), 22 F.Supp. 346, 351, vacated on another ground, 110 F.2d 887 (1st Cir. 1940); Missouri State Life Ins. Co. v. Commissioner, 78 F.2d 778, 781 (8th Cir. 1934); John Hancock Mutual Life Ins. Co., 10 B.T.A. 736, 740, acq. on another point, VII-2 C.B. 20; Estate of Lucy J. Schieffelin, 44 B.T.A. 137, 140 (1941), acq. on another point 1941-1 C.B. 9; I.T. 1611, II-1 C.B. 87.

[172] Section 164(d) I.R.C.; Reg. Sec. 1.164-6.

[173] Just as expenses of sale are treated in a voluntary purchase. Section 1001, I.R.C.

the mortgage debt. The gross bid price is reduced by the amount of foreclosure expenses incurred to determine the net bid price. And the same rule has been applied to a voluntary conveyance transaction in which the value of the property received was reduced by the accompanying legal expenses.[174]

Example: Creditor forecloses a mortgage. Prior to foreclosure, he paid real property taxes of $500 against the property. His expenses of foreclosure amounted to $800 and during foreclosure he paid $400 to discharge a special assessment levied against the property. Assuming that the basis for his mortgage note is $20,000 and that the property was sold for $16,000, we find that his loss is computed as follows:

Gross proceeds realized	$16,000	
Less expenses of foreclosure	800	$15,200
Basis for loan	$20,000	
Plus taxes advanced	500	20,500
Deficiency		$ 5,300
Plus special assessment paid		400
Amount of bad debt deduction		$ 5,700

Had the mortgagee acquired the property in the foreclosure, the result would vary as follows:

1. Bad Debt Deduction

Value of property acquired	$16,000	
Less expense of foreclosure	800	$15,200
Basis for loan	$20,000	
Plus taxes advanced	500	20,500
Amount of bad debt		$ 5,300

2. Basis of Property

Value of property acquired	$16,000
Plus special assessment paid	400
Basis of property acquired	$16,400

I. ASSIGNMENT OF RENTS TO THE MORTGAGEE

Suppose the mortgagor assigns the income from the property to the mortgagee prior to the completion of the foreclosure proceeding. Are the rentals taxed as income to the mortgagee by virtue of the assignment? A similar problem arises if the mortgagee sequesters the rents in the foreclosure action. Are the sequestered rents income to him?

Ordinarily, the mortgagor is given credit against principal or interest on the mortgage debt for the rents collected by the mortgagee out of the property. Hence, the income is still benefiting him. For this reason it has been held that the mortgagee is not taxable on rents received by him which are applied against the mortgage principal.[175]

---

[174]Bowles Lunch, Inc., 33 F.Supp. 235, 240 (Ct.Cl. 1940). Contra, Hadley Falls Trust Co. v. United States, 110 F.2d 887, 893 (1st Cir. 1940).
[175]Hadley Falls Trust Co. v. United States, 22 F.Supp. 346, 353 (D.C.Mass. 1938), vacated on another point, 110 F.2d 887 (1st Cir. 1940).

DISPOSITION OF PROPERTY ACQUIRED BY MORTGAGEE

Nor are rents taxed to a mortgagee who uses them to discharge a lien for real property taxes or other charges against the mortgaged property.[176]

Even if the rents were applied to interest, the mortgagee would not be taxed upon the receipt of the rents as rental income. The rents would be taxed first to the mortgagor who in turn would be entitled to a corresponding deduction for interest paid. The rental payment would then be reportable by the mortgagee as interest income received.

Consequently, we must conclude that the mortgagor remains taxable upon the income from the property, despite an assignment of income or the sequestration of income by the mortgagee.[177]

If the rents are taxed to the mortgagor, he ought to be permitted to deduct depreciation upon the property just as if he had collected the rents directly. This was the result reached in a case in which the mortgagor later recovered the property by way of redemption.[178]

Suppose the mortgagor were not personally liable upon the mortgage debt. The use of the income from the property to discharge the mortgagee debt would not affect his liability. Because the income is not used to discharge his obligation, the rents or other income would not constitute taxable income to him.[179]

J. DISPOSITION OF PROPERTY ACQUIRED BY MORTGAGEE

Regardless of the method by which mortgaged property is acquired by the mortgagee,[180] his basis for it will be its fair market value at the time of acquisition, both for the purpose of measuring depreciation upon the property and for the purpose of computing gain or loss upon a subsequent sale. This rule also applies when the mortgagee bids in the property at foreclosure but it must be remembered that in this case the bid price is presumed to equal fair market value "in the absence of clear and convincing proof to the contrary."[181]

Is the gain or loss realized by the mortgagee in a subsequent sale of the property capital or ordinary in nature? If we assume that the mortgagee is in the business of lending money, as is a bank, savings and loan association, or other financial institution, the property is treated as inventory property and any gain or loss realized will be ordinary in nature.[182]

If the lender is an occasional lender, the property repossessed will be a capital or Section 1231 asset unless it is immediately advertised for sale.[183]

---

[176]Commissioner v. Penn Athletic Club Bldg., 176 F.2d 939 (3rd Cir. 1949).

[177]Clarence E. Day, par. 42,197 P-H B.T.A. Memo (1942). See Murray v. Commissioner, 232 F.2d 742 (9th Cir. 1956).

[178]E. J. Murray, 21 T.C. 1049, 1062 (1954), acq. 1954-2 C.B. 5, aff'd on another ground, 232 F.2d 742 (9th Cir. 1956).

[179]Hilpert v. Commissioner, 151 F.2d 929, 933 (5th Cir. 1945).

[180]Except in the case of a seller-mortgagee. See the rules on reacquisition set forth in this Chapter, Part A.

[181]Reg. Sec. 1.166-6(b)(2) and (c).

[182]Rev. Rul. 74-159, I.R.B. 1974-14, 13; Girard Trust Corn Exchange Bank, 33 T.C. 1343, 1359 (1954), acq. 1955-1 C.B. 4. If the property were held for rental purposes for a substantial period of time, it might qualify for Section 1231 treatment.

[183]Thompson Lumber Co., 43 B.T.A. 726 (1941); Kanawha Valley Bank, 4 T.C. 252, 256 (1944), acq. 1946-1 C.B. 3.

8

Tax Techniques and Advantages in Leasing Real Property

The leasing of real property necessarily involves two parties, the lessor and the lessee, or more commonly, the landlord and the tenant. Each has his own problems concerning the imposition of federal income taxes, and each is entitled to take advantage of various techniques and tax benefits. The aim of this chapter is to outline these problems, techniques, and benefits with reference to a number of typical situations that commonly arise in leasing transactions. Accordingly, the chapter will explore the following topics:

A. *Tax Consequences of Lease Clauses*;
B. *Depreciation of Improvements on Leased Property*;
C. *Costs of Acquiring a Lease*;
D. *Cancellation or Sale of Leases*;
E. *Lease or Purchase?*

A. TAX CONSEQUENCES OF LEASE CLAUSES

A lease contains many provisions and clauses between landlord (lessor) and tenant (lessee). It is the purpose of this article to explore the federal income tax consequences of some of them which may affect the tax position of either or both of the landlord and the tenant.

1. Covenant to Pay Rent

Rentals agreed to be paid by the tenant are ordinary income to the landlord when received (if on the cash method of accounting) or when due (if on the accrual method of accounting).[1] Rentals for this purpose include not only the basic rental but additions thereto such as percentage rentals (measured by the tenant's gross receipts or sales) and cost of living increases. The fact that the landlord may in a later year be required to refund a portion of the percentage or cost of living additional rental does not alter the result; he is taxable on the full amount when received or due.[2] In such later year, the overpaid landlord would be allowed a deduction for the excess.[3]

The tenant can deduct the rentals when paid (if on the cash method) or which become due (if on the accrual method) only if he uses the property in the conduct of a trade or business,[4] or if he holds it for the production of income.[5] Rental of property for the personal use of a tenant (such as his residence) is not deductible.[6]

What if the rental paid is higher or lower than current market levels? If the landlord and tenant are unrelated, the difference between the actual rental paid and going rentals is immaterial: the tenant gets a deduction for the full rental and the landlord gets taxed on the same amount.[7] But if the parties are related, a different tax result will occur.

For example, if the related parties are individuals, an overpayment of rent by the tenant would be a non-deductible gift by him to the landlord.[8] The landlord's receipt of that gift would be non-taxable income.[9] If the rental is too low, the result would be that the landlord was making a gift to the tenant.

If the related landlord and tenant are business entities (whether corporations, partnerships, or sole proprietorships), the Internal Revenue Service has the statutory power to re-allocate the income and deductions between landlord and tenant on a showing that such action is necessary to reflect income accurately or, alternatively, to prevent tax avoidance.[10]

If the related landlord and tenant are shareholder and corporation, the discrepancy between the agreed rental and the fair market rental will be either a dividend (not in excess of earnings and profits) or a contribution to capital. For example, if a share-

---

[1] I.R.C. §§61(a)(5), 451(a). Rents are amounts received by the owner of the property for the use of the property. If services are rendered by the owner, such as in a hotel, motel, or trailer park operation, the income received is not technically rents. Rev. Rul. 72-331, 1972-2 C.B. 513. See also Section 167(k)(3)(c), I.R.C.

[2] Rod Realty Co., T.C. Memo 1967-49; 26 T.C.M. 243 (1967). If the refund is made in the year of receipt (or accrual), it is an offset in that year. In W.W. Millsaps, T.C. Memo 1973-146 (1973), an escrow deposit of rent was held not income until paid out.

[3] I.R.C. §1341 may apply to permit the landlord to recompute his tax in the year of receipt (or accrual) in lieu of a deduction in the year of repayment.

[4] Sections 162(a)(3), 461(a), I.R.C.

[5] Section 212(2), I.R.C.

[6] Section 262, I.R.C. If the tenant uses the property partly for personal and partly for business purposes, an allocation will be required. To the extent that the tenant can show a business use of the leased premises, he is entitled to deduct that portion of the rent.

[7] Audano v. United States, 428 F.2d 251 (5th Cir. 1970); Brown Printing Co. v. Commissioner, 255 F.2d 436 (CA 4, 1958); Stanley Imerman, 7 T.C. 1030 (1946), acq. 1947-1 C.B. 2.

[8] The relationship here assumed between landlord and tenant is personal. If the relationship is other than personal, such as employer-employee, debtor-creditor, mortgagor-mortgagee or buyer-seller, the tax consequences may be different: the excess may then become compensation, interest, or principal payments.

[9] Section 102, I.R.C.

[10] Section 342, I.R.C.

holder leases property to his controlled corporation for an excessive rental, the excess is a dividend to him.[11] That amount of the rental, being a dividend is non-deductible by the corporate tenant.[12]

A striking illustration of this principle appears in the case of a landlord and tenant, each of which is incorporated and is owned by the same controlling stockholder. The excess rental paid by the tenant corporation to its sister landlord corporation is taxed as a dividend to the common shareholder. The tenant corporation gets no deduction for the excess because it is a dividend. The common shareholder, however, has not actually received the excessive payment; that has gone to the landlord corporation which he also owns. The common shareholder is treated as having made a capital contribution of the excessive amount to the landlord corporation.[13] The end result is harsh: (1) the tenant corporation loses the deduction for the excessive rent; (2) the common shareholder is taxed on the excessive rent as dividend income, although he did not receive it; (3) the landlord corporation receives the excessive rent tax-free as a contribution to capital which is non-deductible by the common shareholder.

2. Covenant to Pay Rent in Advance

If a tenant agrees to pay rent in advance of the time period for which it is due, the landlord must report the full advance rental payment as income *when it is received* regardless of his method of accounting.[14] The landlord has no right to postpone the receipt or accrual of this income to the later time period to which the advance payment is to be applied.[15]

The tenant, however, cannot deduct the advance payment at the time he pays it. His deduction is postponed to the period for which the advance rental was paid. The amount of the advance rental then becomes amortizable (deductible on a pro rata basis) over the time period for which it was paid.[16]

If the period for which the "advance" or "additional" rental is not definite, then it is treated as a bonus payment, discussed in the next section.

3. Covenant to Pay Bonus

If the tenant agrees to pay a bonus to the landlord in order to obtain the lease, the landlord has taxable rental income immediately on receipt of the bonus.[17] The same rule applies to additional or advance rentals.

What about the tenant? Because the bonus is not assignable to any particular

---

[11]Limericks, Inc. v. Commissioner, 165 F.2d 483 (5th Cir. 1948); Stanwick's Inc. 15 T.C. 556, aff'd per curiam, 190 F.2d 84 (4th Cir. 1951).
[12]Section 162, I.R.C. Dividends to shareholders are not a business expense of a corporation.
[13]Sparks Nugget, Inc. v. Commissioner, 458 F.2d 631 (9th Cir. 1972).
[14]Regulations §1.61-8(b).
[15]Hyde Park Realty v. Commissioner, 211 F.2d 462 (2nd Cir. 1954); New Capital Hotel, Inc., 28 T.C. 706 (1957), aff'd per curiam, 261 F.2d 437 (6th Cir. 1958).
[16]Norman Baker Smith, 51 T.C. 429 (1968); Lola Cunningham, 39 T.C. 186 (1962); I.R.S. Pub. No. 334 (1972) p. 73. D.K. McColl, ¶41,050 P-H Memo T.C.
[17]Jennings and Co. v. Commissioner, 59 F.2d 32 (9th Cir. 1932); Cowden v. CIR, 289 F.2d 20 (5th Cir. 1961).

portion of the lease, it is recoverable as a pro rata amortization deduction over the life of the lease.[18]

4. Covenant to Pay Decreasing Fixed or Minimum Rental

If a tenant agrees to pay a high rental for the first half-term of his lease and a low rental for the second half-term, what are the results? Under the above authorities, the landlord has rental income as received.

What about the tenant? Can he deduct the rentals as paid? Or must he amortize the difference between the two rental levels over the entire life of the lease? Authority is sparse, but at least one case has upheld the tenant's right to deduct the rentals as paid.[19] Obviously so to do, the tenant must show that the higher fixed or minimum rental in the first half of the lease was not a subterfuge to conceal an advance rental payment. The decrease must be based on economic reality.

It is for this latter reason that rental increases or decreases based on (1) gross receipts, (2) net profits, (3) cost of living, or (4) cost of maintenance are not challenged.

5. Covenant for True Security Deposit by Tenant

It is normal to require the tenant to deposit with the landlord an agreed sum of money, in addition to rent, to guarantee the faithful performance by the tenant of his lease obligations. In the event the tenant violates any of his obligations, the landlord may forfeit the deposit. What result?

If the landlord is required, by state law or otherwise, to escrow the deposit so that he cannot touch it until termination of the lease, the deposit is not income to him at the time the tenant makes the deposit.[20] Nor is it deductible by the tenant at the time of deposit in escrow.[21]

But if an escrow of the deposit is *not* required, what are the tax consequences of the security deposit? Here the deposit is made by payment of cash directly to the landlord. The landlord has the free and unfettered use of the deposit immediately on his receipt of it. For this reason, the Internal Revenue Service has argued that the receipt of the deposit by the landlord is income to him. Because of this position of the Internal Revenue Service, it is possible for a landlord to report such security deposits as immediate income. On return of the deposit to the tenant, the landlord has a deductible expense. It is the author's experience that the Internal Revenue Service does not challenge such treatment.

---

[18] Regulations §1.162-11(a). Main and McKinney Building Co. v. Commissioner, 113 F.2d 81 (5th Cir. 1940), cert. den. 311 U.S. 688; Baton Coal Co. v. Commissioner, 51 F.2d 469 (CA 3, 1931), cert. den. 284 U.S. 674; Jo Alland and Bro., Inc., 1 BTA 631 (1925).

[19] Ryegate Paper Co., ¶61,193 P-H Memo T.C. See Oscar L. Thomas, 31 T.C. 1009 (1959), acq. 1959-2 C.B. 7.

[20] Clinton Hotel Realty Co. v. Commissioner, 128 F.2d 968 (CA 5, 1942). Knowledgeable New York lawyers have advised the author such a deposit must be escrowed under New York law that similar escrow requirements appear in other states. Whether or not such requirements are a matter of state law, they can be made such by the terms of the lease.

[21] Minneapolis Security Building Corp., 38 B.T.A. 1220 (1938).

But the landlord is under an obligation to repay the amount deposited with him on the termination of the lease, provided the tenant has not defaulted. For this reason, the security deposit, *even though not escrowed*, is treated as the equivalent of a loan.[22] Since borrowed money is not income, the security deposit made to the landlord is not income to him. The repayment of the deposit to the tenant is not deductible by the landlord nor income to the tenant. It is simply the repayment of a loan.

What happens if the landlord requires the tenant to forfeit all or a part of the security deposit? The tax consequences arise on forfeiture, as follows:

(1) Failure of tenant to pay rent: taxable income to landlord; deductible rent to tenant.

(2) Failure of tenant to repair premises: recovery of basis to landlord; deductible by tenant.

(3) Imposition by tenant of lien against premises: recovery of basis to landlord; deductible by tenant.

6. Covenant for Security Deposit Applicable to Future Rents

An ambivalent security deposit is one that not only secures the landlord against waste but also can be used by the landlord as rental payment for the final periods of the lease. If the landlord has this discretion, the security deposit is treated as the advance payment of rent: taxable when received.[23]

But a security deposit placed in escrow will protect the landlord from realizing income at the time the deposit is made. Because the escrowed deposit is not immediately reachable by him, it does not become income to him until it is applied to the final rental payments.[24]

7. Covenant to Pay Property Taxes

If the tenant agrees to pay property taxes, the taxes paid are deductible by him. If the taxes are imposed on his trade fixtures, furnishings, equipment, and inventory, the tenant is allowed a property tax deduction for them.[25]

If the tenant pays property taxes on his landlord's property, he is entitled to a business rental deduction.[26] In the case of the tenant, he has a rental deduction for the landlord's taxes he pays whether the taxes themselves are deductible or are not deductible.[27]

---

[22]Warren Service Co. v. Commissioner, 110 F.2d 723 (2nd Cir. 1940); Bradford Hotel Operating Co. v. Commissioner, 244 F.2d 876 (1st Cir. 1957); John Mantell, 17 T.C. 1143 (1952), acq. 1952-1 C.B. 3; See Rev. Rul. 67-47, 1967-1 C.B. 9.

[23]Hirsch Improvement Co. v. Commissioner, 115 F.2d 656 (2nd Cir. 1944), cert. den. 323 U.S. 750 New Capital Hotel, Inc., 28 T.C. 706 (1957), aff'd per curiam, 261 F.2d 437 (6th Cir. 1958); Gilken Corp. v. Commissioner, 176 F.2d 141 (10th Cir. 1949).

[24]Commissioner v. Riss, 374 F.2d 161 (8th Cir. 1967); Clinton Hotel Realty Corp., v. Commissioner, 128 F.2d 968 (5th Cir. 1942).

[25]Section 164, I.R.C.

[26]Section 162, I.R.C.

[27]Regulations §1.162.11. In other words the payment by a tenant of his landlord's non-deductible special assessments are deductible rent to the tenant.

These payments by the tenant are rental income to the landlord.[28] The landlord is allowed an offsetting deduction for real and personal property taxes paid by the tenant on his behalf.[29] But if part of the tenant's payment is for a special assessment that benefits the landlord's property, it is a non-deductible payment made by the tenant on the landlord's behalf.[30]

8. Covenant to Pay Mortgage Service

The tenant may agree to service the landlord's mortgage obligation against the leased property. The results are the same. All of what the tenant pays is deductible rent. But these payments on behalf of the landlord are rental income to him. The landlord can take a wash deduction for the amounts paid by the tenant on his interest obligation. But any payments made by the tenant against the landlord's obligation to pay principal must be capitalized.

9. Covenant to Pay Insurance Premiums

Any payment made by the tenant of insurance premiums on his own property is currently deductible unless the term of the insurance exceeds one year. In that case, the premium is amortizable over the insurance period on a pro rata basis.[31]

If the tenant pays insurance premiums on his landlord's property, he has a current rental deduction. Yet the landlord has rental income against which he is entitled to offset only a deduction for the current year's premium.

All of these last three categories may impose a hardship on the landlord. He may be in receipt of current rental income, on which he is taxable, without having a current offsetting expense deduction.[32]

10. Covenant to Paint, Repair, and Maintain

A tenant's covenant to paint, repair, and maintain the landlord's premises normally should not cause tax difficulty. Theoretically, the amounts paid by the tenant for maintenance, repairs, and painting are rental income to the landlord and deductible rental expense to the tenant. But the landlord washes out his income by a current deduction for the paint, repair, and maintenance paid on his behalf. It is, therefore, normal to treat the tenant's payments as his direct business expenses.

But if the covenant to repair is drawn so broadly that it may require the tenant to replace structural damage, the result may well be different.[33]

---

[28]Ethel S. Amey, 22 T.C. 756 (1954); William A. Clementson, 1968 P-H Memo T.C. ¶68,118.
[29]Rev. Rul. 54-600, 1954-2 C.B. 164.
[30]Young v. Commissioner, 59 F.2d 691 (9th Cir. 1932), cert. den. 287 U.S. 652.
[31]Insurance premiums must be amortized over the life of the insurance protection. Rev. Rul. 70-413, 1970-2 C.B. 103.
[32]Reg. §1.1441-2(a)(2) requires a resident U.S. tenant to withhold on rentals paid both to and *on behalf of* of a non-resident alien landlord.
[33]See the discussion below on Covenant to Restore Premises.

11. Covenant to Reimburse Landlord for Expenses

A covenant to reimburse the landlord for expenses is quite common in shopping center leases. While each tenant may be responsible for the maintenance and upkeep of his own leased premises, the landlord is usually responsible for the maintenance and upkeep of common areas, such as parking, service and mall areas, and for general expenses, such as insurance and taxes. In order to minimize his risk, the landlord frequently will require each tenant to reimburse him for his pro rata share of these general expenses. The landlord generally will be entitled to a deduction at the time the expenses are paid or accrued, unless the payment is made for some benefit, such as insurance protection that is contracted for a period in excess of one year. If so, the landlord's expenditure will be amortizable over the contract period.

When the tenant reimburses the landlord for his share of such expenses, the payment is additional deductible rent to him.[34] The landlord receives the reimbursed amount as additional rental income.[35]

The foregoing analysis would not apply reimbursement of certain extraordinary landlord expenditures. For example, the landlord might agree to put substantial improvements on the premises that had a useful life equal to the term of the lease. In completion, the tenant covenants to reimburse the landlord for the cost of the improvements. In this situation, the reimbursement payment would not be currently deductible; it would be treated as the equivalent of an advance payment of rent and would be amortizable over the term of the lease.[36]

The landlord would be required to treat the payment is the same way; it would be immediate taxable income to him as advance rent.[37] But because the reimbursement payment is taxable income, he is not required to reduce his basis for the improvements by the amount of the payment. The landlord, therefore, gets to depreciate the cost of the improvements over their useful life or over the life of the lease, if shorter.[38]

The same caution should be taken in applying the normal rules of reimbursed landlord expenses to extraordinary expenditures for restoration or demolition which will be discussed below.

12. Covenant to Guarantee Landlord Against Loss

A covenant by the tenant to guarantee the landlord against loss is rare except in a sale and leaseback transaction. But if such a covenant is placed in a lease, the tax effect is that of additional rental. When the tenant pays the amount of the landlord's loss, he has a rental deduction for the amount. The payment is taxable rental income to the landlord.

---

[34] Section 162(a)(3) I.R.C.
[35] Regulations §1.161-8(c). See Regulations §1.1441-2(a)(2) on withholding on such amounts paid to foreign landlords.
[36] Norman Baker Smith, 51 T.C. 429 (1968) I.R.S. Pub. No. 334 (1972), p. 73.
[37] Regulations §1.61-8(b).
[38] Andrew J. Easter, 1964 P-H Memo T.C. ¶64,058 (1964), aff'd per curiam, 338 F.2d 968 (4th Cir. 1965), cert. den. 381 U.S. 912.

13. Effect of Net Lease on Landlord's Interest Deduction

If the tenant covenants to pay the expenses which would normally be the landlord's, it is the tenant who assumes the risk of any increase or decrease in the expenses. The same is true if the tenant covenants to reimburse the landlord for the landlord's out-of-pocket expenditures that the landlord makes on the leases premises; the risk of any increase or decrease in those expenditures is on the tenant.

Under such a net lease (which involves either tenant payment or tenant reimbursement of landlord expenses, or both), the landlord is, in substance, a passive investor. If the landlord has borrowed moneys for the purpose of acquiring, improving, or keeping the lease's property, his interest deduction may be jeopardized. For this purpose, the concept of a "net lease" is carefully defined in the Internal Revenue Code. A statutory "net" lease is one under which the landlord's Section 162[39] deductions are less than 15 percent of the rental income produced by the property.[40] For the purpose of measuring the landlord's Section 162 trade or business expenses, interest, taxes, losses, depreciation, and rentals paid to others are specifically excluded.[41] Reimbursed insurance and repair and maintenance expenses are also excluded.[42]

If the lease is a statutory "net lease," the result is a disallowance of the interest paid by the landlord on the property to the extent that the landlord's interest exceeds $10,000.[43] There are two other phases to the $10,000 basic full allowance. The first is simply: if the landlord makes more out of the property than he spends, the landlord gets the interest deduction in full.[44] Second, to the extent the landlord has a current cash loss (excluding depreciation) he gets the full deduction for interest.[45] Any undeducted interest can be carried forward for possible deduction in future years.[46]

14. Covenant to Restore Property: Wear and Tear not Excepted

If the tenant agrees to restore the property to the landlord at the end of the lease in its condition and value at the commencement of the lease, the landlord may lose his deduction for depreciation.[47]

It is, therefore, essential that the tenant's obligation to restore be subject to the proviso: "other than ordinary wear and tear."

---

[39] Section 162, I.R.C.

[40] Section 163(d)(4) I.R.C. Disallowed interest losses may be carried forward. Section 163(d)(2), I.R.C.

[41] Technically, interest is deductible under Section 163, taxes under Section 164, losses under Section 165, bad debts under Section 166, and depreciation under Section 167. The proposed regulations under Section 163(d)(4), therefore, exclude them from being part of the landlord's trade or business expenses under Section 162.

[42] Section 163(d)(4)(A)(i) parenthetical clause, I.R.C.

[43] If the landlord is married and his wife files a separate return, $12,500 each. Section 163(d)(1)(A), I.R.C.

[44] Section 163(d)(3), I.R.C.

[45] Section 163(d)(3)(B), I.R.C.

[46] Section (d)(3)(C), I.R.C.

[47] Georgia Ry. & Electric Co. v. Commissioner, 77 F.2d 897 (5th Cir. 1935), cert. den. 296 U.S. 601; Commissioner, v. Terre Haute Electric Co., 67 F.2d 697 (7th Cir. 1938), cert. den. 292 U.S. 624; Harry H. Kem, Jr., 51 T.C. 455 (1968), aff'd 432 F.2d 961 (9th Cir. 1944).

15. Covenant to Restore: Wear and Tear Excepted

The tenant's agreement on lease termination to restore the premises to the landlord in the same condition as they were at the date of the original leasing (ordinary wear and tear excepted) has no immediate tax effect. The landlord is entitled to depreciate his investment in the property despite the tenant's obligation to restore.

On termination of the lease, the tenant's expenditures to restore (whether in the nature of repair or capital expenditure) are deductible by him as a current expense. The fact that the expenditure made might result in an improvement to the landlord's property is immaterial to the tenant: because the lease is terminated, he is abandoning the improvement.[48]

The value of the repairs and improvements made by the tenant on termination of the lease are not income to the landlord.[49] Because the landlord receives these restoration expenditures tax-free, he has a zero basis for them and is not entitled to depreciate them.[50]

But suppose the tenant was compelled during the life of the lease to restore the premises because of a structural defect. If the payment were substantial, the tenant would be compelled to capitalize it. He would be entitled to recover the cost over the shorter of its useful life or the term of the lease.[51] What if the restoration expenditure does not result in any increased economic benefit to the tenant? Suppose all that the restoration does is give the tenant back the use of the premises in the same condition he had originally leased them for? At least two courts have held the tenant is entitled to a current business expense despite the fact that the useful life of the restoration exceeded one year.[52] The Internal Revenue Service takes a contrary position.

The tenant's cost of restoration is not income to the landlord when it is made; because the landlord is out of possession of the restored premises, he has not realized any benefit from the restoration.[53] For that reason, the landlord is not entitled to depreciate the cost of the tenant's restoration.

16. Release of Covenant to Restore

What happens if the landlord and tenant decide to liquidate the tenant's obligation to restore the premises by a payment is cash? The tenant's payment in cash is fully deductible as a business expense.[54] But what about the landlord? There are four possibilities and the courts have adopted three and rejected one:

---

[48]Sections 162, 165, I.R.C.
[49]IRC. §109. The only exception to this rule is in a case in which the improvement is intended as a "substitute for rent." Reg. §1.109-1. Restoration of the premises at the end of the lease term is hardly the equivalent of or substitute for rent.
[50]Regulations §1.109-1.
[51]Hotel Kingkade v. Commissioner, 180 F.2d 310 (10th Cir. 1950). But if the tenant is on a month to month lease, he must use useful life. Erlich v. Commissioner, 198 F.2d 158 (1st Cir. 1952). Journal Tribune Publishing Co. v. Commissioner, 348 F.2d 266 (8th Cir. 1965); Atlantic Coast Line RR, 31 B.T.A. 730 (1934), aff'd 81 F.2d 309 (4th Cir. 1936), cert. den. 298 U.S. 656.
[52]Journal Tribune Publishing Co. v. Commissioner, 348 F.2d 266 (8th Cir. 1965); Atlantic Coast Line RR, 31 B.T.A. 730 (1934), aff'd 81 F.2d 309 (4th Cir., 1936), cert. den. 298 U.S. 656.
[53]M.E. Blatt Co. v. United States, 305 U.S. 267 (1938).
[54]Frank and Seder Co. v. Commissioner, 44 F.2d 147 (3rd Cir., 1930).

TAX CONSEQUENCES OF LEASE CLAUSES

(1) Excludable receipt under Section 109 just as if restoration had been made.[55]

(2) Ordinary income as if the equivalent of payment by tenant to cancel lease.[56]

(3) Recovery of basis of leased property that actually had been shown to have been damaged and any balance be taxed as Section 1231 gain.[57]

(4) Recovery of basis of property leased.[58]

The author believes that alternatives (3) and (4) are the proper ones. The only difference between them is whether or not an allocation can be made between that part of the leased property which was damaged and that which was not. But the allocation, if it is possible, should be made on a comparison of the cost of restoration to the value of the leased property. Merely to allow the depreciated basis of the destroyed improvements as an offset to the tenant's in lieu payment[59] ignores both the factors of inflation and the severance damage done to the unrestored premises.

17. Covenant to Restore: Failure Either to Restore or to Pay

Suppose the tenant who is under an obligation to restore does neither. If the damages to the premises were caused by fire or other casualty, the landlord is entitled to a casualty loss under Section 165.[60]

18. Restoration or Reimbursement Covenant

Should the tenant agree to restore or should he agree to reimburse the landlord for the landlord's cost of restoration? The tax consequences are the same to the tenant. He gets a current deduction in either event, provided the restoration does not have a long useful life; in such case, the expenditure may be capitalized as either advance rental or a tenant's improvement. In either case, the capitalized expenditure would be amortizable over the life of the lease.

But it makes quite a difference to the landlord. If the tenant restores the premises himself, the landlord has no income, either immediately,[61] or when the lease terminates.[62] But if the tenant reimburses the landlord for the landlord's cost of restoration, the landlord has ordinary rental income in the amount of the reimbursement. The restoration expenditure becomes deductible by way of depreciation over the useful life of the property, unless the restoration can be shown by the landlord to be attributable to

---

[55] Rejected by Tax Court in Boston Fish Market Corp. 57 T.C. 884 (1972).

[56] Billy Rose's Diamond Horseshoe v. U.S., 448 F.2d 549 (CA 2, 1971)(dicta); Sirbo Holdings, Inc. 61 T.C. No. 77 (1974 on remand from its reversal Sirbo Holdings, Inc. v. Commissioner, 476 F.2d 981 (2nd Cir. 1973).

[57] Adopted by Tax Court in Boston Fish Market Corp., *supra*.

[58] Hamilton & Main, Inc., 25 T.C. 878(1956); Guy L. Waggoner, 15 T.C. 496(1950) acq. 1951-1 C.B. 3.; Washington Fireproof Building Co., 31 B.T.A. 824 (1934).

[59] The rule adopted by the Tax Court in Boston Fish Market Corp., *supra*.

[60] Rev. Rul. 73-41, 1973-1 C.B. 74. The measure of the landlord's loss is the difference between the damage sustained and the amount of a payment later made by the tenant on a judgment obtained against him. The date of the casualty loss was the date of the payment (unless the tenant was insolvent when the fire occurred).

[61] M.E. Blatt Co. v. United States, 305 U.S. 267 (1938).

[62] Regulations §1.109-1.

the current lease only; if so, the restoration expenditure is amortizable over the remaining term of the lease.

The landlord may suffer another serious tax problem on termination of the lease. If, at that time, a tenant pays money to liquidate his obligation to restore, the landlord may be entitled to recovery of basis and Section 1231 treatment. But, if at the time of termination, the only obligation the tenant has to liquidate is one of reimbursement, his payment to the landlord will be rental income taxed at ordinary rates.[63]

19. Covenant to Demolish Existing Improvements

A covenant to demolish may go either way: the tenant agrees to lease the property and demolish the improvements, or the landlord may agree to demolish the improvements if the tenant leases the property. Both are tax-unwise.

The tenant's problems are the simplest. If the tenant covenants to demolish existing improvements, his cost of demolition is part of his cost for the lease. That cost is amortizable over the life of the lease as in any other tenant cost of acquiring a lease.[64] But if the tenant had accepted the lease with the existing improvements and thereafter had demolished an improvement, the tenant would be entitled to a current abondonment loss to the extent of the cost of demolition.[65]

The landlord's problems are harder.

First, if he *agrees* to demolish any improvements, both the undepreciated basis for the improvements and the demolition expense become part of his cost for the new lease.[66] If he had not agreed to demolish the improvements but had done so without connection to the lease, the landlord would have a currently deductible loss.[67] The only exception is in a case in which the landlord bought the property with the intention of demolishing the improvements. In such case, all of the purchase price for the property is allocated to the land. Because no portion of the purchase price is allocated to the improvements, the landlord-owner is entitled to no loss when he demolished them.[68]

If the landlord-owner rents out the property on a temporary basis, he is, however, entitled to a depreciation deduction. The maximum depreciation deduction is the present value of the rentals to be received over the period of their intended use.[69] But no loss deduction on demolition either for unused basis or for cost of demolition is allowable.

Second, suppose the lease itself is silent about any requirement that the landlord demolish. Even in this situation, the landlord may lose his right to take a demolition deduction if the facts show that such demolition was a necessary pre-condition to the

---

[63] See discussion in A-16 and 17 of this chapter.

[64] See discussion in B-15 of this chapter.

[65] Section 165, I.R.C. Because the tenant is renting the property, he has no basis for it. But he can deduct the cost of demolition unless he agreed to do it. See Rev. Rul. 55-110, 1955-1 C.B. 280.

[66] Regulations §1.165-3(b)(2); Houston Chronicle Pub. Co. v. United States, 481 F.2d 1240 (5th Cir. 1973).

[67] Union Bed & Spring Co. v. Commissioner, 39 F.2d 383 (7th Cir. 1930); First National Bank of Evanston, 1 B.T.A. 9 (1924), acq. IV-1 C.B. 2; The Winter Garden, Inc., 10 B.T.A. 71 (1928), acq. VII-2 C.B. 43.

[68] Regulations, §1.165-3(a).

[69] Regulations, §1.165-3(a)(2)(i).

lease itself. An example would be the owner of land with existing improvements who enters into a lease that requires him to erect a new structure. If the evidence shows that the erection of the new structure will necessarily require demolition of the existing improvements, the unrecovered cost basis of the existing improvements and the cost of demolition are not currently deductible; they must be capitalized and amortized over the lease term.[70]

Third, what if the lease *permits the tenant* to raze existing improvements? Is the landlord allowed to write off his unrecovered basis for the improvements at the time the tenant demolishes them? Here the courts appear to be in a hopeless split with the Fifth and Ninth Circuits[71] allowing a demolition loss and the Tax Court and Seventh and Eighth Circuits requiring the unrecovered basis to be amortized over the lease term.[72]

To protect his demolition loss, the owner should demolish the improvements independently of any future lease. The closer the demolition occurs to the new lease, the more likely it is that the owner's right to a demolition loss will become a federal case.

20. Covenant by Landlord to Improve the Leased Property: Turn-key Lease

A covenant to improve property may be made by either the landlord or tenant. If the landlord agrees to improve the property, the cost of the improvement is normally amortizable over the term of the lease.[73] But if the improvement is of general benefit to the property and will outlast the term of the lease, the landlord must depreciate it over its useful life, rather than over the lease term, if shorter.[74]

The improvements made by the landlord are not income to the tenant. The fact that all of the improvements are made to the tenant's specifications so that he can move in with only the turn of a key does not alter the result.[75]

21. Covenant by Landlord to Reimburse Tenant for Improvements Made by Tenant

It is not unusual in office and commercial leases for the landlord to offer certain types of flooring, wall coverings, drapes, electrical and utility outlets, etc. that the new tenant may find unsatisfactory. For example, the landlord is willing to provide floor tile but the tenant wants carpet. The tenant contracts for the carpet and has it installed at his expense. The landlord either reimburses the tenant for the cost of the tile laying he saved or credits the tenant's bill by the same amount.

It is the author's opinion that the payment should be treated as a non-taxable

---

[70]Donald S. Levinson, 59 T.C. 676(1973); Gerald R. Gorman, T.C. Memo 1974-17 (1974).

[71]Hightower v. United States, 463 F.2d 182 (5th Cir., 1972); Feldman v. Wood, 335 F.2d 264 (9th Cir., 1964).

[72]Foltz v. United States, 458 F.2d 600 (8th Cir., 1972); Herman Landerman, 54 T.C. 1042 (1970), aff'd 454 F.2d 338 (7th Cir., 1972); Rev. Rul. 67-410, 1967-2 C.B. 93.

[73]United States v. Wehrli, 400 F.2d, 686 (10th Cir., 1968); New England Tank Ind., Inc., 50 T.C. 771 (1968), aff'd per curiam, 413 F.2d 1038 (1st Cir. 1969).

[74]Regulations §1.167(a)-4. Triangle Realty Co., 12 B.T.A. 867 (1928); See Laurene Walker Berger, 7 T.C. 1339 (1946), acq. 1947-1 C.B.. 1.

[75]O-W-R Oil Co., 35 B.T.A. 452 (1937), by Regulations §1.612-4(a).

reduction in rent to the tenant. The landlord benefits if he credits the tenant's rental obligation rather than reimburses the tenant. If he merely makes a credit, he reduces his income accordingly. But if the landlord makes a cash outlay to reimburse the tenant, the reimbursement will be a capital cost of the lease to the landlord, amortizable over the life of the lease.[76]

One suggested solution to the problem is to push all the extra installation required by the tenant through the landlord.[77] It is assumed that all bills will be paid by the landlord and that the tenant will reimburse the landlord for all leasehold expenses paid in excess of the landlord's commitment. The problems are several. *First*, since the landlord is not the contractor, but a landlord, he receives advance rental income. *Second*, the landlord may add the amount of reimbursed costs to his cost for the lease and amortize that cost over the life of the lease. *Third*, is the extra reimbursement by the tenant additional rental? If so, the tenant gets no current deduction; he must amortize it over the lease term.

The author's advice has been: (1) reduce rent owed to landlord for his allowance; (2) let the tenant pay for his excess improvement costs and take a depreciation or amortization deduction for those payments.

22. Covenant for Tenant's Improvements as Allowance Against Rent

If an agreement is made that the tenant receive an allowance or credit against rent for improvements the tenant wants to make for his benefit, the landlord receives no income. The tenant's improvements are his own and are depreciable over their life or amortizable over the term of the lease. The cost will not include the landlord's allowance or credit.

But, if the improvements are made by the tenant *for the landlord's benefit*, the result is the opposite. The landlord has income to the extent of the value of the improvements on the termination of the lease.[78]

On termination of the lease, the tenant has either fully recovered his cost of improvement by amortization over the lease term or, if the lease is prematurely terminated, he has taken an abandonment loss.[79]

In the absence of a convenant by the tenant to improve the landlord's property, tenant's improvements are received tax-free on the termination of the lease.[80] The tenant is allowed to recover the cost of the improvements over the shorter of the term of the lease or their useful life.[81] The landlord has no income on the receipt of the

---

[76] It has been suggested that reimbursement of cash to a tenant for carpet, drapes, and wall-covering having a useful life of more than one year be treated as taxable income to the tenant. If so, the tenant would have a basis for depreciation or amortization equal to the amount of income. A most unfortunate result for both landlord and tenant. Both pay out cash, but both must apportion their deductions over the useful life or term of lease.

[77] The premise is that the landlord would be a mere agent for the tenant and could wash the tenant's reimbursement against the capital costs paid by him for the tenant's improvements.

[78] Regulations §1.109-1(a).

[79] Section 165, I.R.C.

[80] Section 109, I.R.C.

[81] Regulations §1.167(a)-4.

improved property on termination of the lease.[82] The landlord's tax basis for the improvements is zero.[83]

23. Covenant to Reduce Rent

If a tenant negotiates an agreement to reduce rent, but has to pay an immediate premium for it, the premium paid is immediate rental income to the landlord.[84]

But the payment made to reduce rental income is not immediately deductible by the tenant. It must be capitalized and spread over the remainder of the term of the lease.[85]

24. Covenant to Terminate: Payment by Landlord

Landlord's problems: If a landlord pays a tenant an amount to terminate the lease, the landlord has a non-deductible expenditure. If the landlord makes the payment to get the property for himself, the payment is part of his cost of the property.[86] How should the landlord recover the payment? There are three ways: (1) addition to basis of the property, allocable between land and depreciable improvements on the ratio of respective fair market values; (2) current abandonment lease expense; (3) expenditure recoverable over the remaining term of the lease.

The answer depends upon what the payment was made for. If the payment was made by the landlord to recover the use of the premises for himself, the landlord is entitled to amortize the expenditure over the balance of the life of the canceled lease.[87] But if the landlord made the cancellation payment so that he could sell the property free and clear of the lease, the payment would be a simple addition to basis.[88] And if the landlord bought up the lease in order to make a new lease, the payment is amortizable over the period of the new lease.[89] Finally, if the landlord bought up the lease for the purpose of constructing a new building, the payment is an addition to the cost of the new building (not the land).[90]

In no case can the landlord currently expense his payment to cancel the lease. Because he owns a fee interest in the property, he cannot take an abandonment loss when he pays to buy up the outstanding leasehold. The landlord's payment must therefore be capitalized. How should it be recoverable? Over the life of the old canceled lease? The life of the new lease? The life of new construction? Or ratably allocated between land and improvements?[91]

---

[82] Section 109, I.R.C.
[83] Section 1019, I.R.C.
[84] University Properties, Inc. v. Commissioner, 378 F.2d 83 (9th Cir. 1967).
[85] Rev. Rul. 73-176, 1973-1 C.B. 146.
[86] Peerless Weighing Etc. Corp., 52 T.C. 850 (1968).
[87] Harriet B. Borland, 27 B.T.A. 538 (1933); Herbert-Burwig, 1953 P-H Memo T.C. ¶53,339 (1953).
[88] Shirley Hill Coal Co., 6 B.T.A. 935 (1927).
[89] Montgomery Co., 54 T.C. 986 (1970), acq. 1970-2 C.B. 2; Rev. Rul. 71-283, 1971-2 C.B. 168.
[90] American Spring and Wire Etc., 20 T.C.M. 116 (1961); Houston Chronicle Publ. Co. v. U.S., 339 F.Supp. 1314 (S.D. Tex. 1972); Keiler v. U.S., 395 F.2d 991 (CA 6, 1968), aff'g per curiam below, 285 F.Supp. 521 (W.D. Ky, 1957).
[91] The taxpayer takes the shortest useful life and the Internal Revenue Service the longest, dependent, in each case, on the operation of the net operating loss. IRC §172.

Suppose a landlord merely forgives the rents in order to secure a termination of the lease? The forgiveness should be treated as a reduction in rent: neither taxable to the tenant nor deductible or amortizable by the landlord. But if the foregiveness of rent is for past due or accrued rent, then the tenant, theoretically, should realize income to the extent of the indebtedness forgiven. But that theoretical income would be offset by an equivalent rental or abandonment deduction.[92] It is the landlord who may suffer to the extent he has forgiven past due rents, he has made a lease termination payment amortizable over the remaining life of the lease.[93]

Tenant's problems: What about the tenant's receipt of a payment from the landlord to cancel the lease? By statute, the tenant has a Section 1231 gain receipt,[94] which will be treated as a capital gain to the extent it (and other Section 1231 gains) exceed Section 1231 losses. If the tenant has any unamortized lease costs, he is entitled to deduct them against the cancellation payment before the gain is figured.[95] If the unrecovered lease costs exceed the landlord's payment, the tenant should be entitled to an abandonment loss under Section 165 rather than a Section 1231 loss.

25. Covenant to Terminate: Payment by Tenant

Landlord's problems: The amount paid by a tenant to get out of a lease is ordinary income to the landlord: it is a substitute for the rent he otherwise would have received.[96] The landlord should be entitled to deduct unrecovered lease costs (other than for improvements of continued use to him) against the telescoped rental income, but there is no authority that so states.

Tenant's problems: The amount paid by a tenant to get out of a lease is a deductible expense when paid or accrued.[97] The theory is that the tenant has abandoned his lease. He is, therefore, entitled to deduct immediately both the payment he makes to the landlord and all of his lease costs to the extent not previously recovered.[98]

But the tenant is entitled to these write-offs only if he truly abandons the lease premises. If the tenant makes the payment in order to negotiate a new lease with the same landlord, the payment is part of his cost of the new lease and must be amortized over its term.[99] Also, if the tenant makes the termination payment at the time he purchases the property, the "termination payment" becomes part of his purchase price; it is not separately deductible as a termination payment.[100] The "termination" payment, as part of the cost, is allocable between land and improvements.[101]

---

[92]Except in the case of an accrual method tenant who had previously taken a deduction for the accrued, but unpaid, rentals. The tax benefit rule would saddle him with debt forgiveness income. Section 111, I.R.C.
[93]Cosmopolitan Corp., 1959 P-H T.C. Memo ¶59,122 (1959).
[94]Section 1241, I.R.C.
[95]Rev. Rul. 72-85, 1972-1 C.B. 234.
[96]Hort. v. Commissioner, 313 U.S. 28 (1941).
[97]Cassatt v. Commissioner, 137 F.2d 745 (3rd Cir. 1943); Rev. Rul. 69-511, 1969-1 C.B. 24.
[98]Section 165, I.R.C.
[99]Commissioner v. McCue Bros. etc., 210 F.2d 752 (2nd Cir. 1954), cert. den. 348 U.S. 829; Commissioner v. Golonsky, 200 F.2d 72 (3rd Cir. 1952), cert. den. 345 U.S. 939.
[100]Millinery Center Bldg. Corp. v. Commissioner, 350 U.S. 456 (1956).
[101]Rev. Rul. 60-180, 1960-1 C.B. 114 (where the tenant had previously completely depreciated his own improvements).

B. DEPRECIATION OF IMPROVEMENTS ON LEASED PROPERTY

Improvements to leased property may be made by either the landlord or tenant. This part of Chapter 8 will cover the twin problems of the period over which the cost of the improvements can be recovered and who, landlord or tenant, is entitled to the tax write-off of the cost.

1. Landlord's Improvements

Ordinarily, the landlord is entitled to depreciate the cost of his improvements to the leased premises. But if the tenant's obligation to restore on termination is drawn too broadly, the landlord may lose his rights to take depreciation.[102] Accordingly, the tenant's obligation to restore should specifically except ordinary wear and tear. As long as the burden of the loss from either ordinary wear and tear or obsolescence, or both, is placed upon the lessor, he will be entitled to take a corresponding measure of depreciation on the improvements.[103]

2. Trade Fixtures Installed by Tenant

Generally, a lease permits the tenant to install trade fixtures on the leased premises necessary or incidental to his business. Trade fixtures normally consist of items of machinery, business equipment, and other fixtures to be used in the tenant's business. Because these fixtures are related to the tenant's business, the tenant is generally entitled to remove them on the cancellation or expiration of the lease. Accordingly, their value is never income to the landlord.

If trade fixtures installed by the tenant have a useful life of more than one year, the tenant is required to capitalize their cost. He is permitted to recover their cost over the useful life of the equipment through an allowance for depreciation.[104] If the life is less than one year, the tenant can deduct the entire cost in the year of purchase.

3. Permanent Improvements to Leased Premises by Tenant

If a tenant installs permanent non-removable improvements to the leased property which have a life in excess of one year, he must capitalize the cost. But he is entitled to recover the cost either through an allowance for depreciation over their useful life or through an allowance for amortization over the remaining life of the lease, whichever is the shorter.[105]

---

[102] Georgia Ry & Electric Co. v. Commissioner, 77 F.2d 897 (5th Cir. 1935), cert. den. 296 U.S. 601; Commissioner v. Terre Haute Electric Co., 67 F.2d 697 (7th Cir., 1938), cert. den. 292 U.S. 624. Cf. Harry H. Kem, Jr., 51 T.C. No 44 (1968).

[103] Alaska Realty Co. v. Commissioner, 141 F.2d 675 (6th Cir. 1944); Charles Bertram Currier, T.C. 980, 985 (1946), non-acq. 1950-1 C.B. 5. Rev. Rul. 62-8 1962-1 C.B. 31.

[104] See Eimer & Amend, 2 B.T.A. 603, 607 (1925), acq. V-1 C.B. 2.

[105] Reg. Sec. 1.167(a)-4. If the lessee's interest in a long-term lease of improved property is purchased, it has been held that the purchaser can allocate the lease cost between the building lease and the land lease. The lease cost allocable to the former is amortizable over the life of the building, rather than the lease. 1220 Realty Co. v. Commissioner, 323 F.2d 492 (6th Cir. 1963).

4. Term of Lease: Option to Renew

The term of a lease normally includes options to renew, unless either the landlord or tenant can prove that financial facts forced either or both not to renew.[106] For example, if a tenant constructed a building that had a useful life in excess of the original term, it would be assumed that the tenant would exercise his option to renew.[107]

Section 178 provides three statutory tests for determining whether or not a lease will be renewed. These are respectively: the "sixty percent" test, the "seventy-five percent" test, and the "related parties" test.

a. *Sixty percent test* (useful life of tenant's improvements): If the useful life of an improvement made to the leased premises exceeds the original term of the lease, the term of the renewal option will become part of the original term: the conditions are: (1) the useful life of the improvement exceeds the original term of the lease by at least 60 percent, and (2) the tenant cannot prove it was less probable the lease would be renewed.[108] Does it make a difference if the landlord or the tenant makes the improvement? Yes it does. Under the regulations, only a tenant improvement triggers the addition of the lease options to the original lease term.[109] If there is more than one period of renewal, this test and the following apply separately to each term of renewal.[110]

b. *Seventy-five percent test (lease costs)*: If the cost of acquiring the lease is allocable between the original term and the renewal or renewal options on a ratio of less than 75 percent to the original term and 25 percent or more to the renewal option or options, the adverse rules apply. If so, the term of the renewal option, or options, is added to the original lease term.[111]

How much of a tenant's[112] leasehold cost is allocable to the original term and how much to the renewal option or options is measured by a "fact and circumstance" test. One way of making the test is using present values for the original term and for the renewal option or options. If the rental *is not subject to increase* at the time of the renewal option or options, the lease cost is prorated between the original term and the renewal terms on the present value of each. If 25 percent or more of the present values goes to the options, the options are part of the original term.[113]

What happens if the renewal option or options are on a cost-of-living increase or at an otherwise higher rental? Obviously, the present value of the renewal term is worth more, but the chance of exercise by the lessee worth less. The probable escape is that it is non-probable the tenant will renew. The real escape is that the higher rentals to be

---

[106]IRC §178(c). The test is one of "reasonable certainty" that the lease will be renewed. Reg. §1.162-11(b); Bonwit Teller & Co. v. Commissioner, 53 F.2d 381 (CA 2, 1931), cert. den. 284 U.S. 690.

[107]Alamo Broadcasting Co., 15 T.C. 534 (1950), acq. 1951-1 C.B. 1; Hens & Kelly, 19 T.C. 305 (1953), acq. 1953-1 C.B.

[108]Section §178(a)(1), I.R.C.

[109]Regulations, §1.178-1(b)(1) limits the restriction to improvements made by lessee.

[110]Regulations, §1.178-1(b)(2).

[111]Section 178(a)(2), I.R.C. If the tenant can show a more reasonable probability that the option will not be exercised.

[112]The landlord's tenant costs are ignored under the regulations.

[113]Regulations §1.178-1(b)(5)(ii), Example.

DEPRECIATION OF IMPROVEMENTS

paid are both uncertain and larger in which case the higher and uncertain rentals must substantially diminish the present value of the renewal options.

c. *Related parties renewal of option:* If the landlord and the tenant are related parties, the useful life of the improvement is the measurement of the amortization or depreciation deduction.[114] Related persons (landlord and tenant) are defined, if corporate, as 80 percent or more commonly controlled subsidiary or any so controlled grand-subsidiary and the common parent.[115] In the case of individuals, related persons are the landlord and the tenant's brothers and sisters (whether by whole or by half blood). It also includes the landlord or tenant's "spouse,[116] ancestors, and lineal descendants."[117]

d. *Conclusion:* Both the tenant's costs of acquiring a lease and the life of the improvements will include the period of renewal or renewals, unless the tenant can prove (except in the case of related parties) that there was a reasonable probability of non-renewal. What happens if in fact the lease is not renewed, despite the foregoing presumptions? The termination of the lease will result in a Section 1231 loss of the undepreciated basis in the year the lease expires.[118]

5. Month-to-month Tenancy

But suppose the lease is made between unrelated parties on an indefinite or a month-to-month basis. What measure of depreciation should be taken? Under these circumstances, the tenant is required to capitalize the cost of any improvements added to the property; he is permitted only to depreciate them over their useful life.[119]

6. Premature Termination of Lease or Failure to Renew Option

What happens if the lease is prematurely terminated or the option to renew is not exercised? If the lessee loses his investment in the improvements to the lessor when the lease expires, the lessee is permitted to deduct the amount of his unrecovered cost for the improvements in full in the year of expiration. The amount of the unrecovered cost is treated as a loss incurred by the lessee in the year of cancellation.[120]

7. Tenant's Improvements as Income to Lessor

Does the lessor realize income to the extent of the fair market value of the tenant's improvements at the time the lease is canceled or expires? Or are these improvements received by the lessor without any tax consequence?

---

[114]Section 178(b), I.R.C.
[115]Section 1504(a), I.R.C.
[116]"Spouse" includes an alienated spouse (Regulations §1.267(c)-1(a)(4) but not a divorced one. Section 7701(a)(17), I.R.C.
[117]Regulations §1.178-2(b).
[118]See B-6 of this chapter.
[119]Thatcher Medicine Co., 3 B.T.A. 154, 159 (1925), acq. on another issue, 1938-2 C.B. 32; William Scholes & Sons, Inc. 3 B.T.A. 598 (1925).
[120]Cassatt v. Commissioner, 137 F.2d 745, 749 (3rd Cir. 1943); Robert C. Coffey, 21 B.T.A. 1242 (1931), acq. X-2 C.B. 14. Cf. J.A. Zwetchkenbaum, par. 62,283 P-H Memo T.C. (1962). Strauss v. United States, 199 F.Supp. 845 (W.D. La. 1961).

The answer depends upon whether or not the improvements added by the tenant were intended as a substitute for rent. In other words, if the lessor agrees to take a smaller cash rental in return for the promise of the lessee to erect certain improvements on the leased property, then the value of the property would constitute income to the lessor. Otherwise, the value of these improvements does not constitute income to the lessor either at the time of construction[121] or at the time of forfeiture to the landlord.[122]

Naturally, if the landlord receives the improvements without any tax cost, he has no tax basis for them.[123]

Example: Landlord leases improved property to Tenant for a period of 50 years under a lease calling for the construction of a $500,000 office building by Tenant. Tenant agrees to pay an annual rental of $10,000. The lease provides that the Tenant's improvements become the property of Landlord upon termination or cancellation of the lease. Before the building is completed, Tenant becomes bankrupt and the lease is forfeited. At the time of forfeit, the partially constructed building is worth $100,000. Landlord would not be required to report any part of the $100,000 value for the building in income.[124] Accordingly, Landlord's basis for the building would be zero.[125]

On the other hand, if the value of the tenant's improvements represent the payment of rent in kind, the fair market value of the improvements represents rental income to the landlord at the time of construction.[126] The value of the improvements of construction must, of course, be adjusted to reflect the tenant's right to use the improvements for the remainder of the term.[127]

Correspondingly, if the construction of an improvement by the lessee is treated as the payment of rent, the lessee is entitled to deduct its cost as the equivalent of rent.[128]

C. COSTS OF ACQUIRING A LEASE

The questions relating to the proper tax treatment of the costs of obtaining, renewing, or extending a lease are questions that affect both the lessor and the lessee. In one case, it may be the lessee who makes the expenditure; if so, is the expenditure currently deductible, or must it be capitalized?

But if it is the lessor who makes the payment, must he capitalize the payment? Or is it currently deductible? For the purposes of our analysis, we shall consider first the position of the lessor, then that of the lessee.

1. Lease Expenditures Made by Landlord

Any expenditure made by a landlord for the purpose of obtaining a tenant must be capitalized as a part of his cost of the lease.[129] Among such expenditures are items such

---

[121] M.E. Blatt Co. v. United States, 305 U.S. 267 (1938).
[122] Section 109, I.R.C.
[123] Section 1019, I.R.C.
[124] Reg. Sec. 1.109-(b), Example.
[125] Reg. Sec. 1.1019-1.
[126] Reg. Sec. 1.109-1.
[127] I.T. 4009, 1950-1 C.B. 13 declared obsolete in Rev. Rul. 67-123, 1967-1 C.B. 383 without explanation. Obviously, the Service is now taking the position that the income is not realized by the landlord until lease termination. It has good authority. Helvering v. Brunn, 309 U.S. 461 (1940).
[128] Your Health Club, Inc., 4 T.C. 385, 390 (1944), acq. 1945 C.B. 7.
[129] Young v. Commissioner, 59 F.2d 691 (9th Cir. 1932), cert. den. 287 U.S. 652.

COSTS OF ACQUIRING A LEASE

as brokers' commissions; attorneys' fees, alterations to suit tenants, and other similar expenditures.

But suppose the landlord's expenditures are unsuccessful. In this case, he is entitled to deduct the amount of any such expenditures as a current expense in the year paid or incurred.[130] On the other hand, if the unsuccessful efforts are followed by successful ones, the landlord must capitalize all his expenses unless he can show a reasonable basis for segregating the expenses of the unsuccessful efforts from those that followed.[131]

If the landlord's efforts are successful in producing a lease, his expenditures are treated as a part of his cost for the lease. Accordingly, he is entitled to amortize the cost of such expenditure over the life of the lease.[132]

What if the lease so obtained is canceled or forfeited by the tenant before the expiration of its full term? In this event, the landlord is entitled to deduct the unamortized part of his total lease cost as a loss incurred in the year of cancellation or forfeiture.[133]

If, however, the lessor sells the property, he is not entitled to deduct his unamortized lease costs in the year of sale; these costs are recovered as an addition to his basis for the property sold. Hence, the unamortized lease costs will appear as an offset to the lessor's sale price for the lessor's lease costs become a part of his basis for the new property acquired in the exchange.[134]

2. Allocation of Cost to Outstanding Lease on Acquisition of Property

Suppose, then, a taxpayer purchases property subject to an outstanding lease. Being the new landlord, is he entitled to allocate any part of his purchase price to the lease as its cost? And is he entitled to amortize such cost over the remaining life of the lease?

The cases have assumed, for example, that stockholders who receive leased property from their corporation as part of the assets distributed in liquidation are entitled to amortize the corporation's unrecovered costs for the leases over their remaining life.[135] Accordingly, the stockholders who acquire the property in exchange for their stock should be entitled to apportion a part of their cost to the outstanding lease, measured by the corporation's unrecovered lease costs.[136]

But suppose the corporation itself had no lease costs in connection with the lease being distributed to the stockholders. Under these circumstances, the Commissioner has refused to allow the stockholders to allocate any part of their purchase price (value

---

[130] Watson P. Davidson, 27 B.T.A. 158 (1932), non-acq. XII-1 C.B. 16.
[131] Arthur T. Galt, 19 T.C. 892 (1953), aff'd on this issue, 216 F.2d 41 (7th Cir. 1954). cert. den. 348 U.S. 951.
[132] Tonningsen v. Commissioner, 61 F.2d 199 (9th Cir. 1932); The method of accounting used by the landlord is immaterial. Rev. Rul. 70-408, 1970-2 C.B. 68.
[133] Oliver Iron Mining Co., 13 T.C. 416 (1949), acq. 1950-1 C.B. 4.
[134] Post v. Commissioner, 109 F.2d 135 (2d Cir. 1940); Plaza Investment Co., 5 T.C. 1295, 1297 (1945).
[135] See Wolan v. Commissioner, 184 F.2d 101, 104 (10th Cir. 1950). Plaza Investment Co., 5 T.C. 1295 (1945).
[136] See Cooper Foundation v. O'Malley, 221 F.2d 279, 281 (8th Cir. 1955).

of the stock surrendered) to the lease for the purpose of creating a new allowance for amoritization by the stockholders.[137]

3. Allocation of Carry Over Basis on Death of Lessor

A similar rule has been applied in the case of an inherited interest in a lease. The heir is not entitled to allocate any portion of his carry over basis for the property to the lease for the purpose of amortization.[138] But this flat rule gives rise to theoretical difficulties. Suppose, for example, the decedent wills the leased property to one person and the lease itself to another. In other words, one person inherits the right of reversion on the expiration of the lease and another inherits the right to receive the rentals for the remainder of the lease. If the lease were valued in the decedent-lessor's estate separately from the property itself, would not the new owner of the lease be entitled to amortize his basis for the lease over the remainder of its life? This was the result reached in at least one case in which the ownership of the reversion and of the lease rentals were separated.[139]

Accordingly, the next step was but a matter of time. If the person who receives a lease independently of the reversion is entitled to amortize his basis for the lease, why should not a person who receives both the lease and the reversion be entitled to the same tax benefit? This was the result reached over the Commissioner's objections.[140]

Example: Father leased land to Tenant for 99 years at an annual rental of $120,000. Father thereafter died. The leased property was included in his estate at a valuation of $1,500,000. Daughter inherited the property. At the time she inherited the property, Daughter was able to show that she could rent the property for an annual rental of only $24,000, which was the going market rate. Hence, she proved that the lease inherited by her gave her the right to receive a rental that produced $96,000 of annual rent in excess of the present market rate. This right to receive a rental in excess of the going rate was, of course, a right that would disappear over the life of the lease. On establishing these facts, she was permitted to amortize the premium value placed on the lease at the time of its acquisition by her over the remaining life of the lease. The premium value of the lease was therefore set by the Court at $1,000,000, being measured by the discounted value of $96,000 per year for the remainder of the lease. This value was subject to amortization by Daughter over the life of the lease.[141]

Similarly, on the purchase from the lessor of property subject to a beneficial lease in excess of the going market rental, the purchaser should be entitled to allocate a part of his purchase price to the lease. The amount to be allocated to the lease should be measured by the difference between the purchase price and the appraised market value of the property. This difference would represent the premium paid by the purchaser in order to acquire the lease, as distinguished from the property. Or, to state the question

---

[137] Martha R. Peters, 4 T.C. 1236 (1945); Carnegie Center Co., 22 T.C. 1189, 1193 (1954), acq. on another issue, 1955-1 C.B. 4.
[138] Friend v. Commissioner, 119 F.2d 959 (7th Cir. 1941), cert. den. 314 U.S. 673; Charlotte Leviton Herbert, 25 T.C. 807, 815 (1956), acq. on another issue, 1956-2 C.B. 6; see Rev. Rul. 55-89, 1955-1 C.B. 284. This rule was applied to deny an heir the right to recover by amortization the amount of unrecovered lease cost existing on the date of the lessor's death. Albert L. Rowan, 22 T.C. 865, 875 (1954).
[139] John W.F. Hobbs, 16 T.C. 1259 (1951), non-acq. 1951-2 C.B. 5.
[140] Commissioner v. Moore, 207 F.2d 265, 276 (9th Cir. 1953), cert. den. 347 U.S. 942.
[141] Mayr Y. Moore (on remand), par. 55,219 P-H Memo T.C. (1955).

of valuation differently, the amortizable premium should be measured by the excess of the rentals under the lease over the rentals that the purchaser could obtain for a similar lease if he attempted to lease the property at the time of purchase.

But this allocation of purchase price between the reversion and the lease is not yet law. At present, both the Commissioner and the Tax Court have taken positions contrary to the allowance of any allocation in a case in which the purchaser acquires both the reversion and the lease.[142]

4. Allocation of Cost to Depreciable Improvements on Acquisition of Property Subject to Outstanding Lease

Suppose a taxpayer purchases improved property that is subject to an outstanding lease. Is he entitled to allocate any portion of his purchase price to the improvements for depreciation purposes? Of course he is, you may answer. But the answer may not be so clear; it may depend upon whether it was the landlord or the tenant who constructed the improvements.

If the improvements were constructed by the owner of the property, a new owner is entitled by the regulations to allocate a portion of the purchase price to the improvements (equal to their fair market value) for the purposes of taking depreciation on them.[143]

But suppose the improvements had been constructed by the tenant. Under the regulations only the tenant is entitled to the allowance for depreciation on the improvements.[144] The landlord has not made any investment in the property which he is entitled to recover by depreciation. Suppose, then, the landlord sells his reversion to a new owner. Is the new owner entitled to allocate any part of his purchase price to the improvements constructed by the tenant for the purposes of creating a second deduction for depreciation in himself? Both the Commissioner and the Tax Court have held no. Because the new owner's predecessor, the landlord, had no investment in the improvements, the new owner is not permitted to take depreciation on them on the curious theory that he did not acquire an "economic interest" in the tenant's improvements by the purchase, since the landlord had no such interest to sell him.[145]

These rules result in the peculiar situation that whether a purchaser is entitled to take depreciation on improved property subject to a lease will turn on the historical accident of who built the building. Thus, two taxpayers similarly situated, holding land with a valuable building on it, subject to similar leases, will have substantially different tax situations if the lessee built the building in one case and the lessor-seller built it in the other.

The purchaser of improved property subject to a lease may allocate an appropriate portion of his cost to a building constructed by the tenant. This amount constitutes his investment in the building which he is entitled to depreciate over the remaining life of

---

[142]Freida Bernstein, 22 T.C. 1146, 1151 (1954), aff'd 230 F.2d 603 (2d Cir. 1956). But see Davidson v. Commissioner, 60 F.2d 50, 52 (2d Cir. 1932).
[143]Reg. Secs. 1.167(a)-4, 1.167(a)-5.
[144]Reg. Sec. 1.167(a)-4.
[145]World Publishing Company, 35 T.C. 7 (1960), rev'd 229 F.2d 614 (8th Cir. 1962); Freida Bernstein, 22 T.C. 1146, 1151 (1954), aff'd 230 F.2d 603 (2d Cir. 1956); Albert L. Rowan, 22 T.C. 865 (1954).

the building.[146] The Court recognized that the buyer of the leased property had bought two assets, namely (1) the reversionary interest in the land[147] and (2) the building subject to the lease. The buyer then proved that he had paid substantially more than the fair market value at the time of purchase of the reversion itself. This excess value constituted the price the buyer paid for the leased building. Because the building was a wasting asset, this portion of the price was depreciable over its remaining life. Because the remaining life of the building was the same as the remaining term of the lease, the same result would have been reached had the court allocated the excess price to the value of the lease for amortization purposes as it did here by allocating the excess to the building.

A similar problem arises in the cases of *inherited* property subject to a lease. Again the Commissioner and the courts have consistently held that the heir is not entitled to allocate any portion of his new basis (adjusted carry over basis) to the tenant's buildings or improvements.[148]

The Internal Revenue Service argues that since the lessor has made no economic investment in the improvements made by his lessee to his premises, he cannot take depreciation on them despite the fact that he may have legal title to them.[149]

5. Expenses Paid by Tenant to Obtain Lease

Commissions and other expenditures made by a tenant for the purpose of acquiring a lease are not currently deductible; these expenditures must be capitalized and can be recovered only by amortization over the life of the lease.[150]

This rule applies not only to commissions paid to a broker for services in finding a lease,[151] but also to amounts paid by a tenant for the purchase price of a lease from another party,[152] and to a loss incurred on the sale of unwanted merchandise acquired by the tenant to get the lease.[153]

What if the lease acquired by the new lessee is a lease of property upon which are placed substantial improvements? If the useful life of the improvements to the lessee is shorter than the unexpired term of the lease, can the lessee recover his lease costs over the shorter useful life of the improvements rather than over the longer unexpired term of the lease? A shorter write-off would give the lessee a larger amount of deductions for immediate tax purposes. Traditionally, both the courts and the Commissioner have held that the lessee must use the longer term of the unexpired lease because the lessee does not have any investment of his own in the leased buildings; that is, the lessee

---

[146]World Publishing Company v. Commissioner, 299 F.2d 614 (8th Cir. 1962); Wilshire Medical Properties v. United States 314 F.2d 333 (9th Cir. 1963); Contra Bernstein v. Commissioner, 230 F.2d 603 (2d Cir. 1956).

[147]It was stipulated that the life of the building was no greater than the remaining term of the lease.

[148]Reg. Sec. 1.167(a)(4).

[149]Catherine B. Currier, 51 T.C. 488 (1968).

[150]T.D. 4957, 1939-2, C.B. 87.

[151]King Amusement Co. v. Commissioner, 44 F.2d 709 (6th Cir. 1939), cert. den. 282 U.S. 900; D.N. & E. Walker Co., 4 B.T.A. 142, 146 (1926), acq. VI-2 C.B. 7.

[152]Cooper Foundation v. O'Malley, 221 F.2d 279 (8th Cir. 1955); Ed Foster, 19 B.T.A. 958, 962 (1930), acq. IX-2 C.B. 20.

[153]Rev. Rul. 68-260, 1968-2 C.B. 86.

would not be entitled to any allowance for depreciation on buildings which he does not own.[154]

However, where the lessee was able to show that the economic value of the lease to him would be much less once the buildings had reached the end of their useful lives, the lessee was entitled to recover by annual deductions that portion of his lease cost attributable to the lease of the improvements over the useful life of the improvements. The balance of the lease cost, which was allocable to the lease of the underlying land, could be amortized only over the unexpired term of the lease itself.[155] Because the useful life of the improvements was substantially less than the unexpired term, the lessee obtained the advantage of substantially larger write-offs in earlier years.

If the lease is canceled or terminated prior to the end of its term, the tenant is entitled to deduct the balance of his unamortized cost attributable to the lease in the year of cancellation or termination.[156] But if the lease is merged into the fee or remainder interest by the tenant's purchase of the property from the landlord, then the tenant is not entitled to deduct his unrecovered lease costs; these costs must be added to the tenant's purchase price as a part of his basis for the property.[157]

If the tenant extends the lease by agreement with his landlord prior to its termination, any part of his lease costs not previously recovered must be amortized over the period of the extension.[158] But, ordinarily, the tenant is not required to add the period of a prospective renewal to the period of the original lease, unless it appears reasonably certain that the tenant will actually exercise his option to renew.[159]

Under Section 178, the period of amortization of lease costs will include the period of a renewal provided by option if less than 75 percent of the tenant's lease cost is attributable to the original period of the lease.[160] The apportionment between the original term and the renewal period is to be made "on the basis of the facts and circumstances of each case."[161]

If the renewal option was separately bargained for and the price thereof fixed accordingly, the ratio of lease cost to option cost is readily determined. Evidence of arms'-length sales of similar options or of similar leases without options could also be used to fix an allocation of a lump sum cost of the lease with option.

If no evidence exists that the value of the lease during a renewal term will be substantially different from its value during the remaining original term, we must turn to the method of valuation suggested in the regulations.[162] This method assumes that the value of the lease in any year of the original term is the same as in any year of the term plus renewals. The present value of an annuity paying the yearly value of the lease over a term equal to the remaining original term is divided by the present value of the

---

[154]David Dab, 28 T.C. 933 (1957), aff'd 255 F.2d 788 (2nd Cir. 1958); Reg. Sec. 1.162-11(a).
[155]The 1220 Realty Company v. Commissioner, 322 F2d 495 (6th Cir. 1963).
[156]Guelph Hotel Corp., 7 B.T.A. 1043 (1927), acq. VII-1 C.B. 13; Washington Catering Co., 9 B.T.A. 743 (1927), acq. VII-2 C.B. 41.
[157]Henry Boos, 30 B.T.A. 882 (1934); S.M. 2931, IV-1 C.B. 33.
[158]Pig & Whistle Co., 9 B.T.A. 668 (1927).
[159]Section 178(c), I.R.C. Giumarra Bros. Fruit Co., 55 T.C. 460 (1970), acq. 1971-2 C.B. 2.
[160]Section 178(a)(2), I.R.C.
[161]Reg. Sec. 1.178-1(b)(5)(i).
[162]*Ibid*.

same annuity over the term including renewals. The result is the ratio of the value of the original term to the value of the term plus renewals. It is then presumed that the lease cost is allocable in the same ratio as lease value.

The computation is simplified because it is not necessary to determine the actual yearly value of the lease. This factor cancels out. It is necessary merely to take the ratio of the present values of one dollar annuities at an appropriate rate of interest over the two terms.

Example:[163] Lessee acquires a lease of unimproved property for $100,000. The lease then has 21 years remaining in the original term and contains two renewal options of 21 years each. The lease provides uniform annual rental for the remaining term of the lease and the renewal periods. Assuming that 5 percent is an appropriate rate of interest, standard annuity tables show:

Present value of $1 per year for 21 years: $12.821
Present value of $1 per year for 63 years: $19.075
Value of original term:
$$\frac{\$12,821}{\$19.075} = 67.21 \text{ percent of entire lease}$$

The cost of the original term is presumed to be also 67.21 percent of the entire cost. Unless the tenant can show that it is probable that the lease will not be renewed, amortization must be taken over 63 years since less than 75 percent of the cost is allocable to the original term.

D. CANCELLATION OR SALE OF LEASE

Suppose a lessor pays his lessee a sum of money in order to obtain a cancellation of the lease. Is the payment deductible by the lessor? Is it ordinary income or capital gain to the lessee?

A similar problem arises if a tenant sells his interest in a lease to another. Is the payment received ordinary income or capital gain?

1. Lessor's Payment to Cancel Lease

Any expenditure made by a lessor to cancel a lease must be capitalized by the lessor. He is entitled to recover the amount of his payment only through amortization over the remaining life of the *canceled* lease.[164]

But suppose the lessor wishes to cancel an existing lease in order that he may make a new lease of the property. If this is the lessor's purpose in cancelling the existing lease, his cancellation payment is treated as a part of his cost for the new lease. Accordingly, his period of amortization for the cancellation payment is the period of the *replacement* lease, not the canceled lease.[165]

How about the lessee? Is the payment received by him capital gain or ordinary income? Because the transaction is in the nature of a sale to the lessor of the lease, the

---

[163]Reg. Sec. 1.178-(b)(5)(ii).
[164]Harriet B. Borland, 27 B.T.A. 538, 542 (1933); The Trustee Corporation, 42 T.C. 482 (1964), acq. 1966-2 C.B. 7.
[165]Wells Fargo Bank & Union Trust Co. v. Commissioner, 163 F.2d 521 (9th Cir. 1947). Montgomery Co. 54 T.C. 986, acq. 1970-2 C.B. xx.

CANCELLATION OR SALE OF LEASE

lessee's receipt of the cancellation payment is reportable as gain realized on a sale or exchange.[166] Accordingly, the gain will be taxed as capital gain[167] or as a Section 1231 gain, depending upon the nature of his holding of the lease. The benefits of this favorable tax treatment of the cancellation payment are not extended to a lessee who is "in the business of entering and marketing leases." Thus, if a lease is held by a tenant for sale to customers in the ordinary course of his trade or business, the gain would be taxed as ordinary income.[168]

2. Lessee's Payment to Cancel Lease

Suppose it is the lessee who makes the payment to cancel the lease. How will the payment be treated? Ordinarily, the lessee is entitled to deduct the cancellation payment in full in the year of payment as a business expense.[169]

But this rule does not hold true if the lessee's purpose in cancelling the existing lease is to obtain a new lease. Under these circumstances, the cancellation payment becomes a part of the lessee's cost for the new lease. Accordingly, the lessee must amortize the cancellation payment over the life of the new lease.[170]

If the lessee terminates the lease by the purchase of the fee or remainder interest from the lessor, the lessee is not permitted to allocate any part of his purchase price to the cost of cancelling the lease. The entire payment must be capitalized as part of the lessee's cost of the property acquired.[171]

How about the lessor? Is the payment received by him from the lessee taxable as ordinary income or as gain from the sale of property? Because the lessor has no property interest that is subject to a sale or exchange, the entire amount received by him is treated as ordinary income taxable in full in the year of receipt.[172]

3. Proceeds on Sale or Assignment of Lease

The same rule applies if a tenant sells his leasehold interest to a third party. The transaction is treated as a sale or exchange of the leasehold. Accordingly, the gain will be taxed as capital gain[173] or as a Section 1231 gain,[174] depending upon the nature of the lessee's holding of the leasehold, except in the case of a lessee in the business of acquiring and selling leasehold interests. If he desires to sell his lease to a sublessee, he

---

[166]Section 1241, I.R.C.; Reg. Sec. 1.1241-1.
[167]Commissioner v. McCue Bros. & Drummond, Inc., 210 F.2d 752 (2d Cir. 1954), cert. den. 348 U.S. 829; Commissioner v. Golonsky, 200 F.2d 72 (3rd Cir. 1952), cert. den. 345 U.S. 939 Rev. Rul. 69-511, 1969-2 C.B. 24.
[168]Sen. Rep. No. 1622, 83rd Cong., 2d Sess., 445 (1954).
[169]Cassatt v. Commissioner, 137 F.2d 745, 749 (3rd Cir. 1943).
[170]Pig & Whistle Co., 9 B.T.A. 668 (1927); The same rule applies to payments by a tenant to obtain a lease modification; the amount of the payment must be capitalized and is amortizable over the lease term. Rev. Rul. 73-176, 1972-1 C.B. 146.
[171]Millinery Center Bldg. Corp. v. Commissioner, 350 U.S. 456 (1956).
[172]Hort v. Commissioner, 313 U.S. 28 (1941).
[173]Walter H. Sutliff, 46 B.T.A. 446 (1942), acq. 1942-1 C.B. 16.
[174]See 512 West Fifty-Sixth Street Corp. v. Commissioner, 151 F.2d 942 (2d Cir. 1945); Metropolitan Building Co., 31 T.C. 95 (1959). In Rev. Rul. 72-85, 1972-1 C.B. 234, the Service takes the position that while Section 1231 treatment is proper, the recapture rules of Sections 1250 and 1245 on the basis of a "look-through" apply to the underlying assets leased by the tenant! The reciprocal of this ruling is that the tenant can take double declining amortization of his leasehold costs.

should first cancel the sublease and then assign all his interest to the sublessee; his payment will be capital gain just as if he had sold to a third party.[175]

4. Sublease vs. Sale of Lease

If the tenant assigns less than the full term of his leasehold interest, the transaction is in the nature of a sublease. Accordingly, any money received on the sublease would be taxed to him as rent received from a sublessee.

A difficult problem therefore arises if a lessee assigns a portion of the leased premises to another for the full term of the primary lease. Is the assignment a partial assignment of the primary lease, or is it a sublease? In other words, is the lessee receiving proceeds from the sale of a part of his lease, or is he receiving rent from a subtenant?

The answer to this question depends upon the nature of the instruments employed to effectuate the transaction. In order, then, for the tenant to protect himself on a partial assignment of a portion of the leasehold, he should contemplate taking the following steps.[176]

(1) Use language of assignment and sale in the instrument of conveyance, not language of sublease;

(2) Secure the lessor's consent to a release of the original tenant's liability for the part of the rent allocable to the portion assigned; and

(3) Have the assignee pay the rent for his portion of the leasehold directly to the original landlord, not to the assigning tenant.

Under these circumstances, the assigning tenant should be entitled to report any lump sum payment paid to him on the partial assignment of his leasehold as gain derived from the sale of a portion of his lease, rather than as rent.[177]

E. LEASE OR PURCHASE?

From the viewpoint of the person acquiring property for use in a trade or business, the fundamental advantage of leasing over purchasing is the fact that the entire amount expended for leasing is currently deductible. On the other hand, if the property were purchased, the owner would not be able to deduct any part of the purchase price; the entire cost would be capitalized, and the owner would be permitted to recover only part of his cost, through depreciation of the cost of the improvements over their life. The remainder would be recovered only on disposition of the property.

1. Leasing vs. Purchasing

The comparison, for tax purposes, is between the advantages of an immediate deduction for the entire rental paid as against a postponed deduction for depreciation

---

[175] Samuel D. Miller, 48 T.C. 649 (1967), acq. 1968-4 I.R.B. 5.
[176] Douglas Properties, Inc., 21 B.T.A. 347 (1930).
[177] Compare Voloudakis v. Commissioner, 274 F.2d 209 (9th Cir. 1960) and Fairmount Park Raceway, Inc. par. 62,014 P-H Memo T.C. (1962) with Metropolitan Building Co. v. Commissioner, 282 F.2d 592 (9th Cir. 1960).

for the amount paid for improvements over their useful life. Initially, the former would seem more attractive than the latter.

Example: Manufacturer wants to acquire the use of a neighboring building as an annex to his plant operation. He discovers that he can either rent it or purchase it outright. If he rents the building, the annual rental charge will be $10,000 a year. If he buys the building, the purchase price will be $100,000, of which only $80,000 is properly allocable to the building itself. He anticipates that the building will have a remaining useful life of 20 years and no salvage value. Which course of action should he take?

If Manufacturer rents the building, he is entitled to a rent deduction of $10,000 in the first year of operation. But if he buys the building, his deduction is but $4,000 in the first year on the straight-line method ($80,000/20), or $6,000 on the 150% declining-balance method (80,000 × 7½%) if he is the first user. In addition to the outlay of the purchase price, Manufacturer will be required to pay real property taxes of $1,000, all of which is deductible.

Suppose, in his first year of operations, Manufacturer has a net income, exclusive of the charges for the annex, of $100,000. A comparison of the federal income taxes produced by the different methods of acquiring the property, assuming that Manufacturer is an unmarried individual, is as follows (the two columns on the right refer to ownership):

	Rental	Straight line depreciation	150% declining depreciation
Net Income	$100,000	$100,000	$100,000
Rents Paid	(10,000)		
Depreciation		(4,000)	(6,000)
Taxes Paid		(1,000)	(1,000)
Taxable Income	$ 90,000	$ 95,000	$ 93,000
Tax	$ 46,190	$ 49,640	$ 48,260

Thus, in the first year of business, the example demonstrates that the acquisition of the use of property by rental is less expensive in taxes than by purchase.

And if we also consider the cash outlay in the first year of business, the advantages of rental become even more apparent. If he rents, Manufacturer is required to make a cash outlay of only $10,000. But if he purchases, he is required to make a cash outlay of $100,000 for the property, plus $1,000 for real property taxes. Thus, Manufacturer also loses the use of operating capital, to the extent that it is tied up in the building.

But obviously our analysis is not complete. What is the long-run picture? Suppose we look at the entire 20-year life of the building. If Manufacturer purchases the building, his total costs are the sum of the following: $100,000 for the purchase price, $20,000 for taxes (20 × $1,000), and a paper charge of some $60,000 for the loss of the use of money tied up in the purchase price of the building.[178] Thus, his total costs over the full period will be approximately $180,000. Offset against the cost will be the value of the land owned at the end of 20 years; if we assume its value to be equal only

---

[178]This paper charge of approximately $5,000 in the first year (5 percent of the $100,000 invested) becomes progressively less as Manufacturer recovers his purchase price out of his depreciation allowance. At the end of the period, only $20,000 would still be tied up in the property. So, on a straight-line method of depreciation, the paper charge per year would reduce itself evenly from $5,000 to $1,000, or an average charge of $3,000 per year. On an accelerated method of depreciation, the charge would be reduced faster, and hence the average charge over the period would be less. If the interest rate is 10 percent, the paper charge would be doubled.

to the $20,000 purchase price, the net cost to Manufacturer over the 20-year period will be approximately $160,000.

If Manufacturer rents the building, the rentals for 20 years will amount to $200,000 (20 × $10,000). However, his tax saving, by renting rather than buying and using straight-line depreciation, will be $87,000 [20 × ($62,970 − $58,620)]. Thus, total cost of renting for 20 years will be $113,000.

The result is a substantial saving ($47,000) over the cost of buying. But this example, thus far, may be deceptive. Much will depend on the level of M's future income, appreciation in property values, changing tax rates or structure, the value of capital funds to M, and so forth. A change in any of these factors, or others, can result in large changes in the above figures.

Furthermore, Manufacturer's effective cost of buying can be drastically reduced by means of mortgaging the property. If for example, he maintains a 6 percent mortgage at 90 percent of the value of the property (assuming that straight-line depreciation correctly reflects the declining value of the property) his cost of buying over the 20-year period is reduced to a mere $49,620, again assuming that all other factors remain constant.[179]

Over the long run, then, purchasing property is probably a cheaper way of obtaining its use than leasing it. Nevertheless, each case must be individually and carefully examined, and proper account taken of all factors in reaching a decision.

2. Lease with Option to Purchase

The initial tax advantages of leasing over purchasing have given rise to a hybrid type of transaction that couples the advantages of both: a lease with an option to purchase. Theoretically, such transactions are treated as conventional leases until the option to purchase is exercised; thereafter the transaction is treated as any other type of purchase. In other words, the lessee deducts the payments made under the lease as rental, and the lessor reports these payments as rental income. But after the option is exercised, the option price paid becomes the lessee-purchaser's cost basis for the property; correspondingly, the lessor-seller treats the receipt of the option price as proceeds realized on the sale of his property.

But suppose the parties rig the transaction. Suppose the lessee agrees to pay a rental higher than the fair rental value of the property in consideration for an option price to buy the property for a price below its market value. In effect, part of the rental payments are being used to pay for the purchase price of the property upon the exercise of the option to buy. If the lessee is then permitted to deduct the entire amount of the

---

[179] M will save 90 percent of the paper charge for capital invested, or $54,000. He will also save $56,380 in taxes by means of his interest deduction, as follows: Yearly interest paid is 6 percent of 90 percent, or 5.4 percent, of the value of the property in any year. Straight-line average value over the 20 years is ½ of the sum of $100,000 plus $20,000 or $60,000. Hence, average interest paid is 5.4% × $60,000 = $3,240. Average taxable income is then $100,000 (net income) less $4,000 (depreciation) less $1,000 (property taxes) less $3,240 (interest paid) equals $91,760. The tax on this amount is $60,151, resulting in an average yearly saving of $2,819 over the tax payable without the mortgage. In 20 years, this comes to $56,380. $56,380 plus $54,000 equals $110,380. $160,000 cost of buying less $110,380 saving by mortgaging equals $49,620. If the interest rate is 12 percent, the results are even more favorable toward leasing.

inflated rental, he will be permitted to deduct a part of his ultimate purchase price for the property and thus escape the necessity of capitalizing it.

On the other hand, if the lessor enters into a lease with an option to purchase that has an excessively high rental coupled with an excessively low option price, he will be converting moneys that would be received by him as proceeds on the sale of his property into rent. Thus, he normally will be converting potential capital gain into ordinary income, except in the case of a lessor who is also a dealer in real property. Therefore, the interest of the lessor in the transaction is normally adverse to that of the lessee. To a certain extent, then, the lessor's adverse interest will act as a brake on the promiscuous use of an inflated rental and a depressed option price in these transactions.

But the Commissioner has not been content to rely solely upon the self-interest of the parties to police transactions of this nature. Section 162(a)(3) authorizes a lessee to deduct rent paid for the use of property only if he has no equity in the property being leased. But if the lessee has title or is acquiring title to or an equity in the property, the rents paid by him are not deductible.[180]

Example: Tenant agrees to rent property from Landlord for $12,000 a year, provided Landlord will grant him an option to purchase the property at the end of five years. The parties agree that the value of the property in five years will be $100,000. But before the formal lease is executed, Tenant asks Landlord to add $50,000 of the purchase price to the rental agreement. Thus, the final lease obligates Tenant to pay $22,000 in annual rental, with the option to buy the leased premises in five years for $50,000.

Under these circumstances, the Tenant's deductions for rent paid would be disallowed. These payments were obviously intended to cover the purchase of an equity in the leased property. Tenant would therefore be required to capitalize these payments as the cost of the property and would be entitled to deduct depreciation during the period that he holds the property.[181] The amount received by Landlord from the contract ($50,000 option price plus $110,000 rental) would be treated as proceeds realized upon the sale of the property,[182] together with interest on the unpaid balance of the price over the period of payment. To the extent of the interest shown to be paid by the "Tenant," "Tenant" would be entitled to a corresponding deduction.[183]

What does the Commissioner look for in order to determine whether or not the lessee is acquiring an equity in the property which he has under lease with an option to purchase? Some of the factors that have been deemed important are the following:

(1) The lease-purchase contract permits the lessee to reduce the option price by part or all of the rental payments previously made under the contract.[184]

(2) The total rental payments under the lease exceed the lessor's allowance for depreciation plus the value of the property (less the option price).[185]

---

[180]Haggard v. Commissioner, 241 F.2d 288 (9th Cir. 1956).
[181]See Judson Mills, 11 T.C. 25, 30, 33 (1948), acq. on another point, 1949-1 C.B. 2.
[182]Oesterreich v. Commissioner, 226 F.2d 798 (9th Cir. 1955).
[183]Judson Mills, 11 T.C. 25, 33 (1948), acq. 1949-1 C.B. 2; Wilshire Holding Corp. v. Commissioner, 262 F.2d 51 (9th Cir. 1958); Estate of Starr v. Commissioner, 274 F.2d 294 (9th Cir. 1959).
[184]See Minneapolis Security Building Corp., 38 B.T.A. 1220, 1224 (1938).
[185]Chicago Stoker Corp., 14 T.C. 441, 445 (1950); Estate of Delano T. Starr, 30 T.C. 856 (1958), aff'd on this issue and rev'd on another, 274 F.2d 294 (9th Cir. 1959).

(3) The option price is nominal in relation to the value of the property.[186]

(4) The intent of the parties and their good faith in setting the rental and option amounts seem doubtful in the light of economic circumstances existing at the time the lease was executed.[187]

Although the lease with option to purchase has considerable value in dealings in real estate, it must be used with care. Both the rental payments and the option price should be set by the parties with reference to going market values and rentals for similar properties. And the parties should be prepared to justify their estimates of rent and purchase price if challenge is later made to the transaction by a revenue agent.

---

[186] Oesterreich v. Commissioner, 226 F.2d 798 (9th Cir. 1955); Cf. Breece Veneer and Panel Co. v. Commissioner, 232 F.2d 319 (7th Cir. 1956).
[187] Benton v. Commissioner, 197 F.2d 745, 752 (5th Cir. 1952).

9

Hybrid Financing Through Sales and Leasebacks and The ABC Transaction

We have compared, in Chapter 8, the advantages of leasing property with the advantages of ownership, in Chapter 3. We have analyzed the problems of borrowing funds to acquire property in Chapter 6. But in all of the preceding discussions, we are reminded constantly of the principle that the cost of acquiring ownership is non-deductible; the owner's purchase price (whether paid immediately, borrowed, or paid in installments) must be capitalized and can be recovered in part only through the mechanics of the depreciation allowance for the improvements. On the other hand, rentals paid for the use of property are currently deductible in full. The advantages of an immediate tax write-off are incalculable: their influence may be seen in the mushrooming growth of the property leasing business under our tax motivated economy and also may be seen in the multiplicity of efforts, discussed at the close of the last chapter, to lease property under terms that give the lessor the equivalent of ownership or the right to acquire ownership.

But now we want to discuss two types of transactions that may perhaps yield the non-tax advantages of ownership with the tax advantages of leasing. Or, to put it another way, we now want to explore case law and legal principles to see whether or not there actually is a way to buy property and take a deduction for part or all of the purchase price. The plan of the chapter is as follows:

A. *Sales and Leasebacks;*
B. *Sales and Leasebacks with Option to Repurchase;*
C. *Sales and Leasebacks Between Related Parties;*
D. *The ABC Transaction;*
E. *The ABC Transaction Applied to Real Estate Acquisitions.*

A. SALES AND LEASEBACKS

Suppose an owner of property desires to raise working capital; he can either use his property as security for a loan of funds, or he may sell the property and convert its value into cash. If he needs the use of the property in his business, he will be reluctant to follow the latter course.

But suppose he sells the property and then leases it back from the purchaser. In this event, he will be ensured of the continued use of the property. In effect, he will be able to convert the value of the property into cash and yet be in a position to enjoy the continued use of it. Such a transaction is commonly termed a sale and leaseback of the property.

1. Advantages of Sale and Leaseback

The sale and leaseback transaction has a number of advantages. From the viewpoint of the buyer, it offers a unique opportunity. He is able to purchase investment property with a built-in tenant, namely the seller. And because the lease is normally executed contemporaneously with the sales agreement, the buyer will know exactly what his return on his investment will be.

The transaction also offers unique advantages to the seller. First, he will regain the use of the money that he had previously tied up in the property. And, second, he is guaranteed the continued use of the property for the term of the lease. Any rent that he pays for the use of the premises will, of course, be deductible. The factor of deductibility of rent becomes increasingly important as the owner exhausts his allowance for depreciation on the property. By transferring the property to a new owner, a new basis for depreciation is created in the hands of the purchaser. Some of the benefit of the new allowance for depreciation may inure to the benefit of the seller in the guise of a lesser rental.

The deductibility of rent becomes even more important in the case of non-depreciable property. For example, land devoted to public parking is almost completely non-depreciable; only the surfacing and fencing would be depreciable. Thus, since the owner obtains no immediate tax benefit from owning the property, he might find it advantageous to sell the parking lot and lease it back. The rentals paid by him would qualify for deduction, and he would free his investment in the property for use as working capital in his business.

2. Gain or Loss on Sale of Property

Assuming that we have a sale and leaseback that will be treated as such for tax purposes, the sale of the property gives rise to taxable gain or deductible loss as the case may be.[1] If the property had been put to a business use, this gain or loss would qualify for the benefits of Section 1231. Accordingly, the owner can convert his property into cash at the price of a capital gains tax (and any depreciation recapture

---

[1] Standard Envelope Mfg. Co., 15 T.C. 41 (1950), acq. 1950-2 C.B. 4.

applicable) or with the additional tax benefit of a fully deductible loss (after first offsetting Section 1231 gains).

Example: A department store owns a parking lot that cost $2,500,000 because the lot is located in the center of a city's downtown area. Because the lot is zoned and used for parking, its current market value is substantially below the cost. Accordingly, the store arranges to sell the lot to a syndicate of investors for a price of $460,000, which produces a loss of $2,040,000. At the same time, the syndicate leases the parking lot back to the store for 20 years at an annual rental of $32,200. Despite the fact that the syndicate of investors did not have sufficient cash to pay the purchase price in full, but obtained terms to spread the $260,000 purchase price over the 20-year term of the lease, the entire $2,040,000 loss was held deductible.[2]

Naturally, if the sale of the property produces a deductible loss the seller will want to realize it as a tax benefit in addition to the conversion of his property into cash. As the foregoing example illustrates, he may want to sell merely to obtain the true tax write-off of his loss whether or not he receives the cash for his property immediately on the sale. But if the sale produces gain, the seller may want to avoid it. If his primary purpose is to raise working capital, he may be unwilling to pay a capital gains tax on the transaction; after all, if he borrowed the money and put the property up as security, no tax liability would be incurred.

3. Tax-Free Exchange and Leaseback

To avoid being taxed on the gain on a sale of property to be leasebacked, all that the owner-lessee need do is to enter into a contract of exchange with his buyer-lessor. If the lease is intended to be in exchange for the property and if it is for a term of 30 years or more, then the transaction will qualify as a tax-free exchange under Section 1031. The regulations expressly state that a leasehold of 30 years or more is property of like kind to property held in fee.[3] Accordingly, gain would be recognized to the seller-owner only to the extent of any cash or other boot received.

Example: A chemical company which has its head office in cramped, obsolete quarters on a valuable downtown site is faced with the problem of rebuilding or of moving to new quarters. Its depreciated cost for the old building and land is $500,000. At current values, the property is worth at least $1,500,000 for the underlying land alone. An insurance company desires to acquire the site for the purposes of erecting a modern high-rise office building to house its staff and to rent to tenants. The chemical company agrees to exchange the property for a 30-year leaseback of five floors of the office building. The parties estimate that the market value of the rental of these quarters would be $150,000 per year. For purposes of the exchange, this rental is reduced by $50,000 a year ($1,500,000 price divided by 30 years equals $50,000 per year), so that the leaseback requires the chemical company to pay only $100,000 annual rent over the 30-year term of the lease. Because the chemical company receives back only a 30-year leasehold and no boot, no part of its $1,000,000 gain on the transfer of its old property is taxed. In addition, the chemical company will be entitled to transfer its basis of $500,000 for the old property to its 30-year leasehold and obtain an amortization deduction for the $500,000 over the life of the leaseback because it is a wasting asset.

---

[2]May Department Stores Co., 16 T.C. 547 (1951), acq. 1951-2 C.B. 3.
[3]Reg. Sec. 1.103(a)-1(c)(2).

Thus, an exchange and leaseback affords the owner not only the benefit of avoiding any tax at the time of conveyance but also the right to deduct his cost or other basis for the property conveyed over the life of the leasehold that he acquires in exchange.

4. Losses on Tax-Free Exchange and Leaseback

But in any case in which the owner holds property that is worth less than its depreciated cost, he would want to avoid an exchange of the property. Only a sale (or exchange for unlike property) would cause his loss to be recognized for income tax purposes. If he exchanges his property for a leasehold of 30 years or more, his loss is not recognized.[4] This rule holds true whether or not cash or other boot is received; boot does not cause a loss to be recognized in an exchange in which like kind property is also received.

Example: An electric company owner improved business property which had a depreciated cost of $530,000. It sold the property for $150,000 in cash and immediately leased the property back for 95 years (with right of prior termination after 25 years) at an annual rental of $367,500 per year for the first 25 years and $11,400 per year thereafter. The electric company deducted a loss of $380,000 in the year of sale, but the loss was disallowed. Even though the form of a sale and leaseback had been followed, the transaction was in substance an exchange and leaseback. Accordingly, the electric company was not entitled to deduct its $380,000 unrecovered basis of its property to the leasehold to be recovered through amortization over the life of the lease.[5] The $150,000 of cash received was treated as boot which did not cause any portion of the loss to be recognized.

Obviously, if a conveyance is made in exchange for a leaseback, it logically follows that the cash or other boot paid for the conveyance is not sufficient to itself to pay for the property. In any case in which no boot is received, the only reason that the owner would convey is in exchange for a leaseback at less than going market rentals (i.e., a so-called "premium" lease). And it follows that in any case in which the cash or other boot is *equal* to the current market value of the property conveyed, the property has been sold solely for cash or other boot, as the case may be; the fact that the new owner may have entered into a leaseback of the property is immaterial to the transaction. The leaseback cannot be in exchange for the property because the full market price of the property has already been paid. The owner-lessee has received, independently of the leaseback, all that he is entitled to be paid for his property. Therefore, in any case in which the sale price of the property is equal to its fair market value, the transaction is a sale, upon which gain or loss is recognized in full, regardless of the term of any leaseback.

Example: A department store owned certain improved parcels of real estate at a depreciated cost of $4,770,000. It sold the properties to an outsider for $2,300,000 and deducted a loss of $2,470,000 on its tax return. The outsider leased the properties back at a rental of $138,000 per year for a period of 30 years. The Commissioner disallowed the deduction of the loss on the theory that the 30-year leaseback was in exchange for the property. In the trial of the case, the parties agreed that the fair rental value was $138,000 per annum. Because the properties were sold for their full fair market value, the court found that the 30-year leaseback was *not in*

---

[4] Section 1031(c), I.R.C.; Reg. Sec. 1.1031(c)-1.
[5] Century Electric Co. v. Commissioner, 192 F.2d 155 (8th Cir. 1951), cert. den. 342 U.S. 954.

SALES AND LEASEBACKS

exchange for the conveyance of the properties. Accordingly, the loss deduction was allowed in full; it was incurred in a sale of the property for cash.[6]

As yet, however, we are not justified in assuming that a loss will be allowed on a sale and leaseback regardless of the length of the leaseback merely because the sale was at full market value. The Commissioner apparently takes the position that the presence of a leaseback of 30 years or more will of itself disallow the loss on the sale whether or not the leaseback was in exchange for the property. Whether he will be upheld on this illogical point remains to be seen. In any event, we can conclude that a sale and leaseback of less than 30 years will permit allowance of the loss; we can also conclude that a sale for full market value and a leaseback of 30 years or more will give the owner-lessee a fighting chance in court to deduct a loss on the sale.[7]

5. Rental Deduction to Seller-Lessee

Whether the transaction is a sale and leaseback or an exchange and leaseback, the transferor-lessee is entitled to deduct his annual rental payments as a trade or business expense under Section 162.[8] If the transaction is a sale and leaseback, the rental will presumably be at current market levels. On the other hand, if the transaction were an exchange and leaseback, the transferor-owner presumably would have received a premium lease in exchange, in whole or in part for his property. Accordingly, he would be entitled to deduct his rentals, which would be less than current market levels, and also to deduct the unrecovered portion of his basis for the property conveyed by amortization over the life of the leaseback.[9]

There are two possible exceptions to these rules, each of which will be discussed below. First, if the sale and leaseback is in substance a pure financing transaction, the so-called rental payments will be reclassified as non-deductible repayments of borrowed funds.[10] Second, if the leaseback is between related parties, the rental deduction may be disallowed because it is not "ordinary and necessary."[11]

6. Rental Income to Buyer-Lessor

The rental paid to the transferee-lessor for the use of the property is ordinary income to him. This result is reached whether he acquired the property by purchase (sale and leaseback), by exchange (exchange and leaseback) or by gift (gift and leaseback). As owner of the property, the transferee-lessor is entitled to deduct depreciation and expenses incurred in connection with the property against the rental income received.

---

[6]Jordan Marsh Company v. Commissioner, 269 F.2d 453 (2d Cir. 1959).
[7]See City Investing Co., 38 T.C. 1 (1961), non-acq. 1963-2 C.B. 6 which upheld a deduction for a loss incurred on a sale at market value despite a leaseback of 21 years plus renewal options totaling 204 years. The seller was engaged in "liquidating" its properties, which the court thought significant in justifying the loss deduction.
[8]Skemp v. Commissioner, 168 F.2d 598 (7th Cir. 1948); Brown v. Commissioner, 180 F.2d 926 (3rd Cir. 1950), cert. den. 340 U.S. 814; Albert T. Felix, 21 T.C. 794 (1954). Non-acq. 1956-2 C.B. 10.
[9]See Century Electric Co. v. Commissioner, 192 F.2d 155 (8th Cir. 1951), cert. den. 342 U.S. 954.
[10]Paul W. Frenzel, Par. 63,276 P-H Memo Dec. (1963).
[11]I.L. Van Zandt, 40 T.C. 824 (1963); aff'd 341 F.2d 440 (5th Cir. 1965), cert. den. 382 U.S. 814; Warren Brekke, 40 T.C. 789 (1963).

Again we find that there are two possible exceptions to these rules. First, if the sale and leaseback is reclassified as a financing transaction, then the amounts received will be recovery of loaned funds plus interest, not rental income. Second, if the transaction is disregarded as a sham between related parties, then the amounts disallowed as rental deductions to the lessee are likely to be treated as non-taxable gifts to the lessor. Each of these possibilities will be discussed below.

B. SALES AND LEASEBACKS WITH OPTION TO REPURCHASE

A *true* sale and leaseback with an option in the seller-lessee to repurchase the property after a stated time is treated like any other sale and leaseback for tax purposes. The sale will create Section 1231 gain or loss to the seller; the purchaser, as owner of the fee, will be entitled to deduct depreciation against rental income received on the leaseback. The seller-lessee will have deductible rent on the leaseback. Thus far, the tax consequences are the same as in the case of any other sale and leaseback. The presence of the option to repurchase does not change these relationships between the parties so long as it remains unexercised.

1. Reacquisition by Seller-Lessee on Exercise of Option

But on the exercise of the option, the seller-lessee then resumes his ownership of the property. To the extent of the option price, he becomes a purchaser of the property; the option price must, therefore, be capitalized as his cost for the property. On the other hand, the purchaser-lessor under the sale and leaseback becomes the seller of the property; the amount he receives is treated as the amount received on the sale of rental property, creating Section 1231 gain or loss as the case may be.

But the very presence of the option to repurchase casts substantial doubt on the true nature of the sale and leaseback. Because the seller has the opportunity of reacquiring the property, has he in reality sold it? Or is the possibility of his exercise of the option to repurchase so great that we can say that he merely pledged the property as security for a loan? If the latter is true, the tax consequences of the transactions will be completely altered from those of a sale and leaseback. The seller will become a mere borrower of money and his repayments will be the payment of interest and repayment of principal, not the payment of rents. His buyer-lessor will not be receiving rental income; instead, his receipts will constitute the recovery of borrowed funds with interest.

2. Loan with Security or Sale and Leaseback with Option to Repurchase?

How can we tell which is which? When is a purported sale and leaseback with option to repurchase treated as a true sale and leaseback and when is it reclassified as a loan of funds secured by a temporary conveyance of the property to the lender ("buyer-lessor")?

The answer depends upon the intent of the parties to the transactions.[12] But by

---

[12]Helvering v. F. & R. Lazarus & Co., 308 U.S. 252 (1939); Judson Mills, 11 T.C. 25 (1948), acq. 1949-1 C.B. 2.

intent we do not mean what the parties thought (so-called "subjective intent"); rather we mean what did the parties do (so-called "objective intent"). In other words, what intent would a reasonable, independent, third party ascribe to the parties if he knew what their conduct had been but did not know why they had done it.

For this reason, we must judge the sale and leaseback with option to repurchase transaction on the basis of the conduct of the parties and the terms of their agreement and not upon the basis of what they called it and what they tell us it meant.

What factors tell us that a sale and leaseback with option to repurchase is a true sale and leaseback? *First* of all, the sale price must be equal to the fair market value of the property; if it is either greater or less, suspicion may be aroused. *Second*, the leaseback must be for a rental at current market levels; a greater or less than market rental tends to indicate that the payment is not really rent for the use of the property. *Third*, is the sale and leaseback with an investor in real estate or is it with a commonly recognized financial institution which normally only lends money? *Fourth*, upon whom is risk of loss of the property placed? If the substance of the transaction is such that the buyer-lessor is never really subject to possibility of serious loss during the term of his so-called "ownership" because of the commitments of his seller-lessee-repurchaser, then it is difficult to treat him as the owner of the property for tax purposes. And, *finally*, how much does the seller-lessee have to pay to get the property back? If he can get it back for a song, it would follow that he had never parted with the property but was merely entitled to a reconveyance on completion of his loan repayment. On the other hand, if the option to repurchase is for a substantial price in line with projected market values then there exists a substantial possibility the seller-lessee will not exercise his option and the buyer-lessor will retain the property even after the term of the leaseback has expired.

Example: A contractor owns well-located, unimproved warehouse acreage that an industrial company desires to lease after construction of a modern warehouse built to its specifications. The projected cost of the warehouse structure is $1,200,000. The contractor finds himself unable to borrow the entire $1,200,000 of construction cost. After negotiation with a trust company, the contractor sells the land with a warehouse to be constructed to a trust company for $1,200,000. The trust company immediately leases the property back for a term of 10 years at a rental measured by the amount necessary to amortize the sum of $1,200,000 over 10 years plus 5 percent of the unamortized balance outstanding payable quarterly. At the end of the 10-year term, the contractor has the option to purchase the completed warehouse and underlying land for $120,000, or 10 percent of its original cost. Under these circumstances the sale and leaseback is nothing but a sham; in substance it is only a borrowing of $1,200,000 with interest at 5 percent plus a financing charge of $120,000. The interest and financing charge are deductible to the contractor. The balance of the "rental" payments are non-deductible payments of principal.[13]

Obviously, the reclassification of a transaction from a sale and leaseback to a loan and repayment may have disastrous tax consequences to the seller-lessee, such as the following: (1) Any loss deducted on the "sale" of the property would be disallowed; correspondingly, any gain would be unrecognized; (2) his "rental" payments would be disallowed as deductions, except to the extent that they constitute interest; the balance is non-deductible repayment of principal; (3) offsetting the foregoing disadvantages is

---

[13]Paul W. Frenzel, Par. 63,276 P-H Memo Dec. (1963).

the fact that the seller-lessee will be entitled to continue to take depreciation on the property.

On the other hand, the purchaser-lessor will not be required to report the monthly payments as rental income; these payments will constitute repayment of loaned funds plus interest income. The purchaser-lessor will not be allowed any depreciation because he did not become the owner of the property for tax purposes. Finally, he will have no gain or loss when he reconveys the property to the seller-lessee on the exercise of the option to repurchase because he was never the owner of it. But he will have to account for the option price as receipt of loaned funds or as interest income. It has been the practice of this author to eliminate the option to repurchase. If the seller-lessee wants the property back after the use of the money, the seller-lessee simply does two things: (1) Inflates the purchase price,[14] and (2) Makes the entire purchase debt due at eight or less years.[15]

C. SALES AND LEASEBACKS BETWEEN RELATED PARTIES

A sale and leaseback between related parties is subject to a number of additional pitfalls that do not lie in the path of unrelated parties who enter into a similar transaction. Gains and losses on the sale, for example, may be treated differently from the case of a sale between unrelated parties. The rental deduction of the seller-lessee may be disallowed to the extent that the Commissioner determines that it is a payment for some purpose other than the use of the leaseback property. And, finally, the rental income of the purchaser-lessor may be allocated back to the seller-lessee of the property on the theory that he remained the true owner of the property for tax purposes. Each of these possibilities will be discussed in the succeeding sections.

1. Gain or Loss on Sales Between Related Parties

Gain on a sale between related parties is ordinarily recognized and taxed to the seller; the fact that the parties are related does not shelter the seller from paying a tax on his gain.[16] However, the fact that the parties are related may result in denying the benefits of Section 1231 to the seller. Thus, any gain realized on a sale of depreciable property between husband and wife or between a corporation and a stockholder who owns more than 80 percent of its stock is ordinary income, regardless of the length of the holding period or the trade or business classification in the seller's hands.[17] Similarly, a sale between a partner and a partnership which is owned by him to the extent of more than 80 percent of its capital or profits will give rise to ordinary income in any case in which the property will not be held by the partnership as a capital asset.[18] Thus,

---

[14] Which is a matter of indifference because the purchase price is based on the leaseback.

[15] Commonly known as the "Godfather" clause, attributed to the author.

[16] Except perhaps in a case of a sale between stockholders and their corporation which is reclassified as a tax-free exchange of property for stock or securities under Section 351, I.R.C.

[17] Section 1239, I.R.C. Also between two 80 percent owner corporations.

[18] Section 707(b)(2), I.R.C. This provision also applies to sales between two partnerships each more than 80 percent owned by the same persons.

any sale of property to a partnership that is to be rented back is received by the partnership as a trade or business, not a capital asset; accordingly, if the ownership tests of the Code are met, the gain will be ordinary income. Additionally, if the property is depreciable, the depreciation recapture rules will convert part of the gain realized into ordinary income to the extent of their application.[19]

Losses on sales between related parties are not infrequently denied in full because of the relationship between the buyer and seller. Any loss incurred on a sale between members of a family (brothers and sisters, spouse, ancestors and lineal descendants), between a corporation and a more than 50 percent stockholder (or between two corporations so owned), and between certain trust grantors, fiduciaries and beneficiaries is disallowed.[20] Similarily, a loss on a sale between a partnership and a partner who owns (directly or indirectly) more than 50 percent of the capital or profits of the partnership is disallowed.[21]

2. Gifts and Leasebacks

Because of the problems encountered in taxing the gain or deducting a loss on a sale between related parties, a projected sale and leaseback between members of a family frequently takes the form of a gift and leaseback. The gift eliminates the need of accounting for any gain or loss on the transaction and, accordingly, the adverse rules of the preceding section are of no consequence to the donor-lessee.

Because the donee-lessor receives the property by way of gift, he is not entitled to a new basis for it. His basis for the property is the basis that it had in the hands of his donor, increased by any federal gift tax paid (if the value of the property exceeds its basis to the donor by such amount).[22] Because basis is not adjusted by a gift (except for the possible gift tax increment) the depreciation recapture rules are not applicable.[23]

By its very nature, a gift and leaseback gives rise to some problems of its own. Being among members of a family, it is commonly used as a device to split income in order to save taxes. The property, or the money used to purchase the property, is transferred from the donor to other non-income members of his family who immediately lease it back to the donor in exchange for a lease that hopefully will permit the donor to pay them rental income that he can deduct from his business income. A transaction of this nature has two basic weakness: first, has the donor really transferred the property or has he retained so many of the rights of ownership over it that in substance he is still the owner? And, second, have the donees actually acquired the property or have their rights been so circumscribed because of their youth, age, or legal incapacity that they are not the owners of the property? If either, or both, of the foregoing questions are answered in the negative, the gift and leaseback will be fruit-

---

[19] Sections 1245, 1250, I.R.C. See, also, Rev. Rul. 62-92 1962-C.B. 29, with respect to real property.

[20] Section 267(a)(1), I.R.C. Reference should be made to the language of the section for a definitive description of the relationships covered.

[21] Section 707(b)(1). This provision also applies to sales between two partnerships.

[22] Section 1015, I.R.C. If the value of the property is less than its basis to the donor at the time of the gift, its value becomes the basis of the property to the donee if he thereafter sells it for a loss. For all other purposes, the basis to him is its basis to the donor.

[23] Sections 1245(b)(1) and 1250(d)(1) expressly except transfers by gift.

less; the donor-lessee will not be entitled to deduct his rental income and accordingly his attempt to split his income with members of his family will come to naught.[24]

3. Family Leasebacks as Income Splitting Devices

In any case in which the donor does not part with dominion and control over the income producing property, the income from the property will continue to be taxed to him. This principle has been applied by the Commissioner and the courts to any number of situations: for example, a gift of an interest coupon clipped from a bearer investment bond is not effective to shield the bond owner from being taxed on the interest when the coupon matures in the hands of the donee.[25] Similarly, an anticipatory gift of one year's income by the holder of a life estate does not shield the donor from being taxed on the year's income when received by the donee.[26] Another example is furnished by the creation of a partnership between the owner of a business and his children: the business income is taxable to the owner and not to the partnership so long as the owner retains control over the business assets and the partnership interests of his children.[27] And we find in the field of trusts of income-producing property that the income from the property is taxed to the grantor, not to the trustee (or beneficiaries), in any case in which the grantor has retained effective dominion and control over the trust property through the exercise of power to control beneficial enjoyment, to administer the trust property in his favor, or to reacquire the trust property after a limited trust term.[28]

In any case, then, in which the donor-lessor fails to part with dominion and control over the leaseback property, the income from the property is taxed to him just as if legal title had never been transferred. The form of the gift and leaseback is a nullity for tax purposes.[29] What must be done, then, is to create a transfer of property that effectively deprives the donor of dominion and control over the property. If, for example, the gift is to be made to a family trust, the trust must be one that will be recognized for tax purposes as an entity separate from and independent of its grantor. The mechanics of establishing such a trust are beyond the scope of this book, but reference is made to the requirements of Section 671-677 of the Internal Revenue Code and the regulations thereunder. By the same token, if the gift is to be made to a family partnership, the partnership must be one that will be recognized for tax purposes as an entity separate from and independent of the donor. Reference is made to the requirements of Section 704(e) of the Internal Revenue Code and the regulations thereunder.

It has also been held that a transfer to a guardian (even if the guardian is the

---

[24]White v. Fitzpatrick, 193 F.2d 398 (2d Cir. 1951), cert. den. 343 U.S. 928; I.L. Van Zandt, 40 T.C. 824 aff'd. 341 F.2d (5th Cir. 1965), cert. den. 382 U.S. 814 (1963); Rev. Rul. 54-9, 1954-1 C.B. 20.
[25]Helvering v. Horst, 311 U.S. 112 (1940).
[26]Harrison v. Schaffner, 312 U.S. 579 (1941).
[27]Commissioner v. Tower 327 U.S. 280 (1946); See the statutory tests of family partnerships set out in Section 704(e), I.R.C.
[28]Helvering v. Clifford, 309 U.S. 331 (1940); See the statutory tests of grantor trusts set out in Sections 671-677, I.R.C.
[29]Finley v. Commissioner, 255 F.2d 128 (10th Cir. 1958); Kirschenmann v. Westover, 225 F.2d 69 (9th Cir. 1955), cert. den. 350 U.S. 834.

transferor himself) is also sufficient. The fact that the guardian is subject to State Court reporting and accounting is sufficient to ensure the independence of the guardian.[30]

4. Requirements of a Valid Family Leaseback

But even where the donor transfers the property from his dominion and control, he may, through the mechanism of a leaseback, reacquire such substantial rights that his deduction for rentals will be disallowed. While the income of the family trust or family partnership will not be taxed to him, he may still find that the rentals paid to the lessor are disallowed as a deduction against his business income. The effect of the disallowance of the rental deduction is tantamount to reallocating the rental income of the lessor from the leaseback property back to the donor-lessee any other income of the donee-lessee from property other than the leaseback property. To this extent, the disallowance of rental is a slightly lesser catastrophe than a reallocation of income.

Example: A physician established two trusts, one each, for his minor son and minor daughter. Each trust was for more than 10 years and was irrevocable. At the end of the term, the corpus was to revert to the physician-grantor. While the physician-grantor named himself as trustee, he retained no powers or rights to deal with the trust corpus that would make him taxable on the income from the trusts under Sections 672-677 of the Internal Revenue Code or under *Helvering v. Clifford*.[31] The grantor-donor then transferred his medical building and equipment to the two trusts and paid a reasonable rental to the trusts for the use of the building and equipment in his practice. The Tax Court held that even though the donor-grantor was not taxable on the income of the trusts, he still could not deduct the rental paid to the trusts because, while ordinary, these expenses were not necessary to his practice. It was not necessary that he transfer his medical assets to a trust for his children and lease them back.[32]

But where the trustee is independent of the donor-lessee, the rentals on a gift and leaseback have been held deductible.[33] Why the difference? The courts, in upholding the rental deductions, have emphasized that independent trustees would insist on the payment of reasonable rent for the use of the leaseback property and would also insist upon having the power to dispose of the leaseback property and invest the proceeds in some other property more easily managed in the event the donor-lessee should prove difficult to deal with. Both of these powers would be exercised in a fiduciary capacity in accordance with professional standards if the management of the leaseback property were placed in the hands of an independent trustee. The same observance of fiduciary standards on behalf of the beneficiaries and, if necessary, against the interests of the donor-lessee could hardly be assumed to be present if the donor-lessee named himself as trustee for minor family beneficiaries.

The same question can be raised with respect to other adult members of the family of the donor-lessee if named as holder of legal title on behalf of the donee-lessors. For example, one court has pointed out that a gift and leaseback between an inventor and

---

[30]Brooke v. United States, 468 F.2d 1155 (9th Cir., 1972).
[31]Helvering v. Clifford, 309 U.S. 331 (1940).
[32]I.L. Van Zandt, 40 T.C. 824 (1963), aff'd 341 F.2d 440 (5th Cir. 1965), cert. den. 382 U.S. 814. Robert F. Zumstein, T.C. Memo 1973-45 (1973). Audano v. United States, 428 F.2d 251 (5th Cir. 1970).
[33]Skemp v. Commissioner, 168 F.2d 598 (7th Cir. 1948); Brown v. Commissioner, 180 F.2d 926 (3rd Cir. 1950); Albert T. Felix, 21 T.C. 803 (1954), non-acq. 1956-2 C,B. 10.

his wife was defective because the inventor's wife "was neither equipped nor evidenced any desire to exercise or transfer any rights to the use of either of the properties."[34] Thus, even though the donor's wife was a separate taxpaying entity whose income would not be attributed to the donor, the donor-lessee's rental deductions were disallowed because his donor-lessor was unable to take title to the leaseback property save in name only.

But with an independent trustee competent to act and subject to professional fiduciary standards of administration, a gift and leaseback has been recognized by the courts,[35] including, the Tax Court,[36] although the Commissioner still appears reluctant to agree.[37] But to ensure the validity of a gift and leaseback among family members, the parties must remember that not only should the trustee selected for the family members be independent but he should also be clothed with the powers of an independent trustee including (1) the power to sell or dispose of the leaseback property, at the trustee's discretion and (2) the power to compel the donor-lessee to pay the rent on time in full. The terms of leaseback must be for a reasonable term at a reasonable rental based on current market levels. The leaseback should be for a term that is less than the balance of the useful life of the property to the donor-lessee. If all these conditions are met, the gift and leaseback has an excellent chance of being upheld.

Example: A physician deeded his medical office building to a bank as trustee of an irrevocable trust established for his minor children as beneficiaries. The trust was to last for a term of 20 years or until the prior death of both the physician and his wife. At the end of the trust term, the corpus went to the beneficiaries; it did not revert to the physician. The trustee, on receipt of the medical building, made a determination of its rental value and then leased it back to the physician at a reasonable rental for a term of 10 years. The rentals paid by the physician to the trustee on behalf of his minor children were held deductible.[38]

5. Rental Deduction on Leaseback Between Related Parties

Assuming that we have by-passed the hurdles of the preceding sections so that the sale (or gift) and leaseback is upheld as a valid set of transactions for tax purposes, the rental paid by the seller (or donor)-lessee will normally be deductible if the leaseback property is used in his trade or business.[39] But the fact that the parties are related may still cause adverse tax consequences.

For example, if the rental paid on an otherwise valid leaseback is excessive, the excessive portion of the rental payment may represent something other than deductible rent. Where the parties are related by blood or marriage, the excess portion of the rental

---

[34]White v. Fitzpatrick, 193 F.2d 389 (2d Cir. 1951), cert. den. 343 U.S. 928; Irvine K. Furman, 45 T.C. 360 (1966), aff'd 381 F.2d 22 (5th Cir. 1967).

[35]Skemp v. Commissioner, 168 F.2d 598 (7th Cir. 1948); Brown v. Commissioner, 180 F.2d 926 (3rd Cir. 1950), cert. den. 340 U.S. 814.

[36]Albert T. Felix, 21 T.C. 803 (1954), non-acq. 1956-2 C.B. 10; John T. Potter, 27 T.C. 200 (1956), acq. 1957-2 C.B. 6.

[37]Rev. Rul. 54-9, 1954-1 C.B. 20; Commissioner's non-acquiescence to the result in Albert T. Felix, 21 T.C. 803 (1954) published at 1956-2 C.B. 10.

[38]Skemp v. Commissioner, 168 F.2d 598 (7th Cir. 1940); Alden B. Oakes, 44 T.C. 524 (1965), non-acq. 1967-1 C.B. 3.

[39]Stearns Magnetic Mfg. Co. v. Commissioner, 208 F.2d 849 (7th Cir. 1954); Consolidated Apparel Co. v. Commissioner, 207 F.2d 580 (7th Cir. 1953).

payment would be treated as a non-deductible gift from the lessor to his family lessees.[40] On the other hand, if the parties are a corporate lessee and stockholder-lessors, the excessive rental payment will be treated as a non-deductible dividend to the corporation.[41]

If the leaseback is coupled with an option to reacquire the property, an excessive rental and an unreasonably low option price may convert the rental payment into nondeductible installment payments to reacquire property[42] (or, alternatively, into nondeductible repayments of borrowed funds).[43] This latter possibility appears most frequently in cases involving sales and leasebacks between business enterprises and tax-exempt organizations. If, for example, the selling entity expects to reacquire the business assets, directly or indirectly, then the excess rental paid to the tax exempt organization would be non-deductible payments of the final repurchase price.[44]

Finally, if both the seller-lessee and the purchaser-lessor are related businesses, an excessive rental paid by one to the other is subject to the power of the Commissioner to reallocate items of gross income, deductions or credits under Section 482 of the Internal Revenue Code. The exercise by the Commissioner of his power to reallocate the excessive rental would shift the tax burden on the amount of the excess from the lessor-recipient to the lessee-payor. The income tax liability of both entities would be recomputed just as if the excessive rental had never been paid. The Commissioner's power to reallocate income or deductions is exercisable in any case in which he finds such reallocation "necessary in order to prevent evasion of taxes or clearly to reflect the income of any . . . organizations, trades or businesses . . . owned or controlled directly or indirectly by the same interests . . . ."[45]

D. THE ABC TRANSACTION

In the oil and gas area of law, there are three parties to many sales of oil and gas operating interests.

The typical ABC transaction in the oil and gas business involves three parties: A, who is the owner of the lessee's working interest in an oil and gas property and who desires to sell all of his interest to a new operator. The new operator who desires to purchase A's property is B. But because B does not have sufficient funds of his own to meet the entire purchase price, B calls upon C, a bank or other lending institution, for financial help. The financial help offered by C is not, however, a direct loan of money to B. Instead, C purchases for A an interest in the property that is self-liquidating. That is to say, C's interest is limited to an interest in income for a limited amount; on receipt by C of the agreed amount, C's interest disappears and B becomes sole owner of the working interest as successor to A.

---

[40] See Coe Laboratories, Inc., 34 T.C. 549 (1960), acq. on another ground, 1961-2 C.B. 4.
[41] Potter Electric Signal and Manufacturing Co. v. Commissioner, 286 F.2d 200 (8th Cir. 1961); J.J. Kirk, Inc., 34 T.C. 130 (1960), aff'd 289 F.2d 935 (6th Cir. 1961).
[42] See Starr v. Commissioner, 274 F.2d 294 (9th Cir. 1959).
[43] Paul W. Frenzel, T.C. Memo Dec. 26, 347 (M) (1963).
[44] But only where the sale price is excessive, indicating an attempt to convert future profits into capital gain. Commissioner v. Clay Brown, 380 U.S. 563 (1965); Rev. Rul. 66-153, 1966-1 C.B. 187.
[45] Section 482, I.R.C.

The question is whether or not B's income that is paid to C can be made reportable as C's taxable income. If it is B's taxable income, B has non-deductible payments of principal; if it is C's taxable income, B can exclude from his income the amounts paid to C. But this is not the result.

Under the Revenue Act of 1969, a retained oil payment at the time of the sale of a working interest is treated as a purchase money loan to the buyer of the working interest.[46] The results are two: first, the seller receives as the amount realized on the sale both the price actually paid for the working interest and the principal amount of the retained oil payment. Second, the oil income paid to the holder of the oil payment is included in the working interest owner's income; the payment of that income to the holder of the retained oil payment is a non-deductible repayment of a purchase money mortgage lien on the property. thus, the tax advantages of the ABC transaction to the buyer of the working interest are eliminated.

By these amendments Congress eliminated the former tax advantages of ABC financing over simple borrowing in oil and gas ventures.[47]

E. THE ABC TRANSACTION APPLIED TO REAL ESTATE ACQUISITIONS

An example of the use of ABC financing of a real estate acquisition is as follows:

Example: Buyer to purchase from A certain farmlands for $925,000, subject to a $250,000 "production payment" reserved by A to be paid out of 10 percent of the gross farm income. B also agreed that the "production payment" would bear interest 7 percent.

A then sold the reserved "production payment" to C, which, unfortunately, was not an unrelated entity. C was a series of ten and one-half year trusts set up for the benefit of B's children. B advanced $100,000 to the trusts and a bank loaned the other $150,000 to pay A the full $250,000.

In 1963, B paid $37,400 to the trusts (C). The Tax Court held that the $37,400 was taxable to B, not to C.[48]

Under existing authorities, it is clear that:

(1) A taxpayer who sells his landlord's interest in a leasehold interest only accelerates the rental income.[49]

(2) But if the taxpayer sells the entire fee, he realized Section 1231 gain.

(3) If the taxpayer retains the lease rentals and sells the reversion in the fee, he realizes Section 1231 gain on the reversion.

(4) What happens when the taxpayer sells the reserved rentals?[50] Since he sells all that he has, the taxpayer has capital gain.[51]

---

[46] I.R.C. §636.

[47] The statute is expressly limited to production or retained payments carved out of mineral property. Section 636(a), (b), I.R.C. Obviously, it follows as a matter of logic that real property production payments are to be treated differently. If a statute were necessary in the mineral field, the presumption is that the statute was necessary and applied only to the questions raised in mineral law.

[48] Olin Bryant, 46 T.C. 848, (1966), aff'd 399 F.2d 800 (5th Cir. 1968), Contra, Boys, Inc. of America v. Campbell, 18 AFTR 2d 5200.

[49] Hort v. Commissioner, 313 U.S. 28 (1941).

[50] Blair v. Commissioner holds that the taxpayer has sold his entire interest in the property and therefore is entitled to capital gain on any profit. Blair v. Commissioner, 300 U.S. 5 (1937).

[51] Lake, P.G. Inc. 356 U.S. 160 (1958).

THE ABC TRANSACTION

The conclusion is inescapable. If all that the taxpayer buys is a reversionary interest in property subject to a lease, he is not taxable on current income.[52] Obviously, the taxpayer does not get the benefits of depreciation or interest deductions.[53] For this reason, the ABC transaction, as a method of financing is viable only in two contexts: (1) purchase of undeveloped land and (2) purchase of land underneath a high-rise office or apartment building.[54]

---

[52] The lease has been pre-assigned *by the seller* to a bank or other lending institution prior to purchase.
[53] The buyer is only purchasing the reversion after the expiration of the existing leaseholds.
[54] Obviously, the sale of rentals by the seller will deny the buyer any deduction for depreciation. So the question is one of comparing the relative cost of excluding income from that of including income and taking deductions.

10

Partnerships, Subdivisions, Syndicates, and Real Estate Investment Trusts

In this chapter we shall survey the basic principles applicable to the tax problems of partnerships, subdivisions, syndicates, and the statutory real estate investment trusts. The chapter will therefore be divided into five parts, as follows:

A. *Real Estate Held by Partnerships*;
B. *Special Problems Relating to Limited Partnerships*;
C. *Subdivisions*;
D. *Real Estate Syndicates*;
E. *Real Estate Investment Trusts*.

A. REAL ESTATE HELD BY PARTNERSHIPS[1]

Partnerships may own real estate as a partnership asset just as if they were any other owners. Accordingly, investors in real estate may contemplate the formation of a partnership for the purpose of holding title to real estate. Or a partnership may be recognized for the purpose of carrying on a trade or business. Whatever the purpose, it would be contemplated that the partnership, not the individual partners, will own the property.

At first glance, the use of a partnership may seem an easy and logical choice for the holding of title to real estate. However, while a partnership itself is not a taxable entity,[2] it is required to file a tax return in the nature of an information return. In this

---

[1] For an excellent and comprehensive analysis of the tax aspects of partnerships, see Willis, Arthur B., *Handbook of Partnership Taxation* (Prentice-Hall, Inc., 1971).
[2] Section 701, I.R.C.

return, the partnership is required to report its gross income, its deductible business expenses, its net income, and each partner's share of that net income. But in computing its net income, it is not permitted to take advantage of all of the deductions, exclusions, and credits allowable to an individual. Many items of deduction, exclusion, or credit which have been realized by the partnership must be stated separately on the partnership return, and each partner's share must be separately determined. Among the items required to be stated separately from partnership net income are the following:[3]

(1) Net short-term gain or loss of the partnership;
(2) Net long-term gain or loss of the partnership;
(3) Net Section 1231 gain or loss of the partnership;
(4) Charitable contribution of the partnership;
(5) Dividends received by the partnership;
(6) Foreign income taxes paid by the partnership;
(7) Partially tax-exempt interest received by the partnership:
(8) Recoveries of bad debts, prior taxes, and delinquency amounts received by the partnership; wagering gains and losses of the partnership; soil and water conservation expenditures of the partnership; non-business expenses; and
(9) Any other item of income, deduction, credit, or exclusion that is subject to a special agreement of allocation among the partners or is otherwise subject to special limitation or treatment in the individual tax return of one or more of the partners.

Obviously, these rules requiring the separate itemization of certain items of income, deduction, credit, etc., are designed to prevent the partners from using the partnership form of organization to achieve a tax benefit or to avoid a tax limitation that they would not be entitled to as individuals. In the case of real estate, for example, the partners cannot use the partnership to avoid the limitations upon the deduction of capital losses. Nor can they use it to offset partnership net income by partnership Section 1231 losses. These special items of loss are taken into account only on the partner's individual income tax returns.

Example: Partners A, B, and C organize the ABC partnership. In the current taxable year, the ABC partnership realizes gross income of $70,000, ordinary business deductions of $40,000, net long-term capital losses of $18,000 and Section 1231 losses of $6,000. If A, B, and C are equal one-third partners, their respective shares of these items would be as follows:[4]

Partner	Share	Net Income	Capital Loss	Sec. 1231 Loss
A	1/3	$10,000	$ 6,000	$2,000
B	1/3	10,000	6,000	2,000
C	1/3	10,000	6,000	2,000
		$30,000	$18,000	$6,000

It would not be proper for the partnership, for example, to offset its business net income of $30,000 by either the $6,000 Section 1231 loss or the $18,000 capital loss. Both of these items must be stated separately and reported in the return of each partner as items of Section 1231 loss and of capital loss, respectively.

---

[3] Reg. Sec. 1.702-1(a).
[4] Reg. Sec. 1.704-1(b).

1. Problems of Organizing a Partnership

In the normal course of events, a partnership is organized for business by the transfer of the required business assets to it from the partners. Such a transfer of assets from the partners to the partnership is tax-free; neither gain nor loss will be recognized for tax purposes on the transfer.[5]

Accordingly, the partnership's basis for the contributed property is the same as its basis to the individual partners before the contribution.[6] And each partner is entitled to transfer his basis for his interest in the contributed property to his basis for his partnership interest.[7]

If the contributed property is subject to a liability, the rules may be varied somewhat. If the partnership accepts property subject to a liability, the amount of the liability so assumed is treated as the equivalent of a cash distribution in like amount to the contributing partner or partners. However, each partner is entitled to include his share of partnership liabilities as a part of his basis for his partnership interest. Hence, if the contributing partner's share of the partnership's liabilities is the same as his former share of the liability against the property, the implied distribution of money and the implied increase in basis will cancel each other out.

But suppose the interest of the partner in the contributed property and in the partnership are different. In this event, the implied distribution of money will be either greater or less than the increase in basis. Accordingly, the contributing partner's basis for his partnership will not be identical to his basis for his interest in the property.[8]

Example: A and B organize the AB partnership, each being an equal partner. A contributes apartment worth $40,000, subject to a $20,000 mortgage. B contributes $20,000 cash. If we assume that A's basis for the apartment, prior to contribution, is only $30,000, his basis for his partnership interest is computed as follows:

Basis of property contributed by A		$30,000
Less indebtedness assumed by partnership (implied distribution)	($20,000)	
Plus A's one-half share of partnership liabilities	$10,000	(10,000)
A's basis for partnership interest		$20,000
B's basis for his partnership interest is as follows:		
Basis of money contributed by B		$20,000
Plus B's one-half share of partnership liabilities		10,000
		$30,000

The total of A's plus B's basis for their partnership interests is $50,000, which is equal to their total basis for their properties prior to contribution. The only difference is that $10,000 of A's basis in the property has been transferred to B as a result of B's one-half participation as a partner in the liability against the property.

---

[5] Section 721, I.R.C. The only exception arises in the case of property contributed subject to a liability in excess of its basis to the transferors. Section 752(b), I.R.C.
[6] Section 723, I.R.C. Rev. Rul. 73-391, I.R.B. 1973-39, 7 states that under California law, earned income of each spouse is her or his separate property.
[7] Section 722, I.R.C.
[8] Reg. Sec. 1.722-1.

2. Problems of Depreciation

In the absence of any provision to the contrary in the partnership agreement, the partnership is required to deduct its allowance for depreciation upon partnership property at the partnership's level. In effect, this means that the partners will share the deduction for partnership depreciation among themselves in accordance with their respective interests in partnership profits and losses.[9]

If the partnership purchased the property for cash, this rule is fair; but if the property was contributed to the partnership by the partners, the rule may be eminently unfair.

Example: A and B form the AB partnership. A contributes a building with an agreed value of $25,000 which has an adjusted basis of only $10,000. B contributes $25,000 in cash. A and B agree to share profits and losses equally. If we assume that the first year's allowance for depreciation on the building is $1,000, each partner will have the benefit of $500 of depreciation, because the depreciation is deducted at the partnership level before net profits are ascertained.

Is this fair to B? B contributed $25,000 cash. In return he got a one-half interest in partnership assets, that is, one-half of his $25,000, or $12,500, plus one-half of A's building. This half interest in A's building cost him $12,500. Although he paid $12,500 for his interest in the building, he is entitled, under the above allocation, only to $500 depreciation. On the other hand, A also receives $500 depreciation on his half of the building, which has a remaining basis to him of only $5,000. Thus, while A enjoys a 10 percent depreciation rate, B is far below.

What can be done to eliminate this inequity between the partners? One method would be for A to contribute not the building but an equivalent amount of cash, that is, $25,000. The AB partnership would then purchase the building from A for $25,000. In this event, the partnership's basis for the property would be its cost, or $25,000. Assuming a 10 percent depreciation rate, the partnership would be entitled to deduct $2,500 depreciation per year, split between A and B at $1,250 apiece.

Although this method would achieve substantial equity between A and B, it is at the cost of a tax on the $15,000 gain to A at the time he sells the property to the partnership. And A may not be willing to pay this tax if he can avoid it.

In this event, the Code permits the partners to agree to a special rule of allocation of depreciation on contributed property.[10] The partners may agree to allocate depreciation on contributed property in such manner as to take into account the difference between the adjusted basis of the contributed property and its fair market value at the time of contribution.[11]

Example: Let us assume the facts of the foregoing example. In effect B has paid $12,500 for a half interest in A's building, which has a basis to the partnership of only $10,000. Would it not be proper, therefore, to allocate the first $7,500 of depreciation taken on the building to B and then to split the remainder of the depreciation between them equally? This result may be reached by the placing in the partnership agreement of a special provision for this purpose.

---

[9] Section 704(c)(1), I.R.C.
[10] Section 704(c)(2), I.R.C.
[11] Reg. Sec. 1.704-1(c)(2).

3. Problems of Gain

A similar problem arises in the case of a sale by the partnership of contributed property. The gain or loss on the sale will be allocated among the partners, in the absence of a special agreement, in accordance with their interest in profits and losses.[12] Obviously, such a rule can work serious inequities among the partners.

Example: Assume again the facts of the preceding example. A contributed a building worth $25,000 but having an adjusted basis of only $10,000. B contributed $25,000 in cash. The AB partnership sells the building for $25,000, on which it realizes a taxable gain of $15,000. Because A and B have agreed to be equal partners, the gain of $15,000 is taxed $7,500 to A and $7,500 to B.

But is this fair to B? B contributed $25,000 cash. In return he received a one-half interest in partnership assets, including one-half of A's building, for which he contributed $1,500 in cash. Thus, B, in effect, bought half interest in A's property for $12,500. Thus, when the partnership sells the property, it sells B's one-half interest for $12,500; accordingly, B realizes no actual increase in wealth as a result of the sale. The partnership still has only $50,000, of which $25,000 is his. Why, then, should B be compelled to pay a tax on half of the gain realized on the sale?

The actual economics of this example indicates that it is A's gain which is being realized when the partnership sells the property for its agreed value on contribution by A. Thus, to the extent of the gain that had occurred *prior to contribution* of the property to the partnership, A should be expected to pay the tax. In other words, on the sale in this example, A should be required to report the entire $15,000 gain as his own sale by the partnership. B's liability for any tax on the gain should not commence until gain is realized which is attributable to the partnership's period of holding of the property.

Example: Assume the facts of the preceding example, except the partnership agreement provides (1) that the first $15,000 of gain is allocable to A, (2) that if gain is realized on the sale of the apartment, A can withdraw his share only to the extent it exceeds $15,000, and (3) any gain in excess of $15,000 is allocable equally between A and B. Suppose the apartment is sold for $30,000. The total gain realized is $20,000 ($30,000 less $10,000 basis to the partnership).

Partner Allocation

	Special	*Regular*	*Total*
A	$15,000	$2,500	$17,500
B		2,500	2,500
	$15,000	$5,000	$20,000

Example: Let us suppose further that A and B draw out $5,000 of gain allocated equally between themselves, but that A leaves the $15,000 of pre-contribution gain in the partnership as he has agreed. The partnership now has $50,000 of cash only as its assets. Are their capital accounts in balance?

Partner	*Original Basis*	*Gain Allocable*	*Amount Withdrawn*	*New Basis*
A	$10,000	$17,500	$2,500	$25,000
B	25,000	2,500	2,500	25,000
	$35,000	$20,000	$5,000	$50,000

---

[12] Section 704(c)(1), I.R.C.

Thus we find that A has reported all of the pre-contribution gain, but gain occurring after contribution to the partnership is divided equally. Furthermore, by compelling A to leave his pre-contribution gain in the partnership, the capital of the partnership remains unimpaired at $50,000 and each partner now has a capital account of $25,000 for his one-half interest in $50,000 of assets. Obviously, if A were permitted to withdraw his $15,000 of pre-contribution gain, the partnership could hardly be considered to be an equal one.

Example: Let us assume that A withdraws the entire $17,500 of his gain and B withdraws $2,500. The partnership assets now consist of only $35,000 cash, being B's $25,000 contribution and the $10,000 of cash paid for A's basis for the apartment. How is it divided?

Partner	Original Basis	Gain Allocable	Amount Withdrawn	New Basis
A	$10,000	$17,500	$17,500	$10,000
B	25,000	2,500	2,500	25,000
	$35,000	$20,000	$20,000	$35,000

In the case of depreciation upon contributed property, the 1954 Code permits the partners to allocate pre-contribution gain among themselves to take into account the difference between value and basis at the time of contribution.[13]

A suggested provision to accomplish both of these objectives is as follows:

Depreciation or depletion or both realized by the partnership upon property contributed by a partner to the partnership that has a basis at the time of contribution less that its agreed value for purposes of contribution shall be allocated solely to the partners other than the contributor until such time as the depreciation or depletion, or both as the case may be, allocated to them out of the basis for the contributed property shall equal that fractional part of the original difference between the basis of the property and its agreed value at the time of contribution that the interests of all the partners, other than the contributor, in partnership capital bear to the total capital interest of all the partners in partnership capital.

Additional depreciation or depletion or both realized by the partnership on such property shall be allocated among all the partners according to their respective interests in partnership profits and losses.

Gain or loss realized by the partnership upon the sale or other disposition of such property shall be allocated as follows:

(1) If gain is realized, it shall be allocated first to the contributing partner to the extent of the original difference between the basis of the property and its agreed value at the time of contribution less the amount of depreciation or depletion or both from the property previously allocated to the other partners under the special allocation provision set out above. The contributing partner shall not, however, be entitled to withdraw the amount of such gain specially allocated to him, but shall be required to leave the amount of such gain in the partnership as part of his original contribution. The remainder of the gain, if any, shall be allocated among all the partners in proportion to their interests in partnership profits and losses.

(2) If a loss is realized, it shall be allocated first to the partners other than the contributor to the extent of the original difference between the basis of the property and

---
[13] Section 704(c)(2), I.R.C.; Reg. Sec. 1.704-1(c)(2).

its agreed value at the time of contribution less the amount of depreciation or depletion or both from the property previously allocated to the other partners under the special allocation provision set out above. The remainder of the loss, if any, shall be allocated among all the partners in proportion to their interests in partnership profits and losses.

See schedule annexed for a list of contributed property with a statement of the difference between basis and agreed value at the time of contribution.[14]

4. Undivided Interests in Contributed Property

Suppose the property that is contributed to a partnership was owned by all of the partners prior to contribution in the same proportion that they share interests in the partnership. Under these circumstances, a special allocation agreement for depreciation, depletion, and gain or loss may be unnecessary. The 1954 Code provides that as long as the partners' respective interests in partnership capital and profits and losses remain identical to their former undivided interests in the contributed property, depreciation, depletion, and gain or loss will be allocated among the partners as if they still retained their undivided interests directly in the property.[15]

Example: A and B agree to organize a partnership for the purpose of managing rental property. A, who owns an apartment worth $25,000, agrees to sell a one-half interest to B for $12,500. If A's basis for the apartment is $10,000, he would realize a gain of $7,500 on the sale of an undivided one-half interest to B ($12,500–$5,000 [1/2 basis] = $7,500). A and B then agree to form the AB partnership for the purpose of holding the apartment. Accordingly, each contributes an undivided one-half interest in the apartment to the AB partnership in exchange for his equal one-half partnership interest. The basis of the apartment to the partnership is $17,500, the sum of A's basis for his remaining one-half interest ($5,000) plus B's basis for his newly purchased interest ($12,500). Let us assume, first, that the partnership sells the property for $25,000. How are the depreciation and the gain to be allocated?

Partner	Contribution	Basis in Property	(1) Depreciation	[or]	(2) Gain
A	$12,500	$ 5,000	$ 500		$7,500
B	12,500	12,500	1,250		—0—
	$25,000	$17,500	$1,750		$7,500

5. Partnership Distributions

Partnership distributions are ordinarily tax-free because the tax on income items distributed was or will be paid by the partners through inclusion of their shares of partnership income in their own income. If distribution of property is made by a partnership that continues in operation, the partner receiving the distribution merely takes over the basis of the property to the partnership as his own.[16] But if the distribu-

---

[14] A special allocation agreement that has no business purpose is not controlling for tax purposes. Stanley C. Orrisch, 55 T.C. 395(1970), aff'd 31 AFTR 73, 1069 (9th Cir., 1973); Ruth C. Rodebaugh, T.C. Memo, 1974-34 (1974); Robert L. Brock, 59 T.C. 732 (1973).

[15] Section 704(c)(3), I.R.C.; Reg. Sec. 1.704-1(c)(3). If the partners enter into an agreement specially allocating any of these items, then this statutory provision will not apply.

[16] Section 732(a)(1), I.R.C. The basis to the distributee for the property cannot exceed his basis for his partnership interest less any money received. Section 732(a)(2), I.R.C.

REAL ESTATE HELD BY PARTNERSHIPS

tion is made in liquidation of the partnership, or in liquidation of the distributee partner's entire interest in the partnership, the partner receiving the property is required to transfer his basis for his partnership interest to the property received as its basis in his hands.[17]

What we are concerned with here is the effect of a distribution in liquidation of a partnership or of a partner's interest therein. If money is received in such a distribution, the partner receiving the distribution must first reduce his basis for his partnership interest by the amount of money received; the balance then becomes his basis for the partnership property he receives.[18]

Example: The AB partnership owns two apartments worth $50,000 each and $2,000 cash. It dissolves and distributes Apartment #1 and $1,000 cash to A and Apartment #2 and $1,000 cash to B. Let us assume that A's basis for his partnership interest is $30,000 and the B's basis for his interest is $25,000. A's basis for Apartment #1 is computed as follows:

A's basis for interest in partnership	$30,000
Less cash received	1,000
A's basis for Apartment #1	$29,000
B's basis for Apartment #2 would be computed similarly:	
B's basis for interest in partnership	$25,000
Less cash received	1,000
B's basis for Apartment #2	$24,000

Each of the apartments, as we said, is worth $50,000. Thus, on distribution A receives property worth $51,000 in exchange for his partnership interest, which has a basis of only $30,000. Similarly, on distribution B receives property worth $51,000 in exchange for his partnership interest, which has a basis of only $25,000. Thus, A has realized a gain of $21,000 and B a gain of $26,000 on the distribution. But this is only a "paper" gain because it has not been liquidated into money. Accordingly, no part of either A's or B's gain will be recognized for tax purposes on the distribution.[19]

But, obviously, if either partner's interest had been converted into money on the liquidation of the partnership, he would he would have realized his "paper" profit. Accordingly, gain is recognized for tax purposes on the liquidation of a patnership in any case in which a partner receives money in excess of his basis for his partnership interest.[20]

Example: Suppose, under the facts of the preceding example, the AB partnership had sold one of the apartments for $50,000. Accordingly, on the liquidation of the partnership, there remained only Apartment #2 and $52,000 in cash for distribution. Let assume, then, that A takes $51,000 in cash and B takes Apartment #2, worth $50,000 and $1,000 in cash. A's taxable gain on the distribution would be computed as follows:

Amount received on distribution	$51,000
Less A's basis for interest in partnership	30,000
	$21,000

---

[17] Section 732(b), I.R.C.; Section 761(d), I.R.C.
[18] Reg. Sec. 1.732-1(b).
[19] Section 731(a)(1), I.R.C.
[20] Reg. Sec. 1.732-1(a)(1).

B's position would be the same as in the preceding example; because the money received by him ($1,000) does not exceed his basis for his partnership interest ($25,000), none of the gain will be taxed at the time of the distribution. In effect, the realization of the gain, for tax purposes, will be postponed to the time that B disposes of Apartment #2.

These rules and results would be the same on the liquidation of either partner's interest in the partnership.

The rules as to the realization of losses on distribution are similar, except that losses are recognized only to a partner who receives on distribution no property other than money, unrealized receivables, and inventory.[21]

Example: The AB partnership owns an apartment worth $50,000 and $52,000 in cash. A's basis for his partnership interest is $55,000. Suppose, then, that $51,000 in cash is distributed to A. A's loss of $4,000 would be recognized for tax purposes.

Money received on distribution	$51,000
Less A's basis for interest in partnership	55,000
A's loss on exchange	($4,000)

Suppose B's basis for his partnership interest is also $55,000. If B receives the apartment worth $50,000 plus $1,000 in cash on distribution, B would also realize a $4,000 loss. But no part of the loss would be deductible for tax purposes because B has received property other than money, unrealized receivables, and inventory in the distribution.[22]

But, correspondingly, B's basis for the apartment received on distribution becomes equal to his basis for his partnership interest ($55,000) less the money received ($1,000), or $54,000. Thus, the recognition of his $4,000 loss is postponed to the time that he disposes of the apartment in a taxable sale or exchange.

6. Collapsible Partnerships

The rules relating to collapsible partnerships are designed to prevent partners from converting items that would produce ordinary income if realized by the partnership into capital gain by the sale of a partnership interest or by the distribution of such items to the partners. The theory of these rules is not difficult but their mechanics are most complex.

Consider, for example, the customary case of a partnership on the cash method of accounting that has a large amount of trade accounts receivable and also property for sale to customers that has appreciated substantially over its cost to the partnership. If the partnership collected the accounts receivable, the amounts collected would be ordinary income; and, correspondingly, if it sold the property, the gain realized would be ordinary income.

Suppose, then, before sale of the ordinary income property or collection of the receivables, one of the partners decides to sell his partnership interest. His gain would be measured by the difference between the amount received and his basis for the

---

[21] Section 731(a)(2), I.R.C.
[22] Reg. Sec. 1.731-1(b).

partnership interest. If his holding period for the interest has exceeded six months, the gain would, but for these rules, be taxed as capital gain. But under the collapsible partnership rules, the selling partner must, in effect, break the sale down into two components, the first a sale of his interest in the partnership's "unrealized receivables"[23] and "substantially appreciated inventory"[24] and the second a sale of his interest in the other assets of the partnership. Gain realized on the first portion of the transaction is taxed to him as ordinary income; gain realized on the second portion retains its character as capital gain.

Example: The AB partnership is engaged in the business of real estate development. It has subdivided acreage into 100 lots, of which 30 have been sold. It has recovered its entire basis allocable to the lots sold and the purchasers still owe $30,000 to the partnership for these lots. In addition, the partnership has $50,000 of cash. The 70 remaining lots are worth $210,000, for which the partnership has a basis of $70,000. A then sells his one-half interest in the partnership to B for $145,000. If A's basis for his interest is only $50,000, his gain would be computed as follows:

(1) Gain Realized		
Total received		$145,000
Less basis for partnership interest		50,000
Gain realized on sale		$ 95,000
(2) Gain on Collapsible Partnership Items:		
A's interest in receivables (1/2)		$ 15,000
A's share of gain in inventory:		
A's share of inventory (1/2)	$105,000	
A's share of basis to partnership (1/2)	35,000	70,000
Gain taxed as ordinary income		$ 85,000
(3) Gain on Other Items:		
Total received	$145,000	
Portion allocated to (2)	120,000	$ 25,000
Less basis for partnership interest:		
Total basis	$ 50,000	
Basis allocated to inventory	35,000	15,000
Gain taxed as capital gain		$ 10,000

Thus, of the total $95,000 gain received, $85,000 is taxed as ordinary income and only $10,000 as capital gain.

A similar rule applies in the case of distributions. If, in the case of a distribution, a partner receives less than his aliquot portion of the partnership's unrealized receivable

---

[23] "Unrealized receivables" are defined in Section 751(c), I.R.C., as "any rights (contractual or otherwise) to payment for (1) goods delivered, or to be delivered, to the extent the proceeds therefrom would be treated as amounts received from the sale or exchange of property other than a capital asset, or (2) services rendered or to be rendered . . . to the extent not previously includable in income under the method of accounting used by the partnership." See, also, Reg. Sec. 1.751-1(c).

[24] "Substantially appreciated inventory" is defined in Section 751(c), I.R.C. as "inventory items of the partnership . . . if their fair market value exceeds (A) 120 percent of the adjusted basis to the partnership of such property, and (B) 10 percent of the fair market value of all partnership property, other than money." See, also, Reg. Sec. 1.751-1(d). Inventory items include traditional stock in trade or inventory, other property held for sale to customers in the ordinary course of business, and any other property that is not a capital or Section 1231 asset. This definition has been broadened to include Section 1245 or Section 1250 property to the extent of the Section 1245 or Section 1250 gain therein.

and substantially appreciated inventory, he is deemed to have sold his interest therein to the partnership. Accordingly, he will be treated as having received ordinary income on the sale. Conversely, if the partner takes more than his aliquot portion of these items in the distribution, the partnership will be treated as having sold the excess interest to him. Accordingly, the partnership will be treated as having received ordinary income on the sale.[25]

Another application of the collapsible partnership rules appears in the case of a distribution of these assets to a partner in final liquidation of the partnership. Even if the partner receives no more than his aliquot share of the partnership's unrealized receivables and substantially appreciated inventory, these assets will retain their character as ordinary income items for at least five years. Thus, if the distributee partner at any time disposes of the unrealized receivables, his gain or loss is ordinary income or loss. And, if the distributee partner disposes of property that constituted inventory in the hands of the partnership, whether or not substantially appreciated, any gain or loss incurred will be ordinary in nature if the disposition is within five years of the distribution from the partnership.[26]

B. SPECIAL PROBLEMS RELATING TO LIMITED PARTNERSHIPS

A limited partnership is a partnership in which there are two classes of partners: one class is comprised of the general partners (or general partner) who are the partners who manage the enterprise and who are jointly and severally liable for partnership debts (like a partner in an ordinary partnership). The other class is comprised of the limited partners who have no voice in the control of the partnership business and whose liability for partnership debts is limited to the amount of their agreed contribution. Even if the partnership becomes insolvent, no limited partner can be held liable for partnership debts in excess of the amount he has agreed to contribute to the partnership (unless he has been foolish enough to take over control of the partnership; in that case he is treated just as if he were a general partner).

Because of the unusual nature of a limited partnership, it has unusual tax problems that do not ordinarily apply to regular partnerships.

1. Basis of Limited Partner's Interest

Generally, a partner's basis for his partnership interest includes not only the cash and property (at its basis) he has put up, but also his proportionate share of partnership liabilities.[27] This rule is very helpful in any case in which the acquisition or construction of depreciable property is financed by borrowed money.

Example: The AB partnership constructs a $600,000 office building on a lot that cost it $50,000 some 10 years ago. Their total cash contribution for their partnership interests was $25,000 each. The entire cost of construction was financed by a mortgage loan of $600,000.

---
[25]Reg. Sec. 1.751-1(b).
[26]Section 735(a), I.R.C.
[27]Section 752, I.R.C.

SPECIAL PROBLEMS OF LIMITED PARTNERSHIPS

Assuming a 30-year life, annual depreciation would be $20,000 a year. Suppose income from operations just equals all deductible expenses so that in each year the partnership passes the depreciation write-off of $20,000 through to its partners as deductible losses. At the end of the year, the partners would have realized $60,000 of losses, an amount in excess of their $50,000 cash contribution. If we assume no principal payments have been made on the mortgage loan; what is their capital position?

Partner	Original Basis	Share of Debt	Less Loss	Current Basis
A	$25,000	$300,000	$30,000	$295,000
B	25,000	300,000	30,000	295,000
	$50,000	$600,000	$60,000	$590,000

Had the partners not been entitled to add their share of partnership liabilities to their original basis, they would be denied the right to take losses in excess of the first $50,000. Losses can be deducted by a partner only to the extent of basis.[28]

The rule for a limited partnership is the opposite. A limited partner's basis for his partnership interest is limited to the amount he has agreed to contribute and no more.[29] This rule can have disastrous tax consequences.

Example: If we assume the facts of the preceding example, except that the AB partnership is a limited partnership with A being the general partner and B the limited partner, we have the following strange result. A, because he is generally liable for partnership debts, is permitted to add all of the indebtedness to his basis for his partnership interest.[30] B, the limited partner, is entitled to a basis of only his original $25,000 contribution. In the third year of operation, B would be entitled to deduct only $5,000 of the $10,000 depreciation allocable to him. A, of course, would continue to deduct his $10,000 of depreciation in full. In the fourth and succeeding years, B would be allowed no deduction for depreciation until he made additional contributions to the partnership.

Can this result be avoided? How can limited partners increase their basis for their partnership interest by their share of partnership debt? The Regulations suggest it can be done by arranging the indebtedness so that neither the partnership nor any of the partners is liable for it. In other words, the limited partnership, if it wants to acquire depreciable loss property, must acquire it subject to any liability against it for which none of the partners nor the partnership is liable.

Example: G is a general partner and L is a limited partner in the GL limited partnership. The partnership acquires real property for a $10,000 payment in cash, subject to a mortgage debt of $5,000, which is not assumed by anyone. The basis of the partnership interest of each of G and L is increased by $2,500.[31]

It is therefore imperative, if a limited partnership is used as a vehicle for invest-

---

[28] Section 704(d). Any loss disallowed because it exceeds a partner's basis for his partnership interest can be deducted in the year he makes a new contribution, to the extent of the contribution. Nor can his basis be increased by an indemnity agreement between the limited partner and the general partner. Rev. Rul. 69-223, 1969-1 C.B. 184. *Query:* Can it be increased by an amendment to the limited partnership agreement that each limited partner will bear his pro rata share of any mortgage note deficiency?
[29] Reg. Sec. 1.752-1(e).
[30] Reg. Sec. 1.752-1(e), Example. These regulations were upheld in Curtis W. Kingbay, 46 T.C. 147 (1966) which denied loses actually sustained in excess of $20,000 as deductions.
[31] Reg. Sec. 1.752-1(e), Example.

ment, that depreciable property acquired or constructed be financed through debt which is not a personal liability of either the partnership or the partners. How can this result be accomplished?[32] Two methods quickly suggest themselves. The most difficult, but cleanest, is to negotiate with the lending agency to have it agree to a release of all personal liability and to convenant that it will look only to the property for recovery of its loan in the event of default.

The other solution is to use a dummy or straw man to sign all the loan papers. After the loan papers are signed, the dummy or straw man then deeds the property, subject to the mortgage debt, to the limited partnership. The proceeds of the mortgage loan are then paid to the limited partnership which then proceeds to construct the improvements it needs.

It is lamentable that traps like this one for the unwary are found so frequently in the Internal Revenue Code. If something can be done indirectly through a dummy, what policy is served by denying it if done directly, except that of laying a clever trap?

2. "At Risk" Basis for Deductions

Limited partners engaged in farming are permitted to deduct farm losses only to the extent of the amount of capital that each partner has at risk: that is the amount that he has contributed, agreed to contribute, or has personally agreed to be liable for. For this purpose, farming includes orchards; dairies; beef and sheep ranches; breeding and training ranches; and flower, crop, vegetable and fruit farms. Sections 464, 465.

3. Association Taxable as a Corporation

Because both a limited partnership and a corporation share a number of common corporate characteristics, there is always a danger that a limited partnership will lose its non-taxable partnership status and become taxable as a corporation. These common corporate characteristics are limited liability, associates, an objective to join together to engage in business, and centralized management. How, therefore, do we ensure that our limited partnership remains a partnership and does not become taxable as a corporation?

There are three ways. First, make sure that the general partner is both substantial and has unlimited liability.[33] Second, make sure that partnership interests are not transferable in the sense that a limited partner cannot substitute another person in his place without the agreement of all the partners. Third, make sure the partnership is dissolved on the death, withdrawal, or incapacity of a general partner.[34]

But these steps are not always feasible. Suppose, for example, the general partner is a corporation. It, of course, can never become deceased or disabled. It can, however, withdraw from the partnership. If withdrawal from the partnership causes dissolution (as under the Uniform Limited Partnership Act), then the limited partnership lacks one

---

[32] A non-recourse loan by the general partner to the partnership is not treated as a loan; it is treated as a capital contribution by the general partner. Rev. Rul. 72-135, 1972-1 C.B. 200.

[33] For ruling purposes, the Internal Revenue Service suggests that the corporate general partner have a net worth equal to at least 15 percent of the equity capital and take at least 1 percent of the action. Rev. Proc. 72-13, 1972-1 C.B. 735.

[34] Reg. Sec. 301.7701-2(a)(3).

SPECIAL PROBLEMS OF LIMITED PARTNERSHIPS 315

corporate characteristic: continuity of life despite the sale of a partnership interest by a general partner.[35]

What about limited liability? The mere fact that the limited partner's liability for partnership debts is limited to their agreed contribution is not sufficient of itself to create corporate status.[36] The fact that the general partners have personal liability is quite different from a corporation which has no stockholder whose liability is not limited.

Suppose, however, the general partner is itself a corporation. Because the general partner has achieved limited liability, will the limited partnership be taxed as a corporation? It depends upon whether or not the general partner is a dummy. If the corporation[37] has no other assets than its interest in the partnership, then the partnership has the corporate characteristic of limited liability. On the other hand, if the corporation has substantial assets (other than its interest in the partnership) which can be reached by credits of the partnership, then corporate limited liability is not present.

Finally, if the limited partnership agreement provides that a partner can sell his interest to another and the buyer automatically becomes a partner, then the limited partnership has another characteristic of a corporation: free transferability of an ownership interest, like shares of stock, without the consent or agreement of the other owners. The way to prevent this corporate characteristic from being present is to provide that no limited partner has the right to substitute another in his place as limited partner. It is not necessary to deny the limited partners the right of sale. But if they do sell, all their buyer gets is the right to receive the buyer's share of partnership profits and his share of capital on dissolution. Then the corporate characteristic of freely transferable shares is not present. The buyer is merely an assignee of the limited partner, not a substituted limited partner.[38] Even in the latter case it is helpful if the assignability of a partnership interest is restricted by a right of first refusal, or other option, in the other partners.[39]

But the fact that *one* corporate characteristic is absent from a limited partnership is not enough by itself to save the limited partnership from being taxed as a corporation. The test is whether it has *more* corporate than non-corporate characteristics.[40] To be safe, we recommend, if possible, safeguards on three of the six corporate characteristics: continuity of interest, limited liability, and free transferability of interest.[41]

Also, the general partner must be a person of substance, responsible in either capital[42] or earning power.[43] And the granting of irrevocable powers of attorney by the

---

[35] Reg. Sec. 301.7701-2(b)(3).

[36] Reg. Sec. 301.7701-2(d)(1).

[37] The same rule applies to other persons, such as individuals. If, for example, a lawyer organizes a $2,000,000 limited partnership with his assetless secretary as the only general partner, the resulting partnership has the corporate characteristic of limited liability. Reg. Sec. 301.7701-2(d)(1); Rev. Proc. 72-13, 1972-1 C.B. 735.

[38] Reg. Sec. 301.7701-2(e)(1).

[39] Reg. Sec. 301.7701-2(e)(2).

[40] Reg. Sec. 301.7701-2(a)(3).

[41] Other authorities have gambled on two out of the four non-corporate characteristics of a partnership. See Reg. Sec. 301.7701-2(a)(3). But in a limited partnership, more care should be taken. That is, negative three out of the four common corporate characteristics.

[42] Fifteen percent of equity money up to $250,000.00, ten percent above. Rev. Proc. 72-135, 1972-1 C.B. 200.

[43] For example, it is doubtful that a law firm's secretary should serve as the general partner.

limited partners to the general partner is foolhardy.[44] Also foolhardy are votes by the limited partners to (1) throw out the general partner, (2) elect a new general partner, (3) re-finance, and (4) sell the assets, if the vote is less than unanimous.[45]

C. SUBDIVISIONS

The basic tax problem regarding subdivisions is that usually gains realized on the sale of lots constitute ordinary income to the seller. The very fact of subdividing ordinarily is sufficient in itself to characterize the subdivided lots as property held by the subdivider for sale to customers in the normal course of the business of subdividing. Hence, the seller becomes a dealer.[46]

But there is a question whether or not this rule automatically applies. The real question is what was the primary intent at the time of sale.[47]

There seem to be three minor exceptions to this rule, each of which is confined to a relatively limited fact situation. The first of these arises in the case of a liquidation of land holdings; if it becomes necessary to subdivide the property to hasten the liquidation, the gain realized will not necessarily be converted into ordinary income. Second, the sale of a "remnant" of a subdivision which is not itself suitable for the subdivider's purposes will give rise to capital gain. The third exists under statute. Section 1237 of the Code permits a limited amount of subdividing by one not otherwise a dealer without converting all of the gain to be realized into ordinary income.

1. Effect of Subdividing

An owner who subdivides his land is ordinarily by that fact converted into a dealer in real estate.[48] This is true whether the owner himself does the subdividing or has it done by an agent.[49]

2. Subdivision During Liquidation

An increasing number of courts have come to recognize that not all sales of subdivided land are sales in the ordinary course of business. These sales may be sales

---

[44]It's the same as a corporate proxy. The question presented: If the power limited to the amendment of certificates or the agreement itself?

[45]The concept of a partnership is that each partner is bound by his own agreement. *"Peach tree,"* a private, unpublished ruling, applied this concept to the variations made by the California legislature to the Uniform Limited Partnerships Law. That law was amended to conform to the Uniform Act. *"Apple tree,"* a private ruling, unpublished, holds that an agreement by contract to bind the partners by a 50 percent vote does not ascribe continuity. The California act has since been amended and approved. Rev. Rul. 74-320, 1974-27 I.R.B. p. 29.

[46]Stockton Harbor Industrial Co., v. Commissioner, 216 F.2d 638 (9th Cir., 1954).

[47]"Primary" intent means the *principal* intent *at the time of sale*. Malat v. Riddell, 383 U.S. 569(1966). There is doubt whether the Supreme Court focused on the "principal" intent at the time of purchase, or "meantime" or "at time of sale." But like a dictionary, the Supreme Court said "primary" or "of first importance."

[48]Palos Verdes Corp. v. United States, 201 F.2d 256 (9th Cir. 1952); Mauldin v. Commissioner, 195 F.2d 714 (10th Cir. 1152).

[49]Richards v. Commissioner, 81 F.2d 369 (9th Cir. 1936).

in liquidation of an investment rather than in the course of business. If so, gain derived from the liquidating sales stands a chance of being taxed as capital gain rather than as ordinary income.[50]

Suppose, for example, an individual inherits property that had been previously subdivided. He takes no steps to organize a business to sell off the property but merely waits for offers to buy to be submitted. He does not reinvest the proceeds received on the liquidation of his interest in the subdivision in other real estate. Under these circumstances, it is probable that his gain will be taxed as capital gain.[51]

The burden is, of course, placed upon the owner to show that the sales are truly made in the course of liquidation, not in the conduct of a business. In order to establish the necessary framework of sales in liquidation, the owner should offer proof of the following facts, if it is available:

(1) That the original acquisition of the property was for purposes other than for sale to customers;

(2) That the original purpose in acquiring the land was frustrated by some external circumstance or development other than the desire to make a profit;

(3) That a decision was reached to liquidate the owner's investment in the property;

(4) That it was necessary to subdivide the land in order to accomplish the liquidation; in other words, that the land could not have been sold as raw acreage at a reasonable price;

(5) That the liquidation plan was followed without aggressive selling, advertising, or promotional activities; and

(6) That the liquidation proceeds were not immediately reinvested in similar land in the neighboring area.

Example: Owner was an active real estate developer. He and his partner took title to certain real estate in the names of six rental corporations. These corporations built 194 duplexes, but rentals were slower than expected and the corporations showed consistent losses. More than three years later, O and his partner disagreed over O's proposed improvements to make the duplexes more rentable. All the corporations were dissolved and 186 duplexes were distributed to O as his share of the assets. O then began advertising the duplexes for sale, rather than rental. O opened a model duplex for inspection by customers, hired a staff of salesmen, and did extensive newspaper and radio advertising. O had a real estate broker's license during all this period. O sold 169 duplexes in three years, and the last 17 were exchanged for a ranch. The gain realized by O on these sales was held to be capital gain because O's original primary purpose in acquiring the land and constructing the duplexes was for rental, not for sale. Liquidation of the duplexes after frustration of his rental plan did not turn him into a dealer as to this specific property held for rental.[52]

---

[50]Fahs v. Crawford, 161 F.2d 315 (5th Cir. 1947); Dillon v. Commissioner, 213 F.2d 218 (8th Cir. 1954); Victory Housing No. 2., Inc. v. Commissioner, 205 F.2d 371 (10th Cir. 1953); Curtis Co. v. Commissioner, 232 F.2d 167 (3rd Cir. 1956).
[51]Smith v. Dunn, 224 F.2d 353 (5th Cir. 1955); Beck v. Commissioner, 179 F.2d 688 (7th Cir. 1950); Garrett v. United States, 120 F. Supp. 193 (Ct. Cl. 1954).
[52]Heller Trust v. Commissioner, 382 F.2d 675 (9th Cir. 1967).

3. Sale of Unsuitable Parts

If after a subdivider has completed his subdivision he has land left over which is unsuitable for his purposes, the sale of the unsuitable remnant will create capital gain.[53]

Example: Owner, a real estate subdivider, acquired a 16-acre tract for subdivision and sale. Because of existing streets that were extended into this tract in a straight line, a long narrow strip of land was isolated and could not be subdivided or developed by him. He sold the strip to neighboring owners who could develop it. The gain realized on the sale was held to be capital gain.[54]

It has also been held, over the Commissioner's protest, the a condemnation sale of part of a subdivider's land held for subdivision purposes gives rise to capital gain; once the notice of condemnation is served on the subdivider designating the portion to be taken, that portion is no longer held by him for sale to customers in the ordinary course of business.[55]

4. Subdivisions Under Section 1237

In partial recognition of the force of the liquidation argument outlined in the preceding section, Congress added Section 1237 to the Internal Revenue Code. This section recognizes the right of an owner of property who is not otherwise a dealer to engage in a limited amount of subdivision work without, by that fact, converting himself into a dealer. In other words, his gain upon the sale of the subdivided lots may still qualify for capital gain treatment, if the preceding subdivision work has qualified under the terms of Section 1237.

The benefits of Section 1237 will be available to a seller of subdivided property if the following conditions are met:[56]

(1) The seller was not otherwise a dealer during the year of sale and had never previously held the subdivided land for sale to customers in the ordinary course of business;

(2) The seller had not, directly or indirectly, made any substantial improvements to the property; and

(3) The seller had held the property for at least five years or had acquired the property by inheritance or devise.

Corporations, as well as individuals, may qualify for the benefits of this section; but for a corporation to qualify, it must show that no stockholder is a dealer[57] and that the property was acquired by the corporation through foreclosure of a lien securing an indebtedness owed to it.[58]

---

[53]Charles E. Mieg, 32 T.C. 1314 (1959), acq. 1960-2 C.B. 6; Pasadena Investment Co. v. Phinney, 223 F. Supp. 639 (S.D. Tex. 1963).

[54]Eline Realty Co., 35 T.C. 1 (1960), acq. 1961-1 C.B. 4.

[55]Tri-S Corp., 48 T.C. 316 (1967), aff'd (10th Cir. 1968), 400 F.2d 862; Ridgewood Land Co., T.C. Memo dec. 1972-16, aff'd 477 F.2d 135, (5th Cir. 1973). Contra, Juleo, Inc. v. Commissioner, 483 F.2d 47 (3rd Cir. 1973), cert. den.

[56]Section 1237(a), I.R.C.

[57]Indirect ownership of property held for sale to customers by a stockholder would be sufficient to disqualify the corporation. Section 1237(a), I.R.C.

[58]Section 1237(a),(b)(3), I.R.C.

For the purpose of Section 1237, substantial improvements are any improvements that substantially enhance the value of the land. Among these are such improvements as the construction of shopping centers, the building of commercial or residential buildings, the installation of hard surface roads, the installation of sewers, water, gas, or electric lines, or other utilities. Non-substantial improvements have been defined to include the construction of a temporary field office, surveying, filling, draining, leveling, clearing, and the construction of minimum all-weather access roads.[59]

Substantial improvements made by others which are attributable to the owner will also disqualify the property. Thus, improvements to the property made by his whole or half brothers and sisters, his spouse, or his ancestors or descendants are attributed to him. Similarly, improvements made by a partnership of which he is a partner or by a corporation controlled by him are attributed to him. Improvements made by a lessee in lieu of rent are also attributed to him.[60]

The disqualification for substantial improvements also arises in the case of improvements made by a local governmental unit if the cost of the improvement results in an increase of the owner's basis for the property, as in the case of an improvement made through a special assessment district. And an improvement made by the purchaser of the property under the terms of a contract of sale is also attributed to the owner.[61]

There is one exception to this rule of substantial improvements; if the property has been held by the owner for more than 10 years, the owner can install water, sewer, or drainage facilities or roads without losing the benefit of Section 1237, provided he can show that the lots would not have been marketable at prevailing local prices without the improvements. Also, the owner must elect to forgo any increase in his basis for the property to the cost of these improvements. In other words, he can take no tax benefit from the cost of the improvements by deduction or by capitalization.[62]

What are the benefits of Section 1237? If the tract can qualify, all the gain on the sale of the lots will probably qualify for capital gain treatment. To be specific, we find that if the owner qualifies his subdivision under the above restrictions, he is entitled to realize the following benefits:[63]

(1) Up to the time that six lots are sold from the tract, the gain realized will be taxed as capital gain.

(2) In the taxable year in which the sixth lot is sold, the gain realized on all lots sold in that year and thereafter is taxed as ordinary income to the extent of 5 percent of the selling price and as capital gain to the extent of the excess. The seller is entitled to offset the ordinary income so realized by his selling expenses.[64] Because commissions on sale usually equal, if not exceed, 5 percent of the selling price this rule is no handicap. The seller continues to have all his profit taxed as capital gain.

(3) If, after the sale of a number of lots from the tract, the owner waits for a period of five years before he recommences selling, the original rule will apply.[65]

---

[59] Reg. Sec. 1.1237-1(c)(4).
[60] Reg. Sec. 1.1237-1(c)(2).
[61] Section 1237(a)(2), I.R.C.
[62] Section 1237(b)(3), I.R.C.
[63] Section 1237(b)(1), I.R.C.
[64] Section 1237(b)(2), I.R.C.
[65] Section 1237(d), I.R.C.; Reg. Sec. 1.1237-1(g)(2).

Thus, the benefits of Section 1237 are limited to cases of undeveloped real property which consists of one tract within the meaning of the statute. One tract is defined to include not only one parcel of land, but also two or more parcels that are contiguous or that are seperated by no more than a roadway, street, railroad, or stream, regardless of their times of acquisition.[66] And the use of the section is limited to cases of inherited lands or to cases in which the taxpayer has held the land for at least five years before sale.

The principal difficulty with the section is the restriction imposed upon "substantial improvements." Under the subdivision and map acts of many states and municipalities, the owner must provide street access and utility connections before he can sell the property as subdivided property. In this event, he must wait for a full ten years after acquisition before sale in order to come under the exception to the "substantial improvements" rule. And then he must be willing to put in the improvements as a personal non-deductible expenditure which cannot be recovered out of the selling price of the property for tax purposes. But a computation of the benefits of capital gain versus loss of basis may well be in order.

D. REAL ESTATE SYNDICATES

Under the tax laws there is no separate type of taxable entity known as a "syndicate." Such a syndicate is taxable either as a partnership or as a corporation, unless it qualifies for, and elects treatment as, a Real Estate Investment Trust. The law treating such trusts is discussed in Part E, below. If the syndicate is taxed as a partnership, the burden of the income tax imposed upon the business or the syndicate will be borne directly by the individual members of the syndicate. If the syndicate is taxed as a corporation, the burden of the tax will be imposed directly upon the business entity itself, in addition to a potential second tax to be borne by the members upon a distribution or dividend to them.

Obviously, then, except in situations in which a statutory investment trust is desirable, the members of the syndicate will attempt to organize themselves in such a manner that their venture will be taxed as a partnership rather than as a corporation. Otherwise, it probably would have been more advantageous for them to have incorporated at the beginning of their venture in order to obtain the non-tax benefits of the corporate form of organization.

1. Unincorporated Associations

The definition of a partnership under the Internal Revenue Code includes a "syndicate, group, pool, joint venture, or other unincorporated organization through or by means of which any business, financial operation, or venture is carried on, and which is not, within the meaning of [the Code], a corporation or a trust or estate."[67]

In general, these other types of unincorporated associations taxed as partnerships are distinguished from partnerships by the fact that the former are organized to carry on

---

[66]Section 1237(c), I.R.C.; Reg. Sec. 1.1237-1(g).
[67]Section 761(a), I.R.C.

a specific venture; a partnership, on the other hand, is usually organized for the purpose of carrying on a trade or business involving more than one specific venture. There may be other distinctions in liability, duration, or scope of operation that arise under local law. But, regardless of the terminology used ("pool," "syndicate," "joint venture," etc.), such an association is required to file a partnership tax return as if it had been organized as a partnership.

Examples of the types of unincorporated associations which have been treated as partnerships under the federal income tax are the following:

(1) Investment club of an amateur nature which collects periodic contributions from its members for investment in stock or other securities;

(2) Tenancy in common ownership of real estate held for investment or for the production of income;

(3) Joint venture of taxpayers engaged in the contracting business to make a bid on and to carry out the work on a specific contract;

(4) Limited partnership organized to carry on a trade or business;

(5) Pooling agreement among several taxpayers with respect to patent and licensing rights.

2. Unincorporated Associations Taxed as Corporations

But merely because an association is not incorporated under state law does not guarantee that it will be taxed as a partnership under the federal income tax laws. The Code definition of corporations includes "associations."[68] If the unincorporated association has the principal characteristics of a corporation, it will be taxed as a corporation. By regulation[69] and court precedent, these principal characteristics can be enumerated as follows:

(1) Limited liability of participants;
(2) Centralized management selected by the participants;
(3) Transferability of the interests of participants by assignment or sale;
(4) Continuity of the enterprise despite the withdrawal or death of a participant.

If all, or most, or these characteristics are enjoyed by the participants in an unincorporated association, the probabilities are that the association will be taxed as a corporation. Hence, the drafting of the legal instruments setting up such an association must be done with a great deal of care in order to preserve its right to report its income as if it were a partnership. Among the provisions that should be considered are the following:

(1) Each participant should participate in the policy decisions of the venture;

(2) Any person hired by the venture to implement these decisions should be treated as the employee of, or agent for, the participants, not of or for the venture;

(3) The assignment of a participant's interest shall terminate the venture; the remaining participants and the assignee may be given the option to organize a new association to continue the venture if they so choose;

---

[68] Section 7701(a)(3), I.R.C.
[69] Reg. Sec. 301.7701-2.

(4) Similarly, the death of a participant shall terminate the venture, with the right of the remaining participants to organize a new association;

(5) Each participant shall hold his interest in his own name; no joint tenancies, tenancies by the entireties, or tenancies in common can be permitted; and

(6) Each participant shall be personally liable for his share of the losses, debts, and obligations of the venture.

3. Limited Partnerships

Limited partnerships organized under state law usually permit those partners whose interests are limited to limit their liability for the losses of the partnership to the amount of their capital contributions. In addition, state law usually permits the existence of the partnership to continue despite the death or withdrawal of a limited partner. Also, the limited partners are, by law, forbidden to participate as partners in the management of the partnership's business.[70]

Thus, three elements of a corporation are present in a limited partnership; namely, limited liability as to some of the participants, continuity of interest despite the death of a limited partner, and centralized management in the general partners. Despite this close similarity to a corporation, a limited partnership is entitled to be taxed as a partnership and not as a corporation. But, needless to say, limited partnerships are scrutinized carefully to see that each is organized and operated strictly within the requirements imposed by state law on this form of organization.

Therefore, in order to ensure the tax advantages of a partnership to a limited partnership, the draftsman should be careful to provide a number of safeguards. For example, although the death or withdrawal of a limited partner will not terminate its existence, the partnership agreement should prohibit the assignee or distributee of the former limited partner's interest from participating in the partnership until he has signed a new certificate of limited partnership, to be placed on file as required by law. Also, the agreement should provide specifically that the death, withdrawal, or incompetency of a general partner will operate to dissolve the partnership immediately; the remaining members may retain the right to form a new partnership if they choose to do so.

If the general partner is a corporation, certain guidelines have been stated by the Internal Revenue Service as prerequisites for obtaining a ruling that the limited partnership is not taxed as a corporation. For example, Revenue Procedure 72-13 states:[71]

> The Service will consider a request for a ruling on the classification of an organization as a partnership where it is formed as a limited partnership and a corporation to the *sole* general partner under the following conditions:
> The limited partners will not own, directly or indirectly, individually or in the aggregate, more than 20 percent of the stock of the corporate general partner or any affiliates as defined in section 1504(a) of the Internal Revenue Code of 1954. For the purpose of determining stock ownership in the corporate general partner or its affiliates the attribution rules set forth in section 318 of the Code are applicable.

---

[70]To the extent that state law differs from the Uniform Limited Partnership Act, difficulties will be encountered. Regulations §301.7701-2(b)(3).

[71]Rev. Proc. 72-13, 1972-1 C.B. 735.

If the corporate general partner has an interest in only one limited partnership and the total contributions to that Partnership are less than $2,500,000, the net worth of the corporate general partner at all times will be at least 15 percent of such total contributions or $250,000, whichever is the lesser; if the total contributions to that partnership are $2,500,000 or more, the net worth of the corporate general partner at all times will be at least 10 percent of such total contributions. In computing the net worth of the corporate general partner, for this purpose, its interest in the limited partnership and accounts and notes receivable from and payable to the limited partnership will be excluded.

If the corporate general partner has interests in more than one limited partnership, the net worth requirements explained in the preceding paragraph will be applied separately for each limited partnership, and the corporate general partner will have at all times (exclusive of any interest in any limited partnership and notes and accounts receivable from and payable to any limited partnership in which the corporate general partner has any interest), .02 above for each separate limited partnership.

For purposes of computing the net worth of the corporate general partner in .02 and .03 above, the current fair market value of the corporate assets must be used.

The purchase of a limted partnership interest by a limited partner does not entail either a mandatory or discretionary purchase or option to purchase any type of security of the corporate general partner or its affiliates.

The organization and operation of the limited partnership must be in accordance with the applicable state statute relating to limited partnerships.

Revenue Procedure 74-17 adds the following:[72]

The interests of all of the general partners, taken together, in each material item of partnership income, gain, loss, deduction, or credit is equal to at least one percent of each such item at all times during the existence of the partnership. In determining the general partners' interests in such items, limited partnership interests owned by the general partners shall not be taken into account.

The aggregate deductions to be claimed by the partners as their distributive shares of partnership losses for the first two years of operation of the limited partnership will not exceed the amount of equity capital invested in the limited partnership.

A creditor who makes a nonrecourse loan to the limited partnership must not have or acquire, at any time as a result of making the loan, any direct or indirect interest in the profits, capital, or property of the limited partnership other than as a secured creditor.

4. Common Ownership of Income Real Estate

In general, the common ownership of income-producing real estate results in the automatic formation of a partnership for federal income tax purposes. The regulations recognize that "(m)ere co-ownership of property which is maintained, kept in repair, and rented or leased does not constitute a partnership."[73] But the regulations go on to state, "(t)enants in common, however, may be partners if they actively carry on a trade, business, financial operation or venture and divide the profits therefrom. For

---

[72]Rev. Proc. 74-17, I.R.B. 1974-22. It should be noted that these conditions are not necessarily controlling on audit. See Section 4 of Rev. Proc. 74-17.

[73]Reg. Sec. 1.761-1(a).

example, a partnership exists if co-owners of an apartment building lease space *and in addition provide services either directly or through an agent.*"[74] What services are sufficient to convert common ownership into a partnership? Are the mere "furnishing of heat and light, the cleaning of public entrances, exits, stairways, and lobbies, (and) the collection of trash"[75] sufficient? Arguably not, but the regulations are not clear on this point. For protection, the common owners should, in their first year of association, file a "dummy" partnership return in which they specifically elect not to be treated as a partnership for tax purposes.[76] In this way, the owners will preserve their right to be treated as individual owners of individual interests in the property without the interposition of a partnership entity between themselves and the property.

E. REAL ESTATE INVESTMENT TRUSTS

A group of 100 or more investors may now pool their funds for investment in real estate assets, equities and mortgages, have limited liability, nearly free transferability of interests, and centralized management, and still escape taxation as a corporation. This can be done by organizing a "real estate investment trust" which qualifies for taxation under Section 856 to 858 of the Code.

The statute was designed primarily to benefit the traditional "Massachusetts Trust," which is generally subject to corporate tax as an association. It may also be of value in some other situations.

This very complex statute, containing nearly a dozen arbitrary percentage limitations on the structure and activities of the trust, must be used only with caution and after careful planning. Because of this complexity, our discussion will be confined to the highlights of the statute.

1. Election to Be Taxed as a Real Estate Investment Trust

To obtain tax treatment as a real estate investment trust, the trust must elect such treatment. The election is made merely by computing taxable income as a real estate investment trust in the return for the first year (beginning after 1960) in which such treatment is desired. The trust must, of course, be qualified under the provisions discussed below, but the fact that it also qualified in a prior year or years will not disqualify the election. An election once made is irrevocable for the year in which made and *all* succeeding years.[77]

In effect, an election can be rescinded at any time by simply arranging for the disqualification of the trust under one of the numerous qualification provisions discussed below. Because the result would be to tax the trust as a corporation, such action would appear desirable only where the trust expects to incur substantial net operating

---

[74]*Ibid.* (emphasis added).
[75]Reg. Sec. 1.512(b)-1(c)(2), defining such services as incidentals to the rental of real estate for purposes of exempt organizations. See, also, Reg. ¶1.856-4(b)(3)(i)(b), relating to real estate investment trusts.
[76]Section 761(a), I.R.C.; Reg. Sec. 1.761(a)(2).
[77]Reg. Sec. 1.856-2(b).

REAL ESTATE INVESTMENT TRUSTS

losses. Since the net operating loss carryover and carryback deduction are specifically disallowed to a real estate investment trust,[78] reversion to corporate taxation may be beneficial until the losses end and the carryovers are used up.

Can a trust which was qualified in a prior year (but after 1960) elect treatment as a real estate investment trust retroactively by filing amended returns and claiming refunds? The regulations are silent on this point also. But it is noteworthy that they do not require that the election be made on a return "timely filed."[79]

2. Qualification as a Real Estate Investment Trust

A real estate investment trust is "an unincorporated trust or an unincorporated association . . . which is managed by one or more trustees" and which would be taxable as a corporation but for Sections 856 to 858 of the Code.[80] See Part D of this chapter, for a discussion of the requirements for taxability as a corporation.

To qualify as a real estate investment trust, the association or trust must also meet each of the following 13 tests:

(1) It must be managed by trustees and its property held by them. Agents, employees of the shareholders, lesser fiduciaries, or even the general partners in a limited partnership will not do.[81]

(2) Beneficial ownership must be evidenced by transferable shares of certificates. The transferability requirement is satisfied even though the trustee has a power to prevent transfer or redeem on the good-faith belief that such transfer would result in loss of qualified status.[82]

This requirement, together with that of ownership by 100 or more persons, discussed below, makes it likely that the trust will be subject to the requirements of various securities laws, including both those administered by the Federal Securities Exchange Commission and the state "Blue Sky" laws. Careful consideration must be given to the various filing, registration, licensing and reporting requirements of these laws.

(3) The trust cannot hold property for sale to customers; it cannot be a dealer.[83]

(4) Beneficial ownership must be in at least 100 persons, including trusts, estates, corporations and so forth, during at least 335 (not necessarily consecutive) days of the taxable year.[84]

(5) During the last half of the trust's taxable year, not more than 50 percent of the shares may be owned by five or fewer persons. Although the attribution of ownership rules[85] do not apply to the 100 persons rule, they do apply to the five persons rule.[86]

---

[78] Section 857(b)(2)(E), I.R.C.
[79] Compare Reg. Sec. 1.856-2(b) with Reg. Sec. 1.1372-2(b)(1) (relating to subchapter S election), with Reg. Sec. 1.1361-1(b) (relating to subchapter R election), and with Section 2032(c), I.R.C. (relating to election on timely return to permit use of alternate valuation for estate tax).
[80] Section 856(a), I.R.C.
[81] Reg. Sec. 1.8561-1(a)(1); See Rev. Rul. 72-254, 1972-1 C.B. 207.
[82] Reg. Sec. 1.856-1(d)(2).
[83] Reg. Sec. 1.856-1(d)(4); See Rev. Rul. 73-398, I.R.B. 1973-39, 14.
[84] Reg. Sec. 1.856-1.
[85] Section 544(a), I.R.C.
[86] Reg. Sec. 1.856-1(d)(5).

(6) At least 90 percent of the trust's gross income must be from:
   (a) dividends;
   (b) interest;
   (c) rents from real property;[87]
   (d) net gain from the disposition of interests in stock, securities, real property or real property mortgages; and
   (e) abatements and refunds of real property taxes.[88]

The purpose of this limitation is to insure that the trust is essentially a passive organization rather than an active operating entity.

(7) At least 75 percent of gross income must be from:
   (a) rents from real property;[89]
   (b) interest on obligations secured by mortgages on real property;
   (c) net gain from the disposition of interests in real property or in real property mortgages;
   (d) dividends from, or net gain on disposition of interests in other qualified real estate investment trusts; and
   (e) abatements and refunds of real property taxes.[90]

This limitation is designed to insure that the trust is primarily engaged in real estate investments.

(8) Less than 30 percent of its gross income can be derived from the disposition of:
   (a) stock or securities held for less than six months; and
   (b) real property held for less than four years (except involuntary conversions).[91]

By this limitation, Congress prohibited the use of the trust for subdivision or speculative purposes or for investments in fields outside of real estate.

(9) At the close of each quarter of the taxable year at least 75 percent of the value of the assets of the trust must consist of:
   (a) Interests in real property or in real property mortgages;
   (b) Shares in other qualified real estate investment trusts;
   (c) Government securities; and
   (d) Cash and non-purchased receivables.[92]

(10) The trust cannot hold, at the close of any quarter, the securities of any one issuer (other than government securities) in an amount exceeding 5 percent of the total assets of the trust.[93]

---

[87]Reg. Sec. 1.856-4, pursuant to the statute, provides amazingly complex rules for determining what is "rent from real property." The objective, in general, is to prevent receipt of payment for business done by, or services supplied by, the trust in the guise of rent. Thus, all actual maintenance and servicing of property *must* be done by an "independent contractor" or *all* rents may be deemed not "rents from real property." The trustee can, however, *collect* the rent without it losing its character as "rent." Rev. Rul. 72-353, 1972-2 C.B. 413; Rev. Rul. 73-194, 1973-1 C.B. 335; Rev. Rul. 74-134, I.R.B. 1974-12, 12.

[88]Reg. Sec. 1.856-2(c)(1)(i).

[89]See note 83, *supra*. For this purpose rents includes rents measured by a fixed percentage of gross sales or receipts from merchandise sold or services rendered by a tenant of the trust-landlord. Rev. Rul. 66-379, 1966-2, C.B. 279.

[90]Reg. Sec. 1.856-2(c)(1)(ii).
[91]Reg. Sec. 1.856-2(c)(1)(iii).
[92]Reg. Sec. 1.856-2(d).
[93]Reg. Sec. 1.856-2(d)(2).

(11) The trust cannot hold, at the close of any quarter, more than 10 percent of the outstanding voting securities of any issuer.[94]

If the trust finds itself disqualified under (9), (10) or (11) above, by virtue of changes in its investments, it is allowed 30 days after the end of the quarter in which it fails to meet the requirement to change its investments in order to remain qualified. But if the trust fails to meet the requirements of (9), (10) or (11) solely because of reasons not attributable to a change of investments (e.g., change in market values), and the trust had previously qualified, it remains qualified.[95] Hence, the trust need re-evaluate its asset holdings only in quarters in which it has changed investments.[96]

(12) The trust must distribute at least 90 percent of its taxable income, exclusive of net capital gains. The distribution may take place any time within 12 months after the close of the taxable year, provided the dividend (distribution) is declared before the time for filing the return for the taxable year.[97]

(13) The trust must keep such records as will disclose the actual and the constructive ownership of its stock.[98]

3. Taxation of a Real Estate Investment Trust

The taxable income of a real estate investment trust is taxed at corporate rates. But taxable income is computed with a deduction for dividends distributed. Hence, the trust will pay tax on not more than 10 percent of its income, since it will have distributed 90 percent in order to qualify.

Specifically, the taxable income of the trust is computed as if it were a corporation but excluding (1) net capital gain, (2) certain special deductions (such as the dividends received deduction), and (3) the net operating loss deduction. The deduction for dividends paid (including those to be paid within 12 months of the close of the taxable year, if declared before the return is due) is then taken. The remainder, if any, is subject to tax at the corporate rates.[99]

The excess of net long-term capital gain over net short-term capital loss (referred to herein as net capital gain) is separately treated. The trust may send its shareholders notice that some or all of its dividends are out of capital gains, up to an amount equal to the net capital gain of the trust. The trust is taxed at the rate of 25 percent on its net capital gain less distributed amounts that have specifically been designated as capital gains dividends. Thus, the trust may pass on, without tax to it, all or any part of its net capital gain as it may decide. It is taxed only on what it retains.[100]

Example: T, a qualified real estate investment trust, had net income in 1964 of $110,000, consisting of $100,000 from interest, dividends and rents and $10,000 of net capital gain. It distributed $100,000 to its shareholders, and notified them that 8 percent (or $8,000) of their dividends were out of capital gains dividends and the balance (or $92,000) out of other income. T's tax is computed as follows:

---

[94]*Ibid.*
[95] Section 856(c)(5).
[96] Reg. Sec. 1.856-2(d)(3).
[97] Reg. Sec. 1.857-1(a)(1); 1.858-1.
[98] Reg. Sec. 1.857-1(a)(2); 1.857-6.
[99] Reg. Sec. 1.857-2; 1.857-3.
[100] Reg. Sec. 1.857-2(b); 1.857-4(b).

Net ordinary income	$100,000	
Less dividends out of ordinary income	92,000	
Taxable income	8,000	
Apply corporate rate	22%	$1,760
Net capital gain	10,000	
Less dividends out of capital gains	8,000	
Taxable capital gain	2,000	
Apply capital gains rate[101]	22%	440
Total Tax		$2,200

4. Taxation of Beneficiaries of Trust

The "shareholder" or holder of a beneficial interest in a real estate investment trust must include all regular dividends in his gross income for the taxable year in which they are actually received. These dividends are treated as ordinary income and there is no tracing of the source from which they were declared (except for net capital gains). Accordingly, the beneficiary is not entitled to a dividends received credit, to exclusion of exempt interest or to depreciation deductions.

The entire amount attributable to the current earnings of the trust is ordinary income taxable in full.[102]

Capital gains dividends are long-term capital gains in the hands of the shareholders.[103]

Gain or loss on the disposition of shares in a real estate investment trust is treated in the same way as on the disposition of any corporate stock, with one exception. If a share is held less than 31 days and sold at a loss, the loss is a capital loss to the extent of any capital gains dividends received in respect of that share.[104] This provision was placed in the law to prevent dealers from purchasing shares before dividend date, receiving a capital gain dividend and selling ex-dividend at a loss that, but for this section, would be an ordinary loss.

5. Evaluation of a Real Estate Investment Trust

The real estate investment trust may serve a useful purpose in certain limited areas, but by and large the more traditional forms of ownership are more beneficial. In part this conclusion is due to the unwieldiness of the trust structure and in part to the limited tax advantages offered by the trust.

First, the restricted use under the statute of the trust form of doing business causes a number of unfortunate consequences at least in states that are not accustomed to the use of "Massachusetts" or business trusts. For example, the power of the beneficiaries to select the board of trustees may result in unlimited liability for the beneficiaries. Also, while the Agreement of Trust may not need to be filed with the Secretary of State (as in the case of Articles of Incorporation), the permission of the State Corporate

---

[101] Lesser of regular corporate rate (22 percent) or capital gain rate (25 percent).
[102] Reg. Sec. 1.857-4.
[103] Reg. Sec. 1.857-4(b).
[104] Reg. Sec. 1.857-4(c).

Securities officer (or, alternatively, a registration with the Federal Securities and Exchange Commission) would be required in most cases. And, in any case where the property to be acquired by the trust is unimproved, the State Corporate Securities officer is likely to impose very stringent restrictions on the type of investment that may be made. For example, in California it appears that a real estate investment trust would not be permitted to invest in unimproved property. Another area of difficulty is the federal tax requirement for an independent contractor to furnish services to tenants of the properties owned by the trust. Because of the propensity of certain real estate promoters to charge excessively high fees to their investors for such services, the local Corporate Securities officials may set ceiling rates on the fees to be charged that may be less than a reasonable rate. Accordingly, we find that the desirability of the real estate investment trust has not been sufficiently great to overcome these obstacles except in two cases: first, an existing real estate or office building corporation that has sufficient stockholders to qualify, and, second, a group of real estate developers who need a captive purchaser to bail them out of a projected improvement (such as a shopping center) at a price agreeable to them. In the first case, the use of the trust is an obvious way to save tax money if the corporation is paying dividends to its shareholders. The only question to ask is why Congress thought it essential that the corporation dissolve and turn itself into a trust; a simple election should have been sufficient.[105] In the second case, the use of the trust form is obvious to the developers because its presumed tax advantages will help to sell itself to the investing public to raise sufficient funds to purchase their newly completed project at a profit large enough to encourage them to overcome all of the obstacles outlined above.

Second, the tax advantages are not as great as it might appear. While the corporate tax is eliminated, the "stockholders" do not get the advantage of the "pass through" of deductions for depreciation. Thus, if the trust has losses, this fact does the individual beneficiaries no good. The trust may, of course, make tax-free distributions (assuming no accumulated earnings and profits) to the beneficiaries, but it cannot give them a write-off against other income. In this respect, the partnership or individual form of ownership gives a greater tax benefit. Similarly, the tax benefit of other deductions such as interest and taxes are absorbed at the trust level and cannot be "passed through" to the beneficiaries. Accordingly, an individual investor should think twice before he invests in a real estate investment trust. It is not far different from investing in a real estate corporation that does not qualify hereunder. He must weigh the possibility that the trust will forge ahead faster (because it can exempt itself from the federal income tax) against the possibility that its growth will be hindered (because, unlike a corporation, it cannot accumulate income). Surely, the limited tax benefit to him (capital gains distributions) is hardly sufficient in itself to justify selecting the trust over a corporation.[106]

---

[105] As a matter of fact, the Internal Revenue Service has ruled that a trust formed by way of the transfer of corporate assets under Section 368(a)(1)(F), I.R.C. does not qualify as a real estate investment during that part of its first taxable year that coincided with balance of the predecessor corporation's taxable year. Rev. Rul. 71-218, 1971-1 C.B. 209.

[106] Many states (for example, California) that impose corporate income or franchise taxes based on income have not adopted the real estate investment trust provisions. Hence, the trust would be taxable as a corporation and the distributions taxable to the beneficiaries as dividends to the extent of earnings and profits for state tax purposes.

6. Loss of Qualified Status

The risks of loss of qualification are disastrous. First, the real estate investment trust becomes subject to federal income taxes at the corporate level.[107] Second, any distributions made by the trust to its beneficiaries during the year would be taxable dividends to the extent of the trust's current and accumulated earnings and profits.[108]

---

[107] Morrissey v. Commissioner, 296 U.S. 344(1935), Regulations §301.7701-2(a)(2).
[108] See Rev. Rul. 58-466, 1958-2 C.B. 379 (applicable to sister Section 852).

11
Corporations

The use of the corporate form of ownership in holding, managing, and operating real estate is quite common. And the corporate form is even more common in the case of businesses engaged in the subdivision, development, and sale of real estate. There are many advantages, but just as many disadvantages, to the use of a corporation; only a working knowledge of the advantages and disadvantages will permit an owner to decide whether or not a corporation is the best answer to his particular problem.

The purpose of this chapter is to outline in general terms the tax rules that are applied to the corporate form of ownership. Accordingly, the plan of this chapter is as follows:

A. *Problems of Incorporation;*
B. *Problems of Operation;*
C. *Problems of Sales and Liquidations;*
D. *Problems of Acquisition of Property;*
E. *Use of Corporation in Tax Planning.*

A. PROBLEMS OF INCORPORATION

Once a corporate shell has been organized under state law, the corporation becomes an entity separate from the persons of its incorporators or stockholders. Thus, the incorporators or stockholders face the problem of handling the tax consequences that may arise from the transfer of money or other property to the corporation in order to permit it to engage in business.

Ordinarily, the incorporators handle this transaction by transferring money or other property to the corporation in exchange for its stock or other securities. If this exchange is handled in one manner, it will be treated as a taxable sale, requiring the transferors to report the difference between their basis for the property transferred (other than money) and the value of the stock or other securities received as taxable gain realized on the exchange. But the same exchange may be handled in a different manner that will qualify it for treatment as a tax-free exchange. In this event, neither gain nor loss will be recognized for tax purposes and the stockholders will merely transfer their basis for the property to the stock or other securities received in the exchange.

If only money is transferred to the corporation, the difference between the two types of exchange is merely theoretical. Even if the transfer is cast in the taxable form, no gain or loss will be realized, because money ordinarily has a basis equal to its value.

1. Tax-Free Incorporation

But suppose the incorporators transfer property other than money. If all the incorporators receive is stock for the property, their economic status will not be changed by the transfer; their stock represents nothing more to them than their fractional ownership of the corporation, which possesses no assets other than the transferred property. Because of the lack of economic betterment in such a transfer, Section 351 of the Code permits the exchange to be made without tax consequences, provided the following conditions are met:

(1) The exchange of property is made solely for stock or securities of the corporation; and

(2) The owners of the property are the owners after the exchange of at least 80 percent of the total combined voting power of all classes of stock entitled to vote and of at least 80 percent of the total number of shares of all other classes of stock of the corporation.[1]

If both of these conditions are met, the exchange of property for stock will not result in taxable gain or loss either to the corporation or its new stockholders. The corporation will take the stockholders' basis for the property as its own basis,[2] and the stockholders will be entitled to transfer their basis for the property to the stock received by them in exchange.[3]

Suppose, however, that the stockholders receive other property or money from the corporation in addition to its stock or securities. If the other conditions of a tax-free exchange are met, the receipt of this other property or money will be treated as the receipt of "boot." Gain will be recognized to the stockholders on the exchange only to the extent of the "boot" received. Gain in excess of the "boot" received will not be recognized, nor will losses be recognized.[4]

If "boot" is received and gain is taxed in part on the exchange, appropriate adjustments must be made to basis. The corporation's basis for the property and the stockholders' basis for the stock received will be equal to the stockholders' basis for the property increased by the amount of gain taxed to them in exchange.[5] Correspondingly, the stockholders must reduce their basis for the stock received (apart from the property) by the amount of "boot" received.[6]

---

[1] Sections 351(a), 368(c), I.R.C. For this purpose "stock" is equity ownership and "securities" are evidences of debt such as notes, debentures and bonds.
[2] Section 362(a), I.R.C.
[3] Section 358(a)(1), I.R.C.
[4] Section 351(b), I.R.C.
[5] Section 358(a), 362(a), I.R.C.
[6] Section 358(a)(1)(A), I.R.C.

For these purposes, a transfer of property subject to an outstanding debt by stockholders to their corporation is not treated as "boot," whether or not the corporation assumes liability for the indebtedness.[7] An exception is made for the transfer of property mortgaged in excess of its basis[8] or for the transfer of property which is in avoidance of income taxes.[9]

Example: A and B own income-producing real estate that has a depreciated basis to them of $80,000. The value of the property at the time of the transfer is $120,000. The property is transferred to the AB Corporation in exchange for 200 shares of its stock, 100 shares being issued to each stockholder. The property is burdened by a $30,000 mortgage which the AB Corporation agrees to assume.

Because A and B will own all of the stock of the corporation after the transfer, and because the transfer is made solely for stock, the exchange will qualify under Section 351. Accordingly, the corporation's basis for the property will be the $80,000 basis of A and B. And the basis of A and B for their stock will also be a total of $80,000, or $40,000 apiece.

Thus, the unrealized appreciation of $40,000 locked into the property is not realized by the transfer; the corporation acquires the stockholders' basis for the property for the purpose of its depreciation and for the purpose of determining its gain or loss on a subsequent disposition of the property.

Because the corporation takes over the basis of its stockholders for the property, neither Section 1245 nor Section 1250 will force the recognition of ordinary income or gain attributable to prior depreciation; the result will be different in any case in which gain is taxed on incorporation because of the receipt of "boot" or because of a failure to comply with Section 351. In such a case, depreciation recapture will convert all or a part of the gain into ordinary income.

2. Taxable Incorporation

If the parties to a potential incorporation are willing to pay a tax on the unrealized appreciation in the property to be transferred to a corporation, they may select an alternative method of handling the exchange. Accordingly, the corporation will acquire a new and higher basis for the purpose of measuring its depreciation allowance or for the purpose of determining its gain or loss on a subsequent disposition.

All that need be done is for the stockholders to redesign the exchange so that it will not qualify under Section 351. Stock in excess of 20 percent of the total voting stock, or of other classes of stock, may be issued to an outsider. Or the parties may receive their consideration from the corporation in terms of property other than stock or securities in excess of the total amount of the gain to be recognized.

Example: A and B own income-producing property which has a basis to them of $80,000 but a present value of $120,000. They wish to incorporate but desire that the corporation's basis for the property be stepped up to its fair market value. Corporation C is organized. Corporation C agrees to pay $40,000 in cash to A and B as well as to issue 100 shares of stock apiece to them for the property. After the property is transferred to it, Corporation C borrows $40,000 in cash on

---

[7] Sections 357(a), 1032, I.R.C.
[8] See discussion, Chapter 6, Part F, supra.
[9] Section 357(b), I.R.C.

the property, without liability to A and B,[10] and pays the money to them. The transaction would be a taxable exchange because A and B receive money in addition to their stock. Their gain would be computed as follows:

Consideration received:		
Value of stock issued	$80,000	
Cash received	40,000	$120,000
Less basis for property exchanged		80,000
Gain realized		$ 40,000
Amount of gain taxed:		
Boot received	$40,000	
Less excess of boot over gain	—0—	$ 40,000

Thus, the entire $40,000 gain on the transfer of the property would be taxed. The basis of the stock and the basis for the property would be as follows:

1. Stockholders' Basis for Stock

Basis for property	$ 80,000
Plus gain taxed on exchange	40,000
Total basis, including boot	$120,000
Less boot received	40,000
Basis for stock	$ 80,000

2. Corporation's Basis for Property

Stockholders' basis for property	$ 80,000
Plus gain taxed on exchange	40,000
Corporation's basis for property	$120,000

Unfortunately, losses cannot be similarly realized. Even if property is sold to a corporation for cash, the loss on the sale would be disallowed to owners of more than 50 percent of the stock of the corporation.[11]

3. "Thin" Incorporation

One of the principal disadvantages of the management and operation of property in the corporate form is the fact that the stockholders cannot recover their investment in the corporation without incurring substantial tax liability if the corporation has been profitable. Thus, in the absence of a liquidation of the corporate enterprise, any payments by the corporation to its stockholders will be treated as dividend income to them to the extent of the corporation's earnings and profits. These dividends will be non-deductible payments by the corporation, taxable as ordinary income to the stockholders.

Because of the disadvantages inherent in dividends, the stockholders may wish to take debt securities in place of shares of stock at the time of incorporation in payment for the property transferred to the corporation. Debt securities issued by the corporation

---

[10] If A and B are liable on the corporation's borrowing, the step transaction doctrine may attribute the borrowing to them prior to the exchange; if so, the corporation's basis would be their $80,000 for the property and no gain would be taxed.

[11] Section 267, I.R.C.

can be paid off as the repayment of principal to the creditor-stockholders without any tax consequence to either party.

A second advantage in the use of debt securities rather than stock is the tax treatment of interest paid out by the corporation on the principal amount of the debt. Interest so paid, although taxable to the creditor-stockholders as ordinary income, is deductible by the corporation as interest paid.

Example: A and B desire to incorporate certain income-producing property. The property has a value of $120,000. A and B exchange it for $60,000 worth of stock in Corporation C, plus $60,000 worth of the corporation's 10-year, 5 percent debentures. Because these debentures are considered to be "securities" within the meaning of Section 351, the exchange will be tax-free. Suppose, after a year or two of profitable operation, Corporation C decides to pay off $6,000 of the debentures as well as to pay dividends of $2,000 and interest of $2,700. Of the total of $10,700 paid, Corporation C is entitled to deduct the $2,700 paid as interest. The remainder is treated as a non-deductible payment of principal $6,000 and dividends of $2,000. Correspondingly, the stockholders would be required to report $4,700 as ordinary income ($2,700 interest and $2,000 dividends); the remainder would constitute the repayment of principal.

Had the property been exchanged for $120,000 worth of stock, the total $10,700 would have constituted a dividend to the stockholders (to the extent of the corporation's earnings and profits). As dividends, the $10,700 would have been non-deductible to the corporation in its entirety and taxable as ordinary income to the stockholders in its entirety. Obviously, the total tax burden imposed on both the corporation and the stockholders would be considerably more than if half of the consideration paid for the stockholders' property had been furnished as debt security rather than as stock.

Because of the tremendous tax advantages in using debt securities under these circumstances, the Commissioner scrutinizes such transactions with a great deal of care. If the amount of debt securities issued in the exchange is considerably greater than the stock issued, or if the debt securities are subordinated to the claims of other creditors, the Commissioner may challenge the standing of the debt securities as constituting a bona fide debt of the corporation. If the debt is overly topheavy, (that is, more than 2 or 3 to 1), or if the debt is of such a character that its repayment is unlikely, then it may be merely a second class of stock in disguise. This doctrine is the so-called "thin" incorporation doctrine. It gets its name from the fact that in most cases in which it is applicable, the margin of risk capital is very thin when compared to the debt structure of the corporation.

If the "thin" corporation doctrine is applicable, the debt owing to the stockholders will be treated as if it actually were stock. Any payments on principal would be taxed to the stockholders as dividends; and interest paid on the debt would not be deductible by the corporation, because this interest, in reality, represents the payment of additional dividends.

It is therefore necessary on the formation of a corporation which includes both a debt and an equity structure to make sure that, first, the ratio of debt to equity is not topheavy in favor of debt, and, second, that the debt is evidenced by instruments which indicate that the moneys lent to the corporation are not permanently devoted to the capital of the corporation. In other words, the debt instruments should call for the regular payment of interest, with provision for the repayment of principal as the corporation gets on its feet. And these requirements should be observed in actual operation of the corporation, so that the Commissioner cannot later claim that the owners of the corporation treated their debt interest just as if it were stock.

B. PROBLEMS OF OPERATION

Corporations engaged in business are subject to federal income taxes upon their net income; the rate of taxation imposed is 20 percent on the first $25,000, 22 percent on the next $25,000 of net income and 48 percent upon all excess income.[12]

In computing its net income, a corporation is allowed to take deductions for expenses similar to those allowable to business operated under other forms of ownership.[13] But the corporation is allowed no deduction for dividends paid to its stockholders. Thus, dividends paid by a corporation are subject to a double tax, once at the corporate level at corporate income tax rates and once at the stockholder level at personal income tax rates, less a small dividends received deduction.

Because of this double tax situation, a closely held business or investment corporation is ordinarily used for the purpose of accumulating earnings; its earnings are retained by it without distribution to its stockholders. In this manner, the stockholders hope to avoid or to minimize the tax at the personal level. As long as the corporation retains all of its earnings, no tax can be levied on the stockholders personally. Any appreciation in value of the stock due to the retention of corporate earnings is not taxed to the stockholders until they choose to realize the appreciation by a sale or other disposition of the stock. Then the appreciation will normally be realized as capital gains.

This type of planning for a closely held business or investment corporation is perfectly sound, but Congress has placed a number of hurdles in the path of its realization.

1. Accumulated Earnings Surtax

For instance, Congress has imposed an additional surtax upon corporations caught "improperly" accumulating surpluses. Section 531 imposes a surtax of 27-1/2 percent of the first $100,000 of accumulated taxable income and of 38-1/2 percent on all accumulated taxable income in excess of $100,000. These rates, being imposed on top of the ordinary corporate rate of 48 percent, are designed to be a penalty to force the distribution of earnings to stockholders as dividends subject to their personal income tax rates.

"Improperly" means that the tax applies only to a corporation "formed or availed of for the purpose of avoiding the income tax with respect to its shareholders . . . by permitting earnings and profits to accumulate instead of being divided or distrib-

---

[12] Section 11, I.R.C., effective December 23, 1975.
[13] See Chapter 3, *supra*.

PROBLEMS OF OPERATION 337

uted."[14] At least in theory a corporation can accumulate earnings without limit so long as a [15] purpose in so doing is not to avoid tax on the shareholders.

But Congress has erected formidable barriers to the realization of this theory. Section 533 raises a presumption that any accumulation in excess of the "reasonable needs of the business" is for the forbidden purpose. And the usual presumptions of correctness attached to a determination by the Commissioner remain.

In practice, the corporation faced with an accumulated earnings problem will usually have to be able to show that the accumulation was necessary to meet the reasonable, and the reasonably anticipated,[16] needs of the business in order to avoid or minimize the surtax. Nevertheless, there have been cases in which a corporation has been able to show that, despite substantial accumulations, it lacked the forbidden purpose, as where it was prevented from paying dividends by agreements with creditor banks,[17] state law,[18] or lack of distributable assets.[19] And lack of purpose to avoid tax on the shareholders is directly shown where the sole shareholder had losses which would have permitted dividends to be paid tax-free, enabling the shareholder to use up his losses.[20]

The penalty surtax is imposed upon only so much of the year's taxable income as is retained in excess of the corporation's needs; in the words of the statute, only "accumulated taxable income" is subject to the tax. "Accumulated taxable income" is defined to mean corporate taxable income "minus the sum of the dividends paid deduction . . . and the accumulated earnings credit. . . . "[21] Thus the corporation is entitled to deduct from its taxable income all the dividends paid to stockholders in the year for which the tax imposed for the purpose of determining its "accumulated taxable income."[22]

In this manner, the accumulated earnings surtax is designed to force the distribution of corporate earnings as dividends to stockholders. If earnings are not distributed, they become subject to an additional corporate surtax that may be as severe as the personal income tax imposed upon dividends.

But the definition of "accumulated taxable income" contains another exception. The corporation is entitled to deduct from its taxable income the amount of its "accumulated earnings credit" as well as the "dividends paid deduction." This credit expresses a philosphy diametrically opposed to that of the dividends paid deduction; it recognizes that a corporation has a right to accumulate its earnings for growth. And so,

---

[14] Section 532(a), I.R.C.
[15] Avoidance of tax on the shareholders need not be the dominant purpose; it is sufficient that it be one of the purposes of the accumulation. Trico Products Corp. v. Commissioner, 137 F.2d 424 (2nd Cir. 1943), cert. den. 320 U.S. 799.
[16] Section 537, I.R.C.
[17] Trico Securities Corporation, 41 B.T.A. 306, 317 (1940), non-acq. 1940-1 C.B. 9.
[18] William C. Atwater & Co., 10 T.C. 218, 251 (1948), acq. 1948-1 C.B. 1.
[19] Sauk Investment Co. 34 B.T.A. 732 (1936).
[20] Irvington Investments Co., 32 B.T.A. 1165 (1935), non-acq. XIV-2 C.B. 34.
[21] Section 535, I.R.C.
[22] Section 561, I.R.C. The possibility of consent dividends under Section 565, I.R.C., should not be overlooked.

if the accumulated earnings are within the amount of the credit, they are not subject to the penalty surtax.

The "accumulated earnings credit" is defined to be "an amount equal to such part of the retained earnings and profits for the taxable year as are retained for the reasonable needs of the business. . . ."[23]

The problem, then, is one of fact: when are earnings retained improperly, and when are they retained for the reasonable needs of the business? Only the Commissioner knows, and not even his judgment is final. Among the "reasonable" needs of the business are such matters as the need to finance expansion, the need to meet foreseeable contingencies, and the need to retire debt.[24]

Thus, if a real estate corporation is faced with the need of paying off a mortgage debt, the retention of earnings used to build up the equity of the corporation in the property would not be unreasonable. The use of earnings to pay off a mortgage debt on corporate property would thus be a shield against the imposition of the accumulated earnings surtax.

Regardless of the reasonable needs of the business, every corporation is entitled to accumulate up to $150,000 without penalty.[25] This minimum credit of $150,000 is designed to cover the normal needs of the small corporation; it is only when the accumulation exceeds $150,000 that the corporation can get into trouble under the penalty surtax.

The law further states that any accumulation by a "mere holding or investment company" in excess of $150,000 is deemed to be unreasonable. The term "mere holding or investment company" is defined in the regulations[26] in two parts. "A corporation having practically no activities except holding property and collecting the income therefrom or investing therein shall be considered a holding company." If, in addition to or instead of, merely holding property, the corporation buys and sells "stocks, securities, real estate or other investment properties . . . so that the income is derived . . . also from profits on market fluctuations" the corporation is an investment company for purposes of the accumulated earnings surtax. Thus, it is likely that a real estate corporation actively engaged in managing property would be permitted to retain earnings in excess of $150,000 without the imposition of the penalty surtax, provided the retention is for the reasonable needs of its business.

Ordinarily, the threat of the accumulated earnings surtax is one that will arise in the case of a closely held business corporation only after a number of years of successful operation. And, at the time that the threat becomes serious, the owners of the corporation can take steps to eliminate the possible imposition of the tax. Among other alternatives, they may (1) declare and pay dividends to the extent of the current net income after taxes, (2) sell their stock and thereby convert their interest in the corporation's net earnings, to the extent that they are reflected in an enhanced price for the

---

[23] Section 535(c)(1), I.R.C.
[24] Gazette Telegraph Co., 19 T.C. 692, 707 (1953), acq. 1954-2 C.B. 4, aff'd on another point, 209 F.2d 926 (10th Cir. 1954).
[25] Section 535(c)(2), I.R.C.
[26] Reg. Sec. 1.533-1(c). Here, again the net-net lease may be perilous. The lack of activity of the lessor is an indication it may be a mere holding or investment company.

stock, into capital gain, (3) liquidate the corporation, distribute the property to themselves, and operate the property as individuals, after paying a tax at capital gain rates on the increased value of the corporate property, or (4) file a Subchapter S election if available.

2. Personal Holding Company Tax

Section 541 of the Code imposes an additional corporate tax on certain corporations that can be classified as "personal holding companies." The tax is imposed upon the corporations' "undistributed personal holding company income." The rate of 70 percent imposed is deliberately set high to force corporations subject to the tax to distribute their personal holding company income to their shareholders as dividends.

Because the tax is imposed only upon "undistributed personal holding company income," it can be avoided by the declaration and payment of dividends to the stockholders. Under the statute, the income subject to the tax is the taxable income of the corporation less other income taxes paid, certain other adjustments, and the corporation's "dividends paid deduction."[27] The dividends paid deduction is designed to eliminate from taxable income the amount of dividends paid to stockholders during the year.[28] Under the Code a "personal holding company" is defined as a corporation which meets the following conditions:[29]

(1) 60 percent or more of its *ordinary gross* income is personal holding company income; and

(2) More than 50 percent in value of its outstanding stock is owned by fewer than six individuals.[30] Thus the penalty tax is restricted in its possible application to corporations whose stock is held fairly closely.

"Personal holding company income" is defined to include the following types of income.[31]

(1) Dividends;
(2) Interest;
(3) Royalties (mineral, oil, gas, or copyright royalties are included only if the adjusted ordinary income therefrom is less than 50 percent of the corporation's ordinary gross income, or if the copyright is owned by a shareholder);
(4) Annuities;
(5) Certain produced film rents;
(6) Personal service contract payments;
(7) Rents received for the use of property from a stockholder who owns at least 25 percent in value of the corporation's outstanding stock; and
(8) Rents, if the adjusted income therefrom constitutes less than 50 percent of the corporation's ordinary gross income.

---

[27]Section 545, I.R.C.
[28]Section 561, I.R.C. The possibilities of consent dividends or a dividend carryover under Section 561 and of a deficiency dividend under Section 547 should not be overlooked.
[29]Section 542, I.R.C.
[30]For this purpose the constructive ownership rules of Section 544, I.R.C., must be applied.
[31]Section 543, I.R.C.

Prior to the enactment of the Revenue Act of 1964, it was fairly easy to keep a corporation engaged in rental real estate activities from being classified as a personal holding company subject to the penalty surtax. But the amendments adopted in 1964 make this problem much more difficult. The major reason for this change is because the test for determining whether or not rents constitute personal holding company income is now based on the requirement that the *adjusted income from rents* exceed 50 percent of the corporation's *adjusted ordinary gross income*. Formerly, the test was merely whether or not gross rents exceeded the corporation's gross income from other sources; if it did, the rents were not personal holding company income.

The definition of *adjusted income from rents* is gross rents less (1) depreciation taken, (2) property taxes, (3) interest paid, and (4) rents paid to others.[32] The deduction of these charges from gross rents reduces the figure to an amount scarcely larger than net rentals because these four classes of expenses normally comprise the bulk of the deductions directly attributable to rental properties. This net figure (adjusted income from rents) must exceed the adjusted ordinary gross income of the corporation from all other sources; if it is less than the ordinary gross income from other sources, the rental income will be classed as personal holding company income.

Example: Investors, Inc., a corporation owned directly or indirectly by five individuals, is engaged in the business of owning and operating apartment and office buildings. In addition it has invested substantial sums of money in stocks and securities. In 1963, Investors, Inc., realized $30,000 dividend income and $300,000 gross rental income. The interest, real property taxes, and depreciation charged to the rental properties were $280,000. Despite the fact that dividend income exceeded net rental income, the corporation was not a personal holding company *for 1963* because *gross rentals* exceeded 50 percent of the corporation's gross income. But if we extend these same facts to 1964, we find that Investors, Inc. has willy-nilly become a personal holding company *for 1964*.

	Adjusted ordinary gross income	*Adjusted income from rents*
Gross income from rents	$300,000	$300,000
Dividends	30,000	
Gross income	$330,000	
Less adjustments for interest, real property taxes and depreciation	$280,000	$280,000
Total	$ 50,000	$ 20,000

Because the adjusted income from rents ($20,000) does not constitute 50 percent or more of adjusted ordinary gross income (50 percent of $50,000), the $20,000 adjusted income from rents constitutes personal holding company income. Because the $30,000 in dividends is also personal holding company income, the corporation is a personal holding company for 1964. More than 60 percent of its income, in fact 100 percent, is personal holding company income.

---

[32] Section 543(b)(2), I.R.C. The above definition is oversimplified. The deductions stated above are offset against gross rents only "to the extent allocable, under regulations prescribed by the Secretary or his delegate, to such gross income from rents. Furthermore, gross rents need not be reduced by depreciation taken on tangible personal property "which is not customarily retained by any one lessee for more than three years."

PROBLEMS OF OPERATION

But this is not all. Even if the adjusted income from rents exceeds 50 percent of adjusted ordinary gross income, the adjusted income from rents may still be classified as personal holding company income. Rental income, regardless of its size, automatically becomes personal holding company income to a corporation in any case in which the corporation (1) has *other* personal holding company income and (2) fails to pay out to stockholders a dividend equal to (or in excess of) the amount by which the *other* personal holding company income exceeds 10 percent of its ordinary gross income.

Example: Let us suppose that for 1965 Investors, Inc. adjusts its affairs and manages to cut its charges for interest, real estate taxes, and depreciation from $280,000 to $260,000. If we assume gross rentals of $300,000 and dividends of $30,000, we find that Investors, Inc. meets the 50 percent test. Its adjusted income from rents exceeds 50 percent of its adjusted ordinary gross income, as follows:

	Adjusted ordinary gross income	Adjusted income from rents
Gross income from rents	$300,000	$300,000
Dividends	30,000	
Gross income	$330,000	
Less adjustments for interest, real property taxes and depreciation	260,000	260,000
Total	$ 70,000	$ 40,000

Because $40,000 is more than 50 percent of $70,000, the rents are presumably not personal holding company income. But to ensure this conclusion, we must see if the corporation is required to pay out any dividends. The dividends paid out to stockholders must be equal to (or exceed) the amount by which the other personal holding company income exceeds 10 percent of the corporation's ordinary gross income. The above table shows that the corporation's ordinary gross income is $330,000. 10 percent of this amount is $33,000. Because the dividend income of the corporation ($30,000) is less than 10 percent of its ordinary gross income, no dividends need be paid.

On the other hand, had the dividend income been $39,000, some $6,000 of dividends would be required to be paid to stockholders or else the rental income, even though in excess of 50 percent of adjusted ordinary gross income, would be classed as personal holding company income. The amount of the minimum dividend required to be paid is the amount by which the dividend income ($39,000) exceeds 10 percent of ordinary gross income. Thus, the minimum dividend required to be paid out is $6,000, the amount by which $39,000 exceeds $33,000 (10 percent of $330,000).

Obviously, the foregoing rules will have a substantial impact on the use of real estate corporations to shelter other types of personal holding company income from the penalty surtax. A real estate corporation devoted almost exclusively to real estate operations will be untouched by the foregoing changes, provided it carefully controls the amounts of income received from interest, dividends, and other non-rental sources. Gains realized from sales of properties will not cause any problem, provided the property sold is a capital asset or is property held for use in the taxpayer's trade or business.

But if property is sold which gives rise to ordinary income, then the corporation may fall into the personal holding company category because the income from the sale exceeds the adjusted income from rents. If other personal holding company income is present, we may find that the penalty surtax is applicable. Accordingly, the perennial controversy between the Commissioner and the taxpayer on whether a sale gave rise to capital (or Section 1231) gain or to ordinary income appears to have spread to another area of conflict.

3. Treatment of Dividends Paid

As we have stated, and dividends paid out of current earnings are taxed to the stockholders as dividend income, subject to a small dividends received deduction.[33] The same rule is applicable to a dividend paid out of accumulated earnings that have been retained by a corporation from its income in prior years.[34]

Thus, even if a corporation has no current income in the taxable year, a distribution of money or property will constitute a dividend if earnings and profits have been carried over from prior years. But if the corporation has neither current income nor accumulated earnings and profits, the payment of cash or property to a stockholder will be treated as a payment in partial liquidation of the corporation. The amount received will be applied first to reduce the stockholder's basis for his stock; any amount received in excess of his basis will be reportable by him as gain realized on the sale or exchange of his stock.[35]

Example: A incorporated his real estate holdings several years ago. In the current year, A's corporation had no net income. However it had earnings and profits of $10,000 accumulated for prior years. A's basis for his stock is $120,000. The corporation declares a distribution of $24,000 to him. How will this payment by reported by A?

Total amount paid		$24,000
Less amount paid out of earnings and profits:		
Current earnings	$ —0—	
Accumulated earnings	10,000	10,000
Amount applied against A's basis for his stock		$14,000
Amount taxed as dividend		$10,000

A's basis for his stock would therefore be reduced to $106,000.

4. Treatment of Distributions Out of Accelerated Depreciation Reserves

Prior to the enactment of the Tax Reform Act of 1969, the accelerated methods of depreciation then generally available were frequently not only used to shelter corporate real estate profits from tax but were also used to provide a source of funds from which tax-free distributions could be made. This latter benefit would be available, of course, only in cases in which the corporation had neither current nor accumulated earnings and profits.

Example: A group of individuals incorporated for $200,000 cash. No gain or loss was recognized on the incorporation because it was solely for cash and only stock and securities were

---

[33] Sections 316, 34, 116, I.R.C.
[34] Section 316(a)(2), I.R.C.
[35] Section 301(c), I.R.C.

issued to the investors. The $200,000 was used as a down payment on a new apartment building which qualified for 200 percent declining-balance depreciation. The total cost of the apartment to the corporation was $1,200,000 of which $1,000,000 was properly allocable to improvements. Annual depreciation on a straight-line basis over 40 years would have been $25,000 a year, or $100,000 in the first four years of ownership. The corporation elected double-declining-balance depreciation and took $185,590 of depreciation. During the same four year period, the corporation earned $30,000 a year after all expenses (including interest and taxes) but *before* depreciation. Hence in none of the first four years did it report a profit for tax purposes. Depreciation deductions of $185,590 effectively offset the $120,000 of cash income before depreciation.

Prior to the Tax Reform Act of 1969, in each of the first four years the directors of the corporation could distribute $30,000, (the amount by which the cash income exceeded taxable income) to the shareholders and the distribution would be received tax-free by them. Why? The corporation had neither current nor accumulated earnings. The only effect of the distribution would be a reduction in each shareholder's basis for his stock to the extent of the distribution received by him.[36]

But the Tax Reform Act of 1969 has changed this result. Now the *excess* of accelerated depreciation over straight-line depreciation is to be taken into account in computing the current (and accumulated) earnings and profits of a corporation. The excess is still deductible to reduce the corporation's taxable income, but the excess must be added to earnings and profits.[37] Because earnings and profits determine whether or not a distribution is taxable as a dividend, the result may be a surprise dividend to the shareholders. The fact that the corporation has no taxable income will no longer prevent the distribution from being taxable as a dividend.

Example: Take the facts of the preceding example. In each of the four years, the excess of cash income over expenses is $30,000. Let us assume $30,000 of cash is distributed in *each* of the first four years of the corporation's existence. What result?

In the first year $25,000 of the $30,000 is taxable as a dividend. Why? Accelerated depreciation is $50,000, which exceeds straight-line depreciation of $25,000 by exactly that amount $25,000.

In the second year, the dividend portion of the distribution is $22,500 (excess of accelerated depreciation of $47,500 over $25,000). The third year, the dividend portion is $20,174 (excess of $45,174 accelerated depreciation over $25,000) and in the fourth year, the dividend portion of the $30,000 cash distribution is $17,916 (the excess of the accelerated depreciation deduction of $42,916 over $25,000 straight-line depreciation).

Of the $120,000 previously distributed tax-free, $85,590 has become a taxable dividend.

Accelerated depreciation may still be used to shelter taxable income (except to the extent it is a tax preference item), but it cannot be used to shelter tax-free distribution from a corporation.

This provision applies to excess depreciation on both personal and real property.

5. Treatment of Distribution of "Excess F.H.A. Mortgage Proceeds"

As we saw above, a distribution of money or property by a corporation before it has realized any income is not taxable as a dividend.[38] On the basis of this rule, there has grown up a practice of distributing out to stockholders the excess of money

---

[36] Section 301(c)(2), I.R.C.
[37] Section 312(m), effective June 30, 1972.
[38] This statement is subject to the possible application of the "collapsible corporation" rules outlined below.

borrowed by the corporation over the cost of a construction project; if this distribution is made before any income is earned by the corporation, the distribution is not taxable as a dividend.

The practice would take a form something like the following transaction. A group of owners first transfers a parcel of undeveloped land to a corporation. The corporation, as owner of the land, submits a proposal for the development of the property to the Federal Housing Authority for approval. After obtaining the necessary F.H.A. guarantee, the corporation borrows the estimated cost of construction from a private lending institution, the loan being secured both by a first mortgage on the property and by the F.H.A. guarantee. If the construction is completed more economically than the estimate, the corporation would have surplus cash on hand on completion of the project. This cash would then be distributed to stockholders in a taxable year before any profits were earned by the corporation. Because the distribution was not made from earnings and profits, the amount of the excess mortgage proceeds would be received by the stockholders as a tax-free distribution reducing their basis for their stock.

In the 1954 Code, provision was made to halt this practice. If a distribution is made of excess mortgage proceeds which have been secured, guaranteed, or made by a federal agency, the distribution itself will create earnings and profits. At the time of the distribution, earnings and profits are treated as increased by the excess of the mortgage loan over the corporation's adjusted basis for the property. Thus, the distribution itself would be taxed as a dividend because it was made out of these artificially created earnings and profits.[39]

Example: A, B, and C organize a corporation and transfer unimproved real property to it which has a cost basis of $50,000. The corporation borrows $1,000,000 on the strength of an F.H.A. guarantee. If we assume that $850,000 of the loan is used to build an apartment project the corporation's total basis for the completed project will be $900,000. In this event, if $100,000 of the excess mortgage proceeds are distributed to A, B and C, the distribution would be treated as a taxable dividend. At the time the $100,000 is distributed, the corporation's earnings and profits would be increased by $100,000. Immediately after the distribution, which is taxed as a dividend, the corporation's earnings and profits would be reduced correspondingly by $100,000.[40]

6. Dividend in Kind

Suppose a real estate corporation declares a dividend to stockholders payable in property other than money. How will the dividend be treated? If the value of the property exceeds its basis to the corporation, does the corporation realize a gain? And what will be the measure of the dividend to stockholders?

Let us first assume that the value of the property distributed is not in excess of the corporation's current and accumulated earnings and profits. Under these circumstances, the fair market value of the property at the time of the distribution is taxed as dividend income in full to the stockholders.[41] And, as a corollary, the stockholders' basis for the distributed property is equal to its fair market value.[42] If the property is

---

[39] Section 312(j), I.R.C.
[40] Reg. Sec. 1.312-12, Example.
[41] Section 301(b)(1)(A), I.R.C. The rule in the case of a corporate shareholder may be different.
[42] Section 301(d)(1), I.R.C.

PROBLEMS OF OPERATION 345

distributed subject to a liability, the stockholders are entitled to reduce the value of the property by the amount of the liability for the purpose of measuring their dividend; but their basis for the property is its full value, including the amount of the outstanding liability.[43]

Under these facts, no gain is realized by the corporation on the distribution, provided the property is not distributed in satisfaction of a liability to pay a previously declared cash dividend.[44] Gain, however, will be realized on the distribution of property which is mortgaged in an amount in excess of its basis to the corporation. The amount of the gain under these peculiar circumstances is measured by the excess of the liability against the property over its basis to the corporation.[45] Ordinary income will also be realized to the extent of post-1962 depreciation taken on personal property distributed, or to the extent of the difference between the corporation's basis and the value of the property, if this difference is less than post-1962 depreciation.[46]

But let us assume that the corporation's earnings and profits are not sufficient to cover the entire value of the property to be distributed. Is any adjustment to be made to corporate earnings and profits to reflect the excess of the value of the property over its basis to the corporation? *No*.

Section 312(a) of the 1954 Code clarified this previously muddy area. The property distributed will be taxed as a dividend to the stockholders only to the extent of the available corporate earnings and profits. Thus, the excess of the fair market value of the distributed property over existing earnings and profits will be received as a distribution of capital to be applied in reduction of the stockholders' basis for their stock. In other words, the only adjustment to be made to corporate earnings and profits on such a distribution will be a reduction to the extent of the adjusted basis of the property at the time of distribution.[47]

Example: Corporation C owns, among other assets, an apartment worth $80,000 having an adjusted basis of $30,000. It has accumulated earnings and profits of only $40,000 and has no prospect of any net income in the taxable year. Corporation C distributes the apartment to its stockholders.

1. Effect on Stockholders

Amount of distribution (value of property)	$80,000
Amount taxed as dividend (C's earnings and profits)	40,000
Amount applied against basis for stock	$40,000

2. Effect on Corporation

Accumulated earnings and profits	$40,000
Decrease for distribution (adjusted basis for property distributed)	(30,000)
Accumulated earnings and profits after distribution	$10,000

Thus, if a corporation has only a small amount of earnings and profits, it can normally effect a tax saving by distributing property appreciated in value over its basis

---

[43] Section 301(b)(2),(d), I.R.C.

[44] Section 311(a), I.R.C. But a dividend made payable only in certain property is a dividend in kind and does not result in recognition of gain to the corporation. Natural Gasoline Corp., 21 T.C. 439 (1953), aff'd 219 F.2d 682 (10th Cir. 1955).

[45] Section 311(c), I.R.C.

[46] Section 1245, I.R.C. A similar rule appears in Section 1250.

[47] Reg. Sec. 1.312-1(b).

instead of selling the property and then distributing the proceeds. The property would be taxed only to the extent of available earnings and profits; the remainder would be received in reduction of basis of stock.

C. PROBLEMS OF SALES AND LIQUIDATIONS

The chief problem on the sale of property held by a corporation is the double tax that is imposed on the gain realized if the proceeds are distributed to the stockholders as a dividend. For this reason, two courses of action are normally followed: either the sales proceeds are retained by the corporation, or the sale is handled in liquidation of the corporation in such manner that the only tax imposed upon the gain is the tax at the stockholder level. Or, as another alternative, the stockholders may sell their stock and effect an indirect realization of the corporation's appreciated properties through the receipt of an enhanced sales price for their stock.

1. Sale of Stock

Suppose the stockholders decide to sell their stock in the corporation. On the sale of the stock only one tax will be imposed. The stockholders will be required to pay a tax on the difference between their basis for their stock and the proceeds realized on the sale. And, if the stock has been held for more than six months, the gain realized will be taxed as long-term capital gain.

Example: A incorporates a parcel of real estate. The real estate has a basis to him of $20,000. The incorporation is made as a tax-free exchange and, therefore, A's stock has a basis of $20,000. The corporation borrows money to construct an apartment which has a cost of $80,000. After several years of successful operation, the apartment is worth $120,000, less a $30,000 mortgage debt. A then sells his stock to B for a price of $90,000, which reflects the increased value of the corporation's assets. No tax is incurred by the corporation on the sale. A's gain, treated as long-term capital gain, would be computed as follows:

Proceeds received on sale of stock	$90,000
Less basis for stock	20,000
Gain realized on sale	$70,000

Obviously, the sale of stock method of realizing a gain on a corporation's appreciated assets is a valuable method to the seller. But the purchaser may be chary of buying the stock for a number of reasons. For example, he may not wish to assume A's possible liabilities as a successor stockholder. And he may not be happy with the prospect of buying stock in a corporation that has a substantial amount of accumulated earnings and profits which would prevent distributions to him at other than ordinary income tax rates. Similarly, he may not want to be saddled with substantial amounts of depreciation recapture should he decide to liquidate the corporation. So the prospective buyer will usually offer to take the stock only at a substantial discount from its appraised value.

Also, the seller himself must beware of the possible application of the so-called "collapsible corporation" rules, which, if applicable, would convert his gain into ordinary income.

2. Collapsible Corporation Rules Applied to Sales of Stock

Because of the frequent use of the device of selling a corporation's stock in order to realize in part the appreciation in value of the corporation's assets at capital gain rates, Congress adopted a special provision, now Section 341, to try to prevent any misuse of the device. Thus, if the appreciation in value was due to assets which if sold by the corporation would produce ordinary income, the gain realized by the stockholders is similarly to be treated as ordinary income.[48]

In the case of a sale of stock, Section 341 becomes applicable only if the unrealized appreciation in the corporation's "ordinary income" assets exceeds 15 percent of the corporation's net worth.[49] These "ordinary income" assets include property held by the corporation in the nature of inventory. Trade or business property is not ordinarily included, except under certain special circumstances.[50]

Obviously, then, the collapsible corporation rules should not apply to the sale of stock of a corporation engaged in the business of leasing or renting real estate.[51] Hence, the sale of stock by a stockholder under such circumstances should be entitled to be treated as a transaction giving rise to capital gain or loss.

But an exception exists for situations in which an owner of property attempts to insulate himself from the status of a dealer in real estate by selling stock in a corporation owning real property rather than by selling the real property itself. The definition of "ordinary income" property is broadened to include not only inventory property of the corporation but also trade or business property of the corporation which would be inventory property if held by the selling stockholder. This expanded definition of "ordinary income" property is applicable only to stockholders who own more than 5 percent in value of a corporation's outstanding stock.[52]

Thus, a dealer in real property may not hope to escape the disadvantages of his status by incorporation. A sale by a real estate dealer, at a gain, of stock in a corporation engaged in rental or leasing activities would result in the realization of ordinary income, provided the percentage requirements of ownership and of assets are met.

Nor can a non-dealer preserve his status by incorporating several real estate corporations for the purpose of selling stock rather than real property. A sale of stock by a stockholder owning more than 20 percent in value of the outstanding stock of more than one corporation within a three-year period will be treated as a sale of underlying assets for the purpose of determining the stockholder's status as dealer or investor on subsequent stock sales.[53]

And if non-dealers make the mistake of including a dealer in real property among the stockholders of a real estate corporation, they may pay dearly for their mistake. The dealer status of a stockholder owning more than 20 percent of a corporation's outstanding stock will characterize the holding of any real property of the corporation as

---

[48]Section 341(a), I.R.C.
[49]Section 341(e)(1), I.R.C.
[50]Section 341 (e)(5), I.R.C.
[51]Other than in the case of a sale of stock by a stockholder who owns more than 20 percent in value of the outstanding stock to a related person. Section 341(c)(1), I.R.C.
[52]Section 341(e)(1)(B), I.R.C.
[53]Section 341(e)(1)(C), I.R.C. Certain percentage limitations are applied under the statute.

"ordinary income" assets, not only to the dealer-stockholder himself but also to all other stockholders.[54]

If the corporation is engaged in the business of developing and selling real estate, its land holdings will constitute property "held primarily for sale to customers in the ordinary course of its trade or business."[55] If such property has been held by the corporation for less than three years since its acquisition or improvement, the corporation will be in danger of being held to be a collapsible corporation if it was "formed or availed of principally" for the improvement or purchase of the property "with a view to the sale or exchange of stock by its shareholders (whether in liquidation or otherwise), or a distribution to its shareholders, before the realization by the corporation . . . of a substantial part of the taxable income to be derived from such property . . ."[56]

Presumptively, a corporation is a collapsible corporation if its "ordinary income assets" equal 50 percent or more in value of its total assets and the value of its "ordinary income assets" is 120 percent or more of their basis to the corporation.[57]

Under these circumstances, a stockholder runs a grave risk of having the gain realized on a sale of his stock taxed as ordinary income.[58] His gain will be taxed as ordinary income if the following four conditions are present:[59]

(1) He owns, directly or indirectly, more than 5 percent in value of the corporation's outstanding stock;

(2) The corporation has not itself realized a substantial part of the taxable income to be derived from its Section 341 property;

(3) More than 70 percent of the total gain realized is attributable to the "ordinary income assets" owned by the corporation; and

(4) The sale of stock is made within three years of the date of acquisition or improvement of the property being held by the corporation for sale to customers in the ordinary course of trade or business.

All that can be done under these circumstances is to postpone the sale of stock until more than three years after the date of the acquisition or improvement of the corporation's property. Alternatively, the sale of stock can be postponed until after the corporation has realized "substantially" all, or a substantial part, of the gain attributable to the property by its sale to customers. If, for example, the bulk of the corporation's property held for sale to customers is sold prior to the stockholder's sale of stock, less than 70 percent of his gain on the stock sale will be attributable to the corporation's "ordinary income assets;" hence the gain on his stock will qualify for capital gain treatment.

Or, finally, the corporation can consent, by formal election with Internal Revenue Service under Section 341(f), to have all of its dispositions of property treated as a

---

[54] Section 341(e)(5)(A)(i), I.R.C.
[55] Section 341(b)(3)(B), I.R.C.
[56] Section 341(b)(1)(A), I.R.C.
[57] Section 341(c), I.R.C.
[58] Section 341(a)(1), I.R.C.
[59] Section 341(d), I.R.C.

sale for fair market value, giving rise to capital gain or ordinary income as the case may be. In this manner, the corporation will ultimately realize the complete gain or income in the appreciated assets regardless of the date on which a shareholder may have sold his stock. But by making the election, the corporation will be denied the benefits of the normal tax exemption on such dispostions of property as, for example, on liquidation (Section 336), on sales during liquidation (Section 337), on liquidations in one calendar month (Section 333). Because the corporation is forced to recognize ultimately the gain or income inherent in the property, there is no reason to convert the selling stockholder's capital gain into ordinary income.

3. Liquidation of Corporation and Sale of Property by Stockholders

Another method for selling corporate property without incurring a double tax liability is for the corporation to liquidate and to distribute its property to its stockholders, to be followed by a sale of the property by the stockholders. If the steps are carefully followed, the only tax that will be imposed is a tax at the stockholder level.[60]

The first step is the liquidation of the corporation and the distribution of its properties in kind to the stockholders. The corporation will incur no tax on the liquidating distribution.[61] The stockholders will be compelled to report the difference between their basis and the value of the money and other property received as gain or loss realized on the sale or exchange of the stock.[62] If the stock has been held for more than six months, the gain or loss will be treated as long-term capital gain or loss.

The stockholders then hold title to property having a basis equal to its fair market value.[63] If they then sell the property to another party for a price equal to its value, they will incur no further gain on which to be taxed. Thus, the entire appreciation in value in the property is taxed but once, at the time of the distribution in liquidation.

Example: A owns all of the stock of Corporation C. Corporation C's sole asset is an apartment worth $100,000, which has a basis to the corporation of $30,000. A wishes to liquidate his interest in the apartment. He therefore causes the corporation to be liquidated and the apartment distributed to him. If he has a basis for his stock of $30,000, his gain would be computed as follows:

Value of assets distributed	$100,000
Less basis for stock	30,000
Gain taxed on distribution	$ 70,000

A then places the apartment on the market. After several months he sells it to B for a net price of $105,000. His gain would be computed as follows:

Proceeds received on sale	$105,000
Less basis for apartment	100,000
Gain taxed on sale	$ 5,000

---

[60] United States v. Cumberland Public Service Co., 338 U.S. 451 (1950).

[61] Section 336, I.R.C. But it will have ordinary income to the extent of post-1962 depreciation taken on personal property distributed, (See Section 1245, I.R.C.), and to excess depreciation on real estate. Section 1250.

[62] Section 331, I.R.C.

[63] Section 334(a), I.R.C.

But here again we must be cautious of the possible application of the collapsible corporation rules. If the rules are applicable, A's gain on the liquidating distribution will be converted, in part at least, into ordinary income.

4. Sale of Property in Section 337 Liquidation

Section 337 of the 1954 Code added a new provision to permit a corporation in liquidation, as well as the stockholders, to sell corporate property without incurring the burden of a corporate tax on the sale. Obviously, if the corporate tax could readily be avoided by a distribution of the property to the stockholders before sale, there seemed little reason for Congress to continue to insist that a sale in liquidation by the corporation itself was subject to corporate tax. The distinction between the two types of sale is wholly formal; if the corporation is in the process of liquidation, the sale is actually being made for the benefit of the stockholders to whom the proceeds are to be distributed.

Accordingly, Section 337 permits a sale of property made by a corporation to be free of any corporate tax liability (except recapture of depreciation under Sections 1245 and 1250) if the following conditions are met:

(1) The corporation has adopted a plan of complete liquidation before the sale;

(2) The sale is made during the twelve-month period immediately following the adoption of the plan of liquidation;

(3) All of the assets of the corporation (including the sale proceeds) are in fact distributed to stockholders within the 12 months following the adoption of the plan; and

(4) The property sold is other than its inventory, or installment obligations.[64]

If these conditions are met, no gain or loss will be recognized to the corporation on a sale of property. However, in 1962 Congress enacted an exception to this rule. Section 1245 provides that the *corporation* realizes ordinary income on the sale of personal property to the extent of post-1962 depreciation taken (but limited to the difference between sales price + basis) even when the sale is made in a Section 337 liquidation. A similar exception was made for depreciation recapture under Section 1250.

Gain or loss will also be recognized at the stockholder level at the time of the distribution of the corporation's assets to them; they will report a gain or loss measured by the difference between their basis for their stock and the fair market value of the property distributed to them by the corporation, including the proceeds received on the corporate sale.

Thus, the same benefits are available to stockholders under a Section 337 liquidation and sale procedure as are made available to them if the property is first distributed to them and the sale is then made by the stockholders. Correspondingly, in neither situation can the corporation avoid depreciation recapture.

---

[64]An exception is made for bulk sales of inventory. Section 337(b)(2), I.R.C. For example, a sale of subdivided lots in bulk qualified for non-recognition of gain. The selling corporation was not a collapsible corporation. Jeanese, Inc. v. United States, 341 F.2d 502 (9th Cir. 1965); see Luff Co., The, 44 T.C. 532 (1965), acq. 1965-2 C.B. 5.

PROBLEMS OF SALES AND LIQUIDATIONS

Example: A owns all of the stock of Corporation C. Corporation C's sole asset is an unfurnished apartment which has a basis to the corporation of $30,000. A causes the corporation to adopt a plan of liquidation, and thereafter it sells the property to B for $105,000. Corporation C distributes the sales proceeds to A within 12 months of the adoption of the plan of liquidation. Because the sale and liquidation qualify under Section 337, Corporation C distributes the sales proceeds to A within 12 months of the adoption of the plan of liquidation. Because the sale and liquidation qualify under Section 337, Corporation C is not taxed on the gain realized on the sale. But A is taxed on the difference between the value of the distribution received and the basis for his stock. If we assume his basis to be $30,000, his gain would be computed as follows:

Value of assets distributed	$105,000
Less basis for stock	30,000
Gain taxed on distribution	$ 75,000

If the apartment contains furniture on which C had taken $2,000 of depreciation in 1963 or thereafter, C must report ordinary income of $2,000 in the year of sale despite the fact that the sale qualified under Section 337.[65]

Obviously, Section 337 will serve a useful purpose in the case of small real estate corporations engaged in the business of renting or leasing property. But it may also serve a useful purpose in the case of real estate corporations engaged in the business of developing and selling real estate. In this latter case, the real estate held by a corporation will be in the nature of inventory property, that is, property held primarily for sale to customers in the ordinary course of business. But if the real estate is sold in bulk to one purchaser at one time, the sale, if made during the course of liquidation, will qualify for tax exemption under Section 337.[66]

If the sale can be so qualified for exemption, one of the more difficult problems of a real estate development corporation will be eliminated. Prior to the adoption of Section 337, there was substantial conflict among the courts as to whether or not a real estate dealer could qualify a sale of real estate for capital gain treatment even though the sale was being made as part of a program of liquidation of its holdings. Section 337 may now provide the key; if the sale is made in liquidation of substantially all of the property to one person at one time, it will be exempt from the corporate tax; and upon distribution of the proceeds of the sale to the stockholders, the stockholders are entitled to report the amount received on distribution as amounts received in exchange for their stock.

But the possible application of the "collapsible corporation" rules to this type of transaction should be carefully scrutinized before its use is advised. If the corporation is collapsible within the meaning of Section 341, Section 337 is not available to it.[67]

5. Distribution of Property in "One Month Liquidation"

Under Section 333, an alternative is provided to the normal rules of distribution and liquidation. As we have stated previously, a distribution in complete liquidation is

---

[65] Section 1245 does not apply to "a building or its structural components" but this exception does not reach ordinary furniture. If accelerated depreciation had been taken on the building, there may also be depreciation recapture under Section 1250.

[66] Section 337(b)(2), I.R.C.; See Reg. Sec. 1.337-3. Jeanese, Inc. v. Commissioner, 341 F.2nd 502 (9th Cir. 1965).

[67] Section 337(c)(1), I.R.C.

treated as an exchange of the money and property distributed for the stockholders' stock. Thus, the difference between the value of the property distributed and the stockholders' basis for their stock is capital gain or loss. And the stockholders take the fair market value of the property as their basis for the property received in the liquidation.

But Section 333 provides an elective method of distribution property out of a corporation without paying tax on the gain represented by the excess of the value of the property to be received over the stockholders' basis for their stock. The stockholders merely take over the property of the corporation, substituting their basis for their stock for their basis for the property. Adjustment to basis is made for any money received or gain taxed on the liquidation.

Apparently the corporation will be forced to recognize ordinary income up to the amount of post-1962 depreciation taken on personal property distributed, under Section 1245. Since this gain will be taxed to the corporation rather than the shareholder, the latter will not be entitled to a basis adjustment on account of the recognition of Section 1245 gain.[68]

In order for the liquidation of a corporation and the distribution of its assets to be treated in this manner, certain procedures set up in Section 333 must be religiously followed:

(1) The liquidation must be made pursuant to a plan of complete liquidation, in which all of the stock is to be redeemed or canceled;

(2) All of the assets of the corporation must be distributed to the stockholders within the calendar month in which the plan is adopted;

(3) The first distribution must follow, not precede, the adoption of the plan;

(4) At least 80 percent of the stockholders must file the necessary election required by the regulations within thirty days after the adoption of the plan of liquidation.[69]

If these conditions are met, the electing stockholders are entitled to treat the liquidation distribution as a tax-free transaction, except to the extent of the corporation's earnings and profits to the date of liquidation. To the extent of each stockholder's ratable share of the corporation's earnings and profits, he will be required to report his gain on the distribution as a dividend, subject to tax as ordinary income.

The remainder of the gain realized on the distribution is not recognized for tax purposes unless the amount of money, stock, and securities[70] distributed to a stockholder exceeds his ratable share of the corporation's accumulated earnings and profits. If a stockholder does receive an amount of money, stock, and securities in excess of his share of corporate earnings, an additional amount of the gain realized on the total distribution will be recognized. To the extent of the amount of money, stock, and securities not covered by the dividend, the remainder of the gain will be taxed as capital gain.[71]

---

[68] Section 334(c), I.R.C. Section 1250 may also force recapture of accelerated depreciation of real estate to the corporation.

[69] Reg. Sec. 1.333-3.

[70] If acquired by the corporation after December 31, 1962, Section 333(e)(2), I.R.C. This portion of the gain (in excess of the corporation's earnings and profits) can readily be avoided; all that the corporation need do is to invest the surplus cash, stock or securities in real estate prior to the liquidation.

[71] The rule is different for corporate stockholders. Section 333(f), I.R.C.

PROBLEMS OF SALES AND LIQUIDATIONS

The rules of Section 333 are designed to prevent two things: (1) the stockholders liquidating a corporation with accumulated earnings and profits without paying a tax on the accumulated earnings as if a dividend had been declared, and (2) the stockholders causing a corporation to convert its properties into liquid assets (money, stock, or securities) and then distributing these current assets to the stockholders without there being a tax imposed upon the distribution.

Obviously, these rules restrict the use of the Section 333 cases to situations in which a corporation has little or no accumulated earnings and profits and owns a property that has substantially appreciated in value. In other words, the situation must be such that it is less expensive to pay a dividend tax on a relatively small amount of earnings and profits than to pay a capital gain tax on a relatively large amount of property appreciation.

Once the property has been distributed to the stockholders, their basis for the property received is equal to their basis for their stock;

(1) Increased by the amount of any gain taxed to the stockholders in the liquidation; and

(2) Decreased by the amount of any money received in the liquidation.[72]

Example: Three individuals, A, B, and C own all of the stock of the ABC corporation. The total basis for their stock is $150,000. ABC corporation has assets totaling $405,000, of which $75,000 is cash, $90,000 is stock and securities acquired after December 31, 1962, and $240,000 is real property. ABC corporation dissolves and distributes all of its assets ratably to the three stockholders within the calendar month of the adoption of the plan of liquidation. A, B, and C each sign and file the necessary election within 30 days after the adoption of the plan of liquidation. At the time of dissolution, the ABC corporation has $60,000 of accumulated earnings and profits. How is the liquidation taxed to the shareholders, A, B, and C, and what is the basis of the property to them?

1. Gain Taxed As Ordinary Income

Value of property distributed		$405,000
Less basis for stock		150,000
Total gain realized		$255,000
Less gain in excess of earnings and profits:		
Total gain realized	$255,000	
Accumulated earnings and profits	60,000	195,000
Amount of gain taxed as ordinary income		$ 60,000

2. Treatment of Remainder of Gain

Total gain realized		$255,000
Less gain in excess of money and securities received:		
Total gain realized	$255,000	
Money and securities received	165,000	90,000
Total gain recognized on distribution		$165,000
Less portion taxed as ordinary income		60,000
Gain taxed as capital gain		$105,000

Thus, of the total $225,000 gain realized in the liquidation, only $165,000 is recognized for tax purposes, of which $60,000 is taxed as ordinary income and $105,000 is taxed as capital gain.[73]

---

[72] Section 334(c), I.R.C.
[73] Reg. Sec. 1.333-4(c)(2)(ii).

354   CORPORATIONS

3. Basis of Property to Stockholders

Basis of stock before distribution	$150,000.00
Plus gain recognized on distribution	165,000.00
Adjustment for gain recognized	$315,000.00
Less money received	75,000.00
Basis allocable to property and securities	$240,000.00
Portion allocable to securities	65,454.54
Portion allocable to real estate.	$174,545.46

Again, in planning for a liquidating distribution under Section 333, we should take care not to run afoul of the collapsible corporation provisions. The benefits of Section 333 are expressly denied to a corporation that is collapsible within the meaning of Section 341.[74]

6. Problem of Accelerated Depreciation in "One Month Liquidation"

The recapture rules of Sections 1245 and 1250 are paramount to the distribution rules of Section 333. Hence ordinary income will be recognized to the corporation at the time it distributes depreciable property to its shareholders to the extent of depreciation recapture. The limit placed upon the amount of recapture income realized upon distribution is the excess of the fair market value of the property over its adjusted basis at that time. In other words the distribution is treated as the equivalent of a sale at a price equal to fair market value.[75]

The amount of the depreciation recapture, subject to the above limitation, is, in the case of personal property, all of the depreciation taken since 1961, and, in the case of real property, the excess of accelerated depreciation over straight line depreciation taken since 1963.[76]

The effect of depreciation recapture is two fold. First, it creates taxable income to the corporation. Second, the amount of income thus created is added to the corporation's earnings and profits. And, as we have seen, the distribution is taxed as a dividend to the shareholders to the extent of available earnings and profits.

These considerations make it imperative that the corporation obtain an appraisal of depreciable assets subject to recapture to determine how much exposure, if any, it may have under these rules.

Example: Real estate corporation decides to liquidate in the month of December, 1969, because of the adverse effects the Tax Reform Act of 1969 will have on its operations. Not only will the availability of accelerated depreciation be limited on future acquisitions, but also the new rules relating to earnings and profits will eliminate the possibility of continued tax-free distributions out of depreciation allowances in the future.[77] At the time of liquidation, the earnings and profits account is zero. But an appraisal of its depreciable personal property shows a value of $100,000 in excess of basis. Depreciation since 1961 on this property was greater than the $100,000 potential gain. Thus, the entire $100,000 will be recaptured and taxed as ordinary income to the corporation if the distribution is made. Earnings and profits will be increased by

---

[74] Section 1245(a)(1)(B)(ii), I.R.C.; Section 1250(a)(1)(B)(ii), I.R.C.
[75] Sections 1245 and 1250, I.R.C.
[76] Section 312(m)(2), I.R.C.
[77] To the extent the corporation takes depreciation allowances, it has earnings and profits. Regulations § 312-15(a).

PROBLEMS OF SALES AND LIQUIDATIONS 355

the same $1,000,000 and decreased by the federal income levied thereon. If we assume that the tax is $46,750, earnings and profits will be increased by the net addition of the difference, or by $53,250. Thus, if the distribution is made under Section 333, $53,250 of the gain will be taxed as ordinary income to the shareholders.

A similar rule applies in the case of depreciable real estate, but its effects are ameliorated by two considerations: first, only the excess of accelerated depreciation over straight line is recaptured. Second, the amount of the excess recapture is subject to a percentage depending upon how long the property was held. The former limitation still applies with respect to acquisitions made *after* the effective dates of the 1969 Tax Reform Act, but, in most cases, the second limitation based on a sliding scale percentage of recapture has been eliminated.[78]

Since the effective date of the Tax Reform Act of 1969, accelerated depreciation of property causes another hidden problem. While acceptable methods of accelerated depreciation may be used as a deduction to reduce taxable income, the excess of such accelerated depreciation over straight-line depreciation is treated as an annual addition to the corporation's earnings and profits. If the corporate books and records are not adjusted to reflect this annual addition, they will not show this excess as constituting earnings and profits. Hence, a Section 333 distribution may be undertaken in the belief that it will be tax free whereas in reality a severe dividend tax may be incurred.[79]

Example: Real estate corporation acquires in 1970 a new apartment building (which qualifies for 200 percent declining-balance depreciation) at a cost of $1,200,000, of which $200,000 is allocated to land. The corporation takes total depreciation of $185,590 in the first 4 years of ownership. During the same period allowable straight-line depreciation is $100,000. Its books and records reflect a zero earnings and profits account because the excess of accelerated depreciation deductions over straight-line depreciation was not taken into account.

Obviously, if the shareholders decide to liquidate the corporation and distribute its assets to themselves under Section 333, they are in for a shock. The $85,590 excess of accelerated over straight-line depreciation will be treated as part of the corporation's earnings and profits account and will convert the first $85,590 of gain on the distribution into a dividend, taxable at ordinary rates.

In the foregoing example, a second penalty will be paid. The entire excess of accelerated depreciation over straight-line depreciation will be recaptured because the building was not held for at least 100 months. Thus, the corporation will also realize $85,590 of recapture income taxable at ordinary rates if the property on distribution is worth at least that much more than its depreciated basis to the corporation.

Normally the recapture income would also be added to earnings and profits (less a deduction from earnings and profits for any tax paid on it), but here it would not seem proper to add this recapture income again to earnings and profits because the excess of accelerated income over straight-line income has already been included in earnings and profits.[80]

---

[78] Earnings and profits are taxable as dividend income under a Section 333 liquidation. Section 333(e)(1), I.R.C.

[79] A second hidden addition to earnings and profits is the excess of percentage over cost depletion. Beware in liquidating oil or mineral corporations.

[80] The amendments made by the Tax Reform Act of 1969 are not clear on this question. The regulations promulgated do not clarify the matter. See Senate Report No. 91-552, 91st Cong. 1st Session (November 21, 1969) page 177.

7. Liquidation of a Collapsible Corporation

The collapsible corporation rules apply to distribution in liquidation as well as to sales of stock.

A collapsible corporation is one that was "formed or availed of principally" for the improvement or purchase of property "with a view to the sale or exchange by its stockholders (whether in liquidation or otherwise), or a distribution to its stockholders, before the realization by the corporation . . . of a substantial part of the taxable income to be derived from such property. . . ."[81] And, presumptively, a corporation is considered to be collapsible of its "ordinary income assets" equal 50 percent or more in value of its total assets and the value of these "ordinary income assets" is 120 percent or more of their basis to the corporation.[82]

For our purposes, the "ordinary income assets" of a real estate corporation include all of its property held for sale to customers and all of its contracts for the sale of such property, to the extent that these contracts have not previously been included in the corporation's taxable income.[83]

Under these circumstances, a stockholder who receives a distribution in liquidation of the corporation runs a grave risk of having the gain realized taxed as ordinary income.[84] His gain will be taxed as ordinary income if the following four conditions are met:[85]

(1) He owns, directly or indirectly, more than 5 percent in value of the corporation's outstanding stock;

(2) The corporation has not itself realized a substantial part of the taxable income to be derived from its Section 341 property;

(3) More than 70 percent of the total gain realized is attributable to the "ordinary income" assets of the corporation; and

(4) The distribution is made within three years of the date of acquisition or improvement of the property held for sale to customers.

Obviously, the liquidation of any corporation engaged in the development and sale of real estate can run afoul of these rules. The price for failure here is the conversion of capital gain into ordinary income. About all that can be done is to postpone the liquidation until more than three years after the date of the acquisition or improvement of the property. Or, alternatively, the corporation should sell sufficient of its "ordinary income" property so that less than 70 percent of the stockholder's gain on distribution will be attributable thereto, or so that it has realized a "substantial part" of the income to be derived from the Section 341 property.

On liquidation we can assume that the bulk of such a corporation's assets will consist of trade or business property, which, if sold by the corporation, would qualify for Section 1231 treatment. Such property is included in the definition of Section 341

---

[81] Section 341(b)(1)(A), I.R.C.
[82] Section 341(c), I.R.C. While we use the descriptive term "ordinary income assets," the Code uses the term "Section 341 assets."
[83] Section 341(b)(3), I.R.C.
[84] Section 341(a)(1), I.R.C.
[85] Section 341(d), I.R.C.

property.[86] But all is not lost. Except in the case of certain "tainted" stockholders, a corporation in liquidation will be treated as a collapsible corporation only if the net unrealized appreciation in its "ordinary income assets" exceeds 15 percent of its net worth.[87] For this purpose the scope of "ordinary income assets" does not include trade or business property; it includes only inventory or property held for sale to customers.[88]

Thus, the ordinary and usual liquidation of a real estate corporation engaged in the business of renting or leasing real estate will be free of the collapsible corporation rules. And, similarly, it will be able to utilize the benefits of Section 337 in liquidation[89] or qualify the liquidation for special treatment under Section 333.[90]

The "tainted" stockholder situations referred to above are two. First, if any stockholder owning more than 20 percent in value of the corporation's outstanding stock is a dealer in real estate, all of the corporation's real property will be considered to constitute "ordinary income assets." The interest of the corporation in trade or business real estate will be treated in the same manner as property held for sale to customers for the purpose of applying the provisions of Section 341.[91] And such a stockholder cannot shield his status by having an interest in several corporations, if the liquidations or sales of stock are within three years of one another.[92]

The second situation involves a stockholder who owns more than 5 percent but not more than 20 percent in value of the corporation's outstanding stock. Applied to him, if a dealer, the distribution may be treated as an exchange giving rise to ordinary income, even though to his co-stockholders, if non-dealers, the distribution is taxed as capital gain. In this case the taint is personal; it affects only the stockholder guilty of the taint, not the corporation. If, for example, such a stockholder is a dealer in real estate, all of the corporation's real estate will be considered to be "ordinary income assets" for the purpose of determining whether or not, as it applies to him, the net unrealized appreciation therein exceeds 15 percent of the corporation's net worth.[93]

D. PROBLEMS ON ACQUISITION OF PROPERTY

Property can be acquired by a corporate taxpayer by purchase, by gift, or by exchange of like property. And the tax rules to be applied to such acquisition are exactly the same as in the case of any other type of taxpayer.

But because of the peculiar nature of a corporation, it can acquire property by means not available to other types of taxpayers. It can, for example, acquire property by issuing its stock to the seller in payment of the purchase price. Or it can acquire the property of another corporation by merging or consolidating with it. Or it can acquire

---

[86] Section 341(b)(3)(D), I.R.C.
[87] Section 341(e)(2), I.R.C.
[88] Section 341(e)(5), I.R.C., referred to in the incomprehensible language of the statute as "subsection (e) assets."
[89] Section 341(e)(4), I.R.C. Additional limits are imposed upon the use of Section 337 by this section.
[90] Section 341(e)(3), I.R.C.
[91] Section 341(e)(5)(A)(i), I.R.C.
[92] Section 341(e)(2)(C), I.R.C.
[93] Section 341(e)(2)(B), I.R.C.

property by purchasing the stock of another corporation followed by a liquidation and distribution in kind of the latter's property to the new owner. All of these alternative methods of acquisition have their peculiar rules.

1. Purchase of Property by Issuing Stock

Suppose a corporation decides to acquire property by issuing stock for it. What are the results of the transaction?

The answer will depend upon the relationship of the seller of the property to the corporation. If the only result of the transaction is to make the seller a *minority* stockholder in the corporation, the transfer will be treated as a taxable exchange of unlike property to the seller.[94] In other words, the seller is selling his property in a taxable sale to the corporation. Gain will be recognized to the extent that the fair market value of the stock received exceeds his basis for the property transferred.

Because the exchange is taxable, the basis of the property to the corporation will be its cost, which in this case is the fair market value of the stock exchanged for the property.[95]

Example: A owns a hotel. B corporation, owning a string of hotels, wishes to acquire A's hotel. A sells his equity in the hotel for $250,000 worth of B corporation's preferred stock, which is a minority interest. If the hotel is encumbered by a $750,000 mortgage and A's basis for the property is $900,000, his gain would be computed as follows:

Sale Price:		
Value of stock received	$250,000	
Outstanding mortgage	750,000	$1,000,000
Less A's basis for hotel		900,000
Gain realized on exchange		$ 100,000

Are there any exceptions to this rule which treat the exchange as taxable to the stockholder? There is, of course, the exception mentioned at the beginning of this chapter. If the stock is issued or transferred to persons having control of the corporation after the exchange, the exchange will be tax-free.[96] As we pointed out, the exchange will be tax-free only if two conditions are met:

(1) The exchange is solely for stock or securities in the corporation acquiring the property; and

(2) The transferors of the property are the owners after the exchange of at least 80 percent of the total combined voting power of all classes of stock entitled to vote and of at least 80 percent of the total number of shares of all other classes of stock.

For this purpose, it is possible to have two or more owners of property enter into a plan to transfer jointly their properties to a newly created corporation in exchange for stock. If they act in concert pursuant to a pre-existing plan, the tests of control will be

---

[94] Section 1031(a), I.R.C. No gain would be recognized to the corporation. Section 1032, I.R.C.
[95] Section 1012, I.R.C.
[96] Sections 351(a), 368(c), I.R.C.

judged from the viewpoint of the group as a whole, not from the standpoint of each transferor.[97]

But there is also a second exception. The use of the second exception is confined to a case in which the transferor of the property is also a corporation. In other words, both parties to the exchange must be corporations. This second exception, because it involves the capital structures of two corporations, has come to be known as a "tax-free reorganization."

2. Tax-Free Reorganization

If one corporation, in exchange for its voting stock, acquires substantially all of the properties of another corporation, the transaction is treated as a tax-free exchange.[98] Thus, if both parties to the transaction are corporations, the exchange of the stock of one for the property of the other will be tax-free provided the following conditions are present:[99]

(1) The acquiring corporation must acquire *substantially all* of the property of the transferor corporation;

(2) The acquiring corporation must pay for the property only by the issuance or transfer of its voting stock;[100]

(3) The acquisition must be pursuant to a plan of reorganization adopted by both corporations;

(4) The stockholders of both corporations must have a continuity of interest after the transfer in the acquiring corporation;

(5) There must be a continuity of the business enterprise under the acquiring corporation.

If the exchange is tax-free, the basis of the property to the acquiring corporation will be the same as its basis to its former owner.[101]

Example: Corporation B owns no assets other than an apartment building. The apartment has a basis of $100,000 to Corporation B and a value of $150,000. Corporation A, also engaged in the business of managing and operating apartments, wishes to acquire Corporation B's apartment. Pursuant to a plan of reorganization adopted by both corporations, Corporation B agrees to transfer its apartment to Corporation A in exchange for $150,000 of A's stock. Corporation A takes over and continues to operate B's apartment.

The exchange would be tax-free; hence, Corporation A would now hold the apartment at a basis of $100,000, and no tax would be payable by either Corporation A or B.

---

[97] Reg. Sec. 1.351-1.
[98] Sections 361, 368(a)(1)(C), I.R.C.
[99] Reg. Sec. 1.368-1, et seq. The regulations should be studied for possible variations of this basic transaction.
[100] For this purpose, the assumption of the transferor's liabilities against the property does not count. Reg. Sec. 1.368-2(d).
[101] Section 362(b), I.R.C.

3. Statutory Merger or Consolidation

A merger or consolidation of two corporations under the provisions of state law may also qualify as a tax-free reorganization. The requirements for qualification are similar, except that the consideration paid need not be solely stock, to those mentioned in the preceding section. In other words, the merger or consolidation must be:

(1) Pursuant to state law;[102]

(2) Pursuant to a plan of merger or consolidation adopted by both corporations;

(3) Pursuant to a plan that provides for the continuity of the business enterprise; and

(4) Pursuant to a plan that provides for a continuity of interest of stockholders of both corporations in the resultant corporation.

Example: Corporation A and Corporation B, both engaged in the business of owning and operating apartments, wish to merge. All of the property of Corporation B is thereupon transferred to Corporation A, pursuant to a plan of merger adopted by both corporations. The stockholders of Corporation A retain their stock in the new enterprise, but the stockholders of Corporation B surrender the stock in B for stock of Corporation A issued to them in the merger.[103] Corporation A takes over and manages Corporation B's apartments. The merger would be tax-free and, consequently, Corporation A's basis for the property would be the transferred basis that it had in the hands of Corporation B.[104]

4. Other Types of Tax-Free Reorganizations

Four other basic types of tax-free reorganizations are recognized under Section 368. They are the following:

(1) The exchange of stock of one corporation for the *stock* of another, if the first corporation has or acquires sufficient stock of the second to have control over the second after the exchange. For this purpose, control is defined to mean the ownership of stock possessing at least 80 percent of the total combined voting power of voting stock and at least 80 percent of the total number of shares of all other classes of stock.

(2) The transfer of stock of one corporation for the *property* of a second, but only if the second corporation has control over the first after the exchange. This type of exchange differs from the type previously discussed in that the first corporation need not acquire substantially all of the property of the second. But the stock of the first corporation acquired by the second must immediately be distributed to its stockholders.

(3) The recapitalization of a corporation.

(4) A mere change in its identity, form, or place of organization, however effected.[105]

---

[102] Reg. Sec. 1.368-2(b).
[103] A tax-free exchange under the provisions of Section 354, I.R.C.
[104] Sections 368(a)(1)(A), 362(b), I.R.C.
[105] For those who enjoy labels, these six types of exchanges are known by the letters of the subsections under which they are found in the Code, as follows:
Type A: Statutory merger or consolidation;
Type B: Exchange of stock for stock of a controlled corporation;
Type C: Exchange of stock for substantially all of the property of another corporation;
Type D: Exchange of stock for property of a corporation that has or acquires control;
Type E: Recapitalization; and
Type F: A mere change in identity, form, or place of organization.

5. Acquisition of Stock and Liquidation

Another method of acquiring property is the acquisition of the stock of the corporation owning the property, followed by a liquidation and distribution of the property to the stockholder. If the stockholder acquiring the property is also a corporation, this transaction can be handled in such a way that the liquidating distribution is tax-free and, yet, the stockholder will be entitled to transfer its basis for the stock purchased to the assets received in liquidation.

In order for these objectives to be accomplished, the acquiring corporation must purchase sufficient stock to place itself in "control" of the second corporation. In other words, the acquiring corporation must own or acquire at least 80 percent of the voting power and 80 percent of all the other stock of the second corporation. If this test is met at the time of the distribution in liquidation, the distribution will be tax-free. That is to say, any difference between the value of the assets of the second corporation and the purchase price of the stock to the first corporation will not be recognized as gain or loss on the distribution.[106]

Ordinarily, the corporation receiving the distribution would be required to take over the basis of the property in the hands of the liquidated corporation.[107] But if the liquidation is made pursuant to a plan of liquidation adopted within two years of the date on which the first corporation acquired control of the corporation to be liquidated, the first corporation is entitled to substitute its cost basis for the stock of the second as the basis for the property received in liquidation. In order for this rule to apply, the acquiring corporation must have purchased its interest in the stock of the corporation to be liquidated within the period of 12 months or less.[108]

Example: A Corporation purchases all of the stock of B Corporation for $120,000. B corporation owns an apartment worth $120,000, which has a basis of $80,000. A Corporation causes B Corporation to adopt a plan of complete liquidation within two years of its purchase of the stock. B Corporation dissolves by distributing the apartment to A Corporation in redemption of its stock. No gain or loss would be recognized on the liquidation, but A Corporation would be entitled to adjust its basis for the apartment up to $120,000, the cost of the stock purchased by it.

E. USE OF CORPORATION IN TAX PLANNING

As pointed out earlier, the advisability of the use of the corporate form of ownership depends upon an analysis of the potential tax that would be paid by the business enterprise if it were owned by a corporation or held in some other form of ownership.

1. Comparison of the Advantages and Disadvantages of Corporate Ownership

For purposes of comparison, we might summarize the tax advantages of incorporation as follows:

---

[106] Section 332, I.R.C. The distributions must be completed within three years of the close of the taxable year in which the first distribution was made. An exception to this statement must be made for depreciation recapture under Section 1245 (personal property), and Section 1250 (real property).
[107] Section 334(b)(1), I.R.C.
[108] Section 334(b)(2), I.R.C.

(1) The corporate income tax rate is not progressive, except for the step up from 20 percent on the first $25,000, 22 percent on the next $25,000 and 48 percent on the balance;

(2) The corporate form permits the owner of property to segregate more readily property held for sale to customers in the ordinary course of business from property held for investment;

(3) The corporation may qualify its stockholder-officers for inclusion in pension and profit-sharing plans, employee stock options, and other fringe benefits;

(4) In some cases, not readily available to a real estate investor, the corporation may elect under Subchapter "S" to escape taxation of the corporate level.

In addition to these tax advantages, the use of the corporate form provides a number of business advantages. Among those which we should consider are the following:

(1) Liability of stockholders is limited to capital investor;
(2) Title to property is held in name of only one owner;
(3) Gifts of stock are easier to handle than gifts of undivided interests in property; gifts to minors are more easily handled;
(4) Management of property is centralized in Board of Directors;
(5) There is continuity of enterprise despite death or incompetence of owner;
(6) Advantageous financing may be more readily arranged.

But there are a number of disadvantages and traps that we must keep in mind. Among these are the following:

(1) Losses and depreciation are deductible only against corporate income;

(2) Corporate income cannot be used for the personal purposes of stockholders without the payment of a dividend tax;

(3) There may be an imposition of penalty taxes as for being a personal holding company or for unreasonable accumulations of earnings;

(4) Basis of property owned by corporation is unaffected by the death of a stockholder or a change of stock ownership;

(5) Property is frozen into the corporate structure, making it difficult to take it out without payment of a tax on distribution or liquidation;

(6) Capital losses can be offset only against capital gains, not against ordinary income.

2. Conclusion

Corporate ownership of real estate makes tax sense only if the real estate is held for sale to customers. It is difficult to understand why one would want to incorporate investment real estate.

12

Subchapter S and Straw Corporations

This chapter covers only two topics, as follows:

A. *Subchapter S.*
B. *Straw Corporations.*

A. SUBCHAPTER S

In 1958, Subchapter "S" was added to the Internal Revenue Code for the purpose of permitting certain qualified corporations to elect not to be subject to the corporate income tax.[1] If the election is properly made, a corporation can be exempt from tax on its income. Instead, all of its income, whether or not distributed to its stockholders, is reportable by the stockholders in their individual income tax returns. Each stockholder picks up a proportionate share of the corporation's net income, measured by the ratio of his stockholdings to the total stock outstanding at the end of the corporation's taxable year.

1. Elections

The election is severely limited. Both the corporation and its stockholders must meet the tests prescribed by law, as follows:

(1) The corporation must have not more than ten stockholders;[2]
(2) No stockholder may be a corporation, partnership, or trust;
(3) No stockholder may be a non-resident alien;
(4) The corporation may have only one class of stock;

---

[1] Sections 1372-1377, I.R.C.
[2] For this purpose husband and wife who hold stock as their community property or as joint tenants, tenants by the entireties or tenants in common are treated as one stockholder. Section 1371(c) I.R.C.

(5) The corporation may not be a member of an affiliated group of corporations;

(6) The corporation must be a domestic, not a foreign, corporation;

(7) The corporation must not receive more than 20 percent of its gross receipts from rents, royalties, dividends, interest, annuities, and security sales; and

(8) The corporation must not receive more than 80 percent of its gross receipts from sources outside the United States.

2. Result of Election

If a corporation makes a timely Subchapter S election, it is not required to pay a corporate income tax at the federal level.[3] All income is taxable to the shareholders as individual income, whether or not distributed. Capital gains are similarly treated.[4] However, capital losses are not.[5] Capital losses are a corporate loss deductible by the corporation in the year incurred against capital gains only. Or, by being allowed as a capital loss to the corporation only in a three-year carry-back, five-year carry-forward period.[6]

Operating losses pass through immediately,[7] and do not qualify for the normal carry-forward and carry-back treatment of Section 172.[8] If a stock transfer is made during the taxable year, the net operating loss is prorated between buyer and seller.[9]

3. Basis as a Tax Problem

Losses can be deducted only to the extent of basis. In the case of a Subchapter S corporation, the basis of each shareholder is limited to amount he paid for his stock plus any loans made directly by him to the corporation.[10] A stockholder cannot include in his basis for his investment his pro rata share of debt owed by the corporation to third parties.[11]

4. Conclusion

Because of the limitations on shareholder basis and because of the limitations on the type of income that can be received, Subchapter S is not usually a desirable type of entity in the real estate field.

First, Subchapter S is not available for corporations that receive more than 20 percent of their income from rents. Thus, apartment houses and net leased commercial buildings cannot, if incorporated, elect Subchapter S.

Second, if the corporation renders services in addition to the use of space, a

---

[3] Some states that impose a corporate income or franchise tax based on income (for example, California) do not recognize the Subchapter S election. The result is that the Subchapter S corporation is subject to state corporate taxes and all payments to shareholders are taxable as dividends to them to extent of earnings and profits.

[4] Unless "one-shotted." Section 1378, I.R.C.

[5] Capital losses do not pass through. Section 1374, I.R.C.

[6] Section 1212, I.R.C.

[7] Section 1374, I.R.C. If stock is sold, the sharing of the loss is day to day.

[8] Section 172, I.R.C.

[9] Regulations §1.1374-1(b)(3).

[10] Regulations §1.1374-1(b)(4).

[11] George W. Weibush, 59 T.C. 77(1973), aff'd per curiam, 32 AFTR 2d ¶73-5371 (8th Cir. 1973).

Subchapter S election is available. Illustrations would include hotels, motels, office buildings, (other than on a net lease arrangement) and shopping centers (but only if "significant" services are furnished by the landlord to the tenants).[12]

"Significant" services are defined in the Regulations as follows:[13]

> The term "rents" does not include payments for the use or occupancy of rooms or other space where significant services are also rendered to the occupant, such as for the use or occupancy of rooms or other quarters in hotels, boarding houses, or apartment houses furnishing hotel services, or in tourist homes, motor courts, or motels. Generally, services are considered rendered to the occupant if they are primarily for his convenience and are other than those usually or customarily rendered in connection with the rental of rooms or other space for occupancy only. The supplying of maid service, for example, constitutes such services; whereas the furnishing of heat and light, the cleaning of public entrances, exits, stairways and lobbies, the collection of trash, etc., are not considered as services rendered to the occupant. Payments for the use or occupancy of entire private residences or living quarters in duplex or multiple housing units, of offices in an office building, etc., are generally "rents" under section 1372(e)(5). Payments for the parking of automobiles ordinarily do not constitute rents. Payments for the warehousing of goods or for the use of personal property do not constitute rents if significant services are rendered in connection with such payments.

But even if significant services are furnished by the Subchapter S corporation, the shareholders may well lose out if the corporation attempts to pass large depreciation losses based on the investment of corporate borrowings. These are not part of the shareholder's bases for their stockholdings and may soon become non-deductible at the shareholder level.

Example: ABC Corporation constructs a $5,000,000 shopping center. A, B, and C, individual citizens, each puts $15,000 for his stock in the ABC corporation. After construction, the ABC corporation negotiates a take-out loan of $5,045,000. It pays $5,000,000 on the construction loan and project and distributes $15,000 to each of A, B, and C. The ABC corporation furnishes parking facilities; landscaping; exterior maintenance; garbage removal; security patrol services; heat, light and power; maintenance of escalators, walkways, freight elevators, and underground delivery facilities; street signboard daily changes; window washing; and structural damage insurance from earthquake, fire, or other casualty. In 1975, ABC Corporation elects Subchapter S and incurs a $100,000 operating loss (which includes all the above costs plus real property taxes, interest, and depreciation of $187,500.[14]

Results: (1) No part of the $100,000 operating loss passes through to the shareholders, in 1975;[15] (2) No part of the 1975 operating loss is available to the ABC corporation as a carry-back or carry-forward loss;[16] and (3) No part of the 1975 operating loss is allowable to the shareholders, A, B, or C in any year.[17]

---

[12]It is understood that rulings can be obtained. While no guidelines have been published, a showing that the landlord's Section 162 expenses exceed 15 percent of gross revenues is favorable. See §163(d), [relating to the definitions of investment interest].

[13]Regulations §1.1372-4(b)(vi).

[14]Computed on a 40-year composite life at 150 percent declining-balance method.

[15]Because of the distribution of $15,000 to each of them, their basis for their stock is zero. Hence, no write-off of the loss is available to the stockholders. Section 1374(c)(2); Regulations §1.1374-1(b)(4).

[16]Section 172, I.R.C.

[17]Richard Lee Plowden, 48 T.C. 666 (1967) aff'd 398 F.2d 340 (4th Cir. 1968).

Third: But if the corporation is engaged in the business of developing and selling real estate, the election should be available, provided the other tests are met. In this event, the income derived from the sale of real estate will be taxed directly to the stockholders and not to the corporation. In this respect, an electing corporation is analogous to a partnership.

Similarly, if the corporation is engaged primarily in furnishing services, such as operating a hotel or motel, the election is available. But in both cases, the operation should be profitable. And, finally, if these operations are profitable, would it be better to have them taxed at normal corporate rates than at the rates levied on Subchapter S income passed through to shareholders?[18]

B. STRAW CORPORATIONS

Straw corporations are a necessity in any case in which a lender insists on recourse liability against the purchaser or developer. Lending institutions and sellers sometimes have difficulties when a deal will not close if either does not agree to a waiver of any deficiency against the buyer or developer. But if a buyer or developer cannot take depreciation on that part of his loan or purchase price based on recourse liability, how can he (buyer or developer) generate the cash flow necessary to pay off the loan or purchase price? Ultimately, the problem of the buyer-developer will rest at the door of the lender (in terms of foreclosures) or the seller (in terms of "NO SALE").

1. The "Why" of Non-Recourse Liability

Investors in real estate have several choices;

(a) Individual ownership; both recourse and non-recourse loans are part of basis.[19]

(b) Joint tenancy, tenancy by the entities, or community property ownership: both recourse and non-recourse loans are part of basis.[20]

(c) Partnership ownership: both recourse and non-recourse notes are part of basis.[21]

(d) Limited partnership ownership: only non-recourse liability is allocated pro rata to the limited partners.[22] Unlimited liability (recourse liability) is added solely to the basis of the general partners.[23]

(e) Corporate ownership: neither recourse nor non-recourse liability of the corporation become part of the shareholder's basis.

---

[18] The 50 percent maximum rate on the earned income of individuals does not apply to the "pass-through" of Subchapter S income. Section 1348(b)(1), I.R.C.

[19] Manuel D. Mayerson, 47 T.C. 340 (1966), acq. 1969-1 C.B. 21. Rhoda Mayerson was joined as a petitioner only because she had signed a joint return. She had no separate interest in the property, but a joint and several liability in their return.

[20] The problem here is not of allocation. In a community property state, basis is allocated equally. In a common law state, basis depends on who pays.

[21] Each partner shares pro rata. Regulations §1.752-1(a).

[22] Section 752(d), I.R.C.; Regulations §1.752-1.

[23] Section 752(a), I.R.C.

(f) Subchapter S election by a corporation: neither recourse nor non-recourse liability become part of the shareholders' basis.

(g) Syndicates and pools: the question is one of tax classification between corporate or partnership status.[24]

2. Straw Corporations as a Useful Device

There should be no distinctions between recourse and non-recourse liabilities for sale and purchase purposes.[25] The Internal Revenue Service insists that the liability relieved of be part of the amount realized. But if no liability is relieved, where is the taxable income or gain?[26]

It is noted that liability is a mere matter of form; except on sale. In that case, liabilities are both part of basis and of cost.[27] But how about abandonment?[28]

3. Straw Corporations as Tax Non-Entities

Are straw corporations non-entities for federal income tax purposes? If a straw is a taxable corporation, all of the income and gain are taxed at the corporate level. Any distributions to shareholders are dividends to the extent of earnings and profits.[29] Any excess is capital gain.[30]

To be useful a straw corporation must be a non-entity of tax purposes. To be a non-entity means that the straw corporation files information returns much like an agent.

4. Internal Revenue Service Position

Neither the Internal Revenue Service nor the Tax Court of the United States likes straw corporations. The record that each has made is clear.

If a corporation is organized for the purposes of holding title to real estate, the test of whether or not the corporation will be treated as such for tax purposes is dependent upon whether or not it engages in business activities.

For example, a corporation was organized at the suggestion of the creditor purely for the purpose of permitting the owner of property to pledge the property as security for a bank loan. Afterwards several activities occurred on the property in which the corporation participated technically. It refinanced the mortgage, it entered into a lease of the property and it participated in two lawsuits. It maintained no bank accounts or books of account. It filed corporate tax returns and treated the rents received as income.

---

[24] Regulations §301.7701.
[25] The author has suggested that a non-recourse note can be abandoned. A recourse note? Only if no consideration is received.
[26] Section 111, I.R.C. depends on recovery of cash.
[27] Crane v. Commissioner, 331 U.S. 1 (1967).
[28] The loss of an investment on abandoning it is an ordinary loss. Section 165, I.R.C. It is axiomatic that an abandonment neither forgives nor forgets a bad debt loss by the seller or lender.
[29] Earnings and profits include the excess of accelerated over straight-line depreciation. Section 1250, I.R.C.
[30] Section 331, I.R.C.

When the property was sold, the question was whether the corporation or the controlling shareholder was the seller. The Supreme Court held that the gain must be reported by the corporation.[31]

Authorities are confused. It has been held that avoiding taxes is not a business activity.[32] Also avoiding property from claims or creditors of the shareholders is not a business activity.[33]

A title holding company was held not to engage in business when it merely executed deeds and mortgages on the property.[34] But a title holding company that was formed for the purpose of preventing the creditors of one of the owners from attaching the property was held to have been engaged in business even though the corporate minutes expressly stated that full beneficial interest and control remained in the individuals. One of the corporations had executed a lease. Another corporation borrowed money from outside interest and assigned a leasehold as security for the loan.[35] Collection of oil royalties, leasing, buying additional property, and investigating a decline in royalty receipts were held to be business activities.[36]

Suppose a corporation simply took title to property in exchange for stock and notes. The notes bore interest equal to rental income under a net lease. The corporation collected rents and passed them on to the note holders. It ratified the lease and held directors meetings to fill vacancies on the board. These activities were sufficient to require recognition of the corporation.[37]

5. Ensurance of Straw Corporation Position

Obviously, a straw corporation is one in which the equity owners have no interest. If they do have an equity interest, there is a question.[38]

The answer is to incorporate with persons who have no equity interest in the property.[39]

---

[31] Moline Properties, Inc. v. Commissioner, 319 U.S. 436 (1943).
[32] National Investors, Corp. v. Hoey, 144 F.2d 466 (2nd Circuit 1944).
[33] Jackson v. Commissioner, 233 F.2d 289 (2nd Cir. 1956).
[34] K-C Land Co., TC Memo 1960-35.
[35] Paymer v. Commissioner, 150 F.2d 334 (2nd Cir. 1945).
[36] Hagist Ranch, Inc. Commissioner 295 Fed. 2d 351 (7th Cir. 1961).
[37] Commissioner v. State Adams Corp., 283 F.2d 395 (2nd Cir. 1960), cert. den. 365 U.S. 844 (1961) See also, Joseph Rothafel, T.C. Memo 1965-277.
[38] David F. Bolger, 59 T.C. 760(1973) was appealed by the Internal Revenue Service and the appeal then withdrawn.
[39] A straw corporation should be a true straw. For example, the business purpose of sheltering mortgage loans from state law usury limitations has been held to make the straw corporation a separate taxable entity. *William B. Strong*, 66 T.C. 12 (1975). aff'd F.2d (2nd Cir. 1977).

13

Cooperative and Condominium Housing

A. COOPERATIVE HOUSING CORPORATION[1]

A cooperative housing corporation is a corporation organized for the purpose of constructing, maintaining, and operating apartment units for the primary benefit of its stockholders. Each stockholder's stock carries with it a lease or other evidence of his right to live in a particular apartment. Title to the land and improvements is in the corporation itself and the individual stockholder has no insurable interest in the title to the property. For this reason, construction or improvement loans are generally obtained by the corporation itself, and all of the units in the project are subject to the lien of an over-all mortgage.

1. Benefits of Section 216: Deductions

The purchaser of stock with the right to occupy a unit in a cooperative housing corporation is treated for federal income tax purposes as being the owner of an interest in the property itself. Section 216 of the Internal Revenue Code provides that each stockholder of a qualified cooperative housing corporation may deduct his share of real estate taxes and mortgage interest paid or incurred by the corporation itself. The share of real estate taxes and interest is determined by the proportion that his stock in the corporation bears to the total stock outstanding.

Limitations on Deductions. The deduction by the stockholders of real property taxes and mortgage interest is limited to taxes and interest[2] incurred by the corporation on the land and improvements which are used for cooperative housing purposes. To the extent that the corporation has deductions for real property taxes and interest on

---

[1] This material has been adapted from an article by the author entitled "Tax Aspects of Cooperative and Condominium Housing" published in *Proceedings of the New York University Twenty-Fifth Annual Institute* and produced by permission.

[2] "Points" paid by the cooperative housing pass through to tenant-stockholders as deductible interest. Rev. Rul. 73-15, 1973-1 C.B. 141.

business space rented by the corporation to non-stockholders, no deduction is allowable to the tenant-stockholders.[3]

Double Deduction. Because the corporation has direct ownership of the property in question, it too is allowed a deduction for real property taxes and interest expense incurred by it on the property. In other words, the deduction does not pass through to the stockholders in such a manner that it is denied to the corporation. Both the corporation and the stockholders are entitled to take a deduction for the same items.

Depreciation. Similarly, the tenant-stockholders are entitled to deduct their share of the depreciation deduction taken by the corporation on the building itself.[4] However, depreciation is not allowable to a tenant-stockholder unless the apartment unit is used by the stockholder in his trade or business or is held for the production of income. The amount of the depreciation deduction allowable must be reduced for any depreciation allocable to areas rented out by the corporation for its own account.[5] If the stockholder uses his apartment for personal living purposes, no deduction for depreciation is allowable.[6]

The corporation itself is not entitled to deduct depreciation on its building and other improvements.[7]

Other Expenses. Ordinarily, other expenses incurred by the corporation in operating and maintaining the property are not deductible by the tenant-shareholders. However, where a tenant-stockholder devotes his leasehold interest to a trade or business use, it would follow that any payments made by him to the cooperative corporation for maintenance, repairs, and similar expenses, would be deductible under Section 162 of the Code, independently of Section 216. In addition, any expenses incurred directly by the tenant-stockholder to third parties in maintaining the rented unit would be deductible by him. If the tenant-stockholder makes capital improvements to his leasehold, he will be entitled to deduct depreciation on them as in the case of any tenant's improvements devoted to a business use.[8]

2. Requirements of Section 216

In order for a cooperative housing corporation to qualify its stockholders for the benefits of Section 216, certain basic requirements must be met. First, the corporation may have no more than one class of stock outstanding.[9] Second, each stockholder must be entitled, as a result of his stock ownership, to occupy for dwelling purposes a unit in the property owned by the corporation. It is not essential that the stockholder actually occupy the premises, so long as he has the right to occupy them as against the

---

[3] Reg. § 1.216-1(e), Examples (2), (3).
[4] I.R.C. § 216(c).
[5] Reg. § 1.216-2(b)(ii). Rev. Rul. 73-444, I.R.B. 1973-44, 7.
[6] It appears that a tenant-stockholder may use an accelerated method of depreciation on his share of the building and improvement regardless of the method used by the corporation. All that is required is that the property in the hands of the corporation be property qualifying for accelerated depreciation. Reg. § 1.216-2(b)(i).
[7] Park Place, Inc. 57 T.C. 767 (1972).
[8] Reg. § 1.167(a)-4.
[9] I.R.C. § 216(b)(1)(A). There is an exception for a nominal amount of preferred stock not exceeding $100, and issued to a governmental agency. Reg. § 1.216-1(c). Section 216(b)(4), I.R.C.

corporation.[10] Third, none of the stockholders can be entitled, except on liquidation, to receive any distribution other than one taxable as a dividend.[11] Fourth, and most importantly, 80 percent or more of the gross income of the corporation must be derived from tenant-stockholders.[12]

If these requirements are met, the tenant-stockholders will be entitled to take deductions in their personal returns for their aliquot shares of real property taxes, mortgage interest and, if applicable, depreciation. The cooperative housing corporation itself is not exempt from the corporate income tax. Accordingly, if its receipts from tenant-stockholders and from other sources exceed its expenses, it will have net income subject to taxation.[13]

3. Other Tax Aspects of Ownership

In two other areas, a tenant-stockholder in a cooperative housing corporation is treated just as if he owned an interest in the real property owned by the corporation.

Sale of Stock by Tenant-Stockholder. If he sells his stock and leasehold interest in a cooperative housing corporation, he will be entitled to defer the recognition of gain on the sale under Section 1034 of the Code, provided that he meets the requirements of that section.[14]

The two principal requirements are, first, that the premises sold have been occupied by him as his principal residence on the date of sale and, second, that he acquire a new residence at a cost equal to or in excess of the selling price of the property sold.

---

[10]I.R.C. § 216(b)(1)(B); Reg. § 1.216-1(c)(2). A tenant-stockholder is defined as an "individual" who owns stock in a cooperative housing corporation § 216(b)(2). Yet it is not necessary that *all* of the stockholders be individuals. It has been ruled, for example, that the ownership of 9 percent of a cooperative's outstanding stock by a corporation did not disqualify the cooperative from the benefits of I.R.C. § 216. The corporation planned to use the apartment thus acquired "for the temporary housing of certain of its officers and directors." Rev. Rul. 55-654, (C.B. 1952, 58). However, the corporation would not be entitled to the benefits of I.R.C. § 216 because it cannot be a tenant-stockholder within the meaning of I.R.C. § 216.

Thus, the share of taxes, interest, and depreciation charges incurred by the cooperative on the corporation's unit would not pass through to the corporation. But this result may be of no consequence if the corporation puts the apartment to a business use. The business uses of the apartment will independently entitle the corporation to various income tax deductions in leasing and maintaining the apartment. No deduction for depreciation would be allowable because the corporation's investment is in an intangible stock interest.

[11]I.R.C. § 216(b)(1)(C).

[12]I.R.C. § 216(b)(1)(D). For this purpose amounts received by the Cooperative from tenants to defray expenses such as providing for maid and secretarial service, garage or parking space, utilities, recreational facilities, cleaning and related services are considered to be gross income received from a tenant-stockholders. Rev. Rul. 68-387, I.R.B. 1968-30, 14. Payments received by a cooperative from stockholders who are corporations or partnerships are not considered to constitute income from "tenant-stockholders." Thus if more than 20 percent of the cooperative's gross income were derived from shareholders who were corporations, or partnerships, the cooperative would lose the benefits of I.R.C. § 216. Rev. Rul. 55-654 *supra;* Rev. Rul. 58-421 (C.B. 1958-2, 112) (ruling that the sale of stock and space to a banking corporation and to a real estate partnership for banking and real estate business purposes did not disqualify a cooperative housing corporation, more than 80 percent of the gross income of which was derived from individual tenant stockholders).

[13]See Lake Forest, Inc., Par. 63,039 P-H Memo T.C. (1963). The portion of the stockholder-tenant's payment which is for amortization of the corporation's mortgage indebtedness on the apartment has been treated as non-taxable contributions to the capital of the corporation. Cambridge Apartment Bldg. Corp., 44 B.T.A. 617 (1941) (acq. 1942-2, 2); 874 Park Ave. Corp., 23 B.T.A. 400 (1931) (acq. X-2, 21).

[14]I.R.C. § 1034(f).

For the purposes of applying Section 1034, it does not make any difference whether the new property acquired be property individually owned by the purchaser or an apartment leased to him as a tenant-stockholder in another cooperative housing corporation. The converse is also true. It is possible for the owner of a house to sell his house and qualify for the benefits of Section 1034 by purchasing an interest in a cooperative housing corporation which entitled him to an apartment that he uses as his principal residence.[15]

Condemnation. Similarly, if the property is condemned, the tenant-stockholder may elect to use the benefits of Section 1033 for the purposes of postponing the recognition of gain. In this case, it will be necessary for him to acquire replacement property which is also used for residential purposes within the time prescribed by Section 1033.[16]

Section 121. Another benefit available to a tenant-stockholder in a cooperative housing corporation is the possibility of qualifying for the benefits of Section 121.[17]

These benefits are available to the owner of a residence who is older than 65 and has used the property as his principal residence for periods aggregating at least five of the last eight years before sale. Under Section 121, such an individual is entitled to exclude from income the gain realized on the sale of his residence if the adjusted sales price does not exceed $20,000. If the adjusted sales price exceeds $20,000, the owner is entitled to exclude from income only the portion of the gain which bears the same ratio to the total gain as $20,000 bears to the adjusted sales price.[18]

Limitations on Joint-Tenancy. One benefit denied a tenant-stockholder in a cooperative housing corporation is the possibility of creating a joint tenancy with his wife without making a taxable gift. Under Section 2515, it is possible for a husband, as the sole owner of real property, to create a tenancy by the entireties or a joint tenancy with his wife with right of survivorship without incurring any gift tax liability. For the purposes of the gift tax, the conveyance of the property into the joint tenancy is disregarded. It is only when the joint tenancy is terminated that there is deemed to be a taxable transfer if the property goes in whole or in part to a spouse who had not furnished any part of the original purchase price. However, these benefits are not available to a tenant-stockholder because his interest is not in fact an interest in real property.[19]

It is suggested that if the interest of the owner of the tenant-stockholder interest in the cooperative housing corporation is treated as the equivalent of an interest in real estate, the interest of a tenant-stockholder should qualify for Section 2515 exemption.[20]

4. The Problem of Non-Qualifying Income

The most serious tax problem facing stockholder-tenants in a cooperative housing corporation is the possible loss of the tax benefits because more than 20 percent of the

---

[15] Reg. § 1.1034-1(c)(3).
[16] Reg. § 1.1033(b)(1).
[17] I.R.C. § 121(d)(3).
[18] Reg. § 1.121-5(c).
[19] Rev. Rul. 66-40 (I.R.B. 1966-8, 50).
[20] See, for example, California law as stated in Pitts, Estate of Mae Purdie, 218 Cal. 185 (1933).

gross income of the corporation is derived from non-tenant stockholders. If this occurs, the tenant-stockholders will lose the right to take itemized deductions for their proportionate shares of the corporation's real property taxes, interest and depreciation, and will also lose the possibility of utilizing Sections 121 and 1034 on a sale of their units.

Commercial Rents. Clearly, if the cooperative housing corporation leases out space for commercial purposes to tenants who are not also stockholders, the income derived from these rental units will be non-qualifying income. However, there are other types of receipts that are non-qualifying. For example, rentals received from a commercial tenant who is also a stockholder will be non-qualified income if the tenant is a corporation or partnership.[21]

Another source of non-qualified income to a cooperative housing corporation is that derived from the developer during the period that the developer is engaged in the sale of the community apartments. It is customary for the developer to be organized as a corporation for business and tax reasons. Any amounts paid by the development corporation to the cooperative housing corporation in connection with its retained apartment units will constitute non-qualified income, even though the development corporation is itself a stockholder in the cooperative housing corporation.

Non-Stockholder Lessees. The same result would follow where the cooperative housing corporation itself leases out certain of the unsold apartments. Because the tenants of the unsold apartments are mere lessees, they cannot qualify as stockholder-owners. The rentals paid by them to the cooperative housing corporation are therefore non-qualified income. The probability that either of these possibilities may occur is the greatest at the beginning of occupancy of a new project.

Foreclosure of Stock. For a period of three years after foreclosure, a bank or other lending institution will be treated as tenant stockholder. The purpose of this 1976 amendment is to prevent inadvertent loss of Section 216 benefits because some tenant-stockholders have lost their property by foreclosure.[22]

The mere fact, however, that a cooperative housing corporation does not qualify under Section 216 in its first year will not deprive it of qualification in a later year.

5. Allowable Commercial Use

To what extent, then, can units in a cooperative housing corporation be used for non-residential purposes? Obviously, the corporation can itself lease out units for commercial purposes to a non-stockholder, provided that the rentals from commercial uses do not exceed 20 percent of gross income. The only price paid for such commercial use is the fact that the deductions for interest and taxes allowable to the individual tenant-stockholders must be reduced in proportion to the ratio that commercial income bears to the gross income of the cooperative.[23]

Similarly, the community housing corporation may lease space to a corporation or partnership that owns stock in the cooperative housing corporation. The amount of rentals received from such a corporation or partnership, when added to the amount of

---

[21] Rev. Rul. 58-421 (C.B. 1958-2, 112); Rev. Rul. 55-654, (C.B. 1955-2, 58).
[22] Section 216(b)(5).
[23] Reg. § 1.216-1(b).

rentals received from non-stockholder lessees, cannot exceed 20 percent of the cooperative's gross income.[24]

Commercial Use of Space by Tenant-Stockholders. What about commercial uses of space rented to individual tenant-stockholders? By inference it appears that such use of space by a tenant-stockholder will not affect the qualification of the cooperative housing corporation. While Section 216 refers to cooperative *housing* corporations, the requirement that each of the stockholders be entitled, by reason of his stock ownership, to occupy an apartment for *dwelling* purposes has been interpreted liberally.

It is not necessary that the tenant-stockholder actually use the space for dwelling purposes. All that is required is that he be entitled, as against the corporate lessor, to use the space for dwelling purposes.[25]

Thus, the fact that a tenant-stockholder sublets his apartment to someone else for dwelling purposes will not affect the cooperative's tax status. Similarly, it should follow that a tenant-stockholder's use of space in the cooperative for other commercial purposes, including the conduct of a professional practice or the operation of a commercial business, should not disqualify the cooperative, provided the owner of the business operates it as an individual. Should it be necessary to incorporate the business or have it conducted in the form of a partnership, the corporation or partnership should sublease the space from the individual tenant-stockholder.

To what extent these devices can be used for the purpose of converting a cooperative housing corporation into a cooperative business corporation is uncertain. It may be that the use of the title "cooperative *housing* corporation" in the statute would of itself place a limitation upon the amount of business than can safely be conducted under its form.

6. Non-Exempt Status of Corporation

The community housing corporation is not exempt from the federal income tax. Therefore, if its gross income exceeds its allowable deductions, it will be subject to the federal income tax levied on corporations. In most cases this possibility is not a serious one, because the corporation is entitled to take deductions for interest, depreciation, and taxes against its income. The fact that these items are also deductible by the tenant-stockholders does not affect the right of the corporation itself to take the deduction.

Other items of deductible expense to the corporation would include repairs, maintenance, and other payments, such as those for water, garbage, heat, light, power, and other services. These latter items, being personal, are, of course, not deductible by the tenant-stockholders.

It should be noted that for purposes of determining the gross income of the cooperative, amounts paid by the tenant-stockholders to retire mortgage indebtedness incurred to construct the apartment building are excluded. These amounts are treated as non-taxable capital contributions made to the cooperative housing corporation by its tenant-stockholders.[26]

---

[24] Rev. Rul. 58-421 *supra;* Rev. Rul. 55-654, *supra.*
[25] Reg. § 1.216-1(b)(2).
[26] Park Place, Inc., 57 T.C. 767 (1972).

B. CONDOMINIUM OWNER AS PROPERTY OWNER

1. Definitions

A condominium is simply a plan of ownership which permits individuals to own directly a portion of the building in which they reside and the land underneath it. A condominium provides for the separate ownership by each owner of a unit or apartment in the building and for the common ownership of the underlying land and public or commonly used improvements.

The units are in reality nothing but cubes of space bounded by the floors, walls, and ceilings of each apartment. The commonly used improvements are the balance of the building, including its structural elements and all needed service facilities, including entrances, hallways, elevators, stairs, etc.

2. Correlated Rights and Duties

The owner in a condominium project receives a deed which gives him the title to his unit, described as a cube of space, and a proportionate undivided interest in the common areas. Each owner has obligations toward his co-owners and is entitled to rights from them. For example, if the condominium is a high-rise building, each owner would be entitled to the right of support from the owners below him and also would be under an obligation of support to the owners above him.

C. CONDOMINIUM UNIT HELD FOR PERSONAL RESIDENTIAL USE

If the condominium unit is used by the owner as his personal residence, he will be entitled to take certain itemized personal deductions.[27] Real property taxes assessed against the unit ownership[28] and interest paid on any mortgage liability against the unit[29] are fully deductible by the condominium unit owner. Fire, storm, or other casualty losses suffered with respect to the unit are deductible to the extent that such losses exceed $100.[30]

1. Deductions

Similarly, property taxes assessed against the underlying land and common areas are deductible by the unit owners in accordance with the economic proration of these taxes among them. Interest paid on a mortgage liability against the land and common areas will similarly be prorated. A casualty loss, such as fire damage, to the common areas would also be prorated among the unit owners and each would be entitled to deduct his share.

Two exceptions must be noted. First, if the common areas are incorporated, the taxes, interest, and casualty loss deductions will be those of the corporation, not of the

---

[27] Section 144, I.R.C. An election is required between the optional standard and itemized deductions.
[28] Section 164, I.R.C.; Rev. Rul. 64-1, 1964-1. C.B. 7.
[29] Section 163, I.R.C.
[30] Section 165, I.R.C.

unit owners.[31] Second, if the land is leased, rather than purchased,[32] the amounts paid by the unit owners as ground rent to the landowner are non-deductible personal rentals. It is the landowner who gets to deduct the property taxes against the land and any interest incurred on a mortgage liability against the land.[33]

2. Sale of Unit

If the condominium unit is used as the owner's principal residence, he is treated just like any other home owner on disposition. For example, if he sells at a gain, he may defer the tax on the gain realized by purchasing a new principal place of residence in accordance with the requirements of Section 1034.[34] The new principal residence may be another condominium unit, a single family residence, or stock in a qualified cooperative housing project.[35]

Also, if the owner of a condominium unit is older than 65 at the date of the sale and has used the unit as his principal residence for periods aggregating at least five of the eight years immediately prior to the sale, then he may be entitled to exclude from income all or part of the gain realized on a sale of the property even though he does not buy a new residence to replace the one he sold.[36] The amount of the gain excluded from tax is determined as follows: (1) If the adjusted sales price is $35,000 or less, all of the gain may be excluded; (2) if the adjusted sales price is more than $35,000, the owner may exclude from income that amount of the gain that bears the same percentage relationship to the total gain as $35,000 bears to the adjusted sales price.[37]

If the condominium unit is used as a principal private place of residence and is condemned, or sold under the threat or imminence of condemnation, the owner has a choice of using the benefits of Section 1034 outlined above, or treating the sale as an involuntary conversion to which section 1033 applies. Under the latter section, the owner may defer any gain realized on the conversion sale by purchasing another principal residence within the two taxable years following the close of the taxable year in which the condemnation sale occurred.[38] Section 1034 is also applicable.[39]

---

[31] Unit owner contributions to the corporation to reimburse it for the tax, interest, or casualty deductions are not deductible to the unit owners. Unless the unit owners incur these expenses themselves, they cannot deduct them.

[32] This is a common occurrence in Hawaii and is occurring with some frequency in California and in Puerto Rico and New York.

[33] Estate of Eugene Webb 30 T.C. 1202 (1958). Allen v. Beazley, 157 F.2d 970 (CA 5, 1946).

[34] The three major requirements of Section 1034 are (1) that the condominium unit has actually been used by the owner as his principal residence on the date of sale; (2) that a new principal residence be acquired within one year of the date of sale (18 months, if the new residence is constructed); and (3) that the cost of the new residence equal or exceed the adjusted sales price of the old residence. If the adjusted sales price of the old residence exceeds the cost of acquiring the new residence, gain is recognized to the extent of such difference.

[35] Regulations § 1.1034-1(c)(3) (1970). Or, for that matter, a Winnebago Camper or a North Sea Trawler, provided it be the principal residence of the seller.

[36] Section 121, I.R.C. Rev. Rul. 68-210 1968-1 C.B. 61.

[37] Section 121(b)(1), I.R.C.

[38] Section 1033, I.R.C.

[39] Section 1034(i)(2). Which section should you choose? Section 1034 permits a reduction of the sales price for "fixing-up" expenses within 90 days of the sales contract. But the period of acquisition is 12 months (18 months if a new residence is being constructed). Section 1033 has a 2-year-after-the-year-of

3. Character of Gain or Loss

If a gain is realized on the sale of a condominium unit, it is taxable as a capital gain, long term or short term, as the case may be.[40] The fact that the property was not acquired for profit does not exempt the realized profit from taxation as capital gain. As a capital gain, one-half of the profit on the sale of the unit is excluded from income. The other one-half is taxed as ordinary income, except that the total tax on the included one-half cannot exceed 25 percent on the first $50,000 of total gain (including the excluded one-half) and 35 percent of any excess.[41]

But whether or not the limitation usually called "alternate tax" applies, one-half of the gain is treated as an item of tax preference income and may be subject to the penalty tax levied thereon.[42]

If a loss is realized on its sale, however, the loss is non-deductible because the property was acquired for personal, not profit, purposes.[43] The foregoing holds true even if the property were condemned since a condemnation taking is treated as a sale, not a casualty.[44] Hence, the rules applicable to voluntary sales apply to the involuntary taking of a person's home. If a loss is suffered, it cannot be deducted either as a capital or other loss.[45]

4. Gift of Joint Interest to Spouse

Finally, if the owner is married, he may take title to the property in the joint names of himself and his wife without incurring any federal gift tax liability.[46] Section 2515, which provides the foregoing exception to the application of federal gift tax, applies only to the creation of "tenancies by the entirety" in real property.[47] By statute, the term "tenancy by the entirety" includes a husband-wife joint tenancy with a right of survivorship.[48] The fact that one spouse has paid the full purchase price out of his separate funds is immaterial, unless he elects to report a gift by filing a gift tax return.[49] If the election is not made, federal gift tax liability is not incurred until the tenancy is severed. If severed by death of the husband, then the transfer is subject to federal estate

---

condemnation period, but it does not permit "fixing-up" expenses either to reduce the sales price or to be added to basis. So, if you want to reduce the sales price by your last 3 months gardening expense, plus painting, etc., elect Section 1034. If you want to shop around for 2 years, elect Section 1033. The election cannot be made in the case of "destruction" of the property. Regulations § 1.1034(h)(2)(ii) (1970). In such a case Section 1033 would apply.

[40] Sections 1221, 1223, I.R.C.
[41] Section 1201, I.R.C.
[42] Sections 56-57, I.R.C.
[43] Sections 165, 262, I.R.C.
[44] The author has frequently reflected on the inequity of the denial of loss treatment to the owner of a condemned home. Then it occurred to him that a Section 165 casualty loss is dependent upon the degree of "suddenness" with which the outside force struck. Lightning epitomizes "suddenness." Termites are rather slow, unless you happen to be the owner of the property destroyed. The condemning authority's action is an "Act of God" within the meaning of most leases and contracts. Does a casualty have to be "sudden"?
[45] Section 262, I.R.C. Regulations § 1.262-1(a)(4).
[46] Section 2515, I.R.C.
[47] Section 2515(a), I.R.C.
[48] Section 2515(d), I.R.C.
[49] Section 2515(a), I.R.C.

taxes on the full value. If severed by death of the wife, the transfer is free of estate taxes because we have assumed that all of the purchase price came from the husband. If severed during the lifetime of both husband and wife, a gift, subject to possible gift taxes, will be made to the extent that the wife receives any of the property, or interest therein, at the time of the severance.[50]

D. CONDOMINIUM UNITS HELD FOR BUSINESS USE

If the condominium is utilized by the taxpayer for conducting a trade, business, or the practice of a profession, real property taxes, interest expense, and casualty losses may be deducted whether or not the taxpayer takes the optional standard deduction in lieu of itemizing his personal deductions.[51] Other trade or business expenses, such as the cost of property insurance, repair and maintenance expenses, may also be deducted.[52]

1. Depreciation

In addition, the taxpayer will be entitled to deduct a reasonable allowance for depreciation, which includes accelerated depreciation on new construction not in excess of 150 percent of straight-line depreciation on a declining-balance method.[53] If the condominium unit is rented to others for their personal residential purposes and the unit is new construction in the hands of the owner, then the depreciation deduction is liberalized to include such accelerated methods of depreciation as sum-of-the-years digits and 200 percent declining-balance (double-declining-balance).[54]

2. Limitation on Interest Deduction

If the condominium unit is rented to others, whether for their residential use or for their use in a trade or business (including the practice of a profession), a limitation on the deduction of interest expense will be imposed if the rental terms are such that the relationship is a "net lease." In such a case, interest expense is deductible in full up to $10,000 plus investment income.[55] This limitation on the deduction of investment

---

[50] Section 2515(b), I.R.C.

[51] These are so-called "above the line" deductions, that is, deductions from gross income in order to determine "adjusted gross income." If a charitable deduction is important, the more deductions that can be placed "below the line," the higher adjusted gross income will be and the higher the maximum 50 percent limit on charitable deductions will be. Sections 163-165, I.R.C.

[52] Section 162, I.R.C.

[53] Section 167, I.R.C. The annual excess of accelerated over straight-line depreciation is an item of tax preference income which may be subject to the penalty tax of 10% imposed by the Tax Reform Act of 1969. § 57. No corresponding tax benefit, such as an adjustment to basis or a credit against recapture exposure, is granted the taxpayer.

[54] Section 167(j), I.R.C. The annual excess is an item of tax preference income that may be subject to the 10 percent penalty tax.

[55] Section 163(d), I.R.C. The owner of investment property, including property rented on a "net lease" basis can deduct investment interest (that is, interest paid on obligations to acquire or retain investment property) in full to the extent of $10,000 plus net investment income plus cash expenses over net rental income. The excess can be carried for possible deduction in future years.

interest is not on a "per project" basis. Hence, if the investor has already exceeded the $25,000 limitation on investment interest because of borrowings to invest in the stock market, the investment interest expense incurred to purchase a leased-out condominium unit will be fully subject to the limitations of the 1969 Tax Reform Act.

3. Gain or Loss on Disposition of Unit

If the condominium unit has been held for more than six months and is used by the owner for his own trade or business (including the practice of a profession) or is rented out to others, it constitutes a Section 1231 asset.[56] Thus, any gain or loss realized on the sale of the unit must be aggregated with other Section 1231 gains and losses. Any gain resulting from the 1231 netting computation will be taxed as a long-term capital gain; while a resulting loss will be deductible as an ordinary deduction.[57]

There may be one exception to the foregoing conclusions. If property is rented on a "net lease" within the meaning of the Section 163 limitation on the deduction of investment interest, the asset should be treated as an investment asset, not a Section 1231 trade or business asset. As an investment asset, gains or losses will be capital gains or losses, not subject to Section 1231 netting. Treatment of "net lease" rental property as a capital asset would be beneficial only when a gain is realized on the unit's disposition. The benefit is due to the fact that any gain would not be used to offset 1231 losses for the year. Thus, the probability that the netting process will result in a loss—and ordinary deductions for each 1231 asset—is substantially increased. In the case of a loss, however, treatment of "net lease" rental property as an investment asset would be disastrous. Such a loss would be treated as a capital loss, deductible only against capital gains (including net Section 1231 gains) and, to the extent of 50 percent, or $6,000, of the loss, whichever is less, against $3,000 of the seller's ordinary income.[58]

E. CONDOMINIUM MANAGEMENT AGREEMENTS

Condominium unit owners may enter into an agreement providing for some or all of the following matters:

(1) Maintenance of the exterior and all internal common spaces.

(2) Employment of management staff and other personnel (or making contractual arrangements therefor) such as security, janitorial, gardening, repair, T.V. cable and other services.

(3) Arrangements for supplying and payment of heat, light, water, power, and other utilities.

(4) Management and operation of recreational facilities, such as swimming pools, tennis courts, golf courses, spas, muscle gyms, saunas, and recreational rooms.

(5) Rules of personal conduct applicable to mutual owners living in close proximity, such as noise, smells, lights, practice of a business at home, advertising, and so on.

---

[56] Section 1231(a), I.R.C.
[57] Regulations § 1.1231(b).
[58] Section 1211(b)(1)(C).

The foregoing is a partial compilation of problems that may arise in the common ownership of land.

1. Management, Maintenance and Servicing Agreements

Contracts between mutual owners of commonly owned property for the employment of people to manage, caretake, and otherwise provide service for condominium owners cause no tax problems. If the condominium is wholly residential, the expenses thereof are nondeductible. If the condominium is wholly commercial (for example, a medical-dental building) the expenses are deductible.

Expenditures made under contract providing for painting, gardening, repairing, utility service, and other miscellaneous services, are non-deductible if the condominium is residential. Such expenditures are deductible if the property is commercial.

The contracts discussed in this sub-topic do not give rise to the corporate association problems discussed below because there is no common profit objective. Each owner is on his own.

2. Restrictive Covenants

Agreements of any sort, whether or not tied to the land, or restrictive covenants specifically burdening the land, which set limits on the use of the buyer may make of the land have no federal income tax effect—discrimination is not a taxable event.[59]

3. Recreational Facilities

While the expenses of ordinary operation are non-deductible, the cost of mutually agreed upon operation of recreational facilities creates no tax problem. But the exposure to possible liabilities frequently pressures the unit owners to transfer the common areas and the recreational facilities to a non-profit corporation. By doing so the unit owners hope to limit their liability to their investment. But they pay a tax consequence. The deductions attributable to the property conveyed (property taxes, interest on indebtedness, and casualty losses) are transferred to the non-profit corporation.

In order to avoid this transfer of the deductible items, the author advises that the unit owners retain title and take out a landlord's liability insurance policy. Then the unit owners lease the common places and recreational areas to the non-profit corporation on a net lease basis.

In this way, they retain the deductible items for themselves and the non-profit corporation picks up the tab for the insurance coverage and maintenance (all non-deductible).

Tax problems will arise, however, if the ownership of the recreational facilities is conveyed to a non-profit corporation. The conveyance of the property to such a corporation is tax-free[60] unless the basis allocable thereto is *less* than the mortgage indebted-

---

[59]Problems may arise if the unit owners apply for exemption from federal income taxes under Section 501, I.R.C.
[60]Section 351, I.R.C.

ness against the property. If the mortgage debt exceeds allocable basis, a gain—to the extent of the excess—will be realized and taxed.[61]

The ownership and operation of the recreational facilities of the condominium are of no tax consequence because of various rules. If the corporation operates at a loss, such loss is not deductible by the shareholders. If the corporation operates at a gain, such gain would be non-taxable since the corporation should qualify for an exemption as a Section 501(c)(7) recreational club.[62]

4. Rental to Outsiders

Rental transactions give rise to the most serious tax problem facing condominium owners, whether they participate in a residential or commercial condominium. The problem is a simple one: Will the net rentals be taxed to each owner or will such rentals be taxed first to an association of owners taxable as a corporation?[63] If the latter, the net income will be subject to double taxation. It will be taxed first to the condominium association, and second to the owners on distribution of the net amount after the corporate tax.

The condominium owners who rent their units usually do so through a manager who is under a written contract with the owners. Generally, the manager is empowered to sign a lease for the owner on the best terms and conditions that can be arranged. The question arises as to whether the foregoing arrangement constitutes an association taxable as a corporation.

F. CORPORATE STATUS OF A MANAGEMENT ASSOCIATION

If the unit owners lease out a portion of their property for profit, how can the unit owners avoid being taxed as a corporation?

In order to avoid corporate status, the unit owners must negate at least two of the four common characteristics of a corporation: continuity, transferability, liability, and management.[64]

1. Continuity of Life

No one condominium owner can normally sue for partition, except in the case of destruction in whole or in major part. A condominium is treated under the income tax law as much a product of contractual agreement as it is a conveyance of land. Therefore, in the absence of contrary agreement, death, insanity, and bankruptcy of any member are *not* considered adequate to destroy the "continuity of life" of the association.

---

[61] Section 357(c), I.R.C.

[62] Section 501(c)(7), I.R.C. provides an exemption from taxation for "[c]lubs organized and operated exclusively for pleasure, recreation, and other nonprofitable purposes . . ." Lake Petersburg Association, ¶32,482(M) T.C. Memo (1974) denied Section 501(c)(7) status because of "no social meeting" and exterior maintenance that were of "personal benefit" to unit owners. Rev. Rul. 74-17, I.R.B. 1974-2, 11; Rev. Rul. 74-99, I.R.B. 1974-9, 11.

[63] Regulations § 301.7701-2(a).

[64] Regulations § 301.7701-2(a)(2).

This is a corporate characteristic. In a partnership, any one partner can cause a dissolution under the Uniform Act. In a tenancy in common, any one tenant can normally partition. In a corporation, normally, a 50 percent shareholder can sue to dissolve.

How can the corporate test be violated? Simply by providing a right to expel a unit owner for cause in which case the expelled owner can neither (1) receive the fair market value of his unit, or (2) sue to partition. The fact that such right is seldom exercised because of its consequences seems to be immaterial under the Treasury Regulations.[65]

2. Centralization of Management

The central inquiry regarding centralization of management is who makes the decisions. If the approval and consent of *all* condominium owners is required there is no centralized management. On the other hand if a group of *less than all* of the owners has exclusive authority to make all decisions for the business, centralized management is present.

But business decisions are of two basic kinds. For lack of a better expression, we can divide them into "day-to-day" decisions and "policy" decisions. If all "policy" questions are decided by the entire membership, "day-to-day" decisions can be delegated to a manager (or "board of managers") without fear of having centralized management.[66]

The question, therefore, is what are "policy" questions and what are "day-to-day" questions. "Day-to-day" decisions are decisions that relate to the choice of garbage collectors, gardeners, office procedures, and similar matters. All other decisions, such as the rent to be charged, the term of the lease, and the use of the space should be voted on by the condominium owners either before the execution of the lease or in ratification thereof. If the vote is taken in ratification of the lease, the manager should be careful to make the lease contingent upon such ratification. Normally, neither the contingency nor the ratification is a problem in arranging a lease.

The more limited the authority of the "board of managers," the lesser the chance of being taxed as a corporate association.

3. Limited Liability

Owners of property who rent it out do not have limited liability. Each owner of a condominium unit, and of a tenancy in common in rented property, is directly liable as an owner for what happens on the rented premises.[67] The fact that the owner participated in insurance coverage to indemnify him does not alter his conclusion.

4. Free Transferable Interests

Condominium ownership can be set up with restricted or nonrestricted freedom of transfer. If restricted, for whatever reason, the corporate characteristic of freely transferable interests is absent.[68]

---

[65] Regulations § 301.7701-2(b).
[66] Regulations § 301.7701-2(c)(2).
[67] Regulations § 301.7701-2(d).
[68] Regulations § 301.7701-2(e).

There are several ways by which free transferability can be restricted. One is a mutual buy-sell agreement under the terms of which each owner agrees that he will sell to his co-tenants at a fixed price in the event he decides to sell. Another is to condition any sale upon the consent of a majority of the owner's contenants. Each of these has the economic objection that the owner is subjecting a valuable investment either to a ceiling in price appreciation or to the whim of his co-tenants. A right of first refusal may satisfy these objections. That is, the other co-tenants have a first right to buy a prospective seller's condominium unit on the same terms and conditions as he may negotiate with an outsider. If none of the co-tenants wants to buy at that price, the owner is free to sell to the outsider.

The Treasury Regulations equivocate on the effect of a right of first refusal. Such a right is not sufficient of itself to make the interests not freely transferable. The Regulations state the transferability exists only in modified form. Whether the test of "free" transferability is or is not met or whether such "modified" transferability is a corporate characteristic has not been answered by the Treasury. The Treasury has only to state that if "modified transferability" exists, the corporate characteristic of transferability has *less* significance in determining whether or not the group is taxable as a corporation than otherwise.[69]

The way to solve the problem is to provide that no unit owner can sell his interest without first obtaining the consent of the "board of managers." If the "board of managers" objects to the color of the skin of the prospective purchaser, the free transfer of interests tests is satisfied on the taxpayer's side. On the other hand, if a white can sell to a black, or, a black to a green, free transferability is present. But if all sales require the consent of the "board of managers," there is not free transferability within the meaning of the Internal Revenue Code.[70]

The foregoing provision requiring majority (or board of directors) approval before a sale may be consummated is a common restrictive provision in the articles or bylaws of co-operative corporations organized under Section 216 of the Code. Ironically such "private club" restrictions on condominium ownership will help prevent the co-ownership from being treated as a corporation.[71]

G. TAX CONSEQUENCES OF CORPORATE TAXATION

Because the individual condominium units are not held for a common profit, the gross income and deductions allocable thereto cannot be treated as part of the gross income of deductions of the condominium association. Nor would co-tenancy assessments for non-business purposes, such as the maintenance of recreational facilities, be attributed to the condominium association.

It is the author's practice to sever agreements for the use and occupancy of individually owned space and for the maintenance and care of non-income-producing common space from agreements relating to commonly owned income-producing space. Such separation should not be essential for the separate tax treatment of the latter, but advisable for the simple reason that unsophisticated reviewers of the docu-

---

[69] Regulations § 301.7701-2(e)(1).
[70] Regulations § 301.7701-2(a)(2) and (3).
[71] Such restrictions will prevent qualification for tax exemption under Section 501(c).

ments (such as auditing agents and appellate courts) will not become confused as to the extent of the *common* profit-making activities of the co-owners. Contributions to maintain common space must be explained: why are they not part of the association's gross income?

1. Co-ownership of Rental Units

Corporate treatment is limited to commonly owned property held for profit purposes or for the build-up of cash reserves.

As individual unit owners, the taxpayers are acting independently of one another if each rents out his own unit for business purposes. In such case, unit owners are not acting in concert and cannot be "associates."[72] Nor can the inverse test include commonly owned property held for non-income purposes (elevators, lobbies, hallways, garbage areas, etc., serving residential units only, recreational areas, and similar properties) because even though the common owners are associated, their association is not for a profit.

2. Loss of Deductions

The tax consequences of treating the commonly held rental property of condominium owners as being held by an association taxable as a corporation are disastrous. None of the condominium owners would be entitled to deduct his aliquot portion of the interest, taxes, or depreciation allocable thereto; all of these deductions would be allocated to the corporate association. The rental income received would be taxed to the corporate association at corporate tax rates to the extent it exceeded allocable deductions. Finally, the use of any funds of the corporate association to pay expenses properly allocable to the individual condominium unit owners would be considered a dividend to them which would be taxable as ordinary income.

3. Section 216 Availability

This section permits a pass through to shareholders of (1) interest, (2) property taxes, and (3) depreciation to the extent the shareholder uses the property for trade or business or other profit purposes. The section is not elective and applies if the facts warrant.[73]

Eighty percent or more of the cooperative housing corporation's gross income must be derived from its owners.[74] For this purpose, amounts paid by tenant-stockholders to the cooperative housing corporation to meet mortgage or other lien payments are not part of the corporation's gross income; such amounts are contributions to the corporation's capital.[75] As a consequence, the amount of non-qualified income from outside sources will normally exceed 20 percent of total gross income.

---

[72] Regulations § 301.7701-2(a)(2).
[73] Section 216(a)(c). The corporation must have only one class of stock, each shareholder must have the right to occupy a unit, and no shareholder is entitled to any distribution of earnings except on liquidation.
[74] Section 216(b)(1)(D) I.R.C.
[75] Cambridge Apartment Bldg. Corp., 44 BTA 617 (1941), acq. 1942-2 CB 2; Park Avenue Corp., 23 BTA 400 (1931), acq. X-2 CB 21.

4. Section 528 Availability: Exempt Homeowners' Association

Section 528, adopted in 1976, specifically exempts from income taxation certain qualified homeowners' associations. To qualify, the homeowners' association must meet the following requirements:

(1) The association must be engaged in the acquisition, construction, management, maintenance, or care of property of the association.

(2) 60 percent of its gross income is membership dues, fees or assessments.

(3) 90 percent of the association's expenditures must be for the acquisition, construction, management, maintenance, and care of association property.

(4) No part of the net earnings goes to a private person.

(5) A timely election is filed by the association. If it qualified, the homeowners association will be exempt from tax on the assessments, dues and fees received from members.[76]

However, Section 528(b) imposes a corporate tax on all taxable income over $100 at the rate of 48 percent.[77] Taxable income is defined as gross income (less exempt function income) over its trade or business expenses. Thus, any assessments, dues or fees paid by members for the use of the social or recreational facilities in excess of expenses would be taxable income to the homeowners' association. Such assessments, dues or fees in excess of expenses *are not related* to the exempt functions of the homeowners' association.

It also follows that I.R.C. Section 528(b) levies a 48 percent tax on all of the homeowner associations net interest, dividend and investment income, plus a 30 percent tax on all gains from the sale of assets (less the $100 exclusion; no carryover of losses is permitted).[78] This is a very heavy penalty to pay for the privilege of election. The theory is that individual homeowners are taxable on their dividend and interest income. For that reason, Congress decided to tax the association's dividend and interest income at the highest corporate rate.

Furthermore, any homeowners association that operates recreational facilities for its members will find it difficult to qualify under the 90 percent expenditures test. If more than 10 percent of the expenditures are for non-qualified purposes, the homeowners association election may be lost. For this purpose, qualified expenditures include:

" . . . both current and capital expenditures on association property. For example, qualifying expenditures will include salaries paid to an association manager, secretary and expenses of maintaining association newsletters. Qualifying expenditures will also include expenses for gardening, paving, street signs, security personnel, property taxes assessed on property owned by the association, and current operating expenses of tennis courts, swimming pools, recreation rooms and halls, etc. In addition, expenses for replacement of common buildings equipment and facilities such as replacement of heating, air conditioning, elevators, etc., will qualify. However, . . . expenditures on privately owned property—as opposed to common property—are to qualify only in the limited situation of repair of exterior walls and roofs where the walls and roofs qualify as association property.

---

[76] Section 528(d).
[77] Section 528(b)(1).
[78] Sen. Rep. No. 94-938, 94th Cong. 2nd Sess. (1976), p. 394. There appears to be no backout from the election once made, but the regulations to be issued may clarify this question.

"Investments or transfers of funds to be held to meet future costs are not to be taken into account as an expenditure. For example, transfers to a sinking fund account for the replacement of a roof would not qualify as an expenditure for the 90 percent test."[79]

It follows that an election under Section 528 may either be unavailable, or, if available, more of a tax trap than a tax boon.

5. Overassessments by a Homeowners' Association

Let us suppose the election under Section 528 is not available or is not made. How should overassessments be handled so that they do not become taxable income?

Contribution to Capital. A contribution to the capital of a homeowners association is not taxable income to the association. However, to be excludible from the gross income of the association, three requirements must be met:

(1) A special assessment must be levied by vote of the unit-owner members;[80]

(2) The purpose of the assessment must be for a specific capital expenditure; and

(3) The proceeds of the special assessment must be segregated from general operating revenues; deposit in a separate bank account is sufficient.

Purposes for which a special assessment can be levied include:

(1) Replacement of outdoor pool furniture.[81]

(2) Paving of community parking areas.[82]

(3) Purchase of land for lake and construction of dam, lake and roads.[83]

(4) Replacement of roof and elevators in a high-rise condominium.[84]

(5) Replacement of structural and mechanical equipment, such as ranges, refrigerators, plumbing facilities, washers, dryers and disposals.[85]

The rulings emphasize that the purpose of the special assessment must be to enhance the value of the property, not merely to maintain it. Specific non-qualified purposes are painting, repairs, gardening, and janitorial services.[86]

Return of Overassessment to Members. Can overassessments be returned to members without tax liability to the association? By analogy to the patronage dividend (refund) of cooperatives, the Courts have held such rebates may be made. The form of the refund can be either by repayment or by credit against the following year's assessment.

To the extent that the assessments for the current year exceed, or may exceed, expenses for management, operating, maintaining, and replacing the common elements, the members should hold a meeting in accordance with the following:

---

[79]Sen. Rep. 94-938, 94th Cong. 2nd Sess., p. 396.
[80]Failure to take special membership action was held fatal in *The Edison Club*, 34 T.C.M. 79 (1975). Annual additions to the reserve fund were taxable income to the association.
[81]Rev. Rul. 75-371, 1975-2 C.B. 52.
[82]Rev. Rul. 74-563, 1974-2 C.B. 38.
[83]*Lake Petersburg Association*, 1974 P-H T.C. Memo ¶74,055 (1974).
[84]Rev. Rul. 75-370, 1975-2 C.B. 25.
[85]*Concord Villiage, Inc.*, 65 T.C. 142 at 155 (1975).
[86]Rev. Rul. 75-370, 1975-2 C.B. 25.

"A meeting is held each year by the stockholder-owners of the corporation, at which they decide what is to be done with any excess assessments not actually used for the purposes described above, i.e., they decide either to return the excess to themselves or to have the excess applied against the following year's assessments."

"Held, the excess assessments for the taxable year over and above the actual expenses paid or incurred for the purposes described above are not taxable income to the corporation, since such excess, in effect, has been returned to the stockholder-owners."[87]

6. Separate Entity for Recreational Purposes

Section 501(c)(7) provides an exemption from income tax of clubs organized and operated exclusively for pleasure, recreation and other non-profitable purposes. Regulations §1.201(c)(7)-1 further states:

"In general, this exemption extends to social and recreation clubs which are supported solely by membership fees, dues and assessments. However, a club otherwise entitled to exemption will not be disqualified because it raises revenue from members through the use of club facilities or in connection with club activities."

The Internal Revenue Service has ruled that the developer of a housing development may organize an exempt social and recreational club for the benefit of purchasers of homes in the development. As each owner purchased his home he paid his pro-rata share of the cost of construction of the social and recreational facilities (including a swimming pool) and became a member. However, such a homeowners' social and recreational club may not do any of the following:

(1) Own and maintain residential streets;

(2) Administer and enforce covenants for preserving the architecture and appearance of the housing development;[88] or

(3) Provide the housing development with fire and police protection and a trash collection service; or[89]

(4) Lease lots for personal residential purposes.[90]

Because the activities, revenues and expenditures of a qualified social and recreational club must be kept separate from a homeowner's association, it will be necessary for the social and recreational club to bill its assessments, dues, fees and charges for services separately from those of the homeowners' association. Separate accounting records must be established and maintained for each organization.

7. Separate Business Entity Alternative

If the condominium owners cannot avoid tax treatment as an association taxable as a corporation, they should consider the alternative of incorporating for the purpose of

---

[87]Rev. Rul. 70-604, 1970-2 C.B. 9; Rule repeated in Rev. Rul. 75-371, 1975-2 C.B. 52. In accord, *Park Place, Inc.*, 57 T.C. 767 at 780 (1972). In *Park Place*, the overassessments were held includable in gross income because they were carried on the co-operative corporations books indefinitely. Timely action, by way of refund or credit to the following year's assessments must be made. Accord, *Concord Village, Inc*. 65 T.C. 142 at 154 (1975).
[88]Rev. Rul. 69-281, 1969-1 C.B. 155.
[89]Rev. Rul. 75-494, 1975-2 C.B. 214.
[90]*Lake Petersburg Association*, 1974 P.H. T.C. Memo ¶74,055 (1974).

renting out the commonly owned rental space. The property to be so rented should not be transferred to the rental corporation. It should be retained by the co-owners and leased to the corporation. Each co-owner should individually sign the lease as a tenant in common in order to preserve his status as an individual owner.

The corporation should be organized with a minimal amount of cash, and should then enter into a lease of the rental space from the condominium owners at a rental measured by the maximum fair rental allowable to the owners.

By this arrangement, the owners will get their deductions for interest, taxes, and depreciation because they are the owners of the commonly owned rental space. The corporate lessee should then be able to rent out the quarters on a sublease basis and take a deduction for rentals paid to the condominium unit owners. While these rentals will be taxed to the co-owners, they will not be double-taxed both to the rental corporation and to the co-owners.

To what extent can condominium owners enjoy all the tax benefits of personal deductions for their aliquot share of interest and taxes (plus casualty losses) on their personal units and also rent out commonly owned property to business tenants who will pay for most of the building's services in lieu of taxable rent? The concept is simple, but it is not always easy to execute. It takes a lot of argument to convince a prime tenant that he should pay elevator cost (if he is on the first floor), should pay the cost of the main water meter (which covers all the landscaping), should pay all expenses of maintaining the entrance, lobbies, and hallways, and should provide guards (in his interest) and around-the-clock prestigious doormen. But if his rental is lowered accordingly (*i.e.*, in the amount he has to pay in order to provide the foregoing services), he will understand. In either case, his payments are deductible business expenses. The upstairs condominium unit owners will be pleased, but, hopefully, will not be taxed on these benefits.[91]

---

[91] Bear Valley Mutual Water Co. v. Commissioner, 283 Fed. Supp. 949 (DC, Cal. 1968), aff'd per curiam, 427 F.2d 713 (CA 9, 1970); Anaheim Union Water Co., 321 F.2d 253 (9th Cir. 1963). *Contra*, Chicago & W.R.R. v. Commissioner, 303 F.2d 796 (7th Cir. 1962) (distinguishable because it involved only corporate persons, not individuals).

Table of Cases

Case   *Text Page*

Aaron W. Hardwick, Par. 47,060 P-H Memo T.C. (1947), ...240n
A.B. Culbertson, 14 T.C. 1421, 1424 (1950), ...171n, 173n, 224n
Aberle v. Commissioner, 121 F. 2d 726 (3rd Cir. 1941), ...247n
Ackerman Buick, Inc., T.C. Memo 1973–224 (1973), ...46n
Adolph Schwarcz, 24 T.C. 733, 739, ...31n
Aiken v. Commissioner, 35 F. 2d 620, 624 (8th Cir. 1929), ...178n, 179n
A.J. Schwarzler Co., 3 B.T.A. 535 (1926), ...248n
Alamo Broadcasting Co., 15 T.C. 534 (1950), ...272n
Alaska Realty Co. v. Commissioner, 141 F. 2d 675 (6th Cir. 1944), ...271n
Albert L. Rowan, 22 T.C. 865, 875 (1954), ...276n, 277n
Albert T. Felix, 21 T.C. 794 (1954), ...291n, 297n, 298n
Alden B. Oakes, 44 T.C. 524 (1965), ...298n
Alderson v. Commissioner, 317 F. 2d 790 (9th Cir. 1963), ...121n, 122n, 124n, 125n, 128n
Al Goodman, Inc., 23 T.C. 288, 302 (1954), ...184n
Alice Phelan Sullivan Corp., 381 F. 2d 399 (Ct. Cls., 1969), ...144n
The Alleghany Corporation, 28 T.C. 298 (1957), ...79n
Allen v. Beazley, 157 F. 2d 970, 973 (5th Cir. 1946), ...44n, 376n
Allen v. Courts, 127 F. 2d 127 (5th Cir. 1942), ...192n, 250n
Allen v. Selig, 200 F. 2d 487 (5th Cir. 1952), ...79n
Allen Tobey, 26 T.C. 610 (1956), ...225n
American Central Life Ins. Co., 30 B.T.A. 1182, 1190 (1934), ...241n
American Central Utilities Co., 36 B.T.A. 688 (1937), ...94n
American Spring and Wire Etc., 20 T.C.M. 116 (1961), ...269n
American Valve Co., 4 B.T.A. 1204 (1926), ...76n
Amphitrite Corp., 16 T.C. 1140 (1951), ...193n
Anaheim Union Water Co., 321 F. 2d 253 (9th Cir. 1963), ...388n
Anders, 414 F. 2d 1283 (CA-9, 1969), ...144n
Anders I. Lagreide, 23 T.C. 508 (1954), ...31n
Andrew A. Monaghan, 40 T.C. 680 (1963), ...155, 155n, 156n
Andrew J. Easter, 1964 P-H Memo T.C. ¶64,058 (1964), ...262n
Annie B. Smith, Par. 53,046 P-H Memo T.C. (1953), ...193n
Antone Borchard, 1965 P-H Memo T.C. 65, 297 (1965), ...121n, 125n
A. Raymond Jones, 25 T.C. 1100, 1103 (1956), ...77n
Arch B. Johnson, 42 T.C. 880 (1964), ...138n
Arthur Berenson, 39 B.T.A. 77 (1939), ...252n
Arthur R. Barry, 1971 P-H T.C. Memo ¶71,179, ...30n
Arthur T. Galt, 19 T.C. 892 (1953), ...275n
Atlantic Coast Line RR, 31 B.T.A. 730 (1934), ...264n
Atmore Realty Co., par. 42, 248 P-H Memo B.T.A. (1942), ...229n
Audano v. United States, 428 F. 2d 251 (5th Cir. 1970), ...257n, 297n
A.W. Legg, 57 T.C. 164 (1971), ...165n
Baltimore Baseball Club, Inc. v. United States, 481 F. 2d 1283
    (Ct. Cl. 1973), ...149n, 173n
Bank of Newberry, 1 T.C. 374, 376 (1942), ...222n
Bank of New York v. Commissioner, 147 F. 2d 651 (2d Cir. 1945), ...222n

Bath v. United States, 323 F. 2d 980 (5th Cir. 1963), ...166n
Baton Coal Co. v. Commissioner, 51 F. 2d 469 (CA 3, 1931), ...259n
Bauer v. United States, 144 Ct. Cl. 308, 168 F. Supp. 539 (Ct. Cl. 1958), ...32n
B.C. Cook & Sons, 59 T.C. 516 (1972), ...87n
Bear Valley Mutual Water Co. v. Commissioner, 283 F. Supp. 949 (D.C.Cal. 1968), ..388n
Beck v. Commissioner, 179 F. 2d 688 (7th Cir. 1950), ...317n
Bedell v. Commissioner, 30 F. 2d 622 (2d Cir. 1929), ...181n
Bennet v. Commissioner, 139 F. 2d 961, 965 (8th Cir. 1944), ...235n, 244n
Benton v. Commissioner, 197 F. 2d 745, 752 (5th Cir. 1952), ...286n
Bernard Long, 1 B.T.A. 792 (1925), ...182n
Bernstein v. Commissioner, 230 F. 2d 603 (2d Cir. 1956), ...278n
Bert B. Burnquist, 44 B.T.A. 484 (1941), ...246n, 248n
Bessie Stanly, 40 T.C. 851 (1963), ...166n
Bickerstaff v. Commissioner, 128 F. 2d 366 (5th Cir. 1942), ...147n, 247n
Big "D" Development Corp., 1971 P-H T.C. Memo ¶71,148, ...155n
Billy Rose's Diamond Horseshoe v. U.S., 448 F. 2d 549 (CA 2, 1971), ...265n
Bingham v. Commissioner, 105 F. 2d 971 (2d Cir. 1939), ...233n, 243n
Blackstone Realty Co. v. Commissioner, 22 AFTR 2d 5156 (5th Cir. 1968), ...156n
Blackstone Theater Co., 12 T.C. 801, 805 (1949), ...189n, 192
Blair v. Commissioner, 300 U.S. 5 (1937), ...300n
Blick v. Commissioner, 271 F. 2d 928 (3rd Cir. 1959), ...56n
Bloomington Coca-Cola Bottling Co. v. Commissioner, 189 F. 2d 14
    (7th Cir. 1951), ...129n
Blum v. Commissioner, 133 F. 2d 447 (2d Cir. 1943), ...246n
Bonwit Teller & Co. v. Commissioner, 53 F. 2d 381 (CA 2, 1931), ...272n
Booker, 27 T.C. 932 (1957), ...142n
Bookwalter v. Mayer, 345 F. 2d 476 (8th Cir. 1965), ...151n
Boston Fish Market Corp., 57 T.C. 884 (1972), ...265n
Bourne v. Commissioner, 62 F. 2d 648 (4th Cir. 1933), ...179n
Bowles Lunch, Inc., 35 F. Supp. 235, 240 (Ct. Cl. 1940), ...254n
Boyd A. Veenkant, 1968 P-H T.C. Memo ¶68,119, ...156n
Boys, Inc. of America v. Campbell, 18 AFTR 2d 5200, ...300n
Bradford Hotel Operating Co. v. Commissioner, 244 F. 2d 876 (1st Cir. 1957), ...260n
Brandeis v. Allen, 60 F. 2d 1004 (D.C. Neb. 1932), ...96n
Breece Veneer and Panel Co. v. Commissioner, 232 F. 2d 319 (7th Cir. 1956), ...286n
Briley v. United States, 189 F. Supp. 510 (N.D. Ohio, 1960), ...27n
Brooke v. United States, 468 F. 2d 1155 (9th Cir. 1972), ...297n
Brown v. Commissioner, 180 F. 2d 926 (3rd Cir. 1950), ...291n, 297n, 298n
Brown Printing Co. v. Commissioner, 255 F. 2d 436 (CA 4, 1958), ...257n
Burkhard Inv. Co. v. United States, 100 F. 2d 642 (9th Cir. 1938), ...111n
Burnet v. Logan, 283 U.S. 404,413 (1931), ...93n, 169n, 170n, 176
Burnet v. S. & L. Building Corp., 288 U.S. 406 (1933), ...158n
Burrel Groves, Inc., v. Commissioner, 223 F. 2d 526 (5th Cir. 1955), ...166n
C.A. Cochran, 23 B.T.A. 616, 619 (1931), ...178n, 179n
Cahn v. Commissioner, 92 F. 2d 674 (9th Cir. 1937), ...87n
Caldwell Milling Co., 3 B.T.A. 1232, 1236 (1926), ...84n
Caldwell v. United States, 114 F. 2d 995 (3rd Cir. 1940), ...152n
Cambria Development Co., 34 B.T.A. 1155 (1936), ...170n
Cambridge Apartment Bldg. Corp., 44 B.T.A. 617 (1941), ...371n, 384n
Camp Wolters Enterprises, Inc., 22 T.C. 737, 754 (1954), ...26n, 64n
Cappell House Furnishing Co. V. United States, 244 F. 2d 525
    (6th Cir. 1957), ...137n
Carling Dinkler, 22 B.T.A. 329 (1931), ...93n
Carlisle Packing Co., 29 B.T.A. 514 (1933), ...237n
Carlos Marcello, 1968 P-H Memo T.C. ¶68, 268, ...150n

TABLE OF CASES 391

Carlton v. United States, 20 AFTR 5376 (5th Cir. 1967), ...121n, 122n, 124n
Carnegie Center Company, 22 T.C. 1189, 1193 (1954) 55n, 276n
Carter-Colton Cigar Co., 9 T.C. 219 (1947), ...98n
Casalina Corp., 60 T.C. No. 72 (1973), ...34n
Cassatt v. Commissioner, 137 F. 2d 745, 749 (3rd Cir. 1943), ...270n, 273n, 281n
Catherine B. Currier, 51 T.C. No. 49 (1968), ...75n, 278n
Mrs. C.B. Staton, 1 B.T.A. 1222 (1925), ...111n
Central Cuba Sugar Co., 198 F. 2d 214, 217 (2d Cir. 1952), ...195n
Century Electric Co. v. Commissioner, 192 F. 2d 155 (8th Cir. 1951), ...112n, 290n, 291n
Charles A. Collins, 48 T.C. 45 (1967), ...156n
Charles Bertram Currier, T.C. 980, 985 (1946), ...271n
Charles E. Mieg, 32 T.C. 1314 (1959), ...34n, 318n
Charles F. Neave, 17 T.C. 1237, 1243 (1946), ...27n
Charles H. Black, 45 B.T.A. 204 (1941), ...277n, 228n, 245n
Charles L. Nutter, 7 T.C. 480, 483 (1946), ...246n
Charles M. Howell, 21 B.T.A. 757, 781 (1930), ...193n
Charlotte Leviton Herbert, 25 T.C. 807, 815 (1956), ...276n
Chester B. Knox, 2 B.T.A. 1107, ...65n
Chicago Stoker Corp., 14 T.C. 441, 445 (1950), ...285n
Chicago & W.R.R. v. Commissioner, 303 F. 2d 796 (7th Cir. 1962), ...388n
Chick M. Farha, 58 T.C. 526 (1972), ...163n
City Investing Co., 38 T.C. 1 (1961), ...291n
Clara Driscoll, Par. 44, 021, P-H Memo T.C. (1944), ...196n
Clarence E. Day, par. 42,197 P-H B.T.A. Memo (1942), ...255n
Clarkson Coal Co., 46 B.T.A. 688 (1942), ...240n, 241n
Clifton Investment Co. v. Commissioner, ...133n
Clifton Mfg. Co. v. Commissioner, 137 F. 2d 290 (4th Cir. 1943), ...94n
Clinton Cotton Mills, Inc. v. Commissioner, 78 F. 2d 292, 296 (4th Cir. 1935), ...65n
Clinton Hotel Realty Corp. v. Commissioner, 128 F. 2d 968
    (5th Cir. 1942), ...179n, 259n, 260n
Clinton Park Development Co. v. Commissioner, 209 F. 2d 951 (5th Cir. 1954), ...186n
Coastal Terminals, Inc., 25 T.C. 1053 (1956), ...87n
Coastal Terminals, Inc. v. United States, 320 F. 2d 333 (4th Cir. 1963), ...121n, 125n
Coddon & Bros. Inc., 37 B.T.A. 393, 398 (1938), ...249n, 250n
Coe Laboratories, Inc., 34 T.C. 549 (1960), ...299n
Cohn v. United States, 259 F. 2d 371 (6th Cir. 1958), ...74n
Cole v. United States, 141 F. Supp. 558 (D. Wyo. 1956), ...31n
Colin M. Peters, 1969 P-H Memo T.C. ¶69,052, ...72n, 76n
Colonial Enterprises, Inc., 47 B.T.A. 518, 521 (1942), ...46n
Columbus Die, Tool & Machine Co., Par. 52, 52,312 P-H Memo T.C. (1952), ...134n
Columbus and Greenville R.R., 42 T.C. 834, 848 (1964), ...188n
Commissioner v. Abramson, 124 F. 2d 416 (2nd Cir. 1942), ...231n
Commissioner v. Appleby's Estate, 123 F. 2d 700 (2d Cir. 1941), ...77n
Commissioner v. Babcock, 259 F. 2d 689 (4th Cir. 1958), ...190n
Commissioner v. Clay Brown, 380 U.S. 563 (1965), ...299n
Commissioner v. Crichton, 122 F. 2d 181 (5th Cir. 1941), ...111n
Commissioner v. Daehler, 281 F. 2d 823 (5th Cir. 1960), ...56n
Commissioner v. Duberstein, 363 U.S. 278 (1960), ...251n
Commissioner v. Edwards Drilling Co., 95 F. 2d 719 (5th Cir. 1938), ...94n, 176n
Commissioner v. Fortee Properties, Inc., 211 F. 2d 915 (2d Cir. 1954), ...136n, 190n
Commissioner v. Gazette Telegraph Co., 209 F. 2d 926 (10th Cir. 1954), ...53n
Commissioner v. Golonsky, 200 F. 2d 72 (3rd Cir. 1952), ...270n, 281n
Commissioner v. Green, 126 F. 2d 70 (3rd Cir. 1942), ...247n, 248n
Commissioner v. Harwick, 184 F. 2d 835 (5th Cir. 1950), ...87n
Commissioner v. Highway Trailer Co., 72 F. 2d 913 (7th Cir. 1934), ...87n

Commissioner v. Hoffman, 117 F. 2d 987 (2n Cir. 1941), ...246*n*
Commissioner v. Jacobson, 336 U.S. 28 (1949), ...251*n*
Commissioner v. Jones, 120 F. 2d 828, 830 (8th Cir. 1941), ...248*n*
Commissioner v. Kann's Estate, 174 F. 2d 357 (3rd Cir. 1949), ...176*n*
Commissioner v. Liftin, 317 F. 2d 234 (4th Cir. 1963), ...173*n*
Commissioner v. LoBue, 351 U.S. 243, 76 S. Ct. 800, ...56*n*
Commissioner v. McCarthy, 129 F. 2d 84 (7th Cir. 1942), ...147*n*
Commissioner v. McCue Bros. & Drummond, Inc., 210 F. 2d 752 (2d Cir. 1954), 270*n*, 281*n*
Commissioner v. Minzer, 279 F. 2d 338 (5th Cir. 1960), ...56*n*, 57*n*
Commissioner v. Moir, 45 F. 2d 356 (7th Cir. 1930), ...181*n*
Commissioner v. Moore, 207 F. 2d 265, 276 (9th Cir. 1953), ...276*n*
Commissioner v. National Bank of Commerce, 112 F. 2d 946 (5th Cir. 1940), ...233*n*, 243*n*
Commissioner v. Penn Athletic Club Bldg., 176 F. 2d 939 (3rd Cir. 1949), ...255*n*
Commissioner v. Peterman, 118 F. 2d 973, 976 (9th Cir. 1941), ...229*n*
Commissioner v. P.G. Lake, Inc., 356 U.S. 260 (1958), ...112*n*
Commissioner v. Riss, 374 F. 2d 161 (8th Cir. 1967), ...260*n*
Commissioner v. Sherman, 135 F. 2d 68, 70 (6th Cir. 1943), ...192*n*, 250*n*
Commissioner v. Sisto Financial Corp., 139 F. 2d 253, 255 (2d Cir. 1943), ...234*n*
Commissioner v. Smith, 203 F. 2d 310, 312 (2d Cir. 1953), ...219*n*
Commissioner v. South Texas Lumber Co., 333 U.S. 496, 502 (1948), ...151*n*
Commissioner v. Spreckles, 120 F. 2d 517 (9th Cir. 1941), ...233*n*, 243*n*
Commissioner v. Stanley Co. of America, 185 F. 2d 979 (2d Cir. 1951), ...250*n*
Commissioner v. State Adams Corp., 283 F. 2d 395 (2d Cir. 1960), ...368*n*
Commissioner v. Terre Haute Electric Co., 67 F. 2d 697 (7th Cir. 1938), ...263*n*, 271*n*
Commissioner v. Tower, 327 U.S. 280 (1946), ...296*n*
Commissioner v. Union Pacific Ry Co., 86 F. 2d 637, 639 (2d Cir. 1936), ...182*n*
Commissioner v. West Production Co., 121 F. 2d 9, 11 (5th Cir. 1941), ...240*n*
Commissioner v. Williams, 256 F. 2d 152 (5th Cir. 1958), ...104*n*
Concord Village, Inc., 65 T.C. 142 at 155 (1975), ...386*n*, 387*n*
Consolidated Apparel Co. v. Commissioner, 207 F. 2d 580 (7th Cir. 1953), ...298*n*
Cooper Foundation v. O'Malley, 221 F. 2d 279, 281 (8th Cir. 1955), ...275*n*, 278*n*
Cooperative Publishing Co. v. Commissioner, 115 F. 2d 1017, 1021 (9th Cir. 1940), ...132*n*
Corn Exchange Bank v. United States, 37 F. 2d 34 (2d Cir. 1930), ...94*n*
Corona Flushing Co., 22 B.T.A. 1344 (1931), ...152*n*
Corrine S. Koshland, 19 T.C. 860 (1953), ...187*n*
Cosmopolitan Corp., 1959 P-H T.C. Memo ¶59,122 (1959), ...270*n*
Cotton Concentration Co., 4 B.T.A. 121, 126 (1926), ...131*n*, 133*n*
Cowden v. Commissioner, 289 F. 2d 20 at 24 (5th Cir. 1961), ...173*n*, 258*n*
Crane v. Commissioner, 331 U.S. 1, 11 (1947), ...46*n*, 51*n*, 94*n*, 187*n*, 188*n*,
                                                       189*n*, 197*n*, 199*n*, 200, 200*n*, 231, 367*n*
C.S. Forve, 20 B.T.A. 861 (1930), ...93*n*
Curtis Co. v. Commissioner, 232 F. 2d 167 (3rd Cir. 1956), ...317*n*
Curtis W. Kingbay, 46 T.C. 147 (1966), ...313*n*
C.W. Titus, Inc., 33 B.T.A. 928, 930 (1936), ...94*n*, 173*n*
Dakota Creek Lumber & Shingle Co., 26 B.T.A. 940 (1932), ...182*n*
Dallas Transfer & Terminal Warehouse Co. v. Commissioner,
       70 F. 2d 95 (5th Cir. 1934), ...245*n*
Daniel Hecker, 17 B.T.A. 874, 876 (1929), ...233*n*, 243*n*
Darbs Investment Co. v. Commissioner, 315 F. 2d 551 (6th Cir. 1963), ...172*n*
David Dab, 28 T.C. 933 (1957), ...279*n*
David F. Bolger, 59 T.C. 760 (1973), ...52*n*, 76*n*, 188*n*, 368*n*
Davidson v. Commissioner, 60 F. 2d 50, 52 (2d Cir. 1932), ...277*n*
Davis Co., 6 B.T.A. 281 (1927), ...132*n*
Davis Regulator Co., 36 B.T.A. 437, 443 (1937) 131*n*, 133*n*,
Deal v. Morrow, 197 F. 2d 821, 827 (5th Cir. 1952), ...178*n*, 180*n*

TABLE OF CASES

Denman v. Brumbach, 58 F. 2d 128 (6th Cir. 1932), ...147n
Derby Realty Corp., 35 B.T.A. 335 (1937), ...228n
Detroit Egg Biscuit & Specialty Co., 9 B.T.A. 1365 (1928), ...129n
Dillon v. Commissioner, 213 F. 2d 218 (8th Cir. 1954), ...317n
D.K. McColl, ¶41,050 P-H Memo T.C., ...258n
D.N. & E. Walker Co., 4 B.T.A. 142.146 (1926), ...278n
Dominguez Estate Co., P-H Memo T.C. ¶63, 113, ...132n
Donald S. Levinson, 59 T.C. 676 (1973), ...77n, 267n
Doris D. Havemeyer, 45 B.T.A. 329, 330 (1941), ...221n
Douglas Properties, Inc., 21 B.T.A. 347 (1930), ...282n
Dudley T. Humphrey, 32 B.T.A. 280 (1935), ...173n
Dunigan v. Burnet, 66 F. 2d 201 (D.C. Cir. 1933), ...103–104
Duram Building Corp. v. Commissioner, 66 F. 2d 253 (2d Cir. 1933), ...164n
Durkee, 162 F. 2d 184 (Ca-6, 1947), ...140n
Mrs. E.A. Giffin, 19 B.T.A. 1243 (1930), ...92n, 162n
East Coast Equipment Co. v. Commissioner, 222 F. 2d 676 (3rd Cir. 1955), ...165n
Ed Foster, 19 B.T.A. 958,962 (1930), ...278n
Edison Club, 34 T.C.M. 79 (1975), ...386n
Edna Morris 59 T.C. 21 (1972), ...46n
Edward A. Atlas, par. 45,044 P-H Memo T.C. (1945), ...233n, 243n
Edward F.C. McLaughlin, 43 B.T.A. 528 (1941), ...230n, 231n
Edward F. Dalton, 2 B.T.A. 615 (1925), ...221n
Edward and John Burke, Ltd., 3 T.C. 1031, 1040 (1944), ...229n
Edward S. Phillips, 9 B.T.A. 1016 (1927), ...252n
Edward Warner, 56 T.C. 1126 (1971), ...132n
E.E. Shipp v. Commissioner, 217 F. 2d 401 (9th Cir. 1954), ...80n
E.F. Simms, 28 B.T.A. 988, 1030 (1933), ...235n, 237n
Egbert J. Henschel, Par. 38,187 P-H Memo B.T.A. (1938), ...240n
Ehrman v. Commissioner, 120 F. 2d 607,610 (9th Cir. 1941), ...33n
Eimer & Amend, 2 B.T.A. 603, 607 (1925), ...271n
E.J. Murray, 21 T.C. 1049, 1062 (1954), ...75n, 255n
E.K. Wood Lumber Co., B.T.A. 1013,1024 (1932), ...181n
Electro-Chemical Engraving Co. v. Commissioner, 311 U.S. 513 (1941), ...225n
Eline Realty Co., 35 T.C. 1 (1960), ...318n
Elizabeth Operating Corp., par. 43,434 P-H Memo T.C. (1943), ...251n
Elliot S. Nichols, 1 T.C. 328 (1942), ...239n, 243n
Elverson Corp., 40 B.T.A. 615, 634, ...234n
Elverson Corp. v. Helvering, 122 F. 2d 295 (2d Cir. 1941), ...234n
Emil W. Carlson, 24 B.T.A. 868 (1931), ...185n
Enid Ice and Fuel Co. v. United States (W.D. Okla. 1956), 142 F. Supp. 248n, 486
E.P. Lamberth Est., 31 T.C. 302 (1958), ...161n
E.R. Braley, 14 B.T.A. 1153 (1929), ...111n
Erlich v. Commissioner, 198 F. 2d 158 (1st Cir. 1952), ...264n
Ernest A. Pederson, 46 T.C. 155 (1966), ...58n
Estate of A. Carl Borner, 25 T.C. 584 (1955), ...42n
Estate of Clarence W. Ennis, 23 T.C. 799 (1955), ...171n
Estate of Coid Hurlburt, 25 T.C. 1286 (1956), ...171n
Estate of C. William Meinecke, 47 B.T.A. 634 (1942), ...178n
Estate of Delano T. Starr, 30 T.C. 856 (1958), ...285n
Estate of D.M. Brockway, 18 T.C. 488, 498 (1952), ...42n
Estate of Eleanor H. Davidson, par. 46,259 P-H Memo T.C. (1946), ...221n
Estate of Ernst Zobel, 28 T.C. No. 97 (1957), ...224n
Estate of Eugene Merrick Webb, 30 T.C. 1202 (1958), ...44n, 376n
Estate of Henry H. Rogers, 1 T.C. 629 at 632 (1943), ...157n
Estate of Herbert B. Miller, 24 T.C. 923 (1955), ...157n

TABLE OF CASES

Estate of Isadore L. Myers, 1 T.C. 100.111 (1942), ... 46n
Estate of James R. Jewett, par. 49,163 P-H Memo T.C. (1949), ... 221n
Estate of Lloyd G. Bell, 60 T.C. No. 52 (1973), ... 177n
Estate of Lucy S. Schieffelin, 44 B.T.A. 137,140 (1941), ... 222n, 253n
Estate of Mary G. Gordon, 17 T.C. 427 (1951), ... 179n
Estate of Morris (1971) 55 T.C. 636, ... 135n
Estate of Paul M. Bowen, 2 T.C. 1, 5, (1943), ... 194n
Estate of Resler (1952) 17 T.C. 1085, ... 135n
Estate of Starr v. Commissioner, 274 F. 2d 294 (9th Cir. 1959), ... 285n
Estate of Theodore Gutman, 18 T.C. 112, 121 (1952), ... 219n
Estate of Turney v. Commissioner, 126 F. 2d 712 (5th Cir. 1942), ... 245n
Ethel Black, 35 T.C. 90 (1960), ... 113n
Ethel S. Amey, 22 T.C. 756 (1954), ... 261n
E.T. Weir, 10 T.C. 996 (1948), ... 55n, 102n
Everett Pozzi, 49 T.C. 119 (1967), ... 154n, 166n
Fackler v. Commissioner, 133 F. 2d 509 (6th Cir. 1943), ... 31n
Fahs v. Crawford, 161 F. 2d 315 (5th Cir. 1947), ... 317n
Fairbanks v. United States, 306 U.S. 436 (1939), ... 224n
Fairfield Plaza, Inc., 39 T.C. 706 at 712–714 (1963), ... 97n
Fairmount Park Raceway, Inc. par 62,014 P-H Memo T.C. (1962), ... 282n
Farmers Creamery Co. of Fredericksburg, 14 T.C. 879 (1959), ... 85n
Farmers & Merchants Bank of Cattlesburg, Ky., 59 F. 2d 912 (CA-6, 1932), ... 140n
F.B. Cooper, 31 T.C. 1155 (1959), ... 64n
Feldman v. Wood, 335 F. 2d 264 (9th Cir. 1964), ... 267n
Ferdinand Hotz, 42 B.T.A. 432 (1940), ... 229n
F.H. Wilson, 12 B.T.A. 403,406 (1928), ... 85n
53 West 72d St., Inc., 23 B.T.A. 164 (1931), ... 152n
Finley v. Commissioner, 255 F. 2d 128 (10th Cir. 1958), ... 296n
First National Bank, 43 B.T.A. 456 (1941), ... 50n
First National Bank of Evanston, 1 B.T.A. 9 (1924), ... 77n, 266n
First National Bank of Lawrence County, 16 T.C. 147 (1951), ... 224n
First National Bank of Philipsburg, 43 B.T.A. 456 (1941), ... 235n
First National Corp. v. Commissioner, 147 F. 2d 462 (9th Cir. 1945), ... 96n
Fisher v. Commissioner, 209 F. 2d 513 (6th Cir. 1954), ... 225n
512 West Fifty-Sixth Street Corp. v. Commissioner, 151 F. 2d 942
    (2d Cir. 1945), ... 99n, 281n
F.M. Hubbell & Son Co. v. Burnet, 51 F. 2d 644 (8th Cir. 1931), ... 84n
Foltz v. United States, 458 F. 2d 600 (8th Cir. 1972), ... 267n
Francis Perot's Sons Malting Co., 1 B.T.A. 56, 562 (1925), ... 233n, 243n
Frank A. Newcombe, 54 T.C. 1298 (1970), ... 27n
Frank and Seder Co. v. Commissioner, 44 F. 2d 147(3rd Cir. 1930), ... 264n
Frank v. United States, 44 F. Supp. 729 (D.C. Pa. 1942), ... 192n, 249n, 250n
Frank W. Babcock, 28 T.C. 781 (1957), ... 136n, 190n
Fred Draper, 32 T.C. 545 (1959), ... 104n
Fred Pellar, 25 T.C. 299 (1955), ... 56n
Frederick J. Haynes, 7 B.T.A. 465 (1927), ... 44n
Frederick R. Horne, 5 T.C. 250,256 (1945), ... 111n
Frederick S. Jackson, par. 41,131 P-H Memo B.T.A. (1941), ... 248n
Freida Bernstein, 22 T.C. 1146, 1151 (1954), ... 277n
Fribourg Navigation Co., 383 U.S. 272 (1966), ... 74n
Friend v. Commissioner, 119 F. 2d 959 (7th Cir. 1941), ... 276n
Frito-Lay, Inc. v. United States, 209 F. Supp. 886 (N.D. Ga. 1962), ... 73n
Frost Lumber Industries, Inc., v. Commissioner, 128 F. 2d 693
    (5th Cir. 1942), ... 182n
Fulton Gold Corp., 31 B.T.A. 519 (1934), ... 192n, 252n

TABLE OF CASES

Galvin Hudson, 20 T.C. 734 (1953), ...224n
Garrett v. United States, 120 F. Supp. 193 (Ct. Cl. 1954), ...33n, 317n
Gazette Telegraph Co., 19 T.C. 692, 707 (1953), ...338n
Gehring Publishing Co., 1 T.C. 345, 354 (1942), ...192n, 250n
General American Investors Co., 348 U.S. 434 (1955), ...142n
General American Life Ins. Co., 25 T.C. 1265, 1267 (1956), ...196n
George Antonoplos, 3 B.T.A. 1236 (1926), ...93n
George E. Bailey, 41 T.C. 663 (1964), ...57n
George I. Bumbaugh, 10 B.T.A. 672 (1928), ...181n
George L. Castner Co., Inc., 30 T.C. 1061 (1958), ...173n
George Leavenworth, 1 B.T.A. 754, 757 (1925), ...253n
George R. Newhouse, 59 T.C. 783 (1973), ...236n
George S. Groves, 38 B.T.A. 727, 737 (1938), ...195n
George W. Mitchell, 47 T.C. 120 at 128 (1966), ...24n, 25n, 27n
George W. Weibush, 59 T.C. 77 (1973), ...364n
Georgia Ry. & Electric Co. v. Commissioner, 77 F. 2d 897
    (5th Cir. 1935), ...263n, 271n
Gerald R. Gorman, T.C. Memo 1974–17 (1974), ...267n
Gibbs & Hudson, Inc., 35 B.T.A. 205, 210 (1936), ...154n
Gilford v. Commissioner, 201 F. 2d 735, 736 (2d Cir. 1953), ...31n, 98n, 228n
Gilken Corp. v. Commissioner, 176 F. 2d 141, 145 (6th Cir. 1949), ...179n, 260n
Gillespie v. Commissioner, 128 F. 2d 140 (9th Cir. 1942), ...176n
Girard Trust Corn Exchange Bank, 33 T.C. 1343, 1359 (1954), ...255n
Giumarra Bros. Fruit Co., 55 T.C. 460 (1970), ...279n
Glaser v. United States, 306 F. 2d 57 (7th Cir. 1962), ...42n, 43n
Goodman v. Commissioner, (3rd Cir. 1952) 199 F. 2d 895, ...135n
Graves Bros. Co., 17 T.C. 1499 (1952), ...98n
Grier v. United States, 120 F. Supp. 395, 398 (D. Conn. 1954), ...31n, 32n
Guelph Hotel Corp., 7 B.T.A. 1043 (1927), ...279n
Gus Russell, Inc., 36 T.C. 965 (1961), ...157n
Guy L. Waggoner, 15 T.C. 496 (1950), ...265n
Haden Co. v. Commissioner, 118 F. 2d 285 (5th Cir. 1941), ...249n
Hadley Falls Trust Co. v. United States, 110 F. 2d 887, 893
    (1st Cir. 1940), ...222n, 239n, 253n, 254n
Hadley Falls Trust Co. v. United States (D.C. Mass. 1938),
    22 F. Supp. 346, 351, ...253n, 254n
Haggard v. Commissioner, 241 F. 2d 288 (9th Cir. 1956), ...285n
Hagist Ranch, Inc. v. Commissioner, 295 Fed. 2d 351 (7th Cir. 1961), ...368n
Hale v. Helvering, 85 F. 2d 819, 822 (D.C. Cir. 1936), ...249n
Hamilton & Main, Inc., 25 T.C. 878 (1956), ...265n
Hamlin's Trust v. Commissioner, 209 F. 2d 761 (10th Cir. 1954), ...53n
Hansen v. Commissioner, U.S. (1958), ...94n
Harold A. Jackson, 24 T.C. 1, 14 (1955) 166n
Harold M. Blossom, 38 B.T.A. 1136 (1938), ...230n, 236n
Harold S. Denniston, 37 B.T.A. 834, ...233n, 243n
Harold W. Johnston, 14 T.C. 560, 565 (1950), ...96n
Harold W. Smith, 56 T.C. 263 (1971), ...165n, 177n
Harriet B. Borland, 27 B.T.A. 538 (1933), ...269n, 280n
Harris Hardwood Co., 8 T.C. 847, 881 (1947), ...86n
Harris Trust & Savings Bank, 24 B.T.A. 203 (1928), ...182n
Harris v. United States, 193 F. Supp. 736 (D. Neb. 1961), ...43n
Harrison v. Schaffner, 312 U.S. 579 (1941), ...296n
Harry B. Golden, 47 B.T.A. 94 (1942), ...149n
Harry Brown, 23 T.C. 156 (1954), ...87n
Harry G. Masser, 30 T.C. 741 (1958), ...132n, 132–133

TABLE OF CASES

Harry H. Diamond, 43 B.T.A. 809, 812 (1941), ...227n, 228n
Harry H. Kem, Jr., 51 T.C. 455 (1968), ...263n, 271n
Harsh Investment Corp. v. United States, 323 F. Supp. 409
    D.C. Ore. 1970), ...136n
Harvey J. Johnson, 43 T.C. 736 (1965), ...133n
Hatch v. Commissioner, 190 F. 2d 254 (2d Cir. 1951), ...94n, 172n
Heiner v. Tindle, 276 U.S. 582, 585 (1928), ...26n
Heller Trust v. Commissioner, 382 F. 2d 675 (9th Cir. 1967), ...34n, 170n, 317n
Helvering v. A.L. Killian Co., 128 F. 2d 433 (8th Cir. 1942), ...192n, 250n
Helvering v. American Dental Co., 318 U.S. 322 (1943), ...251n
Helvering v. Brunn, 309 U.S. 461 (1940), ...274n
Helvering v. Clifford, 309 U.S. 331 (1940), ...296n, 297n
Helvering v. F.R. Lazarus & Co., 308 U.S. 252 (1939), ...75n, 292n
Helvering v. Gambrill, 313 U.S. 11, 14 (1941), ...103n
Helvering v. Gordon, 134 F. 2d 685, 687 (4th Cir. 1943), ...147n, 248n
Helvering v. Hammel, 311 U.S. 504 (1941), ...225n, 228n
Helvering v. Horst, 311 U.S. 112 (1940), ...296n
Helvering v. Midland Mutual Life Ins. Co., 300 U.S. 216, 224
    (dictum) (1937), ...236n, 239, 241
Helvering v. Missouri State Life Ins. Co., 78 F. 2d 778, 780
    (8th Cir. 1934), ...244n
Helvering v. Nebraska Bridge Supply & Lumber Co., 115 F. 2d 288, 291
    (8th Cir. 1940), ...231n
Helvering v. New President Corp., 122 F. 2d 92, 97 (8th Cir. 1941), ...239n, 240n
Helvering v. New York Trust Co., 292 U.S. 455 (1934), ...103n
Helvering v. Roth, 115 F. 2d 239, 240 (2d Cir. 1940), ...184n, 224n
Helvering v. San Joaquin Fruit & Investment Co., 297 U.S. 496 (1936), ...55n, 103n
Helvering v. Stormfelz, 142 F. 2d 982 (8th Cir. 1944), ...80n
Henry Boos, 30 B.T.A. 882 (1934), ...279n
Henry Heldt, 16 B.T.A. 1035, 1036 (1929), ...234n
Henry Phipps Estate, 5 T.C. 964 (1954), ...77n
Henry v. Poor, 11 B.T.A. 781 (1928), ...223n
Hens & Kelly, 19 T.C. 305 (1953), ...272n
Herbert Burwig, Par. 53,339 P-H Memo T.C. (1953), ...77n, 269n
Herbert N. Fell, 18 B.T.A. 81, 84 (1929), ...50n
Herbert's Estate v. Commissioner, 139 F. 2d 756 (3rd Cir. 1943), ...224n
Herman Landerman, 54 T.C. 1042 (1970), ...267n
Hightower v. United States, 463 F. 2d 182 (5th Cir. 1972), ...267n
Hilpert v. Commissioner, 151 F. 2d 929, 933 (5th Cir. 1945), ...255n
Hills Estate v. Maloney, 58 F. Supp. 164 (D.C.N.J. 1944), ...177n
Hindes v. United States, F 2d 13 AFTR 2d 376 (5th Cir. 1964), ...157n
Hirsch v. Commissioner, 115 F. 2d 656, 658 (7th Cir. 1940), ...192n, 250n
Hirsch Improvement Co. v. Commissioner, 115 F. 2d 656 (2d Cir. 1944), ...260n
Hirsch Improvement Co. v. Commissioner, 143 F. 2d 912 (2d Cir. 1944), ...179n
Holley v. United States, 246 F. Supp. 553 (D.Nev. 1965), ...151n
Homann v. Commissioner, 230 F. 2d 671 (9th Cir. 1956), ...26n, 64n
Home News Publishing Co., 18 B.T.A. 1008 (1930), ...79n
Honigman v. Commissioner, 466 F. 2d 69 (6th Cir. 1972), ...79n, 85n
Hornberger v. Commissioner, 289 F. 2d 602 (5th Cir. 1961), ...151n
Hort v. Commissioner, 313 U.S. 28 (1941), ...141n, 270n, 281n, 300n
Hotel Astoria, Inc., 42 B.T.A. 759, 762 (1940), ...192n, 252n
Hotel Kingkade v. Commissioner, 180 F. 2d 310 (10th Cir. 1950), ...264n
Houston Chronicle Pub. Co. v. United States, 481 F. 2d 1240 (5th Cir. 1973), ...266n
Houston Chronicle Pub. Co. v. U.S., 339 F. Supp. 1314 (S.D.Tex. 1972), ...269n
Howell v. Commissioner, 140 F. 2d 765 (5th Cir. 1944), ...103n

TABLE OF CASES

Hubinger v. Commissioner, 36 F. 2d 724 (2d Cir. 1929), ...86n
Hulet P. Smith, 1967 P-H T.C. Memo 67–165 (1967), ...27n
Huntington-Redondo Co., 36 B.T.A. 116 (1937), ...193n, 194n, 195n
H.V. Watkins, 1973 P-H Memo T.C. ¶73,167, ...30n
Hyde Park Realty v. Commissioner, 211 F. 2d 462 (2d Cir. 1954), ...258n
Illinois Merchants Trust Co., 4 B.T.A. 103, 106 (1926), ...79n
Imperator Realty Co., 24 B.T.A. 1010 (1931), ...174n
Inaja Land Co., 9 T.C. 727 (1947), ...97n, 140n
Ingle v. Gage, 52 F. 2d 738 (W.D. 740 N.Y. 1931), ...76n
Intercounty Operating Co., 4 T.C. 55, 69 (1944), ...147n
Irvine K. Furman, 45 T.C. 360 (1966), ...298n
Irvington Investments Co., 32 B.T.A. 1165 (1935),..337n
Isabelle B. Krome, Par. 50, 064 P-H Memo T.C. (1950), ...65n
Ivan Irwin, Jr., 45 T.C. 544 (1966), ...153n
Ives Dairy, Inc. v. Commissioner, 65 F. 2d 125 (5th Cir. 1933), ...93n
Jack M. Chesboro, 21 T.C. 123, 130 (1953), ...76n
Jackson v. Commissioner, 172 F. 2d 605 (7th Cir. 1949), ...84n, 85n
Jackson v. Commissioner, 233 F. 2d 289 (2d Cir. 1956), ...368n
Jacob Abelson, 44 B.T.A. 98, 104, ...229n, 230n
Jacobs v. Commissioner, 224 F. 2d 412 (9th Cir. 1955), ...151n, 157n
James Alderson, 38 T.C. 215 (1962), ...121n, 122n
James B. Lapsley, 44 B.T.A. 1105, 1108 (1941), ...200n
James Hammond, 1 T.C. 198 (1942), ...155n
James J. Reilly, 46 B.T.A. 1246, 1251 (1942), ...240n
James McCutcheon & Co., 30 B.T.A. 1177 (1934), ...149n
James Petroleum Corp., 24 T.C. 509, 518 (1955), ...228n
James v. United States, 336 U.S. 213, 81 S.Ct. 105, 1052 (1961), ...184n
Jason L. Honigman, 55 T.C. 1067 (1971), ...79n
J. Bryant Kasey, 54 T.C. 1642 (1970), ...79n
J. Carl Horneff, 50 T.C. No. 10 (1968), ...153n
J.C. Hawkins, 34 B.T.A. 918 (1936), ...228n
J.C. Wynne, 47 B.T.A. 731 (1942), ...166n
J. Darsie Lloyd, 33 B.T.A. 903, 905 (1936), ...176n
Jeanese, Inc. v. United States, 341 F. 2d 502 (9th Cir. 1965), ...350n, 351n
J. Earl Oden, 56 T.C. 569 (1971), ...154n
Jefferson Standard Life Insurance Co. v. United States, 408 Fed. 2d 842
    (4th Cir. 1969), ...83n
Jennings and Co. v. Commissioner, 59 F. 2d 32 (9th Cir. 1932), ...258n
J. Fleet Cowden, 1965 P-H Memo T.C. ¶65,278, ...129n
J.H. Baird Publishing Co., 39 T.C. 608 (1962), ...121n, 125n
J.H. Collingwood, 20 T.C. 937 (1953), ...85n, 86n
J.J. Kirk, Inc., 34 T.C. 130 (1960), ...299n
J.K. McAlpine Land & Development Co., 43 B.T.A. 520, 526 (1941), ...237n
Jo Alland and Bro., Inc., 1 B.T.A. 631 (1925), ...259n
Joell Co., 41 B.T.A. 825, 827 (1940), ...195n
John Charney, par. 34, 543 P-H Memo B.T.A. (1934), ...252n
John D. Riley, 37 T.C. 932 (1962), ...129n
John F. Bayley, 35 T.C. 288 (1962), ...151n
John Hancock Mutual Life Ins. Co., 10 B.T.A. 736 (1928), ...241n, 253n
John Harper, 54 T.C. 1121 (1970), ...151n
John L. Hawkinson, 23 T.C. 933, 943 (1955), ...193n
John L. Sullivan, 17 T.C. 1420, 1425 (1952), ...145n
John Mantell, 17 T.C. 1143 (1952), ...260n
John M. Rogers, 44 T.C. 126 (1965), ...121n
John P. Reaves, 42 T.C. 72 (1964), ...151n

John P. Vidican, 1969 P-H Memo T.C. ¶69,207, ...64n
John Q. Shunk, 10 T.C. 293, 305 (1948), ...93n
John T. Morris, 15 B.T.A. 260 (1929), ...178n
John T. Potter, 27 T.C. 200 (1956), ...298n
John W. Commons, 20 T.C. 900, 903 (1953), ...150n
John W.F. Hobbs, 16 T.C. 1259 (1951), ...276n
Johnson v. Commissioner, 56 F. 2d 58 (5th Cir. 1932), ...173n
Johnson v. Westover, 48 A.F.T. R1671, 1675 (S.D.Cal. 1955), ...65n
Johnson & Co. v. United States, 149 F. 2d 851 (2d Cir. 1945), ...80n
Joliet-Norfolk Farm Corp., 8 B.T.A. 824 (1927), ...173n
Jones v. Commissioner, 209 F. 2d 415 (9th Cir. 1954), ...33n
Jones Lumber Co. v. Commissioner, 22 AFTR 2d 5924 (6th Cir. 1968), ...93n
Jones Lumber Co. v. Commissioner, 29 AFTR 2d 5024 (6th Cir. 1968), ...173n
Jones Lumber Co. v. United States, 404 F. 2d 764 (6th Cir. 1972), ...173n
Jordan Marsh Company v. Commissioner, 269 F. 2d 453 (2d Cir. 1959), ...291n
Joseph P. Abraham, 1970 P-H Memo T.C. ¶70,304 ....46n
Joseph Rothafel, T.C. Memo 1965–277, ...368n
Journal Tribune Publishing Co. v. Commissioner, 348 F. 2d 266 (8th Cir. 1965), ...264n
J. Simpson Dean, 35 T.C. 1083 (1961), ...193n
Judson Mills, 11 T.C. 25, 30, 33 (1948), ...285n, 292n
Juleo, Inc. v. Commissioner, 483 F. 2d 47 (3rd Cir. 1973), ...318n
Julia Stow Lovejoy, 18 B.T.A. 1179 (1930), ...185n
J.W. Elmore, 15 B.T.A. 1210, 1212 (1929), ...152n
Kalbac v. Commissioner, 298 F. 2d 251 (8th Cir. 1962), ...54n
Kanawha Valley Bank, 4 T.C. 252, 256 (1944), ...255n
Katherine B. Bliss, 27 T.C. 770 (1957), ...140n
Katherine H. Watson, 20 B.T.A. 270 (1930), ...152n
Kathryn Lammerding, 40 B.T.A. 589 (1939), ...234n
Kaufman v. Commissioner, 119 F. 2d 901 (9th Cir. 1941), ...244n, 245n
Kaweah Lemon Co., 5 B.T.A. 992 (1927), ...65n
Kay Kimbell, 41 B.T.A. 940, 951 (1940), ...176n
K-C Land Co., TC Memo 1960–35, ...368n
Keiler v. U.S. 395 F. 2d 991 (CA 6, 1968), ...269n
Kentucky Utilities Co. v. Glenn, 21 AFTR 1263 (6th Cir. 1968), ...85n
King Amusement Co. v. Commissioner, 44 F. 2d 709 (6th Cir. 1939), ...278n
Kirschenmann v. Commissioner, 488 F. 2d 270 (9th Cir. 1973), ...152n, 153n
Kirschenmann v. Westover, 225 F. 2d 69 (9th Cir. 1955), ...296n
Kohn v. Commissioner, 197 F. 2d 480 (2d Cir. 1952), ...51n, 235n, 244n
Kornhauser v. United States, 276 U.S. 145 (1928), ...79n
Korth v. Zion's Savings Bank & Trust Co., 148 F. 2d 170 (10th Cir. 1945), ...239n
L.A. Beeghly, 36 T.C. 154 (1961), ...138n
Lake, P.G. Inc., 356 U.S. 160 (1958), ...300n
Lake Forest Inc., Par. 63, 039 P-H Memo T.C. (1963), ...371n
Lake Petersburg Association, 1974 P-H T.C. Memo ¶74,055 (1974), ...386n, 387n
Lake Petersburg Association, ¶32,482 (M) T.C. Memo (1974), ...381n
Lakeland Grocery Co., 36 B.T.A., 289 (1937), ...245n, 250
Landerman v. Commissioner, 454 F. 2d 338 (7th Cir. 1972), ...77n
Lapham v. United States, 178 F. 2d 994 (2d Cir. 1950), ...138n
Larson v. Cuesta, 120 F. 2d 482 (5th Cir. 1941), ...221n, 239n
Laura Massaglia, 33 T.C. 379 (1959), ...72n
Laurene Walker Berger, 7 T.C. 1339 (1946), ...267n
Lee v. Commissioner, 119 F. 2d 946 (7th Cir. 1941), ...172n, 224n
Lee R. Chronister, T.C. Memo 1973-237 (1973), ...87n
Leland Hazard, 7 T.C. 372 (1946), ...28n, 31n, 98n, 228n
Leo A Woodbury, 49 T.C. 180 (1967), ...121n

TABLE OF CASES 399

Leslie Q. Coupe, 52 T.C. 394 (1969), ...122n, 124n
Lewis M. Ludlow, 36 T.C. 102 (1961), ...154n
Liberty Mirror Works, 3 T.C. 1018, 1022 (1944), ...251n
Liftin v. Commissioner, 317 F. 2d 234 (4th Cir. 1963), ...172n
Limericks, Inc., v. Commissioner, 165 F. 2d 483 (5th Cir. 1948), ...258n
Little v. Helvering, 75 F. 2d 436 (8th Cir. 1935), ...221n
Lola Cunningham, 39 T.C. 186 (1962), ...258n
Longview Hilton Hotel Co., 9 T.C. 180 (1947), ...186n
Louis v. Coughlin, T.C. Memo 1973-243 (1973), ...86n
Louis Rubino, Par. 49,288 P-H Memo T.C. (1949), ...173n
Lubken v. United States, 8 AFTR 2d 5073 (S.D.Cal. 1961), ...155n, 163n
Lucas v. North Texas Lumber Co., 281 U.S. 11, 13 (1930), ...94n, 96n, 173n, 178n
Ludlow Valve Mfg. Co. v. Durey, 62 F. 2d 508, 509 (2d Cir. 1933), ...222n
Luff Co., The, 44 T.C. 532 (1965), ...350n
Lutz & Schramm Co., 1 T.C. 682, 688 (1943), ...184n, 185n, 199n, 200n, 237n, 244n
Lynchburg National Bank and Trust Co., 20 T.C. 670 (1953), ...53n, 78n
McCarthy v. Cripe, 201 F. 2d 679, 680 (7th Cir. 1953), ...228n, 229n
McFeely v. Commissioner, 296 U.S. 102, 108 (1935), ...103n
McGah v. Commissioner, 210 F. 2d 769, 771 (9th Cir. 1954), ...33n
McInerney v. Commissioner, 82 F. 2d 665 (6th Cir. 1936), ...157n
Madden Blaine, 56 T.C. 513 (1972), ...80n
Maddux Const. Co., 54 T.C. 1278 (1970), ...34n
Magnolia Development Corp., 1960 P-H Memo T.C. No. 60-177 (1960), ...201n
Magruder v. Supplee, 316 U.S. 394, 398 (1942), ...57n, 63n
Main and McKinney Building Co. v. Commissioner, 113 F. 2d 81
    (5th Cir. 1940), ...259n
Main Properties, Inc., 4 T.C. 364, 384 (1945), ...245n
Malat v. Riddell, 383 U.S. 569 (1966), ...32n, 34n, 316n
Maloney v. Spencer, 172 F. 2d 638, 640 (9th Cir. 1949), ...31n
Mamie E. Eining, 19 B.T.A. 1105, 1107 (1930), ...152n
Mamula v. Commissioner, 346 F. 2d 350 (9th Cir. 1965), ...151n
Manhattan Mutual Life Ins. Co., 37 B.T.A. 1041, 1043 (1938), ...244n
Manuel D. Mayerson, 47 T.C. 340, 353 (1966), ...188n, 366n
Manuel D. Mayerson, Jr., 47 T.C. 348 (1969), ...46n, 52n
Manufacturer's Life Insurance Co., 43 B.T.A. 864, 873 (1941), ...233n, 234n
Margery K. Megargel, 3 T.C. 238, 248 (1944), ...235n
Marion A. Blake, 8 T.C. 546, 555 (1947), ...184n
Marion A. Burt Beck, 15 T.C. 642, 669 (1950), ...79n
Marsh and Marsh, Inc., 5 B.T.A. 902 (1926), ...193n
Martha R. Peters, 4 T.C. 1236 (1945), ...276n
Martin v. Commissioner, 61 F. 2d 942 (2d Cir. 1932), ...163n
Martin v. United States, 119 F. Supp. 468 (D. Ga. 1954), ...31n
Mary Laughlin Robinson, 2 T.C. 305 (1943), ...27n
Mary Y. Moore, par. 55,219 P-H Memo T.C. (1955), ...276n
Massey Motors, Inc. v. United States, 364 U.S. 92, (1960), ...71n, 73n
Massillon-Cleveland-Akron Sign Co., 15 T.C. 79, 85 (1950), ...137n
Mauldin v. Commissioner, 195 F. 2d 714 (10th Cir. 1152), ...316n
May Department Stores Co., 16 T.C. 547 (1951), ...289n
M.E. Blatt Co. v. United States, 305 U.S. 267 (1938), ...264n, 265n, 274n
Mechanics and Merchants Bank v. United States, 164 F. Supp. 246 (Ct. Cl. 1958), ...54n
Megibow v. Commissioner, 218 F. 2d 687 (3rd Cir. 1955), ...85n
Mendham Corporation, 9 T.C. 320, 323 (1947), ...184n, 200n, 201n, 231n
Mercantile Trust Co., 32 B.T.A. 82 (1935), ...120n, 124n, 128n
Merchants National Bank of Mobile v. Commissioner, 199 F. 2d 657, 659
    (5th Cir. 1952), ...224n

TABLE OF CASES

Metropolitan Building Co., 31 T.C. 95 (1959), ...281n, 282n
Metropolitan Properties Corp., 24 B.T.A. 220, 225 (1931), ...186n
Michelin Corp. v. McMahon, 137 F. Supp. 798 (D.C.N.Y. 1956), ...93n
Midco Oil Corporation, 20 T.C. 587 (1953), ...80n
Midland Empire Packing Co., 14 T.C. 635 (1950), ...86n
Millar Brainard, 7 T.C. 1180, 1185 (1946), ...194n
Miller v. Hocking Glass Co., 80 F. 2d 436 (6th Cir. 1935), ...137n
Miller Saw-Trimmer Co., 32 B.T.A. 931, 937 (1935), ...164n, 165n
Miller v. United States, 235 F. 2d 553 (6th Cir. 1956), ...173n
Miller v. United States, 12 AFTR 5244 (S.D.Ind. 1962), ...112n
Millinery Center Bldg. Corp. v. Commissioner, 350 U.S. 456 (1956), ...270n, 281n
Milton S. Yunker, 26 T.C. 161, 170 (1956), ...96n
Minneapolis Security Building Corp., 38 B.T.A. 1220 (1938), ...259n, 285n
Minnie R. Ebner, 26 T.C. 962 (1956), ...154n, 155n
Missouri State Life Ins. Co. v. Commissioner, 78, F. 2d 778, 781 (8th Cir. 1934), ...253n
Moline Properties, Inc. v. Commissioner, 319 U.S. 436 (1943), ...368n
Montell Davis, 11 T.C. 538, 541 (1948), ...98n
Montgomery Co., 54 T.C. 986 (1970), ...269n, 280n
Morgan v. Commissioner, 76 F. 2d 390 (5th Cir. 1935), ...28n
Morris Cohen, 39 T.C. 886 (1963), ...34n
Morrissey v. Commissioner, 296 U.S. 344 (1935), ...330n
Morton v. Commissioner, 104 F. 2d 534, 536 (4th Cir. 1939), ...229n
Motor Products Corp., 47 B.T.A. 983, 1001 (1942), ...222n
Mt. Vernon National Bank, 2 B.T.A. 581 (1925), ...221n
M.P. Klyce, 41 B.T.A. 191 (1940), ...186n
Murray v. Commissioner, 232 F. 2d 742 (9th Cir. 1956), ...255n
Nathan C. Spivey, 40 T.C. 1051 (1963), ...151n, 155n
Nathan Schwartz, par. 51,125 P-H Memo T.C. (1951), ...228n
National Bank of Commerce v. Commissioner, 115 F. 2d 875 (9th Cir. 1940), ...224n
National Investors Corp. v. Hoey, 144 F 2d 466 (2d Cir. 1944), ...368n
National Lumber & Tie Co. v. Commissioner, 90 F. 2d 216 (8th Cir. 1937), ...84n
National Packing Co., 24 B.T.A. 952, 956 (1931), ...66n
Natural Gasoline Corp., 21 T.C. 439 (1953), ...345n
Nebraska Seed Co. v. United States, 116 F. Supp. 740 (Ct. Cl. 1953), ...165n
Neils Shultz, 44 B.T.A. 146, 151 (1941), ...227n, 228n
Neville Coke & Chemical Co., 3 T.C. 113 (1944), ...234n
New Capital Hotel, Inc., 28 T.C. 706 (1957), ...258n, 260n
New England Tank Ind., Inc., 50 T.C. 771 (1968), ...267n
New McDermott, Inc., 44 B.T.A. 1035, 1040 (1941), ...193n
Newaygo Portland Cement Co., 27 B.T.A. 1097, 1105 (1933), ...181n
Nickoll v. Commissioner, 103 F. 2d 619, 621 (7th Cir. 1939), ...228n
Nicholl's Estate v. Commissioner, 282 F. 2d 895 (7th Cir. 1960), ...77n
Nichols v. Commissioner, 141 F. 2d 870, 876 (6th Cir. 1944), ...239n, 241n
Nina J. Ennis, 17 T.C. 465, 470 (1951), ...171n
Norman Baker Smith, 51 T.C. 429 (1968), ...258n, 262n
Norman Cooledge, 40 B.T.A. 1325, 1328 (1939), ...94n, 195n
N.W. Ayer & Sons, Inc. 17 T.C. 631 (1951), ...78n
Oesterreich v. Commissioner, 226 F. 2d 798 (9th Cir. 1955), ...285n, 286n
Olin Alexander, Par. 55,029 P-H Memo T.C., ...98n
Olin Bryant, 46 T.C. 848 (1966), ...300n
Oliver Iron Mining Co., 13 T.C. 416 (1949), ...275n
Oppenheim's, Inc. v. Kavanaugh, 90 F. Supp. 107, 112 (E.D. Mich. 1950), ...137n
Oregon Mesabi Corp., 39 B.T.A. 1033, 1038 (1939), ...85n
Oscar Mitchell, 27 B.T.A. 101, 105 (1932), ...84n
Oscar L. Thomas, 31 T.C. 1009 (1959), ...259n

TABLE OF CASES 401

Osenbach v. Commissioner, 198 F. 2d 235, 237 (4th Cir. 1952), ...224*n*
Ostheimer v. United States, 264 F. 2d 789 (3rd Cir. 1959), ...56*n*, 57*n*
Owen v. United States, 8 F. Supp. 707 (Ct. Cl. 1934), ...93*n*, 171*n*, 173*n*
O-W-R-Oil Co., 35 B.T.A. 452 (1937), ...267*n*
Pacific Fruit Express Co., 60 T.C. no. 68 (1973), ...72*n*
Pacific National Co. v. Welch, 304 U.S. 191 (1938), ...151*n*
Palos Verdes Corp. v. United States, 201 F. 2d 256 (9th Cir. 1952), ...316*n*
Park Avenue Corp., 23 B.T.A. 400 (1931), ...384*n*
Park Chamberlain, 41 B.T.A. 10, 16 (1940), ...247
Park Place, Inc., 57 T.C. 767 (1972), ...374*n*, 387*n*
Parker v. Delaney, 186 F. 2d 455 (1st Cir. 1950), ...189*n*, 198*n*, 200*n*, 201, 232*n*
Parma Co., 18 B.T.A. 429 (1929), ...76*n*
Parsons v. United States, 227 F. 2d 437 (3rd Cir. 1955), ...27*n*
Particelli v. Commissioner, 212 F. 2d 498, 501 (9th Cir. 1954), ...53*n*
Pasadena Investment Co. v. Phinney, 223 F. Supp. 639 (S.D. Tex. 1963), ...318*n*
Paul v. Commissioner, 206 F. 2d 763 (3rd Cir. 1953), ...104
Paul W. Frenzel, Par. 63,276 P-H Memo Dec. (1963), ...291*n*, 293*n*, 299*n*
Paymer v. Commissioner, 150 F. 2d 334 (2d Cir. 1945), ...368*n*
Peerless Weighing Etc. Corp., 52 T.C. 850 (1968), ...269*n*
Pender v. Commissioner, 110 F. 2d 477 (4th Cir. 1940), ...245*n*
Peninsula Properties Co., Ltd., 47 B.T.A. 84, 91, 230*n*, 237*n*
Perry v. Commissioner, 152 F. 2d 183, 187 (8th Cir. 1945), ...170*n*
Peter Jung, Sr., par. 41,411 P-H Memo T.C. (1941), ...224*n*
Philadelphia Park Amusement Company v. United States,
   126 F. Supp. 189 (Ct. Cl. 1954), ...46*n*
Philip F. Tirrell, 14 B.T.A. 1399 (1929), ...132*n*
Philips v. Commissioner, 112 F. 2d 721 (3rd Cir. 1940), ...247*n*
Phillips & Easton Supply Co., 20 T.C. 455, 460 (1953), ...79*n*
Phillips v. Frank, 295 F. 2d 629 (9th Cir. 1961), ...172*n*
Piedmont-Mt. Airy Guano Co., 8 B.T.A. 72 (1927), ...131*n*, 137*n*
Piedmont National Bank of Spartanburg v. U.S., 162 F. Supp. 919
   (WD.S.Cal. 1958), ...78*n*
Pig & Whistle Co., 9 B.T.A. 668 (1927), ...279*n*, 281*n*
Pinkney Packing Co., 42 B.T.A. 823, 829 (1940), ...192*n*, 250*n*
Pioneer Real Estate Co., 47 B.T.A. 886, 889 (1942), ...138*n*
Pitts, Estate of Mae Purdie, 218 Cal. 185 (1933), ...372*n*
Plaza Investment Co., 5 T.C. 1295, 1297 (1945), ...275*n*
Portland Oil Co. v. Commissioner, 109 F. 2d 479 (1st Cir. 1940), ...165*n*
Post v. Commissioner, 109 F. 2d 135 (2d Cir. 1940), ...275*n*
Potter Electric Signal and Mfg. Co. v. Commissioner, 286 F. 2d 200
   (8th Cir. 1961), ...299*n*
P.S. Hiatt, 35 B.T.A. 292, 296 (1937), ...192*n*, 252*n*
Ralph A. Boatman, 32 T.C. 1188 (1959), ...217*n*
Ralph L. Trisco, 29 T.C. 515 (1957), ...30*n*
R.A. Waldrup, 52 T.C. 640 (1969), ...159*n*
Raymond v. Commissioner, 114 F. 2d 140 (7th Cir. 1940), ...177*n*
Raymond Robinson, 54 T.C. 772, ...194*n*
Raytheon Production Corporation, 144 F. 2d 110 (CA-1, 1944), ...140*n*
Real Estate Land Title & Trust Co. v. United States, 309 U.S. 13 (1940), ...76*n*
Realty Operators, Inc., 40 B.T.A. 1051, 1055 (1939), ...248*n*
Rebecca J. Murray, 28 B.T.A. 624, 628 (1933), ...154*n*
Redlands Security Co., 5 B.T.A. 956 (1926), ...65*n*
Regals Realty Co. v. Commissioner, 127 F. 2d 931 (2d Cir. 1942), ...113*n*
Reiner v. United States, 222 F. 2d 770, 772 (7th Cir. 1955), ...31*n*
Rhodes v. Commissioner, 100 F. 2d 966, 969 (6th Cir. 1939), ...147*n*, 247*n*

TABLE OF CASES

Ribbon Cliff Fruit Co., 12 B.T.A. 13, 17 (1928), ... 65n
Rich Lumber Co. v. United States, 237 F. 2d 424 (1st Cir. 1956), ... 178n
Richard Lee Plowden, 48 T.C. 666 (1967), ... 365n
Richards v. Commissioner, 81 F. 2d 369 (9th Cir. 1936), ... 316n
Richardson v. United States, 330 F. Supp. 109 (D.C. Tex. 1971), ... 72n
Richter v. Commissioner, 124 F. 2d 412 (2d Cir. 1942), ... 227n, 247n
Ridgewood Land Co., T.C. Memo Dec. 1972-16, ... 318n
R.M.Waggoner, 9 B.T.A. 629 (1927), ... 181n
Robert C. Coffey, 21 B.T.A. 1242 (1931), ... 273n
Robert K. Fronk, par. 57,240 P-H Memo T.C. (1957), ... 33n
Robert L. Brock, 59 T.C. 732 (1973), ... 308n
Robert F. Zumstein, T.C.Memo 1973-45 (1973), ... 297n
Robert Hays Gries, Par. 50-125 P-H Memo T.C. (1950), ... 194n
Robinson v. Commissioner, 73 F. 2d 769 (9th Cir. 1934), ... 164n
Robinson v. Commissioner, 439 F. 2d 767 (8th Cir. 1971), ... 194n
Rocky Mountain Development Co., 38 B.T.A. 1303 (1938), ... 176n
R. O'Dell & Sons v. Commissioner, 169 F. 2d 247 (3rd Cir. 1948), ... 198n, 200n, 230n
Rod Realty Co., T.C.Memo 1967-49; 26 T.C.M. 243 (1967), ... 257n
Rodney, Inc. v. Commissioner, 145 F. 2d 692 (2d Cir. 1944), ... 195n
Rogan v. Commercial Discount Co., 149 F. 2d 585, 587 (9th Cir. 1945), ... 233n, 243n
Roger's Estate v. Commissioner, 143 F. 2d 695 (2d Cir. 1944), ... 165n
Rogers v. Commissioner, 103 F. 2d 790, 792 (9th Cir. 1939), ... 245n
Rogers v. Commissioner, 377 F. 2d 534 (9th Cir. 1967), ... 122n, 124n
Roland W. Sholund, 50 T.C. No. 48 (1968), ... 154n
Rollin E. Meyer's Estate, 58 T.C. 311 (1972), ... 112n
Rose Licht, 37 B.T.A. 1096 (1938), ... 87n
Rothschild v. Berliner, 43 AFTR 1147 (N.D. Cal. 1950), ... 228n
Rowena S. Barnum, 19 T.C. 401, 408 (1952), ... 28n
Russell T. Smith, 1972, P-H T.C.Memo ¶72,046, ... 30n
Ruth C. Rodebaugh, T.C.Memo 1974-34 (1974), ... 308n
Ruth Iron Co. v. Commissioner, 26 F. 2d 30 (8th Cir. 1928), ... 171n
R. V. Board, 18 B.T.A. 650 (1930), ... 173n
Ryegate Paper Co., ¶61,193 P-H Memo T.C., ... 259n
Rylander v. United States, ¶72,881 P-H Fed. 1956 (D.Cal.1956), ... 31n
Safety Tube Corp., 8 T.C. 757,763 (1947), ... 80n
Sam F. Soter, 1968 P-H T.C.Memo ¶68,043, ... 166n
Samuel D. Miller, 48 T.C. 649 (1967), ... 282n
Sauk Investment Co., 34 B.T.A. 732 (1936), ... 337n
Saunders v. United States, 101 F. 2d 133 (5th Cir. 1939), ... 173n
Sayers F. Harman, 4 T.C. 335,347 (1944), ... 185n
S & B Realty Co., 54 T.C. 863 (1970), ... 132n
Scales v. Commissioner, 211 F. 2d 133 (6th Cir. 1954), ... 151n
Scheuber v. Commissioner, 371 F. 2d 996 (7th Cir. 1967), ... 34n
Schoellkopf v. United States, 6 F. Supp. 225,227 (Ct. Cl. 1934), ... 221n
Scofield's Estate v. Commissioner, 226 F. 2d 154 (6th Cir. 1959), ... 87n
Securities Co. v. United States, 85 F. Supp. 532 (S.D.N.Y. 1948), ... 193n
Securities Mortgage Co., 58 T.C. 667 (1972), ... 239n
Shafpa Realty Corp., 8 B.T.A. 283 (1927), ... 94n, 172n, 224n
Sheldon Land Co., 42 B.T.A. 498,505 (1940), ... 228n
Shellabarger Grain Products Co. v. Commissioner, 146 F. 2d 177, 185 (7th Cir.), ... 251n
Sherwin A. Hill, 40 B.T.A. 376, 380, ... 229n
Shirley Hill Coal Co., 6 B.T.A. 935 (1927), ... 269n
S. H. Kress & Co., 40 T.C. 142 (1963), ... 132n, 134n
Shoemaker-Nash, Inc., 41 B.T.A. 17 (1940), ... 94n
Shubin v. Commissioner, 67 F. 32d 199 (9th Cir. 1933), ... 93n

TABLE OF CASES 403

Shunk v. Commissioner, 173 F. 2d 747 (6th Cir. 1949), ...56n
Sigmund Spitzer, 23 B.T.A. 6 776, 778 (1931), ...186n
Simon v. Commissioner, 285 F. 2d 422 (3rd Cir. 1961), ...184n, 198n, 201n
Simon J. Murphy Co. v. Commissioner, 231 F. 2d 639 (6th Cir. 1956), ...63n
Sirbo Holdings, Inc., 61 T.C. No. 77 (1974), ...265n
Sirbo Holdings, Inc. v. Commissioner, 476 F. 2d 981 (2nd Cir. 1973), ...265n
Skemp v. Commissioner, 168 F. 2d 598 (7th Cir. 1948), ...291n, 297n, 298n
S & L Building Corp., 19 B.T.A. 788, 795 (1930), ...186n
Smith v. Commissioner, 232 F. 2d 142 (5th Cir. 1956), ...34n
Smith v. Commissioner, 324 F. 2d 725 (9th Cir. 1963), ...184n
Smith v. Dunn, 224 F. 2d 353 (5th Cir. 1955), ...317n
Smith & Wiggins Gin, Inc. v. Commissioner (5th Cir. 1965) 341 F. 2d 341, ...136n
Snell v. Commissioner, 97 F. 2d 891, 893 (5th Cir. 1938), ...149n
Society Brand Clothes, Inc., 18 T.C. 304, 317 (1952), ...51n
Solomon Silberblatt, 28 B.T.A. 73 (1933), ...96n
Solomon Wright, Jr., 9 T.C. L 173 (1947), ...98n
Sophia M. Garretson, 10 B.T.A. 1381 (1928), ...179n
South Dakota Concrete Products Co., 26 B.T.A. 1429 (1932), ...87n
Sparks Nugget, Inc. v. Commissioner, 458 F. 2d 631 (9th Cir. 1972), ...258n
Speedway Water Co. v. United States, 100 F. 2d 636, 638 (7th Cir. 1938), ...129n
Spitalny, 430 F. 2d 195 (CA-9, 1970), ...144n
Spring City Foundry Co. v. Commissioner, 292 U.S. 182 (1934), ...93n, 173n
Springfield Industrial Bldg. Co., 38 B.T.A. 1445 (1938), ...245n
S. Rose Lloyd, 32 B.T.A. 887, 890 (1935), ...78n
Stamler v. Commissioner, 145 F. 2d 37 (3rd Cir. 1954), ...227n, 247n
Standard Envelope Mfg. Co., 15 T.C. 41 (1950), ...288n
Stanley C. Orrisch, 55 T.C. 395 (1970), ...308n
Stanley Imerman, 7 T.C. 1030 (1946), ...257n
Stanwick's Inc., 15 T.C. 556, ...258n
Starr v. Commissioner, 274 F. 2d 294 (9th Cir. 1959), ...299n
State Bank of Alcester, 8 B.T.A. 878 (1927), ...172n
Stearns Magnetic Mfg. Co. v. Commissioner, 208 F. 2d 849
 (7th Cir. 1954), ...298n
Stein v. Director, 135 F. Supp. 356 (E.D.N.Y. 1955), ...165n
Stephen T. Wasnok, P-H Memo T.C. ¶ 71,906 (1971), ...31n
Sterling v. Ham, 8 F. Supp. 386 (S.D. Me. 1933), ...170n
Stevens Realty Co., 1967 P-H Memo T.C. ¶67,113, ...72n
Stires Corporation, 28 B.T.A. 1, 6 (1933), ...54n
Stiver v. Commissioner, 90 F. 2d 505, 508 (8th Cir. 1937), ...96n
Stockton Harbor Industrial Co. v. Commissioner, 216 F. 2d 638
 (9th Cir. 1954), ...316n
Stokes v. Commissioner, 124 F. 2d 335 (3rd Cir. 1941), ...246n
Stollberg Hardware Co., 46 B.T.A. 788, 749 (1942), ...187n
Stonecrest Corp., 24 T.C. 659 (1955), ...110n, 161n
Strauss v. United States, 199 F. Supp. 845 (W.D. La. 1961), ...273n
Strollberg Hardware Co., 46 B.T.A. 788, 794 (1942) 51n
Sullivan's Estate v. Commissioner, 175 F. 2d 657 (9th Cir. 1949), ...42n
Susan P. Emery, 17 T.C. 308, 311 (1951), ...31n, 228n
Swastica Oil & Gas Co., 123 F. 2d 382 (CA-6, 1941), ...140n, 142n
Tampa Electric Co., 12 B.T.A. 1002, 1007 (1928), ...86n
Ted F. Merrill, 40 T.C. 66 (1963), ...103n
Tennessee Life Insurance Co. v. Phinney, 280 F. 2d 38
 (5th Cir. 1960), ...63n
T. F. Sanford, 22 B.T.A. (1931), ...93n
Thatcher Medicine Co., 3 B.T.A. 154, 159 (1925), ...273n

TABLE OF CASES

Theodore R. Plunkett, 41 B.T.A. 700, 709 (1940), ...194n
Theron M. Lemly, T.C. Memo Dec. 1973-147 (1973), ...135n
Thomas F. Pendergast, 22 B.T.A. 1259 (1931), ...149n
Thomas H. Thatcher, 45 B.T.A. 64 (1941), ...84n
Thomas J. Avery, 11 B.T.A. 958, 962 (1928), ...52n
Thomas v. Obenchain, 185 F. 2d 455 (5th Cir. 1950), ...220n
Thomas Palmer, 23 B.T.A. 296, 300, ...65n
Thompson Lumber Co., 43 B.T.A. 726 (1941), ...255n
Ticket Office Equipment Co., 20 T.C. 272, 279, ...86n
Tiscornia v. Commissioner, 95 F. 2d 678, 683 (9th Cir. 1938), ...223n
T. K. Harris Co., 38 B.T.A. 383, 387 (1938), ...75n
Thompkins v. Commissioner, 97 F. 2d 396, 401 (4th Cir. 1938), ...229n
Tonningsen v. Commissioner, 61 F. 2d 199 (9th Cir. 1932), ...275n
Town Park Hotel Corp. v. Commissioner, 446 F. 2d 878
    (6th Cir. 1971), ...135n
Triangle Realty Co., 12 B.T.A. 867 (1928), ...267n
Trico Products Corp. v. Commissioner, 137 F. 2d 424
    (2d Cir. 1943), ...337n
Trico Securities Corporation, 41 B.T.A. 306, 317 (1940), ...337n
Tri-S Corp., 48 T.C. 316 (1967), ...318n
Trustee Corporation, 42 T.C. 482 (1964), ...280n
1220 Realty Co. v. Commissioner, 323 F. 2d 492 (6th Cir. 1963), ...271n, 279n
12701 Shaker Blvd. Co., 36 T.C. (1961), ...196n
Twin Ports Bridge Co., 27 B.T.A. 346, 359 (1932), ...52n, 237n
Union Bed & Spring Co. v. Commissioner, 39 F. 2d 383
    (7th Cir. 1930), ...77n, 266n
Union National Bank of Troy v. United States, 195 F. Supp. 382, 384
    (N.D.N.Y. 1961), ...32n
United Pacific Corp., 39 T.C. 721 (1963), ...161n
U.S. v. Causby, 328 U.S. 256 (1946), ...139
United States v. Cumberland Public Service Co., 338
    U.S. 451 (1950), ...349n
United States v. Davis, 370 U.S. 65 (1962), ...46n
United States v. Heasty, 370 F. 2d 525 (10th Cir. 1966), ...42n
United States v. Hendler, 303 U.S. 564 (1938), ...187n
United States v. Koshland, 208 F. 2d 636, 639 (9th Cir. 1953), ...87n
United States v. Marshall, 357 F. 2d 294 (9th Cir. 1966), ...153n
United States v. Wehrli, 400 F. 2d 686 (10th Cir. 1968), ...267n
United States v. Wharton, 207 F. 2d 526 (5th Cir. 1953), ...187n
U.S. v. Winthrop, 417 F. 2d 905 (5th Cir. 1969), ...33n
United Surgical Steel Co., 54 T.C. 1215 (1970), ...165n
University Properties, Inc. v. Commissioner, 378 F. 2d 83
    (9th Cir. 1967), ...269n
Vancoh Realty Co., 33 B.T.A. 918, 926 (1936), ...221n
Van Zandt, 40 T.C. 824 (1963), ...291n, 296n, 297n
Veenstra & De Haan Coal Co., 11 T.C. 964, 967 (1948), ...179n
Vernon Hoven, 56 T.C. 50 (1971), ...103n
Victor B. Gilbert, 6 T.C. 10, 13 (1946), ...94n, 172n, 224n
Victor Shaken, 2 T.C. 785 (1945), ...184n
Victory Glass, Inc., 17 T.C. 381, 386 (1951), ...187n
Victory Housing No. 2, Inc. v. Commissioner, 205
    F. 2d 371 (10th Cir. 1953), ...317n
Vincent, 219 F. 2d 228 (CA-9, 1955), ...143n
Virginia Iron, Coal and Coke Co. v. Commissioner, 99 F. 2d 919
    (4th Cir. 1938), ...178n

TABLE OF CASES 405

Virginia M. Cramer, 55 T.C. 1125, 1132 (1971), ...219n
Voloudakis v. Commissioner, 274 F. 2d 209 (9th Cir. 1960), ...282n
W. A. Ayling, 32 T.C. 704 (1959), ...97n
W. A. Dallmeyer, 14 T.C. 1282, 1289 (1950), ...219n
Wagegro Corp., 38 B.T.A. 1225 (1938), ...153n
W. A. Graeper, 27 B.T.A. 632, 638 (1933), ...76n
Wala Garage, Inc. v. United States, 163 F. Supp. 379
    (Ct. Cl. 1958), ...136n, 191n
Walnut Realty Trust, 23 B.T.A. 850 (1931), ...149n
Walter H. Rich, Par. 36, 166 P-H Memo B.T.A. (1936), ...195n
Walter H. Sutliff, 46 B.T.A. 446 (1942), ...281n
Walter M. Priddy, 43 B.T.A. 18, 29 (1940), ...248n
Walter R. Crabtree, 20 T.C. 841, 848 (1953), ...34n
Walther v. Commissioner, 316 F. 2d 708 (7th Cir. 1963), ...193n
W. A. Mays v. Cambell, Jr., 246 F. Supp. 375 (N.D. Tex., 1965), ...126n
Warner A. Shattuck, 25 T.C. 416, 422 (1955), ...225n
Warner Mountains Lumber Co., 9 T.C. 1171, 1176 (1947), ...84n, 85n
Warren Brekke, 40 T.C. 789 (1963), ...291n
Warren Jones Company, 60 T.C. No. 70 (1973), ...169n
Warren Leslie, Sr., 6 T.C. 488, 493 (1946), ...27n
Warren Service Co. v. Commissioner, 110 F. 2d 723 (2nd Cir. 1940), ...260n
Washington Catering Co., 9 B.T.A. 743 (1927), ...279n
Washington Fireproof Building Co., 31 B.T.A. 824 (1934), ...265n
Waters F. Burrows, 38 B.T.A. 236 (1938), ...252n
Watson v. Commissioner, 62 F. 2d 35 (9th Cir. 1932), ...178n
Watson P. Davidson, 27 B.T.A. 158 (1932), ...275n
Waukesha Malleable Iron Co. v. Commissioner, 67 F. 2d 368, 371
    (7th Cir. 1933), ...152n
W. C. Haden Co. v. Commissioner, 165 F. 2d 588, 590
    (5th Cir. 1948), ...120n, 128n, 235n, 244n
W. Einnie Cadby, 24 T.C. 899 (1955), ...54n
Welch v. Street, 116 F. 2d 953, 955 (1st Cir. 1941), ...231n
Weldon D. Smith, 17 T.C. 135, 144 (1951), ...194n, 195n
Wellman v. United States, 25 F. Supp. 868 (D.C. Mass. 1938), ...252n
Wells Fargo Bank & Union Trust Co. v. Commissioner, 163
    F. 2d 521 (9th Cir. 1947), ...280n
West Production Co., 41 B.T.A. 1043, 1049 (1940), ...240n
Whipple v. Commissioner, 373 U.S. 193 (1963), ...220n
White v. Commissioner, 172 F. 2d 629 (5th Cir. 1949), ...32n
White v. Fitzpatrick, 193 F. 2d 398 (2d Cir. 1951), ...296n, 298n
Whitlow v. Commissioner, 82 F. 2d 569 (8th Cir. 1936), ...93n
Willhoit v. Commissioner, 308 F. 2d 259 (9th Cir. 1962), ...172n
William A. Clementson, 1968 P-H Memo T.C. ¶68,118, ...261n
William B. Howell, 57 T.C. 546 (1972), ...34n
William B. Strong, 66 T.C. 12 (1975), ...368n
William C. Atwater & Co., 10 T.C. 218, 251 (1948), ...337n
William C. Heinemann & Co., 40 B.T.A. 1090, 1093 (1939), ...221n
William C. Hormann, 17 T.C. 903, 907 (1951), ...25n, 27n, 28n
William H. Jamison, 8 T.C. 173, 181 (1947), ...147n
William Holden, 6 B.T.A. 605 (1927), ...181n
William I. Nash, 60 T.C. 503 (1973), ...34n, 78n
William Justin Petit, 8 T.C. 228, 236 (1947), ...80n
William Parris, 20 B.T.A. 320, 326 (1930), ...93n
William Scholes & Sons, Inc. 3 B.T.A. 598 (1925), ...273n
William T. Bivin, 21 B.T.A. 1051 (1930), ...50n

Williams Furniture Corp. 45 B.T.A. 928 (1941), ...137n
Williams v. United States, 219 F. 2d 523 (5th Cir. 1955), ...96n, 155n, 181n
Wilshire Holding Corp. v. Commissioner, 262 F. 2d 51 (9th Cir. 1958), ...285n
Wilshire Medical Properties v. United States, 314 F. 2d 333
    (9th Cir. 1963), ...278n
Winfield A. Coffin, 41 T.C. No. 10 (1963), ...88n
The Winter Garden, Inc., 10 B.T.A. 71 (1928), ...77n, 266n
W. L. Moody Cotton Co. v. Commissioner, 143 F. 2d 712, 714
    (5th Cir. 1944), ...223n
Wolan v. Commissioner, 184 F. 2d 101, 104 (10th Cir. 1950), ...275n
Woodsam Associates, Inc. v. Commissioner, 16 T.C. 649, 654 (1951), ...199n
Woodsam Associates v. Commissioner, 198 F. 2d 357, 359
    (2d Cir. 1952), ...184n, 185, 198n, 200n, 231n
World Publishing Company, 35 T.C. 7 (1960), ...277n
World Publishing Company v. Commissioner, 299 F. 2d 614 (8th Cir. 1962), ...278n
W. W. Hoffman, 40 B.T.A. 459, 462 (1939), ...228n, 248n
W. W. Millsaps, T.C. Memo 1973-146 (1973) 257n
W. Z. Sharp, 8 B.T.A. 399 (1927), ...222n, 253n
Young v. Commissioner, 59 F. 2d 691 (9th Cir. 1932), ...261n, 274n
Your Health Club, Inc., 4 T.C. 385, 390 (1944), ...274n
Zwetchkenbaum, par. 62,283 P-H Memo T.C. (1962), ...273n

Index

A

Abandonment of building, loss deduction and, 77–78
Abandonment of property, 147, 247
   mortgaged in excess of basis, 199–201
   "walk-away," 201
ABC transaction, 299–301
   real estate acquisitions, application to, 300–301
Accelerated depreciation, 67–68
   methods, use of, 74
   and Tax Reform Act of 1969, 355
Accrual basis taxpayer, deferred payment method and, 173
Accumulated earnings surtax, 336–339
Accumulated taxable income, meaning of, 337
Acquiring real property, 35–63
   allocation of tax basis, 52–54
      by contract, 52–53
      in general, 52
      to structure to be demolished, 53–54
   apportionment of taxes, 57–63
      on acquisition other than purchase, 63
      current, 58–59
      excess tax paid, treatment of, 60
      reimbursement for taxes paid, 61–63
      time for deducting, 59–60
   bargain price, acquisition for, 56–57
      by broker without commission, 56–57
      exception for pre-existing relationship, 56
   option, 54–56
      allocation of basis, 55
      to buy from estate, 55
      failure to exercise, 55
      holding period, 55–56
      inherited, 54–55
      purchased, 54
      sale, 55
   tax basis of property, 45–52
      as community property, 50
      as compensation, 50
      on corporate distribution, 51

Acquiring real property (*cont.*)
   tax basis of property (*cont.*)
      for debt, 50–51
      by gift, 47–48
      by gift in contemplation of death, 49
      by inheritance, 48–49
      by purchase, 46
      subject to mortgage, 51–52
      by surviving joint tenant, 50
      by tax-free exchange, 47
   title, taking, 35–45
      corporate ownership, 36–40 (*see also* "Corporate ownership")
      husband and wife, 40–44 (*see also* "Husband and wife ownership")
      individual, 36
      joint tenancy, 44
      partnership, 44–45
      tenancy in common, 44
Adjusted income from rents, meaning of, 340
Advantages in real estate ownership, 19–23
   capital gain, postponed, 22
   casualty losses, 22
   depreciation, 20–21
   election to capitalize or deduct interest and taxes, 22
   equity financing, 20–21
   exchanges, tax-free, 20–21
   leasing vs. ownership, 23
   repair and maintenance, expenses of, 22
   sale of property, 22
   versus stock market investment, 20–21
   and tenants' improvements, 22–23
   title, 23
"All-inclusive" mortgage, installment sales and, 161–162
Allocation of tax basis on acquisition, 52–54 (*see also* "Acquiring real property")
Annuity, private, sales for, 176–178
   estate planning, value for, 178
   "investment," meaning of, 177
"Apple tree" ruling, 316*n*
Apportionment of real estate taxes upon acquisition, 57–63 (*see also* "Acquiring real property")

B

Bargain price, acquisition of property for, 56–57 (*see also* "Acquiring real property")
Basis of property upon acquisition, 45–52 (*see also* "Acquiring real property")
  effect of mortgage upon, 184
  of mortgaged property acquired, 187–189
Beneficiaries of investment trust, taxation of, 328
Bonus to landlord, convenant by tenant to pay, 258–259
"Boot" in tax-free exchange, 47, 114–117, 332–333
  basis of property, 115–117
  effect of, 115
  losses, 115
Broker's own account, purchase of property for, 56–57
Buildings, guideline categories of useful life of, 73
Business, property held for, 25 (*see also* "Trade or business . . .")

C

Cancellation of lease, 280–282 (*see also* "Leasing real property")
Capital assets, gains or losses on, 99–102
Capital gain, postponed, as advantage, 22
Capital improvements, deduction for expenses of, 78–79
Carrying charges, election for, 84–85
Casualty losses on business property, 85–87
  cost of restoration, 86–87
  insurance received, reduction for, 87
  measuring, 86
Casualty losses to real estate, deductibility of, 22
Classification of real property, 23–26
  for income production, 24–25
    what it means, 25
  problems of, 26–34
    "house" and "home," difference between, 26–28
    "investor" and "dealer," 32–34
    in quasi-business use, 28–30
    rental as trade or business, 30–32 (*see also* "Trade or business property . . .")
    vacation home, occasional rental of, 28–30

Classification of real property (*cont.*)
  as residence, personal, 23–24
    condemnation, 24
    and IRC Section 262, 23–24
    new home, purchase of, 24
    owner over 65, 24
    "principle residence," definition of, 24
  for sale to customers, 25–26
  for trade or business, 25
    and Section 1231, 25
    and Section 1250, 25
    tax treatment most favorable, 25
Collapsible corporation, liquidation of, 356–357
  definition on, 356
  "tainted" stockholders, 357
Collapsible corporation rules applied to sales of stock, 347–349
Collapsible partnerships, 310–312
Commissions, 196
Community property, basis of property acquired as, 50
Compensation, basis of property acquired as, 50
Compromise of mortgage debt, 249–252
  gift cancellation, 251
  mortgagee, loss to, 249
  mortgagor, income to, 249–250
    insolvent, 250
    non-assuming, 251-252
    purchase-money, 250
  postponement of income by reduction of basis, 251
  suggestions, 252
Condemnation, inverse, 139–145
  definition, 139
  examples, 139
    "flood plain" in Virginia, 140*n*
    jet flyways, 140
  loss previously taken, 144–145
  "roll over," 144
  nature of action, 139
  no prior loss deduction, 140–141
  partial destruction, 141–144
    fair market value allocation, 143
    gross receipts method allocation, 143–144
    lost income method, 142–143
    relative cost method, 142
  Section 1033, application of, 141, 144
  tax consequences, 139–140
Condemnation of cooperative property, 372
Condemnation expenses, 137–138

INDEX 409

Condemned property, depreciation recapture of under Section 1033, 146–147
Condominium owner, 375–381
  for business use, 378–379
    depreciation, 378
    gain or loss on disposition of unit, 379
    interest deduction, limitation on, 378–379
  corporation, four common characteristics of, 381–383
    business entity alternative, separate, 387–388
    centralization of management, 382
    continuity of life, 381–382
    co-ownership of rental units, 384
    and home owners associations, 385–387
    IRC Section 216, 384
    IRC Section 528, 385–386
    limited liability, 382
    recreation, separate entity for, 387
    tax consequences, 383–388
    transferability, 382–383
  definitions, 375
  management agreements, 379–381
    corporate status, 381–383
    recreational facilities, 380–381
    rental to outsiders, 381
    restrictive covenants, 380
  for residential use, 375–378
    deductions, 375–376
    gain or loss, character of, 377
    gift of joint interest to spouse, 377–378
    IRC Section 1034, 376
    sale of unit, 376
  rights and duties, correlated, 375
Consolidation, corporate, 360
Contingent price, sale for, 175–176
Conversions, involuntary, of real property, 129–138
  into cash, 130–131
  condemnation expenses, 137–138
  election on tax return, 135
  exchange for similar property, tax-free, 129–130
  flowage and other non-exclusive easements, 138
  "like kind" property, 134
  mortgage, effect of, 136
  proceeds that can be sheltered, 133
  replacement property, 133–134
    "functional" test, 133
    period for, 134–135

Conversions, involuntary, of real property (*cont.*)
  and Section 1231, 145–146
  severance damages, 137–138
  single economic unit rule, 132–133
  successor to owner of condemned property, 135–136
  use and occupancy insurance, 136–137
  what it is, 131–132
Cooperative housing corporation, 369–374
  commercial rents, 373
  commercial use, allowable, 373–374
    by tenant-stockholders, 374
  condemnation, 372
  foreclosure of stock, 373
  income, non-qualifying, problem of, 372–373
  joint-tenancy, limitations on, 372
    and IRC Section 2515, 372
  lessees, non-stockholder, 373
  non-exempt status, 374
  sale of stock by tenant-stockholder, 371–372
    definition, 371n
  Section 121, 372
  Section 216, 369–371
    deductions, 369–370
    requirements, 370–371
Corporate distribution, basis of property acquired through, 51
Corporate ownership, 36–40
  and individual, comparison of, 37–40
  and tax preference income, 39–40
Corporation, four common characteristics of, 381
Corporation, partnership's characteristics of, 314–315
Corporations, 331–362
  acquisition of property, problems in, 357–361
    acquisition of stock and liquidation, 361
    merger or consolidation, 360
    stock, issuing, 358–359
    tax-free reorganization, 359
    types, other, 360
  advantages and disadvantages, 361–362
  operation, problems of, 336–346
    accumulated earnings surtax, 336–339
    distribution from accelerated depreciation reserves, 342–343
    distribution of "excess F.H.A. mortgage proceeds," 343–344
    dividend in kind, 344–346

Corporations (*cont.*)
   operation, problems of (*cont.*)
      dividends paid, treatment of, 342
      personal holding company tax, 339–342
   problems, 331–336
      debt securities, 334–335
      taxable, 333–334
      tax-free, 332–333
      "thin," 334–336
   sales and liquidations, problems of, 346–357
      collapsible corporation, liquidation of, 356–357 (*see also* "Collapsible corporations")
      collapsible corporation rules, 347–349
      liquidation and sale of property by stockholders, 349–350
      "one month liquidation," 351–354 (*see also* "One month liquidation")
      Section 337 liquidation, 350–351
      stock, sale of, 346
   tax planning, 361–362
Costs of acquiring lease, 274–280 (*see also* "Leasing real property")
Cost as basis of property in purchase, 46
Customers, property held for sale to, 25–26

D

"Dealer" and "investor," difference between, 32–34
Debt, basis of property acquired for, 50–51
Debt securities, 334–335
Deferred payment sales, 168–175
   advantages and disadvantages, 169–170
   and installment method, comparison of, 169
   obligation, sale of, 174–175
   pledge of obligation, 175
   qualified sales, 170
      negotiable contract of sale, 171
      non-negotiable contract sale, 170–171
      and personal property, 173
      sale subject to mortgage, 174
      sale subject to note secured by mortgage, 171–172
      sale subject to personal note, 172–173
      sales by accrual basis taxpayer, 173
   repossession of property sold, 175
Deficiency judgments, 221 (*see also* "Foreclosure by sale to third party")
Demolition of building, loss deduction and, 77–78
Demolition of existing improvements, covenant by tenant for, 266–267

Depreciation, 64–76
   accelerated depreciation, 67–68
   accelerated methods, use of, 74
      limitations on use of, 69–70
      and low-cost rental housing, 70
   allowance, measuring, 66–67
      allocation, methods of, 67–69
   basis, apportionment of, 65–66
   change of method, 71
   double-declining balance method, 67–68
   improvements, types of, 65
   land not depreciable, 64–65
   limitations on, 64n
   125% declining-balance method, 69
   150% declining-balance method, 69
   salvage value, 73–74
   straight-line method, 67
   sum-of-the-years' digits method, 68
   and tax preference item tax, 74–75
   200% declining-balance method, 69
   useful life, 71–73
      buildings, guideline categories of, 73
      guidelines, IRS, 72
   who is entitled to, 75–76
Depreciation, accelerated, Tax Reform Act of 1969 and, 355
Depreciation of condominium, 378
Depreciation of improvements on leased property, 271–274 (*see also* "Leasing real property")
Depreciation of partnership property, problems of, 305
Depreciation recapture, 104–105
   farm improvements, 107–108
   real estate improvements, 105–107
      Revenue Act of 1969, 106
   under Section 1033, 146–147
   under Sections 1245 and 1250, 354–355
Depreciation as tax advantage, 20–21
Dividend, corporate, in other than money, 344–346
Dividends paid to corporation stockholders, treatment of, 342
Double-declining balance method of depreciation, 67–68, 69
   for new residential housing, 69

E

Easement, sale of, 97
Election to deduct or capitalize expenses, advantage of, 22
"Equitable" apportionment, meaning of, 96–97

INDEX 411

Equity financing as advantage of real estate ownership, 20–21
Erosion, deductibility of, 85
Escrow sales, 180–182
    closing of escrow as general rule for date, 180–181

Escrow sales (*cont.*)
    exception: deposit of purchase price, 181–182
    exception: transfer of possession, 182
Exchange of property mortgaged in excess of basis:
    non-taxable, 198–199
    taxable, 198
Exchange, tax-free:
    as advantage of real estate ownership, 20–21
    basis of property acquired by, 47
    in involuntary conversions, 129–130
    leaseback, 289–290
    losses, 290–291
Exchanges, taxable, 129
Exchanges of like property, tax-free, 111–129
    basis, 113
    "boot," 114–117
        basis of property, 115–117
        effect of, 115
        losses, 115
    holding period, 114
    for investment or trade/business, requirement of, 112
    "like property," meaning of, 111–112
    losses, 113
    mortgage, effect of, 117–118
    mortgages, offsetting, 118–120
    planning, 126–129
    three-cornered, 120–123
        techniques for, 123–126
Expenses incurred with mortgage debt, 196
Expenses of landlord, tenant's reimbursement of, 262
Expenses for repair and maintenance, deductibility of, 22

F

Fair market value allocation in inverse condemnation, 143
Family leasebacks, 294–299
    gain or loss, 294–295
    guardian, role of, 296–297
    as income-splitting devices, 296–297
    rental deduction on, 298–299
    requirements, 297–298

Farm improvements, depreciation recapture and, 107–108
Farming land, soil conservation expenses for, 88
Fertilizer expenses for farmer, deduction for, 89–90
Finders' fees, 196
Foreclosure, assignment of rents to mortgagee and, 254–255
Foreclosure, expenses of, 253–254
Foreclosure by sale to third party, 219–232
    bad debt loss of mortgagee, 219
    business or non-business bad debt, 219–220
    deduction of mortgagee for previously reported income, 223–224
    gain or income to mortgagee, possibility of, 224–225
    loss of mortgagee, determining amount of, 221–223
        "recovery exclusion" meaning of, 222n
    loss of mortgagor on foreclosure sale, 225–227
    gain on sale, 229–230
    nature of, 227–228
    of non-assuming mortgagor, 230–232
    time for deducting, 228–229
    suggestions, 232
    time for deducting, 220–221

G

Gain or loss on sale, computation of, 92 (*see also* "Sales of real property")
    of capital assets, 99–102
    nature of, 97–98
    time for reporting, 95–96
Gain on sale of partnership property, problem of, 306–308
Gift, tax basis of property acquired by, 47–48
Gift cancellation of mortgage debt, 251
Gift in contemplation of death, tax basis for, 49
Gift of property mortgaged in excess of basis, 201–202
Gift tax liability for wife, 41
Gifts and leasebacks, 295–296
Golf course, depreciation and, 65
Gross receipts method allocation in inverse condemnation, 143–144
Guarantee by tenant against loss by landlord, 262
Guardian, family leasebacks and, 296–297

H

Handbook of Partnership Taxation, 302n
Holding period, 102–104
    on tax-free exchange, 114
Home owners associations, exemption of, 385–387
    overassessments by, 386–387
"House" and "home," difference between, 26–28
Housing and Urban Development Act of 1968, 70
Husband and wife ownership, 40–44
    basis after death, 41–42
    comparison of ownership, 43–44
    estate and gift taxes, 41
    joint tenancy, termination of, 42–43

I

Improvements by landlord on leased property, depreciation of, 271
Improvements to leased property by tenant, permanent, depreciation of, 271
Improvements qualifying for depreciation, types of, 65
Improvements to real property, deduction for expenses of, 78–79
Improvements made by tenant, reimbursement of tenant for, 267–268
    as allowance against rent, 268–269
Improvements by tenants as untaxed accretion, 22–23
Income, effect of mortgage upon, 184
Income production, property held for, 24–25
    what it means, 25
Incorporation, problems of, 331–336 (*see also* "Corporations")
Indeterminate price, sale for, 175–178 (*see also* "Price . . .")
Individual ownership, 36
    and corporate, comparison of, 37–40
Inheritance, tax basis of property acquired by, 48–49
Inheritance of property mortgaged in excess of basis, 202
Insect infestations, deduction for, 85
Installment method and deferred payment sale, comparison of, 169
Installment sales, 149–168
    advantages, 149
    bonds of corporate seller, 154
    constructive receipt of payment in year of sale, 154–155
    contract, sale of, 163–164
    disadvantages, 149–150

Installment sales (*cont.*)
    dispositions of contracts, other, 165–166
    gain, reporting, 157–158
    guarantee by financial institution, 167
    of mortgaged property, 158–161
    planning, 155–157
    pledge of installment contract, 165
    qualifying for, 150–151
    repossession of property, 167–168
    and Section 453, 149
    and Section 1038, 167
    selling expenses, 162–163
    substituted security, 166
    types of sales qualifying, 163
    and "wrap-around" mortgage, 161–162
    in year of sale, 151–154
        30% rule, 151–152
Insurance premiums paid by tenant, 261
Insurance received for casualty loss, deductions and, 87
Interest, deduction for, 81–83
    for construction period, 83
    "points," 82–83
    prepaid, 83
Interest of mortgage debt, payment of, 193–196
    delinquent, 195
Internal Revenue Code Sections:
    108, 192–193, 252
    121, 372
    162, 263, 291
    164 (d), 60, 95
    165, 76, 87, 265
    166, 219
    175, 87–90, 108
    178, 272, 279
    216, 369–371, 384
    262, 23–24
    280 A, 29–30
    333, 349
        and "one month liquidation," 351–354
    336, 349
    337, 349, 350–351
        liquidation under, 350–351
    341, 347–349
    351, 352
    357 (c), 209
    453, 149
    461 (c), 59–60
    482, 299
    483, 95, 194
    501, 387
    528, 385–386
    531, 336–337
    533, 337
    541, 339
    732, 308n

# INDEX

Internal Revenue Code Sections (*cont.*)
   856–858, 324–330
   1001 (b), 61–63
   1015, 295n
   1017, 192–193, 252
   1031, 111–112
   1033, 130–138, 141, 144, 372
     and depreciation recapture, 146–147
   1034, 376
   1038, 167, 215–219
   1211, 220
   1231, 25, 98–99, 227–228
     and involuntary conversions, 145–146
   1237, 316–320
   1239, 108–109
   1245, 104–105, 245
     and accelerated depreciation, 354–355
     and liquidation, 350
   1250, 25, 105
     and accelerated depreciation, 350, 354–355
   2515, 372
Inverse condemnation, 139–145 (*see also* "Condemnation, inverse")
"Investment" in annuity, meaning of, 177
Investment interest, definition of, 81
Investment trusts, 324–330
   beneficiaries, taxation of, 328
   election to be taxed as, 324–325
   evaluation, 328–329
   loss of qualified status, 330
   "Massachusetts Trust," 324, 328
   qualification, 325–327
   taxation, 327–328
"Investor" and "dealer," difference between, 32–34
Involuntary conversions, 129–138 (*see also* "Conversions, involuntary . . .")
Involuntary conveyance to mortgagee, 232–238 (*see also* "Strict foreclosure")

J

Jet flyways, inverse condemnation and, 140
Joint tenancy, 44
Joint tenant, surviving, basis of property acquired as, 50

L

Land not depreciable, 64–65
Land-clearing expenses for farmer, deduction of, 89–90
Landlord, non-resident alien, 261n

Landlord's costs for lease, 274–275 (*see also* "Leasing real property")
   tenant's reimbursement of, 262
Landscaping, depreciation and, 65
Lease with option to purchase, 284–286
Lease renewal, 272–273
   conclusion, 273
   by related parties, 273
   "seventy-five percent test," 272–273
   "sixty percent test," 272
Leasebacks, 287–299 (*see also* "Sales and leasebacks")
Leasing real property, 23, 256–286
   cancellation of or sale of, 280–282
     lessee's payment, 281
     lessor's payment, 280–281
     sale or assignment, proceeds on, 281–282 (*see also* "Sale of lease")
   clauses, tax consequences of, 256–270
     advance payment of rent, 258
     bonus, 258–259
     decreasing fixed or minimal rental, 259
     demolition of existing improvements, 266–267
     expenses of landlord, reimbursement of, 262
     guarantee against loss, 262
     improvements by tenant as allowance against rent, 268–269
     insurance premiums, payment of, 261
     landlord, non-resident alien, 261n
     maintenance and repairs, covenant for, 261
     mortgage service, payment of, 261
     net lease, 263
     payment of rent, 256–258
     to reduce rent, 269
     and related parties, 257
     restoration of property, 263–264
     restoration or reimbursement, 265–266
     security deposit by tenant, 259–260
     security deposit applicable to future rents, 260
     taxes, covenant to pay, 260–261
     tenant's improvements, reimbursement for, 267–268
     termination, 269–270
     turn-key lease, 267
   costs of acquiring, 274–280
     allocation to outstanding lease, 275–276
     carry-over basis on death of lessor, allocation of, 276–277
     depreciable improvements subject to outstanding lease, allocation to, 277–278
     of landlord, 274–275
     of tenant, 278–280

Leasing real property (*cont.*)
    depreciation of improvements, 271–274
        improvement by tenants as income to lessor, 273–274
        landlord's, 271
        month-to-month tenancy, 273
        option, failure to renew, 273
        by tenant permanent, 271
        term of lease, option to renew, 272–273 (*see also* "Lease renewal")
        termination of lease, premature, 273
        trade fixtures installed by tenant, 271
    lease or purchase, 282–286
        with option to purchase, 284–286
"Like property" for exchange, meaning of, 111–112
Limited partnerships, 312–316, 322–323
    definition, 312
    interest, basis of, 312–314
    "Peach tree" and "Apple tree" rulings, 316*n*
    "at risk" basis for deductions, 314
    taxable as corporation, 314–316
Liquidations by corporations, problems of, 346–357 (*see also* "Corporations")
Loan processing fees, 82–83 (*see also* "Interest, deduction for")
Loss to mortgagee, determining, 221–223
Loss on sale, computation of, 92 (*see also* "Sales of real property")
    of capital assets, 99–102
    nature of, 97–98
    time for reporting, 95–96
Losses on tax-free exchange, 113
Lost income method in inverse condemnation, 142–143
"Low-cost rental housing," meaning of, 70

M

Maintenance expenses, deductibility of, 22, 78–79
"Massachusetts Trust," 324, 328
Merger, corporate, 360
Mortgage:
    effect on converted property, 136
    effect on tax-free exchange, 117–118
    offsetting, 118–120
Mortgage costs, deductibility of, 185–187
Mortgage financing, tax aspects of, 183–213
    acquiring mortgaged property, 187–193
        basis, 187–189
        condemnation proceeds, reinvestment of, 190–191

Mortgage financing, tax aspects of (*cont.*)
    acquiring mortgaged property (*cont.*)
        condemnation proceeds on property, payment of, 189–190
        payments made by owner on debt, 189
        reduction in mortgage debt, effect of, 191–193
    corporate transactions in property mortgaged in excess of basis, 209–212
        contribution of property, 209–210
        distribution of property, 210–211
        F.H.A. "windfall" profits, 212
    liabilities in excess of basis, 197–202
        abandonment of property, 199–201
        exchange, taxable, 198
        exchange, non-taxable, 198–199
        gift of property, 201–202
        inheritance of property, 202
        sale of property, 197–198
    partnership transactions in property mortgaged in excess of basis, 202–209
        conclusions, 209
        contribution by partner not personally liable for debt, 203–204
        contribution of property, 202–203
        distribution of contributed property, 208
        distribution by partnership, 204–205
        gain, possibility of, 203
        receipt of contribution by partnership, 204
        sale of contributed property, 206–207
        tax-planning, 205–206
    payments, penalties and commissions, 193–196
        commissions, fees and other expenses, 196
        deferred payments, failure to provide for interest on, 194
        delinquent interest, 195
        lump sum payments, 194–195
        prepayment penalties, 196
    placing upon property, 183–187
        basis, effect upon, 184
        cost, 185–187
        disposition, effect to owner upon, 184–185
        income, effect upon, 184
        release of liability as disposition, 185
    tax advantages, 212–213
Mortgage service, payment of by tenant, 261
Mortgaged property, basis of acquisition of, 51–52

INDEX

Mortgaged property, installment sale of, 158–161
Mortgagee, bad debt loss of, 219
    determining amount of, 221–223
        "recovery exclusion," meaning of, 222n
Mortgagee, forclosure by sale to, 238–242
    gain, 240–241
    as hybrid transaction, 238
    income, 241–242
    loss, 238–239
        nature of, 239
        reduction, 240
    mortgagor, gain or loss to, 242
    suggestions, 242
Mortgagee:
    gain or income to in foreclosure, 224–225
    gain or loss to on voluntary conveyance, 243–244
    loss to on involuntary conveyance, 233
        basis to of acquired property, 235
        gain to, 233–235
        second, loss of, 252–253
Mortgagor:
    gain or loss to on voluntary conveyance, 244–245
        insolvent, gain to, 245
        non-assuming, 246–247
        purchase-money, gain to, 245–246
    loss of on foreclosure sale, 225–227
        gain on sale, 229–230
        nature of, 227–228
        non-assuming, gain or loss of, 230–232
        time for deducting, 228–229
    loss of on strict foreclosure, 235–236
        gain, 236–237

N

Net lease, effect of on landlord's interest deduction, 263
"Net-net" lease, status of property and, 31–32
Net operating loss carryover, sale and, 109
"Objective intent," role of in sale and leaseback with option to repurchase, 292–293
Obsolescence, 76–77
"One month liquidation," 351–354
    and accelerated depreciation, 354–355
125% declining-balance method of depreciation, 69
150% declining-balance method of depreciation, 69

O

Operation of real property, 64–90 (see also "Ownership and . . .")
Option, acquisition of property under, 54–56
    allocation of basis, 55
    to buy from estate, 55
    failure to exercise, 55
    holding period, 55–56
    inherited, 54–55
    purchased, 54
    sale, 55
Option to renew lease, depreciation and failure to exercise, 273
Option sales, 178–180
    exercise or failure of, 179
    and sales contract, difference between, 178–179
    seller, advantages to, 180
Orchards, depreciation and, 65
Ownership and operation of real property, 64–90
    assessments, special, 83–84
    carrying charges, 84–85
    casualty losses on business property, 85–87
        cost of restoration, 86–87
        insurance received, reduction for, 87
        measuring, 86
    defense of title, 79–80
    demolition, abandonment or removal of improvements, 77–78
    depreciation, 64–76
        accelerated methods, use of, 69–70, 74 (see also "Depreciation")
        allowance, measuring, 66–67
        basis, apportionment of, 65–66
        change of method, 71
        improvements, types of, 65
        land not depreciable, 64–65
        limitations on, 64n
        and "low-cost rental housing," 70
        methods of allocating allowance, 67–69 (see also "Depreciation")
        salvage value, 73–74
        and tax preference item tax, 74–75
        useful life, 71–73 (see also "Depreciation")
        who is entitled to, 75–76
    interest, 81–83
        for construction period, 83
        "points," 82–83
        prepaid, 83
    obsolescence, 76–77
    protection of income, 79–80

Ownership and operation of real property (*cont.*)
    repairs, maintenance expenses, and capital improvements, 78–79
    soil and water conservation expenses, 87–90
        definition, 87–88
        districts, 89
        election to deduct, 89
        farming land, 88
        fertilizer and land clearing expenses, 89–90
        limitation, 88, 89
    taxes, 81

P

Partnership, 44–45
Partnerships, real estate held by, 302–312
    collapsible, 310–312
        "substantially appreciated inventory," meaning of, 311*n*
        "unrealized receivables," meaning of, 311*n*
    depreciation, problems of, 305
    distributions, 308–310
    gain, problems of, 306–308
    items, separate, 303
    limited, 312–316 (*see also* "Limited partnerships")
    problems of organizing, 304
    undivided interests in contributed property, 308
Partnerships and unincorporated associations, differences between, 320–321
Pasture land, depreciation and, 65
"Peach tree" ruling, 316*n*
Personal holding company tax, 339–342
Personal property, deferred payment method and, 173
Plant disease destruction, deduction for, 85
"Points," 82–83, 187
Postponing tax on real property sale, 148–182
    deferred payment sales, 168–175 (*see also* "Deferred payment . . .")
        advantages and disadvantages, 169–170
        and installment method, comparison of, 169
        qualified sales, 170–173 (*see also* "Deferred payment sales")
    escrow sales, 180–182
        closing of escrow as general rule for date, 180–181
        exception: deposit of purchase price, 181–182
        exception: transfer of possession, 182

Postponing tax on real property sale (*cont.*)
    indeterminate price, sale for, 175–178 (*see also* "Price . . .")
    installment sales, 149–168 (*see also* "Installment sales")
        contract, sale of, 163–164
        of mortgaged property, 158–161
        planning, 155–157
        qualifying for, 150–151
        repossession of property, 167–168
        and Section 1038, 167
        30% rule, 151–154
        types of sales qualifying, 163
        and "wrap-around" mortgage, 161–162
        in year of sale, 151–154
    option sales, 178–180
        exercise or failure of, 179
        and sales contract, difference between, 178–179
        seller, advantages to, 180
"Premium" lease, 290
Prepayment penalties, 196
Price, indeterminate, sale for, 175–178
    for annuity, private, 176–178
        estate planning, value for, 178
        "investment," meaning of, 177
    contingent price, 175–176
    by production, 176
Principal of mortgage debt, payment of, 193–196
Proceedings of the New York University Twenty-Fifth Annual Institute, 369*n*
Production, sales measured by, 176
Property acquired by mortgagee, disposition of, 255
Purchase of property, tax basis and, 46

Q

Quasi-business use of property, problem with, 28–30

R

Reacquisition by seller in satisfaction of indebtedness, 215–219
    bad debt loss, 216
    basis, 217–218
    and IRC Section 1038, 215–219
        holding period, 218
        rules personal to seller, 218–219
    gain, general rule for, 215–216
        character, 217
        extent of, 216–217

INDEX

Reacquisition by seller in satisfaction of indebtedness (*cont.*)
    legal fees, 219
    loss, 216
Recapture of depreciation, 104–105 (*see also* "Depreciation . . .")
Recourse liability, 366–368 (*see also* "Straw corporations")
"Recovery exclusion," meaning of, 222n
Reduction of rent, tenant's negotiation for, 269
Reimbursement of seller for taxes paid, 61–63
Related parties, rentals by, 257
    renewal of lease option, 273
Relative cost method in inverse condemnation, 142
Removal of improvements, loss deduction and, 77–78
Rentals, 256–258 (*see also* "Leasing real property")
Rents, assignment of to mortgagee prior to foreclosure, 254–255
Repair expenses, deductibility of, 22, 78–79
Replacement property for involuntary conversions, 133–134
    "functional" test, 133
    period of, 134–135
Residence, personal, property held as, 23–24
    condemnation, 24
    and IRC Section 262, 23–24
    new home, purchase of, 24
    owner over 65, 24
    "principle residence," definition of, 23–24
Restoration, cost of as measurement for loss, 86–87
Restoration of property by tenant, 263–264
    or reimbursement, 265–266
    release from obligation, 264–265
    wear and tear excepted, 264
Revenue Act of 1969, 106, 300

S

Sale of lease, 280–282
    proceeds on, 281–282
    sublease v. sale, 282
Sale of property, advantageous treatment of, 22
    mortgaged in excess of basis, 197–198
Sales contract and option contract, difference between, 178–179
Sales by corporations, problems of, 346–357 (*see also* "Corporations")
Sales and leasebacks, 287–299
    advantages, 288

Sales and leasebacks (*cont.*)
    exchange, tax-free, and leaseback, 289–290
    losses, 290–291
    "premium" lease, 290
    gain or loss, 288–289
    with option to repurchase, 292–294
        "objective" and "subjective intent," 292–293
        qualifications for, 293
    between related parties, 294–299
        gain or loss, 294–295
        gifts and leasebacks, 295–296
        guardian, role of, 296–297
        as income-splitting devices, 296–297
        rental deduction on, 298–299
        requirements, 297–298
    rental deduction to seller-lessee, 291
    rental income to buyer-lessor, 291–292
Sales of real property, 91–111
    basis allocations between portions of tract, 96–97
    easement, sale of, 97
    "equitable," meaning of, 96–97
    gain or loss, computation of, 92
        capital, 99–102
        nature of, 97–98
        ordinary, treatment of, 98
        Section 1231, treatment of, 98–99
        time for reporting, 95–96
    depreciation recapture, general, 104–105
        farm improvements, 107–108
        real estate improvements, 105–107
    gross sales price, computation of, 93–95
    holding period of property, 102–104
    to related parties, 108–109
    subject to favorable mortgage, 110–111
    timing, 109–110
        net operating loss carryover, 109
Salvage value, 73–74
Second mortgagee, 252–253 (*see also* "Mortgagee, second . . .")
Security, installment sales and, 166–167
Security deposit by tenant, covenant for, 259–260
    applicable to future rents, 260
Seepage destruction, deduction for, 85
"Seventy-five percent test" for lease renewal, 272–273
Severance damages, 137–138
Single economic unit rule in involuntary conversions, 132–133
"Sixty percent test" for lease renewal, 272
Soil and water conservation expenses, deductibility of, 87–90
    definition, 87–88

Soil and water conservation expenses, deductibility of (*cont.*)
    districts, 89
    election to deduct, 89
    farming land, 88
    fertilizer and land clearing expenses, 89–90
    limitation, 88, 89
Stock, corporate, issuing to acquire property, 358–359
Stock in corporation, sale of, 346
Stock market investments, real estate ownership compared to, 20–21
Straight-line method of depreciation, 67
Straw corporations, 366–368
    ensurance of position, 368
    IRS position, 367–368
    as tax non-entities, 367
    usefulness of, 367
    "why" of non-recourse liability, 366–367
Strict foreclosure, 232–238
    mortgagee:
        basis to, 235
        gain, 233–235
        loss, 233
    mortgagor:
        gain, 236–237
        loss, 235–236
    problems, three, 232–233
    suggestions, 237–238
Subchapter S corporations, 363–366
    basis as tax problem, 364
    conclusion, 364-366
        "significant" services, 365
    elections, 363–364
    result of election, 364
Subdivisions, 316–320
    effect of, 316
    during liquidation, 316-317
    under Section 1237, 316–320
        benefits, 319
        exceptions, 319
        substantial improvements, 319
    unsuitable parts, sale of, 318
"Subjective intent," role of in sale and leaseback with option to repurchase, 292–292
Sublease v. sale of lease, 282
"Substantially appreciated inventory," meaning of, 311*n*
Sum-of-the-years' digits method of depreciation, 68
    for new residential housing, 69
Surtax, accumulated earnings, 336–339

Syndicates, real estate, 320–324
    common ownership of income real estate, 322–324
    limited partnerships, 322–323
    unincorporated associations, 320–322
        examples, 321
        taxed as corporations, 321–322

T

"Tainted" stockholders in liquidation, 357
Tax preference income, 39–40
Tax Reform Act of 1969, accelerated depreciation and, 355
    and corporate distributions, 342–343
Taxes, deductibility of, 81
Taxes, property, payment of by tenant, 260–261
Tenancy in common, 44
Tenant, cost to of obtaining lease, 278–280
Tenant-stockholder, definition of, 371*n* (*see also* "Cooperative housing corporation")
Tenant's improvements, reimbursement for, 267–268
    as allowance against rent, 268–269
Tenant's restoration of leased property, 263–264
    release from obligation, 264–265
    restoration or reimbursement, 265–266
    wear and tear excepted, 264
Tenants, tax consideration for, 256–270 (*see also* "Leasing real property")
Termination of lease, premature, depreciation and, 273
Termination of rental, 269–270
Termite damage, deduction for, 85
"Thin" incorporation, 334–336
Third party, foreclosure by sale to, 219–232 (*see also* "Foreclosure. . . ")
30% rule in installment sales, 151–154
Title, defense of, 79–80
Title, how to take, 35–45 (*see also* "Acquiring real property")
    corporate ownership, 36–40
        and individual, comparison of, 37–40
        tax preference income, 39–40
    husband and wife ownership, 40–44
        basis after death, 41–42
        comparison of ownership, 43–44
        estate and gift taxes, 41
        joint tenancy, termination of, 42–43

INDEX

Title, how to take (*cont.*)
    individual, 36
    joint tenancy, 44
    partnership, 44–45
    tenancy in common, 44
Title to real estate, tax advantage in, 23
Trade or business, property held for, 25
    and Section 1231, 25
    and Section 1250, 25
    tax treatment most favorable, 25
Trade or business property, problems with, 30–32
    "net-net" lease, 31–32
Trade fixtures installed by tenant, depreciation of, 271
Transferability in condominium property, 383
Trees and shrubbery, depreciation and, 65
Turn-key lease, tax consequences of, 267
200% declining-balance method of depreciation, 67–68, 69
    for new residential housing, 69

U

Uniform Limited Partnership Act, 314, 322*n*
Unincorporated associations and partnerships, differences between, 320–321
United States Housing Act of 1937, 107
"Unrealized receivables," definition of, 311*n*

Useful life of real property, 71–73
    buildings, guideline categories of, 73
    guidelines, IRS, 72

V

Vacation home, occasional rental of, 28–30
Voluntary conveyance of mortgaged property, 242–248
    abandonment of mortgaged property, 247–248
    basis to mortgagee of property received, 244
    mortgagee, gain or loss to, 243–244
    mortgagor, gain or loss to, 244–245
        insolvent, gain to, 245
        non-assuming, 246–247
        purchase-money, gain to, 245–246
    suggestions, 248

W

"Walk-away," 201
Water conservation expenses, 87–90 (*see also* "Soil and water. . .")
Willis, Arthur B., 302*n*
"Wrap-around" mortgage, installment sales and, 161–162